Certainly few things could be more needed at the beginning of the 21st century than a 'common sense,' 'Bible-its-own-interpreter,' historically accurate exposition of the Book of Revelation. I believe that is what you hold in your hands right now. It is wholesome medicine.

May it be blessed and used to do much good!

—Dr. Stephen P. Westcott,
Bristol, England
2004

Back to the Future – A Study in the Book of Revelation
Copyright © 2004 by Ralph E. Bass, Jr.
LIVING HOPE PRESS

Ralph E. Bass, Jr.,
100 Iverson Street,
Greenville, SC 29615.
LivingHope@digitran.net

ISBN 0-9759547-0-9

Printed in the United States of America

Back

to the

FUTURE

A Study in the
Book of Revelation

Ralph E. Bass, Jr.

LIVING HOPE PRESS
Greenville, SC, USA

To
Ralph E. Bass, Sr.
Mary E. Bass
God bless you in your growing faith,

and with special thanks to
Dr. and Mrs. Daniel Nickles
who kindly helped finance the publication of this book.

Contents

Preface

The researches of many commentators have already thrown much darkness on this subject, and it is probable that, if they continue, we shall soon know nothing at all about it!
—Mark Twain[1]

So, why did I write this commentary?

First, I became a believer in a Dispensational church. A loving pastor and many dear friends nourished my faith there. I embraced this theology for 33 years after my salvation. The number of sermons, Sunday school lessons, and Bible studies on eschatology that I heard were beyond count. Yet, there was a nagging doubt. While pastoring I avoided the subject. But one day I was asked questions on prophecy that I simply could no longer answer with commitment or conviction. It was time to find some real answers. This book began as Sunday school lessons to provide those real answers for others and for myself.

Second, long after the Sunday school lessons ended, the study and the writing continued. I was not satisfied with Sunday school answers; I wanted something definitive for my own benefit and the benefit of others. This work is an effort to provide that substance, that body of learning beyond the Sunday school class for those that demands more, much more.

Third, sadly, there is much in print that I regard as very bad prophetic theology and little that I see as good. It seemed to me that perhaps another work from the loyal opposition of the prevailing opinion was a worthwhile undertaking. Something written from a deep conviction in the sufficiency and trustworthiness of Scripture, yet something far different from

---

[1] C. Marvin Pate, Editor, <u>Four Views on the Book of Revelation</u> (Grand Rapids, MI: Zondervan Publishing House, 1998), 10.

what was commonly dished up to the Church. This is that something.

These are some the reasons this book was written. I prayed as I wrote it that it would honor Christ in its message. I continue to pray that you will be greatly benefited by a careful study of its content.

—Ralph E. Bass, Jr.
June, 2004

Ᏻntroduction

Ꮦhe Book of Revelation has been described as "a riddle wrapped in a mystery inside an enigma, and that efforts to understand it are a waste of time."[2]   Such a view hardly suggests any real hope in understanding its contents. The fact of the matter is any book taken out of its original context becomes difficult to understand, and no book in the entire Bible has suffered more from being removed from its historic context than the Book of Revelation. The contention of this study is that the Book of Revelation is virtually without meaning if its historical context is not given center stage. However, when it is given this perspective, the pages open to our understanding like petals on a beautiful flower.

Methods of Interpretation

Throughout Christian history, the Book of Revelation has been approached in many different ways.

The **Futurists** see in this book a prophecy about times that have not yet come and events that have not yet occurred. Although written to seven churches nearly 2000 years ago, they see in it no significant message to those churches, because to the Futurists, this book is about a future rapture, tribulation and millennium. Dispensational Premillennialists dominate the Futurist's camp.

The denominations that commonly subscribe to this position include independent Baptist, the Mormons, the Armstrong Church of God, the Jehovah's Witnesses and the Seventh Day Adventists. In addition, many that use the term "Bible Church" or "Community Church" and most graduates of Dallas Theological Seminary would be advocates of Dispensational Premillennialism. The Dispensational Premillennialist view is that of the *Left Behind* book series by Tim LaHaye and Jerry Jenkins, two prominent Dispensational authors. Some others who share this view are John Nelson Darby, Arno C. Gaebelein, Donald Grey Barnhouse, H. A. Ironside, Hal Lindsey, Henry M. Morris, Charles C. Ryrie, J. A. Seiss,

---

[2] James B. Jordon, <u>A Brief Reader's Guide to Revelation</u> (Niceville, Fl: Transfiguration Press, 1999), 6.

Charles L. Feinberg, M. R. DeHaan, Lewis Sperry Chafer, Gleason L. Archer, Lehman Strauss, Merrill C. Tenney, Dwight Pentecost and John Walvoord.

The *Historicists* see the message of the book working itself out through the successive eras of history. Generally, each of the seven churches is portrayed as a period of time in church history. Again, this group sees no significant message to the churches to which it was written. Inevitably, advocates of this position tend to see themselves as the last church and generation before Christ comes. Generally, the Reformers of the 16th century were Historicists. One theologian/historian has summed up the weakness of this position by remarking "...while the historicist approach once was widespread, today, for all practical purposes, it has passed from the scene. Its failed attempts to locate the fulfillment of Revelation in the course of the circumstances of history has doomed it to continual revision as time passed and, ultimately, to obscurity...."[3]

Premillennialists have often been fascinated with the Historicist's position and some have attempted to mix the Historicist's and Futurist's positions into one system. A few Amillennialists still subscribe to the Historicist' position as well. Names in this camp would include Albert Barnes, Robert Caringola, Adam Clarke, E. B. Elliott, Matthew Henry, and Fred P. Miller.

The *Spiritualists*, sometimes called *Idealists*, those that advocate a symbolic approach to the book, do not attempt to find individual fulfillments in the visions, but instead take "...Revelation to be a great drama depicting transcendent spiritual realities.... Fulfillment is seen either as entirely spiritual or as recurrent, finding representative expression in historical events throughout the age, rather than in one-time, specific fulfillments."[4] "One group of interpreters holds that there are no historical references in the Revelation at all, hardly even to current events. The symbols represent abstract ideas or general principles which may be seen at work in any age; if there is any reference to current history it is only because figures in current history (like Nero) are good examples of the general principle in question."[5]

---

[3] C. Marvin Pate, Editor, 18.

[4] Steve Gregg, Revelation – Four Views (Nashville, TN: Thomas Nelson Publishers, 1997), 2.

[5] Philip Carrington, The Meaning of the Revelation (London, England: SPCK, 1931), viii.

And again, this group sees no significant message to the early churches to which this book was written. Amillennialists dominate this view and include Henry Alford, William Hendriksen, R.C.H. Lenski, William Milligan, Earl Morey, Leon Morris, S.L. Morris, Rousas John Rushdoony, H.B. Swete, Edward J. Young, Abraham Kuyper, Anthony A. Hoekema, Lewis Berkhof, G.C. Berkouwer, F.D. Maurice and Geoffrey B. Wilson.

The **Preterists** are the next group we will consider. Their position is not well known and even the term they use to identify themselves, Preterism, is foreign to the vocabulary of most Christians. "The word comes from the Latin *praeteritus* ("to go by, pass") which, in turn, is based upon *praeter* ("that which is beyond, past")."[6] This word was chosen because it makes the point that most of the Book of Revelation has, in their view, been fulfilled in what is now, our past.

The *Preterists* see the message to the seven churches as having contemporary significance to the generation to which it was written. They understand that the prophecies of the book were determined for the near future, and were substantially fulfilled by the fall of Jerusalem in A.D. 70. As one author clarifies, "...the sustained attempt to root the fulfillment of the divine prophecies of Revelation in the first century A.D. constitutes the preterist's distinctive approach."[7] Preterists contend, therefore, that because of its first century context, most of the prophecies of Revelation have been fulfilled and are now, two thousand years later, in our past. In other words, "Though the prophecies were in the future when John wrote and when his original audience read them, they are now in *our* past."[8] In this camp you will find Jay E. Adams, R. C. Sproul, Kenneth L. Gentry, Greg L. Bahnsen, Gary DeMar, J. Marcellus Kik, R. T. France, Morris Ashcraft, Philip Carrington, C. Vanderwall, David Chilton, David S. Clark, J. Stuart Russell, Phillip S. Desprez, Moses Stuart and Milton Terry.

In the Preterists camp are found Amillennialists, Historic Premillennialists and Postmillennialists. In other words, you could be an Amillennialist, a Historic Premillennialist, or a Postmillennialist and also be a Preterist. "Some form of preterism could conceivably be incorporated into all of

---

[6] Jay E. Adams, <u>Preterism: Orthodox or Unorthodox?</u> (Stanley, NC: Timeless Texts, 2003), v.

[7] C. Marvin Pate, Editor, 19.

[8] Ibid., 37.

them."[9] This author writes from the Biblical Preterist (partial or orthodox preterist), position in this commentary. Hence the name of this book— *Back To the Future*. It is only by going back some two thousand years, do we come to a time when the prophecies in the Book of Revelation were yet future. Preterists believe that if Christ's words in Matthew 24 are correct, then this position is inevitable.

> *Truly I say to you, this generation will not pass away until all these things take place. (Matthew 24:34, NASB95)*

Dispensationalism

We must note that there is a relatively new eschatological system, recently developed by Edward Irving and John Nelson Darby in the 1830's, called Dispensational Premillennialism, which must also be considered. "It has swept across the modern world, due largely to the wide influence of *The Scofield Reference Bible*, published in 1909. Dispensationalism has become in our day the majority report among evangelical Christians."[10]

Classical Dispensationalism, (as distinguished from Progressive Dispensationalism), differs from Historic Premillennialism in that the Classic Dispensationalists 1) have a pre-tribulation rapture at the beginning of chapter 4 of the book of Revelation. 2) They believe the Church is a mystery wholly unknown and unmentioned in the Old Testament Scriptures, 3) they see the millennium as a period in which Israel picks up its favored people status with God after a parenthesis in which the Church age occurred. In addition, 4) they believe that in a future Millenium, there will be a rebuilt temple in Jerusalem and a return to the Jewish sacrificial system as memorials to the death of Christ.

It is of great significance to the Classic Dispensational Premillennialist that the Jews be viewed as "God's chosen people," as they like to refer to them. Note, it is unsaved Jews who are to them "God's chosen people," not Christians! For them, this preeminent status is unchanged through the ages—Old Testament and New Testament periods alike. The Church is simply a side show, wholly unanticipated and unmentioned in the Old

---

[9] R. C. Sproul, The Last Days According to Jesus (Grand Rapids, MI: Baker Books, 1998), 201.

[10] Ibid., 196.

Testament. For them, the greatness and expanse of the gospel message of the New Testament is to be ended with a return to the narrowness of the gospel message of racial Judaism. The Jewish Temple is to be rebuilt and animal sacrifices are to again take place! And all this is to occur in spite of the once for all sacrifice of Christ at Calvary. In speaking of the Temple mentioned in Ezekiel chapters 40 through 46, Gaebelein says, "The true interpretation is the literal one which looks upon these chapters as a prophecy yet unfulfilled and to be fulfilled when Israel has been restored by the Shepherd and when His glory is once more manifested in the midst of His people. The great building seen in his prophetic vision will then come into existence and all will be accomplished."[11]

Animal sacrifices are to be reinstituted says Pentecost, "To perpetuate the Memorial of Sacrifice."[12]

Rushdoony says that Classical Dispensationalism is simply an,

> ...exaltation of racism into a divine principle. Every attempt to bring the Jew back into prophecy as a Jew is to give race and works (for racial descent is a human work) a priority over grace and Christ's work and is nothing more or less than paganism. It is significant that premillennialism is almost invariably associated with Arminianism, i.e., the introduction of race into prophetic perspectives is accompanied by, and part and parcel of, the introduction of works into the order of salvation.[13]

It is important to note that in academic circles Classic Dispensationalism is in rapid decline as it has been for some thirty years now. It is being quickly replaced with a new, less offensive version of Dispensationalism called Progressive Dispensationalism. For that reason it is important to take note of the differences between these two systems which are so alike at various

---

[11] Arno C. Gaebelein, The Prophet Ezekiel (New York, NY: Our Hope Publishers, 1911), 272.

[12] J. Dwight Pentecost, Things to Come (Grand Rapids, MI: Dunham Publishing Co, 1958), 516.

[13] Rousas John Rushdoony, Thy Kingdom Come (Phillipsburg, NJ: Presbyterian and Reformed Publishing Co, 1971), 134.

points and yet so different at what has traditionally been critical points[14]. As one wit noted, Progressive Dispensationalism "is quickly becoming the dominant position of the Dallas Theological Seminary faculty (we're a few funerals away from the complete dismantling of traditional [Classic] Dispensationalism at that school, which is, of course, the "dispy" capital of the world), even if lay people and fiction authors aren't aware of it."[15]

In light of these concerns, Classical Dispensationalism appears to be in its essential points, foreign to Scripture. The New Testament writers knew nothing of it, for the writers of the New Testament interpret Old Testament passages toward Israel as fulfilled by the Church. For instance, Paul applies the prophecies of the Old Testament to the Church in his epistle to Romans—which the Classical Dispensationalists say cannot be done.[16] As you read this, notice Paul's use of Old Testament Scripture to identify New Testament Christians, the Church.

> *And He did so to make known the riches of His glory upon vessels*
> *of mercy, which He prepared beforehand for glory, even us,*
> *whom He also called, not from among Jews only, but also from*
> *among Gentiles. As He says also in Hosea, "I will call those who*

---

[14] "Progressive dispensationalism is clearly not your father's dispensationalism (nor your favorite televangelist's). Radical changes distinguishing it from its antiquated forbears include:

A rejection of simplistic literalism in hermeneutics. Progressive dispensationalists pretty much adopt a genuine grammatical-historical-theological theory of interpretation — like the rest of the evangelical world.

A revision of the Israel-Church distinction, allowing that Israel and the Church are two phases of the one people of God. Classic dispensationalism argued for a radical distinction between Israel and the Church that would even continue into eternity; revised dispensationalism maintained that distinction only in terms of the earthly outworking of redemption.

A breaking down of the walls of separation between the dispensations. Their dispensations are not discrete, unmixed time frames, but rather evolving stages of historical development. Contained within any particular dispensation are the seeds of the next dispensation so that the dispensations gradually progress (hence the name). This allows that Christ is now enthroned as king — in anticipation of his coming earthly-millennial rule." – Dr. Ken Gentry http://www.monergism.com/thethreshold/articles/topic/dispensationalism.html

[15] In private correspondence with a Dispensational friend.

[16] Charles D. Provan, The Church is Israel Now (Vallecito, CA: Ross House Books, 1987). Presents a very convincing argument demonstrating the error of Dispensationalism in its teaching on the Church.

were not My people, 'My people,' and her who was not beloved,
'beloved.' " "And it shall be that in the place where it was said to
them, 'you are not My people,' there they shall be called sons of the
living God." Isaiah cries out concerning Israel, "Though the
number of the sons of Israel be like the sand of the sea, it is the
remnant that will be saved; for the Lord will execute His word on
the earth [land], thoroughly and quickly." And just as Isaiah
foretold, "Unless the Lord of Sabaoth had left to us a posterity, we
would have become like Sodom, and would have resembled
Gomorrah." (Romans 9:23-29, NASB95)

In this passage above, we see that "The church, consisting of both Jews and
Gentiles, has become the people of God."[17] Paul uses other passages to
drive home this point, that the Church is spiritual Israel, as well.

...and he received the sign of circumcision, a seal of the
righteousness of the faith which he had while uncircumcised, so
that he might be the father of all who believe without being
circumcised, that righteousness might be credited to them....
(Romans 4:11, NASB95)

To understand this point, let's ask a few questions. Who believes but has
not been circumcised? It is the Church, who also has the honor of calling
Abraham their father. You can call them spiritual "Abrahamites" or
spiritual "Israelites." Both are accurate, it is the Church. And consider this
passage:

For this reason it is by faith, in order that it may be in accordance
with grace, so that the promise will be guaranteed to all the
descendants, not only to those who are of the Law, but also to
those who are of the faith of Abraham, who is the father of us all,
(as it is written, "A father of many nations have I made you") in
the presence of Him whom he believed, even God, who gives life to
the dead and calls into being that which does not exist. (Romans
4:16-17, NASB95)

---

[17] Robert G. Clouse, Editor, <u>The Meaning of the Millennium, Historic Premillennialism by</u>
<u>George Eldon Ladd</u> (Downers Grove, IL: InterVarsity Press, 1977), 24.

Abraham is the father of many nations. To Jews, the word nation means "gentile." And it is the Gentiles who have become spiritual Abrahamites by faith. God has rejected the Jews who have rejected Christ; they are *not* His children. Who are His children then? It is the Church. And Paul continues:

> *Therefore, be sure that it is those who are of faith who are sons of Abraham. The Scripture, foreseeing that God would justify the Gentiles by faith, preached the gospel beforehand to Abraham, saying, "All the nations will be blessed in you." (Galatians 3:7-8, NASB95)*

It is by faith that a person becomes a child of Abraham, not simply being born a Jew. The Gentiles, the nations, have believed and have therefore become spiritual Jews. Paul says again:

> *And if you belong to Christ, then you are Abraham's descendants, heirs according to promise. (Galatians 3:29, NASB95)*

If you are a Christian, you are of the seed of Abraham, a spiritual Jew; nothing could be plainer.

> *For he is not a Jew who is one outwardly, nor is circumcision that which is outward in the flesh. But he is a Jew who is one inwardly; and circumcision is that which is of the heart, by the Spirit, not by the letter; and his praise is not from men, but from God. (Romans 2:28-29, NASB95)*

True membership in Israel is a product of an inward faith, and without that faith a Jew is not a part of the Israel of God. With that faith a person is a part of the Israel of God, notwithstanding the fact that he or she is a gentile.

> *...for we are the true circumcision, who worship in the Spirit of God and glory in Christ Jesus and put no confidence in the flesh.... (Philippians 3:3, NASB95)*

Here Paul is rather bold and very plain; he calls Christian people *the true circumcision*. That is, they are true sons of Abraham because their hearts have been circumcised.

> *And those who will walk by this rule, peace and mercy be upon them, and upon <u>the Israel of God</u>. (Galatians 6:16, NASB95)*

And now Paul spells it out. The Gentile church at Galatia, and anywhere else for that matter, is <u>the Israel of God</u>.

Clearly, Paul "applies prophecies to the church which in their Old Testament setting belong to literal Israel; he calls the church the "sons," the "seeds" of Abraham. He calls believers the "true circumcision." It is difficult therefore to avoid the conclusion that Paul sees the church as spiritual Israel."[18]   And yet, the Church is a great mystery to Dispensationalism; it was not foretold in the Old Testament. According to them, it is simply a parenthesis. At the rapture it will go away and God will then get back to his real plan, the true people of God, racial Israel.

The eschatology of Dispensationalism is formed by fitting the New Testament into Old Testament forms, making the New Testament fit into the earthly kingdom concept that the Jews envisioned as their destiny. This was the very idea Christ rejected in His ministry to them. Of course the proper way of understanding the Old Testament is by seeing it in the light of New Testament fulfillment.   In other words, Dispensationalism does theology backwards and thereby gets confused results.

Philip Carrington speaking of Dispensationalism under the name Adventism says, "The study of a modern Adventist sect is of great importance, for it illustrates the psychology and doctrinal ideas of the 'montanist' type of heresy, to which St. John did not belong. ...literal interpretation of symbols, ... puritan legalism, exact predictable dates, ... a catastrophic 'end of the world,' ... are ideas which all hang together and mark the type of mind which is profoundly material at the very moment it prides itself on being spiritual."[19]   Now it is unfair to classify Dispensationalism as a sect like the Seventh Day Adventists, who Carrington was more specifically speaking of, yet Dispensationalism holds many of these doctrines and is not fully in the historic tradition of the Christian Church at these points.

---

[18] Robert G. Clouse, 25.

[19] Philip Carrington, 250-251.

Because of its recent origin, historically, in the two-thousand year period of Christianity, most Christians have not heard of this theory, however, in recent years it has become the dominant explanation of things to come, especially in the U.S. This is not to the benefit of the Church.

The Author and Date[20]

The book clearly identifies the earthly instrument in writing Revelation, saying that Christ *"sent and communicated it by His angel to His bond-servant John"* (1:1). We say "earthly instrument" because "we must remember that the real Author of the book is not the apostle John but God Omniscient Himself."[21]

What this book does not tell us is—which John? There were several in the New Testament world, and because there were several in the early church it would be incumbent upon the earthly author to tell us which one he is, that is, if he were any other than the apostle John. However, "...to say John was sufficient. Any other John would need a descriptive epithet, but there was one John who needed none."[22] Which John would that be? "The external evidence is overwhelmingly in favor of this view, and Justin Martyr, Irenaeus, Tertullian, Hippolytus, and Origen testify direct testimony that the Apocalypse is the writing of the apostle John."[23]

As one author says, "The nature of the book demands the essence of a man who compares in abilities to a fully inspired Peter or Paul. In fact, he must be able to stand beside an Isaiah, Jeremiah, Ezekiel or Zechariah, for the Apocalypse encompasses the fullness of these prophets and more. Only John, the apostle, measures up to the likeness of these notable ones."[24]

---

[20] See Kenneth L. Gentry, Jr., <u>Before Jerusalem Fell</u> (Atlanta, GA: American Visions Publishers, 1998). This book is of considerable importance in any study on the date of Revelation.

[21] William Hendriksen, <u>More Than Conquerors</u> (Grand Rapids, MI: Baker Books 1940, 1967), 45.

[22] David S. Clark, <u>The Message from Patmos</u> (Grand Rapids: Baker Book House, 1989), 13.

[23] Milton S. Terry, <u>Biblical Apocalyptics</u> (New York, NY: Curts & Jennings, 1898), 253.

[24] Arthur M. Ogden, <u>The Avenging of the Apostles & Prophets</u> (Somerset, KY: Ogden Publications, 1991), 3.

Some scholars have questioned this conclusion, noting that John does not characteristically attach his name to his letters, and yet here he does. This objection seems less weighty, however, when the following points are considered. 1) In his epistles, John wrote personal letters to close friends who knew him well. The intimacy and personal nature of the letters did not require additional information on the author. 2) In his Gospel, he probably hand delivered his story to the Christian community in which he lived. Again, eliminating any question as to the authorship. 3) But for the Book of Revelation, he was not "home," and he was writing to seven churches, only one of which knew him well—Ephesus. He simply needed to tell them who was sending the letter. He did not, could not, hand deliver this letter as he was on the Isle of Patmos at the time. Considering also the unique nature of his letter, it is quite possible that he would feel a need to inform his audience with certainty just who the writer was. As a result, John the Apostle is the only serious contender for authorship.

The author Milton Terry succinctly describes the importance of grappling with the date of Revelation saying,

> The great importance of ascertaining the historical standpoint of an author is notably illustrated by the controversy over the date of the Apocalypse of John. If that prophetical book was written before the destruction of Jerusalem, a number of its particular allusions must most naturally be understood as referring to that city and its fall. If, however, it was written at the end of the reign of Domitian (about A.D. 96), as many have believed, another system of interpretation is necessary to explain the historical allusions.[25]

In considering the external evidence on the date of the book, we must take note that many scholars believe that John wrote in the later part of the first century during the reign of Domitian, about A.D. 95-96, well after the destruction of Jerusalem in A.D. 70. Although several of the Fathers make this assertion, all base their position on the comments of one person, Irenaeus bishop of Lyons in France. Irenaeus said this: "We therefore do not run the risk of pronouncing positively concerning the name of the Antichrist, for if it were necessary to have his name distinctly announced at the present time, it would doubtless have been announced by him who saw the Apocalypse; for it is not a great while ago that it [or he] was seen, but

---

[25] Milton S. Terry, <u>Biblical Hermeneutics</u>, 237.

almost in our own generation, toward the end of Domitian's reign."[26] While this statement appears rather straight forward, Terry points out that "...the critical reader will observe that the subject of the verb... *was seen*, is ambiguous, and may be understood either of John or the Apocalypse."[27]

So, the question is this, who or what was *seen*? It may have been John that Irenaeus claims was seen, since the Apostle is reported to have lived to almost one hundred years of age. Actually, the logic of the sentences seems to require this interpretation. If the Revelation was *"seen"* at this late date, how would that have helped determine who the Antichrist was? In and of itself, possessing a copy of the Revelation does not answer that question. On the other hand, if John was *seen*—well certainly he could personally reveal who the Antichrist was! So, clearly, the *seeing* of John is really the only thing that makes sense. If, on the other hand, this passage is stating that John *saw* the Revelation at this time, then that is powerful testimony for a late date. Unfortunately, this quote will never be able to tell us more than it does, which is nothing certain, making this source of questionable force in the argument.

One other possibility exists as to whom Irenaeus was referring when he made reference to Domitian. It is a possibility that he was referring to "(Nero Claudius Caesar) [who] was originally named Lucius <u>Domitius</u> Ahenobarbus,"[28] instead of referring to Titus Flavius <u>Domitianus</u>, commonly known as Domitian. If Nero is here referenced, then there is no confusion in Irenaeus, just in his interpreters. But again the ambiguity cannot be cleared up.

Since the external evidence does not provide satisfaction for the dating, what evidence within the book exists that might resolve this impasse? Consider these points:[29]

---

[26] Ibid., 238.

[27] Ibid., 256.

[28] Paul Lagass and Columbia University, <u>The Columbia Encyclopedia</u>, 6th ed. (New York; Detroit: Columbia University Press, 2000).

[29] Milton S. Terry, <u>Biblical Hermeneutics</u>, 240.

THE WRITING STYLE OF JOHN IN REVELATION VERSUS THE GOSPEL OF JOHN

In the Book of Revelation, John's use of the Greek language is strained; his grammar is poor and his mindset is Hebrew. As one author said, "...while he writes in Greek, he thinks in Hebrew."[30] This is not at all like his gospel, which, although simple in style, is well written in Greek. What explains the difference? The difference can be explained by the fact that John wrote the Revelation in his early years shortly after he removed from Judah to Asia, at a time when his use of Greek was still rather rough. His gospel, however, was written sometime later, after some interaction with the Greek community. By then he had worked off the rough edges of his "foreign accent" and communicated with greater grammatical correctness. This would imply an early date for Revelation.

In fairness, another explanation can be suggested concerning the difference of style in John's gospel and the book of Revelation. That would be the possibility that John used a secretary to write the gospel, that is, he would have dictated it to one with better grammatical skills in Greek than his own. However, while on Patmos, he would not have had access to such help, and therefore wrote Greek with some difficulty. "Employing scribes in the writing of letters and documents was a common practice during the first century, for Paul and Peter even mention their amanuenses by name: Paul refers to Tertius (Rom. 16:22) and Peter mentions Silas (1 Pet. 5:12). But as an exile, John was alone and had to rely on his own authorial ability and thus wrote Greek unaided by native speakers."[31]

So, this point is subject to various explanations; perhaps John's gospel was written first. But if John's gospel was written first, how do we explain the lack of eschatological references in his gospel? The best explanation is that he had covered that material in his earlier Revelation and therefore saw no need to address it again. "Of the fact, however, that john wrote the Apocalypse before he wrote his Gospel, ... there can now, I think, be no

---

[30] R. H. A. Charles, <u>Critical and Exegetical Commentary on the Revelation of St. John</u> (Edinburgh, Scotland: T. & T. Clark, 1920), vol. 1, cxvii-clix.

[31] Simon J. Kistemaker, and William Hendriksen, <u>New Testament Commentary: Exposition of the Book of Revelation</u> (Grand Rapids: Baker Book House, 1953-2001), Vol. 20, 22.

reasonable ground of doubt."[32] It is important to note that all of the other gospel writers do give considerable attention to eschatological issues in their books, only the gospel of John does not.

Along this line of thinking, it must be noted that John evidenced a considerable knowledge of the cities to which he wrote. This would suggest that he had visited them in his ministry—suggesting a later date. And of course, during these visits, he took the time to learn much of these various communities. Some see this as evidence of his prolonged ministry in Asia Minor before he wrote Revelation. On the other hand, an intelligent man would have learned much in a few short years, so there is in this argument no requirement that he minister there for decades.

Perhaps the difference in style between John's Gospel and the Revelation, lies in the nature of the writings, that is, when writing like a Hebrew prophet of old John would naturally have used Hebrew prophetical style, whereas when writing a Gospel, a Greek historical literary style would be mandated. After all, a prophet must write like a prophet.[33]

So, although these points rise to the level of interesting speculation, they are not critical proofs of an early or late date.

THE PERSECUTION OF THE EARLY CHURCH

Clearly, the book of Acts and Revelation portray the persecution in the early Church coming primarily from Judaism, but after the fall of Jerusalem, persecution came primarily from Rome as Jewish opposition quickly faded into the background. This is not to say Nero did not persecute the Church, for certainly he did, and did so in fulfillment to the prophecies found in Revelation. However, the bigger empire wide persecutions came only in the second century. Indeed there were few persecutions during the reign of Domitian, a fact that in itself would seem to exclude his reign from the setting of the Revelation. One scholar takes note of this saying,

---

[32] Moses Stuart, Commentary on the Apocalypse, vol. 2 (New York, NY: Allen, Mornll, and Wardwell, 1845), 11.

[33] Valued insight based on a conversation with, and notes from Dr. Stephen Westcott, Bristol, England.

Less easy to gauge is Domitian's attitude toward Christians and Jews, since reliable evidence for their persecution is difficult to find. Christians may have been among those banished or executed from time to time during the 90's, but the testimony falls short of confirming any organized program of persecution under Domitian's reign. ... As with Christians, such policies did not amount to persecution, but it does help to explain the Jewish fears of expulsion present in the sources. On balance, the tradition of Domitian as persecutor has been greatly overstated, yet given his autocratic tendencies and devotion to Roman pagan religion, it is easy to see how such stories could have evolved and multiplied.[34]

Therefore, we must surmise that this book was written before the fall of Jerusalem, when Jewish antagonism and persecution of the Church were prominent.

The References to Jerusalem and the Temple

The Book of Revelation had to have been written before A.D. 70 because the city of Jerusalem and its Temple are clearly standing as John writes. For testimony to the presence of the city of Jerusalem we read:

> *And their dead bodies will lie in the street of the great city which mystically is called Sodom and Egypt, where also their Lord was crucified. (Revelation 11:8, NASB95)*

And for the existence of the Temple we read:

> *Then there was given me a measuring rod like a staff; and someone said, "Get up and measure the temple of God and the altar, and those who worship in it. Leave out the court which is outside the temple and do not measure it...." (Revelation 11:1-2, NASB95)*

A date later than A.D. 70, the date of the destruction of Jerusalem and its temple, would make these comments by John meaningless.

---

34 John Donahue, http://www.roman-emperors.org/ domitian.htm

We must also note the familiarity of John with the details of the Temple worship and not just it's existence. These details are so numerous that Alfred Edersheim says, "These naturally suggest the twofold inference that the Book of Revelation and the Fourth Gospel must have been written before the Temple services had actually ceased, and by one who had not merely been intimately acquainted with, but probably at one time an actor in them."[35]

THE POLITICAL/HISTORICAL SITUATION IN REVELATION

There are political/historical indicators in the Book of Revelation that demonstrate that it was written before June of A.D. 68. In Revelation 17 we read concerning Rome and its current leader.

> *Here is the mind which has wisdom. The seven heads are seven mountains on which the woman sits, and they are seven kings; five have fallen, one is, the other has not yet come; and when he comes, he must remain a little while. (Revelation 17:9-10, NASB95)*

The seven hills refer to Rome "the city on seven hills" as it was known from antiquity. Seven kings are mentioned, five have died, one is currently reigning, and one will succeed him but will only reign for a short period of time. Consider the history of the kings of Rome at this time.

The Five That "***Have Fallen***"

Julius Caesar	49-44 B.C.
Augustus Caesar	31 BC-A.D.14
Tiberius Caesar	A.D. 14-37
Gaius Caligula	A.D. 37-41
Claudius	A.D. 41-54

The One That "***Is***"

Caesar Nero	A.D. 54-68

The One That Has "***Not Yet Come***"

Galba	A.D. June 68 to January 69

He reigned but "***a little while***"

---

[35] Alfred Edersheim, The Temple (Grand Rapids, MI: Kregel Publications, 1874, 1997), 98.

Following these seven were:

Otho	A.D. 69
Vitellius	A.D. 69
Vespasian	A.D. 69-79
Titus	A.D. 79-81

No other period in Roman history fits John's picture so well, and as a result it appears quite likely that John wrote during the reign of Nero, which ended with his suicide in A.D. 68. Therefore John's book had to have been written before his death in A.D. 68.

THE TIME REFERENCES

The time indicators given in the book require a near date for its fulfillment. Throughout the book, John constantly alerts his readers to the imminent nature of the things that he is discussing with them. Examples include the following...

The Revelation of Jesus Christ, which God gave Him to show to His bond-servants, the things which must soon take place.... (*Revelation 1:1, NASB95*)

...for the time is near. (Revelation 1:3, NASB95)

...I am coming to you quickly.... (Revelation 2:16, NASB95)

I am coming quickly.... (Revelation 3:11, NASB95)

...the third woe is coming quickly. (Revelation 11:14, NASB95)

Behold, I am coming like a thief. (Revelation 16:15, NASB95)

...the things which must soon take place. (Revelation 22:6, NASB95)

And behold, I am coming quickly. (Revelation 22:7, NASB95)

...for the time is near. (Revelation 22:10, NASB95)

Behold, I am coming quickly.... (Revelation 22:12, NASB95)

Yes, I am coming quickly. (Revelation 22:20, NASB95)

Futurists are very aware of these verses but it is essential to their view that these verses be interpreted in such a way as to mean that when He comes it will be quick or sudden, not that it will soon occur. However, the soon occurrence, or nearness, is certainly the overwhelming thought behind these passages. Putting these verses in the greater context of the New Testament we read:

> *Truly I say to you, there are some of those who are standing here who will not taste death until they see the Son of Man coming in His kingdom. (Matthew 16:28, NASB95)*

> *Jesus said to him, "You have said it yourself; nevertheless I tell you, hereafter <u>you will see the Son of Man sitting at the right hand of Power, and coming on the clouds of heaven</u>." (Matthew 26:64, NASB95)*

> *Now these things happened to them as an example, and they were written for our instruction, upon whom <u>the ends of the ages have come</u>. (1 Corinthians 10:11, NASB95)*

> *For yet <u>in a very little while</u>, He who is coming will come, and will not delay. (Hebrews 10:37, NASB95)*

> *You too be patient; strengthen your hearts, for the coming of the Lord is <u>near</u>. (James 5:8, NASB95)*

> *The end of all things is <u>near</u>; therefore, be of sound judgement and sober spirit for the purpose of prayer. (1 Peter 4:7, NASB95)*

> *Children, <u>it is the last hour</u>; and just as you heard that antichrist is coming, even now many antichrists have appeared; from this we know that <u>it is the last hour</u>. (1 John 2:18, NASB95)*

These and other verses drive home the point with force. Matthew, Paul, James, Peter and John all made the same point—the Lord was coming very soon, indeed in their very generation.

CONCLUSION

The external evidence provided little in the way of satisfactory clues for the dating of John's Apocalypse. However, the collective internal evidence all points to the conclusion that John wrote his book before June of A.D. 68, while still learning the Greek language, while Judaism was Christianity's greatest enemy, while Jerusalem and the Temple still stood, while Emperor Nero, still lived, and while "soon," "near," and "quickly" would have still had meaning. As a result, we understand that John wrote the Book of Revelation in approximately A.D. 64-66 when all these historical facts were yet true. To argue otherwise, seems to leave the book open to the charge of fraudulence.

Now, let us relate the early date to the Preterist perspective. The early date allows one to take the "time references" in the Book of Revelation seriously as well as the Olivet Discourse in Matthew 24, which absolutely demands a first century setting. In addition, an early date allows us to take seriously the prophetic nature of the book. Revelation had significance to those that first read it; like the other prophetic books of the Bible; it met a present need in the life of its readers.

The Message, Purpose or Theme of the Book

It has been wisely said that, "...the purpose of a book is the key to its interpretation."[36] And this principle applies especially to the Book of Revelation, which has been terribly misunderstood because commentators are so confused about its purpose.

Fortunately, this is not a guessing game, for the Book of Revelation tells us just what its theme is:

> *Behold, He is coming with the clouds, and every eye will see Him, even those who pierced Him; and all the tribes of the earth [land] will mourn over Him. So it is to be. Amen. (Revelation 1:7, NASB95)*

---

[36] David S. Clark, 15.

The theme of the Book of Revelation is *the coming of Christ*. But that does not necessarily clear everything up, as there are at least six types of *comings* of God mentioned in the Bible. It is essential that we properly understand and, most importantly, distinguish each of them.

THE COMING IN THEOPHANIES

The *first* type of coming of Christ is His coming in Theophanies in the Old Testament.

> *They heard the sound of the Lord God walking in the garden in the cool of the day, and the man and his wife hid themselves from the presence of the Lord God among the trees of the garden (Genesis 3:8, NASB95)*

> *Now when Abram was ninety-nine years old, the Lord appeared to Abram and said to him, "I am God Almighty; Walk before Me, and be blameless. (Genesis 17:1, NASB95)*

THE COMING AT BETHLEHEM

The *second* type of coming of Christ is His incarnation coming at Bethlehem. The Gospels tell the story.

> *'And you, Bethlehem, land of Judah, are by no means least among the leaders of Judah; for out of you shall <u>come</u> forth a Ruler who will shepherd My people Israel.' (Matthew 2:6, NASB95)*

In addition, John mentions it in his first epistle using a different but related word.

> *You know that He <u>appeared</u> in order to take away sins; and in Him there is no sin. No one who abides in Him sins; no one who sins has seen Him or knows Him. Little children, make sure no one deceives you; the one who practices righteousness is righteous, just as He is righteous; the one who practices sin is of the devil; for the devil has sinned from the beginning. The Son of God <u>appeared</u> for this purpose, to destroy the works of the devil. (1 John 3:5-8, NASB95)*

Since the point is obvious and not under doubt by Christians we will not belabor the point. Yet it was a coming by Christ.

THE FINAL COMING AT THE END OF TIME

The *third* type of coming is His Final Coming at the end of time and the only one many Christians consider when discussing this topic and this book of the Bible. We find it mentioned in several verses in the New Testament.

> *They also said, "Men of Galilee, why do you stand looking into the sky? This Jesus, who has been taken up from you into heaven, will <u>come</u> in just the same way as you have watched Him go into heaven." (Acts 1:11, NASB95)*

> *But we do not want you to be uninformed, brethren, about those who are asleep, so that you will not grieve as do the rest who have no hope. For if we believe that Jesus died and rose again, even so God will bring with Him those who have fallen asleep in Jesus. For this we say to you by the word of the Lord, that we who are alive and remain until <u>the coming of the Lord</u>, will not precede those who have fallen asleep. For the Lord Himself will descend from heaven with a shout, with the voice of the archangel and with the trumpet of God, and the dead in Christ will rise first. Then we who are alive and remain will be caught up together with them in the clouds to meet the Lord in the air, and so we shall always be with the Lord. (1 Thessalonians 4:13-17, NASB95)*

> *But now Christ has been raised from the dead, the first fruits of those who are asleep. For since by a man came death, by a man also came the resurrection of the dead. For as in Adam all die, so also in Christ all will be made alive. But each in his own order: Christ the first fruits, after that those who are Christ's <u>at His coming</u>, then comes the end, when He hands over the kingdom to the God and Father, when He has abolished all rule and all authority and power. For He must reign until He has put all His enemies under His feet. The last enemy that will be abolished is death. (1 Corinthians 15:20-26, NASB95)*

This coming is yet in our future for it is the coming at the end of time. More need not be said on this topic at this point, since it is the most familiar of the comings of God.

THE COMING TO THE FATHER - THE ASCENSION

The *fourth* type of coming is Jesus coming to God the Father in heaven. From our point of view we see it as a going from earth to heaven, but the Scripture pictures it as a coming of the Son to the Father after His resurrection and at His ascension.

> *I kept looking in the night visions, and behold, with the clouds of heaven One like a Son of Man was <u>coming</u>, and He <u>came</u> up to the Ancient of Days and was presented before Him. (Daniel 7:13, NASB95)*

This occurred after the resurrection and at His ascension.

A SPIRIT COMING

The *fifth* type of coming is a Spirit coming.

> *I will ask the Father, and He will give you another Helper, that He may be with you forever; that is the Spirit of truth, whom the world cannot receive, because it does not see Him or know Him, but you know Him because He abides with you and will be in you. I will not leave you as orphans; I will <u>come</u> to you. (John 14:16-18, NASB95)*

This occurred at Pentecost with the descent of the Holy Spirit.

THE COMING IN JUDGEMENT

The *sixth* type of coming is a coming of God in judgement. Many examples of this type of coming are found in Scripture.

> *Therefore remember from where you have fallen, and repent and do the deeds you did at first; or else I am <u>coming</u> to you and will remove your lampstand out of its place — unless you repent. (Revelation 2:5, NASB95)*

The Book of Revelation is about a judgement *coming* of Christ; as simple as that may seem, in fact, it is not simple because this *coming* of Christ is not His Second Coming. It is, instead, a judgement coming against Jerusalem,

Israel and as seen in the above verse, His Church. It is typical of many such sign-comings found in the Old Testament. They may be typical and common to Scripture but most Christians have never heard of them. "Cloud-comings are frequent prophetic emblems in the Old Testament. They serve as indicators of divine visitations of judgement upon ancient, historical nations. God 'comes' in judicial judgement upon Israel's enemies in general (Psa. 18:7-15; 104:3), upon Egypt (Isa. 19:1), upon disobedient Israel in the Old Testament (Joel 2:1,2), and so forth."[37]

A COMING JUDGEMENT AGAINST ISRAEL

Jesus Himself made this very point that He was coming in judgement against Israel in His earthly ministry.

> *"Therefore when the owner of the vineyard comes, what will he do to those vine-growers?" They said to Him, "He will bring those wretches to a wretched end, and will rent out the vineyard to other vine-growers who will pay him the proceeds at the proper seasons." .... "Therefore I say to you, the kingdom of God will be taken away from you and given to a people, producing the fruit of it. And he who falls on this stone will be broken to pieces; but on whomever it falls, it will scatter him like dust." When the chief priests and the Pharisees heard His parables, they understood that He was speaking about them. (Matthew 21:40-41, 43-45, NASB95)*

Here Jesus clearly promises He will *come*, but it will be a coming unto judgement. "Our Lord here causes them to pass that sentence of destruction upon themselves which was literally executed about forty years afterwards by the Roman armies."[38] Consider also these passages.

> *...and the rest seized his slaves and mistreated them and killed them. But the king was enraged, and he sent his armies and destroyed those murderers and set their city on fire. (Matthew 22:6-7, NASB95)*

---

[37] Kenneth L. Gentry, The Revelation of Jesus Christ, Biblical Issues Series (NP, 2001), 11.

[38] The Treasury of Scripture Knowledge, Introduction by R.A. Torrey (Oak Harbor, WA: Logos Research Systems, Inc., 1995), Mt. 21:41.

Which is exactly what He did in A.D. 70 with the destruction of Jerusalem. Our point in this section is that there is a coming judgement against Israel, which is what Jesus predicted here.

> *"You serpents, you brood of vipers, how will you escape the*
> *sentence of hell?" Therefore, behold, I am sending you prophets*
> *and wise men and scribes; some of them you will kill and crucify,*
> *and some of them you will scourge in your synagogues, and*
> *persecute from city to city, so that upon you may fall the guilt of*
> *all the righteous blood shed on earth [land], from the blood of*
> *righteous Abel to the blood of Zechariah, the son of Berechiah,*
> *whom you murdered between the temple and the altar. "Truly I*
> *say to you, all these things will come upon <u>this generation</u>.*
> *"Jerusalem, Jerusalem, who kills the prophets and stones those*
> *who are sent to her! How often I wanted to gather your children*
> *together, the way a hen gathers her chicks under her wings, and*
> *you were unwilling. "Behold, your house is being left to you*
> *desolate! "For I say to you, from now on you will not see Me until*
> *you say, 'Blessed is He who <u>comes</u> in the name of the Lord!' "*
> *(Matthew 23:33-39, NASB95)*

How could He have made it clearer? He was coming in judgment upon the very generation that He was speaking to.

In summary, Revelation is about the coming of Christ in judgement against Israel, which will be discussed, in great detail later in this commentary.

The Purposes of this Judgement Coming

IT CLOSES THE OLD COVENANT AND IMPLEMENTS THE NEW COVENANT

The Book of Revelation is primarily about the close of the old covenant that God had with the people of Israel and the implementation of the new covenant, which was made with Christ and His Church. Christ Himself alluded to this in His conversation with the woman at the well.

> *"Our fathers worshiped in this mountain, and you people say that*
> *in Jerusalem is the place where men ought to worship." Jesus*
> *said to her, "Woman, believe Me, an hour is coming when neither*

*in this mountain nor in Jerusalem will you worship the Father.
You worship what you do not know; we worship what we know,
for salvation is from the Jews. But an hour is coming, and now is,
when the true worshipers will worship the Father in spirit and
truth; for such people the Father seeks to be His worshipers."
(John 4:20-23, NASB95)*

While this may be a rather thinly veiled discussion of the coming change in
the covenant, the writer of Hebrews speaks more directly when he tells of
*"removing of those things which can be shaken" "so that those things
which cannot be shaken may remain."* That which can be shaken is old
Israel; that which cannot be shaken is the true worship of Christ in the New
Covenant Church.

> *See to it that you do not refuse Him who is speaking. For if those
> did not escape when they refused him who warned them on earth,
> much less will we escape who turn away from Him who warns
> from heaven. And His voice shook the earth then, but now He has
> promised, saying, "Yet once more I will shake not only the earth,
> but also the heaven." This expression, "Yet once more," denotes
> the removing of those things which can be shaken, as of created
> things, so that those things which cannot be shaken may remain.
> Therefore, since we receive a kingdom which cannot be shaken,
> let us show gratitude, by which we may offer to God an
> acceptable service with reverence and awe; for our God is a
> consuming fire. (Hebrews 12:25-29, NASB95)*

Israel of old had come to the mount of God to receive from Him the Ten
Commandments. The Mount Sinai experience was a frightening one for it
was a mountain that burned with fire. But the coming of God's people to
the heavenly Jerusalem was of greater import says the author of Hebrews.
The first kingdom was temporary and was passing away. The second
kingdom, the new covenant, is permanent and will not pass away. Hebrews
is telling us that God's word speaking the gospel today must be listened to
with even greater attention and faith than Israel did in receiving the law at
the mountain. There they received a covenant that passes away, but now
the Church receives a covenant that never passes away.

The issue here is a faithfulness or faithlessness to God by Israel. God's
relation to Israel is by Covenant or treaty. One kingdom, old Israel, is

replaced with another, the Church. In doing so, one Covenant is replaced with another, the new covenant.

> *When He said, "A new covenant," He has made the first obsolete. But whatever is becoming <u>obsolete and growing old is ready to disappear</u>. (Hebrews 8:13, NASB95)*

These passages in Hebrews are critical to understanding New Testament theology. Although the new covenant had come, with its institution by Christ at the Lord's Supper, yet the old covenant was also in force in this age of transition between Christ first coming at Bethlehem and his judgement coming to Jerusalem in A.D. 70. But this transitionary age would only last one generation, for Christ had *made the first obsolete* (Hebrews 8:13) and it was therefore *ready to disappear* (Hebrews 8:13). Revelation is the story of how God made it disappear.

IT REVEALS THE LORD'S DIVORCE OF ISRAEL AND THE TAKING OF A NEW BRIDE – THE CHURCH

Revelation is about Christ' judgement coming to punish Israel, His former wife, for her spiritual adultery, and the establishment of the new covenant family in His marriage to a new bride, the Church. God's relationship to the Church is the same as God's relationship had been to Israel of the Old Testament; namely, He is the husband of his bride or wife. In the Old Testament we read these passages that make that point with clarity:[39]

> *"Then I passed by you and saw you, and behold, you were at the time for love; so I spread My skirt over you and covered your nakedness. I also swore to you and entered into <u>a [marriage] covenant</u> with you so that you became Mine," declares the Lord God. (Ezekiel 16:8, NASB95)*

> *"How languishing is your heart," declares the Lord God, "while you do all these things, the actions of a bold-faced harlot. When you built your shrine at the beginning of every street and made your high place in every square, in disdaining money, you were not like a harlot. <u>You adulteress wife</u>, who takes strangers instead of her <u>husband</u>!" (Ezekiel 16:30-32, NASB95)*

---

[39] See also Isaiah 62:4; Jeremiah 3:14, 20; Hosea 1:2; 2:2, 7, 16; 5:4, 9:1.

Isaiah, speaking at a time before God divorced Israel says,

> *Thus says the Lord, "Where is <u>the certificate of divorce</u> by which I have sent your mother away? Or to whom of My creditors did I sell you? Behold, you were sold for your iniquities, and for your transgressions your mother was sent away." (Isaiah 50:1, NASB95)*

> *For your husband is your Maker, whose name is the Lord of hosts; and your <u>Redeemer</u> is the Holy One of Israel, who is called the God of all the earth. (Isaiah 54:5, NASB95)*

> *"...not like the covenant which I made with their fathers in the day I took them by the hand to bring them out of the land of Egypt, My covenant which they broke, although I was a <u>husband</u> to them," declares the Lord. (Jeremiah 31:32, NASB95)*

In time, God divorced the ten northern tribes called Israel. God brought a covenant lawsuit against the ten tribes, found her guilty, divorced her, and put her to death for breaking the covenant through her spiritual adulteries. He did so by destroying her as a nation, and sending her survivors into captivity and exile. See how the following verses speak to this experience.

> *And I saw that for all the adulteries of faithless Israel, I had sent her away and given her <u>a writ of divorce</u>, yet her treacherous sister Judah did not fear; but she went and was a harlot also. (Jeremiah 3:8, NASB95)*

> *Therefore, I gave her into the hand of her lovers, into the hand of the Assyrians, after whom she lusted. They uncovered her nakedness; they took her sons and her daughters, but they slew her with the sword. Thus she became a byword among women, and they executed judgements on her. (Ezekiel 23:9-10, NASB95)*

But this theme goes back further than Israel and Judah. Paul draws that to our attention in Galatians chapter four. There he notes the relationship between Hagar and Ishmael who represents the "Present Jerusalem" and Sara and Isaac who represent the "Jerusalem above."

> *But what does the Scripture say?*

"Cast out the bondwoman and her son,
For the son of the bondwoman shall not be an heir with the son of
the free woman." (Galatians 4:30, NASB95)

So this imagery of casting out the rejected that the chosen might fully fill the role of God's true people has deep roots in Scripture. And notice this is between two women there as it is in Revelation—the fornicating harlot—the "present Jerusalem," and the virgin bride—the "Jerusalem above" or as John calls her the "new Jerusalem."

The penalty for harlotry in Scripture is death and the Book of Revelation details how that sentence was carried out on Judah, as it had been earlier on the ten northern tribes. The nation, city, and the temple are going to be destroyed. Old Testament Israel will no longer exist; the old covenant is abolished. God is now married to another, the Church; the new covenant is fully instituted. The Book of Revelation "...predicts the curses which are about to be brought upon the Judaistic system and its people because of their violations of the covenant."[40] "Thus, the theme of Revelation is the execution of God's divorce decree against Israel, her subsequent capital punishment and cremation, followed by his turning to take a new bride, the Church."[41]

But if you or your sons indeed turn away from following Me, and
do not keep My commandments and My statutes which I have set
before you, and go and serve other gods and worship them, then I
will cut off Israel from the land which I have given them, and the
house which I have consecrated for My name, I will cast out of
My sight. So Israel will become a proverb and a byword among
all peoples. And this house will become a heap of ruins; everyone
who passes by will be astonished and hiss and say, 'Why has the
Lord done thus to this land and to this house?' And they will say,
'Because they forsook the Lord their God, who brought their
fathers out of the land of Egypt, and adopted other gods and
worshiped them and served them, therefore the Lord has brought
all this adversity on them.' (1 Kings 9:6-9, NASB95)

---

[40] J. E. Leonard, <u>I Will Be Their God</u> (Chicago, IL: Laudemont Press, 1992), 152.

[41] Kenneth L. Gentry Jr., <u>The Revelation of Jesus Christ</u>, 20.

IT PREDICTS THE POURING OUT OF GOD'S WRATH ON ISRAEL FOR MURDERING HIS SON

Revelation is a pouring out of God's wrath on Israel for murdering God's Son. The Jews demanded Christ's crucifixion and are directly responsible for his murder. Naturally, that act is not without consequence, and that consequence is described in the Book of Revelation.[42]

> So when the chief priests and the officers saw Him, they cried out saying, "<u>Crucify, crucify!</u>" Pilate said to them, "Take Him yourselves and crucify Him, for I find no guilt in Him." (John 19:6, NASB95)

> ...let it be known to all of you and to all the people of Israel, that by the name of Jesus Christ the Nazarene, <u>whom you crucified,</u> whom God raised from the dead—by this name this man stands here before you in good health. (Acts 4:10, NASB95)

> As a result of this Pilate made efforts to release Him, but the Jews cried out saying, "If you release this Man, you are no friend of Caesar; everyone who makes himself out to be a king opposes Caesar." (John 19:12, NASB95)

> And he said to the Jews, "Behold, your King!" So they cried out, "Away with Him, away with Him, crucify Him!" Pilate said to them, "Shall I crucify your King?" The chief priests answered, "<u>We have no king but Caesar.</u>" (John 19:14-15, NASB95)

"...the crucifixion is the beginning of that process of which the destruction of the city is the end."[43]

Our study in the Book of Revelation will clarify the relationship and consequence of the murder of Jesus the Christ of Israel and the destruction of Jerusalem.

---

[42] Acts 2:22, 23, 36; 3:14, 15; 4:8-10; 5:30; 10:39; I Thessalonians 2:14-16.

[43] Philip Carrington, 252.

IT COMMUNICATES HOPE TO THE CHURCH ON THE VERGE OF PERSECUTION

The Book of Revelation, along with its message of doom for Israel, is a message of hope to the church, God's new bride. As Dr. Jay Adams says, "At bottom the book of Revelation is a message of encouragement and exhortation to the churches of Asia Minor in view of portending persecutions of great magnitude."[44] On the verge of persecutions that will prove to be vicious beyond comprehension, the church is forewarned and assured that God is in charge and will from the misery and chaos bring victory to His church. "By predicting events shortly to come in great detail—events they will see transpire before their very eyes exactly as predicted—they will recognize that God is in control of history."[45]

Jay Adams points out an important verse in Daniel that focuses on what God is doing in the period of Revelation.

> *I kept looking, and that horn was waging war with the saints and overpowering them until the Ancient of Days came and judgement was passed in favor of the saints of the Highest One, and the time arrived when the saints took possession of the kingdom. (Daniel 7:21-22, NASB95)*

This passage details several critical points of prophecy. "The three things mentioned in that passage are primary in Revelation. The brief successful persecution of the church; God's vindication of his suffering people by the judgement of the persecutor, and the establishment of the new kingdom of God."[46] Revelation is Daniel 7 come to fulfillment.

IT PICTURES THE CONSUMMATION OF THE AGE – THE ENDING OF THE JEWISH ERA

The destruction of Jerusalem, the theme of the Book of Revelation, is a sovereign act by God that closes the Old Testament sacrificial system. See Hebrews 8-10.

---

[44] Jay E. Adams, The Time is at Hand (Greenville, SC: A Press, 1987), 46.

[45] Jay E. Adams, and Michael W. Carroll, Visions of the Revelation (Virginia Beach, VA: The Donning Company Publishers, 1991), 22.

[46] Jay E. Adams, The Time is at Hand, 48.

... but now once at the consummation of the ages He has been manifested to put away sin by the sacrifice of Himself. (Hebrews 9:26, NASB95)

The Jewish age is about to end. The writer of the book of Hebrews describes his time as *the consummation of the ages*. This is not the end of the world. That is not what he was talking about, but the end of the Jewish era. The sacrificial system is no longer required or even appropriate with the finished work of Christ.

IT PROMOTES THE WORLDWIDE FOCUS OF THE GREAT COMMISSION

The destruction of Jerusalem frees Christianity from Judaism and allows it to turn its focus worldwide in fulfilling its great commission.

And Jesus came up and spoke to them, saying, "All authority has been given to Me in heaven and on earth. Go therefore and make disciples of all the nations, baptizing them in the name of the Father and the Son and the Holy Spirit, teaching them to observe all that I commanded you; and lo, I am with you always, even to the end of the age." (Matthew 28:18-20, NASB95)

For He Himself is our peace, who made both groups into one and broke down the barrier of the dividing wall, by abolishing in His flesh the enmity, which is the Law of commandments contained in ordinances, so that in Himself He might make the two into one new man, thus establishing peace, and might reconcile them both in one body to God through the cross, by it having put to death the enmity. (Ephesians 2:14-16, NASB95)

In the early years of Christianity, the Church was tied to unbelieving Israel. In experiencing the judgement of God for its many sins, Israel is set apart as something other than the people of God. That role is now the exclusive property of the Church. The Church is now free to preach the Gospel to the world, no longer fearing the disapproval of Judaism.

In conclusion, although the purposes of Revelation are multifaceted, they are summed up with admiral simplicity in Revelation 1:7.

> *Behold, He is coming with the clouds, and every eye will see Him,*
> *even those who pierced Him; and all the tribes of the earth [land]*
> *will mourn over Him. So it is to be. Amen. (Revelation 1:7,*
> *NASB95)*

Its Message to the Current Church

When approaching the books of Scripture, a sound tool of interpretation is to remember that the books' messages are directed at historical people in historical circumstances, but that those same messages continue to have relevance for those reading the books today. We have already seen how we can best understand the Book of Revelation when we remember that it was sent to a group of Christians who were warned of God's coming judgement on the enemies of His Church. In the first century, Israel rejected God and was in turn rejected by God. Judaism and the Roman Empire wrecked havoc upon God's people. God responded in judgement on the enemies of His Church.

The reader, seeking to grasp fully the Apocalypse's message, should also call to mind that in other eras, unfaithfulness by God's people and new enemies of the Church, are to be faced with fresh applications from the Book of Revelation. This should be applied to the new and current evil, within and without the Church. Liberalism in the Church corresponds to Israel's unfaithfulness. Roman Catholicism and Islam replaced the religious enemy of Judaism; and Communism and all forms of political totalitarianism have replaced the political enemy of the Roman Empire. How are we to deal with these enemies—and the new ones that will follow? And most importantly, how will God deal with these enemies of His people? Answers and applications from the Book of Revelation will be of incalculable value in determining the actions of the Church to new, yet old enemies.

Therefore, while this commentary focuses primarily on the one historical interpretation, the reader must not cease to apply this book's message to their current experiences.

The Audience of the Book – The Seven Churches in Asia Minor

An interesting question arises when one ponders Revelation. The book was written about the destruction of Jerusalem; that is clear but it may be asked, why was the book then sent to seven churches in Asia Minor? In essence, it was written about a problem in one area, but why then sent to seven churches in another area? Does that make sense and can it be explained?

THE CHURCHES IN ISRAEL ALREADY KNEW OF THE COMING JUDGEMENT

When wondering why the Book of Revelation was sent to the Asia Minor churches, an answer begins to crystallize when one considers that the churches in Israel already had a message of the coming destruction of Jerusalem, namely in the three Synoptic gospels which were written in the early A.D. 60's.[47] That being the case, they did not necessarily need a second (or fourth) warning of its coming destruction. They were equipped with Christ's own explanation of the coming tribulation, and took it so seriously that they responded as Christ had instructed them to and fled at the opportune moment. The churches in Asia would have had access to these gospels as well of course; but the message in those gospels is clearly to and about the Jews of the Covenant. Its application to the broader Church would not necessarily be clear. Revelation broadens that message by sending it to seven churches in Asia.

IT PREPARED THE CHURCH AT LARGE FOR THE COMING JUDGEMENT

Consider what a shock this event was to the Christian world at large. If the young Church had not been warned of this terrible coming tribulation, would they not have been in a state of alarm and shakened in their faith?

But, the judgements spoken of in Revelation are not limited to the Church of the first century. There would be trials for all God's people through the ages. Knowledge of God's dealings with evil and His love for the Church would strengthen faith and engender resolve in the dark days of the Church through the ages.

---

[47] That information is found in Matthew 24, written about 64 A.D., Mark 13, written about 62 A.D. and Luke 21, written about 63 A.D.

It Informed Jewish Christians

The Church, before the fall of Jerusalem in A.D. 70, was predominately a Jewish Church. These Jewish believers in particular would have a heightened interest in Judea and its future. So, no matter where these Christian Jews may have lived in the Roman world, they would want to know God's plan for Israel. Plus we have the example of the Greek churches giving gifts for the persecuted Church in Jerusalem. We therefore have a clear indication how the various regions of the Church showed concern about the condition of the Church in Jerusalem.

It Went to the Center of the Christian Community

Consider the fact that Asia Minor, at this time, was the very center of the Christian community. To be sure, some believers were found to the west in Greece and Rome; others were found to the east and south in Syria, Israel and Egypt. But being in the very center of the then current Christian civilization the Church in Asia Minor was in an ideal place to forward the message to the entire Christian world. Carrington makes this very point saying, "But it is obvious too that the Asian churches must be regarded in some sense as central and representative of all Christendom. .... For a time the primacy of Christendom rested over Ephesus. ... Ephesus, therefore, was leading and guiding Christendom; it actually was central, representative, and primatial."[48]

It Went to John's Particular Flock

At this time, John was the pastor of the church in Ephesus and spiritual leader to Asia Minor. Where else would he be expected to send a message from God but to his congregation and those under his spiritual oversight?

So, we conclude, Asia Minor was the best of all places for such a book to be sent. It sat in the hub of Christianity, amidst a Christian-Jewish people, in the place of coming persecution and amongst John's ministry responsibilities.

---

[48] Philip Carrington, 92.

The Book of Revelation and Its Relationship to the Olivet Discourse[49]

In Matthew 24, Mark 13:1-37, and Luke 21:5-36 we have what is known as Christ's Olivet Discourse. Here Christ deals with God's coming judgement on Israel, Jerusalem, and the Temple. Many theologians have convincingly argued that the Olivet discourse, sometimes called the *little apocalypse*, is the brief version of the Book of Revelation.[50] Milton Terry says, "The things thus destined to come to pass soon after the composition of this book (Revelation) were in substance the same as those of which Jesus discoursed on the Mount of Olives...."[51] Nor should it be assumed that this view is modern or contemporary for it was utilized as early as the fourth century when the church father Eusebius (A.D. 260-340) used Josephus's history of the Jewish War (A.D. 67-70) to illustrate the fulfilling of the Olivet Prophecy (*Eccl. Hist.* 3:5-9)."[52]

And indeed, the Book of Revelation covers the same material as that of the Olivet Discourse.

The Book of Revelation	The Olivet Discourse
Revelation 2-3 Deals with false apostles, persecution, lawlessness, love grown cold, and the duty of perseverance	Matthew 24:3-5, 9-13 Deals with false Christ's and prophets, persecution, lawlessness, love grown cold, and the duty of perseverance
Revelation 4-7 – The Seven Seals Deals with wars, famines, and earthquakes	Matthew 24:6-8 Deals with wars, famines, and earthquakes
Revelation 8-14 – The Seven Trumpets Tells of the Church's witness to	Matthew 24:14-27 Tells of the Church's witness to the world, her flight, the Great

---

49 Excellent studies in Matthew 24 include: Gary DeMar, Last Days of Madness (Powder Springs, GA: American Vision Press, 1999), and Kenneth L. Gentry, Jr., Perilous Times: A Study in Eschatological Evil (Texarkana, AR: Covenant Media Press, 1973).

50 J. Stuart Russell, The Parousia (Grand Rapids, MI: Baker Books, 1887, 1999), 379.

51 Milton S. Terry, Biblical Apocalyptics, 276.

52 C. Marvin Pate, Editor, 53.

the world, her flight into the wilderness, the Great Tribulation, and the False Prophet	Tribulation, and false prophets
Revelation 15-22 – The Seven Chalices Describes the darkening of the Beast kingdom, the destruction of the Harlot, the gathering of eagles over Jerusalem's corpse, and the gathering of the Church into the Kingdom	Matthew 24:28-31 Describes the same events[53]

Having demonstrated in general terms how the Olivet discourse and the Book of Revelation parallel, let's look at some specific examples.

BOTH TEACH A SOON FULFILLMENT

First, the urgency in time is similar between the two. Both teach a soon fulfillment of their prophecies.

> *Truly I say to you, this generation will not pass away until all these things take place. (Matthew 24:34, NASB95)*

> *The Revelation of Jesus Christ, which God gave Him to show to His bond-servants, <u>the things which must soon take place</u>; and He sent and communicated it by His angel to His bond-servant John.... (Revelation 1:1, NASB95)*

BOTH BLEND TWO KEY OLD TESTAMENT PASSAGES

Next, the blending of two key Old Testament passages is similar. Those passages are:

> *I will pour out on the house of David and on the inhabitants of Jerusalem, the Spirit of grace and of supplication, so that they will look on Me whom they have pierced; and they will mourn for*

---

53 David Chilton, <u>The Days of Vengeance</u> (Tyler, TX: Dominion Press, 1987), 20.

Him, as one mourns for an only son, and they will weep bitterly over Him like the bitter weeping over a firstborn. (Zechariah 12:10, NASB95)

I kept looking in the night visions, and behold, with the clouds of heaven One like a Son of Man was coming, and He came up to the Ancient of Days and was presented before Him. (Daniel 7:13, NASB95)

Notice that Christ's statement in Matthew combines these two passages. They are used in such a similar way in both places because they are dealing with the same instance in the New Testament era.

And then the sign of the Son of Man will appear in the sky, and then all the tribes of the earth [land] will mourn, and they will see the Son of Man coming on the clouds of the sky with power and great glory. (Matthew 24:30, NASB95)

Now notice Christ's statement in Revelation doing the same thing.

Behold, He is coming with the clouds, and every eye will see Him, even those who pierced Him; and all the tribes of the earth [land] will mourn over Him. So it is to be. Amen. (Revelation 1:7, NASB95)

BOTH HAVE A THEME OF JUDGEMENT

Three, notice the judgement theme in both. The great tribulation is the central element in both the Olivet Discourse and the Book of Revelation.

For then there will be a <u>great tribulation</u>, such as has not occurred since the beginning of the world until now, nor ever will. (Matthew 24:21, NASB95)

Now compare this verse in Matthew with these two in Revelation.

Behold, I will throw her on a bed of sickness, and those who commit adultery with her into <u>great tribulation</u>, unless they repent of her deeds. (Revelation 2:22, NASB95)

I said to him, "My lord, you know." And he said to me, "These are the ones who come out of the <u>great tribulation</u>, and they have washed their robes and made them white in the blood of the Lamb." (Revelation 7:14, NASB95)

BOTH SPEAK OF THE DESTRUCTION OF THE TEMPLE

Last, look at the role the destruction of the Temple plays in both.

And He said to them, "Do you not see all these things? Truly I say to you, not one stone here will be left upon another, which will not be torn down." (Matthew 24:2, NASB95)

Then there was given me a measuring rod like a staff; and someone said, "Get up and measure the temple of God and the altar, and those who worship in it. Leave out the court which is outside the temple and do not measure it, for it has been given to the nations; and they will tread under foot the holy city for forty-two months." (Revelation 11:1-2, NASB95)

As B. B. Warfield said of Revelation, "…he who can understand our Lord's great discourse concerning the last things (Matt. 24), cannot fail to understand the Apocalypse, which is founded on that discourse and scarcely advances beyond it."[54]

The Outline of the Book

The most obvious outline of the book is found in Revelation ch. 1.

Therefore write the things which you have seen, and the things which are, and the things which will take place after these things. (Revelation 1:19, NASB95)

---

[54] Benjamin B. Warfield, "*The Apocalypse*," in <u>Selected Shorter Writings of Benjamin B. Warfield</u> (Nutley, NJ: Presbyterian and Reformed Publishing Co., 1973), vol. II, 652f.

In addition, we might see Revelation as divided up into seven cycles of judgement, each cycle leading to a description of the Second Coming.[55] It has been noticed that "...more than once, when the end is nearly reached, the writer turns back to the beginning...."[56] So, what we appear to have in Revelation is not a linear unfolding of events but seven climatic cycles telling and retelling the story of God's coming judgement from one angle, then another. "The book cannot be understood as moving directly in chronological order from the time of the apostolic church to the final consummation of all things, for midway through it the birth of Christ and his attempted murder by the satanically controlled powers of the state are described (Rev. 12:1-5)."[57]

As Pate says, "John's spiral structure allows occasional backward glances and a reconsidering of events from different angles, rather than a relentless chronological progression."[58]   Again following this thought further, Rushdoony concludes, "It is thus apparent that the visions are in a sense repetitious in that they cover the same ground, while new, in that they cast further light on the same subject."[59] Interestingly, the Epistle of 1 John, also written by the Apostle John, uses a similar cycle of repetition in its subject matter. Putting the two together we get:

THE THINGS WHICH YOU HAVE SEEN   1

a.	Title and Superscription	1:1-3
b.	Salutation 1:4-6	
c.	Apocalyptic Announcement	1:7-8
d.	Introductory Christophany	1:9-20

THE THINGS WHICH ARE   2-3

I.	To the Church in Ephesus	2:1-7
II.	To the Church in Smyrna	2:8-11

---

55 R. C. Sproul, Editior, New Geneva Study Bible (Nashville, TN: Thomas Nelson Publishers, 1995), 2005.

56 Henry Barclay Swete, The Apocalypse of St. John (Grand Rapids, MI: Wm. B. Eerdmans Publishing Co., 1906), xliii.

57 O. Palmer Robertson, The Israel of God (Phillipsburg, NY, P&R Publishing Co, 2000), 153.

58 C. Marvin Pate, Editor, 38.

59 John Rousas Rushdoony, 141.

Chapter 1
Vision of the Son of Man

The Revelation of Jesus Christ

1:1 The Revelation of Jesus Christ, which God gave Him to show to His bond-servants, the things which must soon take place; and He sent and communicated it by His angel to His bond-servant John.... The Greek word for **revelation (1:1)** is ἀποκάλυψις (*apokalupsis*) or apocalypse, and is made up of ἀπο—"from," and κάλυψις—"to cover, hide, or conceal." When you move "from" cover, hide, or conceal, you move toward "revelation, disclosure, manifestation."[60] As indicated in the word itself, it is not the purpose of the Revelation to hide, but to reveal and therefore we should expect to understand this book. It is not a book of hallucinations; it is a revelation (singular, it is one revelation, not many) from Jesus Christ which was given to Him by the Father. It is not primarily a revelation *about* Jesus Christ; it is a revelation *of* Jesus Christ. It is a prophecy from God the Father, through Jesus Christ, to **His bond-servants (1:1).**

> And he said to me, "Do not seal up the words of the prophecy of this book, for the time is near." (Revelation 22:10, NASB95)[61]

Therefore, we should expect to understand this book for it was written to be understood. However, it will be impossible to do so without constant attention to the Old Testament. As Benjamin Warfield said, "John's Apocalypse need not be other than easy: all its symbols are either obvious natural ones, or else have their roots planted in the Old testament poets and prophets and the figurative language of Jesus and his apostles. No one who knows his Bible need despair of reading this book with profit."[62]

---

60 Thoralf Gilbrant, International Editor, <u>The New Testament Greek-English Dictionary</u> (Springfield, MO: The Complete Biblical Library, 1991), Vol. Alpha-Gamma, 368.

61 Revelation 1:3, 22:6, 18, 19.

62 Benjamin B. Warfield, vol. 2, 652.

The phrase, **which God gave Him (1:1)** "...shows the office of Christ as revealer of the Godhead."[63]   Christ holds and exercises the offices of prophet, priest and king. In the Book of Revelation, we primarily see Him exercising His office of prophet and revealing to us the divine plan of the Father. Although it certainly reveals Him as king and priest as well. Jesus in His high priestly prayer says to the Father "...*the words which You gave Me I have given to them...*" John 17:8: NASB95. The same thing is happening again here in Revelation.

Revelation, then, was given to **show (1:1)**, that is, "to make known the character or significance of something by visual, auditory, gestural, or linguistic means...."[64] Its purpose is not to hide, but to disclose. If its message is hidden, it is contrary to God's purpose. Neither was the message for the apostle John only, but it was for Christ's **bond-servants (1:1)**, especially the seven churches in Asia.

This book, like all the books of the Bible, was written to a contemporary audience. In this case, to seven churches in Asia Minor, a geographic region near the Middle East now called Turkey. Although we instinctively seek to apply Scripture to our own day and life, it is not really possible to do that correctly until we have asked the question, "what message did it have to its original audience?"

Some believe this book, in reality, had little or nothing to say to its original audience, but was instead written for an audience some two or three thousand years in the future, however, the statements of the book assert otherwise. John says that the things contained in the Apocalypse **must soon take place (1:1)**. Look at the Greek word **must (1:1)**, δεῖ (*deî*), it means, "that which must necessarily take place, often with the implication of inevitability."[65] **Must (1:1)**, then, sets the tone by giving the book an air of urgency and immediacy for **things which must <u>soon take place</u> (1:1)**. The future is determined by Divine decree.

John says that these things are about to happen and drives home the point by concluding the introduction with "...*the time is <u>near</u>*..." (1:3). This

---

[63] David S. Clark, 22.

[64] J. P. Louw, <u>Greek-English lexicon of the New Testament: Based on Semantic Domains</u> (New York, NY: United Bible Societies, 1996, c1989), LN 28.47.

[65] J. P. Louw, LN 28.47.

sentiment of immediacy colors the whole book for John, as if to put time sensitive covers around the book. Revelation concludes by saying, *"...the Lord, the God of the spirits of the prophets, sent His angel to show to His bond-servants the things which must <u>soon</u> take place..."* (Revelation 22:6, NASB95). And then he adds, *"<u>Do not seal up the words</u> of the prophecy of this book, for <u>the time is near</u>"* (Revelation 22:10, NASB95). In contrast to John's message, compare his words of impending expectation with those of Daniel. *"But as for you, Daniel, <u>conceal these words</u> and <u>seal up the book</u> until the end of time..."* (Daniel 12:4, NASB95). And these words, *"Go your way, Daniel, for these words are <u>concealed</u> and <u>sealed</u> up until the end time"* (Daniel 12:9, NASB95).

What we have here are instructions for Daniel to *"conceal these words"* and *"seal up the book"* because there will yet be a considerable amount of time before they are fulfilled. How long? Daniel wrote about 530 B.C. These concluding words from Daniel refer to the coming of political leaders and events of the distant future, some of them reaching even to the time of Christ. There was a delay of 344 to 558 years before these events of Daniel were to occur. That being such a long time, and the prophecy having no immediate relevance to Daniel's current audience, he is told to *"seal up the book"* until a later date when all this would come to pass and make sense.

On the other hand, the book of Revelation is nearly 2000 years old and, according to some, we have yet to see the first prophecy fulfilled, even though we are told *"<u>do not seal up the words</u> of the prophecy of this book, for <u>the time is near</u>"* (Revelation 22:10, NASB95). Something is radically wrong here. If 344 to 558 years were so long as to demand a sealing of the book, would not 2000 years require an even stronger message to conceal and seal the book? John, on the other hand, was told not to seal the book because *"the time is near."* Jay Adams makes this very point saying, "Unlike John's, Daniel's prophecy did not constitute a 'contemporary' message, and was therefore sealed until the times of which he wrote. In direct contrast, Jesus told John not to seal the Apocalypse, for the matters it concerns were *'at hand.'* "[66]

This accords with the tone of the New Testament as a whole. As we have seen in the Olivet discourse, Jesus teaches the nearness of the predicted events.

---

[66] J. E. Adams, <u>The Time is at Hand</u>, 52.

> *Truly I say to you, <u>this generation</u> will not pass away until all these things take place. (Matthew 24:34, NASB95)*

> *Truly I say to you, there are some of those who are standing here <u>who will not taste death</u> until they see the Son of Man coming in His kingdom. (Matthew 16:28, NASB95)*

> *Truly I say to you, all these things will come upon <u>this generation</u>. (Matthew 23:36, NASB95)*

The same theme of looming judgement echoes across the pages of many New Testament books. Facing the Sanhedrin, Jesus tells them that some of them would live to see Him come in judgement, a prophecy that could not take place much more than forty years in the future.

> *Jesus said to him, "You have said it yourself; nevertheless I tell you, hereafter you will see the Son of Man sitting at the right hand of Power, and coming on the clouds of heaven." (Matthew 26:64, NASB95)*

Peter preaching at Pentecost, quoted Joel explaining the new tongues phenomena as a sign of the last days of the Jewish age, and the association with this outpouring of the Holy Spirit with the "day of the Lord," a term commonly associated with the judgement of God on Israel.

> *...but this is what was spoken of through the prophet Joel: 'And it shall be in the last days,' God says, 'That I will pour forth of My Spirit on all mankind; and your sons and your daughters shall prophesy, and your young men shall see visions, and your old men shall dream dreams; even on My bondslaves, both men and women, I will in those days pour forth of My Spirit And they shall prophesy. 'And I will grant wonders in the sky above and signs on the earth [land] below, blood, and fire, and vapor of smoke. The sun will be turned into darkness and the moon into blood, before the great and glorious day of the Lord shall come. (Acts 2:16-20, NASB95)*

Notice how these verses in Acts 2 give us a succinct summation of the Book of Revelation, which will bring this age to a close.

Paul speaks to the early church at Rome with a sense of urgency; they are running out of time; something is going to happen soon.

> *Do this, knowing the time, that it is already the hour for you to awaken from sleep; for now salvation is nearer to us than when we believed. The night is almost gone, and the day is near. Therefore let us lay aside the deeds of darkness and put on the armor of light. (Romans 13:11-12, NASB95).*

> *The God of peace will soon crush Satan under your feet. The grace of our Lord Jesus be with you. (Romans 16:20, NASB95)*

Again Paul address another church, Corinth, with the same message of distress, a shortness of time, and a warning of the passing away of the former world of Judaism.

> *I think then that this is good in view of the present distress, that it is good for a man to remain as he is. (1 Corinthians 7:26, NASB95)*

> *But this I say, brethren, the time has been shortened, so that from now on those who have wives should be as though they had none.... (1 Corinthians 7:29, NASB95)*

> *...and those who use the world, as though they did not make full use of it; for the form of this world is passing away. (1 Corinthians 7:31, NASB95)*

To the Colossians Paul warns that God's wrath upon Israel is near because of their persistent sins.

> *Therefore consider the members of your earthly body as dead to immorality, impurity, passion, evil desire, and greed, which amounts to idolatry. For it is because of these things that the wrath of God will come upon the sons of disobedience.... (Colossians 3:5-6, NASB95)*

James says, "...*the coming [parousia] of the Lord is near*" (James 5:8, NASB95). So near in fact that he goes on to say, "...*behold, the Judge is standing right at the door*" (James 5:9, NASB95). Peter boldly says, "*The end of all things is near*..." (1 Peter 4:7, NASB95). The writer of Hebrews makes a similar point saying, "*For yet in a very little while, He who is coming will come, and will not delay* " (Hebrews 10:37, NASB95). Revelation therefore fits perfectly into the tone of the rest of the New Testament, which has as a significant theme, the nearness of events that would change the world.

The word **communicated (1:1)** is the Greek word "signified" σημαίνω (*sēmainō*), the meaning of which is sometimes explained by breaking the English word apart this way: sign-i-fied. Signs and symbols were common and important tools used by God to communicate with His people, and it is of supreme importance that the reader understands this method of teaching used by God in the Book of Revelation. "This term evidently meant a kind of communication that is neither plain statement nor an attempt at concealment. It is figurative, symbolic, or imaginative, and is intended to convey truth by picture rather than by definition."[67] In properly understanding this word, "signified," you have in your hand a major key to understanding the Book of Revelation.

A sign is not the real thing; the thing pointed to by the sign is the real thing and this is the distinction that is often missed, resulting in serious errors of interpretation when the sign is seen as the real thing. Some students of the Book of Revelation call themselves "literalists" and boast in their faithfulness in *literally* taking the Word of God at face value. Their position is that in the Book of Revelation everything should first be interpreted literally, if possible, and only if this proves to be impossible should it be interpreted figuratively. While this may seem to make sense up front, in poetic and apocalyptic literature it is generally not a good idea to interpret a passage literally. Actually, such literature must be interpreted in keeping with the genre of the literature of which it is a class. Words used in poetic genres such as Psalms or the Song of Solomon have less rigid meanings, whereas words used in a theological discourse such as Romans need to be understood and used with greater precision. To confuse these practices leaves the student open to erroneous views which, as discussed above, was far from the intent of the Apostle John in the Book of Revelation.

To take a poetic phrase from the Psalms like, *"But You, O LORD, are a shield about me...."* (Psalm 3:3, NASB95) and interpret it literally, would be a

---

[67] Merrill C. Tenney, Interpreting Revelation (Grand Rapids, MI: Wm. B. Eerdmans Publishing Co., 1957), 186.

serious error. As a metaphor it conveys tender meaning. As a literal statement it is simply wrong; God is not "literally" a shield made of metal. Would we understand the Twenty-third Psalm properly if we were to take it "literally"? Does God really cause us to "lie down in green pastures?" Or is He not promising to meet our need for food and security? Does God literally "anoint my head with oil?" Does my real cup literally "overflow?" Educated people simply do not think this way.

And interestingly, literalists in prophecy are not literalists in common life where literalism would have a far greater likelihood of having a valid application. When the literalist is told to "stop and smell the roses," does he literally stop what he is doing and proceed to find literal and real roses to smell? It is certainly literally possible to stop and smell roses. But no, he understands that this is figurative language meaning to slow down and enjoy life. So, that being the case, where is the "literal if possible and figurative only if impossible" rule? It does not exist in life and it does not exist in any of the poetic and prophetic sections of the Bible. A better rule in this type of literature would be "first look for the figure and only if it cannot be found should the passage be interpreted literally."

Like the Psalms, the Book of Revelation must be interpreted with the literary tools with which it was created. In the Book of Revelation many truths are pointed at with word picture signs. Fortunately, Revelation itself is very helpful here in demonstrating how it and its signs should be understood. In eleven places in the book, John demonstrates how the Revelation is to be interpreted; they are 1:20; 4:5; 5:6; 5:8; 7:13, 14; 12:9; 17:9; 17:12: 17:15; and 17:18. Here we are given a demonstration in interpretation. We read,

> *As for the mystery of the seven stars which you saw in My right hand, and the seven golden lampstands: the seven stars are the angels of the seven churches, and the seven lampstands are the seven churches. (Revelation 1:20, NASB95)*

Do we have literal stars here? No, the *seven stars* are not actually stars but symbols for the *angels of the seven churches*. The *seven golden lampstands* are not literally lampstands but the *seven churches* of Asia.

> *Out from the throne come flashes of lightning and sounds and peals of thunder. And there were seven lamps of fire burning*

> *before the throne, which are the seven Spirits of God....*
> *(Revelation 4:5, NASB95)*

Are the *"seven lamps"* literally seven lamps? No, that is a figurative representation. In giving us the reality behind the figure John tells us that the figure of the *"seven lamps"* is to be understood as the *"seven Spirits of God."*

> *And I saw between the throne (with the four living creatures) and the elders a Lamb standing, as if slain, having seven horns and seven eyes, which are the seven Spirits of God, sent out into all the earth. (Revelation 5:6, NASB95)*

John again gives us another figure of the *"seven Spirits of God,"* but this time the figure is *"seven eyes."* Are they seven literal eyes? No, not at all, but a picture of something else, that something else being the *"seven Spirits of God."*

> *When He had taken the book, the four living creatures and the twenty-four elders fell down before the Lamb, each one holding a harp and golden bowls full of incense, which are the prayers of the saints. (Revelation 5:8, NASB95)*

Are the bowls here literal? No, here John helps us to see that the *"bowls full of incense"* are not literally, bowls full of incense, but rather *"the prayers of the saints."*

John writes in the 12th chapter,

> *And the great dragon was thrown down, the serpent of old who is called the devil and Satan, who deceives the whole world; he was thrown down to the earth, and his angels were thrown down with him. (Revelation 12:9, NASB95)*

Are we dealing with a literal serpent? No, here the symbolism of the great dragon is plain; he is Satan.

> *Here is the mind which has wisdom. The seven heads are seven mountains on which the woman sits.... (Revelation 17:9, NASB95)*

Heads are *heads*, right? Wrong, they are *seven mountains*. They symbolically represent something other than what they are called. We cannot, must not interpret them literally.

> *The ten horns which you saw are ten kings who have not yet*
> *received a kingdom, but they receive authority as kings with the*
> *beast for one hour. (Revelation 17:12, NASB95)*

Are the *ten horns* really *ten horns*? No, the *ten horns* are of course not horns at all but they are symbols for *ten kings*.

> *And he said to me, "The waters which you saw where the harlot*
> *sits, are peoples and multitudes and nations and tongues."*
> *(Revelation 17:15, NASB95)*

Water is water? No, the *waters* are not to be understood literally either for they symbolically stand for *peoples, multitudes, nations and tongues*.

> *The woman whom you saw is the great city, which reigns over*
> *the kings of the earth. (Revelation 17:18, NASB95)*

But the *woman*, she certainly is a *woman*! No, the *woman* is not a *woman* at all but the figure stands for a *great city*.

In these passages we see how John infallibly demonstrates his method of writing and the proper method of interpretation for that writing. He writes figuratively and must be interpreted figuratively. He has gone to extremes to make his point.

John needed to provide his readers with these instructions and insights in his method of writing because of the human tendency to deal concretely with spiritual truths expressed figuratively. Christ also had to work to get His audience to see beyond the sign or symbol in order to grasp the spiritual truth He was attempting to express. For instance, when He said, "*Destroy this temple, and in three days I will raise it up*" (John 2:19, NASB95) the crowds and religious leaders took offense, for they could not grasp the figure of His death and resurrection. Philip Carrington sums up Jesus' reliance on figurative language and expressions nicely by noting that, "The poetry of Jesus has it [figurative language] to a superlative degree; camels are swallowed or passed through needles' eyes; mountains are thrown into the depths of the sea; a man gets a tree-trunk stuck in his eye."[68]

When Christ spoke to Nicodemus about the new birth, Nicodemus, a literalist, missed the figure and tried to apply it to a physical birth (John 3:3-10). When Jesus spoke to the Samaritan woman at the well, He offered her *"living water"* (John 4:10-14, NASB95); but she, thinking literally, inquired about His lack of something to draw the water with. He, however, was speaking figuratively of the Holy Spirit. On another occasion Christ offered His flesh and blood to the crowd.

> *So Jesus said to them, "Truly, truly, I say to you, unless you eat the flesh of the Son of Man and drink His blood, you have no life in yourselves. He who eats My flesh and drinks My blood has eternal life, and I will raise him up on the last day." (John 6:53-54, NASB95)*

But thinking literally they missed the figure, *"As a result of this many of His disciples withdrew and were not walking with Him anymore"* (John 6:66, NASB95). And still on another occasion Christ offered them spiritual freedom,

> *So Jesus was saying to those Jews who had believed Him, "If you continue in My word, then you are truly disciples of Mine; and you will know the truth, and the truth will make you free." (John 8:31-32, NASB95)*

They, however, thinking literally, again missed the figure and insisted that they being children of Abraham were already free. These are just a few of Christ's many uses of figures that drive home critical lessons of spiritual significance. And notice that all these are found in the Gospel of John, the John who wrote Revelation.

Clearly, Christ loved to convey great truths in symbols and figures during His earthly ministry and John duly records that in his gospel. Now once again in the Book of Revelation Christ communicates in figures and John faithfully records the message. So when studying the Book of Revelation,

---

[68] Philip Carrington, 136-137.

keep in mind Christ's use of many "signs" to communicate truth, for that, says John, is how the Apocalypse was written.

It is important to recognize that some that do not embrace or even understand the symbolic nature of the book, often, see those that focus on the symbolic character of the book as enemies of the "true" meaning of the passage. As one author puts it, "to this day, in the minds of many, a non-literal interpretation is synonymous with liberalizing tendencies which are equated with denying the validity of the Word."[69] And another observes "...they think that when we talk about spiritual meanings we are trying to find a low and cunning way out of what the book actually says...."[70] Of course, not only are we not trying to find a way out of what it actually says, we are trying to find out what it actually says! And to understand the figures as figures teaching spiritual truths, is to understand what it actually says. J. Marcellus Kik deals with this issue saying,

> There is just a little misunderstanding in the minds of some people when you state that certain expressions in the Bible are figurative. They feel that it robs them of reality and makes them meaningless. That is not true. Figurative expressions stand for realities. The "Lamb" stands for the reality of the sacrificial atonement of Christ. The "Dragon" stands for the reality of Satan's power over ungodly nations.... The figurative expressions help us to understand the spiritual realities and they help to portray them to the mind.[71]

It must be understood that the dichotomy that prophecy is interpreted either literally or figuratively is incorrect. A Biblically literal method of interpretation makes no such distinction. Instead, a Biblically literal method of interpretation insists that "...symbols be treated as symbols, images as images, and plain indicative statements as indicative statements. The problem rests in correctly identifying the literary genre of each passage."[72] What we have here is not a dichotomy between those who interpret the Bible literally and those who interpret the Bible figuratively or

---

[69] Clarence B. Bass, <u>Backgrounds to Dispensationalism</u> (Grand Rapids, MI: Baker Book House, 1960), 21.

[70] Ibid., 66.

[71] J. Marcellus Kik, <u>An Eschatology of Victory</u> (Nutley, NJ: The Presbyterian and Reformed Publishing Co., 1971), 192.

[72] Kenneth L. Gentry, Jr., <u>Perilous Times: A Study in Eschatological Evil</u>, x.

spiritually (and therefore by implication erroneously). What we have is a distinction between those who apply the genre of Scripture to obtain the literal meaning of each passage, and those who do not believe that the metaphors, symbols, signs, figures of speech, or similes of the author should generally be interpreted figuratively, but rather literally.

It is interesting that those who call themselves "literalists" will in the section on visions and symbols interpret the figures, metaphors and symbols of Revelation literally. But, they will then in the didactic sections reverse themselves and interpret the non-symbols, like the timing words, "*near*," "*quickly*," and "*at hand*" figuratively. Such a confused handling of Scripture is hard to understand, and certainly hard to sympathize with.

1:2 ...*who testified to the word of God and to the testimony of Jesus Christ, even to all that he saw.* By this he means, "...the word of which God is the author and communicator, and the testimony which Christ discloses."[73] Through these attestations John is claiming absolute faithfulness and accuracy in his letter. Notice these words *Revelation* (1:1), *show* (1:1), *communicated* (1:1), and now ***saw (1:2).*** This book was never meant to be an enigma. At every turn we are confronted with words that drive home the point—this message was given clearly that it might be clearly understood.

1:3 *Blessed is he who reads and those who hear the words of the prophecy, and heed the things which are written in it; for the time is near.* Take note that this book was to be a blessing to the hearer not a source of confusion and mental disarray. At every turn we are confronted with indications of God's intent to communicate clearly not obscurely. These readers were expected to understand what it meant and receive blessing as a result. We are as well.

In the New Testament period, there were no printed Bibles and manuscripts were rare, in large part because of the lack of the technological capabilities of the ancient world. To compensate for that, the writings of apostles and other church leaders were, upon reception, read to the congregation and then passed along to the next town where a Christian

---

[73] Moses Stuart, 8.

church existed and where the procedure was repeated. This undoubtedly was the case for the Book of Revelation.[74]

This is the only book in the Bible in which a special blessing is promised to those who read and takes heed of its message. "Doubtless many spurious apocalypses were circulated in the early church, so that the people were wary of any works of that type. In order to ensure a hearing for the book, the first blessing is pronounced upon the reader who would read it publicly and upon the members of the church who would accept and heed its precepts."[75]

As is commonly known, the emphasis on hearing means hearing for the sake of doing. David Chilton sums this point up saying, "No Biblical writer ever revealed the future merely for the sake of satisfying curiosity: The goal was always to direct God's people toward right action in the present."[76]

That blessing was no doubt especially relevant to those about to see and experience the prophecies of the book. Today, it continues to be applicable to every believer who searches its pages, but in order to reap the fullness of the blessing, we must understand exactly what John meant for those seven churches, by grasping the signs and symbols that pepper its pages.

The word, *heed (1:3)*, means "...to continue to obey orders or commandments."[77] The promised blessing is not simply to those that *hear (1:3)*, but to those that *heed (1:3)*. Obedience is a key element in Biblical faith. "When one believes in Christ, he is bound to Him in an obedient, vital relationship. Commitment is an essential element in the act of believing. Faith is not merely intellectual assent."[78] There are many people with itching ears that love to study this book, but Jesus said that wise men go beyond study and do something about what they read.

> *Therefore everyone who hears these words of Mine and acts on them, may be compared to a wise man who built his house on the rock. (Matthew 7:24, NASB95)*

---

[74] David S. Clark, 23.

[75] Merrill C. Tenney, 181.

[76] David Chilton, The Days of Vengeance, 27.

[77] NET Bible Notes, electronic edition (Dallas, TX: Biblical Studies Press, 1998), Re 1:4.

[78] Kenneth L. Gentry Jr., Lord of the Saved (Phillipsburg, NJ: P&R Publishing, 1992), 20.

But how can a book that is beyond understanding be heeded? Why, of course, it cannot be. Clearly Jesus Christ expected the reader to understand its meaning, otherwise what would be the point in instructing him or her to **heed (1.3)** it?

Concerning the phrase *for the time is near (1:3)* see *things which must* <u>*soon take place*</u> (1:1) above.

Message to the Seven Churches

1:4 John to the seven churches that are in Asia: Grace to you and peace, from Him who is and who was and who is to come, and from the seven Spirits who are before His throne.... John begins his circular letter to the churches of Asia Minor with the words, **grace (1:4)** and **peace (1:4)**. This greeting is not especially unique among the writers of the New Testament. It is rather common and the readers would have known that **grace (1:4)** is to be understood objectively as God's favor given in Christ to those who would otherwise deserve eternal damnation. **Peace (1:4)** is that state of reconciliation with God through Christ that is a product of his saving grace. These terms, however, contained more powerful meanings than bare concepts and facts, for they communicated subjective, emotional qualities as well. Because of these objective truths, the readers of these letters had the joy of grace and the serenity of peace. Now to be sure, there is no proper subjective application without a prior and proper objective application. Apart from the objective facts of Christ's redemption, grace and peace are but false and temporary emotional states that have no eternal significance.

The blessings of **grace (1:4)** and **peace (1:4)** come,
1) ...*from Him who is and who was and who is to come (v4)*, (the Father)
2) ...*and from the seven Spirits who are before His throne (v4)*, (the Holy Spirit)
3) ...*and from Jesus Christ, the faithful witness, the firstborn of the dead, and the ruler of the kings of the earth (v5)*. (the Son)

In other words they come from God who is in Trinity. "The words following ἀπο are all taken together as one indeclinable noun, corresponding to and expressive of the Hebrews word ... *Jehovah*...."[79]

If your **grace (1:4)** and **peace (1:4)** come from any other than the self-existent and self-sustaining Trinity, then you are not on solid theological ground. You may simply be experiencing an emotional high of some kind. On the other hand, if you know the God of the Apostle John and do not enjoy **grace (1:4)** and **peace (1:4)**, then you do not possess what is properly yours. Notice that God expects you to have **grace (1:4)** and **peace (1:4)**, even in a world of impending judgement.

The Father is identified as **Him who is and who was and who is to come (v4)**. Later, we will see the Son with the identical title.

There is only one Holy Spirit; however, here He is seen in His sevenfold perfection and called **the seven Spirits (1:4)**. "It is not that the One develops into the Many; the One is Many in himself."[80]

William Milligan explains it this way, "The 'seven Spirits of God' are His one Spirit; the 'seven churches,' His one Church; the 'seven horns' and 'seven eyes' of the Lamb, His one powerful might and His one penetrating glance."[81] So as we have only one Church and one Lamb, so we have only one Holy Spirit.

However, Moses Stuart believes that **the seven Spirits (1:4)** do not refer to the Holy Spirit but instead what we have spoken of here are ministering spirits or presence angels.[82] He refers to Paul's comment in I Timothy.

I solemnly charge you in the presence of God and of Christ Jesus and of His chosen angels, to maintain these principles without bias, doing nothing in a spirit of partiality. (1 Timothy 5:21, NASB95)

[79] Moses Stuart, 15.

[80] Philip Carrington, 90.

[81] William Milligan, The Expositor's Bible, The Book of Revelation, (London: Hodder and Stoughton, 1889), 136.

[82] Moses Stuart, 20-23.

Notice the place of angels in this passage in relation to God and Christ Jesus. The point being that a reference to the Holy Spirit is not necessary every time the Father and Son are mentioned together. "What he says then is this, viz., It is his fervent desire that the blessing of grace and peace my be bestowed on the seven church of Asia—blessings which Jehovah dispenses, by his presence-angels, and by the Mediator the Lord Jesus Christ."[83]

1:5 ...and from Jesus Christ, the faithful witness, the firstborn of the dead, and the ruler of the kings of the earth. To Him who loves us and released us from our sins by His blood.... In this section we see Christ in His three offices as prophet, priest and king. The first description that John records of Jesus is **the faithful witness (1:5)**, which is description of His office of prophet. After the resurrection of Jesus some of his disciples were talking about Jesus. In their description of Jesus they identified Him as *a prophet mighty in deed and word.*

> *And He said to them, "What things?" And they said to Him, "The things about Jesus the Nazarene, who was a <u>prophet</u> mighty in deed and word in the sight of God and all the people...." (Luke 24:19, NASB95)*

In addition, Isaiah has this to say of the coming savior,

> *Behold, I have made him a <u>witness</u> to the peoples, a leader and commander for the peoples. Behold, you will call a nation you do not know, and a nation which knows you not will run to you, because of the Lord your God, even the Holy One of Israel; for He has glorified you. (Isaiah 55:4-5, NASB95)*

And so John bears a message from Jesus to seven gentile communities exactly as this passage presaged. "Peoples" and "nations" were used to refer to gentiles in the Old Testament.

Before we move from Christ as prophet to Christ as king let us take note of His resurrection. Christ's death, burial and resurrection are all parts of His priestly work. This phrase, **the firstborn of the dead (1:5)** of course, refers to His resurrection. "Here the phrase implies that while Jesus is the

---

[83] Ibid., 23.

first to have conquered death, he is also not the last but provides the precedent for the subsequent resurrection of believers who have died."[84] In his book to the Colossian church, Paul uses this very term to describe Jesus.

> *He is also head of the body, the church; and He is the beginning,*
> *the firstborn from the dead, so that He Himself will come to have*
> *first place in everything. (Colossians 1:18, NASB95)*

He, Jesus Christ, is the first to break the bonds of death forever. Others, such as Lazarus, were resurrected, but they saw death again. Christ, however, was raised never to taste death again. The Psalmist makes this point saying,

> *For You will not abandon my soul to Sheol; nor will You allow*
> *Your Holy One to undergo decay. (Psalm 16:10, NASB95)*

Paul also makes clear that Jesus was victorious over the grave.

> *But now Christ has been raised from the dead, the first fruits of*
> *those who are asleep. (I Corinthians 15:20, NASB95)*

Exercising all power, Christ is also **ruler of the kings of the earth (1:5)** and as such, sovereign over His creation. In times of persecution and oppression, like we are about to see unfolded in the Book of Revelation, it is important for the Church to be reminded of God's Lordship over His Creation. These several verses help us see His sovereign lordship over man and the world.

> *In order that the living may know*
> *That the Most High is ruler over the realm of mankind,*
> *And bestows it on whom He wishes*
> *And sets over it the lowliest of men. (Daniel 4:17b, NASB95)*

> *Why are the nations in an uproar*
> *And the peoples devising a vain thing?*
> *The kings of the earth take their stand*
> *And the rulers take counsel together*
> *Against the LORD and against His Anointed, saying,*

---

[84] David E. Aune, Vol. 52A: Revelation 1-5, Rev. 1:5.

"Let us tear their fetters apart
And cast away their cords from us!"
4 He who sits in the heavens laughs,
The Lord scoffs at them. (Psalm 2:1-4, NASB95)

These will wage war against the Lamb, and the Lamb will
overcome them, because He is Lord of lords and King of kings....
(Revelation 17:14, NASB95)

And on His robe and on His thigh He has a name written, "KING
OF KINGS, AND LORD OF LORDS." (Revelation 19:16, NASB95)

Next we read, **to Him who loves us and released us from our sins by His blood (1:5).** These are tremendously encouraging words. Some texts read "washed" instead of **released (1:5)** or "freed," but either translation has ample support from Scripture. For instance, in reference to "washed," a reading found in the Majority Text, we read:

...who gave Himself for us, that He might redeem us from every
lawless deed and <u>purify</u> for Himself a people for His own
possession, zealous for good deeds. (Titus 2:14, NASB95)

...how much more will the blood of Christ, who through the
eternal Spirit offered Himself without blemish to God, <u>cleanse</u>
your conscience from dead works to serve the living God?
(Hebrews 9:14, NASB95)

...and the blood of Jesus His Son <u>cleanses</u> us from all sin. (I John
1:7, NASB95)

On the other hand, references using the metaphor of **released (1:5)** or freed include:

But now having been <u>freed</u> from sin and enslaved to God, you
derive your benefit, resulting in sanctification, and the outcome,
eternal life. (Romans 6:22, NASB95)

When Jesus saw her, He called her over and said to her, "Woman,
you are <u>freed</u> from your sickness." (Luke 13:12, NASB95)

Last the phrase, *from our sins by His blood (1:5)*, "...from the impurity, turpitude of sin, and so (by consequence) from its penalty."[85]

1:6 *...and He has made us to be a kingdom, priests to His God and Father—to Him be the glory and the dominion forever and ever. Amen.* Another expression of Christ's compassion for His people involves His work making them *a kingdom, priests to His God and Father (1:6)*. The King tells us that He has made us a kingdom and He has made us priests to God. "Observe also that the characterization 'kingdom...priests', which was formerly applied to Israel (Ex. 19:6), is now applicable to believers collectively, that is, to the Church. In the Church Israel lives on."[86] This is a critical point; the special standing of Old Testament Israel is now applied to the church.

> *...and you shall be to Me a kingdom of priests and a holy nation. (Exodus 19:6, NASB95)*

John continues this theme in other parts of Revelation.

> *You have made them to be a kingdom and priests to our God; and they will reign upon the earth. (Revelation 5:10, NASB95)*

> *...but they will be priests of God and of Christ and will reign with Him for a thousand years. (Revelation 20:6, NASB95)*

Peter boldly takes the titles and positions once used of Israel, and now gives them to the church.

> *...you also, as living stones, are being built up as a spiritual house for a holy priesthood, to offer up spiritual sacrifices acceptable to God through Jesus Christ.... But you are A CHOSEN RACE, A royal PRIESTHOOD, A HOLY NATION, A PEOPLE FOR God's OWN POSSESSION...now you are THE PEOPLE OF GOD.... (I Peter 2:5, 9-10, NASB95)*

---

85 Moses Stuart, 26.

86 William Hendriksen, 53.

Paul confidently calls gentile Christians *"the Israel of God."*

> *And those who will walk by this rule, peace and mercy be upon them, and upon the Israel of God. (Galatians 6:16, NASB95)*

From these verses we see the reality of our priesthood and our relationship to God as the new Israel. "In referring to the churches as a kingdom of priests, John is making the point that Christians have become the new covenant people through Jesus Christ."[87] This point is much disputed by theologians but is fully clarified by the Scriptures we have referenced. "The idea here is that Christians are the true spiritual Israel in God's promise to Abraham as explained by Paul in Gal. 3 and Rom. 9."[88] After A.D. 70, Old Testament Israel, and the Old Covenant, ceased to exist. The New Testament Church and the New Covenant have replaced them.

...to Him be the glory and the dominion forever and ever (1:6). The word ***glory (1:6)***, δοξα, (dóxa), means, "splendor, brightness, a most glorious condition, most exalted state."[89] ***Dominion (1:6)***, κρατος, (*kratos*), means "force, strength, power, might."[90] We cannot give these things to God; they are His by right, however, in ascribing them to him, we enter into worship counting Him worthy of such praise and recognizing that He and He alone is the proper object of these titles of divinity.

Now look at verses 5 and 6 together. This is homage to Christ equal only to what God the Father receives in Scripture. Here we see "...the same ascriptions of praise to the Lord Jesus as are rendered to God the Father."[91] And how evil this would be if He were not truly equal to God the Father being Himself the Second Person of the Trinity.

---

[87] J. E. Leonard, <u>Come Out of Her My People</u> (Arlington Heights, IL: Laudemont Press, 1991), 29.

[88] Archibald Thomas Robertson, <u>Word Pictures in the New Testament</u> (Nashville, TN: Broadman Press, 1933), Vol. VI, 287.

[89] Ephesians Four Group, <u>Greek Dictionary</u>, electronic ed. (Oak Harbor, WA: Logos Research Systems, Inc., 1997), 2.

[90] Ibid.

[91] Moses Stuart, 29.

1:7 BEHOLD, HE IS COMING WITH THE CLOUDS, and every eye will see Him, even those who pierced Him; and all the tribes of the earth [land] will mourn over Him. So it is to be. Amen. At this point, John gives us the theme of the Book of Revelation. He is ***coming (1:7)*** and He is ***coming (1:7)*** to judge those who murdered Him.

As indicated earlier, the Olivet Discourse, the *little apocalypse,* covers much of the same material as the Book of Revelation. And in Matthew we see this same topic addressed.

> *And then the sign of the Son of Man will appear in the sky (heaven), and then all the tribes of the earth [land] will mourn, and they will see the SON OF MAN COMING ON THE CLOUDS OF THE SKY with power and great glory. (Matthew 24:30, NASB95)*

> *And the high priest said to Him, "I adjure You by the living God, that You tell us whether You are the Christ, the Son of God." Jesus said to him, "You have said it yourself; nevertheless I tell you, hereafter you will see THE SON OF MAN SITTING AT THE RIGHT HAND OF POWER, and COMING ON THE CLOUDS OF HEAVEN. (Matthew 26:63-64, NASB95)*

> *Then they will see the Son of Man coming in a cloud with power and great glory. (Luke 21:27, NASB95)*

So, to what does ***COMING ON/WITH THE CLOUDS (1:7)*** refer? First, note that "The present tense "he comes" describes the event as taking place in the immediate future...."[92] In other words, the implication is for a soon coming, not one greatly delayed; he does not use a future tense. Next, "...we must allow the Bible to direct us to the best interpretation of what ***coming (1:7)*** means based on the context and an evaluation of parallel passages."[93] In doing that let us consider these passages:

---

[92] Robert G. Bratcher, Re. 1:7.

[93] Gary DeMar, 71.

Behold, the LORD is riding on a swift cloud and is about to <u>come</u> to Egypt;
The idols of Egypt will tremble at His presence,
And the heart of the Egyptians will melt within them. (Isaiah 19:1, NASB95)

Then the earth [land] shook and quaked;
And the foundations of the mountains were trembling
And were shaken, because He was angry.
8 Smoke went up out of His nostrils,
And fire from His mouth devoured;
Coals were kindled by it.
9 He bowed the heavens also, and <u>came</u> down
With thick darkness under His feet.
10 He rode upon a cherub and flew;
And He sped upon the wings of the wind.
11 He made darkness His hiding place, His canopy around Him,
Darkness of waters, thick clouds of the skies.
12 From the brightness before Him passed His thick clouds,
Hailstones and coals of fire.
13 The LORD also thundered in the heavens,
And the Most High uttered His voice,
Hailstones and coals of fire.
14 He sent out His arrows, and scattered them,
And lightning flashes in abundance, and routed them.
15 Then the channels of water appeared,
And the foundations of the world were laid bare
At Your rebuke, O LORD,
At the blast of the breath of Your nostrils. (Psalm 18:7-15, NASB95)

The LORD said to Moses, "Behold, I will <u>come</u> to you in a thick cloud...." So it came about on the third day, when it was morning, that there were thunder and lightning flashes and a thick cloud upon the mountain and a very loud trumpet sound, so that all the people who were in the camp trembled. 17 And Moses brought the people out of the camp to meet God, and they stood at the foot of the mountain. 18 Now Mount Sinai was all in smoke because the LORD descended upon it in fire; and its smoke ascended like the smoke of a furnace, and the whole mountain quaked violently. 19 When the sound of the trumpet grew louder and louder, Moses

*spoke and God answered him with thunder. 20 The LORD came
down on Mount Sinai, to the top of the mountain; and the LORD
called Moses to the top of the mountain, and Moses went up.
(Exodus 19:9, 16-20, NASB95)*

Notice the relationship of **coming (1:7)** to judgment. God came in
judgment many times in the Old Testament. He will come again in just
these same terms. Let's look at the individual words as well. Consider these
additional **coming (1:7)** verses:

*The LORD came down to see the city and the tower which the sons
of men had built. (Genesis 11:5, NASB95)*

*So I have come down to deliver them from the power of the
Egyptians, and to bring them up from that land to a good and
spacious land.... (Exodus 3:8, NASB95)*

*For thus says the LORD to me,
"As the lion or the young lion growls over his prey,
Against which a band of shepherds is called out,
And he will not be terrified at their voice nor disturbed at their
noise,
So will the LORD of hosts come down to wage war on Mount Zion
and on its hill." (Isaiah 31:4, NASB95)*

*For behold, the LORD is coming forth from His place.
He will come down and tread on the high places of the earth
[land]. (Micah 1:3, NASB95)*

Now look at these **clouds (1:7)** verses:

*He lays the beams of His upper chambers in the waters;
He makes the clouds His chariot;
He walks upon the wings of the wind;
He makes the winds His messengers,
Flaming fire His ministers. (Psalm 104:3-4, NASB95)*

*In that time it will be said to this people and to Jerusalem, "A
scorching wind from the bare heights in the wilderness in the
direction of the daughter of My people—not to winnow and not to
cleanse,*

12 a wind too strong for this—will <u>come</u> at My command; now I
will also pronounce judgements against them.
13 "Behold, he goes up like <u>clouds</u>,
And his chariots like the whirlwind;
His horses are swifter than eagles.
Woe to us, for we are ruined! (Jeremiah 4:11-13, NASB95)

For the day is near,
Even the day of the LORD is near;
It will be a day of <u>clouds</u>,
A time of doom for the nations.
4 "A sword will <u>come</u> upon Egypt,
And anguish will be in Ethiopia;
When the slain fall in Egypt,
They take away her wealth,
And her foundations are torn down. (Ezekiel 30:3-4, NASB95)

Blow a trumpet in Zion,
And sound an alarm on My holy mountain!
Let all the inhabitants of the land tremble,
For the day of the LORD is <u>coming</u>;
Surely it is near,
A day of darkness and gloom,
A day of <u>clouds</u> and thick darkness. (Joel 2:1-2, NASB95)

Near is the great day of the LORD,
Near and <u>coming</u> very quickly;
Listen, the day of the LORD!
In it the warrior cries out bitterly.
A day of wrath is that day,
A day of trouble and distress,
A day of destruction and desolation,
A day of darkness and gloom,
A day of <u>clouds</u> and thick darkness,
A day of trumpet and battle cry
Against the fortified cities
And the high corner towers. (Zephaniah 1:14-16, NASB95)

These are a lot of references to consider, more than I would normally ask the reader to ponder, however, this point, the coming of Christ, is held in such confusion that I thought it necessary to drive home the point forcefully. This **coming with the clouds (1:7)** in Revelation chapter 1 does not refer to the Final Coming on the Last Day. The point made by these many passages is that the **coming with the clouds (1:7)** in Revelation, like the ones of the Old Testament, is a **coming (1:7)** by God in judgement.

Notice how R.C. Sproul deals with this same topic. He says,

> ...the coming of Christ in A.D. 70 was a coming in judgement on the Jewish nation, indicating the end of the Jewish age and the fulfillment of a day of the Lord. Jesus really did come in judgement at this time, fulfilling his prophecy in the Olivet Discourse. But this was not the final or ultimate coming of Christ. The parousia, in its fullness, will extend far beyond the Jewish nation and will be universal in its scope and significance. It will come, not at the end of the Jewish age, but at the end of human history, as we know it. It will be, not merely a day of the Lord, but the final and ultimate day of the Lord.[94]

Jesus spoke of His judgement **coming (1:7)** in Matthew 21. He said,

> *But when the vine-growers saw the son, they said among themselves, 'This is the heir; come, let us kill him and seize his inheritance.' "They took him, and threw him out of the vineyard and killed him. "Therefore when the owner of the vineyard comes, what will he do to those vine-growers?" They said to Him, "He will bring those wretches to a wretched end, and will rent out the vineyard to other vine-growers who will pay him the proceeds at the proper seasons." Jesus said to them, "Did you never read in the Scriptures, 'The stone which the builders rejected, this became the chief corner stone; this came about from the Lord, and it is marvelous in our eyes'? "Therefore I say to you, the kingdom of God will be taken away from you and given to a people, producing the fruit of it. "And he who falls on this stone will be broken to pieces; but on whomever it falls, it will scatter him like dust." When the chief priests and the Pharisees heard His parables, they understood that He was speaking about them. (Matthew 21:38-45, NASB95)*

---

[94] R.C. Sproul, The Last Days According to Jesus, 158.

Notice that Christ equates His **coming (1:7)** with bringing Israel to *a wretched end,* and didn't the Pharisees see that and react violently to it? In chapter 22 Jesus goes on and says this, *"But the king was enraged, and he sent his armies and destroyed those murderers and set their city on fire"* (Matthew 22:7, NASB95). Later in Matthew, in the little apocalypse, Jesus prophesies *"Truly I say to you, <u>this generation</u> will not pass away until all these things take place"* (Matthew 24:34, NASB95). The point is that the **coming (1:7)** of Jesus and the destruction of Jerusalem are concomitant events. Christ came in A.D. 70 to judge Israel, but that was not the Final Coming at the consummation of the world, that is yet in our future.

"We may observe that our Lord makes 'when the Lord *cometh*' coincide *with the destruction of Jerusalem,* which is incontestably the overthrow of the wicked husbandmen. This passage therefore forms an important key to our Lord's prophecies, and a decisive justification for those who like myself, firmly hold that *the coming of the Lord is,* in many places, to be identified, primarily, with that overthrow."[95]

The meaning of words like "every" as in **every eye (1:7)** has been a cause for confusion for many when interpreting the Bible. It would be helpful to see this word as similar to the meaning of the word "all" in this well know passage, *"Now in those days a decree went out from Caesar Augustus, that a census be taken of <u>all</u> the inhabited earth"* (Luke 2:1, NASB95). Instinctively we know that China and South America were not actually taxed at this time, but that many people in the world were, namely those in the Roman Empire at the time of Christ birth.

People of the ancient world used words like "all" or "every" in much the same loose and carefree way that we do today. When asked who was at the party, the answer often comes back, "everyone!" But it is assumed correctly that "everyone" includes only the "class" under discussion, not the whole city, state, or world. In this case it would be the friends of the two people speaking. The "class" in the census of Luke 2:1 above were all those under the authority of Rome. The "class" here in Revelation is that group of people to whom Christ is coming in judgement, Israel, especially those of Jerusalem, and more especially the leaders of that nation who played a role

---

[95] Henry Alford, <u>The Greek New Testament</u>, 4 vols (Chicago, IL: Moody Press, 1958 [1849-1861]), 1:216-217.

in crucifying Him. In other words, some of these would still be alive when He returns. The ***every eye (1:7)*** would refer to all those within that group of those who crucified Him. Or as John defines the class *"all the tribes of the earth [land]."*

> And then the sign of the Son of Man will appear in the sky, and
> then all the tribes of the earth [land] will mourn, and they will see
> the SON OF MAN COMING ON THE CLOUDS OF THE SKY with power and
> great glory. (Matthew 24:30, NASB95)

To comprehend the statement, ***and all the tribes of the earth [land] will mourn over Him (1:7)***, it is essential to understand that the word, here translated ***earth (1:7)***, is the Greek word γη (*gē*) which should be translated "land" in this passage. The proof of that is found in the word ***tribes***. The ***tribes*** spoken of are the tribes of Israel, and the "land" is the land of Israel.[96] So it is all the tribes in the land of Israel that will mourn over Him. This is because first, these prophecies are directed at them, and second, it is they who will see what a great crime they have committed in killing the Lord of Glory, and they will know that they now are the objects of the wrath of the Lamb.

> Jesus said to him, "You have said it yourself; nevertheless I tell
> you, hereafter you will see THE SON OF MAN SITTING AT THE RIGHT
> HAND OF POWER, and COMING ON THE CLOUDS OF HEAVEN."
> (Matthew 26:64, NASB95)

In what sense will they ***see (1:7)*** this? The passage does not tell us. At a minimum, however, they ***see (1:7)*** it in His judgements on Israel, Jerusalem, and the Temple. It is important to remember that "see" is often used in the Bible and in our lives as "understand." If a teacher explains a complex math concept to a student, he may then ask, "Do you see what I mean by this?" To which the student may reply, "Yes, now I understand." He understands in his mind, but he does not actually see anything. The Scripture also speaks in this way.

---

[96] The words, ***land*** and ***tribes***, are found in relationship with each other 130 times in the Old Testament. In this context, ***land*** *always* means the land Israel, ***tribes*** *always* refers to the tribes of Israel.

Render the hearts of this people insensitive,
Their ears dull,
And their eyes dim,
Otherwise they might <u>see</u> with their eyes,
Hear with their ears,
<u>Understand</u> with their hearts,
And return and be healed. (Isaiah 6:10, NASB95)

...but as it is written,
"They who had no news of Him shall <u>see</u>,
And they who have not heard shall <u>understand</u>." (Romans 15:21,
NASB95)

The Jewish leaders of the first century would no doubt recall Jesus' statement on the day of His trial.

Jesus said to him, "You have said it yourself; nevertheless I tell
you, hereafter you will see the Son of Man sitting at the right
hand of Power, and coming on the clouds of heaven." Then the
high priest tore his robes and said, "He has blasphemed! What
further need do we have of witnesses? Behold, you have now
heard the blasphemy; what do you think?" They answered, "He
deserves death!" (Matthew 26:64-66, NASB95)

Even though forty years had passed many of those leaders of Israel were still alive. "The crucifiers would <u>see</u> Him coming in judgement—that is, they would <u>understand</u> that His coming would mean wrath on the land."[97] Many of them, however, may very well have seen him, literally, on a great horse leading his holy armies against Israel as found described in the 19th chapter of the Book of Revelation. Note this quote from Josephus:

...a certain prodigious and incredible phenomenon appeared; I suppose the account of it would seem to be a fable, were it not related by those that <u>saw</u> it, and were not the events that followed it of so considerable a nature as to deserve such signals; for, before sun-setting, <u>chariots and troops of soldiers in their armor were</u>

---

[97] David Chilton, <u>The Days of Vengeance</u>, 66.

seen <u>running about among the clouds, and surrounding the cities.</u>[98]

This story is not unlike that found in II Kings when the armies of Syria surrounded Elisha in Dothan.

> *Now when the attendant of the man of God had risen early and gone out, behold, an army with horses and chariots was circling the city. And his servant said to him, "Alas, my master! What shall we do?" So he answered, "Do not fear, for those who are with us are more than those who are with them." Then Elisha prayed and said, "O LORD, I pray, open his eyes that he may see." And the LORD opened the servant's eyes and he saw; and behold, the mountain was full of horses and chariots of fire all around Elisha. (II Kings 6:15-17, NASB95)*

There, God was protecting his people, but here in Revelation, God is making war on Jerusalem, the harlot, and the unfaithful wife whom He is divorcing.

Concerning this phrase, ***those who pierced Him (1:7)*** in the Gospels, it is only John that takes note that Jesus was ***pierced (1:7)***.

> *But one of the soldiers <u>pierced</u> His side with a spear, and immediately blood and water came out. (John 19:34, NASB95)*

Interestingly, in the Septuagint, the Greek translation of the Hebrew Old Testament, Zech 12:10, from which our passage comes, is translated "insulted."[99] "John then must have translated the Hebrew original, in this case, for himself. And here it should be noted that in both cases, viz. in the Gospel and in the Apocalypse, the version is exactly the same, as to all the important words. This looks like the same hand in both."[100] In other words, this is one more in a long series of indicators and proofs that the Apostle John wrote the Book of Revelation.

---

[98] Flavius Josephus, <u>The Works of Josephus</u> (Oak Harbor, WA: Logos Research Systems, Inc., 1997), *Wars,* 6:5:3.

[99] Moses Stuart, 30.

[100] Ibid., 30.

The New Testament primarily portrays the Jewish nation as the murderers of Christ and speaks of **those who pierced Him (1:7).** The Romans were fully culpable for their crime, for indeed can one consider a greater breech of justice than what Pilate perpetrated on Christ whom he knew was innocent. But the Jewish people cajoled the Romans into murdering Jesus. The Scriptures make this point clear:

> ...and how the chief priests and our rulers delivered Him to the sentence of death, and crucified Him. (Luke 24:20, NASB95)

> ...this Man, delivered over by the predetermined plan and foreknowledge of God, you nailed to a cross by the hands of godless men and put Him to death. (Acts 2:23, NASB95)

> But you disowned the Holy and Righteous One and asked for a murderer to be granted to you, but put to death the Prince of life, the one whom God raised from the dead, a fact to which we are witnesses. (Acts 3:14-15, NASB95)

> And all the people said, "His blood shall be on us and on our children!" (Matthew 27:25, NASB95)

It is these **who pierced Him (1:7)** who are the special object of God's judgement. No greater crime has been committed since the creation of the world than to murder the Lord of Glory. Certainly that crime will not go unpunished, as Christ Himself predicted.

We read that **all the tribes of the earth [land] will mourn over Him (1:7).** At the Last Supper, Christ quotes from Zechariah, which reads:

> I will pour out on the house of David and on the inhabitants of Jerusalem, the Spirit of grace and of supplication, so that they will look on Me whom they have pierced; and they will mourn for Him, as one mourns for an only son, and they will weep bitterly over Him like the bitter weeping over a firstborn. In that day there will be great mourning in Jerusalem.... (Zechariah 12:10-11, NASB95)

Jesus, placed Zechariah (13:6-7) in the context of His crucifixion, not at some future time of deliverance and salvation thousands of years in the future. "Jesus quotes this prophecy at the Last Super, indicating that it is on the verge of fulfillment. He is warning His disciples of the wounds He will receive that very evening 'in the house of [His] friends....' "[101]

After the crucifixion there was a mourning and repentance; we see this at Pentecost and at other times when the gospel was preached. In addition, there was a mourning that did not include repentance; we see this here in the Book of Revelation but Jesus also predicted it in Matthew 24, where clearly the mourning is one of fear and judgement.

> *And then the sign of the Son of Man will appear in the sky, and then all the tribes of the earth [land] will mourn, and they will see the SON OF MAN COMING ON THE CLOUDS OF THE SKY with power and great glory. (Matthew 24:30, NASB95)*

Both Matthew and Revelation are speaking of the same event. Christ said of this event, "*Truly I say to you, this generation will not pass away until all these things take place* (Matthew 24:34, NASB95)."

Zechariah adds this information as well,

> *In that day a fountain will be opened for the house of David and for the inhabitants of Jerusalem, for sin and for impurity. "It will come about in that day," declares the LORD of hosts, "that I will cut off the names of the idols from the land, and they will no longer be remembered; and I will also remove the prophets and the unclean spirit from the land." (Zechariah 13:1-2, NASB95)*

> *And one will say to him, 'What are these wounds between your arms?' Then he will say, 'Those with which I was wounded in the house of my friends.'*
> *7 "Awake, O sword, against My Shepherd,*
> *And against the man, My Associate,"*
> *Declares the LORD of hosts.*
> *"Strike the Shepherd that the sheep may be scattered;*
> *And I will turn My hand against the little ones.*
> *8 "It will come about in all the land,"*
> *Declares the LORD,*

---

[101] J. E. Leonard, <u>Come Out of Her My People</u>, 30.

"That two parts in it will be cut off and perish;
But the third will be left in it.
9 "And I will bring the third part through the fire,
Refine them as silver is refined,
And test them as gold is tested.
They will call on My name,
And I will answer them;
I will say, 'They are My people,'
And they will say, 'The LORD is my God.' (Zechariah 13:6-9,
NASB95)

As indicated, Jesus quotes this passage at His Last Supper indicating that it is now being fulfilled. The Shepherd was stricken, and now two parts of Israel are about to be *"cut off and perish."* The covenant phrase *"I will say, 'They are My people,' and they will say, 'The Lord is my God' "* is now applied to the *"third part,"* the church, that survives God's judgement.

So it is to be. Amen. (1:7) "...a double expression *of so be it, assuredly, certainly,* one in Greek and one in Hebrew. ... The two words of synonymous import are designed to strengthen the expression of an idea. John means to say, that the coming of the Lord Jesus to punish his enemies and crucifiers, is altogether certain."[102]

Chapter 1 and verse 7 is a critical point in our study of Revelation. A failure to grasp this verse will make it impossible to understand why Revelation was written.

1:8 *"I am the Alpha and the Omega," says the Lord God, "who is and who was and who is to come, the Almighty."* The term the **Alpha and the Omega (1:8)** would be important information to a church on the verge of persecution. The One who is the beginning and the end, the first and the last is speaking to that Church. Nothing is outside His purview. They are under His watchful care. Since it is Jesus **who is to come (1:8)**, it is Jesus who is **the Almighty (1:8)**. "Higher titles than these cannot be bestowed on any being...."[103]

---

[102] Moses Stuart, 31.

[103] Ibid., 33.

The one speaking here is called **the Lord God (1:8)**. Now the question is this, is the Father speaking or the Son? To find that answer let us go back to verse 7. Clearly it is Jesus Christ who was "*pierced*" (1:7) and the one "*who is coming*" (1:7). In Verse 8 the passage continues stating again that He **is to come (1:8)**. This ties verses 7 and 8 together tightly. It is one and the same person in both verses. Since it is Jesus Christ in verse 7 who "*is coming*" (1:7), it is also Jesus Christ in verse 8 **who is to come (1:8)**. Jesus Christ is therefore the **Alpha and the Omega (1:8)**, and therefore **the Lord God (1:8)**. In addition, the phrase **the Almighty (1:8)** is clearly another powerful title of deity. Jesus Christ rightly bears both these titles. "The saying 'who is, who was, who is to come,' with the addition of 'the Almighty,' occurs as a fourfold attestation of God's deity, eternity, presence, and power (1:8; 4:8)."[104]

This phrase, the **Alpha and the Omega (1:8)**, is used later in the Book of Revelation as well referring to Christ as well.

> Then He said to me, "It is done. <u>I am the Alpha and the Omega,</u>
> <u>the beginning and the end."</u> (Revelation 21:6, NASB95)

> <u>I am the Alpha and the Omega,</u> the first and the last, the
> beginning and the end. (Revelation 22:13, NASB95)

And what does this phrase, **who is and who was and who is to come (1:8)**, refer to? "It is merely a paraphrastic explanation of the word Jehovah."[105]

Thus Christ here describes Himself as being the complete and perfect eternal revelation of God. Here He tells us that He is fully equal with the Father and is Himself God. The same phrase which in verse 4 described the Father here designates the Son, "...*from Him who is and who was and who is to come*" (Revelation 1:4, NASB95).[106]

---

[104] Simon J. Kistemaker, and William Hendriksen, Vol. 20, 24.

[105] Ibid., 33.

[106] William Hendriksen, 54-55.

The Patmos Vision

1:9   I, John, your brother and fellow partaker in the tribulation and kingdom and perseverance which are in Jesus, was on the island called Patmos because of the word of God and the testimony of Jesus. The author introduces himself as ***John, your brother (1:9).*** He uses no titles or other identification, which implies he is well known to his readers."[107] This gives significant weight to John the Apostle as the author. Anyone else would need to identify and justify himself and his writing. Only John the Apostle would not.

John tells us that he is a ***fellow partaker in the tribulation and kingdom (1:9).*** Most Christians have been taught to believe that ***the tribulation (1:9)*** is in our future, for John it was in his and their present. John calls them ***fellow partakers (1:9)*** in ***the tribulation (1:9).*** "... he states he has had, or is having, the same experiences they have had (see similar language in Phil 4.14). The phrase *in Jesus* means 'as a follower of Jesus,' 'as a believer in Jesus,' or even 'as a Christian.' "[108]

It appears that John may have been in a prison colony on Patmos, an island used for this purpose by the Romans, or he may simply have relocated to Patmos to avoid the current tribulation and to write. As William Hendriksen says, "He tells us that he was in the isle that is called Patmos for the Word of God and the testimony of Jesus. Does this mean that the apostle had been sentenced to hard labour because he refused to drop incense upon the altar of a pagan priest as a token of worshipping the emperor? We are not sure."[109]

As indicated, John was a ***fellow partaker in the tribulation (1:9).*** Just as Christ had predicted *"Then they will deliver you to <u>tribulation</u>, and will kill you, and you will be hated by all nations because of My name"* (Matthew 24:9, NASB95). John was telling them that "he stood with them on common ground. Every hardship they bore, he endured. Every prospect of martyrdom they faced, he had already contemplated. He was even in the vanguard bearing the first baptism of fire and blood. They would listen to

---

[107] Robert G. Bratcher, Rev. 1:9.

[108] Ibid., Rev. 1:9.

[109] William Hendriksen, 55.

the words of one who suffered in their sufferings, and stood in the forefront of their dangers."[110]

John was also in the **kingdom (1:9)**. He was not waiting for a kingdom, especially not one of Old Testament Jews, as are Classical Dispensationalists. John was already in the **kingdom (1:9)**, as are all believers. John the Baptist had preached that the kingdom of God was at hand, and the apostle John entered that **kingdom (1:9)** through repentance and faith in the Messiah. We do as well. All of God's children are a part of God's **kingdom (1:9)**, not just Jews, and not in some distant point in the future.

> *For He rescued us from the domain of darkness, and transferred us to the kingdom of His beloved Son, in whom we have redemption, the forgiveness of sins. (Colossians 1:13-14, NASB95)*

> *...so that you would walk in a manner worthy of the God who calls you into His own kingdom and glory. (1 Thessalonians 2:12, NASB95)*

> *Listen, my beloved brethren: did not God choose the poor of this world to be rich in faith and heirs of the kingdom which He promised to those who love Him? (James 2:5, NASB95)*

> *...and He has made us to be a kingdom, priests to His God and Father—to Him be the glory and the dominion forever and ever. Amen. (Revelation 1:6, NASB95)*

All this occurred close to the same time that Paul was put to death in Rome, at least within a few short years. It is not clear why John's life was spared and others were martyred. Christ addressed this issue, however, after his resurrection; talking to Peter He said,

> *Truly, truly, I say to you, when you were younger, you used to gird yourself and walk wherever you wished; but when you grow old, you will stretch out your hands and someone else will gird you, and bring you where you do not wish to go. 19 Now this He said, signifying by what kind of death he would glorify God. And*

---

[110] David S. Clark, 27.

*when He had spoken this, He said to him, "Follow Me!" Peter,
turning around, saw the disciple whom Jesus loved [John]
following them; the one who also had leaned back on His bosom
at the supper and said, "Lord, who is the one who betrays You?"
21 So Peter seeing him said to Jesus, "Lord, and what about this
man?" 22 Jesus said to him, "If I want him to remain until I <u>come</u>,
what is that to you? You follow Me!" 23 Therefore this saying
went out among the brethren that that disciple would not die; yet
Jesus did not say to him that he would not die, but only, "If I want
him to remain until I <u>come</u>, what is that to you?" (John 21:18-23,
NASB95)*

The Greek word used here in this passage for "come" is ἔρχομαι,
érchēomai. It is the same word Matthew uses seven times in chapter 24 to
refer to Christ' coming in judgement.

And so, Peter was crucified, and John did remain <u>until Christ came</u> in A.D.
70 just as He said he would. Notice how many passages that previously
made little sense, come to life in the light of a Preterist view of Scripture.
This passage in John 21 has generally been un-interpretable by most
commentators, yet in the light of Christ coming in A.D. 70, it makes perfect
sense.

To **kingdom (1:9)** John adds *...and perseverance which are in
Jesus...(1:9).* Paul expresses himself in a similar way saying, "*If we
endure, we will also reign with Him...*" (2 Timothy 2:12, NASB95). To
endure is to exercise **perseverance (1:9).** To endure and persevere is to
assure that we reign in His **kingdom (1:9).**

**1:10 I was in the Spirit on the Lord's day, and I heard behind
me a loud voice like the sound of a trumpet....** John tells us that he
was **in the Spirit (1:10).** This was probably similar to what Peter and
Paul experienced in the Book of Acts.

*But he became hungry and was desiring to eat; but while they
were making preparations, he fell into a trance; and he saw the
sky opened up.... (Acts 10:10-11, NASB95)*

*It happened when I returned to Jerusalem and was praying in
the temple, that I fell into a trance.... (Acts 22:17, NASB95)*

"The phrase ejn pneuvmati (ἐν πνεύματι) "in the Spirit" is an idiom that refers to the fact that John's revelatory experiences took place not "in the body" but rather "in the spirit," i.e., in a vision trance...."[111]

We must note that this revelation was mediated by God's Holy Spirit. John did not simply have unusual insight into what was about to happen, no, John was *in the Spirit (1:10).*

> *...for no prophecy was ever made by an act of human will, but men moved by the Holy Spirit spoke from God. (2 Peter 1:21, NASB95)*

John continues telling us that all this occurred on *the Lord's day (1:10).* Probably "...this is the Christian day of worship, the first day of the week, the day of Christ's resurrection (see Acts 20.7; 1 Cor 16.2). Only here in the New Testament is the expression *the Lord's day* used, but it is found in early Christian literature: *Didache* 14 (the end of the first century), and Ignatius' *Letter to the Magnesians* 19 (early second century). The same adjective that is translated *the Lord's* is used in the phrase "the Lord's Supper" (1 Cor 11.20)."[112]

From the beginning of the church age, Christians have worshiped on Sunday, *the Lord's day (1:10)*, that is, the day of His resurrection. We are not commanded to do so, although we are given Scriptural indication it was done by the early Church. Consider these verses.

> *On the first day of the week, when we were gathered together to break bread, Paul began talking to them. (Acts 20:7, NASB95)*

> *On the first day of every week each one of you is to put aside and save, as he may prosper, so that no collections be made when I come. (I Corinthians 16:2, NASB95)*

In addition, "Deissmann has proven...from inscriptions and papyri that... "hemera Sebaste" (Augustus Day) was the first day of each month, Emperor's Day on which money payments were made.... It was easy,

---

[111] David Aune, Volume 52a: Revelation 1-5, Rev. 1:10

[112] Robert G. Bratcher, Rev. 1:10.

therefore, for the Christians to take this term, already in use, and apply it to the first day of the week in honour of the Lord Jesus Christ's resurrection on that day...."[113]

However, it is also possible to understand this phrase, **the Lord's day (1:10)**, as "the day of the Lord" meaning the Day of Judgement, which so characterizes the theme of the Book of Revelation.[114]

> *But the day of the Lord will come like a thief, in which the heavens will pass away with a roar and the elements will be destroyed with intense heat, and the earth and its works will be burned up. (2 Peter 3:10, NASB95)*

> *Seek the Lord, all you humble of the earth who have carried out His ordinances; seek righteousness, seek humility. Perhaps you will be hidden in the day of the Lord's anger. (Zephaniah 2:3, NASB95)*

> *Will not the day of the Lord be darkness instead of light, even gloom with no brightness in it? (Amos 5:20, NASB95)*

John tells us that he **heard behind (1:10)** him **a loud voice like the sound of a trumpet (1:10)**. This is very characteristic of God's communication with man.

> *So it came about on the third day, when it was morning, that there were thunder and lightning flashes and a thick cloud upon the mountain and a very loud trumpet sound, so that all the people who were in the camp trembled. (Exodus 19:16, NASB95)*

> *And all the people perceived the thunder and the lightning flashes and the sound of the trumpet and the mountain smoking; and when the people saw it, they trembled and stood at a distance. (Exodus 20:18, NASB95)[115]*

---

[113] Archibald Thomas Robertson, Vol. VI, 290.

[114] I Thessalonians 5:2; II Thessalonians 5:2; II Peter 3:10; I Corinthians 1:8; 5:5; II Corinthians 1:14; Acts 2:20.

[115] See also: Isa 18:3; Joel 2:1; Zechariah 9:14; Ps 47:5; 2 Samuel 6:15; Isaiah 27:13; Joel 2:15; Ps 81:3.

***1:11** ...saying, "Write in a book what you see, and send it to the seven churches: to Ephesus and to Smyrna and to Pergamum and to Thyatira and to Sardis and to Philadelphia and to Laodicea.* John is told to **write (1:11)** this vision **in a book (1:11)**. What kind of **book (1:11)** was he to write in? In Greek it is "βιβλίον (*Biblíon*) ... a papyrus[116] roll as distinguished from a parchment[117] book ... the length of which "may be estimated at 15 feet."[118] Even rolled up it would have been of considerable size.

In addition to these **seven churches (1:11)** we know of at least three others that were in this region, Colosse (Colossians 1:2), Hierapolis (Colossians 4:13), and Troas (II Corinthians 2:12). And there may have been more, in facts, maybe several dozen in the smaller outlying towns. So why were these others not mentioned? Perhaps one answer is the significance of the number seven. Symbolism in the Bible is pronounced, and in the Book of Revelation it is overwhelming. Seven, being the number of perfection or qualitative fullness, may suggest that this letter has significance to the whole church, not simply to a regional church.

A possibility of far weightier significance has to do with the relationship between numbers and covenants, "...the Hebrew word for "swear," *nishba'*, literally translated is, "seven oneself." This means that a covenant oath could not be taken without using the number seven. Such a linguistic link in the original language of the Old Testament indicates that in Scripture, seven is usually a reference to the covenant."[119] As Edersheim says, "the number seven, ... became in Scripture-symbolism the sacred or covenant number."[120] So, here we have God entering into Covenant with His Church,

---

[116] Papyrus -- A plant growing along the Nile in Egypt during biblical times. It was used as writing material. Papyrus scrolls were made by cutting and pressing sections of the papyri plant together at right angles. We get the word "paper" from this word. Many of the biblical manuscripts were on papyrus.

[117] Parchment -- Writing material made from the skins of sheep or calf. Pliny says that it was invented in the 2nd century BC in Pergamum; hence the name parchment from the Latin pergamena (of Pergamum).

[118] Henry Barclay Swete, 14.

[119] J. E. Leonard, I will Be Their God, 33-34.

[120] Alfred Edersheim, 120.

these seven churches representing the whole. This is a very good explanation as to why seven churches were chosen to receive this letter, and not six or eight.

Seven is covenant imagery and all of the Revelation is constructed around the number seven. It is written to seven churches and refers to seven stars, seven candlesticks or lampstands, seven seals, seven bowls, seven plagues, seven thunders, seven trumpets and seven messengers. Revelation is a book about the covenant, the breaking of the covenant, the sanctions of the covenant, and the implementation of the new covenant.

Finally, as to why these particular seven churches, a practical reason emerges when we understand that, "...all the Seven Cities stand on the great circular road that bound together the most populous wealthy, and influential part of the Province.... Planted at these seven centers, the Apocalypse would spread through their neighborhoods, and from thence to the rest of the province."[121]

1:12 *Then I turned to see the voice that was speaking with me. And having turned I saw seven golden lampstands....* Verse 20 speaks of these ***seven golden lampstands (1:12)*** and tells us that *"the seven lampstands are the seven churches"* (1:20). The seven-branched lampstand of the Temple was symbolic of the nation of Israel in covenant with God, the word seven being the number of the covenant as noted above. Here that same lampstand, the heavenly original, is used to symbolize God's covenant with the church. Israel has been rejected and replaced by the Church, for Christ, having divorced His first wife has taken a new bride. In this passage, Christ stands in the midst of His Church, as He at one time stood in the midst of Israel as a cloud by day and a pillar of fire by night.

The lampstand, which stood in the Tabernacle and Temple of old, is symbolic of the nation of Israel in much the same way that the American eagle is symbolic of the United States. Through the use of the ***lampstands (1:12)*** "...John makes it clear that the churches of Asia Minor are members of the covenant. There are seven of them; they are symbolized by

---

[121] Henry Barclay Swete, lvii.

lampstands; Jesus, the Mediator of the new covenant, walks among them and holds their 'angels' or messengers in His hand."[122]

1:13 *...and in the middle of the lampstands I saw one like a son of man, clothed in a robe reaching to the feet, and girded across His chest with a golden sash.* By placing Himself **in the middle of the lampstands (1:13)**, Jesus is stating symbolically that He is in the midst of His Church.

> He is not an absentee Lord. He is an abiding presence and personality ... Unless Christ is in the midst, the church is dead and shorn of power. This vision was of special significance and comfort to those churches in the scenes of blood thru which they were called to pass. In the burning fiery furnace into which they were soon to be thrown, there was One who would walk with them, whose appearance was like to the Son of Man.[123]

Who is the **one (1:13)** who stands among the lampstands **like a son of man (1:13)**? It is Christ, and Daniel, like John, saw Christ in a similar prophetic trance.

> *I lifted my eyes and looked, and behold, there was a certain man dressed in linen, whose waist was girded with a belt of pure gold of Uphaz. His body also was like beryl, his face had the appearance of lightning, his eyes were like flaming torches, his arms and feet like the gleam of polished bronze, and the sound of his words like the sound of a tumult. (Daniel 10:5-6, NASB95)*

The general character of the vision is one of the glory of Christ, the shining face being reminiscent of that which John had seen on the Mount of Transfiguration decades earlier (Matt. 17:2). According to the various expositors, the golden band worn across the chest is an emblem of high rank in the ancient world, and the long, linen garment is probably priestly. White hair is the emblem of age and honor-and possibly wisdom. The flaming eyes convey the idea of piercing vision, and the feet like fine brass suggest the irresistibility

---

[122] J. E. Leonard, Come Out of Her My People, 31-32.

[123] David S. Clark, 28.

of His judgement as He will later tread the "great winepress of the wrath of God" (Rev. 14:19). The two-edged sword from His mouth can hardly refer to anything other than His word (Heb. 4:12; Eph. 6:17), and the meaning of the seven stars is given in verse 20.[124]

...girded across His chest with a golden sash (1:13). Of this sash Alfred Edersheim says, "...it was only put on during actual ministration, and put off immediately afterwards. Accordingly, when in Revelation 1:13, the Savior is seen 'in the midst of the candlesticks,' 'girt about the paps with a golden girdle,' we are to understand by it that our heavenly High Priest is there engaged in actual ministry for us."[125]

1:14 His head and His hair were white like white wool, like snow; and His eyes were like a flame of fire. Here we have a picture of the Ancient of Days, which is found in Daniel 7:9. It is employed by John to make a critical point, Jesus Christ is the Ancient of Days of the Old Testament, or simply Jesus Christ is God.[126]

John next draws our attention to Jesus' eyes; they are as ***a flame of fire (1:14).*** As David Clark says of these eyes, "No night so dark as to dim his vision ... No secret so hidden that it does not blaze before him. No heart that he does not read like an open page. No deed so buried that it does not stand out before him. Nothing so forgotten that it will not come to light."[127]

1:15 His feet were like burnished bronze, when it has been made to glow in a furnace, and His voice was like the sound of many waters. The word ***burnished (1:15)*** means polished and so polished as to ***glow (1:15)*** says John. One is reminded of a passage that Paul quotes found in Isaiah concerning the feet of the messenger of the Messiah or perhaps the Messiah Himself,

---

[124] Steve Gregg, 60.

[125] Alfred Edersheim, 72.

[126] Henry Barclay Swete, 16.

[127] David S. Clark, 28.

> *How lovely on the mountains are the feet of him who brings good*
> *news, who announces peace and brings good news of happiness,*
> *who announces salvation, and says to Zion, "Your God reigns!"*
> *(Isaiah 52:7, NASB95)*

Yet feet that are so lovely to some, bearing the gospel message, are so terrifying to others trampling the grapes of the wrath of God. Here the *feet (1:15)* burn with the fire of a *furnace (1:15)*, encouraging to the Church and its martyrs but terrifying to the enemies of Christ.

Like His feet, so His *voice (1:15)* has a twofold effect on His audience. "Sweet and low as the brook that sings its way through the meadow, or filled with majesty and grandeur as it speaks the language of judgement and fear, as the roar of the angry surf as it thunders upon the shore. For those who hear not the one, Christ reserves the other. There are such contrasts in Christ because there are such contrasts in men."[128]

1:16 In His right hand He held seven stars, and out of His mouth came a sharp two-edged sword; and His face was like the sun shining in its strength. This great king, as described by John, regal beyond imagination, and majesty that exceeds the capacity of language, is poised for battle. With words God calls the universe into existence. With words He judges His creation for John tells us **out of His mouth came a sharp two-edged sword (1:16).** He is not dependent on arms or weapons, as we understand them.

> *And He will strike the earth [land] with the rod of His mouth,*
> *And with the breath of His lips He will slay the wicked. (Isaiah*
> *11:4, NASB95)*

This imagery corresponds with Paul's who says: *'The sword of the Spirit, which is the word of God.'* Israel and Jerusalem are the objects of His war. The description comes from Ezekiel and Daniel where they behold a figure "...who is nothing short of a manifestation of Jehovah, his Word or his

---

[128] Ibid., 28-29.

Angel."[129]   Here John sees Christ "...risen and reigning in his church; despite persecution and suffering...."[130]

Philip Carrington speaks of those he calls "Adventist" or those we more commonly call Dispensationalists saying of them, "The weakness in all Adventist thought is the assumption that God and his Messiah are a long way off; it is the familiar heresy of the "orthodox," a one-sided enthusiasm for the "transcendent." ... The Messiah is not far off in the infinite; with all his transcendent glory he reigns here on earth among his martyrs."[131] The present reign of Christ is a vital teaching of this passage. We are not waiting some day for His return that He might reign. He reigns in His Church *now* by means of His Word.

1:17 When I saw Him, I fell at His feet like a dead man. And He placed His right hand on me, saying, "Do not be afraid; I am the first and the last...." John describes for us his own response at seeing Jesus saying **I fell at His feet like a dead man (1:17).** This is a common reaction and mirrors that of other encounters by God's servants such as Daniel.

> *So I was left alone and saw this great vision; yet no strength was left in me, for my natural color turned to a deathly pallor, and I retained no strength. 9 But I heard the sound of his words; and as soon as I heard the sound of his words, I fell into a deep sleep on my face, with my face to the ground. (Daniel 10:8-9, NASB95)*

Although Isaiah did not fall dead, his experience stresses the central issue of such an encounter—the holiness of God and the sinfulness of man. That experience is expressed in these words,

---

[129] Philip Carrington, 78.

[130] Ibid., 80.

[131] Ibid., 81.

Then I said,
"Woe is me, for I am ruined!
Because I am a man of unclean lips,
And I live among a people of unclean lips;
For my eyes have seen the King, the LORD of hosts." (Isaiah 6:5,
NASB95)

Moses Stuart says of this phrase, **I am the first and the last**, "These are certain predicates of the eternal God...."[132] John makes this point again as he closes this book.

I am the Alpha and the Omega, the first and the last, the
beginning and the end. (Revelation 22:13, NASB95)

1:18 ...and the living One; and I was dead, and behold, I am alive forevermore, and I have the keys of death and of Hades. This phrase, **the living One (1:18)**, is also a divine title. It speaks of the resurrected Christ, who had been raised from death but now lives forever.[133]

...and as the women were terrified and bowed their faces to the
ground, the men said to them, "Why do you seek the living One
among the dead?" (Luke 24:5, NASB95)

Christ conquered death and tells us so saying **I was dead, and behold, I am alive forevermore (1:18).** Perhaps this is the central element in Christianity, the thing that makes it utterly different from all other religions. This victory over death is central to the gospel and is found in several critical passages in the Bible.

...knowing that Christ, having been raised from the dead, is never
to die again; death no longer is master over Him. (Romans 6:9,
NASB95)

The first and the last, who was dead, and has come to life, says
this.... (Revelation 2:8, NASB95)

---

[132] Moses Stuart, 52-53.

[133] Robert G. Bratcher, Rev. 1:18.

Then the angel whom I saw standing on the sea and on the land lifted up his right hand to heaven, and swore by Him who lives forever and ever.... (Revelation 10:5-6, NASB95)

Then one of the four living creatures gave to the seven angels seven golden bowls full of the wrath of God, who lives forever and ever. (Revelation 15:7, NASB95)

Notice how these passages focus on the resurrected life of Christ. A Christ that is not alive, is a Christ that cannot save.

This statement by the resurrected Christ, **I have the keys of death and of Hades (1:18)**, is no mere statement of what is in His possession but rather a proclamation of His power and authority, for to have the keys to something is to own it. When the father gives the keys to the car to his child, that child exercises authority over that vehicle for the time that he has the keys. To be sure this analogy speaks of a temporary empowerment, which the punishment of 'taking away the keys' swiftly alters. Christ's authority, however, is unalterable, since the Father has given him the keys to death and hades in fullness and for eternity. **Hades (1:8)** does not mean "hell" but "the grave." He has authority to unlock the grave and let its inhabitants out! With this power Christ unlocks and opens the gates to eternal bliss to His resurrected saints and judges and sentences His enemies to eternal damnation. Therefore, as Christ Himself warns, the greatest thing to fear is not death, but rather He who can destroy *"both body and soul in hell"* (Matthew 10:28, NASB95).

Then I will set the key of the house of David on his shoulder, when he opens no one will shut, when he shuts no one will open. (Isaiah 22:22, NASB95)

He who is holy, who is true, who has the key of David, who opens and no one will shut, and who shuts and no one opens....
(Revelation 3:7, NASB95)

Then the fifth angel sounded, and I saw a star from heaven which had fallen to the earth [land]; and the key of the bottomless pit was given to him. (Revelation 9:1, NASB95)

Then I saw an angel coming down from heaven, holding the key of the abyss and a great chain in his hand. (Revelation 20:1, NASB95)

1:19 Therefore write the things which you have seen, and the things which are, and the things which will take place after these things. These words, **will take place (1:19)**, sound as if it could be in the distance future; however, the Greek word is μελλω (*mellō*) and is better-translated *"things which are about to take place."* The close proximity of the writer and the message is stressed by this word. These things will not happen in the distant future, they are about to take place now.

1:20 As for the mystery of the seven stars which you saw in My right hand, and the seven golden lampstands: the seven stars are the angels of the seven churches, and the seven lampstands are the seven churches. Jesus now begins to explain to John and his audience *"the things which you have seen"* (1:19). **The seven stars are the angels of the seven churches (1:20).** To some degree it is important to address the question, "who are the **angels (1:20)** that are spoken of?" We should note that the word "**angels**" comes from a Greek word often translated "messenger."

To the angel of the church in Ephesus write.... (Revelation 2:1, NASB95)

Each letter is sent to the angel of that church, not directly to the church itself. It is thought that this *"angel"* could either be a guardian angel assigned to each church or the elder/bishop/pastor of the church. Because each of these angels is apparently expected to pass on the letter to the next church, we have to assume that the *"angel"* or messenger is the pastor. Another possibility that is similar suggests that special delegates or delegations were sent to Patmos who would return to their home church with a copy of the Revelation.[134]

---

[134] Henry Barclay Swete, 21.

Chapter 2
The Seven Letters

A s mentioned in the Introduction, the *Historicists* believes that the message of the book of Revelation is worked out through the ages of history. Generally each of the seven churches is portrayed as a period of time in church history. As a result, they see in this book no significant message to the churches to which it was originally written.

However, we agree with Jay Adams when he says, "There is not even a hint that the seven churches symbolize the future of the history of the church, as some claim. To begin with, their order is strictly geographical and not determined by content. The error of the representative idea is manifest as soon as one recognizes the incontestable fact that they are distinguished from prophecy...."[135]

Milton Terry very pointedly agrees saying, "The notion that we have in these seven epistles a prophetic outline of seven chronological periods of Church history traceable through the Christian centuries may be safely discarded as the fiction of extremists, whose great error consists in spending more effort to discover what may possibly be made out of a sacred writer's words than to make sure of that which the scope and language most naturally require."[136]

Certainly, all these churches see their counterpart in churches of every age in the Church. But, there are not periods of Church history that are identified exclusively with one church.

> The *Seven Churches* are the churches of the actual seven towns. Most of the fantastic schemes which twist the *Revelation* into a forecast of modern history begin by making each of the churches an age in the history of the church universal; for without this indefensible proceeding it would be difficult to get down to modern times at all. All these schemes are contrary to the plain warning of the prophet, *what must quickly come to pass: the time is at hand.*

---

[135] Jay E. Adams, <u>The Time is at Hand</u>, 57-58.
[136] Milton S. Terry, <u>Biblical Apocalyptics</u>, 313.

This argument alone is enough to refute every kind of Adventism.[137]

The world of the seven churches of Asia was a world of emperor worship; Asia was loyal to the Roman emperor like no other part of the empire. Proof of this loyalty was found in their willingness to worship the emperor. Monarchical worship had been practice by the Middle Eastern cultures for centuries. We can see this in the behavior of Nebuchadrezzar king of Babylon and the response of Shadrach, Meshach and Abed-nego to this behavior. But, "In no part of the world, probably, was there such a fervent and sincere loyalty to the emperors as in Asia. Augustus had been a savior to the Asian peoples, and they deified him as the Savior of mankind, and worshipped him with the most wholehearted devotion as the god incarnate in human form, the 'present deity.' "[138] This was the world of the new Christian church. This was the world of the seven letters of the Apocalyptics. In this world Christians must live yet, "...it was to the ancient mind an outrage and an almost inconceivable thing that people could be fellow citizens without engaging in the worship of the same city gods. The bond of patriotism was really a religious bond."[139] The city god, of course, was the emperor. In refusing emperor worship the Christians were charged with disloyalty to their government as well as being atheists.

Message to Ephesus

Ephesus was the most important city in the Roman province of Asia, on the West Coast of what is now Asiatic Turkey. It was situated at the mouth of the Cayster River. A magnificent road 11 meters wide and lined with columns ran down through the city to the fine harbor, which served both as a great export center at the end of the Asiatic caravan-route and also as a natural landing-point from Rome.[140]

---

[137] Philip Carrington, 74. By Adventism the author means Premillennialism.

[138] W. M. Ramsey, The Letters to the Seven Churches (Peabody, Mass: Hendrickson Publishers, 1994), 83.

[139] Ibid., 105.

[140] J. D. Douglas, Editor, The New Bible Dictionary, Third Edition, Logos electronic edition (Wheaton, Illinois: Tyndale House Publishers, Inc. 1962), "Ephesus."

Ephesus also maintained its religious importance under Roman rule. It became a center of the emperor cult, and eventually possessed three official temples, thus qualifying three times over for the proud title 'temple-warden' of the emperors. It is remarkable that Paul had friends among the Asiarchs or leaders of the community... (Acts 19:31). These were officers of the 'commune' of Asia, whose primary function was actually to foster the imperial cult.[141]

There was a large colony of Jews at Ephesus, and they had long enjoyed a privileged position under Roman rule (Jos., *Ant.* 14. 225ff.; 14. 262ff.). The earliest reference to the coming of Christianity there is in *c.* AD 52, when Paul made a short visit and left Aquila and Priscilla there (Acts 18:18-21). Paul's third missionary journey had Ephesus as its goal, and he stayed there for over 2 years (Acts 19:8, 10), attracted, no doubt, by its strategic importance as a commercial, political and religious center. His work was at first based in the synagogue, later he debated in the lecture-hall of Tyrannus, making of Ephesus a base for the evangelization of the whole province of Asia. The spread of Christianity, which refused syncretism, began to incur the hostility of vested religious interests. It affected not only the magic cults which flourished there (Acts 19:13ff) but also the worship of Artemis (Acts 19:27), causing damage to the trade in cult objects which was one source of the prosperity of Ephesus. There followed the celebrated riot described in Acts 19. The city was later the headquarters of the John who had jurisdiction over the seven leading churches of Asia addressed in the Apocalypse. The church in Ephesus is addressed first of the seven (Rev. 2:1-7), as being the most important church in the *de facto* capital, and as being the landing-place for a messenger from Patmos and standing at the head of a circular road joining the seven cities in order.[142]

2:1 To the angel of the church in Ephesus write: The One who holds the seven stars in His right hand, the One who walks among the seven golden lampstands, says this.... John continues with the symbolic expressions ***seven stars (2:1)*** and ***seven golden lampstands (2:1)*** which were introduced in chapter one. The ***seven stars (2:1)*** are the seven angels (1:20), or pastors, and the ***seven golden lampstands (2:1)*** are the seven churches (1:20). Christ identifies

---

[141] Ibid., "Ephesus."

[142] Ibid., "Ephesus."

Himself as *the one who walks among (2:1)* the churches. The meaning is clear; He is active in their care. "As a priest in the temple tends the lamps to keep them from growing dim or going out, Christ moves among the churches to attend to the purity and brightness of the light they give to the world."[143]

2:2 I know your deeds and your toil and perseverance, and that you cannot tolerate evil men, and you put to the test those who call themselves apostles, and they are not, and you found them to be false.... We are next introduced to three words: *deeds (2:2)*, *toil (2:2)*, and *perseverance (2:2)*. In understanding these words and their meaning, it will become evident under what circumstances these believers labored for the gospel of Christ. *Deeds (2:2)* is from ἔργον (*érgon*) and means "to work or labor."[144] *Deeds (2:2)* "are not just specific deeds but the manner of life, the behavior of these people: 'I know the life that you have lived.' "[145] *Toil (2:2)* is from κόπος (*kopos*) and means "a state characterized by troubling circumstances - 'trouble, distress.'"[146] *Toil (2:2)* refers to "their persistent and painful struggles to maintain their Christian profession."[147] The next significant word is *perseverance (2:2)* which comes from ὑπομονή (*uhpomoné*) and means "to continue to bear up despite difficulty and suffering - 'to endure, to put up with.' "[148]

Putting this all together, we see that the Ephesians <u>worked</u> hard in promoting and living their faith. They did so even when <u>distressed</u> and <u>troubled</u> by the Jews and local authorities. And they <u>continued</u> to do so over a long period of time. They were not "flash in the pan" believers or as Jesus described some, seeds that fell among the thorns and stones, making a good start but fizzling out in the long run. For all this, the Lord of the Church commended them.

---

[143] Steve Gregg, 64.

[144] <u>Enhanced Strong's Lexicon</u> (Oak Harbor, WA: Logos Research Systems, Inc., 1995).

[145] Robert G. Bratcher, Rev. 2:2.

[146] Johannes P. Louw and Eugene A. Nida, <u>Greek-English Lexicon of the New Testament Based on Semantic Domains</u> (New York, NY: United Bible Societies, 1988, 1989), LN 22.7.

[147] Robert G. Bratcher, Rev. 2:2.

[148] Johannes P. Louw and Eugene A. Nida, LN 25.175.

The word **tolerate (2:2)** speaks of bearing or carrying a heavy burden. The Ephesian church was not tolerating evil among their members, but instead was trying to help their members overcome it. When a few refused the help offered and became belligerent about their sin; this church refused to tolerate those that had thereby so clearly defined themselves as evil. Indeed, such recalcitrant men and women are a burden to many churches, a burden the church should not tolerate or bear. And this is an important lesson; many churches are afflicted with evil in their midst, but because they don't want "waves," they put up with, **tolerate (2:2)**, evil people. When Christians put self first, instead of Christ's testimony and the purity of His Church, they become very tolerant. The world demands that we tolerate their sin; Christ praises those that refuse to do so.

We are told that they **put to the test (2:2)** these so-called **apostles (2:2)**. Now "the verb 'to test' means to apply certain procedures in order to determine the truth or falsity of a claim."[149] We do not know what procedures they used. The church in each generation is presented with self-proclaimed apostles and prophets and other religious charlatans. Perhaps the procedures differ over time, but the need of putting these religious leaders to the test remains.

"The rulers of the church were not afraid to discipline evil men. They knew the importance of heresy trials and excommunications, and it seems that this church had a good share of both: Its rulers had tested the false 'apostles,' and had convicted them."[150] Paul prepared them for these times when he said to them,

> *Be on guard for yourselves and for all the flock, among which the*
> *Holy Spirit has made you overseers, to shepherd the church of*
> *God which He purchased with His own blood. I know that after*
> *my departure savage wolves will come in among you, not*
> *sparing the flock; and from among your own selves men will*
> *arise, speaking perverse things, to draw away the disciples after*
> *them. (Acts 20:28-30, NASB95)*

Paul, on his way to Jerusalem to meet with the leaders of the church there, was not sure he would ever see the Ephesians again. He left them this

---

[149] Robert G. Bratcher, Rev. 2:2.

[150] David Chilton, The Days of Vengeance, 94-95.

warning. In applying this warning, we may ask, how are we to know which ones to endure and which ones to show no patience with? We are required to "test" those who make spiritual claims. From these early tests came our *Apostles Creed, Nicene Creed* and eventually the *Westminster Confession of Faith*, and these documents provide a test of orthodoxy today. In addition, to this material in Revelation, John makes this point again in his epistle.

> *Beloved, do not believe every spirit, but test the spirits to see whether they are from God, because many false prophets have gone out into the world. (1 John 4:1, NASB95)*

The Ephesians had well heeded this advice. "Ephesians alone does not mention a single doctrinal issue that needed apostolic correction."[151]

2:3 *...and you have perseverance and have endured for My name's sake, and have not grown weary. Name (2:3)* stands for the person, and here the person is Christ. They are suffering for Christ's sake; that is, they are suffering because they are determined to be faithful Christians.[152]

2:4 *But I have this against you, that you have left your first love.* And yet all is not well for Jesus says, *I have this against you (2:4)*. As Henry Barclay Swete says, "Patience and unremitting toil in His cause are not all that Christ requires, and indeed are of little value, if the spirit of love is absent. But at Ephesus love was waning, perhaps as the result of the controversies through which the Church had passed."[153] Fighting for the purity of the church can fray the edges of love. And for that reason, perhaps it is no surprise that the one church that was so successful in their fight against error should be the one church rebuked for failing to love. "The strives of theologians and the cry 'First purity, then peace,' translated into 'Purity without peace,' have been in every age the scandal and the weakness of the Church."[154] This should serve as a warning to all those that love the purity of doctrine, especially those that are in leadership

---

151 Ibid., 94.

152 Robert G. Bratcher, Rev. 2:3.

153 Henry Barclay Swete, 26.

154 William Milligan, 46.

positions entrusted with the well being of the flock. Continue to love the truth of the Scripture, but deal with error in love as well. "Christ does not criticize the Ephesians for being 'too orthodox,' but for leaving, forsaking the love which they had at first. The question of 'doctrine *versus* love' is, Biblically speaking, a non-issue.... Christians are required to be both orthodox and loving...."[155]

2:5 *Therefore remember from where you have fallen, and repent and do the deeds you did at first; or else I am coming to you and will remove your lampstand out of its place—unless you repent.* There is but one biblical response to sin, and that is to **repent (2:5)**. Excuses, even the best of them, as in defending the church against heresy, are not acceptable and run the risk of judgement from the head of the Church. "The very nature of Christianity is one of separation from sin and the world, and separation to Christ and holiness."[156] True repentance produces this holiness.

Notice the relationship between repentance and **deeds (2:5)**. Christ knows of no repentance that produces no change in the believer's life. In our day, repentance is very often viewed as feeling sorry for some behavior, and certainly, sorrow is not inappropriate at such times. However, real repentance always goes beyond sorrow to life-changing behavior. Being sorry in itself it not always that hard, change, on the other hand, is indeed hard. This is the point of real repentance; actions always follow. John the Baptist made the same point when he said to the Pharisees and Sadducees, *"Therefore bear fruit in keeping with repentance..."* (Matthew 3:8, NASB95).

Notice how Jesus uses the word **coming (2:5)**. He is not referring to His Second Coming; He is referring to a judgement coming. An understanding of this type of *coming*, mentioned here and in Revelation 2:16, 3:3 and 3:11 is critical to a proper understanding of much of Scripture. A failure to grasp this concept will cause you to see the Second Coming at every point the word *coming* is mentioned. And if you do that, you will grossly misinterpret the Bible at critical points.

---

[155] David Chilton, The Days of Vengeance, 96.

[156] Ralph E. Bass, Jr., Hope For Today's Problems (Greenville, SC: Living Hope Press, 2002), 300.

Notice that these four comings are dependent on the conduct of the church. If they were to repent, He would not come. If they did not repent, He would come, but at different times based on the spiritual condition of that church. "Now if these four 'comings' are each dependent on the conduct of the different churches, they must all be at different dates; they cannot refer to one colossal outward 'coming' on the clouds of heaven, visible to all."[157] And they did not; they referred to a judgment coming. This reminds us that it is not only Israel and Jerusalem that is subject to judgment comings, clearly, the Church is as well. Often "where the Messiah says *I am coming, he refers to an invisible spiritual visitation....*"[158] And one must ask, "Where are those seven churches today?"

2:6 *Yet this you do have, that you hate the deeds of the Nicolaitans, which I also hate.* It is a shock for many uninformed and immature Christians to read that Jesus **hates (2:6)**. However, the Scripture is abundantly clear that God does indeed **hate (2:6)** evil, and we are to do so as well. But we must make it clear that it is evil we hate, and nothing else.

> *You hate all who do iniquity. (Psalm 5:5, NASB95)*

> *Hate evil, you who love the LORD.... (Psalm 97:10, NASB95)*

> *I hate and despise falsehood,*
> *But I love Your law. (Psalm 129:163, NASB95)*

> *The fear of the LORD is to hate evil;*
> *Pride and arrogance and the evil way*
> *And the perverted mouth, I hate. (Proverbs 8:13, NASB95)*

> *Hate evil, love good,*
> *And establish justice in the gate! (Amos 5:15, NASB95)*

---

[157] Philip Carrington, 96.

[158] Ibid, 97.

Also let none of you devise evil in your heart against another, and do not love perjury; for all these are what I hate,' declares the LORD. (Zechariah 8:17, NASB95)

"For I hate divorce," says the LORD, the God of Israel. (Malachi 2:16, NASB95)

In our era, one of the attacks of those that hate God is to accuse the child of God of hating. Generally, when this accusation is made the Christian begins to back pedal, assuring all listening that he does not hate. But how can a believer do this? Is it a virtue not to hate? As Henry Swete says, "Hatred of evil deeds ... is a true counterpart of the love of good, and both are Divine ... To share His hatred of evil is to manifest an affinity of character with Him, which is a sign of grace in Churches and in individuals."[159] It is a responsibility of God's people to have similar affections as God, to both love righteousness and hate evil.

The **Nicolaitans (2:6)** are mentioned as a licentious sect by Irenaeus, an influential early Church Father. "The Nicolaitanes," he says, "are the followers of that Nicolas who was one of the seven first ordained to the diaconate by the apostles. They lead lives of unrestrained indulgence. The character of these men is very plainly pointed out in the Apocalypse of John, where they are represented as teaching that it is a matter of indifference to practice adultery, and to eat things sacrificed to idols."[160]

Whether Irenaeus makes a proper association with this heresy and one of the first deacons with a similar name is not certain. "The clue to the real meaning of this term is found in the identification of the Nicolaitans with 'the teaching of Balaam' in Revelation 2:14–15. Not only is it possible that 'Nicolaitan' is a Greek form of 'Balaam' (as understood by the rabbis), but, more important, this interpretation fits both the text and the first-century situation."[161] The identification of the Nicolaitans is largely speculation though it is based on some convincing inferences.

---

[159] Henry Barclay Swete, 28.

[160] Philip Schaff, History of the Christian Church (Oak Harbor, WA: Logos Research Systems, Inc., 1997), Vol. II, Chapter XI, #122.

[161] W.C. Kaiser, Hard Sayings of the Bible (Downers Grove, IL: InterVarsity Press, 1997, c1996), 759-761.

The Nicolaitans, then, appear to be a group that corrupted God's people by suggesting compromise with the culture of the day. Rather than worship God and him alone, they suggested that it was appropriate to engage in patriotic ceremonies (such as feasts associated with the worship of the emperor) and other cultural institutions (for example, trade guilds, something like our modern unions or professional associations, and their worship). It is possible that either as part of these ceremonies or as a separate area of compromise they also permitted the use of prostitutes (perhaps as an accepted part of the "business ethic" of their day). Jesus (who is speaking through John) was not impressed. In fact, he threatened judgement on the church.[162]

2:7 He who has an ear, let him hear what the Spirit says to the churches. To him who overcomes, I will grant to eat of the tree of life which is in the Paradise of God. The believer is expected to **overcome (2:7)**. However, the Christ who is ordering him or her to a certain course of action is also empowering that person through His Holy Spirit to accomplish that for which He will reward them from **the tree of life (2:7)**.

So, in the power of the Holy Spirit, the believer is expected to be faithful in the face of opposition. In being an overcomer, "the question is not one of victory or defeat. The question is victory or treason."[163] For fighting a good fight, he is given the privilege of eating from the **tree of life (2:7)**, in other words, eternal life. Failure to overcome would imply a refusal or inability to eat from **the tree of life (2:7)**, in other words, eternal damnation.

> On either side of the river was the tree of life, bearing twelve kinds of fruit, yielding its fruit every month; and the leaves of the tree were for the healing of the nations. (Revelation 22:2, NASB95)

> If we endure, we will also reign with Him; if we deny Him, He also will deny us.... (II Timothy 2:12, NASB95)

---

[162] Ibid., 759-761.

[163] David Chilton, The Days of Vengeance, 99.

Message to Smyrna

Smyrna, was a city in the Roman province of Asia, which is on the Aegean shore of what is now Asiatic Turkey. It was the natural port for the ancient trade route through the Hermus valley, and its immediate hinterland was very fertile. Smyrna was a faithful ally of Rome long before the Roman power became supreme in the East Mediterranean. Under the empire it was famous for its beauty and for the magnificence of its public buildings. The gospel probably reached Smyrna at an early date, presumably from Ephesus (Acts 19:10). The 'angel of the church in Smyrna' is the recipient of this the second (Rev. 2:8-11) of the letters to the 'seven churches in Asia'. As in other commercial cities, the church encountered opposition from the Jews. But in Smyrna the opposition was extreme.[164]

2:8 And to the angel of the church in Smyrna write: The first and the last, who was dead, and has come to life, says this.... These are words of comfort. Here Christ reiterates His deity and resurrection to this church. This is, no doubt, to encourage those who are about to follow Him in martyrdom. Because He is God and knows the beginning from the end, because He has determined both, they can rest in His sovereign purpose for their lives. Because He has conquered death, they can rest in His promise of the resurrection. It was He, who had earlier said,

> *I am the resurrection and the life; he who believes in Me will live even if he dies, and everyone who lives and believes in Me will never die. (John 11:25-26, NASB95)*

2:9 I know your tribulation and your poverty (but you are rich), and the blasphemy by those who say they are Jews and are not, but are a synagogue of Satan. Their *poverty (2:9)* is associated with the *tribulation (2:9)* they are suffering. It was common in the Jewish community, and Smyrna had a very large Jewish community, to economically boycott those that had been put out of the synagogue. "Smyrna had the largest Jewish population of any Asian city. If this was written prior to A.D. 70, then it was a period in which the main adversaries of Christianity were Jews. The church there was understandably harassed

---

[164] J. D. Douglas, Editor, <u>The New Bible Dictionary</u>, "Smyrna."

more than most."[165] This is perhaps the main reason the Christians in Jerusalem were suffering such economic deprivation, and for this reason Paul took offerings from the Gentile churches for their support. If the Jews had political power, they would go beyond boycott and seize the property of dissenters, a practice on which the author of Hebrews remarks in his epistle.

> *For you showed sympathy to the prisoners and accepted joyfully the seizure of your property, knowing that you have for yourselves a better possession and a lasting one. (Hebrews 10:34, NASB95)*

The result of this tribulation was **poverty (2:9)**, and yet Christ called them **rich (2:9)**. Paul says something similar,

> *...as poor yet making many rich, as having nothing yet possessing all things. (II Corinthians 6:10, NASB95)*

Christ puts between the crosshairs of His condemnation a group in Smyrna for whom He uses these startling words, **those who say they are Jews and are not, but are a synagogue of Satan (2:9)**. They considered themselves real Jews, which Christ denies flatly, and they thought they were God-worshippers, a claim, which in the most jarring terms Christ also rejects. In what sense were these people not Jews? They were, no doubt, born into Jewish families, who traced their lineage back to Abraham. What these people failed to consider, however, Paul addressed in Romans this way.

> *For he is not a Jew who is one outwardly, nor is circumcision that which is outward in the flesh. But he is a Jew who is one inwardly; and circumcision is that which is of the heart, by the Spirit, not by the letter; and his praise is not from men, but from God. (Romans 2:28-29, NASB95)*

It was not many years after this that Polycarp was arrested and brought before the Proconsul at Smyrna; it was the *Jews* that were the most furious of the entire multitude in demanding his condemnation. When the mob, after he was sentenced to death, set about gathering fuel to burn him, it was

---

[165] Steve Gregg, 67.

the *Jews* that ran to procure the fuel. And when, inasmuch as the burning failed, and the blessed martyr had been run through with various weapons, it was the *Jews* that urged the magistrate to refuse to give his dead body to the Christians for burial.[166]

We have an important issue here. There are many today that say that the Jews are "God's chosen people." The church is but an interruption in God's main plan. The "real" people of God are Jews. But not according to the Apostle John, these Jews rejected and murdered Christ and in doing so rejected Abraham as well, for "...*Abraham rejoiced to see My day, and he saw it and was glad*" (John 8:56, NASB95). But these Jews were not "glad;" indeed, they crucified the Lord of Glory. We must recognize that non-believing Jews are covenant-breaking apostates, not "God's chosen people." This is the same crowd that Christ dealt with some thirty years earlier.

> *They answered and said to Him, "Abraham is our father." Jesus said to them, "If you are Abraham's children, do the deeds of Abraham. "But as it is, you are seeking to kill Me, a man who has told you the truth, which I heard from God; this Abraham did not do. "You are doing the deeds of your father." They said to Him, "We were not born of fornication; we have one Father: God." Jesus said to them, "If God were your Father, you would love Me, for I proceeded forth and have come from God, for I have not even come on My own initiative, but He sent Me. "Why do you not understand what I am saying? It is because you cannot hear My word. You are of your father the devil, and you want to do the desires of your father. He was a murderer from the beginning, and does not stand in the truth because there is no truth in him. Whenever he speaks a lie, he speaks from his own nature, for he is a liar and the father of lies." (John 8:39-44, NASB95)*

It is these same Jews that Christ now calls **a synagogue of Satan (2:9).** They were of Satan (the devil) then and they are now. "Even the martyrdom of Polycarp at Smyrna, a generation later, was distinguished by the fierce zeal with which the excited Jewish calumniators urged it on."[167]

---

[166] Moses Stuart, 69.

[167] Milton S. Terry, <u>Biblical Apocalyptics</u>, 297.

At the martyrdom of Polycarp it was noticed that the Jews of Smyrna not only made common cause with the heathen but also outdid them in efforts to prepare fuel for the fire.[168] These Jews not only rejected Christ, but they did their best to cooperate with the pagan mob, to bring about the destruction of the Asian Church.[169]

"Who then is the true Jew? Who belongs to the true Israel? According to the clear teaching of the New Testament, the person (regardless of his ethnic heritage) who has been clothed with Jesus Christ is the inheritor of the promises to Abraham, and possesses the blessings of the Covenant."[170]

> *Therefore, be sure that it is those who are of faith who are sons of Abraham. (Galatians 3:7, NASB95)*

> *For you are all sons of God through faith in Christ Jesus. For all of you who were baptized into Christ have clothed yourselves with Christ. There is neither Jew nor Greek, there is neither slave nor free man, there is neither male nor female; for you are all one in Christ Jesus. And if you belong to Christ, then you are Abraham's descendants, heirs according to promise. (Galatians 3:26-29, NASB95)*

William Hendriksen apply sums up our point stating, "How anyone can say that the Jews of today are still, in a very special and glorious and preeminent sense, God's people, is more than we can understand. God Himself calls those who reject the Saviour and persecute true believers 'the synagogue of Satan.' They are no longer His people."[171]

2:10 Do not fear what you are about to suffer. Behold, the devil is about to cast some of you into prison, so that you will be tested, and you will have tribulation for ten days. Be faithful until death, and I will give you the crown of life. It is the **devil (2:10)** that animates his servants, both Jews and Gentiles, to oppose Christ. For the believers of Smyrna, new persecutions were on the horizon,

---

[168] Henry Barclay Swete, xciii.

[169] Ibid., xciii.

[170] David Chilton, The Days of Vengeance, 102.

[171] William Hendriksen, 65.

and for a certain **ten-day (2:10)** period things were to be particularly bad. Whether this was actually a ten-day period of brutal persecution or whether the number ten has symbolic significance cannot be determined with certainty, but some scholars have noted that St. John often links ten with persecution as in the ten-horned monster.[172]   This type of historical phenomena was not unprecedented as one is reminded of a one-day period of planned persecution for the people of God in the book of Esther.

> *Letters were sent by couriers to all the king's provinces to destroy,*
> *to kill and to annihilate all the Jews, both young and old, women*
> *and children, in one day, the thirteenth day of the twelfth month,*
> *which is the month Adar, and to seize their possessions as*
> *plunder. (Esther 3:12, NASB95)*

God chose to intervene and deliver Israel from this persecution, but He does not determine to do so for Smyrna. Here He expects them to suffer for His name's sake.

We are not privy to the details of this tribulation, but as the text tells us that **the devil is about to cast some of you into prison (2:10).** But, "imprisonment was not recognized by the law as a punishment for crime in the Greek or the Roman procedure. The state would not burden itself with the custody of criminals, except as a preliminary stage to their trial, or in the interval between trial and execution. Fine, exile, and death constituted the usual range of penalties."[173] So, to be cast **into prison (2:10)** was often tantamount to a death sentence. "Prison was thought of by the writer of the letter as the prelude to execution, and was understood in that sense by his readers."[174] For this reason they were encouraged to be **faithful until death (2:10)** and promised a **crown of life (2:10)** for doing so. Nothing, however, is promised to those who recant their testimony.

2:11 He who has an ear, let him hear what the Spirit says to the churches. He who overcomes will not be hurt by the second death. John speaks of the **second death (2:11)** here and in Revelation 20.

---

[172] Revelation 12:3; 13:1; 17:3: 17:7; 17:12: 17:16.

[173] W. M. Ramsey, W.M., 199.

[174] Ibid., 200.

> *Blessed and holy is the one who has a part in the first*
> *resurrection; over these the second death has no power....*
> *(Revelation 20:6, NASB95)*

The Scriptures are quite clear about the meaning of the **second death (2:11)**; it is the lake of fire.

> *But for the cowardly and unbelieving and abominable and*
> *murderers and immoral persons and sorcerers and idolaters and*
> *all liars, their part will be in the lake that burns with fire and*
> *brimstone, which is the second death. (Revelation 21:8, NASB95)*

Message to Pergamum

Pergamum, was a city of the Roman province of Asia, which is in the West of what is now Asiatic Turkey. It occupied a commanding position near the seaward end of the broad valley of the Caicus, and was probably the site of a settlement from a very early date. It became important only after 282 BC, when Philetaerus revolted against Lysimachus of Thrace and made it the capital of what became the Attalid kingdom, which in 133 BC was bequeathed by Attalus III to the Romans, who formed the province of Asia from it. The first temple of the imperial cult was built in Pergamum (c. 29 BC) in honor of Rome and Augustus. The city thus boasted a religious primacy in the province, though Ephesus became its main commercial center.

Pergamum is listed third of the 'seven churches of Asia' (Rev. 1:11): the order suits its position in geographical sequence. This was the place 'where Satan's throne is' (Rev. 2:13). The phrase has been referred to the complex of pagan cults, of Zeus, Athena, Dionysus and Asclepius, established by the Attalid kings, that of Asclepius Soter (the 'saviour', 'healer') being of special importance. These cults are illustrative of the religious history of Pergamum, but the main allusion is probably to emperor worship. This was where the worship of the divine emperor had been made the touchstone of civic loyalty under Domitian. It marked a crisis for the church in Asia. Antipas (v. 13) is probably cited as a representative (perhaps the first) of those who were brought to judgement and execution here for their faith.

This letter is the primary source for the Nicolaitans, who are emphatically equated with Balaam, and seem to be a party that advocated compromise under pagan pressures.

Here Christ possesses the real and ultimate authority, symbolized by the 'sharp two-edged sword' (v. 12), in the place where the Roman proconsul exercised the 'power of the sword' in judgement. The church is blamed for tolerating a party whose teaching would subvert it into idolatry and immorality like that of Balaam. A small town (Bergama) still stands on the plain below the acropolis of the ancient city.[175]

2:12 And to the angel of the church in Pergamum write: The One who has the sharp two-edged sword says this.... It is Christ who has the **sharp two-edged sword (2:12)**, as was read earlier in 1:16.

> *In His right hand He held seven stars, and out of His mouth came a sharp two-edged sword.... (Revelation 1:16, NASB95)*

> *And He will strike the earth [land] with the rod of His mouth, And with the breath of His lips He will slay the wicked. (Isaiah 11:4, NASB95)*

In discussing **the sharp two-edged sword (2:12)**, W. M. Ramsey provides these insightful thoughts,

> In the Roman estimation the sword was the symbol of the highest order of official authority, with which the proconsul of Asia was invested. The "right of the sword" was roughly equivalent to what we call the power of life and death ... and governors of provinces were divided into a higher and a lower class, according as they were or were not invested with this power. When the divine author addresses Pergamum in this character, his intention is patent, and would be caught immediately by all Asian readers of the apocalypse. He wields that power of life and death, which people imagine to be vested in the proconsul of the province.[176]

---

[175] J. D. Douglas, Editor, The New Bible Dictionary, "Pergamum."
[176] W. M. Ramsey, 214.

The meaning of this introduction to the church would be this: "He, who has power by a single word to chastise, or even to destroy, addresses you; harken then to his warnings!"[177]

So, these words may be spoken here both as comfort and warning to this church. It is comforting to know that Christ will prevail in His conflict with evil. It is a warning to those in the church that are failing in their mission. To that failure He says, *"Therefore repent; or else I am coming to you quickly, and I will make war against them with the sword of My mouth"* (2:16).

2:13 *I know where you dwell, where Satan's throne is; and you hold fast My name, and did not deny My faith even in the days of Antipas, My witness, My faithful one, who was killed among you, where Satan dwells.* Pergamum was noted for its many pagan temples. Where most communities had one major temple, at Pergamum there were temples to Zeus, Minerva, Apollo, Venus, Bacchus, and Aesculapius. The latter was the god of healing, and we get the medical emblem of a snake on a pole from this ancient cult. In addition, as early as 29 BC there was a temple there to the worship of the Roman Emperor Augustus. As a result emperor worship was particularly prevalent in this community. It is to these many temples that the phrase **Satan's throne (2:13)** has reference.

> Here were to be seen the many pagan altars and the great altar of Zeus. All these things may have been in the mind of Christ when He called Pergamum the place 'where Satan dwells'. ... Pergamum was the capital of the province and, as such, also the centre of emperor-worship. Here the government was carried on and here believers were asked to offer incense to the image of the emperors and to say, 'Caesar is Lord.'[178]

The church is praised because it has have not succumbed to these many "faiths" but instead have held true to Christ's **faith (2:13)**. Among the different definitions and meanings of faith in the Bible, the faith referred to here is a series of beliefs or doctrines that are strongly held by its adherents.

---

[177] Moses Stuart, 71.

[178] William Hendriksen, 66.

A faith is not simply a warm fuzzy feeling a person gets when he goes to church on Sunday, but rather a set of convictions that affects the warp and woof of a person's life and behavior. The combination of these strongly held beliefs and the resulting behavioral changes that result at times in persecution can engender the question, "Is this worth dying for?" They answered that question in the affirmative in Pergamum where their faith required them to avoid worship in the numerous satanic centers. Here they were "confessing Him alone as Savior, Mediator and Lord, proclaiming ... His identity as the link between heaven and earth...."[179]

We don't know anything about **Antipas (2:13)** other than what we are told in verse 13. And what we are told by the King of Glory is that he was Christ's **faithful one (2:13)**, quite a praise indeed. Who killed him and why, we are not told. As was so often the case, however, we can guess that it was by government approval, if not by government action. Historically, the two great enemies of Christianity in the first century were Judaism and humanistic Statism.

2:14 But I have a few things against you, because you have there some who hold the teaching of Balaam, who kept teaching Balak to put a stumbling block before the sons of Israel, to eat things sacrificed to idols and to commit acts of immorality. In verses 14 and 15, John clarifies for us the teachings of **Balaam (2:14)**. **Balaam (2:14)** was an OT character who had an encounter with the Jewish nation as it prepared to enter the Holy Land at the end of their Exodus journey. After being dissuaded in a forceful and quite unforgettable way from acting against Israel, he instructed Balak to attack Israel, not outright, but by enticing them with idolatrous festivals and immorality. So Israel succumbed to the "partying" mindset, and fell into sin. Now Satan is working this same strategy in Pergamum by way of the *Nicolaitans* (2:15), which we have seen at Ephesus. Although Ephesus would not tolerate this crowd, those at Pergamum are not so wise.

2:15 So you also have some who in the same way hold the teaching of the Nicolaitans. The **teaching of the Nicolaitans (2:15)** "...was evidently an attempt to effect a reasonable compromise with

---

[179] David Chilton, The Days of Vengeance, 107.

the established usages of Greco-Roman society and to retain as many as possible of those usages in the Christian system of life."[180]

> ...it is highly probable that the Nicolaitans either already had, or soon would have, reached the conclusion that they might justifiably comply with the current test of loyalty, and burn a little incense in honor of the emperor. The church was not disloyal ... then why should its members make any difficulty about proving their loyalty by burning a few grains of incense? A little incense was nothing. An excellent and convincing argument can readily be worked out, and then the whole ritual of the state religion would have followed as matter of course. Christ and Augustus would have been enthroned side by side ... and everything that was vital in Christianity would have been lost ... either it must conquer and destroy the imperial idolatry, or it must compromise and in so doing be itself destroyed.[181]

A.T. Robertson, the great Greek scholar tell us, "These early Gnostics practiced licentiousness as a principle since they were not under law, but under grace...."[182] We in our generation also have an entrenched group in our churches that boast of being under grace and not law. Sadly, their lives often evidence licentiousness as well. Now, of course, there is no dichotomy between the law of God and grace, but there is one between man's laws, rules and regulations and grace. These man made laws and regulations we repudiate but in doing so we do not throw out the baby with the bath water. Law in and of itself is an aspect of the nature of God. The revelation of that law is an aspect of the grace of God. Unfortunately, many that think they are honoring God by repudiating the "law" miss this point. You do not repudiate the law of God and still honor God. As a result, much of modern day Christianity is lawless, repudiating God's law in a confused attempt to magnify grace. Such theology simply magnifies lawlessness. Believers become a law unto themselves, restrained at best only by some of the books of the New Testament—but not necessarily the Gospels and Revelation, which are for different dispensations.

---

[180] W. M. Ramsey, 219.

[181] Ibid., 220.

[182] Archibald Thomas Robertson, Vol. VI, 305.

2:16 Therefore repent; or else I am coming to you quickly, and I will make war against them with the sword of My mouth. This is a serious threat. Notwithstanding the faithfulness of this church in other areas, this defect is so great that Christ threatens war on this congregation. In the light of this passage, we marvel at those churches that allow immorality in their midst without rebuke. The doctrines of Balaam and the Nicolaitans are alive and well in modern Christianity. Couples are divorcing for every reason imaginable, church members are subject to the fraudulent business schemes and scams of other church members, contracts are broken and lawsuits result. In many cases there is one common element in all this, the failure of the church's leadership to respond to the problems by means of Biblical discipline.

Again let us notice that the **coming (2:16)** of Christ does not necessarily refer to His Second Coming. It often refers to a judgement coming as in Revelation 2:5 and 3:3. Miss this point and every **coming (2:16)** will offer the major theological challenge of fitting the incident into the Second Coming, where in many cases it does not belong. As Gary DeMar says, "These are judgement comings that were threatened on a particular church at a particular time similar to Jesus' promised coming in judgement against apostate Judaism in the first century. The passages that describe the coming of Christ to first-century churches are not descriptive of the 'second coming' (consummating coming) of Christ...."[183]

2:17 He who has an ear, let him hear what the Spirit says to the churches. To him who overcomes, to him I will give some of the hidden manna, and I will give him a white stone, and a new name written on the stone which no one knows but he who receives it.

> As the manna was laid up in the ark, no one could even approach it but the high-priest, who, once in each year, went into the most holy place in order to make atonement. Yet even he could not taste of it. But under the new dispensation, where all are to be made 'kings and priest unto God,' Christians may enter for themselves into the most holy place, (for the veil is rent), and may even partake of the manna deposited there. Yet all this, it will be remembered, is but

---

[183] Gary DeMar, 72.

118

imagery employed in order to portray the ample and delightful enjoyment of the faithful in the world to come.[184]

Of course the true manna, of which the Old Testament is but a type is Christ Himself. And it is He that is promised as our eternal heritage.

Jesus then said to them, "Truly, truly, I say to you, it is not Moses who has given you the bread out of heaven, but it is My Father who gives you the true bread out of heaven." (John 6:32, NASB95)

The true **manna (2:17)** was for the true Israel. God now takes that **manna (2:17)** from racial Israel and gives it to spiritual Israel, the Church. Ignatius, an early Church father wrote in A.D. 107. "It is absurd to speak of Jesus Christ with the tongue, and to cherish in the mind a Judaism which has now come to an end. For where there is Christianity there cannot be Judaism."[185]

Paul uses this word **stone (2:17)** in a unique way in his personal testimony saying,

And this is just what I did in Jerusalem; not only did I lock up many of the saints in prisons, having received authority from the chief priests, but also when they were being put to death I cast my vote against them. (Acts 26:10, NASB95)

This use of the word **stone (2:17)** comes from the practice of casting votes using white and black stones. Although Paul does not use the word **white (2:17)**, that is clearly implied in that he voted "yes" to putting Christians to death. That would require a white stone versus a black one. "This old word for pebble ...was used in courts of justice, black pebbles for condemning, white pebbles for acquitting."[186] To the overcomers, those that cast their vote for Christ in this life, He promises to cast His vote for them in the life to come.

---

[184] Moses Stuart, 77.

[185] Philip Schaff, (2000). The Ante-Nicene Fathers, electronic ed. (Garland, TX: Galaxie Software), Vol. 1, The Apostolic Fathers, Chapter 10.

[186] Archibald Thomas Robertson, 307.

This **new name (2:17)**, the one that goes on this **stone (2:17)**, reflects something of the character of the person being named. Here Christ may give either a new name to the believer, reflecting an aspect of the Christian's faithful character, or He may give a new name—a revelation—of Himself to the Christian, a sort of special secret between the two of them. It would be a secret that reflects something of the character of God that no one knows but that person alone. I don't think it would be unlike God to give a special treasure to every believer in this way. And how could God run out of names that reflect His Holy character, He that is eternal in all His qualities?

Most importantly, a name given to a person represents ownership. The beast puts his name on his followers.

> *And he causes all, the small and the great, and the rich and the poor, and the free men and the slaves, to be given a mark on their right hand or on their forehead, and he provides that no one will be able to buy or to sell, except the one who has the mark, either the name of the beast or the number of his name. (Revelation 13:16-17, NASB95)*

Christ does the same thing.

> *There will no longer be any curse; and the throne of God and of the Lamb will be in it, and His bond-servants will serve Him; they will see His face, and His name will be on their foreheads. (Revelation 22:3-4, NASB95)*

Message to Thyatira

Thyatira was a city in the Roman province of Asia, in the West of what is now Asiatic Turkey. It occupied an important position in a low-lying 'corridor' connecting the Hermus and Caicus valleys. It was a frontier garrison, first on the West frontier of the territory of Seleucus I of Syria, and later, after changing hands, on the East frontier of the kingdom of Pergamum. With that kingdom, it passed under Roman rule in 133 BC. But it remained an important point in the Roman road-system, for it lay on the road from Pergamum to Laodicea, and thence to the East provinces. It was also an important center of manufacture; dyeing, garment-making, pottery and brass-working are among the trades known to have existed there. A large town (Akhisar) still stands on the same site.

The Thyatiran woman Lydia, the 'seller of purple' whom Paul met at Philippi (Acts 16:14), was probably the overseas agent of a Thyatiran manufacturer; she may have been arranging the sale of dyed woolen goods which were known simply by the name of the dye. This 'purple' was obtained from the madder root, and was still produced in the district, under the name 'Turkey red,' into the present century.

The Thyatiran church was the fourth (Rev. 1:11) of the 'seven churches of Asia'. Some of the symbols in the letter to the church (Rev. 2:18-29) seem to allude to the circumstances of the city. The description of the Christ (v. 18) is appropriate for a city renowned for its brass-working. The terms of the promise (vv. 26-27) may reflect the long military history of the city. 'Jezebel' (the name is probably symbolic) was evidently a woman who was accepted within the fellowship of the church (v. 20). Her teaching probably advocated a measure of compromise with some activity, which was implicitly pagan. This is likely to have been membership of the social clubs or 'guilds' into which the trades were organized. These bodies fulfilled many admirable functions, and pursuance of a trade was almost impossible without belonging to the guild; yet their meetings were inextricably bound up with acts of pagan worship and immorality.[187]

2:18 And to the angel of the church in Thyatira write: The Son of God, who has eyes like a flame of fire, and His feet are like burnished bronze, says this.... Thyatira was the least significant of the seven churches, interestingly however, it has the longest letter written to it.

The Son of God (2:18), this is John's earlier description in 1:14-15. Emperor worship in Thyatira gave homage to the Roman emperor as "the Son of God." "An inscription from Asia (Revelation's territory) *circa* 9 C.E. extols Augustus as savior and son of God."[188] Here Christ is confronting that worship and stating that it is He who is the true Son of God.

Thyatira was a center for bronze making; Christ uses their familiarity with this substance to make a point about His power when He said **who has**

---

[187] J. D. Douglas, Editor, The New Bible Dictionary, "Thyatira."

[188] M. Eugene Boring, Revelation, A Bible Commentary for Teaching and Preaching (Louisville, KY: John Knox Press, 1989), 20.

eyes like a flame of fire, and His feet are like burnished bronze (2:18). "Both of these characteristics suggest impending judgement. His piercing vision sees all and can therefore not fail to judge rightly, whereas His feet, with which He will tread upon the wicked in the winepress of God's wrath (14:19f; Isa. 63:1-4), are irresistible strength, like brass. Jesus will judge the wicked in the church (vv. 22f) with a judgement none can thwart or resist."[189]

2:19 I know your deeds, and your love and faith and service and perseverance, and that your deeds of late are greater than at first. Unlike the Ephesian church, Thyatira was not lacking in love. However, also unlike the Ephesian church, Thyatira was compromising with doctrinal and moral issues. Because Thyatira was not actively dealing with that portion of their church involved in moral sins, they were not confronted with the challenge of disciplining in love. They simply were not disciplining. As a result their relationships were not frayed with conflict. However, they were not pure in doctrine and practice either, like the Ephesians. What we must learn from all this is that neither extreme is acceptable to Christ. We don't ignore error for love's sake as they did in Thyatira; neither do we sacrifice love for the sake of doctrinal or moral purity as they did in Ephesus. Because Christ expects us to have both and will enable us in that pursuit, we therefore can.

2:20 But I have this against you, that you tolerate the woman Jezebel, who calls herself a prophetess, and she teaches and leads My bond-servants astray so that they commit acts of immorality and eat things sacrificed to idols. Notice that we have the same sins here that we had in Ephesus with the Nicolaitans and in Pergamum with Balak and Balaam. Moral impurity was a way of life within these pagan cultures. Sexual *immorality (2:20)* goes by many words and history indicates the church's susceptibility to this category of sinfulness, but Christ demands that we not be deceived. We can also notice that Christ identifies the source of the problem with a woman, to whom He gives the name *Jezebel (2:20)*, the name of the wife of King Ahab in the Old Testament, both of whom were enemies of the people of God. The *Jezebel (2:20)* of Revelation tried, and perhaps succeeded, in packaging her sin with a religious aura. She "called" herself a *prophetess (2:20)*;

---

[189] Steve Gregg, 71.

122

Christ identified her as an idolatrous pagan. Christ makes it clear, there will be no compromise between His church and immorality. That is a lesson we must not fail to note in our day of guiltless sexual immorality.

Compare this woman of Thyatira with another mentioned in Acts. "*A woman named Lydia, from the city of Thyatira, a seller of purple fabrics, a worshiper of God, was listening; and the Lord opened her heart to respond to the things spoken by Paul*" (Acts 16:14, NASB95). Both were women of influence, and probably both had considerable economic power. But how different was their impact on the church.

2:21 I gave her time to repent, and she does not want to repent of her immorality. Jezebel needed to **repent (2:21)**, and Christ in His goodness gave her opportunity to do this.

> *Or do you think lightly of the riches of His kindness and tolerance and patience, not knowing that the kindness of God leads you to repentance? But because of your stubbornness and unrepentant heart you are storing up wrath for yourself in the day of wrath and revelation of the righteous judgement of God, who will render to each person according to his deeds.... (Romans 2:4-6, NASB95)*

2:22 Behold, I will throw her on a bed of sickness, and those who commit adultery with her into great tribulation, unless they repent of her deeds. Punishment follows steadfast refusal to **repent (2:22)**. Here the consequences of being stiff necked, are some sort of physical affliction that she and her "lovers" would experience. The **bed (2:22)** is much different than she and her lovers expected; it is a **bed of sickness (2:22)** and **great tribulation (2:22)**.

> *For then there will be a great tribulation, such as has not occurred since the beginning of the world until now, nor ever will. (Matthew 24:21, NASB95)*

> *I said to him, "My lord, you know." And he said to me, "These are the ones who come out of the great tribulation, and they have washed their robes and made them white in the blood of the Lamb. (Revelation 7:14, NASB95)*

It would appear that the **great tribulation (2:22)** mentioned here is the same as the one mentioned later in Revelation. They appear to be one and the same event. This **great tribulation (2:22)** has a primary focus on Israel and Jerusalem but a powerful secondary one on all believers in the Roman Empire. Whereas Christ promises to deliver some, the 144,000, others especially those that are not faithful to Him are threatened with this tribulation.

2:23 And I will kill her children with pestilence, and all the churches will know that I am He who searches the minds and hearts; and I will give to each one of you according to your deeds. Sin cannot be hidden from God. Not only does God know open and visible sins, but He **searches the minds and hearts (2:23)** of man.

> *I, the Lord, search the heart,*
> *I test the mind,*
> *Even to give to each man according to his ways,*
> *According to the results of his deeds. (Jeremiah 17:10, NASB95)*

Because God **searches the minds and hearts (2:23)**, it is incumbent upon us to guard our minds and hearts from thoughts that displease Christ and lead to greater sins.

> *Watch over your heart with all diligence, for from it flow the springs of life. (Proverbs 4:23, NASB95).*

2:24 But I say to you, the rest who are in Thyatira, who do not hold this teaching, who have not known the deep things of Satan, as they call them—I place no other burden on you. Probably this crowd saw their "freedom" spring from an understanding of the "deep things of God." Jesus here calls these things, **the deep things of Satan (2:24)**. This suggests a fascination with quasi-Gnostic teachings that said that familiarity with and practice of paganism resulted in greater sanctification. "Connecting this with what we already know of her teaching, it seems that her doctrine was a proto-Gnostic teaching that Christians would attain new and greater levels of sanctification by immersion into the depths of Satanism: worshiping idols, committing fornication, entering to the fullest extent into the depravities of the heathen around them—sinning that grace might abound."[190]

To be sure Paul makes reference himself to "the deep things of God," *"For to us God revealed them through the Spirit; for the Spirit searches all things, even the depths of God"* (1 Corinthians 2:10, NASB95). But he hardly had in mind the debauchery that apparently accompanied Jezebel's teaching. Instead, Christ makes it clear, that this doctrine is nothing but the *"deep things of Satan."*

2:25 *Nevertheless what you have, hold fast until I come.* Jesus tells this church to ***hold fast until I come (2:25).*** This refers "to those of their number who were holding to the truth against the Jezebel pagan philosophies and Nicolaitane doctrines...."[191] They are doing right in their opposition to this evil. They must not grow weary in this holy task.

2:26-27 *He who overcomes, and he who keeps My deeds until the end,* TO HIM I WILL GIVE AUTHORITY OVER THE NATIONS; 27 AND HE SHALL RULE THEM WITH A ROD OF IRON, AS THE VESSELS OF THE POTTER ARE BROKEN TO PIECES, *as I also have received authority from My Father....* Here Jesus refers to the great Messianic Psalm two,

> *Ask of Me, and I will surely give the nations as Your inheritance,*
> *And the very ends of the earth as Your possession.*
> *'You shall break them with a rod of iron,*
> *You shall shatter them like earthenware. (Psalm 2:8-9, NASB95)*

In Psalm Two, the Father is giving to the son the inhabitants of all the earth. In our passage here, Christ, who has received this as His inheritance, is saying to the Church "I will give him an exalted station, with abundance and honor like those of kings...."[192] Now such a promise and gift must have looked very unlikely to these new Believers.

---

[190] David Chilton, The Days of Vengeance, 115.

[191] Foy E. Wallace, Jr., The Book of Revelation (Fort Smith, AR: Foy E. Wallace, Jr. Publications, Inc., 1997), 95-96.

[192] Moses Stuart, vol. II, 84.

...the promise sets the true and victorious Christian in the place and dignity of the Roman emperor. Rome was the only power on earth that exercised authority over the nations, and ruled them with a rod of iron, and smashed them like potsherds; to the Roman State that description is startlingly applicable. Accordingly the promise here designates the victor as heir to a greater, more terrible, more irresistible strength than even the power of the mighty empire with all its legions.[193]

"The point of the quotation here is that the Christian overcomers, in this age, are promised a share in the messianic reign of Jesus Christ, in time and on earth. In spite of all opposition, God has set up His King over the nations. Those who are obedient to His commands will rule the world, reconstructing it for His glory in terms of His laws."[194] This promise to rule and reign is reiterated to this early Church in several verses that follow in Revelation. Consider these:

And she gave birth to a son, a male child, who is to rule all the nations with a rod of iron; and her child was caught up to God and to His throne. (Revelation 12:5, NASB95)

From His mouth comes a sharp sword, so that with it He may strike down the nations, and He will rule them with a rod of iron; and He treads the wine press of the fierce wrath of God, the Almighty. (Revelation 19:15, NASB95)

Has this happened or will it happen? In fact, it has happened. In the fourth century Christianity became the official religion of the Roman Empire. In this capacity, it did **rule all nations with a rod of iron (2:27)**. That is, Christian laws replaced pagan laws and the population of the empire was required by law to obey these regulations or face sever punishment. By way of example, such laws would include a prohibition of infanticide and homosexuality. In addition, there is every reason to believe that under the providence of God Christ will again, and even more fully so, rule the nations both in time and eternity.

---

[193] W. M. Ramsey, 243.

[194] David Chilton, The Days of Vengeance, 117.

For the earth will be full of the knowledge of the Lord as the waters cover the sea. (Isaiah 11:9, NASB95)

In saying, **as I also have received authority from My Father (2:27)** "...he transmits to his victorious followers the same authority he had received from God."[195]

2:28 ...**and I will give him the morning star. 'He who has an ear, let him hear what the Spirit says to the churches.'** Many years earlier the Jews were promised a **star (2:28)**.

I see him, but not now; I behold him, but not near; a star shall come forth from Jacob, a scepter shall rise from Israel, and shall crush through the forehead of Moab, and tear down all the sons of Sheth. (Numbers 24:17, NASB95)

That **star (2:28)** has now come, for Jesus Christ is that **star (2:28)**.

I, Jesus, have sent my angel to give you this testimony for the churches. I am the Root and the Offspring of David, and the bright Morning Star. (Revelation 22:16, NASB95)

Their "reward, then, is the Son of God Himself under the symbol of the morning star."[196]

---

[195] Robert G. Bratcher, Rev. 2:28.

[196] J. Massyngberde Ford, Revelation, *The Anchor Bible* (New York, NY: Doubleday Co., 1975), 407.

Chapter 3
The Seven Letters

Message to Sardis

Sardis was a city in the Roman province of Asia, in the West of what is now Asiatic Turkey. It was the capital of the ancient kingdom of Lydia, the greatest of the foreign powers encountered by the Greeks during their early colonization of Asia Minor. Its early prosperity, especially under Croesus, became a byword for wealth; its riches are said to have derived in part from the gold won from the Pactolus, a stream that flowed through the city. The original city was an almost impregnable fortress-citadel, towering above the broad valley of the Hermus, and nearly surrounded by precipitous cliffs of treacherously loose rock. Its position as the center of Lydian supremacy under Croesus was ended abruptly when the Persian king Cyrus besieged the city and took the citadel (546 BC), apparently by scaling the cliffs and entering by a weakly defended point under cover of darkness. The same tactics again led to the fall of the city in 214 BC, when it was captured by Antiochus the Great. Though it lay on an important trade route down the Hermus valley, it never regained under Roman rule the spectacular prominence it had had in earlier centuries. In AD 26 its claim for the honor of building an imperial temple was rejected in favor of its rival Smyrna. There is now only a small village (Sart) near the site of the ancient city.

The letter to 'the angel of the church in Sardis' (Rev. 3:1-6) suggests that the early Christian community there was imbued with the same spirit as the city, resting on its past reputation and without any present achievement, and failing, as the city had twice failed, to learn from its past and be vigilant. The symbol of 'white garments' was rich in meaning in a city noted for its luxury clothing trade: the faithful few who are vigilant shall be arrayed to share in the triumphal coming of their Lord.

Important current excavations have brought much to light, including a superb late synagogue. Sardis had evidently been for centuries a principal center of the Jewish Diaspora.[197]

---

[197] J. D. Douglas, Editor, The New Bible Dictionary, "Sardis."

The ***seven Spirits (3:1)*** are the same which in 1:4, are said to be 'before the throne;' in 4:5, they appear as 'seven lamps of fire burning before the throne,' and in 5:6, as 'seven eyes sent forth into all the earth.' These are all so many different apocalyptic conceptions of the one Holy Spirit, proceeding from God and Christ.[198] The role of the number ***seven (3:1)*** should be pursued, after all, there is but one Holy Spirit. Seven emphasized the perfection or fullness of a thing. When Joseph interpreted the dreams of Pharaoh's chief baker and chief cupbearer the number seven played a central role stressing the perfect character of the good and bad days to come. Here the perfect character and complete work of the Holy Spirit is made with clarity in the use of this number.

In chapter 1 and verse 20 we have Christ's interpretation as to what ***the seven stars (3:1)*** represent; they are the seven churches in Asia.

> *As for the mystery of the seven stars which you saw in My right hand, and the seven golden lampstands: the seven stars are the angels of the seven churches, and the seven lampstands are the seven churches. (Revelation 1:20, NASB95)*

3:1 To the angel of the church in Sardis write: He who has the seven Spirits of God and the seven stars, says this: 'I know your deeds, that you have a name that you are alive, but you are dead.' Once a church has a good reputation in the public eye, it is possible to mechanically continue in the same activities but lose the original motivation that made it great. The incentive to good ***deeds (3:1)*** can shift from a desire to serve and please God to simply a desire to maintain the good public face that the church has come to enjoy.[199] Sardis had come to terms with its pagan environment.[200] We read in James that a person can have some sort of faith, yet without the works ordained by Christ, it is a dead faith.

---

[198] Milton S. Terry, Biblical Apocalyptics, 305.

[199] Steve Gregg, 73.

[200] Robert H. Mounce, 112.

Even so faith, if it has no works, is dead, being by itself. (James 2:17, NASB95)

For just as the body without the spirit is dead, so also faith without works is dead. (James 2:26, NASB95)

But in addition, a person, or church, can have works, and yet have a dead faith.

3:2 Wake up, and strengthen the things that remain, which were about to die; for I have not found your deeds completed in the sight of My God. Sardis is here told to **wake-up (3:2)**. Twice during the history of Sardis, the acropolis had fallen into the hands of an enemy, as a result of a lack of vigilance on the part of its citizens.[201] Sardis had been captured because the guards of the city slept while on duty. Here Christ is using this historical precedent to remind them of the danger of failing to be vigilant. The story of this church is a duplication of past experiences; the character of these people remains unchanged. Their faults are yet the same; and therefore their fate must be the same.[202] Unless they **wake up (3:2)**, they will **die (3:2)**.

Sardis is not totally dead, but certain things are **about to die (3:2)**. Although the Lord has not written off the entire church yet, there is a real and immediate danger. As a result, the elders at Sardis must begin now to **strengthen the things that remain (3:2)**.[203] It seems the Christians at Sardis had begun to do things as Christians but had lost their enthusiasm and not finished what they had begun.[204]

3:3 So remember what you have received and heard; and keep it, and repent. Therefore if you do not wake up, I will come like a thief, and you will not know at what hour I will come to you. The English word **what (3:3)** as in **what you have received (3:3)** is in reality the Greek word "how."   It is the word πῶς, *pos*, and is an "interrogative particle of manner" meaning "how," "by what means," "after

---

[201] Henry Barclay Swete, 49.

[202] W. M. Ramsey, 278.

[203] David Chilton, <u>The Days of Vengeance</u>, 120.

[204] Robert G. Bratcher, Rev. 3:2.

what manner," or "in what way."[205]   So, they are not being asked to remember *what* they believed, but *how* they received the gospel message. Yet we are not told the context of the "how." Was it in the midst of persecution and at much personal cost to them? It is left unsaid, yet, so important, that they are to call it to mind.

Christ says that He **will come like a thief (3:3)**. Addressing the question of which coming is under discussion Robert Bratcher says, "...this is a coming to punish them, not the final coming."[206] This is an important point, as mentioned before; there are many judgement comings in the Bible but only one consummation coming at the end of time.

In this admonition there is a biting allusion to two tragic past instances when the city was taken by surprise: by a night attack from Cyrus of Persia and under Antiochus the Great. The Sardians are bidden to undergo conversion, i.e. a genuine return to commitment to God, which they had received and heard. Otherwise, they will be surprised by a third (night) attack—from Christ Himself.[207] This is typical apocalyptic terminology similar to what Christ used in the Olivet Discourse. Its message is threatening.

> *Therefore be on the alert, for you do not know which day your Lord is coming. But be sure of this, that if the head of the house had known at what time of the night the thief was coming, he would have been on the alert and would not have allowed his house to be broken into. (Matthew 24:42-43, NASB95)*

3:4 But you have a few people in Sardis who have not soiled their garments; and they will walk with Me in white, for they are worthy. A few in Sardis (3:4) are praised for not soiling their **garments (3:4)**. Sardis was known for its wool and garment making industries. As a result, this comment was sure to catch their attention. They had pride in their community industry and the guilds would have taken care to insure the quality of this industry. However, they had not

---

[205] James Strong, The Exhaustive Concordance of the Bible: electronic ed., G4459 (Ontario, Canada: Woodside Bible Fellowship, 1996).

[206] Robert G. Bratcher, Rev. 3:3.

[207] J. Massyngberde Ford, 412.

taken adequate care to insure the quality of their spiritual condition and walk with God. "Clean white garments are very natural emblems of innocence, and have been extensively spoken of as such among many nations. Hence to be clothed with polluted garments, i.e. garments soiled, stained, etc., is an emblem of a character which is soiled or polluted...."[208]

3:5-6 *He who overcomes will thus be clothed in white garments; and I will not erase his name from the book of life, and I will confess his name before My Father and before His angels. ⁶ He who has an ear, let him hear what the Spirit says to the churches.* Christ promises these people that He **will not erase** their **name from the book of life (3:5)**. This verse is also mentioned in the last verses of Revelation.

> *...and if anyone takes away from the words of the book of this prophecy, God will take away his part from the tree of life and from the holy city, which are written in this book. (Revelation 22:19, NASB95)*

There are two ways one could look at this verse. The <u>first</u> would be that people could lose their salvation and have their names erased from the book of life. There is a principle in biblical interpretation that says that an obscure passage is to be interpreted in the light of clear passages. Putting that hermeneutic into practice here, we must reject that explanation as being in conflict with the great mass of Scripture that teaches eternal security.

> *Jesus said to them, "I am the bread of life; he who comes to Me will not hunger, and he who believes in Me will never thirst.... 37 All that the Father gives Me will come to Me, and the one who comes to Me I will certainly not cast out.... 39 This is the will of Him who sent Me, that of all that He has given Me I lose nothing, but raise it up on the last day. 40 For this is the will of My Father, that everyone who beholds the Son and believes in Him will have eternal life, and I Myself will raise him up on the last day." (John 6:35-40, NASB95)*

---

[208] Moses Stuart, vol. II, 89.

My sheep hear My voice, and I know them, and they follow Me; and I give eternal life to them, and they will never perish; and no one will snatch them out of My hand. "My Father, who has given them to Me, is greater than all; and no one is able to snatch them out of the Father's hand." (John 10:27-29, NASB95)

Now may the God of peace Himself sanctify you entirely; and may your spirit and soul and body be preserved complete, without blame at the coming of our Lord Jesus Christ. 24 Faithful is He who calls you, and He also will bring it to pass. (1 Thessalonians 5:23-24, NASB95)

Well, if it is not possible to lose your salvation, then what does this mean? A second possible interpretation would be to see in this phrase a metaphor speaking of the apparent loss of salvation by those who are apparent Christians, but not actually so.

They went out from us, but they were not really of us; for if they had been of us, they would have remained with us; but they went out, so that it would be shown that they all are not of us. (1 John 2:19, NASB95)

In a similar way these are the ones on whom seed was sown on the rocky places, who, when they hear the word, immediately receive it with joy; 17 and they have no firm root in themselves, but are only temporary; then, when affliction or persecution arises because of the word, immediately they fall away. (Mark 4:16-17, NASB95)

To conclude this point: The threat stated by Jesus Christ here is very real. Those who are in the Book of Life—i.e., who are baptized Church members professing Christ, and are thus counted as, and treated as, Christians—must remain faithful to Christ. If they apostatize into heresy, immorality, or simply the "secularization" that plagued Sardis, they will be erased, written out of the record of the redeemed. But the Christian who overcomes these temptations, thus demonstrating that Christ has truly purchased him for His own, is in no danger—his name will never be erased.[209]

---

[209] David Chilton, The Days of Vengeance, 125.

These words remind us of what Christ Himself said earlier,

> *Therefore everyone who confesses Me before men, I will also* *confess him before My Father who is in heaven. 33 But whoever* *denies Me before men, I will also deny him before My Father who* *is in heaven. (Matthew 10:32-33, NASB95)*

Message to Philadelphia

Philadelphia was a city in the Roman province of Asia, in the West of what is now Asiatic Turkey. It was perhaps founded by Eumenes, king of Pergamum, in the 2nd century BC, and certainly named after his brother Attalus, whose loyalty had earned him the name Philadelphus. It was situated near the upper end of a broad valley leading down through Sardis to the sea near Smyrna; and it lay at the threshold of a very fertile tract of plateau country, from which much of its commercial prosperity derived. The area was subject to frequent earthquakes. A severe one in AD 17 destroyed the city; and as the shocks continued intermittently the people took to living outside the city. After an imperial bounty had helped it to recover, the city voluntarily assumed the new name of Neocaesarea. Later, under Vespasian, it took another imperial name, Flavia. The city was remarkable for the number of its temples and religious festivals.

The letter to 'the angel of the church in Philadelphia' (Rev. 3:7-13) probably alludes to some of the circumstances of the city. As Philadelphus was renowned for his loyalty to his brother, so the church, the true Philadelphia, inherits and fulfills his character by its steadfast loyalty to Christ (vv. 8, 10). As the city stands by the 'open door' of a region from which its wealth derives, so the church is given an 'open door' of opportunity to exploit (v. 8; *cf.* 2 Cor. 2:12). The symbols of the 'crown' and the 'temple' (vv. 11-12) point to a contrast with the games and religious festivals of the city. In contrast with the impermanence of life in a city prone to earthquakes, those who 'overcome' are promised the ultimate stability of being built into the temple of God. As at Smyrna, this church had met rejection from the Jews in the city (v. 9), but the conqueror shall enjoy final acceptance by the Lord whose name he had confessed (v. 8), signified again by the conferring on him of the divine names (v. 12), which recall the new names taken by the city from the divine emperors. Ignatius later visited the city on his way from Antioch to martyrdom in Rome, and sent a letter to the church there. [210]

3:7 And to the angel of the church in Philadelphia write: He who is holy, who is true, who has the key of David, who opens and no one will shut, and who shuts and no one opens, says this.... The word ***true (3:7)*** identifies Christ as "...he who will perform all his promises or keep his word."[211]

Jesus also claims to have ***the key of David (3:7)***. Luke comments, *"He will be great and will be called the Son of the Most High; and the Lord God will give Him the throne of His father David..."* (Luke 1:32). The meaning is the same here. Christ is David's greater son. Keys are symbolic of authority in Scripture; Christ has the authority to act like that scion of David, the lion of the tribe of Judah. In filling this role, He is not a usurper, but has legitimate claim to the throne, as the ***key (3:7)*** indicates.

This phrase, ***who opens and no one will shut, and who shuts and no one opens (3:7)***, designates "...complete and entire control, i.e. supreme dominion. One, who had this power over a house, would have the supreme control of it. So here; the Messiah who is ὁ ἅγιος καὶ ὁ ἀληθινός, [the holy and true one] has power to perform all his promises, for his control is supreme and entire."[212]

3:8 I know your deeds. Behold, I have put before you an open door which no one can shut, because you have a little power, and have kept My word, and have not denied My name. He that has the keys has opened the door for the enjoyment of some privilege.[213] That privilege is designated with the words ***I know your deeds. Behold, I have put before you an open door which no one can shut (3:8)***. The next two verses tell us what those privilege entail.

These words, ***you have a little power (3:8)***, show that they were not what the world would call a strong and influential church. It is likely that

---

[210] J. D. Douglas, Editor, <u>The New Bible Dictionary</u>, "Philadelphia."

[211] Moses Stuart, vol. II, 90.

[212] Ibid., vol. II, 91.

[213] Ibid., vol. II, 91.

the "best" families in town were not members. In that sense they had **little power (2:8)**. Consider these similar words by Paul:

> *For consider your calling, brethren, that there were not many wise according to the flesh, not many mighty, not many noble; but God has chosen the foolish things of the world to shame the wise, and God has chosen the weak things of the world to shame the things which are strong.... (1 Corinthians 1:26-27, NASB95)*

When brought before the civil magistrates, and accused of practicing a religio non-licita [an unlicensed religion], they were required to renounce and denounce the name of Christ; the church of Philadelphia had refused to do this. Instead, Christ says, they **have kept My word, and have not denied My name (3:8)**. Clearly, they had met persecution and danger with steadfastness and with constancy.[214]

3:9 Behold, I will cause those of the synagogue of Satan, who say that they are Jews and are not, but lie—I will make them come and bow down at your feet, and make them know that I have loved you. The **Jews (3:9)** were the first and most violent persecutors of the Church.[215] As such Christ addresses them saying, **behold, I will cause those of the synagogue of Satan, who say that they are Jews and are not, but lie—(3:9)**. These are not simply Jews; they are, according to Christ, **the synagogue of Satan (3:9)**, they are the enemies of the Cross. This has a familiar ring to it; it is not unlike a statement Christ made to the Jews of His day.

> *You are of your father the devil, and you want to do the desires of your father. He was a murderer from the beginning, and does not stand in the truth because there is no truth in him. Whenever he speaks a lie, he speaks from his own nature, for he is a liar and the father of lies. (John 8:44, NASB95)*

The Jews were the enemies of the early church. Christ here promises victory of the church over their enemies saying, **I will make them come and bow down at your feet, and make them know that I have**

---

[214] Moses Stuart, vol. II, 93.

[215] See previous notes on Revelation 2:9.

loved you (3:9). The metaphor of *bow down (3:9)* suggests victory over an enemy. The Jews will suffer defeat; the church will experience victory.

The church in Thyatira was given a similar promise.

> *...and he shall rule them with a rod of iron, as the vessels of the potter are broken to pieces, as I also have received authority from My Father. (Revelation 2:27, NASB95)*

The economic and political elite in the community were not Believers. As a result, the church was suffering discrimination and persecution. Christ promises them that in time these will all change, the Church will rise to the ascendancy. In time Constantine did make Christianity the official religion of the Roman Empire. And notwithstanding the desire of the pagan community for legalized prostitution, animal sacrifice, and sodomy, they will bow at the feet of the Christian leaders of society to a higher moral standard. If they do not, they will acquiesce by means of a rod of iron.

3:10 Because you have kept the word of My perseverance, I also will keep you from the hour of testing, that hour which is about to come upon the whole world, to test those who dwell on the earth. Christ predicted that His people would experience persecution, and at the same time He made it clear that a proper spiritual relationship with Him required <u>endurance,</u> or *perseverance (3:10)* as it is here called.

> *You will be hated by all because of My name, but it is the one who has endured to the end who will be saved. (Matthew 10:22, NASB95)*

> *If we endure, we will also reign with Him; if we deny Him, He also will deny us.... (2 Timothy 2:12, NASB95)*

One thing is certain; judgement is *about to come (3:10)*. And although a major part of it is focused on Jerusalem, another part is coming upon *the whole world (3:10)*, i.e. the Roman Empire. This means either that He would exempt them from the severe trials of persecution which would soon come upon Asia and experienced by all the countries around them, or it means that He would mitigate those trials.

Dispensationalism, on the other hand, views this verse as the most significant proof in Scripture that the Church will be raptured before the Tribulation.[216] Yet this verse does not say that this church, or any church, will be taken physically from the planet. It does not say that this is an end of the world scene. In fact, the context forbids such an assumption. And if it did, what value would this promise be to the Philadelphian church? Clearly they did not actually live to see a pre-tribulation rapture. What comfort was this to them?

We might also ask how this matches up with Christ instruction, recorded by this same John:

> I do not ask You to take them out of the world, but to keep them *from the evil one. (John 17:15, NASB95)*

Clearly, Jesus was not teaching a pre-tribulation rapture here. Christ prayer is to keep us from, not take us out. If this is the most significant Scripture teaching the pre-tribulation rapture, certainly this position has little to commend itself to the Christian.

3:11 I am coming quickly; hold fast what you have, so that no one will take your crown. In verse 11 we see another one of the many instances in which Christ indicates that he is **coming quickly (3:11)**. His coming and His judgements are near. Because His coming is near, the encouragement to **hold fast (3:11)** is meaningful. But a holding on that requires several centuries or millennia before it's reward is realized is much more difficult to apprehend; indeed, it would have been utterly depressing to those who first received the letter and were admonished to wait that length of time. Can you imagine Him saying, "I am coming in a couple or three thousand years, so hold on and be comforted by these words?" In the midst of the persecution they were suffering, what comfort does that bring?

This comment, **so that no one will take your crown (3:11)** sounds very much like, *"And I will not erase his name from the book of life"* spoken

---

[216] Keith A. Mathison, <u>Dispensationalism, Rightly Dividing the People of God?</u> (Phillipsburg, New Jersey: P&R Publishing, 1995), 118.

in 3:5 to the Church at Sardis. And the comments made there about eternal security are applicable here as well.

3:12-13 *He who overcomes, I will make him a pillar in the temple of My God, and he will not go out from it anymore; and I will write on him the name of My God, and the name of the city of My God, the new Jerusalem, which comes down out of heaven from My God, and My new name.* [13] *He who has an ear, let him hear what the Spirit says to the churches.* This idea can best be understood in the light of the culture of that era. "Those in Philadelphia who were faithful servants of the culture of the state had their names inscribed on pillars in the temple of some god; for noted priests, a memorial pillar was added to demonstrate that they were the support of the edifice."[217] The Bible in several places refers to God's people using "temple" language as well.

> ...you also, as living stones, are being built up as a spiritual house for a holy priesthood, to offer up spiritual sacrifices acceptable to God through Jesus Christ. (1 Peter 2:5, NASB95)

> Or what agreement has the temple of God with idols? For we are the temple of the living God; just as God said, "I will dwell in them and walk among them; and I will be their God, and they shall be My people." (2 Corinthians 6:16, NASB95)

> Do you not know that you are a temple of God and that the Spirit of God dwells in you? If any man destroys the temple of God, God will destroy him, for the temple of God is holy, and that is what you are. (1 Corinthians 3:16-17, NASB95)

> Or do you not know that your body is a temple of the Holy Spirit who is in you, whom you have from God, and that you are not your own? (1 Corinthians 6:19, NASB95)

> ...and recognizing the grace that had been given to me, James and Cephas and John, who were reputed to be pillars, gave to me

---

[217] Rousas John Rushdoony, Thy Kingdom Come, 125.

*and Barnabas the right hand of fellowship, so that we might go to
the Gentiles and they to the circumcised. (Galatians 2:9, NASB95)*

Here Christ is using an easily recognizable practice of the pagan culture, the building of a Temple, to drive home a spiritual point from which the Christians of Philadelphia could take encouragement. Truly the believer is secure in his salvation as we are assured by Christ's words, **and he will not go out from it anymore (3:12)**.

Of course temples and pillars regularly had the name of their god inscribed on them, so it would not seem strange for Jesus to say, **I will write on him the name of My God, and the name of the city of My God, the new Jerusalem, which comes down out of heaven from My God, and My new name (3:12)**. In addition, slave owners often had their names branded or tattooed on their slaves. This was not always a degrading thing. For instance, if the slave's master were of renown in the community, that brand or name gave that slave a certain status. Often the emperor's slaves were men of power and wealth in the bureaucracy, and were feared by others as a result. Christ here promises to put His mark, His **name (3:12)**, on His people and thereby to make clear whose property we are.

Possessing the name of the **new Jerusalem (3:12)** would give its owners the right of entry into the blessed city, which refers to both the Church now and heaven later. In addition, Christ has been given a **new name (3:12)** that in turn is affixed to His people. This passage does not say what that name is, though something like "Redeemer" might be an appropriate idea.

*The nations will see your righteousness, and all kings your glory;
and you will be called by a new name which the mouth of the
Lord will designate. (Isaiah 62:2, NASB95)*

*To them I will give in My house and within My walls a memorial,
and a name better than that of sons and daughters; I will give
them an everlasting name which will not be cut off. (Isaiah 56:5,
NASB95)*

Message to Laodicea

Laodicea was a city of Southwest Phrygia, in the Roman province of Asia, in the West of what is now Asiatic Turkey. It was founded by the Seleucid Antiochus II in the 3rd century BC, and called after his wife Laodice. It lay in the fertile valley of the Lycus (a tributary of the Maeander), close to Hierapolis and Colossae, and was distinguished by the epithet 'on Lycus' from several other cities of the name. It was at a very important cross-road: the main road across Asia Minor ran West to the ports of Miletus and Ephesus about 160 km away and East by an easy incline on to the central plateau and thence towards Syria; and another road ran North to Pergamum and South to the coast at Attalia.

This strategic position made Laodicea an extremely prosperous commercial center, especially under Roman rule. When destroyed by a disastrous earthquake in AD 60 it could afford to dispense with aid from Nero. It was an important center of banking and exchange. Its distinctive products included garments of glossy black wool, and it was a medical center noted for ophthalmology. The site had one disadvantage: being determined by the road-system, it lacked a sufficient and permanent supply of good water. Water was piped to the city from hot springs some distance South, and probably arrived lukewarm. The deposits still encrusting the remains testify to its warmth. The site of Laodicea was eventually abandoned, and the modern town (Denizli) grew up near the springs.

The gospel must have reached Laodicea at an early date, probably while Paul was living at Ephesus (Acts 19:10), and perhaps through Epaphras (Col. 4:12-13). Although Paul mentions the church there (Col. 2:1, 4:13-16), there is no record that he visited it. It is evident that the church maintained close connections with the Christians in Hierapolis and Colossae. The 'letter from Laodicea' (Col. 4:16) is often thought to have been a copy of our Ephesians which had been received in Laodicea.

The last of the Letters to the seven churches of Asia (Rev. 3:14-22) was addressed to Laodicea. Its imagery owes relatively little to the OT, but contains pointed allusions to the character and circumstances of the city. For all its wealth, it could produce neither the healing power of hot water, like its neighbor Hierapolis, nor the refreshing power of cold water to be found at Colossae, but merely lukewarm water, useful only as an emetic (an agent that causes vomiting). The church was charged with a similar uselessness: it was self-sufficient, rather than half-hearted. Like the city, it thought it had 'need of nothing'. In fact it was spiritually poor, naked and blind, and needed 'gold', 'white garments' and 'eyesalve' more effective than its bankers, clothiers and doctors could supply. Like citizens inhospitable to a traveler who offers them priceless goods, the Laodiceans had closed their doors and left their real Provider outside. Christ turns in loving appeal to the individual (v. 20).[218]

3:14 To the angel of the church in Laodicea write: The Amen, the faithful and true Witness, the Beginning of the creation of God, says this.... The word **Amen (3:14)** "...was the confession of the praise of God which was laid on the community and which the community was to affirm by its answer. And it was the confession of the blessing of God which was pronounced to the community and which the community was to make operative by its Amen. Apart from divine service it was to be used in response to any prayer or praise uttered by another. The concluding Amen signified concurrence."[219] Christ is God's **amen (3:14)** to His promises.

> *For as many as are the promises of God, in Him they are yes;*
> *therefore also through Him is our Amen to the glory of God*
> *through us. (2 Corinthians 1:20, NASB95)*

This is the second time Christ identifies Himself as the "*faithful witness*" (see 1:5). To the church at Philadelphia Christ also identifies Himself as He "*who is true*" (3:7). Here both titles, **the faithful and true Witness (3:14)**, are combined. "The object of employing these designations here seems to be, to remind the church addressed that the comminations (denunciations) of its Lord and Master are to be believed, as well as his promises."[220]

This phrase, **the Beginning of the creation of God (3:14)**, does not mean that God created Christ first. Christ, being God, is not a created being. "It should not be assumed that this makes Christ out to be a created thing. The Greek word translated "Beginning" is *arche*, which carries the

---

[218] J. D. Douglas, Editor, The New Bible Dictionary, "Laodicea."

[219] Gerhard Kittel and Gerhard Friedrich, The Theological Dictionary of the New Testament (Grand Rapids, MI: Wm. B. Eerdmans Publishing Company, 2000, c1964), Vol. 1, Page 336.

[220] Moses Stuart, vol. II, 97.

concept of the 'beginning, origin, active cause.' Rather than the 'first thing created,' the expression could be understood to mean 'he who is the Origin (Source, Creator) of the creation of God.'[221] "The Greek word *archē*, translated "beginning" in this verse, here carries the meaning of 'one who begins,' 'origin,' 'source,' or 'first cause.' The English word *architect* is derived from *archē*. This verse says that Jesus is the architect of all creation."[222]

The word can also refer to "an authority figure who initiates activity or process, *ruler, authority*."[223] Christ is the *ruler **of the creation of God (3:14)*** as well as its *source* and *architect*.

> *He is the image of the invisible God, the firstborn of all creation. For by Him all things were created, both in the heavens and on earth, visible and invisible, whether thrones or dominions or rulers or authorities—all things have been created through Him and for Him. He is before all things, and in Him all things hold together. He is also head of the body, the church; and He is the beginning, the firstborn from the dead, so that He Himself will come to have first place in everything. (Colossians 1:15-18, NASB95)*

This very word ἀρχή, *archē*, beginning, is used of God in Revelation 21 as well.

> *And He who sits on the throne said, "Behold, I am making all things new." And He said, "Write, for these words are faithful and true." 6 Then He said to me, "It is done. I am the Alpha and the Omega, the beginning and the end. I will give to the one who thirsts from the spring of the water of life without cost." (Revelation 21:5-6, NASB95)*

---

[221] Steve Gregg, 79.

[222] Norman L. Geisler, and Ron Rhodes, When Cultists Ask: A Popular Handbook on Cultic Misinterpretations (Grand Rapids, Mich.: Baker Books, 1997), 305.

[223] William Arndt, Walter Bauer, F. Wilbur Gingrich, and Frederick W. Danker, A Greek-English Lexicon of the New Testament and Other Early Christian Literature (Chicago, IL: University of Chicago Press, 1979).

Notice the one speaking is sitting *"on the throne"* (21:5). In Revelation 4:9 and 20:11 the One sitting on the throne was God the Father. It is said of Him that He is *"the beginning [ἀρχή, archē], and the end"* (21:6). So if arche refers to having a beginning, then God Himself has a beginning, which is nonsense. "It cannot mean a created being, for God the Father is also a creature.... Hence, 'beginning' should be understood in the absolute sense of Beginner or Source of all things."[224]

So in summary we see that "...the One who speaks to Laodicea is the Amen, the great Guarantor of the Covenant, the infallible Witness who is Truth Himself, with all the authority possessed by the creator and King of the universe. And He has come to bear testimony against His church."[225]

3:15 I know your deeds, that you are neither cold nor hot; I wish that you were cold or hot. This interesting phrase is terribly misunderstood by most commentators and therefore by most Christians.

> Laodicea was 'lukewarm, and neither hot nor cold.' This has often been interpreted as if hot meant godly enthusiasm and cold meant ungodly antagonism; but there is another explanation which suits the historical and geographical context better. Laodicea was situated between two other important cities, Colossae and Hieropolis, Colossae, wedged into a narrow valley in the shadow of towering mountains, was watered by icy streams which tumbled down from the heights. In contrast, Hieropolis was famous for its hot mineral springs that flowed out of the city and across a high plain until it cascaded down a cliff that faced Laodicea. By the time the water reached the valley floor, it was lukewarm, putrid, and nauseating. At Colossae, therefor, one could be refreshed with clear, cold, invigorating drinking water; at Hieropolis, one could be healed by bathing in its hot, mineral-laden pools. But at Laodicea, the waters were neither hot (for health) nor cold (for drinking).[226]

[224] Norman L. Geisler, and Ron Rhodes, 305.

[225] David Chilton, The Days of Vengeance, 125.

[226] C. J. Hemer, "Seven Cities of Asia Minor," in R. K. Harrison, ed., Major Cities of the Biblical World (Nashville, TN: Thomas Nelson Publishers, 1985), 246ff.

3:16 So because you are lukewarm, and neither hot nor cold, I will spit you out of My mouth. Christ is not saying that being **cold (3:16)** spiritually is better than being **lukewarm (3:16)** spiritually. "He is not saying that outright apostasy is preferable to middle-of-the-roadism...."[227] He is saying that cold water has a use and hot water has a use, but the Laodiceans have no use. They have become complacent in their lives. To the community in which they live, they have no spiritual value. They cannot invigorate as a cold cup of water; neither can they heal as a hot mineral spring. They are simply without benefit to the community in which they live.

We have all heard preaching which insists that God would rather have a believer cold spiritually if they will not be hot spiritually, using this verse for support. However, that is foolish preaching and certainly not found in this verse, or any passage in the Bible for that matter. In the spiritual spectrum, lukewarm is far better than cold, notwithstanding the fact that it is not as good as hot. This passage is teaching that God wants us to be useful either as cold water is useful or as hot water is useful. But lukewarm water is of no use. It is not fit to drink or heal.

The threat, ***I will spit you out of My mouth (3:16)***, is similar to that to the other churches. As God has made war on the inhabitants of Palestine, made war on the Israel, and will soon make war on Judah, as the Book of Revelation makes clear, if need be, He will make war on the Church.

> *Do not defile yourselves by any of these things; for by all these the nations which I am casting out before you have become defiled. 25 'For the land has become defiled, therefore I have brought its punishment upon it, so the land has spewed out its inhabitants. 26 'But as for you, you are to keep My statutes and My judgements and shall not do any of these abominations, neither the native, nor the alien who sojourns among you 27 (for the men of the land who have been before you have done all these abominations, and the land has become defiled); 28 so that the land will not spew you out, should you defile it, as it has spewed out the nation which has been before you. (Leviticus 18:24-28, NASB95)*

---

[227] David Chilton, <u>The Days of Vengeance</u>, 134.

The threat to the Church is very real. Uselessness engenders the question *"why does it even use up the ground?"* (Luke 13:7, NASB95). And with that question comes the concomitant judgement *"cut it down"* (Luke 13:7, NASB95).

3:17 Because you say, "I am rich, and have become wealthy, and have need of nothing," and you do not know that you are wretched and miserable and poor and blind and naked.... Apparently this church had become **rich (3:17)** and **wealthy (3:17)**, either through the prosperity of the community or the conversion of wealthy people in that community. However, the Laodiceans quickly lost that attitude characterized by Christ as *"poor in spirit"* (Matthew 5:3, NASB95), instead, they had become "poor in Spirit."

The church of Smyrna, on the other hand, was in dire economic straits. However, because of their love for Christ they were called "rich." Here a church that thinks it is rich is told that in reality they are **wretched, miserable, poor, blind,** and **naked (3:17)**. These would be the qualities of many of the castoffs of society, the beggars that could not care for themselves. People who were "wealthy" would often look down upon this very class of people. But here the tables are turned on them. It is you, who are in such beggarly straits, says Christ. It is they who are in danger of being the castoffs of Christ.

3:18 I advise you to buy from Me gold refined by fire so that you may become rich, and white garments so that you may clothe yourself, and that the shame of your nakedness will not be revealed; and eye salve to anoint your eyes so that you may see. Although they were encouraged to **buy from Me (3:18)**, what they needed to buy was free.

> *Ho! Every one who thirsts, come to the waters;*
> *And you who have no money come, buy and eat.*
> *Come, buy wine and milk*
> *Without money and without cost. (Isaiah 55:1, NASB95)*

"...for though his mercies are without money or price the arrogant and self-conceited must needs pay the heaviest of all prices—humiliation and surrender of themselves. They must renounce their self-conceit and pride, and be made to feel that they are indeed poor and needy."[228] The meaning of the verse is: I counsel thee to obtain from me true and unadulterated riches, i.e. spiritual gifts, and graces, so that thou may be rich in the true sense of the word.[229] So often Christians, like Christ Himself, are thought of as being unkind and mean spirited, if not downright hateful, if they reprove sin and discipline their members. But Christ does that very thing here, and it is a most loving act for Him to condescend to give sinners an opportunity to change and conform their lives to His righteous standard.

3:19 Those whom I love, I reprove and discipline; therefore be zealous and repent. It is Christ Himself who makes it clear that love drives Him to this end, as it should us. By contrast, we can see that those who do not reprove and discipline know little of the love of Christ, notwithstanding how many prayer meetings and sing-alongs they attend.

3:20 Behold, I stand at the door and knock; if anyone hears My voice and opens the door, I will come in to him and will dine with him, and he with Me (3:20). This verse has been taken out of context innumerable times to call sinners to repentance and faith in Christ as Savior. In reality it is a call to Christians to wake up and hear the Savior of the Church, and let Him be the Lord He insists on being. He promises fellowship with those that obey. "...this verse, in context, actually expresses Christ's feeling of being an outsider from His own church, desiring to be invited back in.... Dining with Christ may have eucharistic connotations: Although Jesus may not be attending the Church's love feast, He will commune privately with any individual who welcomes Him."[230]

3:21-22 He who overcomes, I will grant to him to sit down with Me on My throne, as I also overcame and sat down with My Father on His throne. ²² 'He who has an ear, let him hear what the Spirit says to the churches.' Overcoming is a most important theme in Revelation. The overcomer will "*...eat of the tree of life which is in the Paradise of God*" (Revelation 2:7, NASB95), "*...will not be hurt by the second death...*" (Revelation 2:11, NASB95), will be given "*...some of the hidden manna... a white stone, and a new name written on*

---

228 Milton S. Terry, <u>Biblical Apocalyptics</u>, 312.

229 Moses Stuart, vol. II, 102.

230 Steve Gregg, 80.

the stone which no one knows but he who receives it" (Revelation 2:17, NASB95). The overcomer is defined by Christ as *"...he who keeps My deeds until the end..."* (Revelation 2:6, NASB95). Such a person will receive *"...authority over the nations..."* (Revelation 2:26, NASB95), he will *"...be clothed in white garments..."* (Revelation 3:5, NASB95). Christ says of him *"...I will not erase his name from the book of life, and I will confess his name before My Father and before His angels"* (Revelation 3:5, NASB95). In addition, Jesus says, *"I will make him a pillar in the temple of My God..."* (Revelation 3:12, NASB95) and *"I will grant to him to sit down with Me on My throne, as I also overcame and sat down with My Father on His throne"* (Revelation 3:21, NASB95). And finally the Lord says, *"He who overcomes will inherit these things, and I will be his God and he will be My son"* (Revelation 21:7, NASB95).

Obviously, overcoming is of major importance to our Lord.[231] Revelation 12 clarifies who the "overcomer" is:

> *And they overcame him because of the blood of the Lamb and because of the word of their testimony, and they did not love their life even when faced with death. (Revelation 12:11, NASB95)*

The church was facing imminent persecution. This is one of the reasons the book was written, to shore up the church during the dark days ahead. "...the existence of an 'overcoming' passage in every one of the seven letters again substantiates the argument that this book was written to people about to suffer persecution and death."[232]

---

[231] 2:7; 2:11; 2:17; 2:26; 3:5; 3:12; 3:21

[232] Jay E. Adams, The Time is at Hand, 58.

Chapter 4
The Throne Room

The church was on the verge of massive persecution, indeed it had already begun. Where would it all end? Was God really in charge? Did He really care? Would the righteous be vindicated and the wicked punished? "Widespread persecution was breaking out everywhere; greater still was yet in the offing. Lest there be doubt in any Christian's mind, the Savior graciously draws back the curtain of heaven (or to use the exact figure of the text, opens the door) and gives John a reassuring glimpse of the Divine control and care."[233]

Chapters 4 and 5 give us a picture of a powerful and caring God who, indeed, is in control. It would all work out because God was directing the affairs of men. "...John is ushered into the heavenly throne room just at the very time when the righteous Judge is about to mete out judgement against the evildoers. In a very real sense, this chapter sets the theme for all that follows: *God will soon avenge his own.*"[234]

Chapters 4 and 5 serve as a heavenly introduction to this part of the book. Chapter 6 begins the judgements.

Scene in Heaven

In the introduction we explained the purpose of The Book of Revelation. It is important to reiterate that here. This book is about the close of the old covenant through God's punishment of Israel, His former wife, for her spiritual adultery, and the establishment of the new covenant in His marriage to a new bride, the Church. Formerly, God punished the ten northern tribes called Israel for her sin. God brought a covenant lawsuit against the ten tribes, found her guilty, divorced her, and put her to death for breaking the covenant. He did so by destroying her as a nation, and sending her survivors into captivity and exile.

---

[233] Ibid., 60.
[234] Ibid., 61.

The penalty for harlotry in Scripture is death. In the Book of Revelation, that sentence is now being carried out on Judah as it was earlier on the ten northern tribes. The nation, the city, and the temple are being destroyed; its survivors will be sent into captivity and exile. Old Testament Israel no longer exists; the old covenant is abolished. God has now married another, the Church; the new covenant is now fully instituted.

With that in mind, in chapter 4 we see the court in session where this judicial process is about to unfold.

> We are introduced...to a heavenly courtroom scene. The Judge sits on the throne (v2) where, as we shall see in chapter 5, He is about to hand down sentence upon the accused. The plaintiffs are the martyrs of Christ, whose complaint against their persecutors is recorded later in the vision (6:9). The accused (Jerusalem) is about to be condemned.... The seven-sealed book (5:1) is God's sentence against Jerusalem, and the subsequent breaking of the first six seals depicts the Jewish crisis of A.D. 66-70: the war between the Jews and Rome, issuing in the utter destruction of the Jewish capital, state, and religious system.[235]

4:1 *After these things I looked, and behold, a door standing open in heaven, and the first voice which I had heard, like the sound of a trumpet speaking with me, said, "Come up here, and I will show you what must take place after these things."* The phrase *after these things (4:1)* used twice in verse one shows the close proximity of time and action that accrued between chapter 3 and the events of chapter 4. "The root meaning of meta [after] is 'mid' or 'midst.... The word...primarily denotes association and accompaniment."[236] So what happens in chapter 4 is in the "midst" of and in "association and accompaniment" with chapter 3. In other words, there is no two thousand-year delay found between the two chapters, as the Dispensational Premillennialists insists. Chapter 4 immediately accompanies chapter 3 in its fulfillment, and indeed, as chapter 3 has been long fulfilled, so has chapter 4.

---

[235] Steve Gregg, 84.

[236] Thoralf Gilbrant, Vol. Lambda-Omicron, 164-165.

The popular image of "going to heaven" involves entering heaven through St. Peter's pearly gate. However, the Biblical picture given here is of an entrance by means of a ***door standing open in heaven...(4:1)***. If I may allow my imagination a little freedom, I see a massive door, or doorway, perhaps several miles high, consisting of two doors that fold inward. It is an awesome picture of magnificent splendor and glory. It is an eternal invitation to the people of God.

This would be a good time to remember that Jesus identified Himself with, and as, a door. How appropriate, that we should remember that detail at this point of entrance into heaven.

> So Jesus said to them again, "Truly, truly, I say to you, I am the door of the sheep. ... I am the door; if anyone enters through Me, he will be saved, and will go in and out and find pasture." (John 10:7, 9, NASB95)

The ***first voice (4:1)*** that John had heard was introduced to us in 1:10 and proved by description to be Jesus Christ. Christ now continues His revelation to John by transporting him to heaven. The purpose of John's transport to heaven is for him to learn about ***what must take place after these things (4:1)***. Christ will now reveal the near future to John.

This would be an appropriate place to mention that in the Dispensational system, it is here that the rapture of the Church takes place. Several things can be said of this position.

First, and most importantly, the text does not say that the rapture of the Church takes place at this point. It is simply assumed by Dispensationalists that it does so because that is what their position requires. Empty assumptions make poor theology.

Second, the Dispensationalists assert that the phrase found earlier in Revelation "*I am coming quickly*" (Revelation 3:11, NASB95) implies the rapture is at hand and then before chapter 4, it actually takes place. However, we find the same phrase in Revelation 22:7, 12, and 20. But, both chapters 3 and 22 cannot refer to the rapture. If the rapture occurred in chapter 3 then it cannot occur again in chapter 22.[237] In addition, the

---

[237] See the commentary on Revelation 3:11 for additional thoughts on this subject.

Dispensationalists tell us that we are now living in the Laodicean Church age, the last church mentioned in chapter 3. But note, the phrase *I am coming quickly* is spoken to the church at Philadelphia. Wrong church age! You would think someone would have noticed.

Three, they make much of the fact that the word Church does not occur again in Revelation until chapter 22:16. To them this means that the Church is not on earth but in heaven and all the chapters from 4-21 are for Jews only, not for the Church. However, the word Church is not mentioned as being in heaven either! So what does this really prove? That the Church is not on earth *and* not in heaven! And consider this, although chapters 4-21 are said to be descriptive of the new Jewish age, please note that neither Jew, Jews nor Israel are mentioned even one time in these chapters. By Dispensational logic, we must conclude that the Jews are also here raptured and are no longer on earth either! I don't think so.

Also, note the use of "Church" in chapter 22, "*I, Jesus, have sent My angel to testify to you these things for the <u>churches</u>. I am the root and the descendant of David , the bright morning star.*" (Revelation 22:16, NASB95). Jesus starts off addressing the Church in chapter 1, and He ends the book doing the same. What has changed? He starts off saying He is going to come quickly, He ends up saying the same thing (22:7, 12, 20), there is continuity here. But the Classical Dispensationalists want to take chapters 4-19 from the Church; by that I mean, they want to say that these chapters are not about the Church and are not for the Church. The fact of the matter is the whole book of Revelation is to and about the Church and it takes more than an argument from silence to rob the Church of its great possession, the Word of God.

Classical Dispensationalists are masters at denying to the Church the whole counsel of God. They dismiss all the Old Testament as being in another "dispensation" and therefore not applicable to, or authoritative for, the Church. They do the same to the gospels and especially the Sermon on the Mount and the Lord's Prayer. Now they would conclude by robbing the Church of one more of its precious gifts from God, the Book of Revelation. But no, this theology, Classical Dispensationalism, must not be allowed to decimate the Scriptures. The entire Bible is the treasure of the Church, Genesis, Matthew and Revelation, no less than Galatians and Ephesians.

4:2 *Immediately I was in the Spirit; and behold, a throne was standing in heaven, and One sitting on the throne.* Here, again, John tells us he was ***in the Spirit (4:2)***. As John was ***in the Spirit (4:2)*** on ***the Lord's day (1:10)*** worshiping God, he was, while in this state of worship, transported to heaven, his body however still on earth. He then appears before the throne of God.

St. Paul had a similar experience. He records his accession this way: *"I know a man in Christ who fourteen years ago—whether in the body I do not know, or out of the body I do not know, God knows—such a man was caught up to the third heaven"* (2 Corinthians 12:2, NASB95). Unlike John, Paul does not tell us what he saw.

The word ***sitting (4:2)*** suggests to the Hebrew mind both ruling and judging; to us it has something of the notion of presiding; as such He appears to be the bishop of the presbytery of heaven.[238]

4:3 *And He who was sitting was like a jasper stone and a sardius in appearance; and there was a rainbow around the throne, like an emerald in appearance.* Here we see that "the whole universe is seen in a blaze of light going forth from the Throne. But God himself remains hidden in that light. The knowledge of God remains eternally inexhaustible to man, even in heaven, so that His very revelation underscores His inexhaustibility and incomprehensibility."[239] Paul tells us that God "... *dwells in unapproachable light, whom no man has seen or can see. To Him be honor and eternal dominion! Amen"* (1 Timothy 6:16, NASB95). Here John gives us a more detailed description of that light.

He starts with the precious gems, with their particular qualities and colors which are designed to teach, and impress us with various characteristics and qualities related to God and His rule. First mentioned is the ***jasper (4:3)*** "a precious stone of various colors, purple, cerulean, green, etc. Here, no doubt, the red or purple is intended, in order to designate the resplendence of the divine Majesty. So also sardius means a precious stone of blood-red or carnation hue. Both images together denote the powerful

---

[238] Philip Carrington, 111.

[239] Rousas John Rushdoony, 130.

splendor which beamed from him who sat upon the throne."[240] It was typical of regents in ages past to wear red/purple robes. That may be the exact idea before us. Here God is pictured in His majestic royal robes of crimson by the colors of the precious gems that surround Him.

Around this throne awash in hues of red is a magnificent **rainbow (4:3)** in shades of **emerald (4:3)** green. Compare John's vision with that of Ezekiel's:

> *Now above the expanse that was over their heads there was something resembling a throne, like lapis lazuli in appearance; and on that which resembled a throne, high up, was a figure with the appearance of a man. Then I noticed from the appearance of His loins and upward something like glowing metal that looked like fire all around within it, and from the appearance of His loins and downward I saw something like fire; and there was a radiance around Him. As the appearance of the rainbow in the clouds on a rainy day, so was the appearance of the surrounding radiance. Such was the appearance of the likeness of the glory of the Lord. And when I saw it, I fell on my face and heard a voice speaking. (Ezekiel 1:26-28, NASB95)*

We should not expect the appearances of God to be exactly the same from scene to scene. Just as David or Solomon would appear with different royal dress and jewels, so the heavenly model of their glory would appear in glorious diversity as well.

The **rainbow (4:3)** instantly reminds us of the covenant of God with Noah. So here we are visually made aware that God is a covenant making and covenant keeping God. And indeed, the Mosaic Covenant, or treaty, has been broken by Israel; therefore, the covenant curses of Leviticus 26 and Deuteronomy 28 are about to be administered.

4:4 Around the throne were twenty-four thrones; and upon the thrones I saw twenty-four elders sitting, clothed in white garments, and golden crowns on their heads. We are next introduced to those that **sit (4:4)** on **thrones (4:4)**; they appear to be

---

[240] Moses Stuart, vol. II, 110.

representatives of the Church in heaven and not other created beings, like angels. The fact that they are called *elders (4:4)* is an important indication of this. "Nowhere else in the Bible is the term elder given to anyone but men, and from earliest times it has stood for those who have rule and representation within the Church.... Thus, the elders in Revelation would appear, at face value, to be representatives of God's people, the senate sitting in council around their bishop."[241] Perhaps they are the sons of Jacob and the Apostles of Christ representing "the worship of mankind offered through its spiritual leaders."[242] But perhaps it is simply 24 glorious heroes of the faith. "The word Elder is a magnificent word. It suggests men of kingly character and function sitting in senate and ruling justly."[243]

Added to this is the significance that these elders sit on *thrones (4:4)*. "We have already been told in this prophecy that Christians are reigning with Christ (1:6), that they wear crowns (2:10; 3:11), that they have been granted kingly authority with Him over the nations (2:26-27), that apostates will be forced to bow before them (3:9), and that they are seated with Christ on His Throne (3:21)."[244]

In our effort to identify these *elders (4:4)* we note that "in the worship of the Old Covenant there were twenty-four divisions of priest (I Chron. 24) and twenty-four divisions of singers in the Temple (I Chron. 25).... What St. John sees is simply the Presbytery of Heaven: the representative assembly of the Royal Priesthood, the Church."[245]

The Throne and Worship of the Creator

4:5 Out from the throne come flashes of lightning and sounds and peals of thunder. And there were seven lamps of fire burning before the throne, which are the seven Spirits of God.... When God came down to Mt. Sinai to establish His covenant with Israel we read of similar phenomenon.

---

[241] David Chilton, The Days of Vengeance, 151.

[242] Philip Carrington, 113.

[243] Ibid, 113.

[244] David Chilton, The Days of Vengeance, 151.

[245] Ibid., 151-152.

> *... there were thunder and lightning flashes and a thick cloud*
> *upon the mountain and a very loud trumpet sound, so that all the*
> *people who were in the camp trembled. And Moses brought the*
> *people out of the camp to meet God, and they stood at the foot of*
> *the mountain. Now Mount Sinai was all in smoke because the*
> *Lord descended upon it in fire; and its smoke ascended like the*
> *smoke of a furnace, and the whole mountain quaked violently.*
> *When the sound of the trumpet grew louder and louder, Moses*
> *spoke and God answered him with thunder. The Lord came*
> *down on Mount Sinai.... (Exodus 19:16-20, NASB95)*

The covenant making God will now deal with a covenant breaking people. Although He is ending one covenant, He is at the same time making another. The writer of the book of Hebrews uses similar Mount Sinai type language. He then ties this language in with the founding of a new covenant by Jesus.

> *For you have not come to a mountain that can be touched and to*
> *a blazing fire, and to darkness and gloom and whirlwind, 19 and*
> *to the blast of a trumpet and the sound of words which sound was*
> *such that those who heard begged that no further word be spoken*
> *to them. 20 For they could not bear the command, "If even a*
> *beast touches the mountain, it will be stoned." 21 And so terrible*
> *was the sight, that Moses said, "I am full of fear and trembling."*
> *22 But you have come to Mount Zion and to the city of the living*
> *God, the heavenly Jerusalem, and to myriads of angels, 23 to the*
> *general assembly and church of the firstborn who are enrolled in*
> *heaven, and to God, the Judge of all, and to the spirits of the*
> *righteous made perfect, 24 and to Jesus, the mediator of a new*
> *covenant, and to the sprinkled blood, which speaks better than the*
> *blood of Abel. (Hebrews 12:18-29, NASB95)*

Following the description of the throne we read, **and there were seven lamps of fire burning before the throne, which are the seven Spirits of God (4:5).** In verse one we are presented with the voice of Christ, in verse three we see the glory of the Father, now in verse five we are introduced again to the sevenfold Spirits of God. So here again, as in so many other cases in the New Testament, we are given a subtle picture of God in Trinity. It is the Triune God who made the first covenant; it is the same Triune God that now abolishes that covenant with Israel and makes a New Covenant with the Church.

The Tabernacle and the Temple on earth were in their details representative of the heavenly original. In the Tabernacle there was a Laver (Exodus 30:17-21) holding large amounts of water and also called a Sea in I Kings 7:23-26. Here the priests were to wash in preparation to serving before God "*so that they will not die.*" So, as the heavenly original represented cleanliness, those that approach God must likewise "*wash with water,*" that is be washed by Christ, as He Himself washed the disciples' feet. The *sea of glass (4:6)* is representative of the necessary cleanliness of any that would approach His presence.

"The Seer ... sees between himself and the Throne a vast surface which flashes back the light that falls upon it, like the Aegean when on summer days he looked upon it from the heights of Patmos. ... But the Sea of glass is not only a striking and splendid feature in the scene; it suggests the vast distance which, even in the case of one who stood at the door of heaven, intervened between himself and the Throne of God."[246]

4:6 ...and before the throne there was something like a sea of glass, like crystal; and in the center and around the throne, four living creatures full of eyes in front and behind. In verse six, "the whole imagery is to be conceived thus: The throne, on which the divine Majesty is seated, rests upon four living creatures, who form its animated and moving basis."[247] These four living creatures have the divine quality of being omniscient, as that is what *full of eyes in front and behind (4:6)* would suggest. We are reminded here of a phrase in 2 Chronicles that gives us a similar image, the image of the all-seeing eyes of God.

> *For the eyes of the Lord move to and fro throughout the earth....*
> *(2 Chronicles 16:9, NASB95)*

4:7 The first creature was like a lion, and the second creature like a calf, and the third creature had a face like that of a man, and the fourth creature was like a flying eagle. All the powers of creation are summed up in these creatures found in *(4:7)*. They stand as guards to the Throne of God. "The four forms suggest whatever is noblest,

---

[246] Henry Barclay Swete, 70.

[247] Moses Stuart, vol. II, 112-113.

strongest, wisest, and swiftest in animate Nature. Nature, including Man, is represented before the Throne, taking its part in the fulfillment of the Divine Will, and the worship of the Divine Majesty."[248]

"These living bearers of the Almighty's throne…serve him with great power [lion], with patient obedience [ox], with quickness of intelligence and reason [man], and with rapidity and perspicacity [eagle]…."[249]

This picture of **the four living creatures (4:8)** is very close to that seen by Ezekiel.

> *As I looked, behold, a storm wind was coming from the north, a great cloud with fire flashing forth continually and a bright light around it, and in its midst something like glowing metal in the midst of the fire. 5 Within it there were figures resembling four living beings. And this was their appearance: they had human form. 6 Each of them had four faces and four wings. 7 Their legs were straight and their feet were like a calf's hoof, and they gleamed like burnished bronze. 8 Under their wings on their four sides were human hands. As for the faces and wings of the four of them, 9 their wings touched one another; their faces did not turn when they moved, each went straight forward. 10 As for the form of their faces, each had the face of a man; all four had the face of a lion on the right and the face of a bull on the left, and all four had the face of an eagle. (Ezekiel 1:4-10, NASB95)*

4:8 And the four living creatures, each one of them having six wings, are full of eyes around and within; and day and night they do not cease to say, "HOLY, HOLY, HOLY is THE LORD GOD, THE ALMIGHTY, WHO WAS AND WHO IS AND WHO IS TO COME." The fact that they are *full of eyes around and within (4:8)*, stated twice now in this section, suggest their omniscience and duty to guard the throne with ever-diligent care. In addition to the six wings, the holy praise of the creatures *(4:8)* reminds us of Isaiah's vision.

---

[248] Henry Barclay Swete, 71-72.

[249] Moses Stuart, vol. II, 113.

In the year of King Uzziah's death I saw the Lord sitting on a throne, lofty and exalted, with the train of His robe filling the temple. 2 Seraphim stood above Him, each having six wings: with two he covered his face, and with two he covered his feet, and with two he flew. 3 And one called out to another and said, "Holy, Holy, Holy, is the LORD of hosts, The whole earth is full of His glory. (Isaiah 6:1-3, NASB95)

Another picture of six winged creatures is found on the mercy seat, which was placed on top of the Ark of the Covenant.

The cherubim shall have their wings spread upward, covering the mercy seat with their wings and facing one another; the faces of the cherubim are to be turned toward the mercy seat. (Exodus 25:20, NASB95)

"The living creatures contribute to the glory and impressiveness of the scene. They may be regarded...as parts of a great composite picture of the presence-chamber of the Almighty...."[250]

For details on the phrase, "**HOLY, HOLY, HOLY is THE LORD GOD, THE ALMIGHTY, WHO WAS AND WHO IS AND WHO IS TO COME**" **(4:8)** see the commentary on 1:8.

4:9 And when the living creatures give glory and honor and thanks to Him who sits on the throne, to Him who lives forever and ever.... Isaiah predicted this scene (4:9-11) of the elders seeing the glory of the Lord in the context of judgement on Jerusalem.

Then the moon will be abashed and the sun ashamed,
For the Lord of hosts will reign on Mount Zion and in Jerusalem,
And His glory will be before His elders. (Isaiah 24:23, NASB95)

The words **glory (4:11)** δόξα (*doxa*) and **honor 4:12)** τιμή (*timē*), and **thanks (4:11)** εὐχαριστέω (*eucharisteō*) are instructive in how God is properly worshiped. One problem associated with prayer is that man often approaches God in the "gimmee, gimmee" mode. It is certainly not wrong

---

[250] Milton Terry, <u>Biblical Apocalyptics</u>, 319.

to ask things from God. However, if things start going well in that person's life, prayers often diminish. This passage is instructive of the importance and centrality of worship in prayer. When things go well and the 'gimmee' list is dimished by the provision of God, prayer still goes on for it is essential that we take time to worship God every day. These words give us instruction in how we can do that in our prayers.

Glory (4:11). Man cannot create glory and give it to God "but implicitly mankind exalts God in His true essence because of His power and might."[251] Man in his fallen state instinctively hates to ascribe to God glory. But instead he

> *...exchanged the glory of the incorruptible God for an image in the form of corruptible man and of birds and four-footed animals and crawling creatures. (Romans 1:23, NASB95)*

To properly worship God it is necessary to ascribe fame, renown, splendor, and glory to Him.

Honor (4:11). To honor God is to ascribe "worth" or "value" to Him. The word honor has its origin in the idea of worth. In fact our English word "worship," i.e. worth-ship, drives home this point. This word is used of money in Scripture. Men find worth or value in many things, certainly they do in money, but all too rarely in God. But Christ taught that true value demands that man *"...upon finding one pearl of great value, he went and sold all that he had and bought it"* (Matthew 13:46, NASB95). Man worships many things but until he values Christ to the point that he sells all to obtain Him, then he does not truly worship at all. To properly worship God it is necessary to ascribe worth, value, and honor to Him.

Thanks (4:11). To thank God properly, requires that we take careful note of what He is being thanked for. We are thankful to God for the grace He has bestowed on us in salvation. The word used, εὐχαριστέω (*eucharisteō*), here translated *thanks (4:11)*, is derived from the Greek word χαρις (*charis*) or "grace." Grace means "favor." "And because a favor deserves an obligation of thanks, the verb developed the meaning 'to be thankful,' hence

---

[251] Thoralf Gilbrant, Vol. Delta-Epsilon, 167.

'to give thanks, return thanks'."[252] To properly worship God it is necessary to express thankful gratitude for the favor He bestowed on us in Christ.

4:10 *...the twenty-four elders will fall down before Him who sits on the throne, and will worship Him who lives forever and ever, and will cast their crowns before the throne, saying....* Only God can rightly accept worship. The one *who sits on the throne (4:10)* here accepts that worship. "...to worship is to acknowledge the unique status and worth of the one being worshiped, and the relationship of that one to the worshiper."[253] One is the Creator; the other is the creation.

True and real worship recognizes that every good thing we have has its source in God and rightly belongs to Him with the result that these elders *cast their crowns before the throne...(4:10)*. "...this action acknowledges that God is the supreme King, who rules over them. *Crowns (4:10)* represent their power, authority to rule as kings, and so here they surrender their power to God."[254]

4:11 *Worthy are You, our Lord and our God, to receive glory and honor and power; for You created all things, and because of Your will they existed, and were created.* In addition, proper veneration requires that God be worshiped as the powerful creator that He is. We read *for You created all things, and because of Your will they existed, and were created (4:11)*. Creation is testimony to the power or omnipotence of God.

> We are also men of the same nature as you, and preach the gospel to you that you should turn from these vain things to a living God, who <u>made</u> the heaven and the earth and the sea and all that is in them. (Acts 14:15, NASB95)
>
> ...and swore by Him who lives forever and ever, who <u>created</u> heaven and the things in it, and the earth and the things in it, and the sea and the things in it, that there will be delay no longer.... (Revelation 10:6, NASB95)

---

[252] Ibid., Vol. Delta-Epsilon, 657.

[253] Robert G. Bratcher, Rev. 4:10.

[254] Ibid., Rev. 4:10.

The heavens are telling of the glory of God; and their expanse is declaring the work of His hands. (Psalm 19:1, NASB95)

Failure to worship God as the powerful creator of heaven and earth is failure to worship God as He designs Himself to be worshiped. This passage gives us considerable insight in how God is worshiped by his creation in heaven, and considerable help in how to shape our own worship of Him here on earth. It is interesting that one of the great battles the Church fights in a God hating world is the battle of God as Creator of heaven and earth. But such a battle is worthy of the name Christian for He created all things, **and because of Your will they existed, and were created (4:11)**.

Chapter 5
The Book and the Lamb

Chapter 5 is God's official divorce decree of Israel. She will no longer be His wife. "After God issues his divorce decree (chap.5), he puts the harlotrous Jerusalem away by capital punishment (chaps. 6-11; 14-18) and hosts the royal wedding feast (19:7-20); thereupon the new Jerusalem appears 'as a bride beautifully dressed for her husband (21:2).' "[255]

The Book with Seven Seals

5:1-2 *I saw in the right hand of Him who sat on the throne a book written inside and on the back, sealed up with seven seals. ² And I saw a strong angel proclaiming with a loud voice, "Who is worthy to open the book and to break its seals?"* There are at least two possibilities as to how this **book (5:1)** is to be understood.

1) The **book (5:1)** may instead be a *scroll*. Ezekiel describes such a scroll saying,

> *Then I looked, and behold, a hand was extended to me; and lo, a scroll was in it. When He spread it out before me, it was written on the front and back, and written on it were lamentations, mourning and woe. (Ezekiel 2:9-10, NASB95)*

Normally, a scroll was not written on the back. The papyrus reed, which was used to make up the scroll, ran horizontal on the front and vertical on the back. As a result, the front was easy to write on, but the back was difficult to do so because of the vertical texture. To use the back implied either a lack of writing material, not a possibility here in our heavenly context, or an abundance of content so pressing in its urgency that every inch had to be used to get it all down. In other words, this scroll implies that the charges and evidence against Israel were overwhelming.

---

[255] C. Marvin Pate, Editor, 87.

The seven seals would be located across the overlapping edge of the rolled up scroll. All of the seals would need to be broken before the scroll could be read. Under this scenario, the breaking of seals provide a backdrop from which the book will later be read. "A careful reading of the passage shows that during the seal-breaking, no action takes place. The most that chapters 6 and 7 do is introduce the reader to the main characters, forces, and circumstances with which the rest of the section is concerned. They are preparatory to the action which will take place once the book is opened."[256]

2) Instead, we may have here a folded up ***book (5:1)***. "The Hebrew document which resembles the apocalyptic scroll most closely is the *get mqussar*, the tied (folded and sealed) deed."[257] The document would have as many seals as there were folds. "The document in Revelation must have had seven folds."[258] Most interestingly, it is said that the folded *get* originated with priests who wished to divorce their wives. As we have stated earlier, Revelation is about God divorcing Israel and marrying the Church. "...the fact that it was used in divorce cases is interesting.... It might easily be a bill of divorce; the Lamb divorces the unfaithful Jerusalem and marries the new Jerusalem."[259]

As each seal was broken at each fold, God brought a new punishment against Israel in proportion to her spiritual harlotries.

The fact that there are seven seals is significant. "Seven is the number of covenant. The Hebrew word for seven, 'sheba,' is the root of the word 'nishba' which means to take an oath, to swear or to covenant. To swear or covenant means literally to seven oneself."[260] So, what we are dealing with here is a covenant issue. "If the sealed scroll is the Lamb's bill of divorce, the seals and the trumpets, in contrast to the vials, reveal disciplinary punishment or warnings to give the wife time to repent."[261]

We have two reasonable options as to what this ***book (5:1)*** is. One, what we see in the right hand of Him who sat on the throne is the book of the

---

[256] Jay E. Adams, <u>The Time is at Hand</u>, 62-63.

[257] J. Massyngberde Ford, 92.

[258] Ibid., 93.

[259] Ibid., 93.

[260] J. E. Leonard, <u>Come Out of Her My People</u>, 30.

[261] J. Massyngberde Ford, 94.

Book of the Covenant. These seven seals open the book, which brings judgement on Israel, just as prophesied in the book of the covenant (the Torah) itself.

> *If also after these things you do not obey Me, then I will punish you seven times more for your sins. (Leviticus 26:18, NASB95)*

> *If then, you act with hostility against Me and are unwilling to obey Me, I will increase the plague on you seven times according to your sins. (Leviticus 26:21, NASB95)*

> *...then I will act with hostility against you; and I, even I, will strike you seven times for your sins. (Leviticus 26:24, NASB95)*

> *...then I will act with wrathful hostility against you, and I, even I, will punish you seven times for your sins. (Leviticus 26:28, NASB95)*

It is now time for these prophecies to be completely fulfilled. Israel is now to be punished seven times just as God said it would, if it violated the covenant.

Two, "...the scroll with seven seals is the sentence handed down by the Judge against Jerusalem for its part in shedding 'all the righteous blood' of the martyrs' (Matt. 23:35). John has entered the courtroom at the end of the trial, just in time to hear the sentence delivered...."[262]

Now, these two points of view are in fact not far apart. Both see the legal environment in which the book is presented and both see judgements forthcoming from opening the **book (5:1)**. "It is a scroll of judgement. It is the record of what the heavenly court has determined to do about the inhuman persecution of God's flock. It is a decree containing God's verdict concerning the charges preferred by the martyrs against their persecutors."[263] Again, let us remember Ezekiel's comment on his book, they explain the one before us nicely,

---

[262] Steve Gregg, 92, referencing the view of Jay E. Adams.

[263] Jay E. Adams, <u>The Time is at Hand</u>, 64.

...and written on it were lamentations, mourning and woe.
(Ezekiel 2:9-10, NASB95)

That indeed sums up the content of the Book of Revelation.

> When viewed against the backdrop of the theme of Jewish judgement, personages (a harlot and a bride), and the flow of Revelation (from the sealed scroll to capital punishment for "adultery" to a "marriage feast" to the taking of a new "bride" as the "new Jerusalem"), the covenantal nature of the transaction suggests that the seven-sealed scroll is God' " divorce decree against his Old Testament wife for her spiritual adultery. In the Old Testament God "marries" Israel (see esp. Ezek. 16:8, 31-32), and in several places he threatens her with a "bill of divorce" (Isa. 50:1; Jer. 3:8).[264]

Here that threat has come to reality.

5:3 And no one in heaven or on the earth or under the earth was able to open the book or to look into it. At first, there is found no one **in heaven or on the earth (5:3)** or even **under the earth (5:3)** that is qualified to be mediator of the covenant and set in motion the judgements it contains. Christ once said, *"He who is without sin among you, let him be the first to throw a stone at her"* (John 8:7, NASB95). Those of the redeemed in the heavenly court could not say that they had not sinned. The angels, on the other hand, were not qualified to sit in judgement having never successfully withstood the temptations of sin. So, at first, there were found in heaven none that were worthy to cast the first stone.

5:4-5 Then I began to weep greatly because no one was found worthy to open the book or to look into it; 5 and one of the elders said to me, "Stop weeping; behold, the Lion that is from the tribe of Judah, the Root of David, has overcome so as to open the book and its seven seals." John is deeply moved, and begins to **weep greatly (5:4)** in response. Perhaps we can speculate that John is grieved that sin will go unpunished as a result of this lack of a worthy one to

---

[264] C. Marvin Pate, Editor, 51-52.

open the book (5:4) and administer the justice of judgement. But at this very point it is pointed out that there is one who has *overcome (5:5)* or "conquered" and thereby *worthy (5:4)*. That one who has conquered is 1) from *the tribe of Judah (5:5)*, and 2) *the Root of David (5:5)*.

5:6   And I saw between the throne (with the four living creatures) and the elders a Lamb standing, as if slain, having seven horns and seven eyes, which are the seven Spirits of God, sent out into all the earth. John increases the details concerning the One that he sees. He is 1) *a Lamb (5:6)*, 2) *as if slain (5:6)*, 3) *having seven horns (5:6)*, 4) and *seven eyes (5:6)*, 5) the eyes are *the seven Spirits of God (5:6)*. This one is none other that Jesus Christ Himself.

> The "Lamb" in the Book of Revelation is the one slain for our salvation (Rev. 5:6), before we were even born (13:8). He alone is found worthy (5:12) and is worshiped (5:8), not we because of our works. In fact, the saints are clothed in the white robes of his righteousness (7:9). Indeed, believers are washed in the blood of the Lamb (7:14). And he alone is the fountain of salvation (7:17). Any victory the saints have is through his merits (12:11). And the saved are the fruit of his work, not ours (14:4). Thus we are his followers (14:4) and sing his praises (5:8–10; 15:3).[265]

"Jesus is the Lamb of God with respect to His sacrificial role, *a Lamb standing, as if slain (5:6)*; this is *not* a description of His nature, as sentimental Arminianism would have it, with its lamb-like Jesus 'meek and mild.' In His nature, Jesus is the Lion of the Tribe of Judah, the self-assured and authoritative ruler."[266]

In the Revelation, Christ is referred to as a lamb thirty times. "This is a powerful confirmation of the authorship of this book. St. John is the only Evangelist who calls our Lord by this name. In his Gospel only we read, that John the Baptist, '*looking upon Jesus as he walked,*' exclaimed,

---

[265] Norman L. Geisler, and Ron Rhodes, Page 306.

[266] Rousas John Rushdoony, They Kingdom Come, 136.

'Behold the Lamb of God which taketh away the sin of the world.' "[267] This passage is found in John 1:29.

Horns (5:6) are a common symbol of power and they are here used with the number seven to make the point that Christ is omnipotent. Likewise the **eyes (5:6)** are symbols of knowledge; the seven fold eyes being symbolic of His omniscience.

This is now the third time the Spirit of God is identified **the seven Spirits of God (5:6)**. Here those seven Spirits are further identified as the **eyes (5:6)** of Christ.

> *John to the seven churches that are in Asia: Grace to you and peace, from Him who is and who was and who is to come, and from the seven Spirits who are before His throne.... (Revelation 1:4, NASB95)*

> *To the angel of the church in Sardis write: He who has the seven Spirits of God and the seven stars, says this: 'I know your deeds, that you have a name that you are alive, but you are dead. (Revelation 3:1, NASB95)*

5:7 And He came and took the book out of the right hand of Him who sat on the throne. The authority and personal qualifications allow this One to approach to the very presence of the Father and take from him **the book (5:7)**. Although it can be easily imagined that the four living creatures that stood in eternal vigilance about the throne would allow none to enter this special place where the Father Himself abode, yet the Son enters by right of family relationship. He is equal with the Father. Clearly the deity of Jesus Christ is here again drawn to our attention in this picture of the Son's intimacy with the Father.

"From this moment on it is the throne of God and of the Lamb (22:1). God governs the universe through the Lamb. That is Christ's reward and our comfort. It means that there is the beginning of a new era in heaven (20:4); and also on earth (20:2, 3). A most significant moment in history is this

---

[267] Phillip S. Desprez, The Apocalypse Fulfilled (London: Longman, Brown, Green and Longmans, 1854), 35.

coronation; the Mediator's investiture with the office of King over the universe."[268]

Let's notice something very interesting found in verses 1-7. First we read of the Father in verse 1, *"Him who sat on the throne"* (5:1). Next in verses 5 we read of *"the Lion that is from the tribe of Judah"* (5:5). Last we read of *"the seven Spirits of God"* (5:6). Without using the word Trinity, John has again subtly put before us the persons of the Triune God. There is a sense in which the Trinity is a mystery in the Bible, yet in the New Testament that mystery is unfolded and the deity of the Father, Son and Holy Spirit are clearly revealed.

5:8 When He had taken the book, the four living creatures and the twenty-four elders fell down before the Lamb, each one holding a harp and golden bowls full of incense, which are the prayers of the saints. The act of taking **the book (5:8)** has a dramatic impact on **the four living creatures and the twenty-four elders (5:8)**. They all **fell down (5:8)** before the **lamb (5:8)** in acts of veneration and worship. Again, nothing could be clearer at this point than is the deity of Jesus Christ. Such behavior on the part of the heavenly court would be nothing short of treason if Christ were anything other than God Himself. How strange it is that so many find it so hard to discover the deity of Christ in Scripture.

Notice the importance of **the prayers of the saints (5:8)**.

> *May my prayer be counted as incense before You;*
> *The lifting up of my hands as the evening offering. (Psalm 141:2,*
> *NASB95)*

Notwithstanding their ephemeral quality, they are not lost to God. They are precious to him and stored as it were in **golden bowels (5:8)** in His presence. He takes note of them and acts on them in due course.

5:9 And they sang a new song, saying, "Worthy are You to take the book and to break its seals; for You were slain, and purchased for God with Your blood men from every tribe and

---

[268] William Hendriksen, 91.

tongue and people and nation. Through the ages men have composed a *new song (5:9)* for momentous events. Such is now the case in heaven. "They sing a new song. It is new because never before had such a great and glorious deliverance been accomplished and never before had the Lamb received this great honour."[269]

The reason Christ is *worthy (5:9)* is set before us in song. It was He who was 1) *slain (5:9)*, who 2) *purchased (5:9)* with His *blood (5:9), men from every tribe, tongue, people, and nation (5:9)*.

The phrase *purchased for God with Your blood...(5:9)* means "by means of your blood," "by means of your death," referring to the verb "you were slain." As in 1:5, *blood (5:9)* stands for violent death, or sacrifice.[270]

Christ did not purchase all men on the earth, but some men *from (5:9)* the tribes, tongues, people and nations. To take *from (5:9)* is to take some and leave others. If He had purchased all, then all, of necessity, would have been saved.

We should take note of the importance of music in worship. Not only on earth, but also in heaven God is worshiped in song. Our singing before the morning service is not simply a preparation for worship; it is worship. That being the case it is incumbent upon us that our singing reflect the fact that we are worshiping. All the enthusiasm, praise, joy and holy awe that can be brought to the song service should be employed in the worship of God.

We might also note that the singing by the creatures and elders is accompanied by instruments (harps). Because the Old Testament and Heaven are filled with vocal and instrumental music, the argument against the use of instruments in the New Covenant, by some, sounds a bit dispensational—by that I mean a non-continuity (a major characteristic of Dispensationalism) between the Old Testament and the New Testament. But clearly there is continuity here between the Old and New Testaments in the use of instruments.

---

[269] Ibid., 91.

[270] Robert G. Bratcher, Rev. 5:10.

5:10 You have made them to be a kingdom and priests to our God; and they will reign upon the earth. It is not man's eternal destiny to live in a non-material heaven. For that reason it is said that ***they will reign upon the earth (5:10).*** Man's heaven is a reconstituted Garden of Eden on a New Earth. Man is a material being and will ever be so throughout all eternity, except for a brief period between his death and resurrection. Man was created to ***reign upon the earth (5:10).*** However, this is not to suggest that man is to reign only in eternity. He is called to reign in time and eternity.

> *Then God said, "Let Us make man in Our image, according to Our likeness; and let them rule over the fish of the sea and over the birds of the sky and over the cattle and over all the earth, and over every creeping thing that creeps on the earth...." God said to them, "Be fruitful and multiply, and fill the earth, and subdue it; and rule over the fish of the sea and over the birds of the sky and over every living thing that moves on the earth." (Genesis 1:26, 28, NASB95)*

Angels Exalt the Lamb

5:11 Then I looked, and I heard the voice of many angels around the throne and the living creatures and the elders; and the number of them was myriads of myriads, and thousands of thousands.... The ***voice (5:11)*** John hears consists of an innumerable choir and the great number of the voices surprises John. He stops to note with awe the tens of millions who join in the song. What an awesome experience it must have been.

5:12 ...saying with a loud voice, "Worthy is the Lamb that was slain to receive power and riches and wisdom and might and honor and glory and blessing." Notice; there are seven attributes ascribed to Christ here. It is not to be assumed that the Lamb is not worthy to receive other ascriptions of honor, like admiration, praise, or grandeur. Instead we should see in this selection of seven attributes an indication of the fullness or completeness of honor that is rightly His as evidenced in the use of seven. It should also challenge us in our worship. We can get in a rut in how we approach and praise God. In this verse we have a demonstration of the various, although not exhaustive, ways we can praise God that He might *receive power and riches and wisdom and might and honor and glory and blessing (5:12)*.

5:13-14 And every created thing which is in heaven and on the earth and under the earth and on the sea, and all things in them, I heard saying, "To Him who sits on the throne, and to the Lamb, be blessing and honor and glory and dominion forever and ever." 14 And the four living creatures kept saying, "Amen." And the elders fell down and worshiped. To the first multitude is added an additional chorus of voices. *Every created thing (5:13)* joins in worship to the *Lamb (5:13)*. Why this unusual focus on praise, power, worship, and eternal dominion?

> The Church in St. John's day was about to experience a time of severe testing and persecution. Already they were seeing what, in a sane age, could scarcely be imagined: a union between Israel and the antichristian Beast of Rome. These Christians needed to understand history as something not ruled by chance or evil men or even the devil, but ruled instead from God's Throne by Jesus Christ. They needed to see that Christ was reigning now, that He had already wrested the world from Satan's grasp, and that even now all things in heaven and earth were bound to acknowledge Him as King. They needed to see themselves in the true light: Not as forgotten troops in a lonely outpost fighting a losing battle, but as kings and priests already, waging war and overcoming, predestined to victory, with the absolute assurance of conquest and dominion with the High King over the earth. They needed the Biblical philosophy of history: that all of history, created and controlled by God's personal and total government, is moving inexorably toward the universal dominion of the Lord Jesus Christ. The new and final age of history has arrived; the New Covenant has come. Behold, He has conquered![271]

We began this section in verse eight observing that *"the twenty-four elders fell down before the Lamb"* (5:8). Now as we conclude this segment we read that *the elders fell down and worshiped (5:14)*. In the throne room of God the Lamb receives worship from those that sit around the very

---

[271] David Chilton, The Days of Vengeance, 180.

throne of God. Such an act, if not a proper function on their part, would be an act of treason. Only God can receive worship. Certainly these elders would not be defying God the Father to His face, robbing Him of His glory and giving worship to someone other than God Himself. Yet here, in the very presence of Him who sits on the throne, Jesus Christ is worshiped. Clearly, the deity of Christ is evident in this passage for He is equal with the Father, and with the Father worthy of worship.

Chapter 6
The Opening of the Seals

We now enter on a discussion of the seals. Seals one through four and the sixth equate to Christ's words in the Olivet Discourse as recorded in Luke 21.

> When you hear of wars and disturbances, do not be terrified; for these things must take place first, but the end does not follow immediately. Then He continued by saying to them, nation will rise against nation and kingdom against kingdom, and there will be great earthquakes, and in various places plagues and famines; and there will be terrors and great signs from heaven. (Luke 21:9-11, NASB95)

Jesus gives us the short version. John here fleshes out the story and gives us greater details. "John and Christ are evidently describing the same events, to happen at the same time, on the same city, and in nearly the same terms."[272]

The seals open with four horsemen. These horsemen are not to be viewed as successive; that is, one follows the other after a period of time. Instead they are concurrent, "they all belong to the same age; they are parts of the same affair; they all go together, conquest, war, famine, death."[273] All these forces of judgement fall on Israel and Jerusalem at the same time. Although concurrent, of necessity, they are described one at a time.

The Book Opened; The First Seal—Conquest

6:1 Then I saw when the Lamb broke one of the seven seals, and I heard one of the four living creatures saying as with a voice of thunder, "Come." In the order to **come (6:1)**, there are two possibilities as to who is here addressed. In the *first*, it is John who is called to come and see the actions of the horseman. In the *second*, it is a cry to the

---

[272] David S. Clark, 54.
[273] Ibid., 54.

horseman, not John. It is a call for the horseman to come forth and do that which he as been assigned to do.

6:2 *I looked, and behold, a white horse, and he who sat on it had a bow; and a crown was given to him, and he went out conquering and to conquer.* The identity of the rider has generated a considerable amount of interest. There are several possibilities as to who this person is on the *white horse (6:2)*.

One, he is the Antichrist with his demonic forces attempting to make Satan's influence felt across the world and instituting the Great Tribulation. This option is typical of those that hold to Dispensationalism although not the only one they might favor.

Two, He is Christ leading His heavenly armies in judgement on Israel for their violation of the old covenant and their murder of their prophesied Messiah, the Lord of Glory Himself. The fact that the rider is crowned is especially important. This One has already conquered and has been crowned as a result of His victories.

> *And I saw heaven opened, and behold, a white horse, and He who sat on it is called Faithful and True, and in righteousness He judges and wages war. His eyes are a flame of fire, and on His head are many diadems; and He has a name written on Him which no one knows except Himself. He is clothed with a robe dipped in blood, and His name is called The Word of God. (Revelation 19:11-13, NASB95)*

> *Then I looked, and behold, a white cloud, and sitting on the cloud was one like a son of man, having a golden crown on His head and a sharp sickle in His hand. (Revelation 14:14, NASB95)*

The use of the phrase **conquering and to conquer (6:2)** is also significant. Christ has already been identified as the one who has conquered.

> *He who overcomes, νικάω (nikaō, conquers), I will grant to him to sit down with Me on My throne, as I also overcame (νικάω, nikaō, conquered) and sat down with My Father on His throne. (Revelation 3:21, NASB95)*

...and one of the elders said to me, "Stop weeping; behold, the Lion that is from the tribe of Judah, the Root of David, has overcome νικάω (nikaō, conquered) so as to open the book and its seven seals." (Revelation 5:5, NASB95)

So Christ, the warrior King, comes to make war on His enemies. The **white horse (6:2)** is symbolic of His rank as general of His armies. The **bow (6:2)** is symbolic of His mission, which is to conquer; the **crown (6:2)** is symbolic of His status, which is King. He leads for His army of judgement, war, famine, and death.

However, one compelling reason for not seeing this rider as Jesus Christ would be that to do so makes Him simply one of four with a mission commensurate to the other riders. "It is tempting to identify him with the Rider on the white horse in xix. 11ff., whose name is 'the Word of God'.... But the two riders have nothing in common beyond the white horse.... Rather we have here a picture of triumphant militarism."[274] Also, it would be somewhat strange for Jesus to both *open* the seal and then *be* the seal. That point in itself probably excludes this possibility.

Three, he is Vespasian, the Roman general and soon to be Emperor of Rome. Under orders from Nero, in A.D. 66 he begins the war, three and a half years later Jerusalem falls and the war is over. "The entire imagery of this first picture points suggestively to the opening of the Roman war against Jerusalem...."[275]

The **white horse (6:2)** is symbolic of both leadership and victory. "Leaders of armies frequently rode on horses of this colour.... Particularly did victors use them in a triumphal procession...."[276] The bow, a weapon that is used from afar, is indicative of his role in pursuing the battle at a distance, steadily destroying the Jews in their various cities and forcing the survivors ever closer to Jerusalem. "The fact that the victorious rider had a bow suggests that in the first stages of this bitter and decisive war the fighting was at a distance, not a close hand-to-hand struggle, such as a use of the sword implies. The war began by capturing the outlying towns of

---

[274] Henry Barclay Swete, 86.

[275] Milton S. Terry, Biblical Apocalyptics, 327.

[276] Moses Stuart, vol. II, 152.

Palestine, preparatory to the siege of the great central city, Jerusalem."[277] The **crown (6:2)** may have reference to the fact that he is soon crowned Emperor after Nero's death. "It should also be noted here, that the conqueror in this case is not the Lamb himself, as in 19:11, but the Generalissimo (so to speak) of the invading army. The Lamb evidently remains in his antecedent position, in order to break the remainder of the seals."[278]

The rider here in Revelation 6 and the one in Revelation 19 are often identified as one and the same person. However, as strong as the case for identification between the two may appear to be on the surface, in fact "...the only feature common to both riders is the color of the horse. They differ in the weapons they carry (bow in 6:2, sword in 19:15), in the crowns they wear (wreath, Gr. stephanos, in 6:2, and diadems Gr. diadema, in 19:12), and in many other details."[279]

Four, he is simply one of the angles of God going forth to do God's service, similar to number three above but without identifying the rider as Vespasian. He is similar to the next three riders and has no more specific identification than do the other riders. Notwithstanding the apparent strength of the arguments for the first three possibilities, this appears to be the best explanation. If it were more than this, then the next three riders would have to be more than they are universally portrayed as being.

The Second Seal—War

6:3-4 *When He broke the second seal, I heard the second living creature saying, "Come." 4 And another, a red horse, went out; and to him who sat on it, it was granted to take peace from the earth [land], and that men would slay one another; and a great sword was given to him.* The second, the **red horse (6:4)**, is symbolic of the blood shed in war. This rider is **to take peace from the earth [land] (6:4)**. This peace is to be taken from the "land" not the **earth (6:4)**. It is the land of Israel that is spoken of. At this time in the Roman world there was a great peace over the Roman Empire call

---

277 Milton S. Terry, Biblical Apocalyptics, 327.

278 Moses Stuart, vol. II, 153.

279 J. Massyngberde Ford, 105.

the *Pax Romana* or Peace of Rome. This comes to an end in *the land* of Israel at this point.

Now the weapon changes from the bow to a **sword (6:4).** Here we have the close hand to hand combat that is demanded in the use of the sword. And it is not any sword that he uses; it is a **great sword (6:4)** implying the immense destruction and death that it is to cause.

The phrase **that men would slay one another (6:4)** suggests civil war on top of the foreign war that Rome and Israel have made on each other. And indeed, this is exactly the condition in Judah and Jerusalem at this time.

> ... every city was divided into two armies encamped one against another, and the preservation of the one party was in the destruction of the other; (463) so the daytime was spent in shedding of blood, and the night in fear, —which was of the two the more terrible; for when the Syrians thought they had ruined the Jews, they had the Judaizers in suspicion also; and as each side did not care to slay those whom they only suspected on the other, so did they greatly fear them when they were mingled with the other, as if they were certainly foreigners. (464) Moreover, greediness of gain was a provocation to kill the opposite party, even to such as had of old appeared very mild and gentle towards them; for they without fear plundered the effects of the slain and carried off the spoils of those whom they slew to their own houses, as if they had been gained in a set battle; and he was esteemed a man of honor who got the greatest share, as having prevailed over the greatest number of his enemies. (465) It was then common to see cities filled with dead bodies, still lying unburied, and those of old men, mixed with infants, all dead, and scattered about together; women also lay amongst them, without any covering for their nakedness: you might then see the whole province full of inexpressible calamities, while the dread of still more barbarous practices which were threatened, was everywhere greater than what had been already perpetrated.[280]

---

[280] Flavius Josephus, *Wars,* 2:18:2. See also 4:3:2; 4:3:10; 4:6:2 for more information of the civil war of the Jews.

The Third Seal—Famine

6:5-6 *When He broke the third seal, I heard the third living creature saying, "Come." I looked, and behold, a black horse; and he who sat on it had a pair of scales in his hand. 6 And I heard something like a voice in the center of the four living creatures saying, "A quart of wheat for a denarius, and three quarts of barley for a denarius; and do not damage the oil and the wine."* The next is **a black horse (6:5)**. "...black is the colour indicative of distress, misfortune, or mourning...."[281] "The symbol is not difficult of interpretation. It signifies the deepening horrors of the war. Famine follows on the heels of war and slaughter."[282] The **scales (6:5)** are to demonstrate the shortage of food. The quart was the daily ration of wheat for one person. A **denarius (6:6)** was a day's wage. "...the denarius was the standard daily wage for a rural worker (see Matt 20.2). This was a very high price for a quart of wheat or three quarts of barley, perhaps as much as ten times the normal price, and indicates a severe shortage as a result of war."[283] To feed a family one would need to buy **barley (6:6)** instead, a less desirable and less nutritious grain. Famine is one of the curses promised by God for breaking his covenant.

> *When I break your staff of bread, ten women will bake your*
> *bread in one oven, and they will bring back your bread in*
> *rationed amounts, so that you will eat and not be satisfied.*
> *(Leviticus 26:26, NASB95)*

Josephus gives us some detail as to how the famine developed.

> The madness of the seditious did also increase together with their famine, and both those miseries were every day inflamed more and more; (425) for there was no corn which anywhere appeared publicly, but the robbers came running into, and searched men's private houses; and then, if they found any, they tormented them, because they had denied they had any; and if they found none, they tormented them worse, because they supposed they had more

---

[281] Moses Stuart, vol. II, 154.

[282] J. Stuart Russell, 390.

[283] Robert G. Bratcher, Rev. 6:6.

carefully concealed it. (426) The indication they made use of whether they had any or not, was taken from the bodies of these miserable wretches; which, if they were in good case, they supposed they were in no want at all of food; but if they were wasted away, they walked off without searching any farther; nor did they think it proper to kill such as these, because they saw they would very soon die of themselves for want of food. (427) Many there were indeed who sold what they had for one measure; it was of <u>wheat</u>, if they were of the richer sort, but of <u>barley</u>, if they were poorer. When these had so done, they shut themselves up in the inmost rooms of their houses, and ate the corn they had gotten; some did it without grinding it, by reason of the extremity of the want they were in, and others baked bread of it, according as necessity and fear dictated to them; (428) a table was nowhere laid for a distinct meal, but they snatched the bread out of the fire, half-baked, and ate it very hastily.[284]

"The Jews in Jerusalem suffered terrible food shortages during the Roman siege. Though initially there was enough food stored up to last a long time, the warring factions in the city, out of sheer spite, regularly destroyed the grain stores of the opposing factions! Thus food became so scarce that Josephus records at least one case of a mother eating her infant."[285] This is exactly what God promised Israel if they rejected His Lordship of their nation.

> *Then you shall eat the offspring of your own body, the flesh of your sons and of your daughters whom the Lord your God has given you, during the siege and the distress by which your enemy will oppress you. (Deuteronomy 28:53, NASB95)*

Unlike the grains, there is to be no shortage of **oil and wine (6:6)**. What is this about? Surely one goes with the other! But Josephus tells us how this happened. He speaks of one called John Gischala, the leader of one of the factions warring inside Jerusalem. He says of John, "...he emptied the vessels of that sacred wine and oil, which the priests kept to be poured on the burnt offerings, and which lay in the inner court of the temple, and

---

[284] Flavius Josephus, *Wars*, 5:10:2.

[285] Steve Gregg, 110.

distributed it among the multitude...."[286] And, in addition, Titus, during the siege of Jerusalem, ordered "...that olive groves and vineyards were not to be ravaged."[287]

So the Apostle John, prophesying of what would soon take place, takes note that in spite of the presence of a famine, there would be ample *oil and wine (6:6)*. Which is exactly what happened when John Gischala distributed the enormous stores used in the temple worship to the multitude and Titus protected the groves and vineyards.

The Fourth Seal—Death

6:7-8 When the Lamb broke the fourth seal, I heard the voice of the fourth living creature saying, "Come." 8 I looked, and behold, an ashen horse; and he who sat on it had the name Death; and Hades was following with him. Authority was given to them over a fourth of the earth [land], to kill with sword and with famine and with pestilence and by the wild beasts of the earth [land]. The Greek word translated *ashen (6:8)* actually denotes pallid yellowish green.[288] "The ghastly specters of Death and Hades now follow in the train of famine and war."[289]

The word *Hades (6:8)* does not mean hell; it simply means the place of the unseen dead, which may be heaven or hell. "Hades (*haides*, alpha privative, and *idein*, to see; in combination it means "the unseen") is the abode of the dead...."[290] "Hades (hell) means the grave, the actual pit dug in the earth, and hence never means more than death or the abode of death."[291]

We read of one of the covenant curses in Deuteronomy twenty-eight.

---

[286] Flavius Josephus, *Wars*, 5:13:6.

[287] J. Massyngberde Ford, 107.

[288] Steve Gregg, 114.

[289] J. Stuart Russell, 392.

[290] Archibald Thomas Robertson, Vol. VI, 342.

[291] Philip Carrington, 160.

*Your carcasses will be food to all birds of the sky and to the beasts
of the earth, and there will be no one to frighten them away.
(Deuteronomy 28:26, NASB95)*

Sword, famine, and pestilence or disease is easy to understand as products
of this war, but what of **wild beasts (6:8)**? I think we need to look at
Ezekiel, as did John, and see that John is using a Biblical formula to make
his point.

*For thus says the Lord God, "How much more when I send My
four severe judgements against Jerusalem: sword, famine, wild
beasts and plague to cut off man and beast from it!" (Ezekiel
14:21, NASB95)*

It isn't that wild animals didn't kill and eat the Israelites as they fled from
the Romans, hiding in caves and other places where they would be exposed
to this sort of thing. No doubt this happened. However, probably John was
using a literary figure from Ezekiel to make a point. That point being, Israel
and Jerusalem will suffer destruction at God's hands in the judgements He
sends on the land. It will be so great that no one will be left to bury the dead
bodies. Therefore the **beasts of the earth (6:8)** will consume them.

So all hope of escaping was now cut off from the Jews, together
with their liberty of going out of the city. Then did the famine
widen its progress, and devoured the people by whole houses and
families; (513) the upper rooms were full of women and children
that were dying by famine; and the lanes of the city were full of the
dead bodies of the aged; the children also and the young men
wandered about the marketplaces like shadows, all swelled with
the famine, and fell down dead wheresoever their misery seized
them. (514) As for burying them, those that were sick themselves
were not able to do it; and those that were hearty and well were
deterred from doing it by the great multitude of those dead bodies,
and by the uncertainty there was how soon they should die
themselves, for many died as they were burying others, and many
went to their coffins before that fatal hour was come! (515) Nor
was there any lamentation made under these calamities, nor were
heard any mournful complaints; but the famine confounded all
natural passions; for those who were just going to die, looked upon
those that were gone to their rest before them with dry eyes and
open mouths. .... Now the seditious at first gave orders that the

dead should be buried out of the public treasury, as not enduring the stench of their dead bodies. But afterwards, when they could not do that, they had them cast down from the walls into the valleys beneath.

However, when Titus, in going his rounds along those valleys, saw them full of dead bodies, and the thick putrefaction running about them, he gave a groan; and spreading out his hands to heaven, called God to witness that this was not his doing: (520) and such was the sad case of the city itself.[292]

Thus says the Lord God, "Now I will spread My net over you with a company of many peoples, and they shall lift you up in My net. I will leave you on the land; I will cast you on the open field. And I will cause all the birds of the heavens to dwell on you, and I will satisfy the beasts of the whole earth with you. I will lay your flesh on the mountains and fill the valleys with your refuse. I will also make the land drink the discharge of your blood As far as the mountains, and the ravines will be full of you." (Ezekiel 32:3-6, NASB95)[293]

In studying the first four seals we see that they "find fulfillment in the war which began about A. D. 66, swept over Galilee and Samaria, laid waste all the cities and villages of Palestine, and became intensified with all those scenes of blood and famine and woe which made the siege and final overthrow of Jerusalem by the Romans one of the most horrible events of human history."[294]

The Fifth Seal—Martyrs

"The fifth seal may be seen as the key to the whole chapter for it looks backward to the concept of the "martyr" Lamb in ch. 5 and forward to the number of those sealed and the configuration of angels in ch. 7. It confirms that all the seals are in the context of the just judgement of God."[295]

---

[292] Flavius Josephus, *Wars*, 5:12:4.

[293] See also Isaiah 18:4-6; 56:9-10; Jeremiah 7:32-34; 12:8-9; 16:4; Ezekiel 33:27; 39:17.

[294] Milton S. Terry, Biblical Apocalyptics, 332.

[295] J. Massyngberde Ford,110.

6:9 *When the Lamb broke the fifth seal, I saw underneath the altar the souls of those who had been slain because of the word of God, and because of the testimony which they had maintained....* When an animal was sacrificed, the blood of the sacrifice, which was considered the life of the victim, ran down to the base of the altar; thus the life would literally be **underneath the altar (6:9)**.[296] "The vision finds its explanation in the custom of pouring out the blood of sacrificial victims at the base of the altar...."[297] Paul uses some of the same kind of language when he describes his coming martyrdom.

> But even if I am being poured out as a drink offering upon the sacrifice and service of your faith, I rejoice and share my joy with you all. (Philippians 2:17, NASB95)

> For I am already being poured out as a drink offering, and the time of my departure has come. (2 Timothy 4:6, NASB95)

The word **maintained (6:9)** is the Greek word ἔχω (*echō*) which means *to have* or *hold*.[298] The grammatical form of this word is important. The tense is imperfect. "The imperfect tense generally represents continual or repeated action."[299] In other words, "that the martyrs were once merely in possession of the word, etc., would not have occasioned their death; it was their steadfast adherence to it, which caused them to be sacrificed on the altar of religion."[300]

"It must be kept in mind that these calamities of the Jewish people were announced in most explicit terms by Jesus as a judgement upon that wicked generation for its guilt in shedding the righteous blood of saints and

---

[296] Gene Fadeley, 19.

[297] Milton S. Terry, <u>Biblical Apocalyptics</u>, 327.

[298] Walter Bauer, William F. Arndt, F. Wilbur Gingrich and Frederick W. Danker, <u>A Greek-English Lexicon of the New Testament and Other Early Christian Literature</u> (Chicago, IL: University of Chicago Press, 1979).

[299] <u>Tense Voice Mood</u> (Ontario: Woodside Bible Fellowship, 1994).

[300] Moses Stuart, vol. II, 161.

prophets.... Hence the significance of placing the martyr scene of verses 9-11 in the midst of these pictures of retributive judgement."[301]

> *Therefore, behold, I am sending you prophets and wise men and scribes; some of them you will kill and crucify, and some of them you will scourge in your synagogues, and persecute from city to city, so that upon you may fall the guilt of all the righteous blood shed on earth, from the blood of righteous Abel to the blood of Zechariah, the son of Berechiah, whom you murdered between the temple and the altar. Truly I say to you, all these things will come upon this generation. Jerusalem, Jerusalem, who kills the prophets and stones those who are sent to her! How often I wanted to gather your children together, the way a hen gathers her chicks under her wings, and you were unwilling. Behold, your house is being left to you desolate! (Matthew 23:34-38, NASB95)*

"Not only is the symbolism of blood-revenge the same; but it points out what later study will confirm; it is the land of Israel, and in particular the Temple at Jerusalem which is to suffer."[302]

The next thing we can note from this passage is that with the right kind of eyes, souls or immaterial beings can be seen. There is some kind of spiritual body that those, who are without material bodies, partake of. We are *not* absorbed into the Spirit of the universe. We maintain our personalities and humanness even without our material bodies, although we are certain to be reunited with them on the last day.

> *But now Christ has been raised from the dead, the first fruits of those who are asleep. For since by a man came death, by a man also came the resurrection of the dead. (1 Corinthians 15:20-21, NASB95)*

"...the psychology of John did not admit the extinction of the soul by the death of the body."[303]

---

[301] Milton S. Terry, Biblical Apocalyptics, 332-333.

[302] Philip Carrington, 132.

[303] Moses Stuart, vol. II, 160.

6:10 ***...and they cried out with a loud voice, saying, "How long, O Lord, holy and true, will You refrain from judging and avenging our blood on those who dwell on the earth?"*** In this verse, we will considered two prominent ideas in the text: 1) the blood offering of the martyrs death and 2) the just retribution for that death. "The twin ideas of Blood-offering and Blood-revenge must be kept in mind if we are to understand Revelation."[304]

This verse, "...would indicate that these persecutors were still alive on earth."[305] This is therefore another indicator of the first century context in which this book has its fulfillment. Christ had predicted it, and in His prediction the timing is specified; it is the first century in which the fulfillment is to take place, it is *this generation*.

"The destruction of Jerusalem in that generation was the sentence of the divine Judge in response to the cries of the blood (souls) of the righteousness ones slain by her leaders."[306] It is as if these believers died as sacrifices to God, their death being raised to this very high level by having their blood poured out *"underneath the altar"* (6:9). It is the work of Christ at Calvary that the Church celebrates. This is a work whereby Jesus pours out His blood as an eternal sacrifice for the sins of His children. On the one hand, it is not to be understood in any way that the sacrifice of His martyrs adds to this work. Yet on the other, it is God Himself who uses this analogy of the death of His Son and the death of His saints to elevate them in their commitment to Him in their death.

On another note, Milton Terry explains, "...the cry for judgement and vengeance is not to be understood as the expression of bitter and vindictive feelings, but a call for the Judge of all the earth to do that which is due to his holiness and truth."[307] This thought is echoed by J. Massyngberde Ford, "...God delivers a man from his enemies; that is the basic idea behind all the subsequent uses and nuances. Retribution in the sense of punishing the

---

[304] Philip Carrington, 133.

[305] David S. Clark, 56.

[306] Steve Gregg, 118.

[307] Milton S. Terry, Biblical Apocalyptics, 331.

wicked does enter into the picture but the idea of vengeance in the sense of personal satisfaction does not."[308]

6:11 And there was given to each of them a white robe; and they were told that they should rest for a little while longer, until the number of their fellow servants and their brethren who were to be killed even as they had been, would be completed also. The **white robes (6:11)** are symbolic of the purity of those who were martyred and their actual victory over evil.

> ...when the priests reached the canonical age they came up to the Temple to have their claims tested. If their genealogies were found correct, they then underwent a physical examination; if they were found to be without blemish, they were accepted as priests and given a White Robe. If St. John has this in his mind, then the White Robe given to the martyrs is the recognition of their claim to priesthood....[309]

The martyrs are told to **rest for a little while longer (6:11)**. "...here *rest* means not only not having to work or strive, but also to be free of anxiety and distress over the punishment of their killers. They must be patient. God's vengeance will not be immediate but will come soon."[310]

> ...now, will not God bring about justice for His elect who cry to Him day and night, and will He delay long over them? I tell you that He will bring about justice for them quickly.... (Luke 18:7-8, NASB95)

Let us also take note of one other important point taught in this passage; souls don't sleep at death, bodies do. "The point is obvious. They were not asleep. They were very conscious, especially of events on earth."[311] We can clearly see in this passage the conscience state of believers after death and without their bodies, which lie asleep in the grave. In Luke 16 in the story of the rich man and Lazarus we also see the conscience state of the dead with

---

[308] J. Massyngberde Ford, 100.

[309] Philip Carrington, 143.

[310] Robert G. Bratcher, Rev. 6:11.

[311] C. Jonathin Seraiah, <u>The End of All Things</u> (Moscow, Idaho: Cannon Press, 1999), 139.

Abraham and the rich man in conversation with each other. The concomitant lesson to be learned here is that it is bodies that are resurrected on the last day from this state of sleep, not souls, which never did sleep. Our resurrection on that last day is a physical one, not a spiritual one. I make note of this here because of the teaching of the unorthodox Preterist, or as they are sometimes called, pantelist.[312] They erroneously teach that the final resurrection occurred in A.D. 70, they have no resurrection of the bodies of the dead on the last day. In fact they have no last day. For them it is souls that sleep and are resurrected, contrary to the clear teaching of this and other passages in Scripture. Theirs is the error of Hymenaeus and Philetus.

> But avoid worldly and empty chatter, for it will lead to further ungodliness, and their talk will spread like gangrene. Among them are Hymenaeus and Philetus, _men who have gone astray from the truth saying that the resurrection has already taken place, and they upset the faith of some_. (2 Timothy 2:16-18, NASB95)

The Sixth Seal—Terror

6:12-17 It would be helpful to look at this section in parallel with Jesus' comments from Matthew 24 and Luke 23. Remember, the Olivet Discourse is the "Little Apocalypse."

6:12 I looked when He broke the sixth seal,	
and there was a great earthquake; and the sun became black as sackcloth made of hair,	"But immediately after the tribulation of those days the sun will be darkened,
and the whole moon became like blood;	and the moon will not give its light,
13 and the stars of the sky fell to the earth [land],	and the stars will fall from the sky,

---

[312] Pantelism: the false doctrine that all biblical prophecy has been fulfilled.

as a fig tree casts its unripe figs when shaken by a great wind.	*and the powers of the heavens will be shaken." (Matthew 24:29, NASB95)*
14 The sky was split apart like a scroll when it is rolled up, and every mountain and island were moved out of their places.	
15 Then the kings of the earth [land] and the great men and the commanders and the rich and the strong and every slave and free man hid themselves in the caves and among the rocks of the mountains; 16 and they said to the mountains and to the rocks, "Fall on us and hide us from the presence of Him who sits on the throne, and from the wrath of the Lamb; 17 for the great day of their wrath has come, and who is able to stand?"	*"Then they will begin to say to the mountains, 'Fall on us,' and to the hills, 'Cover us.' " (Luke 23:30, NASB95)*

Notice how these two passages are parallel. They are telling the same story. One is the short version, the other the more complete one. What is meant by the one, is meant by the other.

But, we are again confronted with the question of a "literal" interpretation of Revelation. We dealt with this topic in the early sections of this book, but in considering this passage, let's make this additional observation as well: "If they are to be taken literally, there is no room for any more apocalypse, or any more history; the physical structure of the universe is at an end."[313] Now in fact the world does not come to an end at this point, there are 16 chapters yet ahead of us. So, they may not be understood literally; how then shall we understand them? As Carrington says, "The problem has to be

---

[313] Philip Carrington, 135.

solved for the whole book. Either it is the work of an inspired poet dealing with invisible ideals and forces and principles, and expressing them in an imaginative system of starry symbols; or else it is the work of a narrow-minded, materialistic, adventist fanatic...."[314] So, which is it?

But before we look at the details of this passage, let us make a couple of points; one, we must let Scripture be our guide in understanding Scripture. Many Christians are quicker to study their daily newspaper than they are to look at the total revelation of Scripture in order to understand obscure phrases or signs. We must not do that here. The Old Testament is a mine of prophetic material that we must not fail to carefully consider. Two, it is important to note that in Scripture there are formula statements or phrases employed to convey critical information pictorially. We do the same in our language. For instance, if a student were to take a test that he had not properly prepared himself for, looking at the first few questions, he might say to his friends, "My whole life just passed before my eyes" or "My whole world came to an end." What he would be saying in metaphoric, picturesque, and stylized language would be that he experienced considerable confusion and fear when he saw the difficulty of the questions and was certain he was going to die (fail the test) right there. Illustrations like this could be multiplied a hundredfold. The point is language is often very symbolic, pictorial and stylized. It is designed to convey both information and emotion. It is critical that we keep that in mind in our study of this book.

6:12-14 *I looked when He broke the sixth seal, and there was a great earthquake; and the sun became black as sackcloth made of hair, and the whole moon became like blood;* [13] *and the stars of the sky fell to the earth, as a fig tree casts its unripe figs when shaken by a great wind.* [14] *The sky was split apart like a scroll when it is rolled up, and every mountain and island were moved out of their places.* In this section we read of the apparent destruction of the universe. The **sun (6:12)** is darkened, the **moon (6:12)** becomes like **blood (6:12)**, and **stars (6:13)** fall to the **earth (6:13)**. "In ancient Jewish thought the obedience of the cosmic order was to be copied by the obedience of the faithful to the commands of God; cf. Ps 19. If the commandments were broken, the constellations, would forsake their order

---

[314] Ibid, 135.

and creation would begin to disintegrate."[315]   That is what is happening here. The Law has been broken, indeed the Lawgiver has been murdered and the universe, symbolically speaking, is disintegrating, at least the universe that the Jews knew is coming apart. "In apocalyptic thought cosmic catastrophe is a consequence of sin...."[316]

The style of language used here is often call de-creation language, meaning the judgement of God would be so severe that it would appear that God would be de-creating the universe. This is common to the Old Testament; we see it used in several judgement scenes.

Babylon:

> *For the stars of heaven and their constellations will not flash forth their light; the sun will be dark when it rises and the moon will not shed its light. (Isaiah 13:10, NASB95)*

Egypt:

> *"And when I extinguish you, I will cover the heavens and darken their stars; I will cover the sun with a cloud and the moon will not give its light. All the shining lights in the heavens I will darken over you and will set darkness on your land," declares the Lord God. (Ezekiel 32:7-8, NASB95)*

Idumea:

> *So their slain will be thrown out, and their corpses will give off their stench, and the mountains will be drenched with their blood. And all the host of heaven will wear away, and the sky will be rolled up like a scroll; all their hosts will also wither away as a leaf withers from the vine, or as one withers from the fig tree. For My sword is satiated in heaven, behold it shall descend for judgement upon Edom and upon the people whom I have devoted to destruction. (Isaiah 34:3-5, NASB95)*

---

[315] J. Massyngberde Ford, 111.

[316] Ibid., 111.

We are here confronted with this same de-creation language in Revelation. This is no more to be taken literally in Revelation than it was in Isaiah or Ezekiel. It is symbolic language describing in picturesque style the utter destruction coming upon those nations God is going to judge.[317]

We read that **there was a great earthquake (6:12)**. Now, "...earthquakes are frequently one of the great events marking the end of the age (see Isa 29.6; Joel 2.10; Hag 2.6; Mark 13.8)."[318] Isaiah used an **earthquake (6:12)** as an illustration of the destruction that God would bring upon Jerusalem in its first destruction in 586 BC.

> *From the Lord of hosts you will be punished with thunder and earthquake and loud noise, with whirlwind and tempest and the flame of a consuming fire. (Isaiah 29:6, NASB95)*

However, there is no record of an actual **earthquake (6:12)** during this period. But that is not necessary; it was not an actual **earthquake (6:12)** that God is here threatening. It is stylized language meaning—a coming upheaval and destruction on Jerusalem. This is illustrated in Ezekiel.

> *In My zeal and in My blazing wrath I declare that on that day there will surely be a great earthquake in the land of Israel. The fish of the sea, the birds of the heavens, the beasts of the field, all the creeping things that creep on the earth, and all the men who are on the face of the earth will shake at My presence; the mountains also will be thrown down, the steep pathways will collapse and every wall will fall to the ground. (Ezekiel 38:19-20, NASB95)*

"The earthquake is the symbol of revolution, the shaking up of the nations in their various places. It is the figure of the agitations, upheavals, resulting in the revolutions and wars.... It is the symbol of divine judgement on the nations persecuting the cause of the Lamb."[319] As indicated, an **earthquake (6:12)** is often used as a prophetic formula for the coming destruction of a society. It is so used here in Revelation.

---

[317] See also Isaiah 2:10; 34:4; Ezekiel 32:3-8; Joel 2:10, 31; 3:15.

[318] Robert G. Bratcher, Rev. 6:12.

[319] Foy E. Wallace, Jr., 153.

Many Christians expect a literal fulfillment to this passage *(6:12-17)* in the coming years. They have been told that only a literal one does justice to Scripture; that believing in a literal fulfillment is a true expression of Biblical faith. But how many of these Christians have taken the time to search through a concordance of the Old Testament for these very words and phrases? How many of the authors of books promoting a literal fulfillment have done so? But as we stated earlier, the Bible serves as a rich pool of information interpreting itself. Consider these other passages that shed light on these metaphors.

Against Tyre Isaiah says,

> *Then the moon will be abashed and the sun ashamed,*
> *For the Lord of hosts will reign on Mount Zion and in Jerusalem,*
> *And His glory will be before His elders. (Isaiah 24:23, NASB95)*

And in prophecies designed for A.D. 70 Joel says,

> *Before them the earth quakes,*
> *The heavens tremble,*
> *The sun and the moon grow dark*
> *And the stars lose their brightness. (Joel 2:10, NASB95)*

> *I will display wonders in the sky and on the earth [land],*
> *Blood, fire and columns of smoke.*
> *The sun will be turned into darkness*
> *And the moon into blood*
> *Before the great and awesome day of the Lord comes. (Joel 2:30-*
> *31, NASB95)*

"In Acts 2:20 we find Peter interpreting the apocalyptic eschatological language of Joel 2:31 about the sun being turned into darkness and the moon into blood as pointing to the events of the day of Pentecost as also *"the great day of the Lord."* Peter's interpretation of Joel should make us cautious about too literal an exegesis of these grand symbols."[320]

---

[320] Archibald Thomas Robertson, Vol. VI, 345.

*The sun and moon grow dark
And the stars lose their brightness. (Joel 3:15, NASB95)[321]*

We have recorded here several Old Testament passages that make prophecies similar to our passage here in Revelation. But in none of these situations did the **sun (6:12)** actually **become black (6:12)**, or did the **moon (6:12)** actually **become like blood (6:12)**, or was the **sky (6:13)** actually **rolled up (6:14)**, but in all of them the threat of God's displeasure and coming judgement is powerfully portrayed with these symbols. And indeed, judgement did come; governments, rulers, authorities, officials and nations were destroyed, just as these signs portrayed.

"In the imagery of this sixth seal mountains and islands—both Jewish and Gentile persecuting authorities, Palestinian and Romans—would be overthrown, moved out of their places, their power dissipated."[322] The key to interpreting all these symbols is to determine the meaning given them by the inspired writers of the Old Testament. To ignore these illustrations and interpretations and to seek meaning in nuclear holocaust, star wars, cobra helicopters, global warming, or some other modern phenomena, is to violate both God's Word and common sense. As is so often the case with many modern day writers on prophecy, there is an appalling disrespect for, as well as a profound ignorance of, the Word of God.

6:15 Then the kings of the earth [land] and the great men and the commanders and the rich and the strong and every slave and free man hid themselves in the caves and among the rocks of the mountains... The phrase **kings of the earth (6:15)**, which is used here, can equally well be translated **rulers of the land (6:15)**, and in fact, it is only the rulers of Israel who would fear the Great Glory on his Throne, and the Lamb who symbolizes the Warrior Messiah.[323]

6:16 ...and they said to the mountains and to the rocks, "Fall on us and hide us from the presence of Him who sits on the throne, and from the wrath of the Lamb...." "What sinners dread

---

[321] Consider these passages as well: Amos 8:9, Haggai 2:6, 7, 21, 22.

[322] Foy E. Wallace, Jr., 155.

[323] Philip Carrington, 138.

most is not death, but the revealed Presence of God."[324]   Christ spoke of these days as soon coming upon Israel both in His Olivet Discourse and while being led to Golgotha.

> *But Jesus turning to them said, "Daughters of Jerusalem, stop weeping for Me, but weep for yourselves and for your children. For behold, the days are coming when they will say, 'Blessed are the barren, and the wombs that never bore, and the breasts that never nursed.' Then they will begin to say to the mountains, 'Fall on us,' and to the hills, 'Cover us'." (Luke 23:28-30, NASB95)*

Fall on us and hide us from the presence of Him who sits on the throne... (6:16) "... is a quotation from Hosea describing the men of high places—kings, nobles, warriors, captains and conquerors—all of whom were to be humbled with men of low station, calling to the mountains for cover."[325]   Jesus referred to this same passage when confronted by those women who were weeping for Him.

Josephus records a variation of this when he says,

> So now the last hope which supported the tyrants, and that crew of robbers who were with them, was in the caves and caverns under ground; whither, if they could once fly, they did not expect to be searched for; but endeavored, that after the whole city should be destroyed, and the Romans gone away, they might come out again, and escape from them. This was no better than a dream of theirs; for they were not able to lie hid either from God or from the Romans.[326]

6:17 ...for the great day of their wrath has come, and who is able to stand? These words, **has come (6:17)**, imply the immediacy of the coming of Christ. And indeed, He did immediately come in judgement on Jerusalem.

---

[324] Henry Barclay Swete, 94.

[325] Foy E. Wallace, Jr., 156.

[326] Flavius Josephus, *Wars*, 6:7:3. See also 3:7:36; 3:2:3; 3:7:35; 5:3:1; 6:9:4; 7:2:1.

So, this ends the sixth seal. As the curtain of God's judgement rises upon defiant Israel, this is the background upon which the rest of the play is to be enacted. "It was a grand providential epoch; the close of an aeon; the winding up of a great period in the divine government of the world. The material catastrophe was but the outward and visible sign of a mighty crisis in the realm of the unseen and the spiritual."[327]

No more fitting conclusion could be given to this chapter than to read the covenant curses of Leviticus 26. Does this passage not clarify our chapter?

> *But if you do not obey Me and do not carry out all these commandments, 15 if, instead, you reject My statutes, and if your soul abhors My ordinances so as not to carry out all My commandments, and so break My covenant, 16 I, in turn, will do this to you: I will appoint over you a sudden terror, consumption and fever that will waste away the eyes and cause the soul to pine away; also, you will sow your seed uselessly, for your enemies will eat it up. 17 I will set My face against you so that you will be struck down before your enemies; and those who hate you will rule over you, and you will flee when no one is pursuing you.*
>
> *18 If also after these things you do not obey Me, then I will punish you seven times more for your sins.*
> *19 I will also break down your pride of power; I will also make your sky like iron and your earth like bronze. 20 Your strength will be spent uselessly, for your land will not yield its produce and the trees of the land will not yield their fruit.*
>
> *21 If then, you act with hostility against Me and are unwilling to obey Me, I will increase the plague on you seven times according to your sins. 22 I will let loose among you the beasts of the field, which will bereave you of your children and destroy your cattle and reduce your number so that your roads lie deserted.*
>
> *23 And if by these things you are not turned to Me, but act with hostility against Me, 24 then I will act with hostility against you; and I, even I, will strike you seven times for your sins. 25 I will also bring upon you a sword which will execute vengeance for the*

---

[327] J. Stuart Russell, 399.

covenant; and when you gather together into your cities, I will send pestilence among you, so that you shall be delivered into enemy hands. 26 When I break your staff of bread, ten women will bake your bread in one oven, and they will bring back your bread in rationed amounts, so that you will eat and not be satisfied.

27 Yet if in spite of this you do not obey Me, but act with hostility against Me, 28 then I will act with wrathful hostility against you, and I, even I, will punish you seven times for your sins. 29 Further, you will eat the flesh of your sons and the flesh of your daughters you will eat. 30 I then will destroy your high places, and cut down your incense altars, and heap your remains on the remains of your idols, for My soul shall abhor you. 31 I will lay waste your cities as well and will make your sanctuaries desolate, and I will not smell your soothing aromas. 32 I will make the land desolate so that your enemies who settle in it will be appalled over it. 33 You, however, I will scatter among the nations and will draw out a sword after you, as your land becomes desolate and your cities become waste. 34 Then the land will enjoy its sabbaths all the days of the desolation, while you are in your enemies' land; then the land will rest and enjoy its sabbaths. 35 All the days of its desolation it will observe the rest which it did not observe on your sabbaths, while you were living on it.

36 As for those of you who may be left, I will also bring weakness into their hearts in the lands of their enemies. And the sound of a driven leaf will chase them, and even when no one is pursuing they will flee as though from the sword, and they will fall. 37 They will therefore stumble over each other as if running from the sword, although no one is pursuing; and you will have no strength to stand up before your enemies. 38 But you will perish among the nations, and your enemies' land will consume you. 39 So those of you who may be left will rot away because of their iniquity in the lands of your enemies; and also because of the iniquities of their forefathers they will rot away with them. (Leviticus 26:14-39, NASB95)

"Four times in these verses God states that He will punish the people seven times for violation of the covenant. John uses four horsemen to execute God's wrath in Revelation, and it comes in a series of Sevens. Clearly, John is making a connection between the judgements in Leviticus and those in Revelation."[328]

Do you think God forgot about these warnings? Or did He actually keep His word and do what this passage says? If so, when did He do that? Was it not A.D. 70? Is not Revelation 6 and what follows simply God keeping His promises laid out in Leviticus 26? Clearly, that is exactly what is happening here!

---

[328] J. E. Leonard, <u>Come Out of Her My People</u>, 50-51.

Chapter 7

The Great Tribulation

"The last words in chapter 6 were: *'The great day of His wrath has come, and who is able to stand?'* ... The present vision answers this question. Those who survived the holocaust of A.D. 70 were those who possessed the seal of God (Eph. 1:13), that is, the Jewish believers in Christ."[329]

In chapter 6, we learned that "the first six seals represent the early stage of the Jewish war, wherein Vespasian fought his way through Galilee toward Jerusalem. But before he has an opportunity to besiege Jerusalem the action pauses as these angels seal the 144,000 from the twelve tribes of Israel...."[330] Why does the action stop? "The purpose of the interlude before breaking the seventh seal is to secure God's people who will receive the seal of the living God...."[331]

An Interlude

7:1 After this I saw four angels standing at the four corners of the earth [land], holding back the four winds of the earth [land], so that no wind would blow on the earth [land] or on the sea or on any tree. As we conclude chapter 6 of Revelation, we are at a point in the drama when the hammer of judgement is about to fall. Then, surprisingly, there is a pause in the story. The four angels standing at **the four corners of the earth [land] (7:1)**, holding back **the four winds of the earth [land] (7:1)** inaugurate the pause and hold back the judgement. Something must happen first before the hammer drops.

Notice the sovereign control of God in the midst of the chaos of chapter 6. We are reminded of a passage in Job that illustrates God's total control over his creation.

---

329 Steve Gregg, 128.

330 C. Marvin Pate, Editor, 56.

331 J. Massyngberde Ford, 120.

> *And I said, 'Thus far you shall come, but no farther; and here*
> *shall your proud waves stop'? (Job 38:11, NASB95)*

The blowing of the **winds (7:1)** suggest the judgement of God. His judgements are often thought of as great storms. But these storms of judgement blow only at his commands. The tragedies of nature or war are in God's sovereign disposition. Although judgement is ordered, it waits His timing. There is something that must occur first.

7:2-3 And I saw another angel ascending from the rising of the sun, having the seal of the living God; and he cried out with a loud voice to the four angels to whom it was granted to harm the earth [land] and the sea, 3 saying, "Do not harm the earth [land] or the sea or the trees until we have sealed the bond-servants of our God on their foreheads." Ezekiel addressed a scene similar to this one at the first destruction of Jerusalem in 586 B.C. At that time, as well as this, "God took care to identify His own and to separate them for safety during the holocaust."[332]

> *The Lord said to him, "Go through the midst of the city, even*
> *through the midst of Jerusalem, and put a <u>mark</u> on the foreheads*
> *of the men who sigh and groan over all the abominations which*
> *are being committed in its midst." But to the others He said in my*
> *hearing, "Go through the city after him and strike; do not let your*
> *eye have pity and do not spare. Utterly slay old men, young men,*
> *maidens, little children, and women, but do not touch any man on*
> *whom is the <u>mark</u>; and you shall start from My sanctuary." So*
> *they started with the elders who were before the temple. (Ezekiel*
> *9:4-6, NASB95)*

It is this deliverance and salvation promised to the disciples of Christ which is symbolically shadowed forth in the episode to the sixth seal. The imagery by which it is described is evidently taken from the scene beheld in vision by the prophet Ezekiel (chap. IX.), where 'the men that sigh, and that cry for all the abominations of Jerusalem,' have 'a mark set upon their foreheads,' which was to

---

[332] Steve Gregg, 126.

ensure their safety when the executioners of divine justice went forth to slay the inhabitants of the city.[333]

But when you see Jerusalem surrounded by armies, then recognize that her desolation is near. 21 Then those who are in Judea must flee to the mountains, and those who are in the midst of the city must leave, and those who are in the country must not enter the city; 22 because these are days of vengeance, so that all things which are written will be fulfilled. 23 Woe to those who are pregnant and to those who are nursing babies in those days; for there will be great distress upon the land and wrath to this people; 24 and they will fall by the edge of the sword, and will be led captive into all the nations; and Jerusalem will be trampled under foot by the Gentiles until the times of the Gentiles are fulfilled. (Luke 21:20-24, NASB95)

We should note that this mark is originally found in the Exodus story of the Passover where the possession of the mark over the lintel and the two doorposts of the home. This mark guaranteed the safety of those that possessed it.

The blood shall be a sign for you on the houses where you live; and when I see the blood I will pass over you, and no plague will befall you to destroy you when I strike the land of Egypt. (Exodus 12:13, NASB95)

It has that meaning here as well.

The **seal (7:2)** could not be seen by people; only God and His angelic host could see this **seal (7:2)** and thereby tell who were His. Indeed, all Christians, past and present, possess a similar and invisible seal.[334]

Do not work for the food which perishes, but for the food which endures to eternal life, which the Son of Man will give to you, for on Him the Father, God, has set His seal. (John 6:27, NASB95)

---

[333] J. Stuart Russell, 403.

[334] See also: Ephesians 1:13; 4:30; II Timothy 2:19.

Now He who establishes us with you in Christ and anointed us is God, who also <u>sealed</u> us and gave us the Spirit in our hearts as a pledge. (2 Corinthians 1:21-22, NASB95)

A Remnant of Israel—144,000

7:4-8 *And I heard the number of those who were sealed, one hundred and forty-four thousand sealed from every tribe of the sons of Israel: 5 from the tribe of Judah, twelve thousand were sealed, from the tribe of Rueben twelve thousand, from the tribe of Gad twelve thousand, 6 from the tribe of Asher twelve thousand, from the tribe of Naphtali twelve thousand, from the tribe of Manasseh twelve thousand, 7 from the tribe of Simeon twelve thousand, from the tribe of Levi twelve thousand, from the tribe of Issachar twelve thousand, 8 from the tribe of Zebulun twelve thousand, from the tribe of Joseph twelve thousand, from the tribe of Benjamin, twelve thousand were sealed.* Before we take a look at what this verse means, let's take a moment to clarify what it does not mean. It does not refer to Jehovah's Witnesses.

The Jehovah's Witnesses teach that there are two groups, a heavenly one—the anointed class, the 144,000 and an earthly one, the great multitude. Apparently, it has taken nearly 2,000 years for the 144,000 quota to be filled up. Indeed, virtually no one in the first 1,900 years of the Church was qualified to be members of this group. Only with the arrival of the sect of the Jehovah's Witnesses were qualified believers found that could make up its number, and then it quickly filled up with its members. Such arrogance, indeed such hatred of historic Christianity, is not to be missed. After the 144,000 number were filled up then the reminder of the Jehovah's Witnesses fall into the great multitude class. The 144,000 go to heaven; the great multitude inherits the earth, according to their theology. However, the Scripture does not teach a two-tiered or two-flock doctrine of salvation. At the end of time there is a bodily resurrection of all people. All the damned go to Hell; all God's children go to heaven.

> Jehovah's Witnesses say the 144,000 refers to the anointed class of believers who have a heavenly destiny (cf. Rev. 14:1–3) (*Reasoning from the Scriptures,* 1989, 166–67). .... Scripture teaches that *all* who believe in Jesus Christ can look forward to a heavenly destiny,

not just some select group of 144,000 (see Eph. 2:19; Phil. 3:20; Col. 3:1; Heb. 3:1; 12:22; 2 Peter 1:10–11). Jesus affirmed that all believers will be together in "one flock" under "one shepherd" (John 10:16). There will not be two "flocks"—one on earth and one in heaven.[335]

Now the question remains, what does this passage refer to?

There is no generally accepted explanation of the twelve tribes that are named. In the Old Testament the tribes are named for ten of Jacob's twelve sons (Rueben, Simeon, Judah, Issachar, Zebulun, Dan, Benjamin, Naphtali, Gad, and Asher) and the two sons of Joseph (Manasseh and Ephraim). Two of Jacob's sons, Levi and Joseph, do not have tribes named after them. In this list Levi and Joseph are named as tribes; Dan and Ephraim are not listed.[336]

So, what do we make of this list? The tribes of Israel represent the holy seed. The family of God continues to be remembered by these tribal symbols, even though they literally may no longer exist. But one thing does exist, the people of God.

Why 144,000? We are told that this number refers to twelve thousand from each of the tribes of Israel. Thousand is almost always used symbolically in Scripture. Consider these verses:

Know therefore that the Lord your God, He is God, the faithful God, who keeps His covenant and His lovingkindness to a thousandth generation with those who love Him and keep His commandments.... (Deuteronomy 7:9, NASB95)

May the Lord, the God of your fathers, increase you a thousand-fold more than you are and bless you, just as He has promised you! (Deuteronomy 1:11, NASB95)

---

335 Norman L. Geisler, and Ron Rhodes, 307.

336 Robert G. Bratcher, Rev. 7:8.

How could one chase a thousand, and two put ten thousand to flight, unless their Rock had sold them, and the Lord had given them up? (Deuteronomy 32:30, NASB95)[337]

It is used here symbolically as well. It refers to a perfect Israel fully present, God having lost none. "The number 144,000 is obviously symbolic.... St. John pictures for us the ideal Israel, Israel as it was meant to be, in all its perfection, symmetry, and completeness; the holy Army of God, mustered for battle according to her thousands."[338]

"In the Old Testament a Thousand is a rough name for a subdivision of the tribe, consisting theoretically of a group of families; it is a 'clan.'"[339] As twelve tribes would be all the tribes, so twelve clans would be all the clans. The use of the term 144,000, all 12 clans and all 12 tribes, would then state that every one was there, all the clans and all the tribes, none were missing. The whole group of those whom God is about to deal with is present.

Notice that these are called **sons of Israel (7:4)**, Jewish-Christians. We are told that in this marking they were **sealed (7:4)**. This is a term found often in Scripture.

Now He who establishes us with you in Christ and anointed us is God, who also <u>sealed</u> us and gave us the Spirit in our hearts as a pledge. (2 Corinthians 1:21-22, NASB95)

In Him, you also, after listening to the message of truth, the gospel of your salvation—having also believed, you were <u>sealed</u> in Him with the Holy Spirit of promise.... (Ephesians 1:13, NASB95)

Do not grieve the Holy Spirit of God, by whom you were <u>sealed</u> for the day of redemption. (Ephesians 4:30, NASB95)

Nevertheless, the firm foundation of God stands, having this <u>seal</u>, "The Lord knows those who are His," and, "Everyone who names

---

[337] Exodus 20:6; Deuteronomy 7:9; Joshua 23:10; Job 9:3; Psalm 50:10, 84:10, 90:4, 105:8; Ecclesiastes 7:28; Isaiah 7:23, 30:17, 60:22; 2 Peter 3:8.

[338] David Chilton, <u>The Days of Vengeance</u>, 206.

[339] Philip Carrington, 140.

the name of the Lord is to abstain from wickedness." (2 Timothy
2:19, NASB95)

Sealing was proof of ownership, similar to our branding of cattle. In
addition, it was proof of authenticity, similar to the metallic and wax seals
on fine bottles of wine. God authoritatively identifies all his children, and I
might add, not just this group of 144,000 alone, all Believers carry His
brand and mark of authenticity. He identifies those who are the real
McCoy, as only He can do.

What He does here is put his authentic seal on His children in Jerusalem,
marking them off for preservation. "This mark was to save them from the
slaughter about to be executed on the guilty. In a similar way the mark of
the blood of the paschal lamb on the dwellings of Israel turned away the
destroying angel from the door...."[340] So what we have is a great multitude
of Jewish believers marked by God that the death angel might pass over
them. God did something similar to this in Egypt.

> *The blood shall be a sign for you on the houses where you live;*
> *and when I see the blood I will pass over you, and no plague will*
> *befall you to destroy you when I strike the land of Egypt. (Exodus*
> *12:13)*

As God marked the house of Israel for survival in the midst of judgement at
the time of the Exodus, so now God marks his people for survival while he
judges a new Egypt, Jerusalem.

> *...the great city which mystically is called Sodom and Egypt,*
> *where also their Lord was crucified. (Revelation 11:8)*

We see a similar marking in Ezekiel. God protected those *"men who sigh*
and groan over all the abominations which are being committed...." On
the others a death sentence was passed. So we have here in Revelation.

> *The Lord said to him, "Go through the midst of the city, even*
> *through the midst of Jerusalem, and put a mark on the foreheads*
> *of the men who sigh and groan over all the abominations which*
> *are being committed in its midst." But to the others He said in my*

---

[340] Milton S. Terry, Biblical Apocalyptics, 336.

hearing, "Go through the city after him and strike; do not let your eye have pity and do not spare. Utterly slay old men, young men, maidens, little children, and women, but do not touch any man on whom is the mark; and you shall start from My sanctuary." So they started with the elders who were before the temple. (Ezekiel 9:4-6, NASB95)

"One of the most remarkable things about the siege of Jerusalem was the miraculous escape of the Christians. It has been estimated that over a million Jews lost their lives in that terrible siege, but not one of them was a Christian."[341] Eusebius, the historian of the early church, says this of these Believers.

But the people of the church in Jerusalem had been commanded by a revelation, vouchsafed to approved men there before the war, to leave the city and to dwell in a certain town of Perea called Pella. And when those that believed in Christ had come thither from Jerusalem, then, as if the royal city of the Jews and the whole land of Judea were entirely destitute of holy men, the judgement of God at length overtook those who had committed such outrages against Christ and his apostles, and totally destroyed that generation of impious men. But the number of calamities which every where fell upon the nation at that time; the extreme misfortunes to which the inhabitants of Judea were especially subjected, the thousands of men, as well as women and children, that perished by the sword, by famine, and by other forms of death innumerable, - all these things, as well as the many great sieges which were carried on against the cities of Judea, and the excessive sufferings endured by those that fled to Jerusalem itself, as to a city of perfect safety, and finally the general course of the whole war, as well as its particular occurrences in detail, and how at last the abomination of desolation, proclaimed by the prophets, stood in the very temple of God, so celebrated of old, the temple which was now awaiting its total and final destruction by fire, - all these things any one that wishes may find accurately described in the history written by Josephus.[342]

---

[341] J. Marcellus Kik, 96.

[342] Early Church Fathers - Nicene/Post Nicene Part 2, Volume One (Garland, TX: Galaxie Software, 1999), Vol. 1, Eusebius, Book 3, Chapter 5.

...it is obvious that these 144,000 Christian Jews who are sealed against the destruction ought to be identified with those who escaped to Pella in accordance with Christ's command (Luke 21:20-24) when they saw Jerusalem surrounded by Roman armies. No other group of Jewish Christians can fit the picture. Consequently, their identification is certain."[343]   "...before the Jewish war reaches and overwhelms Jerusalem, God providentially causes a brief cessation of hostilities, allowing the Jewish Christians in Judea to escape (as Jesus urges in Matt. 24:16-22). This happened when the emperor Nero committed suicide (A.D. 68), causing the Roman generals Vespasian and Titus to cease operations and withdraw for a year because of the turmoil in Rome. We know from the church fathers Eusebius and Epiphanius that Christians fled to Pella before the war overwhelmed Jerusalem...."[344]

A Multitude from the Tribulation

***7:9** After these things I looked, and behold, a great multitude which no one could count, from every nation and all tribes and peoples and tongues, standing before the throne and before the Lamb, clothed in white robes, and palm branches were in their hands....* It appears a second and larger group is now in view. The first were clearly Jewish and limited in number; they were marked for protection from the great tribulation. The second is much larger and unnumbered and they have received no mark of protection for the current tribulation. Indeed they have been martyred (7:14) and are now in heaven. They are not from the Jewish church, as was the first group, but *from every nation and all tribes and peoples and tongues (7:9)*.

We can see from the fact that it is *all tribes and peoples and tongues (7:9)*, not just Jews that suffer this *"great tribulation"* (7:14), that the great tribulation is not exclusively the period of the destruction of Jerusalem. But, instead, it soon extends across the Roman Empire.

---

343 Jay E. Adams, The Time is at Hand, 65.

344 C. Marvin Pate, Editor, 57.

A large group of Jews have been sealed for delivery from this persecution in Jerusalem proper. However, across the Roman Empire a greater multitude of believers will soon suffer martyrdom. Having seen so many others escape, they must now die. Is God fair; is He truly in charge? "Lest they question the wisdom or equity of God, the problem is anticipated and answered. They are shown that it is just as much God's will for some to be slain as for others to be sealed...."[345]

We are told that they are **clothed in white robes (7:9).**

> "...when the priests reached the canonical age they came up to the Temple to have their claims tested. If their genealogies were found correct, they then underwent a physical examination; if they were found to be without blemish, they were accepted as priests and given a White Robe. If St. John has this in his mind, then the White Robe given to the martyrs is the recognition of their claim to priesthood...."[346]

> *...and He has made us to be a kingdom, priests to His God and Father (1:6).*

7:10 ...and they cry out with a loud voice, saying, "Salvation to our God who sits on the throne, and to the Lamb." Roman emperors claimed theocratic titles, including that of savior. However, these faithful ones refused to ascribe to Caesar "savior," limiting it to Christ only, and sealed their testimony with their blood. In doing so, they sealed their death warrants.

7:11-12 And all the angels were standing around the throne and around the elders and the four living creatures; and they fell on their faces before the throne and worshiped God, 12 saying, "Amen, blessing and glory and wisdom and thanksgiving and honor and power and might, be to our God forever and ever. Amen." Here we have a picture of a series of great concentric circles of the inhabitants of heaven. On the outer ring stand all

---

[345] Jay E. Adams, <u>The Time is at Hand</u>, 65.

[346] Philip Carrington, 143.

the angels. Nearer the throne is the twenty-four elders; still nearer are the four living creatures; and before the throne are the whiterobed martyrs.[347]

The fact that gentile believers are now given special attention would suggest that the view of the author has changed both geographically and chronologically. This great tribulation is not limited to Israel and the years leading up to A.D. 70, but comes upon God's people everywhere in the Roman world.

7:13 Then one of the elders answered, saying to me, "These who are clothed in the white robes, who are they, and where have they come from?" The **white robes (7:13)** of the saints are significant. "The white robes of these priests thus correspond to the white robe of their High Priest; and just as His robe is said to be 'dipped in blood,' so theirs are washed and made white in the blood of the Lamb."[348]

> It is in victory that the faithful finally arrive in the presence of God and of the Lamb. They appear, not weary, battered and worn, but victorious. The white robe is the sign of victory; a Roman General celebrated his triumph clothed in white. The palm is also the sign of victory. When, under the might of the Maccabees, Jerusalem was freed from the pollutions of Antiochus Epiphanes, the people entered in with branches and fair boughs and palms and psalms (2 Maccabees 10:7).[349]

7:14 I said to him, "My lord, you know." And he said to me, "These are the ones who come out of the great tribulation, and they have washed their robes and made them white in the blood of the Lamb. We are told that this is **the great tribulation (7:14)**.

It is not tribulation in general of which he is speaking but of that tribulation which Jesus foretold when he said, "In those days there

---

347 William Barclay, *Daily Study Bible Series*: <u>The Revelation of John</u> - Revised Edition (Louisville, KY: Westminster John Knox Press, 2000, c1976), Volume 2, Chapters 6-22, Rev. 7:12.

348 David Chilton, <u>The Days of Vengeance</u>, 206.

349 William Barclay, Volume 2, Chapters 6-22, Rev. 7:14.

will be such tribulation as has not been from the beginning of the creation which God created until now, and never will be" (Mark 13:19; Matthew 24:21). Nowadays we read this passage as speaking about tribulation in general and in that sense find it very precious; and we are right to read it so because the promises of God are for ever. At the same time it is right to remember that originally it referred to the immediate circumstances of the people to whom John was writing.[350]

Notice that the early church was not instructed in, nor were they expecting, a rapture to remove them from the persecutions and martyrdom of the Roman Empire. Instead, they were instructed that persecutions were coming:

> *Indeed, all who desire to live godly in Christ Jesus will be persecuted. (2 Timothy 3:12, NASB95)*

> *These things I have spoken to you, so that in Me you may have peace. In the world you have tribulation, but take courage; I have overcome the world. (John 16:33, NASB95)*

> *Through many tribulations we must enter the kingdom of God. (Acts 14:22, NASB95)*

> *Who will separate us from the love of Christ? Will tribulation, or distress, or persecution, or famine, or nakedness, or peril, or sword? (Romans 8:35, NASB95)*

> *Beloved, do not be surprised at the fiery ordeal among you, which comes upon you for your testing, as though some strange thing were happening to you; 13 but to the degree that you share the sufferings of Christ, keep on rejoicing, so that also at the revelation of His glory you may rejoice with exultation. (1 Peter 4:12-13, NASB95)*

In our day, Christians, mainly Americans, have been taught that this sort of thing is not God's plan for His Church. In fact, it has been God's plan

---

[350] Ibid., Volume 2, Chapters 6-22, Rev. 7:14.

through the ages that believers seal their testimony with their blood. Escapism is not taught in Scripture, perseverance until death is.

But the one who endures to the end, he will be saved. (Matthew 24:13, NASB95)

God is the great saviour, the great deliverer of his people. And the deliverance, which he gives, is not the deliverance of escape but the deliverance of conquest. It is not a deliverance that saves a man from trouble but one which brings him triumphantly through trouble. It does not make life easy, but it makes life great. It is not part of the Christian hope to look for a life in which a man is saved from all trouble and distress; the Christian hope is that a man in Christ can endure any kind of trouble and distress, and remain erect all through them, and come out to glory on the other side.[351]

The churches of the first century were on the brink of the greatest Tribulation of all time. Many would lose their lives, their families, their possessions. But St. John writes to tell the churches that the Tribulation is not a death, but a Birth (cf. Matt. 24:8), the prelude to the establishment of the worldwide Kingdom of Christ. He shows them the scene on the other side: the inevitable victory celebration.

In Nero's Circus Maximus, the scene of his bloody and revolting slaughters of Christians—by wild beasts, by crucifixion, by fire and sword—there stood a great stone obelisk, silent witness to the valiant conduct of those brave saints who endured tribulation and counted all things loss for the sake of Christ. The bestial Nero and his henchmen have long since passed from the scene to their eternal reward, but the Obelisk still stands, now in the center of the great square in front of St. Peter's Basilica. Chiseled on its base are these words, taken from the overcoming martyrs' hymn of triumph:

---

[351] Ibid., Volume 2, Chapters 6-22, Rev. 7:14.

CHRISTUS VINCIT
CHRISTUS REGNAT
CHRISTUS IMPERAT

--which is, being interpreted: Christ is conquering; Christ is reigning; Christ rules over all.[352]

It would be appropriate at this point to point out the Dispensationalist's view of this passage. In their thinking, the rapture of the Christian Church occurred between chapters 3 and 4 of Revelation; of course, we saw that such was not the case. In chapter 7, they understand the 144,000 to be "Godly" Jews that are not raptured but remain on *earth* preaching the gospel of the kingdom, not the gospel of Christ. (How you can be "godly" but reject Christ as Savior is not explained.) Theirs is not the gospel of the Church of Jesus Christ; this is truly, another gospel. Theirs is the gospel that would have saved Israel if they had accepted Christ as King. Now that the Church is gone by means of their pre-tribulation rapture, God can now get back to His *real* agenda, an earthly Israel and an earthly Kingdom.

Supposedly, the *great multitude* of verse 9 is the saving product of their bloodless, post-rapture, gospel. To be more correct, there is blood in their gospel, but it is not the blood of Christ; it is the blood of the reinstituted sacrifices in the rebuilt Temple.

However, this passage, among many others, proves the error of their teachings. Notice the words of verse 14, ***these are the ones who come out of the great tribulation, and they have washed their robes and made them white in the blood of the Lamb (7:14)***. It is the gospel of the Church of Jesus Christ, ***the Lamb (7:14)*** (theoretically the Church is not on earth to preach it) that brings this multitude to faith for it is ***the blood of the Lamb (7:14)*** in which they trust. "This can only mean that they have accepted, not that 'gospel of the kingdom' which, as defined by Scofield, makes no mention of the Cross, but 'the gospel of the grace of God' which is 'the good news that Jesus Christ...has died on the Cross for the sins of the world.' "[353]

So, in fact, the Church has not yet been raptured at this point in Revelation.

---

[352] David Chilton, The Days of Vengeance, 223-224.

[353] Oswald T. Allis, 233.

7:15 For this reason, they are before the throne of God; and they serve Him day and night in His temple; and He who sits on the throne will spread His tabernacle over them.

There is a very significant fact hidden here. Serving God day and night was part of the task of the Levites and the priests (1 Chronicles 9:33). Now those who are before the throne of God in this vision are, as we have already seen in verse 9, drawn from every race and tribe and people and tongue. Here is a revolution. In the earthly Temple in Jerusalem no Gentile could go beyond the Court of the Gentiles on pain of death. An Israelite could pass through the Court of the Women and enter into the Court of the Israelites, but no further. Beyond that was the Court of the Priests, which was for priests alone. But in the heavenly temple the way to the presence of God is open to people of every race. Here is a picture of heaven with the barriers down. Distinctions of race and of status exist no more; the way into the presence of God is open to every faithful soul.[354]

7:16-17 They will hunger no longer, nor thirst anymore; nor will the sun beat down on them, nor any heat; 17 for the Lamb in the center of the throne will be their shepherd, and will guide them to springs of the water of life; and God will wipe every tear from their eyes. Christians were not only martyred for their faith; many were enslaved for it as well which is what this description in 7:16-17 pictures.

In the early days many of the Church's members were slaves. They knew what it was to be hungry all the time; they knew what thirst was; they knew what it was for the pitiless sun to blaze down upon their backs as they toiled, forbidden to rest. Truly for them heaven would be a place where hunger was satisfied and thirst was quenched and the heat of the sun no longer tortured them. The promise of this passage is that in Christ is the end of the world's hunger, the world's pain, and the world's sorrow.[355]

---

354 William Barclay, Volume 2, Chapters 6-22, Rev. 7:15.

355 Ibid., Volume 2, Chapters 6-22, Rev. 7:16.

Chapter 8
The Seven Trumpets

Prelude to the Seven Trumpets

The unfolding of the Book of Revelation demonstrates a climatic spiral in its various sections. We have completed the seals, now we will continue our spiral ascent around the central theme of Revelation, God's judgement on His unfaithful wife, Judah. As we ascend higher and higher, the climactic element intensifies. In the Seals, we saw judgement on 1/4 of those subjects discussed. Here in the Trumpets, we will see that intensified to 1/3; judgement is building. These judgements reflect the Egyptian plagues. The message is that in both the Old Testament and now in the New Testament, Egypt is afflicted that the true Israel of God might go free. Specifically, the corrupt Judaism of Christ's era is now marked off for judgement, that the Church enfolded within its corrupt vestiges might be freed to worship the true God in the purity of Christ's revelation found in the New Testament.

So, there are at least two ways to look upon this new material in Chapter 8. One is that it represents new information, an ongoing panorama, but now moving from background material to actual war by God upon Israel. Adams who says, "Chapter 8 is the real beginning of the judgement prophecy" favors this point. "The time has now come for judgement to fall upon the first enemy. The saints are sealed; the book is open; the angel's action announces the beginning of judgement."[356]   Another possibility would be to recognize that "it is not a continuous and progressive sequence of events, but a continually recurring representation of substantially the same tragic history in fresh forms and new phases."[357] That is, each of the seals, trumpets, and bowls are but several views and facets of the one story of God's judgement on Judah.   As mentioned earlier, this is sometimes called a climactic spiral.   With that thought in mind, we could see Revelation divided into several cycles of judgement, each cycle leading to a description of a judgement coming of Christ to Israel and Jerusalem.

---

[356] Jay E. Adams, The Time is at Hand, 66.

[357] J. Stuart Russell, 406.

8:1 ***When the Lamb broke the seventh seal, there was silence in heaven for about half an hour.*** Perhaps this stillness was "the silence of dreadful suspense, fearful expectation, and a calm before the storm."[358] Clark agrees saying, "It is the lull before the storm; it is the suspense of dread before the breaking out of some great and portentous event. There is a sense of something great and fearful about to happen. One holds his breath in the intensity of expectation."[359]

And, in addition, it was "related to the length of time required for a priest to enter the Temple, offer up the incense, and return."[360] This task usually required about one-half hour to complete. What we would have then is the original model or paradigm (Hebrews 8:5; 9:23) of what happened on earth. Edersheim describes this period of Temple worship this way; "It is this most solemn period, when throughout the vast Temple buildings deep silence rested on the worshipping multitude, while within the sanctuary itself the priest laid the incense on the golden altar, and the cloud of 'odours' (Rev 5:8) rose up before the Lord, which serves as the image of heavenly things in this description (Rev 8:1, 3, 4)...."[361] As Philip Carrington says, "...the prayers of the saints are answered. The Seven Trumpets begin to sound."[362]

8:2 ***And I saw the seven angels who stand before God, and seven trumpets were given to them.*** In the Old Testament ***trumpets (8:2)*** were used to gather before the Lord for war, for worship and for marching orders while in the wilderness.

> As of old the sound of the trumpet summoned the congregation before the Lord as the door of the Tabernacle, so 'His elect' shall be summoned by the sound of the trumpet in the day of Christ's coming (Matthew 24:31), and not only the living, but those also who had 'slept' (I Corinthians 15:52)—'the dead in Christ' (I

---

[358] Foy E. Wallace, Jr., 167.

[359] David S. Clark, 63.

[360] David Chilton, The Great Tribulation (Tyler, TX: Institute for Christian Economics, 1997), 88.

[361] Alfred Edersheim, The Temple Its Ministry and Services (Garland, Texas: Electronic edition by Galaxie Software, 2000), Chapter 8, 'Offering the Incense.'

[362] Philip Carrington, 151.

Thessalonians 4:16). Similarly, the heavenly hosts are marshaled to the war of successive judgments (Revelation 8:2; 10:7), till, as the seventh angel sounded, 'Christ is proclaimed King Universal....'[363]

As indicated, one use of **trumpets (8:2)** was as a signal to prepare for and enter into battle.[364] We see this in the book of Joshua where Israel is instructed to sound the trumpet once a day for seven days and then seven times on the day of battle. This is the day of battle. The trumpets will now sound seven times. "At the long blast of the Trumpet the walls of Jericho fell flat; and the Seven Trumpets of the *Revelation* are also a prelude to the fall of a great city."[365]

> The imagery of the whole section which now follows ... appears to have been suggested by the record of the seven trumpets which sounded the fall of Jericho. Those trumpets sounded the doom of the first great Canaanitish city which stood in the way of the conquest of the promised land; these sound the doom of the great city, which spiritually is called Sodom and Egypt..., and which stood in the way of the free progress of the word of God and the testimony of Jesus Christ.[366]

"The seven trumpets held by the seven messengers in Revelation 8 signal a warning that the curses contained in the covenant (Deut. 28-29) are about to take effect."[367]

8:3 *Another angel came and stood at the altar, holding a golden censer; and much incense was given to him, so that he might add it to the prayers of all the saints on the golden altar which was before the throne.* We are next presented with *a golden censer (8:3).* A censer was a small metal bowl or pan in which the incense was burned. It had a handle so that the priest could hold it and carry it to

---

[363] Alfred Edersheim, The Temple, 191.

[364] David S. Clark, 63.

[365] Philip Carrington, 152.

[366] Milton S. Terry, Biblical Apocalyptics, 342-343.

[367] J. E. Leonard, Come Out of Her My People, 59.

the altar.[368] The ***prayers of all the saints (8:3)*** were found in this ***censer (8:3)***. As you can see, the Bible makes the prayers of the saints out to be a big thing in God's eyes.

8:4 And the smoke of the incense, with the prayers of the saints, went up before God out of the angel's hand. Earlier we read about the elders with their "*golden bowls full of incense, which are the prayers of the saints*" (5:8). Soon, the prayers of the martyrs requesting that a holy God judge and avenge "*those who dwell on the earth [land]*" (6:10) followed this. Now again we read about ***the prayers of all the saints (8:4)***. "The church is thus given a vivid picture of the power of prayer, and also of the necessity for praying for judgement and for justice. The church is too often remiss in this central aspect of intercession. Its prayers are pietistic and humanistic, unconcerned with God's justice and unduly concerned with escape rather than battle."[369] Here we have God's response to those prayers.

> ...*will not God bring about justice for His elect who cry to Him day and night, and will He delay long over them? (Luke 18:7, NASB95)*

But, it is important to remember that Christians are told to not take "*your own revenge, beloved, but leave room for the wrath of God, for it is written, "VENGEANCE IS MINE, I WILL REPAY," says the Lord*" (Romans 1219, NASB95). God keeps His word; He will now repay.

8:5 Then the angel took the censer and filled it with the fire of the altar, and threw it to the earth [land]; and there followed peals of thunder and sounds and flashes of lightning and an earthquake. These prayers are now about to be answered. How? ***Fire from the altar (8:5)*** is the tool by which holy judgement is inflicted on Jerusalem. "The prayers of the saints return to the earth in wrath."[370]

The irony of this passage becomes obvious when we keep in mind that it is a prophecy against apostate Israel. In the worship of the

---

[368] Robert G. Bratcher, Rev. 8:3.

[369] Rousas John Rushdoony, <u>Thy Kingdom Come</u>, 152.

[370] J. Massyngberde Ford, 131.

Old Testament, the fire on the altar of burnt offering originated in heaven, coming down upon the altar when the Tabernacle and the Temple were made ready (Lev. 9:24; 2 Chron. 7:1). This fire, started by God, was kept burning by the priest, and was carried from place to place so that it could be used to start other holy fires (Lev. 16:12-13; cf. Num. 16:46-50; Gen. 22:6). Now, when God's people were commanded to destroy an apostate city, Moses further ordered: "You shall gather all its booty into the middle of its open square and burn all its booty with fire as a whole burnt offering to the LORD your God" (Deut. 13:16; Jud. 20:40; cf. Gen 19:28). The only acceptable way to burn a city as a whole burnt sacrifice was with God's fire—fire from the altar. Thus, when a city was to be destroyed, the priest would take fire from God's altar and use it to ignite the heap of booty which served as kindling, so offering up the entire city as a sacrifice. It is this practice of putting a city "under the ban," so that nothing survives the conflagration (Deut 13:12-18), that the Book of Revelation uses to describe God's judgement against Jerusalem.[371]

God has put Jerusalem under the ban. A holy ***fire from the Altar (8:5)*** is now used to ignite the city bringing the covenant curses upon Israel as He had promised. We have a similar picture of destruction to the city of Jerusalem in 586 B.C. by Ezekiel.

> *And He spoke to the man clothed in linen and said, "Enter between the whirling wheels under the cherubim and fill your hands with coals of fire from between the cherubim and scatter them over the city." And he entered in my sight. Now the cherubim were standing on the right side of the temple when the man entered, and the cloud filled the inner court. Then the glory of the Lord went up from the cherub to the threshold of the temple, and the temple was filled with the cloud and the court was filled with the brightness of the glory of the Lord. Moreover, the sound of the wings of the cherubim was heard as far as the outer court, like the voice of God Almighty when He speaks. It came about when He commanded the man clothed in linen, saying, "Take fire from between the whirling wheels, from between the cherubim," he entered and stood beside a wheel. Then the cherub stretched*

---

[371] David Chilton, <u>The Days of Vengeance</u>, 223-232.

out his hand from between the cherubim to the fire which was between the cherubim, took some and put it into the hands of the one clothed in linen, who took it and went out. The cherubim appeared to have the form of a man's hand under their wings. Then I looked, and behold, four wheels beside the cherubim, one wheel beside each cherub; and the appearance of the wheels was like the gleam of a Tarshish stone. As for their appearance, all four of them had the same likeness, as if one wheel were within another wheel. When they moved, they went in any of their four directions without turning as they went; but they followed in the direction which they faced, without turning as they went. Their whole body, their backs, their hands, their wings and the wheels were full of eyes all around, the wheels belonging to all four of them. The wheels were called in my hearing, the whirling wheels. And each one had four faces. The first face was the face of a cherub, the second face was the face of a man, the third the face of a lion, and the fourth the face of an eagle. Then the cherubim rose up. They are the living beings that I saw by the river Chebar. Now when the cherubim moved, the wheels would go beside them; also when the cherubim lifted up their wings to rise from the ground, the wheels would not turn from beside them. When the cherubim stood still, the wheels would stand still; and when they rose up, the wheels would rise with them, for the spirit of the living beings was in them. Then the glory of the Lord departed from the threshold of the temple and stood over the cherubim. When the cherubim departed, they lifted their wings and rose up from the earth in my sight with the wheels beside them; and they stood still at the entrance of the east gate of the Lord's house, and the glory of the God of Israel hovered over them. (Ezekiel 10:2-19, NASB95)

This picture in Ezekiel is now repeating itself several hundred years later, the Jews having not learned the lessons of disobedience, and indeed having murdered the Lord of Glory.

"The prayers of the saints are accepted; consequently the power of [the] persecutors is about to come to an end."[372] Jesus, in His earthly ministry, referred to this when He said, *"I have come to cast fire upon the earth*

---

[372] Moses Stuart, vol. II, 183.

[land]; and how I wish it were already kindled!" (Luke 12:49, NASB95). That day had now arrived. It is of course "reminiscent of the brimstone and fire which the Lord rained upon Sodom and Gomorrah...."[373] Which is a very appropriate illustration seeing John refers to Jerusalem saying, *"And their dead bodies will lie in the street of the great city which mystically is called Sodom and Egypt, where also their Lord was crucified"* (Revelation 11:8, NASB95).

Josephus tell us of a prodigious storm in the night, with utmost violence, and very strong winds, with the largest showers of rain, and continual lightnings, terrible thundrings, and amazing concussions and bellowings of the earth, that was in **an earthquake (8:5)**. These things were a clear indication that some destruction was coming upon men, when the system of the world was put into this disorder; and anyone would guess that these wonders foreshewed some grand calamities that were coming.[374]

8:6   **And the seven angels who had the seven trumpets prepared themselves to sound them.**   "God is now ordering the trumpets of holy war blown against Israel herself."[375]

> Here we have a picture of the elemental forces of nature hurled in judgement against the world. At each blast on the trumpet, a different part of the world is attacked; the destruction that follows is not total, for this is only the prelude to the end. First, the blast of destruction falls on the earth [land] (verse 7); then it fall upon the sea (verses 8 and 9); then it falls upon the fresh water rivers and springs (verses 10, 11); then it falls on the heavenly bodies (verse 12).[376]

These first four plagues, which fall on nature, remind us of the plagues on Egypt. In essence, as God attacked Egypt and its false gods through the destruction of the land of Egypt, so here God is attacking apostate Israel the same way, by destroying the land itself, all in keeping with the covenant sanctions threatened in Deuteronomy 28 and Leviticus 26. The reader is

---

[373] J. Massyngberde Ford, 131.

[374] Flavius Josephus, *Wars,* 4:4:5.

[375] David Chilton, The Great Tribulation, 95.

[376] William Barclay, Volume 2, Chapters 6-22, Rev. 8:6.

not to miss the obvious. Plagues on nature are acts by God in judgement on the false gods of that land. Notice, the new spiritual Egypt, "...*the great city which mystically is called Sodom and Egypt, where also their Lord was crucified*" (Revelation 11:8, NASB95) is being judged, as was the old one. Both the old and the new Egypt are afflicted that the true Israel of God might go free. This new Egypt, "*where also their Lord was crucified*" (11:8), is, like the old Egypt, the great enemy of the true Israel. In both cases, God destroys these Egypts that He might deliver His people to freedom and service to Himself.

First Trumpet: Vegetation Struck

8:7 *The first sounded, and there came hail and fire, mixed with blood, and they were thrown to the earth [land]; and a third of the earth [land] was burned up, and a third of the trees were burned up, and all the green grass was burned up (8:7).* This first plague destroys a large part of the vegetation of the land of Israel. We see some fulfillment in this from Josephus. He says

> ...nor did the Romans, out of the anger they bore at this attempt, leave off either by night or by day, <u>burning</u> the places in the plain, or <u>stealing</u> away the cattle that were in the country, and <u>killing</u> whatsoever appeared capable of fighting perpetually, and leading the weaker people as slaves into <u>captivity</u>: (63) so that Galilee was all over <u>filled with fire and blood</u>; nor was it exempted from any kind of misery or calamity....[377]

> And now the Romans, although they were greatly distressed in getting together their materials, raised their banks in one and twenty days, <u>after they had cut down all the trees that were in the country that adjoined to the city, and that for ninety furlongs round about</u>, as I have already related. <u>And truly the very view itself of the country was a melancholy thing; for those places which were before adorned with trees and pleasant gardens were now become a desolate country every way, and its trees were all cut down</u>: nor could any foreigner that had formerly seen Judea and the most beautiful suburbs of the city, and <u>now saw it as a desert</u>, but lament

---

[377] Flavius Josephus, *Wars,* 3:4:1.

and mourn sadly at so great a change: for the war had laid all the signs of beauty quite waste....378

This is not a literal **hail (8:7)**. It is a symbolic one, one using a symbol that cannot fail to picture the judgement that God, through the Romans, will now bring on the land.

Second Trumpet: The Seas Struck

8:8 *The second angel sounded, and something like a great mountain burning with fire was thrown into the sea; and a third of the sea became blood....* First let us understand which **great mountain (8:8)** is under discussion here. Look how Jeremiah uses the term in his condemnation of Babylon, a city that was built on a desert-like plain, not in the mountains.

> *"Behold, I am against you, O destroying mountain,*
> *Who destroys the whole earth," declares the Lord,*
> *"And I will stretch out My hand against you,*
> *And roll you down from the crags,*
> *And I will make you a burnt out mountain.*
> *26 They will not take from you even a stone for a corner*
> *Nor a stone for foundations,*
> *But you will be desolate forever," declares the Lord. (Jeremiah*
> *51:25-26, NASB95)*

Consider also the history of identifying God's people with a mountain such as Mt. Sinai and Mt. Zion. In addition, Israel is called *"the mountain of Your inheritance"* (Exodus 15:17, NASB95). Now put this together with Christ's message about prayer and a mountain:

> *Now in the morning, when He was returning to the city, He*
> *became hungry. 19 Seeing a lone fig tree by the road, He came to*
> *it and found nothing on it except leaves only; and He said to it,*
> *"No longer shall there ever be any fruit from you." And at once*
> *the fig tree withered. 20 Seeing this, the disciples were amazed*
> *and asked, "How did the fig tree wither all at once?" 21 And Jesus*

---

378 Ibid., *Wars*, 6:1:1. See also 3:4:1; 3:7:1; 3:7:8; 5:6:2; 5:12:2; 5:12:4; 6:5:1; 7:5:5.

*answered and said to them, "Truly I say to you, if you have faith
and do not doubt, you will not only do what was done to the fig
tree, but even if you say to this mountain, 'Be taken up and cast
into the sea,' it will happen. 22 And all things you ask in prayer,
believing, you will receive." (Matthew 21:18-22, NASB95)*

This is a passage that has made little sense to many Christians, for certainly
none of us have every known a believer who prayed such a prayer. But wait,
notice the context in which it was spoken: *first* we have the Triumphal
Entry, *next* we see the Cleansing of the Temple, and *last* we have the story
of the Barren Fig Tree. In this context, Christ is presenting Himself to Israel
as their Messiah. In that capacity He is cleansing his own temple. He then
illustrates Israel's rejection of His rule in the story of the barren fig tree. It is
at this point He mentions prayer and casting **this mountain (8:8)**; not
mountains in general, but **this mountain (8:8)**, as He looked at
Jerusalem, into the sea, the Gentile world. And so we see it here fulfilled in
A.D. 70. The prayers of the saints and the prayers of the martyrs for
vengeance on Jerusalem have been heard. Fire from the Altar is mixed with
these prayers and cast to the land, putting Israel under the ban.

It is certainly right that believers find comfort in God's righteous judgement
on His and their enemies, however, it is important that we do not "delight"
in the death of the wicked; God does not.

*Say to them, 'As I live!' declares the Lord God, 'I take no pleasure
in the death of the wicked, but rather that the wicked turn from
his way and live. Turn back, turn back from your evil ways!
Why then will you die, O house of Israel?' (Ezekiel 33:11, NASB95)*

As God calls His enemies to repentance, so should we. A hardened heart
that takes *pleasure in the death of the wicked* is out of step with Scripture.

*If I have the gift of prophecy, and know all mysteries and all
knowledge; and if I have all faith, so as to remove mountains, but
do not have love, I am nothing. (1 Corinthians 13:2, NASB95)*

God wants us to be something, not nothing. We cannot be that something
for God, even if we do remove mountains, if we have no love for our
enemies. He loved His enemies and that is why you, His former enemy, are
reading this commentary today.

This mountain, this new Babylon, is now to be destroyed, as was old Babylon earlier. It is to be **thrown into the sea (8:8)**. "Sea" in Scripture, when used metaphorically, speaks of the Gentile world. Israel, the new "*destroying mountain*" is to be set ablaze by fire from God's altar and its survivors are to be cast into the sea, or amongst the Gentile world. They would no longer have a country of their own. "Jesus was instructing His disciples to pray imprecatory prayers, beseeching God to destroy Israel, to wither the fig tree, to cast the apostate mountain into the sea."[379]

> Using ancient Babylon as a backdrop for Jerusalem ... He says in effect, 'I will stretch out my hand against you and roll you down...and I will make you a burnt out mountain.' God has rejected Israel's religious system, and the fire of His presence is departed from her. She is no longer burning, but is burnt out. In days to come she will be literally burned out as the invading Roman armies set fire to her. The place where heaven and earth come together, where God meets with man, is no longer the earthly Jerusalem. She is to be thrown down into *the sea*; she will become one with the Gentiles as her people are dispersed throughout the whole earth.[380]

> *How Babylon has become an object of horror among the nations! The sea has come up over Babylon; she has been engulfed with its tumultuous waves. (Jeremiah 51:41-42, NASB95)*

8:9 ...*and a third of the creatures which were in the sea and had life, died; and a third of the ships were destroyed.* Looking at this verse from another perspective, we note that Josephus sheds additional light on this second plague on the **sea (8:9)** when he says,

> ...because the adjoining region had been laid waste in the war, and was not capable of supporting them, they determined to go off to sea. (416) They also built themselves a great many piratical ships, and turned pirates upon the sea near to Syria, and Phoenicia, and Egypt, and made those seas unnavigable to all men. ....

---

[379] David Chilton, The Great Tribulation, 99.

[380] J. E. Leonard, Come Out of Her My People, 63.

Now as those people of Joppa were floating about in the sea [in their boats], in the morning there fell a violent wind upon them; it is called by those that sail there "the black north wind," (423) and there dashed their ships one against another, and dashed some of them against the rocks, and carried many of them by force, while they strove against the opposite waves, into the main sea; for the shore was so rocky, and had so many of the enemy upon it, that they were afraid to come to land; nay, <u>the waves rose so very high, that they drowned them;</u> (424) nor was there any place whither they could fly, nor any way to save themselves; while they were thrust out of the sea, by the violence of the wind, if they staid where they were, and out of the city by the violence of the Romans; and much lamentation there was when the ships were dashed against one another, and a terrible noise when they were broken to pieces; (425) and some of <u>the multitude that were in them were covered with the waves, and so perished</u>, and a great many were embarrassed with shipwrecks; but some of them thought, that to die by their own swords was lighter than by the sea, and so <u>they killed themselves before they were drowned;</u> (426) although the greatest part of them were carried by the waves, and dashed to pieces against the abrupt parts of the rocks, <u>insomuch that the sea was bloody a long way, and the maritime parts were full of dead bodies</u>; for the Romans came upon those that were carried to the shore, and destroyed them....[381]

In a different section he adds to this description saying,

But now, when the vessels were gotten ready, Vespasian put upon shipboard as many of his forces as he thought sufficient to be too hard for those that were upon the lake, and set sail after them. Now those which were driven in to the lake could neither fly to the land, where all was in their enemies' hand, and in war against them, nor could they fight upon the level by the sea, (523) for their ships were small and fitted only for piracy; they were too weak to fight with Vespasian's vessels, and the mariners that were in them were so few, that they were afraid to come near the Romans, who attacked them in great numbers. (524) However, as they sailed round about the vessels, and sometimes as they came near them,

---

[381] Flavius Josephus, Flavius, *Wars*, 3:9:2-3.

they threw stones at the Romans when they were a good way off, or came closer and fought them; (525) yet did they receive the greatest harm themselves in both cases. As for the stones they threw at the Romans they only made a sound one after another, for they threw them against such as were in their armor, while the Roman darts could reach the Jews themselves; and when they ventured to come near the Romans, they became sufferers themselves before they could do any harm to the other, and were drowned, they and their ships together. (526) As for those that endeavored to come to an actual fight, the Romans ran many of them through with their long poles. Sometimes the Romans leaped into their ships, with swords in their hands, and slew them; but when some of them met the vessels, the Romans caught them by the middle, and destroyed at once their ships and themselves who were taken in them. (527) And for such as were drowning in the sea, if they lifted their heads up above the water they were either killed by darts [arrows], or caught by the vessels; but if, in the desperate case they were in, they attempted to swim to their enemies, the Romans cut off either their heads or their hands; (528) and indeed they were destroyed after various manners everywhere, till the rest, being put to flight, were forced to get upon the land, while the vessels encompassed them about [on the sea]: (529) but as many of these were repulsed when they were getting ashore, they were killed by the darts upon the lake; and the Romans leaped out of their vessels, and destroyed a great many more upon the land: one might then see the lake all bloody, and full of dead bodies, for not one of them escaped. (530) And a terrible stink, and a very sad sight there was on the following days over that country; for as for the shores, they were full of shipwrecks, and of dead bodies all swelled; and as the dead bodies were inflamed by the sun, and putrefied, they corrupted the air, insomuch that the misery was not only the object of commiseration to the Jews, but to those that hated them, and had been the authors of that misery. (531) This was the upshot of the sea fight....[382]

---

[382] Ibid., *Wars*, 3:10:9. See also 4:7:6

Third Trumpet: The Waters Struck

8:10 The third angel sounded, and a great star fell from heaven, burning like a torch, and it fell on a third of the rivers and on the springs of waters. We saw a similar comment earlier "...and *the stars of the sky fell to the earth [land], as a fig tree casts its unripe figs when shaken by a great wind*" (Revelation 6:13, NASB95). At that time we looked at various Old Testament prophecies which talked about stars and the host of heaven.

> *For the stars of heaven and their constellations*
> *Will not flash forth their light;*
> *The sun will be dark when it rises*
> *And the moon will not shed its light. (Isaiah 13:10, NASB95)*

> *And when I extinguish you,*
> *I will cover the heavens and darken their stars. (Ezekiel 32:7-8, NASB95)*

> *Before them the earth [land] quakes,*
> *The heavens tremble,*
> *The sun and the moon grow dark*
> *And the stars lose their brightness. (Joel 2:10, NASB95)*

> *The sun and moon grow dark*
> *And the stars lose their brightness. (Joel 3:15, NASB95)*

Although in none of these situations did the heavenly lights actually darken or fall to earth, yet in all of them the threat of God's displeasure and coming judgement is powerfully portrayed. And indeed, judgement did come; governments, rulers, authorities, and officials were destroyed, just as these symbols portrayed.

Specifically, a ***star (8:10)*** in the Scripture often refers to a great person or city. Jesus is called a star.

> *A star shall come forth from Jacob,*
> *A scepter shall rise from Israel,*
> *And shall crush through the forehead of Moab,*
> *And tear down all the sons of Sheth. (Numbers 24:17, NASB95)*

Isaiah calls Babylon a star as well.

> *How you have fallen from heaven,*
> *O star of the morning, son of the dawn!*
> *You have been cut down to the earth,*
> *You who have weakened the nations! (Isaiah 14:12, NASB95)*

Babylon is pictured as falling from heaven because it was a great and important city that was to be brought low in judgement. The same picture is before us here. Jerusalem, the city of the great King, has been found unworthy of its exalted state and is now consigned to judgement. The phrase **burning like a torch (8:10)** describes the severity of its destruction, for nothing destroys as does fire.

The recurring phrase of a **third (8:10)** reminds us of Zechariah.

> *"It will come about in all the land,"*
> *Declares the Lord,*
> *"That two parts in it will be cut off and perish;*
> *But the third will be left in it.*
> *9 And I will bring the third part through the fire,*
> *Refine them as silver is refined,*
> *And test them as gold is tested.*
> *They will call on My name,*
> *And I will answer them;*
> *I will say, 'They are My people,'*
> *And they will say, 'The Lord is my God.'" (Zechariah 13:8-9,*
> *NASB95)*

Although ultimately two parts are to perish, at this point in the judgements of God only one part, or a third, has so far perished.

8:11 The name of the star is called Wormwood; and a third of the waters became wormwood, and many men died from the waters, because they were made bitter. This passage also tells us that the name of the star is **Wormwood (8:11)**. Consider Jeremiah's words on this subject.

Why is the land ruined, laid waste like a desert, so that no one passes through? 13 The Lord said, "Because they have forsaken My law which I set before them, and have not obeyed My voice nor walked according to it, 14 but have walked after the stubbornness of their heart and after the Baals, as their fathers taught them, 15 therefore thus says the Lord of hosts, the God of Israel, behold, I will feed them, this people, with <u>wormwood</u> and give them poisoned water to drink. 16 I will scatter them among the nations, whom neither they nor their fathers have known; and I will send the sword after them until I have annihilated them." (Jeremiah 9:12-16, NASB95)

This is the exact picture we have here in Revelation of poisoned water, figuratively, being given to rebellious Israel. The result is *"I will send the sword after them until I have annihilated them"* and *"I will scatter them among the nations"* which is exactly what is happening in Revelation. We see it again in another passage of Jeremiah.

Therefore thus says the Lord of hosts concerning the prophets,
'Behold, I am going to feed them <u>wormwood</u>
And make them drink poisonous water,
For from the prophets of Jerusalem
Pollution has gone forth into all the land. (Jeremiah 23:15, NASB95)

Wormwood was the name of a plant, distinguished for intense bitterness, and used to denote anything offensive and nauseous. The use of it to designate either food or water was a sign of extreme suffering. In this connection the name of the falling star was called Wormwood, for the bitter effects accompanying the downfall of the powers here symbolized, which attended the siege and destruction of Jerusalem. It was so revolting that even the mental picture of the physical putrefaction turns to nausea, the bitterness of which only wormwood cold signify.[383]

The symbolism of the Star Wormwood may be draw from the episode at a place called Mara (Bitter), where the only water was too bitter to drink; at the command of Moses, palm trees were

---

[383] Foy E. Wallace, Jr., 173.

thrown into the water and it was sweetened. Here we have the reverse; the sweet and healing waters of earth are made bitter by admixture with Wormwood. The Fallen Star is a kind of Anti-Moses; just as the law of righteousness entered into the world through Moses, so sin entered into the world through the Star. Sin embittered the sweet waters; justice restored them.[384]

To be more literal, it is of importance to remember that invading armies would often block up, fill up, and poison the water supply during war. Poison was especially destructive because both man and beast were destroyed by its effect, not only immediately, but also for weeks, months, perhaps years to come, making the war even more devastating. And it was not only the attacking army that did this in the attempt to utterly destroy their enemy, but the defending army would also do this in an effort to deny water to the approaching foe. We read of Hezekiah's war with Sennacherib,

> *Now when Hezekiah saw that Sennacherib had come and that he intended to make war on Jerusalem, 3 he decided with his officers and his warriors to cut off the supply of water from the springs which were outside the city, and they helped him. 4 So many people assembled and stopped up all the springs and the stream which flowed through the region, saying, "Why should the kings of Assyria come and find abundant water?" (2 Chronicles 32:2-4, NASB95)*

We can be sure that the Romans, being the exceptional soldiers they were, **fell on a third of the rivers and on the springs of waters (8:10)** with the result that a great deal of the waters of Israel **became wormwood, and many men died from the waters, because they were made bitter (8:11)**.

Fourth Trumpet: The Heavens Struck

8:12 The fourth angel sounded, and a third of the sun and a third of the moon and a third of the stars were struck, so that a third of them would be darkened and the day would not shine for a third of it, and the night in the same way. The sixth seal

---

[384] Philip Carrington, 156.

covered similar material. *"I looked when He broke the sixth seal, and there was a great earthquake; and the sun became black as sackcloth made of hair, and the whole moon became like blood; 13 and the stars of the sky fell to the earth [land], as a fig tree casts its unripe figs when shaken by a great wind"* (6:12-13, NASB95). So here we have either a new description of those judgements, or new judgements are revealed with similar symbols.

It is essential to search for the analogies of Scripture that the authors of its various books use to paint the picture that their purpose demands. However, there is no New Testament book that demands this more than does the Revelation. In this book we see illusion after illusion, metaphor after metaphor, and symbol after symbol drawn from the Old Testament. It is impossible for us to understand what this Jew, John, meant without immersing ourselves in his Bible, the Old Testament. "As we have so often seen, John is so steeped in the Old Testament that its visions come to him as the natural background of all that he has to say."[385] The first three trumpets have amply made this point. Number four before us does so again. "...by means of all analogous images, of plague and wrath, the sacred writer aims to make the most profound impression of the great and terrible day of the Lord which is near at hand."[386] John clearly alludes to Isaiah and the other prophets that identify the great powers, leaders, and kings of a culture with the sun, moon and stars.

> *Behold, the Lord lays the earth [land] waste, devastates it,*
> *distorts its surface and scatters its inhabitants.*
> *3 The earth [land] will be completely laid waste and completely despoiled, for the Lord has spoken this word. 4 The earth [land] mourns and withers, the world fades and withers, the exalted of the people of the earth [land] fade away. 5 The earth [land] is also polluted by its inhabitants, for they transgressed laws, violated statutes, broke the everlasting covenant. 6 Therefore, a curse devours the earth [land], and those who live in it are held guilty. Therefore, the inhabitants of the earth [land] are burned, and few men are left.*
> *21 So it will happen in that day, that the Lord will punish the host of heaven on high, And the kings of the earth [land] on earth [land]. 22 They will be gathered together like prisoners in the*

---

[385] William Barclay, Volume 2, Chapters 6-22, Rev. 8:12.

[386] Milton S. Terry, <u>Biblical Apocalyptics</u>, 348.

dungeon, and will be confined in prison; and after many days
they will be punished. *23 Then the moon will be abashed and the
sun ashamed, for the Lord of hosts will reign on Mount Zion and
in Jerusalem, and His glory will be before His elders. (Isaiah
24:1,3-6,21-23, NASB95)*

> ...ruler after ruler, chieftain after chieftain of the Roman Empire
> and the Jewish nation was assassinated and ruined. Gaius,
> Claudius, Nero, Galba, Otho, Vitellius, all died by murder or
> suicide; Herod the Great, Herod Antipas, Herod Agrippa, and most
> of the Herodian Princes, together with not a few of the leading
> High Priests of Jerusalem, perished in disgrace, or in exile, or by
> violent hands. All these were quenched suns and darkened
> stars.[387]

A great deal of Josephus' account of the destruction of Israel deals with the
death of its various leaders, men who would have kept Israel from their war
with Rome, or men who would have arranged a quick and amiable peace if
allowed to do so. However, the zealots and "robbers" as Josephus calls
them, time and time again plotted against and murdered those religious
and political leaders who would have saved Israel from the utter destruction
it suffered.

In addition, **darkened (8:12)** or darkness itself has special meaning in
Scripture.

> At the crucifixion of Jesus darkness fell at midday, not figuratively
> as in the passage quoted above, but in actuality. Darkness signals
> the awful judgement of God, the withdrawing of His light from a
> nation or people, and at Calvary God's judgement fell upon Christ
> and He bore the sins of the world.

> Allowing Scripture to interpret Scripture, we see that the pictures
> presented by the first three plagues are one and the same.
> Jerusalem, appearing under the pseudonym of "Babylon," is
> destined for judgement. The great mountain will be cast down; the

---

[387] Frederic W. Farrar, The Early Days of Christianity (Chicago, IL: Belford, Clarke and Co,
1882), 519.

great star will fall, the lights will go out for the unfaithful nation which broke the covenant of God.[388]

8:13 *Then I looked, and I heard an eagle flying in midheaven, saying with a loud voice, "Woe, woe, woe to those who dwell on the earth [land], because of the remaining blasts of the trumpet of the three angels who are about to sound!"* In Rev 8 the **eagle (8:13)** may represent the invading Roman army, used as an instrument of Yahweh as He had used political forces in the past to discipline His people. The **eagle (8:13)** was the national symbol of the armies of Rome and was always perched upon the unit banners and flags carried by the Roman Legions. The **eagle (8:13)** is ready to swoop down on its prey.[389] We read in Deuteronomy chapter 28 of the curses and judgements that God will bring against Israel if they apostatize.

> *Because you did not serve the Lord your God with joy and a glad heart, for the abundance of all things; therefore you shall serve your enemies whom the Lord will send against you, in hunger, in thirst, in nakedness, and in the lack of all things; and He will put an iron yoke on your neck until He has destroyed you. The Lord will bring a nation against you from afar, from the end of the earth [land], as the <u>eagle</u> swoops down, a nation whose language you shall not understand, a nation of fierce countenance who will have no respect for the old, nor show favor to the young. (Deuteronomy 28:47-50, NASB95)*

Though the Chaldeans are frequently described under the figure of an eagle, yet these verses especially predict the desolations brought on the Jews by the Romans; who came from a country far more distant than Chaldea; whose conquests were as rapid as the eagle's flight, and whose standard bore this very figure; who spake a language to which the Jews were then entire strangers, being wholly unlike the Hebrew, of which the Chaldee was merely a dialect; whose appearance and victories were terrible; and whose yoke was a yoke of iron; and the havoc which they made tremendous.[390]

---

[388] J. E. Leonard, <u>Come Out of Her My People</u>, 68.

[389] J. Massyngberde Ford, 140.

[390] <u>The Treasury Of Scripture Knowledge</u>, Dt 28:49.

Chapter 9
Trumpets Five and Six

The first four trumpets, in ch. 8, introduced us to what we may call "acts of God," that is, cosmic disturbances uncontrollable by man. Here in ch. 9 the fifth and sixth trumpets are blown, these trumpets introduce hostile powers both from the under world and from the earth.[391]

The Fifth Trumpet—the Bottomless Pit

9:1 Then the fifth angel sounded, and I saw a star from heaven which had fallen to the earth [land]; and the key of the bottomless pit was given to him. As has been pointed out in the past, a falling **star (9:1)** in apocalyptic literature normally refers to a great leader or city. Here that star is referred to as **him (9:1)** confirming that point.

Christ had spoken earlier using similar terminology: *"And He said to them, "I was watching Satan fall from heaven like lightning"* (Luke 10:18, NASB95). Isaiah used comparable language:

> How you have fallen from heaven,
> O star of the morning, son of the dawn!
> You have been cut down to the earth,
> You who have weakened the nations! (Isaiah 14:12, NASB95)

This fallen star is Satan. The time of this fall is not given, so we can only speculate; perhaps this was soon after creation, or more likely it was during the ministry of Christ. Observe the perfect πεπτωκότα, fallen, as indicating that the star was already fallen from heaven when John first saw it around A.D. 64-66.[392]

But although he has lost his exalted heavenly residence, he has not lost all his power. For here we read that he was **given (9:1)** the **key of the**

---

[391] J. Massyngberde Ford,146.

[392] Milton S. Terry, <u>Biblical Apocalyptics</u>, 349.

234

bottomless pit (9:1). To be **given (9:1)** a key means to be given authority. We are told of Christ that He is the One "...*who has the key of David, who opens and no one will shut, and who shuts and no one opens...*" (Revelation 3:7). Although Satan does not have "*all authority*" (Matthew 28:18), as does Christ, nevertheless he has been **given (9:1)** considerable authority as illustrated by the key **given (9:1)** to him **of the bottomless pit (9:1).**

9:2 He opened the bottomless pit, and smoke went up out of the pit, like the smoke of a great furnace; and the sun and the air were darkened by the smoke of the pit. He uses this key to open the **pit (9:2).** Out of it come those who were formerly impounded in this damnation, the demons of Hell. We are given a picture of the horror of this place, with the words **smoke went up out of the pit, like the smoke of a great furnace; and the sun and the air were darkened by the smoke of the pit (9:2).** In five different places in the book of Revelation the abode and damnation of evil is called the lake of fire[393], which is the image we are given here.

9:3-4 Then out of the smoke came locusts upon the earth [land], and power was given them, as the scorpions of the earth [land] have power. 4 They were told not to hurt the grass of the earth [land], nor any green thing, nor any tree, but only the men who do not have the seal of God on their foreheads. From this place of damnation and smoke **came locusts upon the earth [land] (9:4).** The **locusts (9:4)** are no more biological locusts than was the "star" an astronomical star. What are being released are the demons of Hell. "They may appropriately denote the unclean spirits of demons, which were permitted to come forth in those days of vengeance and possess and torment the men who had given themselves over to all wickedness."[394] With their release from Hell they are given specific power illustrated by reference to **the scorpions of the earth [land] (9:3).** Both the locusts and scorpion apparently illustrate their mission.

---

393 Revelation 19:20; 20:10, 14, 15; 21:8.

394 Milton S. Terry, Biblical Hermeneutics (Grand Rapids, MI: Academie Books, Zondervan Publishing, nd), 471-472.

During His earthly ministry, Jesus warned Israel that His exorcism ministry would have only a temporary effect if the people do not repent. In fact, he warns them by parable that their own generation would experience a renewed outburst of demonic affliction.[395]

> *Now when the unclean spirit goes out of a man, it passes through waterless places seeking rest, and does not find it. Then it says, 'I will return to my house from which I came'; and when it comes, it finds it unoccupied, swept, and put in order. Then it goes and takes along with it seven other spirits more wicked than itself, and they go in and live there; and the last state of that man becomes worse than the first. <u>That is the way it will also be with this evil generation</u>. (Matthew 12:43-45, NASB95)*

Although these scorpions are given great power, their power and mission does not focus on nature for **they were told not to hurt the grass of the earth [land], nor any green thing, nor any tree (9:4)**. These elements have been covered in the previous four trumpets. Instead they are told that their mission is to hurt **men who do not have the seal of God on their foreheads (9:4)**. In chapter 7 we were introduced to this *seal of God*. As we learned in chapter 7, those there sealed are Christian Jews who lived in the land of Israel at the time of the Jewish-Roman War of A.D. 70. It should be remembered that this mark was similar to the Passover mark on the lintel and doorposts.

> *The blood shall be a sign for you on the houses where you live; and when I see the blood I will pass over you, and no plague will befall you to destroy you when I strike the land of Egypt. (Exodus 12:13, NASB95)*

Both then and again now, this mark guaranteed the safety of those that possessed it. It is also of interest that Christ spoke of scorpions prophetically during His ministry. He said concerning His children, *"Behold, I have given you authority to tread on serpents and scorpions, and over all the power of the enemy, and nothing will injure you"* (Luke 10:19, NASB95).

---

395 C. Marvin Pate, Editor, 60.

It is not unreasonable to see the fulfillment of this statement at this point in the Revelation. Nothing can injure these saints because God seals them. So we see, the demons of Hell are limited in their power. The unbelievers have no protection from their onslaught; but these demons are specifically forbidden from injuring God's children. He has put his seal of protection upon them. We see this protective care in Job's life earlier, "*Then the Lord said to Satan, 'Behold, all that he has is in your power, only do not put forth your hand on him'*" (Job 1:12). And again we read, "*So the Lord said to Satan, "Behold, he is in your power, only spare his life*" (Job 2:6). Compare this to John's teaching in his first epistle, "*... He who was born of God keeps him, and the evil one does not touch him*" (I John 5:18).

9:5 *And they were not permitted to kill anyone, but to torment for five months; and their torment was like the torment of a scorpion when it stings a man.* The author is specific; this **torment (9:5)** will last for *five months (9:5)*, not more, not less. By the time of the last siege, the war had been in progress for over three years. The last scene now unfolds, and it lasts exactly *five months (9:5)*. "Titus began the siege of Jerusalem in April, 70. The defenders held out desperately for *five months*, but by the end of August the temple area was occupied and the holy house burned down."[396] "Simon and his followers, ultimately with the cooperation of John's forces and the Zealots against their common enemy, held out against fierce Roman assaults on the city wall and fortified temple for *five months*. By September, the temple was well as the rest of the city had fallen to the Romans, who butchered the helpless Jews and plundered and burned the whole city."[397]

> And now, as the city was engaged in a war on all sides, from these treacherous crowds of wicked men, the people of the city, between them, were like a great body torn in pieces. (28) The aged men and the women were in such distress by their internal calamities, that they wished for the Romans, and earnestly hoped for an external war, in order to their delivery from their domestic miseries. (29) The citizens themselves were under a terrible consternation and fear; nor had they any opportunity of taking counsel, and of

---

[396] F. F. Bruce, New Testament History (Garden City, NY: Anchor Books, 1969), 382.

[397] Richard A. Horsley, Bandits, Prophets & Messiahs (Harrisburg, PA: Trinity Press International, PA,1999), 125.

changing their conduct, nor were there any hopes of coming to an agreement with their enemies; nor could such as had a mind flee away; (30) for guards were set at all places, and the heads of the robbers, although they were seditious one against another in other respects, yet did they agree in killing those that were for peace with the Romans, or were suspected of an inclination to desert to them, as their common enemies. (31) They agreed in nothing but this, to kill those that were innocent. The noise also of those that were fighting was incessant, both by day and by night; but the lamentation of those that mourned exceeded the other; (32) nor was there ever any occasion for them to leave off their lamentations, because their calamities came perpetually one upon another, although the deep consternation they were in prevented their outward wailing; but, being constrained by their fear to conceal their inward passions, they were inwardly tormented, without daring to open their lips in groans. (33) Nor was any regard paid to those that were still alive, by their relations; nor was there any care taken of burial for those that were dead; the occasion of both which was this, that everyone despaired of himself; for those that were not among the seditious had no great desires of anything, as expecting for certain that they should very soon be destroyed; (34) but, for the seditious themselves, they fought against each other, while they trod upon the dead bodies as they lay heaped one upon another, and taking up a mad rage from those dead bodies that were under their feet, became the fiercer thereupon. (35) They, moreover, were still inventing somewhat or other that was pernicious against themselves; and when they had resolved upon anything, they executed it without mercy, and omitted no method of torment or of barbarity.[398]

These demons are not allowed to kill these godless Jews, **they were not permitted to kill anyone (9:5)**, not because God is protecting them in some way, but because in some way death is a release from their misery.

The entire generation became increasingly demon-possessed; their progressive national insanity is apparent as one reads through the New Testament, and its horrifying final stages are depicted in the pages of Josephus' *The Jewish War* the loss of all ability to reason,

---

[398] Flavius Josephus, *Wars*, 5:1:5.

the frenzied mobs attacking one another, the deluded multitudes following after the most transparently false prophets, the crazed and desperate chase after food, the mass murders, executions, and suicides, the fathers slaughtering their own families and the mothers eating their own children. Satan and the host of hell simply swarmed throughout the land of Israel and consumed the apostates.[399]

Josephus adds this to the story of Jerusalem's plight saying,

The madness of the seditious did also increase together with their famine, and both those miseries were every day inflamed more and more; (425) for there was no corn which anywhere appeared publicly, but the robbers came running into, and searched men's private houses; and then, if they found any, they tormented them, because they had denied they had any; and if they found none, they tormented them worse, because they supposed they had more carefully concealed it.[400]

9:6 And in those days men will seek death and will not find it; they will long to die, and death flees from them. It is not surprising that man would seek death under such circumstances. Indeed, fallen man is instinctively suicidal. God told man in the garden that if he ate the forbidden fruit he would die. Man looked God right in the eye, as it were, and ate it anyway. Surely, this was a suicidal act. Since that time, man has habitually pursued suicide, religious, moral, social, political, economic, physical and more. However, in the providence of God even this desperate act will be denied them.

9:7 The appearance of the locusts was like horses prepared for battle; and on their heads appeared to be crowns like gold, and their faces were like the faces of men. It is well known that **horses prepared for battle (9:7)** were often given protective coverings, including a shield for the breast, and they often had ornaments on their bridle as well.

---

[399] Chilton, David, The Great Tribulation, 246.

[400] Flavius Josephus, *Wars*, 5:10:2.

9:8-10 *They had hair like the hair of women, and their teeth were like the teeth of lions.* 9 *They had breastplates like breastplates of iron; and the sound of their wings was like the sound of chariots, of many horses rushing to battle.* 10 *They have tails like scorpions, and stings; and in their tails is their power to hurt men for five months.* It is not clear if this picture, *they had hair like the hair of women (9:8)*, is a picture of homosexuality or not. "The demonic character of the locusts is brought out by mixing both species and sexes. The faces are human, but not necessarily male; the word is *anthropos* [mankind], not *aner* [male]."[401]

On the other hand, Josephus gives us this picture of violent homosexual activity in Jerusalem at this very time that may illustrate this demonic activity.

> They also devoured what spoils they had taken, together with their blood, <u>and indulged themselves in feminine wantonness</u>, without any disturbance, till they were satiated therewith; while <u>they decked their hair, and put on women's garments</u>, and <u>were besmeared over with ointments; and that they might appear very comely, they had paints under their eyes</u>, and <u>imitated not only the ornaments, but also the lusts of women</u>, and were guilty of such intolerable uncleanness, that they invented unlawful pleasures of that sort. <u>And thus did they roll themselves up and down the city, as in a brothel-house</u>, and defiled it entirely with their impure actions; nay, while <u>their faces looked like the faces of women</u>, they killed with their right hands; and <u>when their gait was effeminate, they presently attacked men, and became warriors, and drew their swords from under their finely dyed cloaks, and ran every body through whom they alighted upon.</u>[402]

9:11-12 *They have as king over them, the angel of the abyss; his name in Hebrew is Abaddon, and in the Greek he has the name Apollyon.* 12 *The first woe is past; behold, two woes are still coming after these things.* We are not left in the dark as to who is the king over this vicious army of demons. It is Satan himself. "We

---

[401] J. Massyngberde Ford, 151.

[402] Flavius Josephus, *Wars,* 4:4:10.

recognize in the woe of the fifth trumpet an apocalyptic symbolizing of the demonical possessions and mad fury which came upon the Jewish people, and especially upon their leaders, during the last bitter struggle with Rome."[403]

The Sixth Trumpet—Army from the East

9:13 Then the sixth angel sounded, and I heard a voice from the four horns of the golden altar which is before God.... It is important to view this scene in context with the previous one, the fifth trumpet. Between them we see

> ...a two-fold catastrophe: 1. the tormenting locusts which brought the demonic plagues; 2. the armies of the Euphrates which brought the demonic wars. The swarms of locusts were said to hurt men; while the armies of the Euphrates were said to kill men. The two-fold vision of destruction symbolized famine and sword. The first part of the vision to hurt men was accomplished in the ravages of pestilence by famine; the second part of the vision to kill men was executed in the devastations of war by the sword.[404]

A voice comes from the direction of the *four horns of the golden altar which is before God (9:13)*.

9:14 ...one saying to the sixth angel who had the trumpet, "Release the four angels who are bound at the great river Euphrates." These, *four angels (9:14)*, are, of course, evil angels. The term ***bound (9:14)*** or *imprisoned* would require this meaning. Just as four angels had earlier been identified with control over the four corners of the *earth [land]* (Revelation 7:1), so here these four angels take on the same meaning or quality, only they control evil as certainly as the previous angels controlled the winds of the *earth [land]*.

There are two possible reasons why reference is made to ***the great river Euphrates (9:14).*** One is because the Euphrates was the traditional place and direction of Israel's greatest enemies, Assyria, the captor of Israel,

---

[403] Milton S. Terry, <u>Biblical Apocalyptics</u>, 351.

[404] Foy E. Wallace, Jr., 190.

the ten northern tribes, and Babylon, the captor of Judah and Benjamin, the two southern tribes. No enemies engendered a greater fear in Jews than these two. They killed thousands of Jews, destroyed the land and its cities, and carried the few survivors off into captivity. And yet, this is exactly what God is now doing to the Jews—killing thousands, destroying its land and cities, and carrying its few survivors off to another land. A more apt image than this could not be found for God to drive home His point. "The River Euphrates was the scene of Israel's captivity six hundred years before. From the River Euphrates had come Sennacherib and Nebuchadrezzar, destroyers of Samaria and Jerusalem; by now the Euphrates has become a mere symbol for the quarter from which judgement is to come on Jerusalem."[405]

Two, Rome obtained many of its troops from garrisons stationed on the Euphrates at this time, as well as many other auxiliary troops from the subject countries of this area. Thousands would come from the region of the Euphrates in this war against the Jews. Josephus says of Titus, "And when he had staid (sic) three days among the principal commanders, and so long feasted with them, he sent away the rest of his army to the several places where they would be every one best situated; but permitted the tenth legion to stay, as a guard at Jerusalem, and did not send them away beyond Euphrates, where they had been before."[406]

9:15 *And the four angels, who had been prepared for the hour and day and month and year, were released, so that they would kill a third of mankind.* In this world of confusion, chaos, and apparent unrelated and random evil, it is important to note that God has prepared every moment to fulfill His divine purpose. These demons of Satan were God's demons and had been ***prepared (9:15)*** to fulfill His ends at the appointed time. ***The hour and day and month and year (9:15)*** had now arrived. For this purpose they had been restrained, and for this purpose they are now released.

At this point we should look at Daniel's prophecy.

---

[405] Philip Carrington, 165.

[406] Flavius Josephus, *Wars,* 7:1:3.

Then after the sixty-two weeks the Messiah will be cut off and have nothing, and the people of the prince who is to come will destroy the city and the sanctuary. And its end will come with a flood; even to the end there will be war; desolations are determined. (Daniel 9:26, NASB95)

Christ was *"cut off"* at Calvary. The *"people of the prince"* are of course the Roman army of Caesar. Their mission is to *"destroy the city and the sanctuary."* And all this was recorded hundreds of years earlier and now at the appointed *hour and day and month and year* it is coming to pass. The result was that destruction came *"with a flood."*

Earlier, during the fifth trumpet, we read that *"they were not permitted to kill anyone"* (9:9). Here we see that this restraint has been removed **so that they would kill a third of mankind (9:15).**

9:16 The number of the armies of the horsemen was two hundred million; I heard the number of them. Two hundred million (9:16) is a number designed to terrorize. And indeed, that is its achieved result. As Carrington says, "...it is the empire of hell."[407] There never has been such an army and apparently never will be one. Indeed, in Desert Storm there were only about 500,000 U.S. soldiers in that whole war and in that very area. In the war known as Iraqi Freedom there were even fewer troops than this. But the number appears to have another meaning than the number of Roman soldiers from that area; it appears to suggest the number of demons that were released on Israel and Jerusalem. Remember the story of the demon possessed man from Gerasenes (Luke 8:30)? He was possessed by a legion of demons. A legion was from 5,000 to 6,000 men, and all this is in but one man! At 6,000 demons per person, it would only require a little over 33,000 inhabitants of Judah to justify these numbers. In reality 1.1 million people were killed in the war and many thousands more taken into captivity.

9:17-18 And this is how I saw in the vision the horses and those who sat on them: the riders had breastplates the color of fire and of hyacinth and of brimstone; and the heads of the horses are like the heads of lions; and out of their mouths

---

[407] Philip Carrington, 167.

proceed fire and smoke and brimstone. A third of mankind was killed by these three plagues, by the fire and the smoke and the brimstone which proceeded out of their mouths. John now begins to explain the appearance of this foe. Two things are to be noted here; first, he talks only briefly about *the riders (9:17)*, and then only to tell us the color of their *breastplates (9:17)*, red, blue, and yellow, nothing about their weaponry.

Second, the *horses (9:17)* do all the destruction of this enemy. And the description of these horses is something beyond imagination. He begins by discussing their *heads (9:17)*, which are *the heads of lions (9:17)* but they breathe out *fire and smoke and brimstone (9:17)*. These three colors seem to have some relationship to the colors of the rider's breastplates, red, blue, and yellow.

Creatures that breathe out fire, smoke, and brimstone are entrenched in our folklore. But more than that, they are mentioned in Scripture. Job speaks of the Leviathan and says,

> *His sneezes flash forth light,*
> *And his eyes are like the eyelids of the morning.*
> *Out of his mouth go burning torches;*
> *Sparks of fire leap forth.*
> *Out of his nostrils smoke goes forth*
> *As from a boiling pot and burning rushes.*
> *His breath kindles coals,*
> *And a flame goes forth from his mouth. (Job 41:18-21, NASB95)*

The memory of such creatures was far more vivid then than it is now some 2,000 years later. Now they are but entertaining fairy tales, then they conjured up pictures of terror. And indeed, that is exactly the point, they were intended to evoke images of dread. This enemy in size and weaponry is not capable of opposition. Destruction is certain.

9:19 For the power of the horses is in their mouths and in their tails; for their tails are like serpents and have heads, and with them they do harm. Additional detail is given of these dreaded creatures. Not only is their head lion and dragon-like, but their *tails are like serpents (9:19)* as well. No ambush or subterfuge of this enemy is possible. Defeat is assured on every side. Joel gives us fascinating detail.

A fire consumes before them
And behind them a flame burns.
The land is like the garden of Eden before them
But a desolate wilderness behind them,
And nothing at all escapes them
Their appearance is like the appearance of horses;
And like war horses, so they run. (Joel 2:3-4, NASB95)

Before we leave this point, we should take note of Josephus's description of the advancing troops fresh from the Euphrates garrisons. It cannot be uncertain that this event did not play a critical role in creating the picture found here in chapter 9 of Revelation.

> So the soldiers, according to custom, opened the cases wherein their arms before lay covered, and marched with their breastplates on; as did the horsemen lead their horses in their fine trappings. (351) Then did the places that were before the city shine very splendidly for a great way; nor was there anything so grateful to Titus's own men, or so terrible to the enemy as that sight; (352) for the whole old wall and the north side of the temple were full of spectators, and one might see the houses full of such as looked at them; nor was there any part of the city which was not covered over with their multitudes; (353) nay, a very great consternation seized upon the hardiest of the Jews themselves, when they saw all the army in the same place, together with the fineness of their arms, and the good order of their men....[408]

9:20-21 The rest of mankind, who were not killed by these plagues, did not repent of the works of their hands, so as not to worship demons, and the idols of gold and of silver and of brass and of stone and of wood, which can neither see nor hear nor walk; 21 and they did not repent of their murders nor of their sorceries nor of their immorality nor of their thefts. We read of the rest of mankind (9:20) which would refer the current survivors of this holocaust. Having long repudiated God and His law, the Jews who ostensibly worship the true God of heaven and earth are here revealed as being not one bit different than idol worshiping pagans. Notice how these

---

[408] Ibid., 5,9,1.

sins describe a breaking of both tables of the law. First, we have the worship demons, and the idols of gold (9:20), which is a breaking of the first table of the law. Next, we have their unwillingness to repent of their murders nor of their sorceries nor of their immorality nor of their thefts (9:20-21), which is a breaking of the second table of the law. These evil people have thoroughly repudiated God and His Law-Word and when judged for their sin, they continue in their defiance and still refuse to repent. "To represent all such guilt and apostasy of the Jewish nation at that time as a flagrant violation of both tables of their fundamental law is in perfect accord with the methods of biblical apocalyptics."[409]

That the Jews prided themselves on the fact that they did not practice idolatry is irrelevant. God who sees the heart judges them guilty of the sin they most proudly deny they are guilty of.

> *Therefore consider the members of your earthly body as dead to immorality, impurity, passion, evil desire, and greed, which amounts to idolatry. (Colossians 3:5, NASB95)*

> *For this you know with certainty, that no immoral or impure person or covetous man, who is an idolater, has an inheritance in the kingdom of Christ and God. (Ephesians 5:5, NASB95)*

---

[409] Milton S. Terry, Biblical Apocalyptics, 356.

Chapter 10
The Mighty Angel and Eating the Little Book

The Angel and the Little Book

10:1 I saw another strong angel coming down out of heaven, clothed with a cloud; and the rainbow was upon his head, and his face was like the sun, and his feet like pillars of fire.... John's description of this ***strong angel (10:1)*** identifies Him as Jesus Christ, although some have looked upon this as simply a very special and exalted angel, but nothing more. The phrase ***coming down out of heaven, clothed with a cloud (10:1)***, however, reminds us of several Old Testament passages that identify this phenomenon as the behavior of God.

> *Whenever Moses entered the tent, the pillar of <u>cloud</u> would <u>descend</u> and stand at the entrance of the tent; and the Lord would speak with Moses. (Exodus 33:9, NASB95)*

> *The Lord <u>descended</u> in the <u>cloud</u> and stood there with him as he called upon the name of the Lord. (Exodus 34:5, NASB95)*

> *Then the Lord <u>came down</u> in the <u>cloud</u> and spoke to him; and He took of the Spirit who was upon him and placed Him upon the seventy elders. And when the Spirit rested upon them, they prophesied. But they did not do it again. (Numbers 11:25, NASB95)*

> *Then the Lord <u>came down</u> in a pillar of <u>cloud</u> and stood at the doorway of the tent, and He called Aaron and Miriam. When they had both come forward.... (Numbers 12:5, NASB95)*

The phrase ***clothed with a cloud (10:1)***, call to mind the Glory Cloud of Jehovah.[410]

---

410 Revelation 1:7; Psalm 97:2; 104:3; Isaiah 19:1; Lamentations 3:44; Daniel 7:13; Luke 21:27.

> *It came about as Aaron spoke to the whole congregation of the sons of Israel, that they looked toward the wilderness, and behold, the glory of the Lord appeared in the cloud. (Exodus 16:10, NSAB95)*

> *The Lord said to Moses: "Tell your brother Aaron that he shall not enter at any time into the holy place inside the veil, before the mercy seat which is on the ark, or he will die; for I will appear in the cloud over the mercy seat." (Leviticus 16:2, NASB95)*

In addition, the phrase **rainbow was upon his head (10:1)** reminds us of the description of God on His throne in Revelation 4.

> *And He who was sitting was like a jasper stone and a sardius in appearance; and there was a rainbow around the throne, like an emerald in appearance. (Revelation 4:3, NASB95)*

His face was like the sun (10:1) reminds us of Christ appearance in chapter 1.

> *In His right hand He held seven stars, and out of His mouth came a sharp two-edged sword; and His face was like the sun shining in its strength. (Revelation 1:16, NASB95)*

And **his feet like pillars of fire (10:1)** correspond to Revelation 1:15.

> *His feet were like burnished bronze, when it has been made to glow in a furnace.... (Revelation 1:15, NASB95)*

Some might question why Christ would be called an angel and, indeed, suggest that this in itself make it impossible for this heavenly creature to be the Lord. However, the phrase "angel of the Lord" is used 68 times in the Bible, many of them clearly referring to God Himself. So, that objection is of no significance, and after all, the word angel simply means messenger, it does not mean in itself a created being with wings. So we conclude, this is Jesus Christ Himself.

You will remember that the **coming (10:1)** with **a cloud (10:1)** motif is common to those sections of Scripture that focus on God's judgment. The material that follows fits that theme well.

10:2 *...and he had in his hand a little book which was open. He placed his right foot on the sea and his left on the land....* What is this **little book (10:2)**? In Revelation 5:1 we were introduced to a book that was in the "*right hand of Him who sat on the throne.*" That similarity would be one more reason for seeing this angel as "*Him who sat on the throne,*" or Christ. This first book was "*written inside and on the back, sealed up with seven seals.*" Our current "*little book*" appears to be the very same book, still in the hand of Christ. The reduced size is explained by the fact that so much of it has been unscrolled and read so far, for we are told that this book **was open (10:2)**, unlike the one in chapter 5 which was closed and sealed. So the book has been progressively unscrolled and therefore not much is left; we are coming to the conclusion of that book. Ezekiel in this case, as in so many cases in Revelation, provides the clue as to the meaning of the **book (10:2)**.

> "*Then I looked, and behold, a hand was extended to me; and lo, a scroll was in it. When He spread it out before me, it was written on the front and back, and written on it were lamentations, mourning and woe." (Ezekiel 2:9-10, NASB95)*

Notice the words **"lamentations, mourning and woe"** these words sum up Revelation nicely and explain the content of the book (10:2).

This angel, Christ, **placed his right foot on the sea and his left on the land (10:2)**. The phrase **the land (10:2)** in Scripture usually refers to Israel. On the other hand, **sea (10:2)** often refers to the Gentile world.

> *Alas, the uproar of many peoples*
> *Who roar like the roaring of the seas,*
> *And the rumbling of nations*
> *Who rush on like the rumbling of mighty waters!*
> *13 The nations rumble on like the rumbling of many waters....*
> *(Isaiah 17:12-13, NASB95)*

For Christ to place His feet upon the **sea (10:2)** and the **land (10:2)** imply His sovereignty over all the peoples of the earth, Jews and Gentiles, seeing they are all under His feet. Warriors and kings put their feet on the necks of their enemies as signs of their power over their adversaries.

> *When they brought these kings out to Joshua, Joshua called for all
> the men of Israel, and said to the chiefs of the men of war who had
> gone with him, "Come near, put your feet on the necks of these
> kings." So they came near and put their feet on their necks.
> (Joshua 10:24, NASB95)*

So, Christ, from this place of power and authority speaks to both the Jews
and the Romans.

**10:3 ...and he cried out with a loud voice, as when a lion roars;
and when he had cried out, the seven peals of thunder uttered
their voices.** We see again from this description of the angel, additional
evidence that this is Christ.

> *For thus says the Lord to me, "As the <u>lion</u> or the young lion growls
> over his prey, against which a band of shepherds is called out,
> and he will not be terrified at their voice nor disturbed at their
> noise, so will the Lord of hosts come down to wage war on Mount
> Zion and on its hill." (Isaiah 31:4, NASB95)*

How utterly specific is Isaiah when he says, *so will the Lord of hosts come
down to wage war on Mount Zion and on its hill* (Isaiah 31:4, NASB95).
That is exactly what is before us in Revelation. Jeremiah adds these
thoughts,

> *Therefore you shall prophesy against them all these words, and
> you shall say to them,
> The Lord will roar from on high
> And utter His voice from His holy habitation;
> He will roar mightily against His fold.
> He will shout like those who tread the grapes,
> Against all the inhabitants of the earth. (Jeremiah 25:30,
> NASB95)*

**10:4 When the seven peals of thunder had spoken, I was about
to write; and I heard a voice from heaven saying, "Seal up the
things which the seven peals of thunder have spoken and do
not write them."** One of the first thoughts that come to mind after
reading this sentence is if we are not to know what is said, why tell us about
it in the first place?

First of all John, was supposed to hear this message. God wanted him to be aware of certain things that He did not want the early Church or us to know. And as such, that is between God and John and no one else. Paul had a similar experience. He says he *"was caught up into Paradise and heard inexpressible words, which a man is not permitted to speak"* (2 Corinthians 12:4, NASB95).

Second, this passage drives home an important point. There are many things that God has not revealed about the future, but that does not mean that He does not fully know them and direct them Himself. It is comforting to remember He fully knows the end from the beginning.

Third, the fact that John is told to **seal up the things which the seven peals of thunder have spoken and do not write them (10:4)** is especially interesting in that at the close of the book he tells John *"do not seal up the words of the prophecy of this book, for the time is near"* (Revelation 22:10, NASB95). So we might conjecture that whatever was said involved the distant future, not the immediate future which was not sealed.

10:5-6 *Then the angel whom I saw standing on the sea and on the land lifted up his right hand to heaven, 6 and swore by Him who lives forever and ever, WHO CREATED HEAVEN AND THE THINGS IN IT, AND THE EARTH AND THE THINGS IN IT, AND THE SEA AND THE THINGS IN IT, that there will be delay no longer....* The fact that the angel here took an oath or **swore by Him who lives forever and ever (10:6)** is another indicator, to some, that this is not Christ, for according to them, Jesus would not take an oath. However, the nature of our relationship with God is by covenant whereby *"by Myself I have sworn, declares the Lord"* (Genesis 22:16, NASB95).[411] In other words, God takes an oath that He will keep the covenant.

At Christ's trial, he was put under oath by the high priest. Up to that point, He had remained quiet. But at that point, He responded to the oath.

---

[411] Exodus 6:8; Numbers 14:30; Isaiah 45:23; Jeremiah 49:13; Ez 20:5; Amos 6:8; Hebrews 6:13-20.

> *But Jesus kept silent. And the high priest said to Him, "I adjure*
> *You by the living God, that You tell us whether You are the Christ,*
> *the Son of God." Jesus said to him, "You have said it yourself;*
> *nevertheless I tell you, hereafter you will see the Son of Man*
> *sitting at the right hand of Power, and coming on the clouds of*
> *heaven." (Matthew 26:63-64, NASB95)*

These verses, and others by way of passing, prove that it is not improper for a Christian to take an oath in a court of law, as some foolishly claim. When the high priest said, "I adjure[412] you" he was saying, "I put you under oath." There are three institutions created by God—the family, the state and the church. These three have a right to put its members under lawful oaths. No one else does. Indeed, it can be said that any others that require an oath do so at the expense of one of the other lawful institutions of God. We see secret societies, for instance, that require oaths. Without question, the loyalty of those members to their family, their church and their government is compromised by that oath. As a result, secret societies employ religious rituals and, historically, their members have had their loyalty to home, church and state questioned, often with justifiable reason.

However, an oath to home, church and state is within the proper function of that particular God-ordained institution. Husbands and wives swear oaths to each other upon marriage. Church members take oaths when becoming a part of a church. In addition, the officers of the church take even more binding oaths upon installation into their respective offices. The state legitimately requires oaths of its soldiers and in its courts. Here Christ is put under a legitimate oath by the high priest. He does not deny his right to require it. He responds with a truthful answer; He is the Christ, the Son of God. Proper oaths are a proper function of God-ordained institutions, but it is an improper function if required by institutions that are not created by God.

The oath stated **that there will be delay no longer (10:6)**. It did not state that *"there should be time no longer"* as the King James Version translates the passage. What is said is that God's patience has come to an end. The final curtain has drawn; the last act is being played out. There will

---

412 "To command solemnly under or as if under oath or penalty of a curse." http://www.m-w.com/cgi-bin/ dictionary?book=Dictionary&va=adjure

be no interruption to this final scene. It is not something that will take place 2,000 or 3,000 years in the future. It will take place right now!

> "The delay which is now to end is the period between the crucifixion and the actual destruction of city, temple and priesthood, which took place nearly forty years later. Forty years were given Jerusalem to hear the prophets who were sent to it and to accept the atonement of Christ as Passover Lamb. Its refusal to do so necessitated that God bring the sacrificial system, so cherished by Jerusalem, to a forcible end, since it now constituted rebellion and blasphemy against the one perfect Sacrifice, God's own Son."[413]

God had delayed his judgment for 40 years; it would be delayed no longer.

In Jewish culture the number 40 was considered a round number implying fullness or completeness. The number 40 seems to be used by God to represent a period of testing or judgment – that is the length of time necessary to accomplish some major part of God's plan in his dealings with people or nations. That is exactly how the 40-years from Christ death in A.D. 30 to the destruction of Jerusalem in A.D. 70 should be viewed.

* It rained for 40 days during the great flood (Gen. 7:4)
* Isaac was 40 years old when he married Rebecca (Gen. 25:20)
* Esau was 40 years old when he married Judith (Gen. 26:34)
* Moses was on Mt. Sinai with God for 40 days (Ex. 24:18)
* Moses was again with God for 40 days and 40 nights (Ex. 34:28)
* Moses was 40 years old when he first visited his people (Acts 7:23)
* Moses' life was divided into 40-year segments (Deut. 34:7)
* The spies scouted the Promised Land for forty days (Numbers 13:25)
* Israel wandered in the desert for 40 years (Numbers 13:33-34)
* The maximum number of lashes with the whip was 40 (Deut. 25:3)
* Caleb was 40 years old when he spied out the land of Canaan (Joshua 14:7)
* God allowed the land to rest for 40 years on three occasions (Judges 3:11; 5:31; 8:28)
* Israel did evil; God gave them to their enemy for 40 years (Judges 13:1)
* Eli judged Israel for 40 years (1 Sam. 4:18)

---

[413] J. E. Leonard, Come Out of Her My People, 77.

* Goliath taunted Israel's army for 40 days (1 Sam. 17:16)

* Saul reigned over Israel for 40 years (Acts 13:21)

* David reigned over Israel for 40 years (2 Sa. 5:4)

* Solomon reigned over Israel for 40 years (1 Kings 11:42)

* God gave Nineveh 40 days in which to repent (Jonah 3:4)

* Jesus was in the wilderness for 40 days of fasting and prayer (Matthew 4:2)

* Jesus was in the tomb apparently for 40 hours (part of Friday – say 3 PM, all day Saturday, part of Sunday, about 7 AM)

* Jesus remained on earth with his disciples after his resurrection for 40 days (Acts 1:3)[414]

Now, one more time, God worked in a 40-year cycle in giving the Jews this time to respond to the Gospel. Of course many did; the early coverts to "the way" were all Jews seeking their Messiah. However, the great majority hated, then murdered, the Lord of Glory.

> *... they have both seen and hated Me and My Father as well. (John 15:24, NASB95)*

Certainly God intended for His people to understand that this 40-year period was like many of the others, a special time of opportunity and testing. We should see the hand of God in this early period of the growth of the Church. This, like so many others, was a particular time set apart by God. That time is now over. There will be no further delay.

We should also take note of the importance of worshiping God as creator. ***"...WHO CREATED HEAVEN AND THE THINGS IN IT, AND THE EARTH AND THE THINGS IN IT, AND THE SEA AND THE THINGS IN IT..." (10:6)***. The creation of the world by God in under unremitting attack by those that hate the Lord of Glory. This passage drives home the importance of recognizing God as creator in worship, and suggests the impossibility of true worship when God's sovereign role of creator is denied.

10:7 ...but in the days of the voice of the seventh angel, when he is about to sound, then the mystery of God is finished, as He preached to His servants the prophets. Notice that this passage

---

[414] Notes by Jim Stephenson, Pastor of *Horizon Church*, Greenville, SC.

starts by telling us when *the mystery of God is finished (10:7)*. The "when" is defined as *in the days of the voice of the seventh angel, when he is about to sound (10:7)*. What is this time and why this time? First let's read what happens at this time.

> Then the seventh angel sounded; and there were loud voices in heaven, saying, "The kingdom of the world has become the kingdom of our Lord and of His Christ; and He will reign forever and ever." (Revelation 11:15, NASB95)

Up till the transitional age from the birth of Christ to the death of Judaism at the destruction of Jerusalem in A.D. 70, Satan was "*the god of this world....*" (2 Corinthians 4:4, NASB95). A sovereign God had given him free reign over the globe everywhere but Israel. This is about to change. As of the seventh trumpet, Christ's kingdom will come in power and with it *the mystery of God (10:7)*.

This oath continues with the statement *the mystery of God is finished (10:7)*. What "mystery" is finished or completed by this oath? Remember, in the Bible mystery does not mean mysterious; it instead refers to something that was formerly unknown, but is now being made known. So, what was unknown, has been made known, and is now completed? It is the mystery that God has called out for himself a people other than Israel. That mystery had been introduced to us by the ministry of Peter at Cornelius' house, and by Paul's ministry to the Gentiles. Paul elaborates in his letter to the Ephesians,

> ...that by revelation there was made known to me the <u>mystery</u>, as I wrote before in brief. 4 By referring to this, when you read you can understand my insight into the <u>mystery</u> of Christ, 5 which in other generations was not made known to the sons of men, as it has now been revealed to His holy apostles and prophets in the Spirit; 6 to be specific, that the Gentiles are fellow heirs and fellow members of the body, and fellow partakers of the promise in Christ Jesus through the gospel, 7 of which I was made a minister, according to the gift of God's grace which was given to me according to the working of His power. 8 To me, the very least of all saints, this grace was given, to preach to the Gentiles the unfathomable riches of Christ, 9 and to bring to light what is the

*administration of the <u>mystery</u> which for ages has been hidden in
God who created all things.... (Ephesians 3:3-9, NASB95)*[415]

With the final destruction of Judaism, the previous Jewish age has come to a final end; ***the mystery of God is finished (10:7)***. For us, the "last days" of Judaism have come and gone. "Remember, the 'last days' extended only until the coming of the great and glorious day of the Lord (Acts 2:20). That day was the day of judgment in A.D. 70."[416]

The ***mystery (10:7)*** having been fully revealed is now, with the destruction of the Old Testament forms and shadows, completely implemented. Jews and Gentiles are now one people called the Church. There is no more Biblical Judaism; Biblical Israel is now the Church. Joel referred to this time saying,

*It will come about after this
That I will pour out My Spirit on all mankind;
And your sons and daughters will prophesy,
Your old men will dream dreams,
Your young men will see visions.
29 Even on the male and female servants
I will pour out My Spirit in those days.
30 I will display wonders in the sky and on the earth [land],
Blood, fire and columns of smoke.
31 The sun will be turned into darkness
And the moon into blood
Before the great and awesome day of the Lord comes.
32 And it will come about that whoever calls on the name of the Lord
Will be delivered;
For on Mount Zion and in Jerusalem
There will be those who escape,
As the Lord has said,
Even among the survivors whom the Lord calls. (Joel 2:28-32)*

We see this whole passage fulfilled in the years following the resurrection of Christ. Carefully follow Joel and note these five points, first, at Pentecost God's Spirit is poured out (Acts 2). Second, the heavenly wonders are

---

[415] Ephesians 2:12, 19, 3, 6:19; Romans 2:28-3:2; 16:25; Colossians 1:25-27.

[416] Jay E. Adams, <u>Signs & Wonders In the Last Days</u> (Woodruff, SC: Timeless Texts, 1977), 16.

fulfilled as explained in earlier passages (Revelation 6:12-17; 8:10; 9:1). Third, *"the great and awesome day of the Lord"* has come in judgement, which is what Revelation as a whole is all about. Fourth, the gospel message goes out to *"whoever"* that is, the Gentile world as well as the Jewish one. That, of course, is the mystery not previously understood by Israel, because it was not thoroughly revealed by God until after the resurrection of Christ. Fifth, God has marked out *"those who escape"* in the 144,000 (Revelation 7). Joel 2:28-32 has been fully fulfilled.

In addition to the passage in Joel 2 quoted by Peter as fulfilled, consider these other passages that make clear, the "last days" have come and gone. But please understand, in saying this, we are referring to the "last days" of the Old Covenant or Jewish era, not to the last days of the world itself. "The last days (or end of days) were the last days of the *Old Testament* era, the last days of the era in which Joel and Peter were living."[417]

Peter says that the coming and appearance of Christ in the world was in *"these last times"* and says, *"the end of all things is near."* The *"all things"* did not mean the end of the world; clearly the world did not end at that time. But the Jewish era did end; the Old Covenant was replaced with the New Covenant.

> For He was foreknown before the foundation of the world, but has appeared in these last times for the sake of you. (1 Peter 1:20, NASB95)

> The end of all things is near; therefore, be of sound judgement and sober spirit for the purpose of prayer. (1 Peter 4:7, NASB95)

The author of Hebrews calls the days of Christ and the early years of the New Testament church *"these last days"* and *"the consummation of the ages."*

> God, after He spoke long ago to the fathers in the prophets in many portions and in many ways, in these last days has spoken to us in His Son, whom He appointed heir of all things, through whom also He made the world. (Hebrews 1:1-2, NASB95)

---

[417] Jay E. Adams, Signs & Wonders In the Last Days, 15.

*Otherwise, He would have needed to suffer often since the
foundation of the world; but now once at <u>the consummation of
the ages</u> He has been manifested to put away sin by the sacrifice
of Himself. (Hebrews 9:26, NASB95)*

And the Apostle Paul agrees calling the apostolic era *"the ends of the ages."*

*Now these things happened to them as an example, and they
were written for our instruction, upon whom <u>the ends of the ages
have come</u>. (1 Corinthians 10:11, NASB95)*

And John, the author of Revelation, himself clarifies the era by saying that
his day is *"the last hour."* Not the last hour of the Church age, which was
not what he was writing about, but the last hour of the Jewish age
characterized by the coming of the antichrist, Nero.

*Children, <u>it is the last hour</u>; and just as you heard that antichrist
is coming, even now many antichrists have appeared; from this
we know that <u>it is the last hour</u>. (1 John 2:18, NASB95)*

"It is a serious error, therefore, when learned exegetes persist in assuming
that the phrase "the last days," as employed in the Scriptures, means the
period of the new Christian dispensation."[418] If this is not grasped, then
Biblical prophecy can never be understood. Most of the Book of Revelation
is not about the last days of the Church; it is about the last days of the
Jewish era. "This Apocalypse depicts the end of the Old Testament cultus
and the consequent beginning of the new kingdom of God among men."[419]

**10:8-9 Then the voice which I heard from heaven, I heard
again speaking with me, and saying, "Go, take the book which
is open in the hand of the angel who stands on the sea and on
the land." 9 So I went to the angel, telling him to give me the
little book. And he said to me, "Take it and eat it; it will make
your stomach bitter, but in your mouth it will be sweet as
honey."** John is told to **take the book ... and eat it (10:8-9).** He is
then informed that **it will make your stomach bitter, but in your**

---

[418] Milton S. Terry, <u>Biblical Apocalyptics</u>, 361.

[419] Ibid., 375.

mouth it will be sweet as honey (10:9). "For Israel sins would be "sweet" in the act of commitment but the consequence would be bitter."[420] This bittersweet concept is illustrated in Job and Proverbs:

> *Though evil is sweet in his mouth and he hides it under his tongue,*
> *though he desires it and will not let it go, but holds it in his mouth,*
> *yet his food in his stomach is changed to the venom of cobras*
> *within him. (Job 20:12-14, NASB95)*

> *Stolen water is sweet; and bread eaten in secret is pleasant. But*
> *he does not know that the dead are there, that her guests are in*
> *the depths of Sheol. (Proverbs 9:17-18, NASB95)*

Ezekiel had a very similar experience.

> *Then I looked, and behold, a hand was extended to me; and lo, a*
> *<u>scroll</u> was in it. 10 When He spread it out before me, it was*
> *written on the front and back, and written on it were*
> *lamentations, mourning and woe. 1 Then He said to me, "Son of*
> *man, eat what you find; eat this scroll, and go, speak to the house*
> *of Israel." 2 So I opened my mouth, and He fed me this scroll. 3*
> *He said to me, "Son of man, feed your stomach and fill your body*
> *with this scroll which I am giving you." Then I ate it, and it was*
> *sweet as honey in my mouth. (Ezekiel 2:9-3:3, NASB95)*

Notice the "*lamentations, mourning and woe*" to which Ezekiel refers. These are the same topics we have on our scroll here in Revelation. The fact that sin is to be judged is a sweet message and experience for John; the fact that it would happen to his own nation was a bitter message.

10:10 I took the little book out of the angel's hand and ate it, and in my mouth it was sweet as honey; and when I had eaten it, my stomach was made bitter. After **eating it (10:10)**, John says, **my stomach was made bitter (10:10).** This is not a difficult picture to interpret. As children of God it is right that we are a compassionate people and experience sorrow, [**my stomach was made bitter (10:10)**], for those that suffer pain but our character cannot be so lopsided that we do

---

420 J. Massyngberde Ford, 164.

not see the propriety of God's judgement on sin, [*in my mouth it was sweet as honey (10:10)*]. John was here experiencing both joy and sorrow.

> Old Israel had turned from the true God to worship idols and demons; she had become a harlot and a persecutor of the saints, and had to be destroyed. And while St. John could rejoice in the victory of the Church over her enemies, it would still be a wrenching experience to see the once-holy city leveled to rubble, the Temple torn down and burned to ashes, and hundreds of thousands of his relatives and countrymen starved and tortured, murdered, or sold into slavery.[421]

10:11 And they said to me, "You must prophesy again concerning many peoples and nations and tongues and kings." John's commission extended beyond Israel. The Roman Empire and its allies continue to be a part of his purview, and most importantly, the Church of Jesus Christ across the world must hear this message of judgement and hope. The contents of the Book of Revelation are not limited to the destruction of Jerusalem in A.D. 70.

---

[421] David Chilton, <u>The Days of Vengeance</u>, 268-269.

Chapter 11
The Two Witnesses and the Seventh Trumpet

In the previous chapters we were introduced to the court in heaven followed by the opening of the seals, the 144,000, and the trumpets. Ch. 10 discusses the little scroll and bridges the gap between heaven and earth by the angelic messenger who places his feet on the sea and the earth, 10:2, and delivers an earthly commission to the prophet, 10:9, 11. The judgment expressed in eating the bitter scroll works it way out in ch. 11 in three ways: the measuring of the temple, the two witnesses, and the seventh trumpet which announces the triumph of the kingdom of God.[422]

The Two Witnesses

11:1 Then there was given me a measuring rod like a staff; and someone said, "Get up and measure the temple of God and the altar, and those who worship in it. Before we begin our exegesis[423] of the passage, let us look at a typical Dispensational take on the episode. Lehman Strauss says, "...looking ahead to the rebuilt temple in Jerusalem...."[424] And Charles C. Ryrie says, "Apparently the temple ... will be rebuilt...."[425] How is that apparent? There is nothing in the Bible suggesting that there will be another Temple after its destruction in A.D. 70 and much in Hebrews suggesting that there will *not* be one. Simply put, it is apparent because it is necessary to the presuppositions of Dispensationalism. It is not so stated in this passage. The point is this, the Dispensationalists recognize that there must be a Temple for this passage to be fulfilled. Since currently there isn't one, presto, it will be rebuilt. But here is a thought; this passage finds fulfillment in the destruction of the Temple in A.D. 70!

---

422 J. Massyngberde Ford, 173.

423 "to explain, interpret ... an explanation or critical interpretation of a text." www.m-w.com/cgi-bin/ dictionary?book=Dictionary&va=exegesis.

424 Lehman Strauss, The Book of Revelation (Neptune, NY: Loizeaux Brothers, 1964), 210.

425 Charles C. Ryrie, The Ryrie Study Bible (Chicago, Il: Moody Press, 1976), 1907.

And take note of another point, this passage clearly teaches that this Temple is to be destroyed during the Tribulation. But Dispensationalism teaches us that there is a Temple during the Millenium, which follows their later day Great Tribulation. That means that there must be *two* rebuilt Temples, one for the (their) coming Great Tribulation that is destroyed and another for the coming Millenium. Actually, I have never heard a Dispensationalist take note of this point and recognize that their theology must make room for not one rebuilt Temple, but two!

Well, let's return to the text and note what it actually says. The purpose in ***measuring the temple of God (11:1)*** was to designate which part was for preservation. "...to measure expresses the thought of preservation, not of destruction."[426] Although the temple proper was rather small, the temple complex was quite large. It was the temple only, consisting of the holy place and the Holy of Holies, which is being symbolically measured for protection. And not only is the temple being measured but those that worship there are as well. As Carrington says, "...it can only represent the body of true believers who form the spiritual temple in which God dwells. ... while the *Outer Court* will be the non-christian Jews who are 'given' into the power of the gentiles."[427]

This symbolic measuring is to determine who "measures up" to God's standard. In fact, the entire temple was destroyed, not just the court of the gentiles. However, God's people were not destroyed, they were delivered. The rest who did not "measure up" were destroyed. This measuring of the Temple "has to do with the building up of the spiritual temple of the true believers—that is to say, of the primitive Jerusalem church.... This inner circle within the old Israel is regarded by St. John as the true Israel recognized by God. The Outer Court, which is given over to the gentiles, symbolizes the other Jews who rejected Christ and are not being built into his spiritual temple."[428]   "The Naos [inner Temple], then, means the community of men in whom God dwells...."[429]

---

[426] William Milligan, 169.

[427] Philip Carrington, 182.

[428] Ibid., 185-186.

[429] Ibid., 184.

Compare this section, which follows the sixth trumpet with chapter 7:1-8, which follows the sixth seal. In chapter 7 we see the 144,000 marked for protection, here we see the true worshipers of God measured for protection by God. Both tell the same story in a cyclic fashion, one marking, and the other measuring; interesting.

11:2 *Leave out the court which is outside the temple and do not measure it, for it has been given to the nations; and they will tread under foot the holy city for forty-two months.* The words *leave out (11:2)* miss the point. The Greek word is ἐκβάλλω (*ekballō*) that is better translated "throw out." "In the New Testament the expression "throw out, outside" almost always applies to excommunication or exclusion...."[430] "Excommunication ... is in the Seer's mind...."[431] What we should understand here is that the nation Israel is excommunicated. The Jews are no longer the people of God, the Church now fills that role. Israel figuratively and Jerusalem literally have been thrown out, excommunicated, and given over to the gentiles. This word "throw out" is the very same Greek word used when the Pharisees threw out the man born blind. *"They answered him, "You were born entirely in sins, and are you teaching us?" So they put him out [threw him out]"* (John 9:34, NASB95). There can be no misunderstanding what was meant here for we read earlier, "*His parents said this because they were afraid of the Jews; for the Jews had already agreed that if anyone confessed Him to be Christ, he was to be put out of the synagogue*" (John 9:22, NASB95). This formerly blind man was excommunicated for his testimony. So also, here in Revelation, except for the inner group of believers, the mass of the nation is now excommunicated.

During His earthly ministry Jesus gave direction to His Church explaining to them how to handle problems within there midst. But if all fails he says, *let him be to you as a Gentile and a tax collector*" (Matthew 18:17, NASB95). And that is exactly what God is now doing to the Old Testament Church. God considers them as gentiles, traitors to God, a veritable "*synagogue of Satan*" (Revelation 2:9, NASB95). They are now cast out from His presence, they are no longer the people of God; the Church now fills that role.

---

[430] J. Massyngberde Ford, 176.

[431] William Milligan, 174.

The fact that the court outside the temple is not measured is indicative that it is not under the protection of God. Indeed we are told that it was **given to the nations (11:2)**. The result would be that the nations, or gentiles, would **tread under foot the holy city (11:2)**. That is, they would destroy the Temple and Jerusalem. The time frame for this destruction is given as **forty-two months (11:2)**. "Vespasian received his commission from Nero, and declared war on Jerusalem February, A.D. 67. The siege ended with the fall of Jerusalem, the burning of the city and temple, in August, A.D. 70. This computation of dates yields the forty-two months for Jerusalem to be 'trodden under foot.'"[432] Luke's account of the Olivet Discourse includes a comment about this scene referring to this period of destruction in Jerusalem as *"the times of the Gentiles."* "The *"times of the Gentiles"* in Luke are times of judgement on Jerusalem, not times of salvation to the Gentiles."[433]

> But when you see Jerusalem surrounded by armies, then recognize that her desolation is near. Then those who are in Judea must flee to the mountains, and those who are in the midst of the city must leave, and those who are in the country must not enter the city; because these are days of vengeance, so that all things which are written will be fulfilled. Woe to those who are pregnant and to those who are nursing babies in those days; for there will be great distress upon the land and wrath to this people; and they will fall by the edge of the sword, and will be led captive into all the nations; and Jerusalem will be trampled under foot by the Gentiles until <u>the times of the Gentiles</u> are fulfilled. (Luke 21:20-24, NASB95)

The *times of the Gentiles* were *fulfilled* when the Romans completed the destruction of Jerusalem, which took them 42 months. "The 'times of the Gentiles' refers to the four kingdom nations depicted in Daniel 2. Rome is obviously the fourth and final kingdom to oppress the Jews. With the destruction of the temple and the city of Jerusalem, the 'time of the Gentiles' is completed...."[434]

---

[432] Foy E. Wallace, Jr., 215.

[433] Milton S. Terry, <u>Biblical Apocalyptics</u>, 367.

[434] Gary DeMar, <u>Last Days of Madness</u>, 124.

We mentioned in the introduction to this book that this incident, showing the presence of the Temple in Jerusalem, is proof positive that the Book of Revelation was written before the Temple was destroyed in A.D. 70. After A.D. 70 this scene could not take place, for the Temple was not there to measure.

"As those who received not the seal of God were given over to destruction, so likewise those who are represented by the portions of the sanctuary not measured are, along with the holy places, given over to the nations to trample under foot."[435] Between the Sixth and Seventh Seals 144,000 saints were set apart for preservation. Now between the Sixth and Seventh Trumpets we again read that God's people are set apart for preservation. This is another indication that the trumpets reduplicate the seals, telling the same story another way.

> History tells us that about A.D. 65, as a result of Jewish rebellion against Rome, Cestius Gallus marched against the cities of Judea, eventually coming to Jerusalem. His siege was successful and the city was ready to surrender when, for some inexplicable reason, Gallus turned back his troops and departed. Christians in Jerusalem, some of whom had come from other towns to celebrate Passover there, apparently recognized that Jesus' prophecy was being fulfilled when the Romans marched around the city. Before the next army, led by Vespasian, returned to make an assault, followers of Jesus escaped to Pella and other neighboring towns. Historians report that no Christians were trapped and destroyed in the siege of Jerusalem which was eventually completed in A.D. 70.[436]

In a few verses we are introduced to the Seventh Trumpet. It is at this point that we become aware that the temple, which had so recently been marked for protection, has been figuratively transferred from Jerusalem to heaven. That which was marked for protection has been protected and the original temple and people are safe.

And the temple of God which is in heaven was opened; and the ark of His covenant appeared in His temple, and there were

---

[435] Milton S. Terry, <u>Biblical Apocalyptics</u>, 366.

[436] J. E. Leonard, <u>Come Out of Her My People</u>, 79.

flashes of lightning and sounds and peals of thunder and an
earthquake and a great hailstorm. (Revelation 11:19, NASB95)

Milton Terry takes note of this point, "...after the seventh trumpet sounds, and the destructive judgement falls, and the kingdom of Christ is inaugurated, behold, the temple of God is opened in the heaven, and in it once more appears the long-lost ark of his covenant."[437]

So, those who are still in search of the Ark of the Covenant are wasting their time. It no longer exists on earth; either God has preserved it and translated it to heaven, or He has allowed the earthly type to be destroyed that the heavenly ante-type might receive the glory designed for it.

Josephus gives us an account of some of the frightening things that occurred during the siege of Jerusalem. One of these incidents may address our passage here, for he tells of what could be a description of God's Spirit abandoning the polluted and condemned earthly Temple.

> Thus were the miserable people persuaded by these deceivers, and such as belied God himself; while they did not attend nor give credit to the <u>signs that were so evident</u>, and did so plainly foretell their future desolation, but, like men infatuated, without either eyes to see or minds to consider, did not regard the denunciations that God made to them. Thus there was a star resembling a sword, which stood over the city, and a comet, that continued a whole year. Thus also before the Jews' rebellion, and before those commotions which preceded the war, when the people were come in great crowds to the feast of unleavened bread, on the eighth day of the month Xanthicus, [Nisan,] and at the ninth hour of the night, so great a light shone round the altar and the holy house, that it appeared to be bright day time; which lasted for half an hour. This light seemed to be a good sign to the unskillful, but was so interpreted by the sacred scribes, as to portend those events that followed immediately upon it. .... Moreover, the eastern gate of the inner [court of the] temple, which was of brass, and vastly heavy, and had been with difficulty shut by twenty men, and rested upon a basis armed with iron, and had bolts fastened very deep into the firm floor, which was there made of one entire stone, was

---

[437] Milton S. Terry, <u>Biblical Apocalyptics</u>, 365.

seen to be opened of its own accord about the sixth hour of the night. Now those that kept watch in the temple came hereupon running to the captain of the temple, and told him of it; who then came up thither, and not without great difficulty was able to shut the gate again. This also appeared to the vulgar to be a very happy prodigy, as if God did thereby open them the gate of happiness. But the men of learning understood it, that the security of their holy house was dissolved of its own accord, and that the gate was opened for the advantage of their enemies. So these publicly declared that the signal foreshadowed the desolation that was coming upon them. Besides these, a few days after that feast, on the one and twentieth day of the month Artemisius, [Jyar,] a certain prodigious and incredible phenomenon appeared: I suppose the account of it would seem to be a fable, were it not related by those that saw it, and were not the events that followed it of so considerable a nature as to deserve such signals; for, before sun-setting, chariots and troops of soldiers in their armor were seen running about among the clouds, and surrounding of cities. Moreover, at that feast which we call Pentecost, as the priests were going by night into the inner [court of the temple,] as their custom was, to perform their sacred ministrations, they said that, in the first place, they felt a quaking, and heard a great noise, and after that they heard a sound as of a great multitude, saying, "Let us remove hence.[438]

And so God and His Spirit removed themselves from what was once His temple, but has now been given up to judgement. The real temple is residing in the hearts of His people. "Measuring the holy and excluding the outsiders precedes the seventh trumpet just as the sealing of the elect preceded the seventh seal."[439] Again, we see the repetitive nature of the trumpets to the seals.

11:3 And I will grant authority to my two witnesses, and they will prophesy for twelve hundred and sixty days, clothed in sackcloth. With these words we enter upon one of the most complex sections in the Bible. Russell refers to this section as "one of the most

---

[438] Flavius Josephus, *Wars*, 6:5:300.

[439] J. Massyngberde Ford, 177.

difficult problems contained in Scripture...."[440] And Clark, after recounting the story, says, "this is a highly figurative passage and while it means something, is to be taken symbolically rather than literally."[441]

To begin, we are told of **two witnesses (11:3)** that will prophesy **twelve hundred and sixty days (11:3)**, which is 42 months, or 3½ years. The Greek word for "witness" is the word from which we get our English word martyr. And indeed, we will see that these two do become martyrs. Their mission is to **prophesy (11:3)**. They are **clothed in sackcloth (11:3)**, which is "the appropriate garb of prophets at a time of impending woes."[442] And of course, this is a time of impending woes. The question, as to why **two witnesses (11:3)** instead of one or ten, should be asked? Perhaps the answer is found in Deuteronomy

> *A single witness shall not rise up against a man on account of any*
> *iniquity or any sin which he has committed; on the evidence of*
> *two or three witnesses a matter shall be confirmed.*
> *(Deuteronomy 19:15, NASB95)*

A person could not be put to death under God's law on the testimony of one witness.[443] Israel was about to be put to death. Capital punishment required two witnesses. These two witnesses are now introduced. Having born proper witness to Israel's capital crimes, the death sentence can now be righteously carried out upon Israel.

11:4 These are the two olive trees and the two lampstands that stand before the Lord of the earth. This picture **the two olive trees (11:4)** comes from Zechariah 4.

> *He said to me, "What do you see?" And I said, "I see, and behold,*
> *a lampstand all of gold with its bowl on the top of it, and its seven*
> *lamps on it with seven spouts belonging to each of the lamps*
> *which are on the top of it; also <u>two olive trees</u> by it, one on the*

---

[440] J. Stuart Russell, 431.

[441] David S. Clark, 76.

[442] Milton S. Terry, <u>Biblical Apocalyptics</u>, 369.

[443] John 8:17; Hebrews 10:28.

right side of the bowl and the other on its left side." (Zechariah 4:2-3, NASB95)

In context, we see that these two men mentioned in Zechariah are Joshua the priest and Zerubabel the governor. In Zechariah's day, one was the head of the church; the other was the head of the state. In some sense, the two men in Revelation 11 are related to, or have something in common with, these men. "John's vision reproduces Zechariah's, and whatever Zechariah meant, that evidently John means. Now as we study Zechariah we find that he means by these two figures the head of the state and the head of the church."[444]

Of course, in Christ the offices of prophet and king are combined and, perhaps, in this line of thinking we can find meaning in this passage. Joshua and Zerubabel had a common mission. That mission was to rebuild the fallen Temple. But of course, it is Christ who is the Temple and the One who said, "*Destroy this temple, and in three days I will raise it up*" (John 2:19, NASB95). So, although Joshua and Zerubabel build an earthly Temple, it is Christ who raises up the fallen tabernacle of David in His own body. This role in building the Temple appears to be the significance that these two men bear to this passage.

11:5-6 And if anyone wants to harm them, fire flows out of their mouth and devours their enemies; so if anyone wants to harm them, he must be killed in this way. ⁶ These have the power to shut up the sky, so that rain will not fall during the days of their prophesying; and they have power over the waters to turn them into blood, and to strike the earth [land] with every plague, as often as they desire. Our picture immediately changes with the addition of these characteristics and powers. They represent the powers that Elijah (I Kings 17-18; Luke 4:25) and Moses (Exodus 7 ff.) exercised in their ministries. Elijah called down fire from heaven to devour the soldiers sent to capture him and he shut up the sky to produce a great drought in Israel. But notice that in this case fire does not fall from heaven but *fire flows out of their mouth (11:5)*. Moses Stuart ask the question, "but is this to be understood literally of fire actually

---

[444] David S. Clark, 76.

breathed out, or tropically[445] of words which like a burning fire would wither and consume?"[446] Based on Jeremiah's similar use of the word fire, a good case can be made for a figurative application.

> *"Is not My word like fire?"* declares the Lord, *"and like a hammer which shatters a rock?"* (Jeremiah 23:29, NASB95).

Moses turned the Nile to blood and struck the land of Egypt with several plagues. Again here, we see the religious head of the land in his day, Elijah, and the political head and founder of the nation, Moses. And again, Christ filled both these roles. So, we move from men known for their role in *construction* of the Temple in the ministries of Joshua and Zerubabel, to men known for their role in *destruction* and judgement in the ministries of Elijah and Moses. As Joshua and Zerubabel rebuilt the Temple, so Elijah and Moses judged Israel and the nations. Christ was the rebuilt Temple; Christ is the judge of Israel and the nations.

"Revelation, then, combines the two witnesses, Moses and Elijah, Joshua and Zerubabel, priest and king, in the one person of Jesus Christ."[447]

The presence of Moses and Elijah reminds us of Christ' Transformation in which these two appeared with Christ. They appear to represent the combined authority of the Law and the Prophets. In the story of the rich man and Lazarus, Abraham says to the rich man who is seeking a representative to go to his brothers, *"They have Moses and the Prophets; let them hear them"* (Luke 16:29, NASB95). That appears to be a part of the message here as well. It is the law and the prophets that are murdered by Israel by their utter refusal to hear them and the Christ they foretold.

11:7 When they have finished their testimony, the beast that comes up out of the abyss will make war with them, and overcome them and kill them. The next thing we learn is that after these two men have completed their **testimony (11:7)**, the **beast (11:7) kills them (11:7)**. This is our first introduction of the word **beast** in the book of Revelation. This beast is identified as he that **comes out of the**

---

[445] Figuratively, metaphorically.

[446] Moses Stuart, vol. II, 230.

[447] J. E. Leonard, <u>Come Out of Her My People</u>, 86-87.

abyss (11:7). This can be no other than Satan himself. This is not to suggest that Satan personally kills them, but that his earthly representative, Rome, kills them. "What is done by Satan's agency, is attributed to him...."[448] Of course, Rome killed Christ as well, a point not to be missed here.

11:8 And their dead bodies will lie in the street of the great city which mystically is called Sodom and Egypt, where also their Lord was crucified. Having murdered them, they magnify their hatred and contempt for them by denying them a proper burial, **their dead bodies will lie in the street (11:8)**. The place of their death is Jerusalem, the place where **their Lord was crucified (11:8)**. Christ, of course, lay dead in Jerusalem as well. However, because of the evil character of Jerusalem it is now called **Sodom and Egypt (11:8)**, a city and nation that experienced God's utter destruction for their sins in previous centuries. God and His prophets used the title of **Sodom (11:8)**, one of the filthiest names a community could be called, on several other occasions in the Old Testament to describe Jerusalem.

> *Hear the word of the Lord, you rulers of Sodom; give ear to the instruction of our God, you people of Gomorrah. (Isaiah 1:10, NASB95)*

> *"As I live," declares the Lord God, "Sodom, your sister and her daughters have not done as you and your daughters have done. Behold, this was the guilt of your sister Sodom: she and her daughters had arrogance, abundant food and careless ease, but she did not help the poor and needy. Thus they were haughty and committed abominations before Me. Therefore I removed them when I saw it." (Ezekiel 16:48-50, NASB95)*

Likewise Israel is compared to Egypt in a similarly unfavorable way.

> *She did not forsake her harlotries from the time in Egypt; for in her youth men had lain with her, and they handled her virgin bosom and poured out their lust on her. (Ezekiel 23:8, NASB95)*

---

[448] Moses Stuart, vol. II, 233.

So what we have are two cultures, which were destroyed by God for their sin. It is these very cultures that God identifies Israel with at this point in their history. The allusion could not be clearer; as these were the objects of God's former judgement, so now, Israel, whose behavior is exactly like **Sodom and Egypt (11:8)**, is now the object of God's judgement. "...Sodom persecuted righteous Lot, and Egypt oppressed the Israelites; and the Lord displayed his righteous judgements against both, as he was now about to do in respect to Jerusalem."[449] "...here is the key to the whole book. The spirit of evil has always prevailed here; and spiritual men recognize it as the real enemy. Jerusalem, not Rome, is the real enemy of the prophet."[450]

This is the first of eight references to **the great city (11:8)** that are found in Revelation. Revelation 17:18 tell us that **the great city (11:8)** is one and the same as *"The woman ... which reigns over the kings of the earth"* (Revelation 17:18, NASB95). The **great city (11:8)** is the *great harlot* (17:1). This connection tells us here in advance that the Babylon we will meet in chapter 17 is none other than Jerusalem.

11:9-10 *Those from the peoples and tribes and tongues and nations will look at their dead bodies for three and a half days, and will not permit their dead bodies to be laid in a tomb. 10 And those who dwell on the earth [land] will rejoice over them and celebrate; and they will send gifts to one another, because these two prophets tormented those who dwell on the earth [land].* There was a great mixed multitude in Jerusalem at this time for the crowd, which came for the Passover, was trapped by the Romans when they besieged the city. "...just before the siege began large numbers of Jewish pilgrims went up there as usual for the Passover festival."[451] Included with the locals were Jews and gentile proselytes from *"Parthians and Medes and Elamites, and residents of Mesopotamia, Judea and Cappadocia, Pontus and Asia, Phrygia and Pamphylia, Egypt and the districts of Libya around Cyrene, and visitors from Rome, both Jews and proselytes, Cretans and Arabs..."* (Acts 2:9-11, NASB95). This crowd made

---

[449] Ibid., vol. II, 234.

[450] Philip Carrington, 190.

[451] F.F. Bruce, Israel & the Nation (Downers Grove, IL: Intervarsity Press, 1997), 225.

up *those from the peoples and tribes and tongues and nations (11:9)*.

Their joy will be so great that the inhabitants of the **earth (11:10)**, or better, *land*, will **rejoice over them and celebrate; and they will send gifts to one another (11:10)**, ostensibly because the torments brought by these two are now brought to an end.

11:11-12 But after the three and a half days, the breath of life from God came into them, and they stood on their feet; and great fear fell upon those who were watching them. 12 And they heard a loud voice from heaven saying to them, "Come up here." Then they went up into heaven in the cloud, and their enemies watched them. They come to life, and like John, the author of the book of Revelation, they hear a message **come up here (11:12)**. At this point, in full view of their **enemies (11:12)**, they are caught up **into heaven in the cloud (11:12)**.

How are we to understand all this? To begin, these *two prophets* (11:10) represent both church and state.

> Civil and religious authority go far to restrain the evil passions and deeds of men. And in the social and civil convulsions that destroyed Jerusalem when the Jewish state was crushed, when the temple was burned, and the leaders of state and church were slain, it would look as if the power of law and religion had perished; the witnesses to social order and moral restraint were slain. And there were men then, and there are some still, who are glad when all authority and restraint are dead, and anarchy and license revel rampant.[452]

True law and true religion are ever the enemy of evil. Both law and religion opposed the anarchists and rebels that engulfed Jerusalem. These prophets (11:10) were hated by the insurrectionists and when opportunity came, they were both slain. At that point, joy spread amongst the leaders of the various rebel parties in Jerusalem. God, willing to give these men the due punishment their actions deserve, removes all vestiges of law and religion

---

[452] David S. Clark, 76-77.

from Israel. As these men were symbols of the Law and the Prophets, so now God's witnesses, the Law and the Prophets are removed from Israel; this is a critical point. God has abandoned Israel; He has left them no spiritual witness, a just judgement for their innumerable sins. This is not to suggest that God has left Himself without Law and Prophet, only that they have been removed from natural Israel. They are removed from there to live in spiritual Israel, the church.

As strange as this passage is, it is not alone in Scripture. We have two other "resurrection" stories concerning Israel in the Old Testament.

> *O Lord our God, other masters besides You have ruled us;*
> *But through You alone we confess Your name.*
> *14 The dead will not live, the departed spirits will not rise;*
> *Therefore You have punished and destroyed them,*
> *And You have wiped out all remembrance of them.*
> *15 You have increased the nation, O Lord,*
> *You have increased the nation, You are glorified;*
> *You have extended all the borders of the land.*
> *16 O Lord, they sought You in distress;*
> *They could only whisper a prayer,*
> *Your chastening was upon them.*
> *17 As the pregnant woman approaches the time to give birth,*
> *She writhes and cries out in her labor pains,*
> *Thus were we before You, O Lord.*
> *18 We were pregnant, we writhed in labor,*
> *We gave birth, as it seems, only to wind.*
> *We could not accomplish deliverance for the earth,*
> *Nor were inhabitants of the world born.*
> *19 Your dead will live;*
> *Their corpses will rise.*
> *You who lie in the dust, awake and shout for joy,*
> *For your dew is as the dew of the dawn,*
> *And the earth will give birth to the departed spirits. (Isaiah 26:13-*
> *19, NASB95)*

> *The hand of the Lord was upon me, and He brought me out by the*
> *Spirit of the Lord and set me down in the middle of the valley; and*
> *it was full of bones. 2 He caused me to pass among them round*
> *about, and behold, there were very many on the surface of the*
> *valley; and lo, they were very dry. 3 He said to me, "Son of man,*

*can these bones live?" And I answered, "O Lord God, You know."
4 Again He said to me, "Prophesy over these bones and say to
them, 'O dry bones, hear the word of the Lord.' 5 "Thus says the
Lord God to these bones, 'Behold, I will cause breath to enter you
that you may come to life. 6 'I will put sinews on you, make flesh
grow back on you, cover you with skin and put breath in you that
you may come alive; and you will know that I am the Lord.' "*

*7 So I prophesied as I was commanded; and as I prophesied,
there was a noise, and behold, a rattling; and the bones came
together, bone to its bone. 8 And I looked, and behold, sinews
were on them, and flesh grew and skin covered them; but there
was no breath in them. 9 Then He said to me, "Prophesy to the
breath, prophesy, son of man, and say to the breath, 'Thus says
the Lord God, "Come from the four winds, O breath, and breathe
on these slain, that they come to life." ' " 10 So I prophesied as He
commanded me, and the breath came into them, and they came
to life and stood on their feet, an exceedingly great army. 11 Then
He said to me, "Son of man, these bones are the whole house of
Israel; behold, they say, 'Our bones are dried up and our hope has
perished. We are completely cut off.' 12 "Therefore prophesy and
say to them, 'Thus says the Lord God, "Behold, I will open your
graves and cause you to come up out of your graves, My people;
and I will bring you into the land of Israel. 13 "Then you will
know that I am the Lord, when I have opened your graves and
caused you to come up out of your graves, My people. 14 "I will
put My Spirit within you and you will come to life, and I will place
you on your own land. Then you will know that I, the Lord, have
spoken and done it," declares the Lord.' (Ezekiel 37:1-14, NASB95)*

So, although natural Israel is about to die, spiritual Israel will live again, and
does so in the Church.

We can summarize this section by observing these points:
1. They were preeminently witnesses, that is, martyrs for the Christian
   faith.
2. They are represented as Two Witnesses rather than any other number
   because of the analogy of the two olive trees, and especially because it
   requires two witnesses to establish testimony for a death sentence.

3. They were anointed, like Joshua and Zerubabel, to build the new Church, and they were in fact the candlesticks that were destined to supplant and supersede the old defunct Judaism.
4. They were notably gifted with power to work miracles, and were divinely supported until their work was finished.
5. Their resurrection and triumphant going up into heaven is an apocalyptic picture of what Jesus had repeatedly assured his followers.[453]

11:13 And in that hour there was a great earthquake, and a tenth of the city fell; seven thousand people were killed in the earthquake, and the rest were terrified and gave glory to the God of heaven. Perhaps, as additional testimony of God's pleasure with His prophets and displeasure of the inhabitants of Jerusalem, there follows a **great earthquake (11:13)** in which **a tenth of the city (11:13)** falls and **seven thousand people (11:13)** die. In keeping with so many other parallels with the life of Christ,

> *And behold, the veil of the temple was torn in two from top to bottom; and the earth shook and the rocks were split. The tombs were opened, and many bodies of the saints who had fallen asleep were raised; and coming out of the tombs after His resurrection they entered the holy city and appeared to many. (Matthew 27:51-53)*

The only redeeming feature found in its inhabitants is this, like the Roman centurion they give **glory to the God of heaven (11:13)**.

> *Now the centurion, and those who were with him keeping guard over Jesus, when they saw the earthquake and the things that were happening, became very frightened and said, "Truly this was the Son of God!" (Matthew 27:54)*

---

[453] Milton S. Terry, <u>Biblical Apocalyptics</u>, 374.

11:14 *The second woe is past; behold, the third woe is coming quickly.* We are now informed that all this has been **the second woe (11:14)**, apparently, in some sense, a part of the sixth trumpet. "It is not easy to identify the third woe, which "is soon to come." No disaster falls upon humanity after the blowing of the seventh trumpet. Many believe that the disasters and sufferings that come at the outpouring of the seven bowls of God's anger (chapter 16) are the third woe; but the writer himself does not say so."[454]

The Seventh Trumpet—Christ's Reign Foreseen

11:15 *Then the seventh angel sounded; and there were loud voices in heaven, saying, "The kingdom of the world has become the kingdom of our Lord and of His Christ; and He will reign forever and ever."* To begin with, let's note that the sounding of the seventh trumpet is not the last trump, "this seventh trumpet is the last of this series of seven, but not the last absolutely, and is not to be confused with the "last trump" of 1 Co 15:52."[455]

To continue, it should not be doubted that Christ is Lord over His creation and that His kingdom is now and always has been in power and authority. However, Paul refers to Satan as *"the god of this world"* (2 Corinthians 4:4, NASB95). As a result, this passage refers to the time when **the kingdom of the world (11:15)** becomes visibly what in fact it actually is, **the kingdom of our Lord and His Christ (11:15)**. In fact, it is a little difficult to imagine when **the kingdom of the world (11:15)** was not **the kingdom of our Lord (11:15)** except in an eschatological sense in which this is corrected at the end of the world. "...the Greek word for *kingdom* here does not mean a region or country ruled by a king but the power to rule as king: kingship, sovereignty, dominion. God and his Messiah have now taken complete control over the world. The underlying thought is that they have defeated Satan and his servants, who had been allowed to rule for a while."[456]

---

[454] Robert G. Bratcher, Rev. 11:14.

[455] Jerome H. Smith, editor, The New Treasury of Scripture Knowledge, electronic edition (Nashville, TN: Logos Library System, Thomas Nelson, 1997, c1997).

[456] Robert G. Bratcher, Rev. 11:15.

11:16-17 *And the twenty-four elders, who sit on their thrones before God, fell on their faces and worshiped God, 17 saying, "We give You thanks, O Lord God, the Almighty, who are and who were, because You have taken Your great power and have begun to reign.* We read a similar statement at the end of the fifth cycle in chapter 19, *"Then I heard something like the voice of a great multitude and like the sound of many waters and like the sound of mighty peals of thunder, saying, "Hallelujah! For the Lord our God, the Almighty, reigns"* (Revelation 19:6, NASB95). This sounds very much like our current text. Again, this might, to some, look like an end of the world picture; the kingdom has now come in all its visibility; but it is not. Having died, been resurrected, ascended to heaven and defeated His enemy and murderers, Christ has begun a universal reign. This ascendancy of Christ will continue until God's purposes are fully achieved. Those purposes are clarified in Isaiah 9.

> *They will not hurt or destroy in all My holy mountain, for the earth will be full of the knowledge of the Lord as the waters cover the sea. (Isaiah 11:9, NASB95)*

Notice that the phrase, **who are and who were (11:17)**, is not concluded by the phrase "and who is to come" found in Revelation 1:4, 8, and 4:8. Why? Because that which was then future, His judgement coming, has now arrived, prophecy has become history; *He has come.*

11:18 *And the nations were enraged, and Your wrath came, and the time came for the dead to be judged, and the time to reward Your bond-servants the prophets and the saints and those who fear Your name, the small and the great, and to destroy those who destroy the earth [land].* The nations were **enraged (11:18)** at the Jews because God put it in their heart to carry out His purpose for Judaism. For this reason they gathered in the Land to destroy Judaism. We are reminded in this passage of Psalm 2,

> *Why are the nations in an uproar and the peoples devising a vain thing? The kings of the earth take their stand and the rulers take counsel together against the Lord and against His Anointed.... Then He will speak to them in His anger and terrify them in His fury....*

> *You shall break them with a rod of iron, you shall shatter them*
> *like earthenware. (Psalm 2:1-2,5,9, NASB95)*

The Romans rage against Jerusalem, and the Jews and the Romans rage against Christ, both having put Him to death. But His judgement has come and He now breaks them "*with the rod of iron,*" and He will "*dash them in pieces.*"

The reference, ***the time came for the dead to be judged (11:18)***, is not of the final judgement at the resurrection as this passage is at an intermediate point in the story in Revelation. This has reference to those that died as martyrs mentioned in Revelation 6:9-11. This judgement would refer to "the time in which they will be avenged or vindicated."[457] Judgement can refer to both condemnation and acquittal. Here it refers to acquittal. They were judged by man, found guilty, and put to death. They are now judged by God, found innocent, and rewarded for their faithfulness. But while they are acquitted, their persecutors are "destroyed."

As God destroyed Babylon for destroying Judea in earlier years, so God will devastate the Romans, ***those who destroy the earth [land] (11:18)***, for demolishing Jerusalem in the first century. In their efforts to destroy Judea, in a very spectacular way they destroyed the land itself.

> And now the Romans, although they were greatly distressed in getting together their materials, raised their banks in one-and-twenty days, after they had cut down all the trees that were in the country that adjoined to the city, and that for ninety furlongs round about, as I have already related. (6) And, truly, the very view itself of the country was a melancholy thing; for those places which were before adorned with trees and pleasant gardens were now become a desolate country every way, and its trees were all cut down: (7) nor could any foreigner that had formerly seen Judea and the most beautiful suburbs of the city, and now saw it as a desert, but lament and mourn sadly at so great a change; (8) for the war had laid all signs of beauty quite waste; nor, if anyone that had known the place before, had come on a sudden to it now, would he have

---

[457] Moses Stuart, vol. II, 242.

known it again; but though he were at the city itself, yet would he have inquired for it notwithstanding.[458]

God forbade Israel to destroy the land of a besieged enemy.

> *When you besiege a city a long time, to make war against it in order to capture it, you shall not destroy its trees by swinging an axe against them; for you may eat from them, and you shall not cut them down. For is the tree of the field a man, that it should be besieged by you? (Deuteronomy 20:19, NASB95)*

Rome violated this law and was to be judged for it.

11:19 And the temple of God which is in heaven was opened; and the ark of His covenant appeared in His temple, and there were flashes of lightning and sounds and peals of thunder and an earthquake and a great hailstorm. The temporary residence of the ark on earth has ended **and the ark of His covenant appeared in His temple (11:19)** which is now in heaven.

> The Temple on earth has lost what status it had. It never did contain the ark, which was lost when Nebuchadrezzar destroyed Solomon's Temple. It was a confident hope of some apocalyptic writers that in the Great day it would be restored; but St. John holds out no hope of any such restoration. God's covenanted presence is no longer the City of David; it is a universal covenant now "in Heaven,' visible to all mankind, and available for all. The earthly, local, temple is to be destroyed.[459]

---

[458] Flavius Josephus, *Wars*, 6:1:5.

[459] Philip Carrington, 193.

Chapter 12

The Woman, the Red Dragon and Michael

The Woman, Israel

12:1 A great sign appeared in heaven: a woman clothed with the sun, and the moon under her feet, and on her head a crown of twelve stars.... Our passage starts with the phrase, ***a great sign (12:1)***, yet the whole book of Revelation is one of signs.

> *The Revelation of Jesus Christ, which God gave Him to show to His bond-servants, the things which must soon take place; and He sent and communicated it (sign-a-fied-it, σημαίνω, [sēmainō]) by His angel to His bond-servant John. (Revelation 1:1, NASB95)*

But this is a ***great sign (21:1)*** that is, a most important one. What makes it so important? The answer is the subject, which it signifies, that subject being Christ. John's allusion is from Isaiah.

> *Then the Lord spoke again to Ahaz, saying, 11 "Ask a sign for yourself from the Lord your God; make it deep as Sheol or high as heaven.... 14 Therefore the Lord Himself will give you a sign: Behold, a virgin will be with child and bear a son, and she will call His name Immanuel." (Isaiah 7:10-11, 14, NASB95)*

"St John is therefore announcing the birth of the male child, the warrior king, foretold by ...Isaiah."[460] From Genesis to Revelation the picture of ***the woman (12:1)*** remains rather unchanged.

> *And I will put enmity*
> *Between you and the woman,*
> *And between your seed and her seed;*
> *He shall bruise you on the head,*

---

460 Ibid., 205.

And you shall bruise him on the heel."
16 To the woman He said,
I will greatly multiply
Your pain in childbirth,
In pain you will bring forth children;
Yet your desire will be for your husband,
And he will rule over you. (Genesis 3:15-16, NASB95)

There have been many "women" in Israel that in some way remind us of this promise. There have been Eve, Sara, Rebekah, Jochebed, Hannah, other Old Testament saints, and eventually Mary. But in one sense it is all the spiritual seed, Godly Israel, that brings forth this child. So, the woman here is spiritual Israel.

The image of a woman, a bride, a wife, has been central to God's relationship to Israel.

It is impossible to understand the *Revelation* at all without fixing clearly in the mind this conception of the Bride of God which is fundamental to so many of the prophets. It applies first to the early Israel of the wanderings in the desert, a period often thought of as the "honeymoon" of Israel and Jehovah; and, secondly it applies to the ideal Israel, the souls in Israel who remain faithful to their God. The actual Israel is too often the faithless wife, the harlot who has gone a-whoring after strange gods.[461]

The woman, spiritual Israel, whether the Old Testament Church or the New Testament Church, **appeared in heaven (12:1)**. Why the heavenly scene? Heaven is the natural and eternal place to view the Church of God. This world is not our home, the heavenly one is.

They are not of the world, even as I am not of the world. (John 17:16, NASB95)

...and raised us up with Him, and seated us with Him in the heavenly places in Christ Jesus.... (Ephesians 2:6, NASB95)

---

[461] Ibid., 207.

Therefore if you have been raised up with Christ, keep seeking the things above, where Christ is, seated at the right hand of God. Set your mind on the things above, not on the things that are on earth. For you have died and your life is hidden with Christ in God. (Colossians 3:1-3, NASB95)

We read that she was **clothed with the sun, and the moon under her feet, and on her head a crown of twelve stars (12:1)**. Joseph had a dream in which the sun, moon, and stars fell down and worshiped him (Genesis 37:9-11). The sun was his father, the moon his mother, and the twelve stars were his brothers. We can see in these same figures in our passage allusions of glory for the holy people that bring forth this child. "*Sun...moon...stars.* This imagery is frequently identified with the nation Israel because of Joseph's dream in Gen 37."[462]

"The twelve stars may have reference to the twelve tribes of Israel. The true Israel, the Zion of God, gives us the incarnate Christ. Out of the bosom of the church comes Jesus Christ into the world as the promised Messiah who was to be the 'seed of the woman.'"[463]

Carrington concludes, "These symbols ... associate the Woman with the true Israel, the glorious Bride of Jehovah; the figure Twelve alone is sufficient to do this...."[464]

So, the woman here is Spiritual Israel. "She is the true people of God, the faithful remnant, the persecuted prophetic minority...."[465]

12:2 ...and she was with child; and she cried out, being in labor and in pain to give birth. With these words Christ is born. "God's people have failed him and are rejected; but there has always been an inner circle, a faithful remnant of visionaries and idealists, who remain true to him. They cry; they groan; they are bringing something to birth—something better than the crude imperialism and commercialisms of the world. From this inner Israel the Messiah is born."[466]

---

[462] The NET Bible Notes, electronic edition (Dallas, TX: Biblical Studies Press, 1998), Rev. 12:12.

[463] David S. Clark, 83.

[464] Philip Carrington, 207.

[465] Ibid., 208.

[466] Ibid., 208.

The Red Dragon

12:3 *Then another sign appeared in heaven: and behold, a great red dragon having seven heads and ten horns, and on his heads were seven diadems.* The **great red dragon (12:3)** is clearly Satan. From the Garden of Eve onward the devil has been identified with the serpent or dragon. John saves us from speculation and says, *"And the great dragon was thrown down, the serpent of old who is called the devil and Satan"* (Revelation 12:9, NASB95). Earlier Isaiah said,

> *In that day the Lord will punish Leviathan the fleeing serpent, with His fierce and great and mighty sword, even Leviathan the twisted serpent; and He will kill the dragon who lives in the sea. (Isaiah 27:1, NASB95)*

In Daniel 7 we read of four beasts that collectively had *seven heads and ten horns.*

> Babylon, Medo-Persia, Greece, and Rome were all stages in the Dragon's attempt to establish his illicit empire over the world.... He was the great Beast, of which they had been only partial images. It was he who had been the age-long enemy of the people of God. In all Israel's struggles against Beasts, through all the attempts by human empires to destroy the Seed of the Covenant, the Dragon had been their foe. He wore the diadems of the persecuting empires.[467]

So, John here identifies this beast as the power behind all the beasts that attack God's people with the description, ***having seven heads and ten horns, and on his heads were seven diadems (12:3)***.

---

[467] David Chilton, The Great Tribulation, 303-304.

12:4 And his tail swept away a third of the stars of heaven and threw them to the earth [land]. And the dragon stood before the woman who was about to give birth, so that when she gave birth he might devour her child. "St. John has already associated stars with angels, a familiar Biblical connection... now he symbolically describes the fall of Satan and the evil angels.... The Dragon's "stars" are the fallen angels, who joined him in rebellion."[468]

> *For if God did not spare angels when they sinned, but cast them into hell and committed them to pits of darkness, reserved for judgement.... (2 Peter 2:4, NASB95)*

> *And angels who did not keep their own domain, but abandoned their proper abode, He has kept in eternal bonds under darkness for the judgement of the great day.... (Jude 6, NASB95)*

> *And the great dragon was thrown down, the serpent of old who is called the devil and Satan, who deceives the whole world; he was thrown down to the earth [land], and his angels were thrown down with him. (Revelation 12:9, NASB95)*

> *And He said to them, "I was watching Satan fall from heaven like lightning." (Luke 10:18, NASB95)*

The **child (12:4)** that Satan attempted to murder was Christ. Satan's tool in this attempted murder was Herod.

> *Then when Herod saw that he had been tricked by the magi, he became very enraged, and sent and slew all the male children who were in Bethlehem and all its vicinity, from two years old and under, according to the time which he had determined from the magi. (Matthew 2:16, NASB95)*

The Male Child, Christ

12:5 And she gave birth to a son, a male child, who is to rule all the nations with a rod of iron; and her child was caught up

---

[468] Ibid., 306.

to God and to His throne. Christ **is to rule (12:5)** His creation. Man does not recognize this and indeed rebels against His rule, but He is still the sovereign God and He does rule. However, in His own providence He does not immediately judge man and force him to bow. One day He will.

"To rule all nations with an iron scepter marks two things; first the universality of his reign, and second the strength or irresistible power of it. An iron scepter is one with can neither be broken nor resisted."[469] The Jews had proclaimed *"We do not want this man to reign over us"* (Luke 19:14, NASB95) and *"We have no king but Caesar"* (John 19:15, NASB95). However, Paul had said *"...at the name of Jesus every knee will bow, of those who are in heaven and on earth and under the earth..."* (Philippians 2:10). And so it will be. It may take a *rod of iron*, but in God's time it will happen.

Since the purpose of the vision is not to retell the life of Christ, but to reveal its sequel with reference to the warfare of His church, after the birth of Christ, the narrative skips to the ascension saying, **and her child was caught up to God and to His throne (12:5).**[470] It should be noted that it was the **child (12:5)** that **was caught up to God (12:5)**, not the Woman. I say this for some Roman Catholic theologians use this verse to attempt to prove the bodily assumption of Mary. The desperation of using this verse to prove this doctrine clearly demonstrates the weakness and falsity of the teaching.

> The "woman" does not represent Mary but rather the nation of Israel. For this woman there is "a place prepared for her by God, where she might be taken care of for 1260 days" (Rev. 12:6) during the tribulation period before Christ returns to earth (cf. Rev. 11:2–3). Christ, not the "woman," was "caught up to God and his throne" (Rev. 12:5). It is pure eisegesis (reading a viewpoint into the text), to see Mary's bodily assumption here. Likewise, to argue that Mary, though not being caught up here, is pictured in heaven in the celestial imagery is equally farfetched. Nothing in this text would entail a belief in her bodily assumption before the resurrection of the rest of the saints (1 Thess. 4:13–18).[471]

---

[469] Moses Stuart, vol. II, 255.

[470] Steve Gregg, 257-258.

[471] Norman L. Geisler, and Ron Rhodes, 309.

12:6 Then the woman fled into the wilderness where she had a place prepared by God, so that there she would be nourished for one thousand two hundred and sixty days. In chapter 7 we read about the 144,000 who were sealed so that they would not experience the judgement that God was about to pour out on Jerusalem. This is the same picture. Here we read, **then the woman fled into the wilderness where she had a place prepared by God (12:6)**. Here God protects the woman, which is spiritual Israel or the Church. Christ warned the Church.

> But when you see Jerusalem surrounded by armies, then
> recognize that her desolation is near. 21 Then those who are in
> Judea must flee to the mountains, and those who are in the midst
> of the city must leave, and those who are in the country must not
> enter the city; 22 because these are days of vengeance, so that all
> things which are written will be fulfilled. 23 Woe to those who are
> pregnant and to those who are nursing babies in those days; for
> there will be great distress upon the land and wrath to this
> people; 24 and they will fall by the edge of the sword, and will be
> led captive into all the nations; and Jerusalem will be trampled
> under foot by the Gentiles until the times of the Gentiles are
> fulfilled. (Luke 21:20-24, NASB95)

The Church headed the warning and fled **into the wilderness (12:6)** and was thereby spared the *days of vengeance*. "...the Woman's flight into the wilderness is a picture of the flight of the Judean Christians from the destruction of Jerusalem...."[472] "According to Eusebius (bk. Iii, chap. v), 'the whole body of the church in Jerusalem, commanded by a divine revelation,' fled to Pella, beyond the Jordan."[473]

This period, **one thousand two hundred and sixty days (12:6)** is the same period the prophets of chapter 11 prophesied or 42 months. It is the amount of time that Israel was *given to the nations* (11:2), that is given up to judgement by the Romans. "Vespasian received his commission from Nero, and declared war on Jerusalem February, A.D. 67. The siege ended

---

[472] David Chilton, The Great Tribulation, 309.

[473] Milton S. Terry, Biblical Apocalyptics, 385.

with the fall of Jerusalem, the burning of the city and temple, in August, A.D. 70. This computation of dates yields the forty-two months for Jerusalem to be 'trodden under foot.'"[474] When this period ended, the threat by Satan's tool, Rome, would pass and God's people, the converted Jews, would move back into the world, but no longer as Jews. That chapter was forever closed; they are now simply Christians.

Michael

12:7 And there was war in heaven, Michael and his angels waging war with the dragon. The dragon and his angels waged war.... At this point we have a parenthetic section, "...St. John unveils this scene in order to explain the preceding verse—to show why the Woman had to flee into the wilderness. Once that is explained, in verses 7-12, he returns to the theme of the flight of the Woman. ... Chronologically, this explanatory section fits in between verses 5 and 6."[475]

Who is *Michael (12:7)*? He is mentioned in Daniel 10:13, 21 and 12:1 as well as Jude 9. There are two possibilities. One is that he is an angel of very high rank. The second is that he is Christ.

However, the greater probability favors identification with Christ. He appears in heaven immediately after the child is caught up to heaven. The picture is one of Christ conquering Satan, as is the actual case, and not merely some angel conquering Satan.

In Daniel 10:13, 10:21 and 12:1 Michael is presented as fighting for God on earth as the captain of the Lord's host and is called the great prince. In Daniel, He is pictured in the midst of a great tribulation fulfilling the role now discussed in Revelation.

> *Now at that time Michael, the great prince who stands guard over the sons of your people, will arise. And there will be a time of distress such as never occurred since there was a nation until that time; and at that time your people, everyone who is found written in the book, will be rescued. (Daniel 12:1, NASB95)*

---

[474] Foy E. Wallace, Jr., The Book of Revelation, 215.

[475] David Chilton, The Great Tribulation, 311.

Here Michael is engaged in a ***war in heaven (12:7)***. That being the case, a rebellion by some of the angelic host would appear to be the cause. It is not Satan that wages the war; it is Michael and his heavenly forces that do so. God is not on the defense; He never reacts to events around Him, He only acts.

Jude 9 refers to Michael as an archangel and from that many have incorrectly thought that Michael was simply a higher member of the angelic host. However, archangel means "Chief of the Angels, an expression equivalent to 'Captain of the Lord's hosts'.... This would ... identify Michael with the Angel of the Lord ... a figure who is, in most cases, a pre-incarnate appearance of Christ."[476] "The word archangel, then, by all the rules, ought to mean captain of the angels, an idea to be compared with the 'Captain of the Lord's host' of Joshua v. 15, which applies to an angel who is clearly a manifestation of Jehovah; if may even be compared with 'Lord of host,' and it may perhaps have meant that manifestation of God in which he appears as leader of the armies of Israel or of the heavens."[477]

So it appears that "...in Daniel Michael is the militant leader of Israel against the forces of persecution; in Revelation he is the militant leader of Christianity and all the forces of God against persecution and all the forces of evil."[478]

12:8 ...and they were not strong enough, and there was no longer a place found for them in heaven. Notwithstanding his best efforts, Satan cannot stand against Michael. Similar to the phrase "this town's not big enough for the both of us," so heaven was not big enough for God and Satan. There was and is no room for Satan in heaven.

12:9 And the great dragon was thrown down, the serpent of old who is called the devil and Satan, who deceives the whole world; he was thrown down to the earth [land], and his angels were thrown down with him. Because he was *not strong enough* (12:8) to stand against Michael, we are told three times that he was

---

[476] Ibid., 312.

[477] Philip Carrington, 221-222.

[478] Ibid., 224.

thrown down (12:9) to earth along with his defeated army. Christ said something very similar in His ministry.

> *And He said to them, "I was watching Satan fall from heaven like lightning." (Luke 10:18, NASB95)*[479]

"According to Jewish sources…he was hurled down from heaven because he tried to place his throne beside God's…."[480] "Note the three-fold use of ballo [βάλλω, *ballō thrown down*] (cast out, or cast down) in this one verse. Ekballo is a technical word for excommunication."[481] Excommunication in the Church has its pattern in heaven. As God insists on holiness in heaven, so He insists on holiness in his Church. Churches that fail to excommunicate those that live worldly lives or hold false doctrines prove themselves to be in greater league with Satan than with God. His example should not be neglected.

This is not the final battle that will be fought at the end of time. This battle has already occurred and been won. In Revelation 9:1 we earlier noted that that passage had reference to Satan.

> *Then the fifth angel sounded, and I saw a star from heaven which had fallen to the earth; and the key of the bottomless pit was given to him. (Revelation 9:1, NASB95)*

As is so often the case in Revelation, we see events that appear to be retold from different perspectives. In 9:11 we are told that this *star* had *fallen to the earth.* Hear we are told that he ***was thrown down (12:9).*** Interestingly, the gospels give us prior information about this subject.

> *Now judgement is upon this world; now the ruler of this world will be cast out. (John 12:31, NASB95)*

> *…because the ruler of this world has been judged. (John 16:11, NASB95)*

---

[479] See also, Matthew 12:28-29; John 12:31, 16:11, 17:15; Acts 14:16, 26:18; Romans 16:20; Colossians 2:15; II Timothy 2:16; Hebrews 2:14; I John 3:8, 4:3-4, 5:18.

[480] J. Massyngberde Ford,.206.

[481] Ibid., 194.

The epistles follow this theme with these additional comments.

> *When He had disarmed the rulers and authorities, He made a public display of them, having triumphed over them through Him. (Colossians 2:15, NASB95)*

> *Therefore, since the children share in flesh and blood, He Himself likewise also partook of the same, that through death He might render powerless him who had the power of death, that is, the devil.... (Hebrews 2:14, NASB95)*

> *The Son of God appeared for this purpose, to destroy the works of the devil. (1 John 3:8, NASB95)*

12:10 Then I heard a loud voice in heaven, saying, "Now the salvation, and the power, and the kingdom of our God and the authority of His Christ have come, for the accuser of our brethren has been thrown down, he who accuses them before our God day and night." Now that Satan has been utterly defeated and evicted from heaven:

1. **Salvation (12:10)** has been achieved.
2. The great **power (12:10)** of God has been demonstrated.
3. The **Kingdom of our God (12:10)** has arrived.
4. The **authority of His Christ (12:10)** has been displayed.

"So the meaning here seems to be that the resurrection and ascension of Christ was the staggering blow to Satan's kingdom, and foretokened the ultimate overthrow of his power. When Christ arose from the dead and ascended to the throne of God it was [an] eviction-notice served on Satan."[482]

> *Then the seventh angel sounded; and there were loud voices in heaven, saying, "The kingdom of the world has become the kingdom of our Lord and of His Christ; and He will reign forever and ever." (Revelation 11:15, NASB95)*

---

[482] David S. Clark, 84.

12:11 And they overcame him because of the blood of the Lamb and because of the word of their testimony, and they did not love their life even when faced with death. "The force of the statement is that they were willing to pay the price of martyrdom in order to be faithful to Jesus Christ."[483] Earlier John dealt with another group that had experienced a victory during *the great tribulation* much like what we read about here. We read:

> And he said to me, "These are the ones who come out of the great tribulation, and they have washed their robes and made them white in the blood of the Lamb." (Revelation 7:14, NASB95)

We appear to have here a repetitive picture of those who had to pay the ultimate price for their faith in Christ. We are given little information about Satan's creation and the origin of evil. This much seems to be true: Satan and the other angels were originally created holy, upright, and good.

> God saw all that He had made, and behold, it was very good. (Genesis 1:31, NASB95)

Sometime between their creation and the temptation of Adam and Eve a number of angels rebelled against God, refusing to continue in the position He had created for them.

> And angels who did not keep their own domain, but abandoned their proper abode, He has kept in eternal bonds under darkness for the judgement of the great day.... (Jude 6, NASB95)

> For if God did not spare angels when they sinned, but cast them into hell and committed them to pits of darkness, reserved for judgement.... (2 Peter 2:4, NASB95)

Those who rebelled were condemned and will be cast, at the last day, into the lake of fire along with everyone who follows their example of rebellion.

> And the devil who deceived them was thrown into the lake of fire and brimstone, where the beast and the false prophet are also;

---

[483] Robert G. Bratcher, Rev. 12:11.

*and they will be tormented day and night forever and ever.
(Revelation 20:10, NASB95)*

The period of history between the ascension of Christ and the last day (the Day of Judgement) will be a period of *"the increase of His government"* and *"of peace"* as Isaiah says below.

For a child will be born to us, a son will be given to us; and the government will rest on His shoulders; and His name will be called Wonderful Counselor, Mighty God, Eternal Father, Prince of Peace. There will be no end to the increase of His government or of peace, on the throne of David and over his kingdom, to establish it and to uphold it with justice and righteousness from then on and forevermore. The zeal of the Lord of hosts will accomplish this. (Isaiah 9:6-7, NASB95)

The victory accomplished on the cross is carried out through the people of God.

The God of peace will soon crush Satan under your feet. The grace of our Lord Jesus be with you. (Romans 16:20, NASB95)

Ask of Me, and I will surely give the nations as Your inheritance, and the very ends of the earth as Your possession. You shall break them with a rod of iron, You shall shatter them like earthenware. (Psalm 2:8-9, NASB95)

Nevertheless what you have, hold fast until I come. He who overcomes, and he who keeps My deeds until the end, to him I will give authority over the nations; and he shall rule them with a rod of iron, as the vessels of the potter are broken to pieces, as I also have received authority from My Father.... (Revelation 2:25-27, NASB95)

Believers today are not to be passive, waiting for God to "do something." We are to be "doing something" ourselves to extend the authority of Christ over the nations. It is certain that those who teach Christians to refrain from exercising dominion in this world clearly weaken the hands of those that seek to expand the Kingdom. The view of Dispensationalists that defeat is certain in this world "...leads many Christians to have a short-termed, pessimistic, predestined, mentally confused view of the future; it leads to absolute paralysis in the Christian community with regard to how we should relate to the society around us."[484] Lewis Sperry Chafer, one of the major leaders of classic Dispensationalism says that the child of God should be delivered from "...undertaking the impossible world-transforming program belonging to the dispensation which is to come."[485] Clearly, he has marginalized Christianity from having any significant impact on the world. Indeed, his theology and counsel has become a self-fulfilling prophecy.

Instead of the Dispensational theology of defeat, we should relate to our world and culture in such a way that both in time and eternity Christ will say that we **overcame (12:11)**, not that we quit.

12:12 For this reason, rejoice, O heavens and you who dwell in them. Woe to the earth [land] and the sea, because the devil has come down to you, having great wrath, knowing that he has only a short time. The heavens **rejoice (12:12)** and the earth experiences **woe (12:12)** for the same reason, Satan is thrown down (12:9) from heaven to the earth.

> There is here the echo of the ancient story of a primeval war in heaven. Satan was an angel who conceived "the impossible thought" of placing his throne higher than that of God (2 *Enoch* 29:4, 5) and was cast out of heaven. The Babylonians had a similar story of Ishtar, the goddess of the morning star. She, too, rebelled against God and was cast down from heaven.
>
> In the Old Testament Satan is an angel under God's command and with access to his presence. In *Job* we find Satan numbered amongst the sons of God and possessing access to his presence (Job 1:6–9; 2:1–6); and in *Zechariah* we also find Satan in the presence of God (Zechariah 3:1, 2).[486]

---

[484] Joseph R. Balyeat, <u>Babylon, The Great City of God</u> (Sevierville, TN: Covenant House Books, 1991, 1995), 22-23.

[485] Lewis Sperry Chafer, <u>Major Bible Themes</u> (Chicago, Il; Moody Press, 1944), 97-98.

[486] William Barclay, Volume 2, Chapters 6-22, Rev. 12:12.

We are told that he has only a ***short time (12:12)***—to do what?

> What event, then could the short time be waiting until? The next significant event in the history of the Church would be the destruction of Israel in A.D. 70, at which time Satan was bound and cast into the abyss. Satan knew he only had a short time (forty years) to stop the Church from growing up. This is why he is said (after realizing he is cast down and only has a short time to work) to go "off to make war on...those who keep the commandments of God and bear testimony to Jesus" (12:17); he wants to destroy the New Covenant Church.[487]

12:13 And when the dragon saw that he was thrown down to the earth [land], he persecuted the woman who gave birth to the male child. Satan's defeat at the hands of Christ enrages him. He cannot win in heaven but he hopes to win on earth. His object of enmity is the holy seed, and ***the woman (12:13)***, whereby the holy seed comes. No doubt Cain was aroused to hatred of Abel through Satan's effort to destroy that holy seed. This malicious effort continued through the Old Testament to include Moses and eventually Christ Himself. And so it continues today. Satan hates the Church because the Church is the holy creation of God to do his righteous purpose. "Since he could not destroy the omnipotent Son of God he persecutes the church to show his hate toward Christ and every thing that is his."[488]

The ***dragon (12:13)*** persecutes the church, then and now, and does so precisely because he cannot attack Christ Himself. We are God's warriors on the front line of the battle. In our story here, ***the woman (12:13)***, which was so recently Mary the mother of Christ, has now changed to the Church, for again it is the holy people, whether Israel, Mary or the Church, that produced the holy offspring. Satan now persecutes the Church in his hatred of Christ. "There is no doubt in the minds of commentators that the Woman now represents the primitive church and its persecution in Jerusalem...."[489]

---

487 C. Jonathin Seraiah, 95.

488 David S. Clark, 84.

489 Philip Carrington, 224.

***12:14 But the two wings of the great eagle were given to the
woman, so that she could fly into the wilderness to her place,
where she was nourished for a time and times and half a time,
from the presence of the serpent.*** Notice the implied comparison,
"The Devil is represented as a crawling serpent; but the church as flying on
wings."[490] When referencing the **great eagle (12:14)**, we note that God
used a similar phrase when speaking of His deliverance of the new nation
Israel from Egypt.

> *You yourselves have seen what I did to the Egyptians, and how I
> bore you on eagles' wings, and brought you to Myself. (Exodus
> 19:4, NASB95)*

So God supernaturally intervenes in the life of the new Church, as He did in
the life of Israel, by delivering her from the destructive aims of Satan. "...the
seer of Revelation represents God's hovering protection and imparted
strength in the flight of the woman from besieged Jerusalem into the
wilderness, as God did for Israel in the exodus from Egypt...."[491] Christ had
prophesied that this would soon occur.

> *Therefore when you see the abomination of desolation which was
> spoken of through Daniel the prophet, standing in the holy place
> (let the reader understand), then those who are in Judea must flee
> to the mountains. (Matthew 24:15-16, NASB95)*

> Here we see how the providences of the world are on the side of
> God's church. The stars in their courses fought against Sisera,
> which may refer to the storms that helped Israel win her battle;
> and here the earth puts forth her helping hand to save God's people
> and God's cause. The God of the church is the God of nature, and
> the God of providence; and he can command them in any exigency
> that may arise.[492]

Time and times and half a time (12:14) is a way of saying "...a year,
two years, and half a year, an expression used in Daniel 7.25; 12.7, to

---

[490] David S. Clark, 85.

[491] Foy E. Wallace, Jr., 281.

[492] David S. Clark, 85.

indicate a limited period of intense suffering. It is the same as forty-two months or 1,260 days (see verse 11.2–3)."[493]

The Church, in this case the church in Jerusalem, flees by God's design and purpose from the soon destruction of Israel and Jerusalem. She flees to Pella and is there protected for the 3-½ year Jewish war.

> The numerical designation for a time, and times and half a time was equivalent to the forty and two months of chapter 11:2, and the thousand two hundred and threescore days of chapters 11:3 and 12:6, and they were equal to the same thing. They all refer...to the mathematically calculated period of twelve hundred and sixty days between Nero's order to Vespasian in the declaration of war and the completion of the siege and destruction of Jerusalem which brought an end to the Jewish state and the system of Judaism.[494]

12:15 *And the serpent poured water like a river out of his mouth after the woman, so that he might cause her to be swept away with the flood.* The *water (12:15)* may be the Roman armies that attempted to round up all the inhabitants of Israel in its net, crowding them into Jerusalem for better control and assured destruction. Waters often mean "people" in the Bible.

> *And he said to me, "The waters which you saw where the harlot sits, are peoples and multitudes and nations and tongues."*
> *(Revelation 17:15, NASB95)*

"...the river may symbolize either the nations which come to Jerusalem, or the soldiers who besiege it...."[495]

12:16 *But the earth helped the woman, and the earth opened its mouth and drank up the river which the dragon poured out of his mouth.* The *"land,"* or *earth (12:16), helped the woman (12:16)*. This land which was such a curse to the Romans, demanded their full attention. By demanding such attention, it simply was not able to

---

493 Robert G. Bratcher, Rev. 12:14.

494 Foy E. Wallace, 282.

495 J. Massyngberde Ford, 203.

control every segment of Jews that desired to flee from this war. One such group was the Church in Israel or more specifically, Jerusalem. In this way the land helped the woman by focusing the Romans' attention from the escapees to the rebels. "Nor is it incongruous to suppose, that the civil and military power of the Romans, bearing down with great force upon the Jews at this period, and obliging them to seek their own personal safety, instead of pursuing schemes of vengeance upon Christians, is symbolized here by *the earth's helping the woman.*"[496]

> *But now, thus says the Lord, your Creator, O Jacob, and He who formed you, O Israel, do not fear, for I have redeemed you; I have called you by name; you are Mine! When you pass through the waters, I will be with you; and through the rivers, they will not overflow you. (Isaiah 43:1-2, NASB95)*

12:17 So the dragon was enraged with the woman, and went off to make war with the rest of her children, who keep the commandments of God and hold to the testimony of Jesus. God had decided to protect the Jewish church for a season, however, He does not protect the Gentile church, or the **rest of her children (12:17)**, in like manner. The result is that Satan turns his attention to the rest of the Mediterranean world that God in His sovereignty has not protected from Satan's fury. It is at this time that great persecutions break out in the Roman Empire against Christians.

Notice that **her children (12:17)** are defined as those that 1) **keep the commandments of God (12:17)** and 2) **hold to the testimony of Jesus (12:17)**. "These two marks excite the wrath of the devil then and always."[497] Satan today would be hard pressed to identify God's **children (12:17)** through these two characteristics. Indeed, a great deal of the Church today glories in not being under **the commandments of God (12:17)**, but instead being under grace; a dichotomy not taught in Scripture. But John makes clear in his epistles what he makes clear here as well; the child of God is a keeper of God's commandments.

---

[496] Moses Stuart, 263.

[497] Archibald Thomas Robertson, Vol. VI, 397.

By this we know that we have come to know Him, if we <u>keep His commandments</u>. The one who says, "I have come to know Him," and does not keep His commandments, is a liar, and the truth is not in him.... (1 John 2:3-4, NASB95)

For this is the love of God, that we <u>keep His commandments</u>; and His commandments are not burdensome. (1 John 5:3, NASB95).

Chapter 13

The Beast from the Sea and from the Land

The Beast Out of the Sea

13:1 And the dragon stood on the sand of the seashore. Then I saw a beast coming up out of the sea, having ten horns and seven heads, and on his horns were ten diadems, and on his heads were blasphemous names. As we saw in chapter 12, the *dragon (13:1)* is Satan. There he made war on the woman (spiritual Israel), but with very limited success. He now stands on the *sand of the seashore (13:1)* (the Gentile world) and, as it were, calls for his demonic tool.

The *beast (13:1)* is described *as coming up out of the sea (13:1)*. The *sea (13:1)* is often a biblical metaphor for the Gentile world as compared to the *land* or the Jewish world. In addition, if you were in Jerusalem or even Patmos where John wrote the book, the *sea (13:1)* would be to your West in the direction of Rome. So this beast is not Jewish in character but in general, Gentile and in particular, Roman. This beast is depicted with the same terms used to describe the dragon in 12:3 from which he draws his power. The Book of Revelation appears to refer to the beast both as a person and a government. This is not uncommon. We often refer to words and actions of the president of a company or a country as the words and actions of that company or country itself.

As John later tells us in Revelation:

> The ten horns which you saw are ten kings who have not yet received a kingdom, but they receive authority as kings with the beast for one hour. These have one purpose, and they give their power and authority to the beast. (Revelation 17:12-13, NASB95)

It would appear that these "kings" are sub monarchs to the Roman Emperor, much as King Herod was subject to the Roman emperor. F.F. Bruce illustrates this relationship saying of Herod, "In theory he was an

300

independent king, enjoying an alliance with the Roman state. In fact, he was bound to respect and carry out he will of the Roman people in all his policies...."[498] These "kings" or governors of the Roman provinces give their full support, both supplies and soldiers, in persecuting the Church throughout the empire.

> The ten provinces may be Italy, Achaea, Asia, Syria, Egypt, Africa, Spain, Gaul, Britain, and Germany. The *diadems* on the horns are royal crowns, not *stephanoi*, that is victors' wreaths. They suggest governors who shared in the imperial power and those who were subject to Rome, such as Herod, and yet retained the title of "king." However, the blasphemous names are on the heads, not the horns, because it was the emperors who were declared divine, not the provincial governors and kings. The blasphemous names must be the divine titles which the Romans emperors arrogated to themselves....[499]

But it would also be important to remember that "...in St. John the number Ten has a connection with persecution, so that a monster with ten horns might in itself suggest a persecuting power, whether in Jerusalem or in Rome."[500] We see this idea illustrated in the message to the Church in Smyrna.

> *Do not fear what you are about to suffer. Behold, the devil is*
> *about to cast some of you into prison, so that you will be tested,*
> *and you will have tribulation for ten days. Be faithful until death,*
> *and I will give you the crown of life. (Revelation 2:10, NASB95)*

The **seven heads (13:1)** refer to seven Roman emperors. The **blasphemous names (13:1)** would refer to the titles of deity used by the Romans emperors. We read in Exodus 28:36-38 that the high priest was to engrave on his turban *"Holy to the Lord"* and wear this in his service to God. So the Roman emperors ascribed to themselves **blasphemous names (13:1)** calling themselves "...*Augustus* or *Sebastos*, meaning *One*

---

[498] F.F. Bruce, Israel & the Nation, 190.

[499] J. Massyngberde Ford, 220.

[500] Philip Carrington, 229.

to be worshiped; they also took on the name *divus* (god) and even *Deus* and *Theos* (God)."[501]

"The dragon is the antithesis of God, but the sea beast is the antithesis of the Lamb.... Later in Revelation one learns that the beast "was and is not and is to come" (17:9), a blasphemous parody on the name of God...."[502]

> *"I am the Alpha and the Omega," says the Lord God, "who is and who was and who is to come, the Almighty." (Revelation 1:8, NASB95)*

13:2 And the beast which I saw was like a leopard, and his feet were like those of a bear, and his mouth like the mouth of a lion. And the dragon gave him his power and his throne and great authority. This **beast (13:2)** is described with the animals used by Daniel to refer to Greece, Medo-Persia, and Babylon. So it would appear, in the use of these various ascriptions, that this fourth kingdom of Daniel is worse than the three kingdoms combined that proceeded it. Again, it is the **dragon (13:2)**, or Satan, that **gave him his power and his throne and great authority (13:2)**. Josephus refers to this power or **great authority (13:2)** saying that the Romans were "the lords of the habitable earth...."[503]

13:3 I saw one of his heads as if it had been slain, and his fatal wound was healed. And the whole earth [land] was amazed and followed after the beast.... There are two major explanations of this crucial passage. They are:

In one view, the world of Satan is defeated at Calvary.

> Daniel had prophesied that in the days of the Romans rulers, Christ's Kingdom would crush the Satanic empires and replace them, filling the earth. Accordingly, apostolic testimony proclaimed that Christ's Kingdom had come, that the devil had been defeated, disarmed, and bound, and that all nations would

---

[501] David Chilton, <u>The Great Tribulation</u>, 328.

[502] J. Massyngberde Ford, 219.

[503] Flavius Josephus, *Wars*, 4:3:10.

begin to flow toward the mountain of the Lord's House. ... For a time, therefore, it looked as if a coup were taking place: Christianity was in the ascendant, and soon would gain control. Satan's head had been crushed, and with it the Roman Empire had been wounded to death with the sword of the Gospel.[504]

However, through the persecutions of the early Church, the evil empire of Satan revives from the dead.

In another view, probably the correct one, the head slain was Nero, and with him the Roman Empire came close to destruction. "At the death of Nero, the Roman Empire was thrown into violent convulsions of civil war and anarchy, in which three emperors succeeded one another within a single year. Historians consider it astonishing that the empire stabilized and survived this period that might easily have spelled the end of the imperial rule."[505] It was with the coming of Vespasian to power that the empire's *fatal wound was healed (13:3)* and the empire continued to live on.

This view would see Revelation 17:10 as additional information on this subject. Here we read,

> *...and they are seven kings; five have fallen, one is, the other has not yet come; and when he comes, he must remain a little while. (Revelation 17:10)*

Seven kings are mentioned, five have died, one is currently reining which is the one who is about to suffer the *fatal wound (13:3)*, and one will succeed him but will only reign for a short period of time.

The Five That *"Have Fallen"*

Julius Caesar	49-44 B.C.
Augustus Caesar	31 BC-A.D.14
Tiberius Caesar	A.D. 14-37
Gaius Caligula	A.D. 37-41
Claudius	A.D. 41-54

---

504 David Chilton, <u>The Great Tribulation</u>, 330-31.

505 Steve Gregg, 282.

The One That "**Is**"
Caesar Nero   A.D. 54-68

The One That Has "**Not Yet Come**"
Galba   A.D. June 68 to January 69
He reigned but "**a little while**"

Following these seven were:
Otho   A.D. 69
Vitellius   A.D. 69
Vespasian   A.D. 69-79
Titus   A.D. 79-81

The phrase used by John is **as if it had been slain (13:3)**. In other words the beast, Rome, came to the very door of death, but did not die. Of this period an ancient historian says, "I am entering on the history of a period rich in disasters, frightful in its wars, torn by civil strife, and even in peace full of horrors. Four emperors perished by the sword. There were three civil wars; there were more with foreign enemies; there were often wars that had both characters at once."[506] Again Tacitus says, "This was the condition of the Roman state when Serius Galba, chosen consul for the second time, and his colleague Titus Vinius entered upon the year that was to be for Galba his last <u>and for the state almost the end</u>."[507]

As Philip Carrington says, "The Heads, like the Horns, represent kings (as we are told later); and the Head that received a mortal wound represents Nero, who initiated the persecutions. He committed suicide, and in his death the Roman Empire received a mortal blow. Three rival generals fought for the throne; but though the Empire staggered, it did not go under. It survived. *The Mortal Wound was healed.*"[508]

Josephus speaks of Rome at this time as "laid waste"[509] and near "ruin."[510] He goes on to say "every part of the habitable earth under them (the Romans) was in an unsettled and tottering condition."[511]

---

[506] Tacitus, <u>The Complete Word of Tacitus</u>, Histories 1:2 (New York, NY: Random House, Inc., The Modern Library, 1942), 420.

[507] Tacitus, Histories 1:11, 425.

[508] Philip Carrington, 230.

[509] Flavius Josephus, *Wars,* 4:10:2.

"Many have suggested that the wound of the whole beast may refer to the anarchy of A.D. 69 which followed Nero's death, the year of the four emperors (Galba, Otho, Vitellius, Vespasian), and the healing to the accession of Vespasian.... Only with the accession of Vespasian did the monster come to life again."[512] F.F. Bruce adds, "Rome, they thought, was on the verge of destruction by civil warfare; the empire was about to break up."[513]

We are told that **his fatal wound was healed (13:3)**. The healing of the Beast, Rome, came about in the form of the Roman general Vespasian putting an end to the civil and foreign wars and bringing stability again to the Roman government at a time when most had given up hope that the empire would survive. Josephus puts this healing this way, "So upon his confirmation of Vespasian's entire government, ... and upon the <u>unexpected deliverance of the public affaires of the Romans from ruin</u>...."[514]

13:4 ...they worshiped the dragon because he gave his authority to the beast; and they worshiped the beast, saying, "Who is like the beast, and who is able to wage war with him?" Again, after these seven reigned, the Empire revived under Vespasian. His power, and that of his son Titus, in establishing himself in Rome and destroying his enemies in Judea (**who is able to wage war with him? (13:4)**) amazed all. The result was that Rome became stronger than ever and all **worshiped the beast (13:4)**, except Christians.

13:5-6 There was given to him a mouth speaking arrogant words and blasphemies, and authority to act for forty-two months was given to him. 6 And he opened his mouth in blasphemies against God, to blaspheme His name and His tabernacle, that is, those who dwell in heaven. The **blasphemies (13:5)** of the Roman Empire are seen 1) in it its treatment of God's

---

[510] Ibid., *Wars*, 4:11:5.

[511] Ibid., *Wars*, 7:4:2.

[512] J. Massyngberde Ford, 221.

[513] F.F. Bruce, <u>Israel & the Nation</u>, 224.

[514] Flavius Josephus, *Wars*, 4:11:5.

tabernacle (13:6) in Jerusalem, 2) its treatment of His Church, and 3) in the titles of deity and worship they required of the citizens of Rome.

In this verse, the Majority Text (MT) reads *and he was given authority to make war for forty-two months (13:5)*. "Note the passive "was given" or "allowed," that is, by the dragon with God's tolerance, for nothing can happen outside the divine plan."[515] There is a limit to the Beast's authority.

> *And I saw the beast and the kings of the earth and their armies*
> *assembled to make war against Him who sat on the horse and*
> *against His army. And the beast was seized, and with him the*
> *false prophet who performed the signs in his presence, by which*
> *he deceived those who had received the mark of the beast and*
> *those who worshiped his image; these two were thrown alive into*
> *the lake of fire which burns with brimstone. (Revelation 19:19-20,*
> *NASB95)*

As for the *forty-two months (13:5)*, "...it is interesting that Nero's persecution of the Church did in fact last a full 42 months, from the middle of November 64 to the beginning of June 68. This period of 42 months thus corresponds (but is not necessarily identical) to the 42 months/1,260 days of 11:2-3 and the 'time, times, and half time' of 12:14."[516]

13:7 It was also given to him to make war with the saints and to overcome them, and authority over every tribe and people and tongue and nation was given to him. The phrase **make war with the saints (13:7)** tells us these comments are not in reference to apostate Judea but refer to the Church instead, *the saints (13:7)*. Daniel chapter 7 covers Rome and the point before us. Especially notice verse 21.

> *Then I desired to know the exact meaning of the fourth beast,*
> *which was different from all the others, exceedingly dreadful,*
> *with its teeth of iron and its claws of bronze, and which devoured,*
> *crushed and trampled down the remainder with its feet, ²⁰ and the*
> *meaning of the ten horns that were on its head and the other horn*

---

[515] J. Massyngberde Ford, 212.

[516] Steve Gregg, 290.

which came up, and before which three of them fell, namely, that horn which had eyes and a mouth uttering great boasts and which was larger in appearance than its associates. ²¹ *"I kept looking, and that horn was waging war with the saints and overpowering them* ²² *until the Ancient of Days came and judgement was passed in favor of the saints of the Highest One, and the time arrived when the saints took possession of the kingdom.* ²³ *"Thus he said: 'The fourth beast will be a fourth kingdom on the earth, which will be different from all the other kingdoms and will devour the whole earth and tread it down and crush it.* ²⁴ *'As for the ten horns, out of this kingdom ten kings will arise; and another will arise after them, and he will be different from the previous ones and will subdue three kings.* ²⁵ *'He will speak out against the Most High and wear down the saints of the Highest One, and he will intend to make alterations in times and in law; and they will be given into his hand for a time, times, and half a time.* ²⁶ *'But the court will sit for judgement, and his dominion will be taken away, annihilated and destroyed forever.* ²⁷ *'Then the sovereignty, the dominion and the greatness of all the kingdoms under the whole heaven will be given to the people of the saints of the Highest One; His kingdom will be an everlasting kingdom, and all the dominions will serve and obey Him.' (Daniel 7:19-27, NASB95)*

Rome expanded its empire till it did have power over **every tribe and people and tongue and nation (13:7)**. Under the providence of God, Rome was given power to persecute the Church. Rome did **make war with the saints (13:7)** and did **overcome them (13:7)** for a time.

The Roman historian Tacitus gives us some detail on how the Beast made **war with the saints (13:7)**.

Consequently, to get rid of the report, Nero fastened the guilt and inflicted the most exquisite tortures on a class hated for their abominations, called Christians by the populace. Christus, from whom the name had its origin, suffered the extreme penalty during the reign of Tiberius at the hands of one of our procurators, Pontius Pilatus, and a most mischievous superstition, thus checked for the moment, again broke out not only in Judaea, the first source of the evil, but even in Rome, where all things hideous and shameful from every part of the world find their center and become popular. Accordingly, an arrest was first made of all who pleaded guilty; then, upon their information, <u>an immense multitude was convicted</u>, not so much of the crime of firing the city, as of hatred against mankind. Mockery of every sort was added to their deaths. Covered with the skins of beasts, they were torn by dogs and perished, or were nailed to crosses, or were doomed to the flames and burnt, to serve as a nightly illumination, when daylight had expired. Nero offered his gardens for the spectacle, and was exhibiting a show in the circus, while he mingled with the people in the dress of a charioteer or stood aloft on a car. Hence, even for criminals who deserved extreme and exemplary punishment, there arose a feeling of compassion; for it was not, as it seemed, for the public good, but to glut one man's cruelty, that they were being destroyed.[517]

13:8 *All who dwell on the earth [land] will worship him, everyone whose name has not been written from the foundation of the world in the book of life of the Lamb who has been slain.* The word **earth [land] (13:8)** either refers to the known earth of the period of the Roman Empire, or to the land of Israel.

We see a similar statement in Luke 2:1 referring to the Roman Empire. *"And it came to pass in those days, that there went out a decree from Caesar Augustus, that <u>all the world</u> should be taxed."* The entire Roman world is what is taxed. And all in this Roman world, except believers, do worship the emperor. The salvation of each soul has been determined from all eternity, **the foundation of the world (13:8)**, because God has elected his people from all eternity.

> *...He chose us in Him before the foundation of the world, that we would be holy and blameless before Him. (Ephesians 1:4, NASB95)*

13:9 *If anyone has an ear, let him hear.* This phrase makes reference to what is about to be said, not what was just said. It is our equivalent to using underlining, Italics or bold type in the text to follow.

---

[517] Tacitus, Annals 15:44.

13:10 *If anyone is destined for captivity, to captivity he goes; if anyone kills with the sword, with the sword he must be killed. Here is the perseverance and the faith of the saints.* John takes these ideas from Jeremiah 15.

Jerusalem had defied God and had brought judgement on itself. So much so that God says that even if Moses and Samuel pleaded their cause it would do no good. In response, the people of Jerusalem ask Jeremiah where they might go since God had rejected them. Jeremiah answers by saying,

> *Thus says the Lord: Those destined for death, to death; and those destined for the sword, to the sword; and those destined for famine, to famine; and those destined for captivity, to captivity. (Jeremiah 15:2, NASB95)*

One of the complaints of Rome after Christianity came to power was that before Christianity, when Rome worshiped the idols of their pagan past, they were strong and powerful. Now they suffered attacks from every part of their empire. They believed that the Christians were to be blamed for these failures. However, in fact, it was God who was dealing treacherously with the Roman beast for their persecution of His Church.

> *Woe to thee that spoilest, and thou wast not spoiled; and dealest treacherously, and they dealt not treacherously with thee! When thou shalt cease to spoil, thou shalt be spoiled; and when thou shalt make an end to deal treacherously, they shall deal treacherously with thee. (Isaiah 33:1, NASB95)*

Here Isaiah refers to the nations around Jerusalem that dealt treacherously with Judah. They might temporarily succeed in their evil purpose, but shortly "*they shall deal treacherously with thee.*" So it was with Rome. They have dealt treacherously with Jerusalem. Soon God will deal treacherously with them. It is they who will be killed by the sword and go into captivity.

This very special message was meant to give comfort to the Church, **here is the perseverance and the faith of the saints (13:10)**. "Awareness of the fact that it is God's will that many of them be imprisoned and slain calls for endurance and faith on their part."⁵¹⁸ Their torment would be short and those that tormented them would surely be paid back in turn.

The Beast out of the Land

13:11   Then I saw another beast coming up out of the earth [land]; and he had two horns like a lamb and he spoke as a dragon. The use of the phrase ***the earth [land] (13:11)*** tells us that this beast is homegrown, unlike the beast out of the sea (or the Gentile world), which is Rome. "...the phrase *the land*, as used by the writers of Scripture and especially the prophets, often refers to the promised land; i.e., the land of Palestine...." ⁵¹⁹ "...'land' is synonymous with Israel in Jewish writings."⁵²⁰

The fact that he had ***two horns (13:11)*** and not ten indicates his subordinate relationship to the first beast. A horn is representative of power. The first beast had much power, the second only a limited amount. In addition, the ***two horns (13:11)*** are ***like a lamb (13:11)***, and unlike the leopard, bear and lion of the first beast, the lamb disarms his audience. The ***lamb (13:11)*** is an animal of peace; he appears to be harmless. But this lamb is a fraud for he speaks like ***a dragon (13:11)***; that is, he acts with evil and violence.

"The appearance of the land-monster is very subtle. Inspired by the concept of Behemoth and conscious of the fact that that which is from the land is a 'home product,' the author shows the merging of the two forces, the Roman Empire and the apostate Jews. The alliance will appear all the more dramatically in the picture of the harlot. The land-monster is a 'wolf in sheep's clothing....' "⁵²¹

13:12   He exercises all the authority of the first beast in his presence. And he makes the earth [land] and those who dwell in it to worship the first beast, whose fatal wound was healed. This second beast has little authority in his own right, but he acts with great authority for he serves ***the first beast (13:12)*** and obtains his ***authority***

⁵¹⁸ Robert G. Bratcher, Rev. 13:10.

⁵¹⁹ J. E. Leonard, Come Out of Her My People, 97.

⁵²⁰ J. Massyngberde Ford, 212.

⁵²¹ Ibid., 223.

(13:12) from him. His job is one of **worship (13:12)**. This beast is identified in chapter 19 of Revelation as the false prophet. He serves a religious purpose. "Satan, the Primal Serpent, has his Messiah, who is himself incarnate; he must also have his Prophet. Pseudo-prophets were expected as well as Pseudo-christs."[522]

> *And the beast was seized, and with him the false prophet who performed the signs in his presence, by which he deceived those who had received the mark of the beast and those who worshiped his image; these two were thrown alive into the lake of fire which burns with brimstone. (Revelation 19:20, NASB95)*

In his insistence on **worship (13:12)**, the beast brings the people of God into conflict with this religious system.

This phrase, **whose fatal wound was healed (13:12)** refers us back to 13:3 and helps us ascertain even more surely the identity of the beast out of the sea. That beast is certainly the Roman Empire, which received the fatal wound.

13:13 He performs great signs, so that he even makes fire come down out of heaven to the earth [land] in the presence of men. It is always the nature of false religion to certify itself with signs and wonders. Elijah called the bluff of this religious crowd by challenging them to a contest of power with the understanding that *"the God who answers by fire, He is God"* (I Kings 18:24). However, Elijah knowing that they were tricksters and powerless to perform true miracles, warns them in the preparation of their sacrifice to *"put no fire under it"* (I Kings 18:23). These priests of the Emperor cult are guilty of the same subterfuge. No real miracle takes place. Christ had warned about this crowd during His sermon on this very period.

> *For false Christ's and false prophets will arise and will show great signs and wonders, so as to mislead, if possible, even the elect. (Matthew 24:24, NASB95)*

---

[522] Philip Carrington, 231.

"...few oriental religions were without ingenious illusions of this kind; talking images and fire from heaven were common enough, and they were expected by the Jews at the coming of Antichrist."[523]

13:14   And he deceives those who dwell on the earth [land] because of the signs which it was given him to perform in the presence of the beast, telling those who dwell on the earth [land] to make an image to the beast who had the wound of the sword and has come to life. As Christ had warned earlier, so Paul also warned of this crowd during his ministry saying:

> *...the one whose coming is in accord with the activity of Satan, with all power and signs and false wonders, and with all the deception of wickedness for those who perish, because they did not receive the love of the truth so as to be saved. For this reason God will send upon them a deluding influence so that they will believe what is false, in order that they all may be judged who did not believe the truth, but took pleasure in wickedness. (2 Thessalonians 2:9-12, NASB95)*

Again, the phrase **who had the wound of the sword and has come to life (13:14)** identifies who this land beast images; it is Rome. See 13:3 above.

...to make an image to the beast who had the wound of the sword and has come to life (13:14). What was this image? A.T. Robinson suggest one possibility, "This *image*...of the emperor could be his head upon a coin...an image painted or woven upon a standard, a bust in metal or stone, a statue, anything that people could be asked to bow down before and worship."[524]

13:15   And it was given to him to give breath to the image of the beast, so that the image of the beast would even speak and cause as many as do not worship the image of the beast to be killed. At this point another miraculous scene is accredited to the false prophets of the first beast. It is the power to animate the image of the beast

---

[523] Ibid., 232.

[524] Archibald Thomas Robertson, Vol. VI, 404.

with speech. The purpose of this fraud is to cause the populace to worship the image of the beast. A failure to do so results in death.

This type of religious fraud was as common then as is fraud in many faith healing services today. The ancients were knowledgeable of the magic arts and trickery, and used them in the service of evil. The book of Acts gives us a small taste of this phenomenon.

> Now there was a man named Simon, who formerly was practicing magic in the city and astonishing the people of Samaria, claiming to be someone great.... (Acts 8:99, NASB95)

> But Elymas the magician (for so his name is translated) was opposing them, seeking to turn the proconsul away from the faith. (Acts 13:8, NASB95)

> It happened that as we were going to the place of prayer, a slave-girl having a spirit of divination met us, who was bringing her masters much profit by fortune-telling. (Acts 16:16, NASB95)

> And many of those who practiced magic brought their books together and began burning them in the sight of everyone; and they counted up the price of them and found it fifty thousand pieces of silver. (Acts 19:19, NASB95)

We read in one early account of Simon Magus a boast, "I have flown through the air; I have been mixed with fire, and been made one body with it; I have made statues move; I have animated lifeless things."[525] So here in this story, we see here either the actual fulfillment of this prophecy in early Church history, or something very much like it. "The superstition of talking and moving statues was widespread at this time.... Ventriloquism or a hidden operator explains the phenomenon."[526]

13:16 And he causes all, the small and the great, and the rich and the poor, and the free men and the slaves, to be given a mark on their right hand or on their forehead.... A mark

---

[525] Milton S. Terry, Biblical Apocalyptics, 400.

[526] J. Massyngberde Ford, 225.

(13:16) would show ownership and was common in ancient history. This was not unlike the branding of cattle that is a familiar picture to us today. Branding just this very way in years past marked slaves. "Animals and slaves were often branded with the owner's name...."[527]

In the Scripture we find a similar marking of slaves. If a slave had served out his time and was to be released, he could petition the master to keep him on as a permanent slave and part of the household. If this was acceptable to the master...

> *...then his master shall bring him to God, then he shall bring him to the door or the doorpost. And his master shall pierce his ear with an awl; and he shall serve him permanently.... (Exodus 21:6, NASB95)*

Often the pierced ear was filled with an earring as well. In fact, in the ancient world nose rings and earrings were signs of being under authority to another. This practice seems to have had its origin in the nose ring of a bull. The large ring, in the very sensitive area of the nose, allowed the difficult animal to be controlled without much effort. The ring demonstrated that he was under submission or authority to another. Women and slaves, who were also under submission or authority to others, commonly wore nose and ear rings as well.

In addition to slaves, soldiers often branded themselves with symbols to show they were loyal to their commander or general. This brand or tattoo was worn as a badge of honor, especially if the legion or general were famous for their achievements.

Certain religions followed this practice as well. For instance, certain Hindus wear a red dot on their forehead testifying to their religious practice and commitment. This type of marking is forbidden in Scripture.

> *You shall not make any cuts in your body for the dead nor make any tattoo marks on yourselves: I am the Lord. (Leviticus 19:28, NASB95)*

---

[527] Archibald Thomas Robertson, Vol. VI, 405.

However, there was one type of mark or cutting that was required in the Old Testament and that was the mark of circumcision.

> *...and he received the sign of circumcision, a seal of the*
> *righteousness of the faith which he had while uncircumcised, so*
> *that he might be the father of all who believe without being*
> *circumcised, that righteousness might be credited to them....*
> *(Romans 4:11, NASB95)*

In the New Testament circumcision is replaced by baptism which has the same purpose in identifying the person as belonging to God. Notice that our baptismal formula says that we are baptized into the name of the Father, Son and Holy Spirit. We are marked spiritually with His name.

The point to note here is that a person is identified as a servant of another by means of marks associated with his or her body, even invisible ones as in baptism. But the mark is there because God places one on His children. He can see it.

> *Nevertheless, the firm foundation of God stands, having this <u>seal</u>,*
> *"The Lord knows those who are His," and, "Everyone who names*
> *the name of the Lord is to abstain from wickedness." (2 Timothy*
> *2:19, NASB95)*

And indeed that sums up the purpose of the mark; it identifies a person with his or her master. God does that, and so does Satan. The devil's mark is on his children just as surely as God's is on His family. This is not the first time we read of a seal or mark on the forehead. In Revelation 7:3 we read:

> *Do not harm the earth [land] or the sea or the trees until we have*
> *sealed the bond-servants of our God on their foreheads.*
> *(Revelation 7:3, NASB95)*

Their seal, as children of God, identifies them as bondservants of God. And as we stated, the sons and daughters of Satan are also identified. "In our present passage the marking of those who worshiped the beast is a blasphemous parody of the protective sealing of the faithful in Rev 7:1-3."[528]

---

528 J. Massyngberde Ford, 215.

Then another angel, a third one, followed them, saying with a loud voice, "If anyone worships the beast and his image, and receives a mark on his forehead or on his hand, 10 he also will drink of the wine of the wrath of God, which is mixed in full strength in the cup of His anger; and he will be tormented with fire and brimstone in the presence of the holy angels and in the presence of the Lamb. 11 And the smoke of their torment goes up forever and ever; they have no rest day and night, those who worship the beast and his image, and whoever receives the mark of his name." (Revelation 14:9-11, NASB95)

13:17 ...and he provides that no one will be able to buy or to sell, except the one who has the mark, either the name of the beast or the number of his name. Now we know that the bondservants of God received a mark or seal visible only in the spiritual world. These received a similar mark visible only in the spiritual world. The reason for noting that the mark was placed on the *forehead (13:17)* and **hand (13:17)** was to make the point that they were servants in *thought* and *deed.*

We also notice that the Old Testament instructs the believer to identify himself with God and His Word through the means of the hand and head, which symbolizes his deeds and thoughts.

You shall bind them as a sign on your <u>hand</u> and they shall be as frontals on your <u>forehead</u>. (Deuteronomy 6:8, NASB95)

You shall therefore impress these words of mine on your heart and on your soul; and you shall bind them as a sign on your <u>hand</u>, and they shall be as frontals on your <u>forehead</u>. (Deuteronomy 11:18, NASB95)

In addition, we know that those that sacrificed to the Roman god's did receive a "receipt" from the officiating authority proving their loyalty to Rome and Caesar in faith (thought) and behavior (deed). This would have been the visible sign of another and invisible one placed by Satan. One thing is certain, without the receipt or mark one could not buy or sell. "...official certificates of loyalty were issued to those who had complied with the law and taken part in the ritual of the imperial religion. These certificates form an apt parallel to the 'mark of the beast....' "[529] And whose name would have been on the receipt? Remember, the mark is a name. It would be the name of Caesar Nero.

"Revelation 13 makes the point that there can be no compromise. Those who choose to appease the beast will be marked for his possession. They will be more successful in the world's terms that those who refuse the mark for, as Jesus put it, no person can serve both God and materialism (Matt. 6:24). But the inestimable cost of such a choice is exclusion from the covenant."[530]

13:18 Here is wisdom. Let him who has understanding calculate the number of the beast, for the number is that of a man; and his number is six hundred and sixty-six. The **beast (13:18)** referred to here is the first beast mentioned, the beast out of the sea, Rome. This beast has a number that is calculated from the name **of a man (13:18)** "...which excludes demonic beings, philosophical systems, political movements or empires, or anything other than a specific, individual, human person."[531] The number calculated from that name is **six hundred and sixty-six (13:18)**. It is not six, six, six and it does not refer to social security cards, bar codes, or mailing addresses. It refers to a man's name. And this would be a man the readers of John's letter would know!

This number is the object of more eschatological nonsense than perhaps any other part of Scripture. It has been applied to most every person of significance in western history, all foolishly so. The amazing thing is, there are really few possibilities for this number, in reality only one, and that is the Emperor Nero.

One of the major evidences for identifying the beast with Nero is this information about *the number of his name* (v.17). John obviously did not expect his readers, who had *understanding* (v.18) to have any difficulty in identifying the beast, since they

---

[529] W. M. Ramsey, 79.

[530] J. E. Leonard, Come Out of Her My People, 107.

[531] R. C. Sproul, The Last Days According to Jesus, 185.

could simply calculate the meaning of this cryptogram. Using English characters, the Hebrew form of "Caesar Nero" is Nrwn Qsr (pronounced "Neron Kaiser"). The value of the seven Hebrew letters is 50, 200, 6, 50, 100, 60, and 200, respectively. The total is thus 666.[532]

And again we read, "A surprising unanimity is found among commentators who have adopted this method; the name is NERON KAISAR (the Greek form of it) and the letters are given their Hebrew values...."[533]

Interestingly, many somewhat defective early manuscripts have the number 616 instead of 666 in this passage. Now the question arises, what solution to this two number tradition could explain both numbers? Carrington says of Neron Kaisar, "This also satisfies a reading found in some Latin authorities, 616; for the Latin way of spelling the name is NERO CAESAR; and the omission of the second Nun gives a total of 616."[534] In essence, the copyist, knowing the answer to be Nero, but not understanding Hebrew or really understanding how the number 666 got there, simply put in the number that provided what he knew to be the correct answer, Nero. I don't know of another solution that explains both 666 and 616. This is a rather decisive point and therefore powerful testimony that the proper answer is indeed Nero. As Bruce M. Metzger says, "Perhaps the change was intentional, seeing that the Greek form Neron Caesar written in Hebrew characters (*nrwn qsr*) is equivalent to 666, whereas the Latin form Nero Caesar (*nrw qsr*) is equivalent to 616."[535]

Obviously, there was a rather significant element of political subversion in naming the reigning Emperor a satanic beast, so the writer had to be careful. However, the readers were expected to be able to figure out this simple code. Of course the Latin/Greek readers would be mystified by it, for it was a Latin name transliterated into Hebrew letters and the number calculated using these Hebrews letters, but the message is given to the reader in Greek. But the Hebrew/Greek readers would easily decipher it, and no doubt they did. Remember, the very early Church were primarily Hebrews who spoke Greek. The beast was clearly Nero.

---

[532] Steve Gregg, 302.

[533] Philip Carrington, 234.

[534] Ibid., 235.

[535] Bruce M. Metzger, <u>A Textual Commentary on the Greek New Testament</u> (Stuttgart: United Bible Societies, 1975), 750.

Chapter 14

The Lamb and the 144,000 on Mount Zion

The Lamb and the 144,000 on Mount Zion

In chapter 13, we read of the beast and his terror upon the people of God. In chapter 16, we read about the judgement of the bowls. But unexpectedly in chapters 14 and 15, we are admitted to heavenly scenes. Why?

> John was writing to Christians who were having their daily trials and temptations. The allurements of heathen immorality were before their eyes every day; the threat of bodily harm, and the pressure of economic privation were goading them to give up their virtue and their faith. These scenes of heaven and the happiness of the redeemed were to show that God had better things to bestow than the world could afford. These scenes were for the moral effect, and the spiritual incentive to the tempted, persecuted, struggling church.[536]

14:1 Then I looked, and behold, the Lamb was standing on Mount Zion, and with Him one hundred and forty-four thousand, having His name and the name of His Father written on their foreheads. The **Lamb (14:1)** is of course Jesus Christ. In the last chapter we had another lamb, a fraud, the false prophet who gave his service to the beast. Perhaps you have seen or heard of old the TV program, *What's My Line?*, that concluded with the statement, "Will the real John Doe please stand up." This is the real **Lamb (14:1)**, and He is **standing (14:1)** up!

The **Mount Zion (14:1)** mentioned here is the eternal Zion found in Heaven. Jerusalem in general and the Temple mount area in particular were the original **Mount Zion (14:1)**. However, in Revelation, and much

---

536 David S. Clark, 94.

of the New Testament, **Mount Zion (14:1)**, is now in heaven. "The *Mount Zion* is here to be understood as the heavenly Zion, the seat of the new Jerusalem which is above, and which is our mother (Gal. 4:26)."[537] The earthly one is under the ban, or curse, by God and is under siege by the Romans. The heavenly original is, however, the place of this meeting and worship. The writer of the book of Hebrews has this same heavenly Jerusalem, or **Mount Zion (14:1)**, in mind in his book. Paul does as well in Galatians.

> But you have come to Mount Zion and to the city of the living God, the heavenly Jerusalem, and to myriads of angels...." (Hebrews 12:22, NASB95)

> But you have come to Mount Zion and to the city of the living God, the heavenly Jerusalem, and to myriads of angels.... (Hebrews 12:22, NASB95)

> But the Jerusalem above is free; she is our mother. (Galatians 4:26, NASB95)

The next question deals with the identity of this **one hundred and forty-four thousand (14:1)**. Are they the same as those in chapter 7? Those in chapter 7 are clearly Jewish Christians that have been sealed for physical protection during the tribulation that is coming upon the whole land of Israel. We have in chapter 7 a great multitude of Jewish believers marked by God that the death angel might pass over them.

This group in chapter 14, however, appears to have sealed their testimony with their blood. They are sealed for eternal salvation, but not from martyrdom. "...they represented the select company of martyrs, purchased by the blood of martyrdom, and having been redeemed from the earth they therefore belong to heaven where they had been caught up unto God."[538] They are standing with Christ in the heavenly Zion singing songs of victory. Who exactly are they? They are martyrs from the gentile church of the first century. They are identified with the phrase **one hundred and forty-four thousand (14:1)**, which in chapter 7 refers to Israel, because that

---

[537] Milton S. Terry, Biblical Apocalyptics, 403.

[538] Foy E. Wallace, Jr., 306.

term makes a critical point generally missed in twentieth century evangelical Christianity, that is this; Christians are *the Israel of God*.

> *And those who will walk by this rule, peace and mercy be upon them, and upon the Israel of God. (Galatians 6:16, NASB95)*

Here a critical term, 144,000, is used to connect God's people from the Jewish community with God's people from the gentile world. The twelve times twelve in each case makes the point that all God's people are marked for eternal security, and in the case of chapter 7, earthly protection during the tribulation. So, "they are also a special group: the Remnant-Church of the first generation."[539]

The phrase **having His name and the name of His Father written on their foreheads (14:1)** is not something that can be seen by earthly eyes, just as the mark of the beast could not necessarily be seen by earthly eyes.

> *Nevertheless, the firm foundation of God stands, having this seal, "The Lord knows those who are His...." (2 Timothy 2:19, NASB95)*

As Paul said, *The Lord knows those who are His*, because they are sealed with His own name, as Satan knows his children, because they are sealed with his evil mark.

No doubt you have heard of cults like the Jehovah's Witnesses who identify themselves as *the* 144,000. Although there are hundreds, even thousands, of errors in the teachings of these cults, the great error here is to take this passage out of the context of the first century and make it apply to distant peoples and ages not even remotely considered by the Apostle John. Dispensationalists do the very same thing. Once Revelation is removed from its historical context and original audience, you can make it say anything you want.

---

[539] David Chilton, The Great Tribulation, 355.

14:2 And I heard a voice from heaven, like the sound of many waters and like the sound of loud thunder, and the voice which I heard was like the sound of harpists playing on their harps. One author describes this **voice from heaven (14:2)** saying, "In the perfection of rhythm it was as the flowing of many waters; in the mighty volume it was as the peal of great thunders; in the sweetness of melody, it was as if it were attuned to the strings of an hundred and forty-four thousand harps."[540]

14:3 And they sang a new song before the throne and before the four living creatures and the elders; and no one could learn the song except the one hundred and forty-four thousand who had been purchased from the earth [land]. Why is it **no one (14:3)** in heaven could **learn (14:3)** this **song (14:3)**? "That no one could learn their song was doubtless because it was the song of redemption; the angels might look with admiration and wonder on the work of redemption, but they have no experience of it. They can never sing: 'for he hath redeemed us by his blood.' The redeemed can sing a song that the angels cannot sing."[541]

14:4 These are the ones who have not been defiled with women, for they have kept themselves chaste. These are the ones who follow the Lamb wherever He goes. These have been purchased from among men as first fruits to God and to the Lamb. There is little question that this **chaste (14:4)** condition refers to spiritual chastity. "That these pious ... are called 'virgins' (chaste) indicates nothing about their marital status. Scripture nowhere extols celibacy as a superior virtue. In fact, the Apocalypse represents the spotless Lamb himself in terms of marriage a few chapters later. Their virginity is purely spiritual ... bespeaking their fidelity and faithfulness to God."[542] "Fornication and harlotry, throughout the Bible, are potent metaphors for apostasy and idolatry...while religious fidelity is called chastity...."[543] "To go a whoring after other gods, is an idea too common in the O. Testament, and

---

[540] Foy E. Wallace, Jr., 307.

[541] David S. Clark, 94.

[542] Jay E. Adams, <u>The Time is at Hand</u>, 74.

[543] David Chilton, <u>The Great Tribulation</u>, 356.

too familiar, to need explanation."[544] This army of believers has not whored after other gods; they have kept themselves from idolatry, especially from the worship of the beast; they are spiritually chaste.

The use of sexual terms might also allude to the immoral religious practices of heathens in Israel and the Mediterranean world. "...these verses may refer to men who have not polluted themselves with women in the sexual rites practiced in the heathen temples such as those at Ephesus...."[545] However, it clearly does not refer to marriage. "The use of this word [*defiled (14:4)*] rules out marriage, which was not considered sinful."[546]

To *follow the Lamb (14:4)* has consequence and often, on this earth, very negative ones. "...they have rushed into danger when duty called, and they have resisted all the allurements of the world to separate them from him."[547]

> *For you have been called for this purpose, since Christ also suffered for you, leaving you an example for you to follow in His steps.... (1 Peter 2:21, NASB95)*

These that *have been purchased from among men (14:4)* are not simply those that were saved first, but those that were martyred first in the history of the church. There are those in the Church today that see this event as yet future, more than two thousand years after these words were spoken. Apparently they believe this passage is about the rapture and these *first fruits (14:4)* are those that are raptured first, compared to others who will not be raptured until after the millennium. How well Adams puts it when he says, "How artificial to twist 'first fruits' into the very *last* fruits of the Christian era!"[548] The Dispensationalists want to make these believers, here called the *first fruits (14:4)*, those that are raptured 2,000 or more years after this was spoken. Of course, this is another of the many indicators and proofs that this book was written for and about the early church. The *first fruits (14:4)* have long ago been harvested through martyrdom and presented to God. They were truly *first fruits (14:4)* not

---

[544] Moses Stuart, vol. II, 293.

[545] J. Massyngberde Ford, 337-340.

[546] Archibald Thomas Robertson, Vol. VI, 409.

[547] Moses Stuart, vol. II, 294.

[548] Jay E. Adams, <u>The Time is at Hand</u>, 74.

last fruits. For this reason they cannot be Jehovah's Witnesses, Seventh Day Adventist or Dispensational Premillennialists, all of which, if even believers, would be far closer to last fruits than first fruits.

14:5 And no lie was found in their mouth; they are blameless. The great sin of those with the mark of the beast is the idolatrous worship of a created being. With their mouths they ascribe power and majesty and glory to this creature. Such praise and worship is a *lie (14:5)*. Those with God's name on their forehead do not so lie.

> *Professing to be wise, they became fools, and exchanged the glory of the incorruptible God for an image in the form of corruptible man and of birds and four-footed animals and crawling creatures. Therefore God gave them over in the lusts of their hearts to impurity, so that their bodies would be dishonored among them. 25 For they exchanged the truth of God for a lie, and worshiped and served the creature rather than the Creator, who is blessed forever. Amen. (Romans 1:22-25, NASB95)*

Vision of the Angel with the Gospel

14:6 And I saw another angel flying in midheaven, having an eternal gospel to preach to those who live on the earth [land], and to every nation and tribe and tongue and people.... The word, *gospel (14:6)*, means "good news" and it has been questioned whether this gospel is the good news that God is judging the beast and his allies, or is this the gospel of Christ?

Those in favor of the former position note that an angel preaches this gospel not a man. Presumably, angels cannot preach the gospel of Christ. In addition, Christ and his death, burial and resurrection are missing from the message.

Those in favor of the latter position point out that the word *eternal (14:6)* here suggests the everlasting gospel of Christ, not a temporal judgement.

We notice that this gospel is first preached to those who live on the *earth (14:6)* or in the *land (14:6)*, that is, Israel. Next, it is preached *to every nation and tribe and tongue and people (14:6)*, that is, the rest of the known world of that day. In fact, this is the very order of gospel preaching that Christ gave his disciples, first Israel, then the rest of the world.

> *...but you will receive power when the Holy Spirit has come upon you; and you shall be My witnesses both in Jerusalem, and in all Judea and Samaria, and even to the remotest part of the earth. (Acts 1:8, NASB95)*

This passage has another point of significance to make. Christ taught that the "end," i.e. judgement on Israel, would not come until the gospel had been effectively preached in this manner.

> *This gospel of the kingdom shall be preached in the whole world as a testimony to all the nations, and then the end will come. (Matthew 24:14, NASB95)*

This end "had reference to the end of the Jewish state...."[549] However, many use this verse as proof that the material of Matthew 24 is for a time yet future. They say that the gospel has not been preached in such a way as to fulfill Matthew 24:14. Yet, this passage in Revelation indicates that Matthew 24 was fulfilled in the first century. Several other passages in the New Testament make the same point.

> *First, I thank my God through Jesus Christ for you all, because your faith is being proclaimed <u>throughout the whole world</u>. (Romans 1:8, NASB95)*

> *...because of the hope laid up for you in heaven, of which you previously heard in the word of truth, the gospel which has come to you, <u>just as in all the world</u> also it is constantly bearing fruit and increasing, even as it has been doing in you also since the day you heard of it and understood the grace of God in truth.... (Colossians 1:5-6, NASB95)*

> *...if indeed you continue in the faith firmly established and steadfast, and not moved away from the hope of the gospel that you have heard, <u>which was proclaimed in all creation under</u>*

---

549 Foy E. Wallace, Jr., 308.

> <u>heaven</u>, *and of which I, Paul, was made a minister. (Colossians 1:23, NASB95)*

You may ask how the gospel reached such extremes so quickly. First, note that we know little of the ministries of most of the Apostles. How far their ministries led them, we simply do not know, but indications are they reached India and perhaps even China. Second, take note of those who heard the gospel preached on that first Pentecost after Christ's resurrection.

> *Now there were Jews living in Jerusalem, devout men from every nation under heaven. 6 And when this sound occurred, the crowd came together, and were bewildered because each one of them was hearing them speak in his own language. 7 They were amazed and astonished, saying, "Why, are not all these who are speaking Galileans? 8 "And how is it that we each hear them in our own language to which we were born? 9 "Parthians and Medes and Elamites, and residents of Mesopotamia, Judea and Cappadocia, Pontus and Asia, 10 Phrygia and Pamphylia, Egypt and the districts of Libya around Cyrene, and visitors from Rome, both Jews and proselytes, 11 Cretans and Arabs—we hear them in our own tongues speaking of the mighty deeds of God. (Acts 2:5-8, NASB95)*

Notice, for instance, that the city of Rome is on this list. An Apostle did not evangelize Rome. Paul wrote them his famed letter before he or any other Apostle ever visited them. Those who responded in faith to Peter's gospel message at Pentecost evangelized Rome. Certainly all the nations listed likewise had the gospel witness quickly imparted to them by the recent converts of Peter's preaching. So the gospel was truly preached **to every nation and tribe and tongue and people (14:6)** in the forty years after Christ resurrection and then the "end" came, the destruction of Jerusalem, just as Christ said.

Next we have the content of this gospel message. As indicated, it does not directly mention Christ's life, death, burial and resurrection, the major points of the gospel message. However, let us look at what it does mention.

***14:7** ...and he said with a loud voice, "Fear God, and give Him glory, because the hour of His judgement has come; worship Him who made the heaven and the earth [land] and sea and springs of waters."* **Fear God (14:7):** Mary, speaking of the Christ said,

> *And His mercy is upon generation after generation / Toward those who fear Him. (Luke 1:50, NASB95)*

Christ, speaking of Himself said,

> *But I will warn you whom to fear: fear the One who, after He has killed, has authority to cast into hell; yes, I tell you, fear Him! (Luke 12:5, NASB95)*

Give Him glory (14:7): After one of Christ' miracles,

> *But when the crowds saw this, they were awestruck, and glorified God, who had given such authority to men. (Matthew 9:8, NASB95)*

The hour of His judgement has come (14:7): When Jesus foretold His death He said,

> *Now judgement is upon this world; now the ruler of this world will be cast out. (John 12:31, NASB95)*

Worship Him who made the heaven and the earth and sea and springs of waters (14:7): Paul preached a similar message and said,

> *... We are also men of the same nature as you, and preach the gospel to you that you should turn from these vain things to a living God, who made the heaven and the earth and the sea and all that is in them. (Acts 14:15, NASB95)*

So, it is not impossible to see that this is the Christian gospel told in broad outlines. Yet, it is more likely that this is the "good news" of the coming judgement on God enemies.

14:8 *And another angel, a second one, followed, saying, "Fallen, fallen is Babylon the great, she who has made all the nations drink of the wine of the passion of her immorality."* This brings us to an important question, who is this **Babylon (14:8)** that is *fallen (14:8)*? Two possibilities exist. One, it is Jerusalem. Two, it is Rome. Each has solid defenders. However, a careful study of chapter 17 appears to make the case for Jerusalem as the Babylon of Revelation. "... this great city is no other than Jerusalem, the murderer of prophets, full of hypocrisy and extortion and all uncleanness, the hold of a generation of vipers, and drunken with the superstition and spiritual idolatry and schemes of world power."[550] We will deal with this subject in greater detail in chapter 17 of Revelation.

One thing is certain, the city is being condemned for playing the harlot. This is a common metaphor for idolatry in scripture. John takes the picture of Babylon as *fallen (14:8)* from Isaiah.

> *...And one said, "Fallen, fallen is Babylon; and all the images of her gods are shattered on the ground." (Isaiah 21:9, NASB95)*

Just as Babylon of old was judged and destroyed for her idolatry, so now the new Babylon is being judged for her idolatry.

Doom for Worshipers of the Beast

14:9 *Then another angel, a third one, followed them, saying with a loud voice, "If anyone worships the beast and his image, and receives a mark on his forehead or on his hand...."* In Revelation 13:12-17 we were introduced to the **mark (14:9)** of the **beast (14:9)**. We now revisit that subject.

14:10 *...he also will drink of the wine of the wrath of God, which is mixed in full strength in the cup of His anger; and he will be tormented with fire and brimstone in the presence of the holy angels and in the presence of the Lamb.* There is an unambiguous response for those who worship the beast and receive his mark; **he will be tormented with fire and brimstone (14:10)**; it is

---

[550] Milton S. Terry, <u>Biblical Apocalyptics</u>, 407.

eternal damnation. No hope is given. Notice that eternal damnation is a public event. They will be **tormented ... in the presence of the holy angels and in the presence of the Lamb (14:10)**. "The punishment of the wicked is made even greater by the fact that they can see the blessed state of the angels and the Lamb."[551]

14:11   And the smoke of their torment goes up forever and ever; they have no rest day and night, those who worship the beast and his image, and whoever receives the mark of his name. Isaiah made a similar observation.

> *Then they will go forth and look*
> *On the corpses of the men*
> *Who have transgressed against Me.*
> *For their worm will not die*
> *And their fire will not be quenched;*
> *And they will be an abhorrence to all mankind. (Isaiah 66:24,*
> *NASB95)*

Christ also made a similar point in His story of the rich man and Lazarus.

> *In Hades he lifted up his eyes, being in torment, and saw*
> *Abraham far away and Lazarus in his bosom. And he cried out*
> *and said, 'Father Abraham, have mercy on me, and send Lazarus*
> *so that he may dip the tip of his finger in water and cool off my*
> *tongue, for I am in agony in this flame.' But Abraham said,*
> *'Child, remember that during your life you received your good*
> *things, and likewise Lazarus bad things, but now he is being*
> *comforted here, and you are in agony. 'And besides all this,*
> *between us and you there is a great chasm fixed, so that those*
> *who wish to come over from here to you will not be able, and that*
> *none may cross over from there to us.' (Luke 16:23-26, NASB95)*

"That the blessed in heaven have cognizance of the wicked and their sufferings, seems to be plainly disclosed.... And the consciousness on the part of the malignant persecutors in the world of woe, that those whom they had pursued unto death were looking down on their torments, from a state

---

[551] Robert G. Bratcher, Rev. 14:10.

of inconceivable happiness above, would doubtless be a circumstance of great aggravation."[552] As great as the suffering of the dammed may be, ignorance of heaven would alleviate it some. But the awareness, indeed a view itself of the eternally blessed, would make hell horrible beyond description. How blessed and wonderful are those that, by God's grace, chose the way of Christ, who denied themselves and turned from temporal bliss and reward, because they saw a city whose maker and founder was God.

> *...for he was looking for the city which has foundations, whose architect and builder is God. (Hebrews 11:10, NASB95)*

We are told that **they have no rest day and night (14:11).** "...the restless unrest which is of the nature of evil is magnificently contrasted with the unresting rest of the blessed."[553]

If ever a believer needed courage to bear up under the difficulties of living the Christian life, it would be during periods in which property, and life itself, are the price needed to stay the course. And what would give that perseverance? One such motivation would be a reminder of what happens to those who compromise with sin and Satan. That reminder we just read in this verse.

14:12   Here is the perseverance of the saints who keep the commandments of God and their faith in Jesus. The reality of eternity and hell is set before the believer to encourage him or her to **keep the commandments of God and their faith in Jesus (14:12).** When people **keep the commandments of God (14:12)** they demonstrate that they possess a true **faith in Jesus (14:12).** Lawless believers are an oxymoron. Although the modern Church is full of people who violate every one of the ten commandments, true Christianity knows nothing of this kind of faith. "The perseverance of the saints is necessarily bound up in the fact that they keep the commandments of God and the faith of Jesus. In opposition to all forms of creature worship, Christians keep the

---

[552] Moses Stuart, vol. II, 299.

[553] Philip Carrington, 249.

commandments; they keep the faith. The New Testament knows nothing of a lawless Christianity...."[554]

14:13   And I heard a voice from heaven, saying, "Write, 'Blessed are the dead who die in the Lord from now on!' " "Yes," says the Spirit, "so that they may rest from their labors, for their deeds follow with them." It is no surprise that those that **die in the Lord (14:13)** are blessed.   Paul quoted Isaiah, who also made this very point,

> *Things which eye has not seen and ear has not heard, and which have not entered the heart of man, all that God has prepared for those who love Him. (1 Corinthians 2:9, NASB95)*

However, what is a surprise, or at least a point of confusion, is why this is **from now on (14:13)**, as if dying in the Lord prior to this point wasn't particularly blessed.   Well, John's style, grammar and vocabulary in Revelation have bothered readers from early times.

But, perhaps the solution is not so difficult. I understand John as saying simply this, **from now on (14:13)**, that is from the point of their death, they receive the blessings of being with Christ in heaven, something they did not possess while on this earth, but something all believers experience who die in the Lord. This thought is confirmed by the next phrase.

Rest (14:13) is something the persecuted church saw precious little of. Yet an eternal rest awaited them. Compare this statement with John's earlier statement,

> *And the smoke of their torment goes up forever and ever; they have no rest day and night, those who worship the beast and his image, and whoever receives the mark of his name. (Revelation 14:11, NASB95)*

One rest now but will never do so again for all eternity. Another knows no rest and is much wearied with persecution, but will soon see God *"wipe away every tear from their eyes; and there will no longer be any death;*

---

[554] David Chilton, The Great Tribulation, 366.

there will no longer be any mourning, or crying, or pain" (Revelation 21:4). Theirs will be an eternal rest.

"There seems to be no middle way; one either adores the beast and is doomed or one accepts with patient endurance the persecution of the beast, obeys the commandments of God, dies in Him, and receives reward for one's good works...."[555]

Merrill Tenney makes this interesting point,

> The apparently unlimited power of the beast and his steady victory over the saints of God would tend to be utterly discouraging to them. How could they continue to believe in the sovereignty and goodness of God if He let them suffer without attempting to rescue them? What difference would there be between their fate and the death of anybody else? The beatitude asserts that they will be compensated by rest and reward. It is intended to encourage those who are under persecution.[556]

Both the **deeds (14:13)** of the believer and the unbeliever follow them into eternity.

> *But when the Son of Man comes in His glory, and all the angels with Him, then He will sit on His glorious throne. All the nations will be gathered before Him; and He will separate them from one another, as the shepherd separates the sheep from the goats; and He will put the sheep on His right, and the goats on the left. Then the King will say to those on His right, 'Come, you who are blessed of My Father, inherit the kingdom prepared for you from the foundation of the world. For I was hungry, and you gave Me something to eat; I was thirsty, and you gave Me something to drink; I was a stranger, and you invited Me in; naked, and you clothed Me; I was sick, and you visited Me; I was in prison, and you came to Me.' Then the righteous will answer Him, 'Lord, when did we see You hungry, and feed You, or thirsty, and give You something to drink? And when did we see You a stranger, and invite You in, or naked, and clothe You? When did we see You*

---

[555] J. Massyngberde Ford, 249.

[556] Merrill Tenney, 181.

sick, or in prison, and come to You?' The King will answer and say to them, 'Truly I say to you, to the extent that you did it to one of these brothers of Mine, even the least of them, you did it to Me.' Then He will also say to those on His left, 'Depart from Me, accursed ones, into the eternal fire which has been prepared for the devil and his angels; for I was hungry, and you gave Me nothing to eat; I was thirsty, and you gave Me nothing to drink; I was a stranger, and you did not invite Me in; naked, and you did not clothe Me; sick, and in prison, and you did not visit Me.' Then they themselves also will answer, 'Lord, when did we see You hungry, or thirsty, or a stranger, or naked, or sick, or in prison, and did not take care of You?' Then He will answer them, 'Truly I say to you, to the extent that you did not do it to one of the least of these, you did not do it to Me.' These will go away into eternal punishment, but the righteous into eternal life. (Matthew 25:31-46, NASB95)

The Reapers

We have two "gatherings" spoken of in this section. One is apparently of grain; the other is of grapes. These two stories appear to be restating what we read in 14:4 about the *first fruits* and in 14:10 about those who *will drink of the wine of the wrath of God, which is mixed in full strength in the cup of His anger.*

14:14 Then I looked, and behold, a white cloud, and sitting on the cloud was one like a son of man, having a golden crown on His head and a sharp sickle in His hand.[557] Here we are introduced to the one who directs the affairs of men for blessing or for curses. He was first introduced to us in Daniel.

I kept looking in the night visions,
And behold, with the clouds of heaven
One like a Son of Man was coming,
And He came up to the Ancient of Days
And was presented before Him.
14 And to Him was given dominion,

---

[557] Refer to the notes on Revelation 1:7 in this commentary.

Glory and a kingdom,
That all the peoples, nations and men of every language
Might serve Him.
His dominion is an everlasting dominion
Which will not pass away;
And His kingdom is one
Which will not be destroyed. (Daniel 7:13-14, NASB95)

The description, **one like a son of man, having a golden crown on His head (14:14)**, identifies Him; He is the Lord. He, who once wore a crown of thorns, now wears a victor's crown.

His enemies I will clothe with shame,
But upon himself his crown shall shine. (Psalm 132:18, NASB95)

We were introduced to this one earlier in Revelation.

Behold, He is coming with the clouds, and every eye will see Him,
even those who pierced Him; and all the tribes of the earth [land]
will mourn over Him. So it is to be. Amen. (Revelation 1:7,
NASB95)

However this is not His Second Coming; this coming "is similar to those conditional visitations promised in the letters to the Seven Churches."[558] This is a coming in judgement. In taking note of the promised comings in judgement on the Seven Churches in Revelation, we should note that judgement comings are not limited to Judaism. They are promised to a compromising and dead Church as well. And Christ in Judgement has indeed visited all of those Seven Churches. Not one of them survives today. And so it goes through the ages, Christ visits His Church and removes their lampstand. I am sure they never miss it! It's not like they were actually using it.

14:15-16 And another angel came out of the temple, crying out with a loud voice to Him who sat on the cloud, "Put in your sickle and reap, for the hour to reap has come, because the harvest of the earth [land] is ripe." ¹⁶ Then He who sat on the

---

[558] Philip Carrington, 251.

cloud swung His sickle over the earth [land], and the earth [land] was reaped. This ingathering is not unto judgement—as is the next one. "The gathering of the elect is symbolized by the Harvest of the Land; the judgement of the sinners is symbolized by the Vintage."[559] It has two possible meanings.

1) This may represent the great mass of martyrs discussed earlier in this chapter.

> *Blessed are the dead who die in the Lord from now on! "Yes," says the Spirit, "so that they may rest from their labors, for their deeds follow with them." (Revelation 14:13)*

Christ Himself predicted this event in Matthew 24.

> *And then the sign of the Son of Man will appear in the sky, and then all the tribes of the earth [land] will mourn, and they will see the Son of Man coming on the clouds of the sky with power and great glory. 31 And He will send forth His angels with a great trumpet and they will gather together His elect from the four winds, from one end of the sky to the other. (Matthew 24:30-31, NASB95)*

We saw verse 30 of Matthew 24 fulfilled in chapter 1 of Revelation. In verse 31 we are told that *He will send forth His angels with a great trumpet and they will gather together His elect from the four winds*. This section here would be that ingathering of the elect. This would reflect the great persecution beginning at this time in the Gentile church. "The harvest of grain represented the gathering of the faithful saints...."[560] "The harvest seems to be the faithful souls."[561]

They are gathered to God in this harvest in martyrdom and death.

2) Another possibility would be a salvation of deliverance before the hammer of judgment falls on Jerusalem. "The thought ... is the separation

---

559 Ibid., 252.

560 Foy E. Wallace, Jr., 317.

561 J. Massyngberde Ford, 238.

of the righteous from the wicked before vengeance falls on the wicked."[562]
This would be the flight of the Christians after the failure of Cestius Gallus
to take the city and before Vespasian and Titus arrive to actually do so.
"The simplest explanation is that the Harvest in Revelation means the
escape of the Christian community from the horrors of the siege of
Jerusalem."[563]

This first option seems to be the best however.

14:17-18 *And another angel came out of the temple which is in
heaven, and he also had a sharp sickle. [18] Then another angel,
the one who has power over fire, came out from the altar; and
he called with a loud voice to him who had the sharp sickle,
saying, "Put in your sharp sickle and gather the clusters from
the vine of the earth [land], because her grapes are ripe."*
Another ingathering now takes place. This one is of **grapes (14:18)**. In
the previous section we saw the ingathering of God's people. Now we see
the ingathering of the lost; "for the concomitant of the gathering of the
Church is the excommunication of Israel."[564] "The gathering of the elect is
symbolized by the Harvest of the Land; the judgement of the sinners is
symbolized by the Vintage."[565]

It is Israel that is ripe for judgement. John the Baptist made reference to
this near judgement in Matthew 3.

> But when he saw many of the Pharisees and Sadducees coming
> for baptism, he said to them, "You brood of vipers, who warned
> you to flee from the wrath to come?" (Matthew 3:7, NASB95)

> The axe is already laid at the root of the trees; therefore every tree
> that does not bear good fruit is cut down and thrown into the fire.
> As for me, I baptize you with water for repentance, but He who is
> coming after me is mightier than I, and I am not fit to remove His
> sandals; He will baptize you with the Holy Spirit and fire. His

---

[562] Philip Carrington, 253.

[563] Ibid., 253.

[564] David Chilton, The Great Tribulation, 373.

[565] Philip Carrington, 252.

winnowing fork is in His hand, and He will thoroughly clear His threshing floor; and He will gather His wheat into the barn, but He will burn up the chaff with unquenchable fire. (Matthew 3:10-12, NASB95)

Here we are introduced to an angel who has **a loud voice (14:18)** and **power over fire (14:18)**. "Fire is the usual emblem of destruction. The angel who has power over it, is here commissioned to give commandment for the excision of the enemies of God."[566] However, "not just 'over fire,' as most translations render it, but over *the* fire, the fire burning on the altar; and he comes specifically from the altar of the saints' prayers in order to render judgement, to bring about the historical response to the worship and the prayers of the Church."[567]

The focus here is on the word *ripe (14:18)*. In recent days Israel was not ripe for judgement although that day was drawing near. Matthew presents a picture of Israel nearly ripe forty years earlier when Jesus says *"fill up"* and then made it clear that the audience Christ spoke to then was the one that would experience the fall of God's judgement.

Fill up, then, the measure of the guilt of your fathers. (Matthew 23:32, NASB95)

...so that upon you may fall the guilt of all the righteous blood shed on earth [land], from the blood of righteous Abel to the blood of Zechariah, the son of Berechiah, whom you murdered between the temple and the altar. (Matthew 23:35, NASB95)

Paul is also anticipating this near judgement; he writes,

They are not pleasing to God, but hostile to all men, hindering us from speaking to the Gentiles so that they may be saved; with the result that they always fill up the measure of their sins. But wrath has come upon them to the utmost. (1 Thessalonians 2:15-16, NASB95)

---

[566] Moses Stuart, vol. II, 302.

[567] David Chilton, The Great Tribulation, 374.

14:19 *So the angel swung his sickle to the earth [land] and gathered the clusters from the vine of the earth [land], and threw them into the great wine press of the wrath of God.* The metaphor continues with the ingathering of the grapes. They are put **into the great wine press of the wrath of God (14:19)**. This is clearly an ingathering of judgement by God upon evil. The fact that **the land (14:19)** is mentioned demonstrates that this judgement refers to Judah. This is further demonstrated by the use of **city (14:20)**, that being none other but Jerusalem.

> It is plain, then, that the coming of our Lord has to do, in this vision, with the destruction of *a particular city*; that it cannot mean the general judgement of mankind, and the gathering of all human beings before his bar; that his coming must be local not general; particular, not universal; that it is connected with the destruction of a particular city; and *the only city that he came to destroy was Jerusalem.*[568]

> Listen to another parable. There was a landowner who planted a vineyard and put a wall around it and dug a wine press in it, and built a tower, and rented it out to vine-growers and went on a journey. When the harvest time approached, he sent his slaves to the vine-growers to receive his produce. The vine-growers took his slaves and beat one, and killed another, and stoned a third. Again he sent another group of slaves larger than the first; and they did the same thing to them. But afterward he sent his son to them, saying, 'They will respect my son.' But when the vine-growers saw the son, they said among themselves, 'This is the heir; come, let us kill him and seize his inheritance.' They took him, and threw him out of the vineyard and killed him. Therefore when the owner of the vineyard comes, what will he do to those vine-growers? They said to Him, "He will bring those wretches to a wretched end, and will rent out the vineyard to other vine-growers who will pay him the proceeds at the proper seasons." Jesus said to them, "Did you never read in the Scriptures, 'The stone which the builders rejected, this became the chief corner stone; this came about from the Lord, and it is marvelous in our

---

[568] Phillip S. Desprez, 412.

eyes'? Therefore I say to you, the kingdom of God will be taken away from you and given to a people, producing the fruit of it. And he who falls on this stone will be broken to pieces; but on whomever it falls, it will scatter him like dust. When the chief priests and the Pharisees heard His parables, they understood that He was speaking about them. (Matthew 21:33-45, NASB95)

And He was! But the Dispensationalists can't seem to grasp what even the Pharisees could see clearly. We have before us now the fulfillment of this prophecy. Judgement has now come. "If they have drunk Babylon's wine of harlotry, lusted after other gods, then they must drink God's wine of wrath unmitigated, and they will be tormented night and day before the Lamb and his angels. The cup or wine of God's wrath is a familiar OT symbol.... It indicates the fearful punishments which God will visit upon evildoers...."[569]

14:20 And the wine press was trodden outside the city, and blood came out from the wine press, up to the horses' bridles, for a distance of two hundred miles. We are told that this happens **outside the city (14:20)**. Which **city (14:20)**? Earlier in 11:8 we read,

And their dead bodies will lie in the street of the great city which mystically is called Sodom and Egypt, where also their Lord was crucified. (Revelation 11:8; NASB95)

The phrase "where also their Lord was crucified" makes it absolutely clear that this city is Jerusalem. Additionally, the writer of Hebrews says this,

Therefore Jesus also, that He might sanctify the people through His own blood, suffered outside the gate. 13 So, let us go out to Him outside the camp, bearing His reproach. 14 For here we do not have a lasting city, but we are seeking the city which is to come. (Hebrews 13:12-14, NASB95)

Now we can't be sure who influenced who here. Did the writer of Hebrews read Revelation or the other way around, or both a third source? Yet, it appears to me that the writer of Hebrews is following Revelation, and

---

[569] J. Massyngberde Ford, 248.

indeed much in Hebrews echoes Revelation. But, either way, the city in Hebrews is, without question, Jerusalem, suggesting the same city for Revelation. We will read of a city later in chapters 16:19 and 17:18 of Revelation. All three of these passages appear to make reference to Jerusalem, and each strengthens the others likelihood of being the one and same city, Jerusalem.

The phrase **up to the horses' bridles (14:20)** refers to how high the blood sprinkled or spattered as the judgement of God swept across the land. This point is illustrated in a war scene in Isaiah.

> *I have trodden the wine trough alone,*
> *And from the peoples there was no man with Me.*
> *I also trod them in My anger*
> *And trampled them in My wrath;*
> *And their lifeblood is sprinkled on My garments,*
> *And I stained all My raiment.*
> *4 "For the day of vengeance was in My heart,*
> *And My year of redemption has come. (Isaiah 63:3-4, NASB95)*

Again, blood is trodden under foot. And here the sprinkling or spattering of blood upon the garments is so great that the Lord of Host notes, "*I stained all My raiment.*" That is, there was a great slaughter of God's enemies and blood spattered over a great distance.

The point is simply this, the fact that we are dealing with a metaphor here in Revelation 14 does not require that we understand that the **blood (14:20)** is five feet deep. It is simply a picturesque way of saying that "this whole land was, figuratively speaking, deluged with blood during the Jewish war which ended in the destruction of Jerusalem."[570] So great was the slaughter that as the horses rode through the blood, it splattered as far [up] as the **horses' bridle (14:20)**.

But what of the phrase, **for a distance of two hundred miles (14:20)**, what does it mean? Was the blood five feet deep for 1600 stadia or two hundred miles? No. The meaning is clear. The war will be thorough. It will cover the whole land. None will escape judgement. Rome attacked Israel from Alexandria, Egypt, to Jewish communities in modern day

---

[570] Milton S. Terry, <u>Biblical Apocalyptics</u>, 413.

Lebanon and Syria, a distance of two hundred miles. That's the meaning here; the blood of the Christ-hating Jews was shed in abundance from one end of the land to the other. "The distance of the blood flow is 1600 stadia, which is roughly the length of the land as a Roman province: The *Itenerarum* of Antonius of Piacenza records Palestine's length as 1664 stadia. This prophecy refers to the enormous blood flow in Israel during the Jewish war."[571]

Josephus gives us a little insight into the great bloody slaughter that took place in Israel at this time. "...insomuch that the sea was bloody a long way, and the maritime parts were full of dead bodies; for the Romans came upon those that were carried to the shore, and destroyed them...."[572] "...one might then see the lake all bloody, and full of dead bodies, for not one of them escaped."[573] "...the whole of the country through which they had fled was filled with slaughter, and Jordan could not be passed over, by reason of the dead bodies that were in it, but because the lake Asphaltitis was also full of dead bodies, that were carried down into it by the river."[574] "...and blood ran down over all the lower parts of the city, from the upper."[575] "And now the outer temple was all of it overflowed with blood...."[576]

> ...insomuch that in any persons who came thither with great zeal from the ends of the earth, to offer sacrifices at this celebrated place, which was esteemed holy by all mankind, fell down before their own sacrifices themselves, and sprinkled that altar which was venerable among all men, both Greeks and Barbarians, with their own blood; (18) till the dead bodies of strangers were mingled together with those of their own country, and those of profane persons with those of the priests, and the blood of all sorts of dead carcasses stood in lakes in the holy courts themselves.[577]

"...but they ran every one through whom they met with, and obstructed the very lanes with their dead bodies, and made the whole city run down with

---

[571] C. Marvin Pate, Editor, 72.

[572] Flavius Josephus, *Wars*, 3:9:3.

[573] Ibid., *Wars*, 3:10:9.

[574] Ibid., *Wars*, 4:7:6.

[575] Ibid., *Wars*, 4:1:10.

[576] Ibid., *Wars*, 4:5:1.

[577] Ibid., *Wars*, 5:1:3.

blood, to such a degree indeed that the fire of many of the houses was quenched with these men's blood."[578]

What about the phrase, **outside the city (14:20)**? What John is telling us is that at this point Israel is drenched in blood everywhere except Jerusalem. It will be much later before Jerusalem will fall to Titus.

"On a historical level one might suggest that the author predicted, or his work reflected, conditions in Palestine. In A.D. 66 Vespasian (with Titus), after strengthening his forces, captured nearly all the cities in Galilee which were held by the Zealots. Then he marched to Caesarea and Jerusalem. It was at this time that the whole of Palestine suffered <u>bloodshed, with the exception of the Holy City</u>."[579]

We can therefore conclude that "the Harvest symbolizes the safe gathering together of the elect, those that love God; the Vintage symbolizes the vengeance of blood that is to come upon the unfaithful nation."[580]

---

[578] Ibid., *Wars*, 6:8:5.

[579] J. Massyngberde Ford, 250.

[580] Philip Carrington, 254.255.

Chapter 15
The Seven Last Plagues

A Scene of Heaven

In chapters 4 and 5 of Revelation, we have an introduction and prelude to the <u>seven seals</u>. In chapter 8:1-6, we have an introduction and prelude to the <u>seven trumpets</u>. Now here in chapter 15, we have an introduction and prelude to the <u>seven bowls</u>. In the structure of the book we see three clearly defined judgements and three clearly defined introductions. Each takes time to play out; each creates a dramatic anticipation to the coming judgement.

15:1 Then I saw another sign in heaven, great and marvelous, seven angels who had seven plagues, which are the last, because in them the wrath of God is finished. These **seven plagues (15:1)** are very similar to the seven trumpets found in chapters 8-14. They appear to be a repetition of that same scene from a different angle. As a repetition, they are either given to provide some new information but from a different perspective, or they are given to drive home the point of the inevitability of the coming events. This happened to Pharaoh when he dreamed of the seven fat cows and the seven scrawny cows and then again dreamed of the seven full heads of grain and the seven withered heads of grain. They both told the same story and were apparently given to emphasize the certainty of the coming famine. That is evidently what we have here. The repetition is to emphasize the inevitability and certainty of the coming judgement.

The use of "seven" in these judgements reminds us of God's prophecy against Israel in Leviticus, if they failed to keep the covenant.

> If then, you act with hostility against Me and are unwilling to obey Me, I will increase the plague on you <u>seven</u> times according to your sins. (Leviticus 26:21, NASB95)

And so we see this prophecy fulfilled here in the book of Revelation. I would think that God intended Judaism to make that association.

15:2 And I saw something like a sea of glass mixed with fire, and those who had been victorious over the beast and his image and the number of his name, standing on the sea of glass, holding harps of God. Those **standing on the sea of glass (15:2)** are the 144,000 of the last chapter. "They appear to be the same people as the redeemed remnant portrayed in 14:1-5."[581]

We were first introduced to the **sea of glass (15:2)** in chapter 4.

> ...and before the throne there was something like a sea of glass, like crystal; and in the center and around the throne, four living creatures full of eyes in front and behind. (Revelation 4:6, NASB95)

To this picture is added the phrase **mixed with fire (15:2)**. We have two possible explanations for the significance of fire. In some way the two blend together. One, fire is a symbol of judgement. The martyrs have come through the fire of judgement and now they stand **victorious over the beast and his image and the number of his name (15:2)**. Second, it is the color red from the **fire (15:2)** that is the point made here "as if reflecting the vast sea of blood from the wine press of God's wrath mentioned just before (XIV, 20)."[582] These martyrs came through a sea of blood, theirs and the blood of their enemies that came from the *great wine press of the wrath of God* (14:19).

The martyrs are now **holding harps of God (15:2)**. Heavenly choirs play a prominent role in Revelation.

> When He had taken the book, the four living creatures and the twenty-four elders fell down before the Lamb, each one holding a harp and golden bowls full of incense, which are the prayers of the saints. (Revelation 5:8, NASB95)

> And I heard a voice from heaven, like the sound of many waters and like the sound of loud thunder, and the voice which I heard

---

[581] Ibid., 257.

[582] Milton S. Terry, Biblical Apocalyptics, 414.

was like the sound of harpists playing on their harps. (Revelation 14:2, NASB95)

Echoes of these heavenly originals are the temple choirs of the Old Testament. Music plays a prominent role in Biblical worship, on earth and in heaven.

15:3-4 *And they sang the song of Moses, the bond-servant of God, and the song of the Lamb, saying,*
"Great and marvelous are Your works,
O Lord God, the Almighty;
Righteous and true are Your ways,
King of the nations!
Who will not fear, O Lord, and glorify Your name?
For You alone are holy;
For all the nations will come and worship before You,
For Your righteous acts have been revealed."

The fact that they sang **the song of Moses (15:3)** drives home the judgement element before us in this chapter. The song of Moses is a song of victory; it celebrates the destruction of God's, and Israel's, enemies. In the same way, those that have come through the tortures and torments of the beast in victory now celebrate their victory in song.

> *Then Moses and the sons of Israel sang this song to the Lord, and said,*
> *"I will sing to the Lord, for He is highly exalted;*
> *The horse and its rider He has hurled into the sea.*
> *2 "The Lord is my strength and song,*
> *And He has become my salvation;*
> *This is my God, and I will praise Him;*
> *My father's God, and I will extol Him.*
> *3 "The Lord is a warrior;*
> *The Lord is His name....*
> *7 "And in the greatness of Your excellence You overthrow those who rise up against You;*
> *You send forth Your burning anger, and it consumes them as chaff....*
> *13 "In Your lovingkindness You have led the people whom You have redeemed;*

In Your strength You have guided them to Your holy habitation....
17 "You will bring them and plant them in the mountain of Your
inheritance,
The place, O Lord, which You have made for Your dwelling,
The sanctuary, O Lord, which Your hands have established.
18 "The Lord shall reign forever and ever. (Exodus 15:1-3,7,13,17-
18, NASB95)

This is not only the song of Moses, for the One greater than Moses has come to deliver His people. This is preeminently **the song of the Lamb (15:3)**.

The song that John quotes for us here is not itself a repeat of the song of Moses but borrowing from an array of Scriptural passages it weaves together a new song of victory and worship before God.

15:5-6 *After these things I looked, and the temple of the tabernacle of testimony in heaven was opened, and the seven angels who had the seven plagues came out of the temple, clothed in linen, clean and bright, and girded around their chests with golden sashes.* Not only is the **temple (15:5)** mentioned here, it is referenced by its fuller name **the temple of the tabernacle of testimony (15:5)**. Now the phrase **tabernacle of testimony (15:5)** refers to the two tablets of the law of God, the Ten Commandments. So, we see that not only is New Testament Christianity worked out in the Ten Commandments as its proper standard for Godly living, as is seen in the Sermon on the Mount, but even in heaven itself this holy standard maintains its central place in the eternal temple of God. Dispensationalism teaches that we live not under law but under grace. They reference Romans 6 to support this point.

For sin shall not be master over you, for you are not under law
but under grace. (Romans 6:14, NASB95)

However, what is missed is that Paul is teaching that salvation is not obtained by keeping the Law, but that salvation is by God's grace. Dispensationalism extends this from the realm of justification into the realm of sanctification. That is they see no role for the Law of God in our sanctification. The result is lawlessness. The Law of God, Old Testament or New Testament was never a means of salvation. However, the Law of God,

Old Testament or New Testament is always the standard of holiness and obedience to God. We are not under Law as a means of salvation, but of utter necessity, the Law of God is God's standard of holiness.

So we see that God's law is grace and both grace and law have been the gift of God from creation. Dispensationalists are right when they dismiss man's law and the perversions of God's law but they are wrong when they dismiss the law of God itself. Only God can tell us, through divine revelation, which parts are fulfilled and therefore, through a change in the covenant, are no longer binding. Man cannot arbitrarily do that. What God has not clearly changed remains in force.

15:7 Then one of the four living creatures gave to the seven angels seven golden bowls full of the wrath of God, who lives forever and ever. We were introduced to the *four living creatures* *(15:7)* in chapter 4 and in a context similar to our own here.

> ...and before the throne there was something like a sea of glass,
> like crystal; and in the center and around the throne, four living
> creatures full of eyes in front and behind. (Revelation 4:6,
> NASB95)

These creatures were mentioned several times in chapters 4 and 5 right before the opening of the seals but have not been heard from since. Now right before the *seven angels who had seven plagues, which are the last, because in them the wrath of God is finished* (15:1) we see them again. So they appear both to open and to close the various judgements found in this book.

15:8 And the temple was filled with smoke from the glory of God and from His power; and no one was able to enter the temple until the seven plagues of the seven angels were finished. This filling of the **temple (15:8)** with the **smoke** of **the glory of God (15:8)** is indicative of His presence.

> Then the cloud covered the tent of meeting, and the glory of the
> Lord filled the tabernacle. Moses was not able to enter the tent of
> meeting because the cloud had settled on it, and the glory of the
> Lord filled the tabernacle. (Exodus 40:34-35)

Until these plagues had been completed, and Jerusalem was utterly destroyed, no one could enter the temple. "...none could appear in intercession before God to avert the doom of destruction pronounced on Jerusalem, that once 'faithful city turned harlot,' and the fallen Babylon of apostasy."[583]

---

[583] Foy E. Wallace, Jr., 325.

Chapter 16
Pouring out of the Bowls

Six Bowls of Wrath

The bowl judgements have not only a decided similarity with the previous trumpets; they have a similar correspondence with God's judgement on Egypt. It is ironic that the plagues that were once signs of God's judgement on Egypt are now signs of God's judgement on the new Egypt, Jerusalem.

> And their dead bodies will lie in the street of the great city which mystically is called Sodom and Egypt, where also their Lord was crucified. (Revelation 11:8, NASB95)

This mystical Sodom and Egypt is Jerusalem.

16:1 Then I heard a loud voice from the temple, saying to the seven angels, "Go and pour out on the earth [land] the seven bowls of the wrath of God." Isaiah records an earlier **loud voice (16:1)**. His was a warning of a soon destruction, so is this *loud voice*.

> A voice of uproar from the city, a voice from the temple, the voice of the Lord who is rendering recompense to His enemies. (Isaiah 66:6, NASB95)

First Bowl: Loathsome Sores

16:2 So the first angel went and poured out his bowl on the earth [land]; and it became a loathsome and malignant sore on the people who had the mark of the beast and who worshiped his image. Let us compare this first bowl with the first trumpet.

> The first sounded, and there came hail and fire, mixed with blood, and they were thrown to the earth [land]; and a third of the earth [land] was burned up, and a third of the trees were burned up, and all the green grass was burned up. (Revelation 8:7, NASB95)

349

One thing stands out; both judgements are upon the **land (16:2)**. Other than that, they differ. The bowl judgement afflicts people; the trumpet judgement afflicts plant life. This is not to say that both did not happen at the same time, simply that one focuses on man, the other on man's environment.

We can see similarities with this bowl judgement and Moses' judgement on Egypt.

> *Then the Lord said to Moses and Aaron, "Take for yourselves handfuls of soot from a kiln, and let Moses throw it toward the sky in the sight of Pharaoh. It will become fine dust over all the land of Egypt, and will become boils breaking out with sores on man and beast through all the land of Egypt." (Exodus 9:8-9, NASB95)*

The **loathsome and malignant sore (16:2)** here in Revelation corresponds to the *boils breaking out with sores on man and beast* in Exodus 9. However, in Revelation this judgements seems to be limited to those **who had the mark of the beast and who worshiped his image (16:2)**. Two marks are listed in Revelation, the mark of the beast in chapter 13 and the mark of the Father in chapter 14. Those that received that mark of the beast, were specifically apostate Israel. They are now singled out for judgement for their apostasy.

Compare this judgement with that mentioned in Deuteronomy 28, that passage that delineates the penalty for breaking the covenant.

> *The Lord will smite you with the <u>boils</u> of Egypt and with <u>tumors</u> and with the <u>scab</u> and with the <u>itch</u>, from which you cannot be healed. 35 The Lord will strike you on the knees and legs with sore <u>boils</u>, from which you cannot be healed, from the sole of your foot to the crown of your head. (Deuteronomy 28:27,35 NASB95)*

In the Old Testament those with leprosy were to be removed from the camp. Their disease was an affront to God. They were not allowed to be a part of the community of God.

> *Then the Lord spoke to Moses, saying, "Command the sons of Israel that they send away from the camp every leper and*

everyone having a discharge and everyone who is unclean because of a dead person." (Numbers 5:1-2, NASB95)

These **loathsome and malignant sores (16:2)** are the proof that God has rejected Israel. They must now be cast out of the camp of God, Jerusalem.

We have little in specific historical information on the fulfillment of this prophecy. However, it is not hard to imagine the condition of a city filled with dead bodies, restricted in access to clean water, limited in quality and quantity of foods, and afflicted with the ever-present threat of death from enemies within and without Jerusalem. I think we would not be surprised to learn that they were afflicted with **loathsome and malignant sores (16:2)** under these circumstances, although we no doubt would be surprised to learn that they were not so afflicted.

Second Bowl: The Sea Turns to Blood

16:3 The second angel poured out his bowl into the sea, and it became blood like that of a dead man; and every living thing in the sea died. Again, in keeping with our format, let's look at the second bowl in the light of the second trumpet judgement.

The second angel sounded, and something like a great mountain burning with fire was thrown into the sea; and a third of the sea became blood, 9 and a third of the creatures which were in the sea and had life, died; and a third of the ships were destroyed. (Revelation 8:8-9, NASB95)

The **sea (16:3)** becoming **blood (16:3)** and the sea creatures dying is the theme of both of these judgements. They correspond to Moses turning the Nile to blood.

So Moses and Aaron did even as the Lord had commanded. And he lifted up the staff and struck the water that was in the Nile, in the sight of Pharaoh and in the sight of his servants, and all the water that was in the Nile was turned to blood. 21 The fish that were in the Nile died, and the Nile became foul, so that the Egyptians could not drink water from the Nile. And the blood was through all the land of Egypt. 22 But the magicians of Egypt did the same with their secret arts; and Pharaoh's heart was hardened, and he did not listen to them, as the Lord had said. 23 Then Pharaoh turned and went into his house with no concern even for this. 24 So all the Egyptians dug around the Nile for water to drink, for they could not drink of the water of the Nile. 25 Seven days passed after the Lord had struck the Nile. (Exodus 7:20-25, NASB95)

In the study of the second trumpet (8:8-9), we saw that the "great mountain" was Jerusalem and the sea was the Gentile world. In addition, we also referenced some of Josephus' material on two sea battles that took place at that time. These were battles characterized by immense bloodshed. The same story is told here. The picture references the Jews who took to the sea to fight the Romans. In referencing them John says, **every living thing in the sea died (16:3)**. This does not refer primarily to fish, as it did in Egypt during that plague. Instead it refers primarily to the Jews who took to the sea to fight or run from the Romans. They all died. Josephus says,

> ...one might then see the lake all bloody, and full of dead bodies, for not one of them escaped. And a terrible stink, and a very sad sight there was on the following days over that country; for as for the shores, they were full of shipwrecks, and of dead bodies all swelled; and as the dead bodies were inflamed by the sun, and putrefied, they corrupted the air, insomuch that the misery was not only the object of commiseration to the Jews, but to those that hated them, and had been the authors of that misery.[584]

Third Bowl: The Waters Turn to Blood

16:4 Then the third angel poured out his bowl into the rivers and the springs of waters; and they became blood. This third bowl is to be compared with the third trumpet:

> *The third angel sounded, and a great star fell from heaven, burning like a torch, and it fell on a third of the rivers and on the springs of waters. (Revelation 8:10, NASB95).*

---

[584] Flavius Josephus, *Wars,* 3:10:9.

In both cases *the rivers and the springs of waters (16:4)* were contaminated. Like the last bowl, this one reminds us of the first Egyptian plague in which the water was turned to blood.

In our study of the third trumpet (8:10-11), we took note of the role water played in warfare, especially in an arid area. Armies typically poisoned water supplies to deny them to the enemy. This no doubt occurred in Israel at this time.

16:5 And I heard the angel of the waters saying, "Righteous are You, who are and who were, O Holy One, because You judged these things...." The phrase *who are and who were (16:5)* is another ascription to God as being eternally self-existent. Similar phrases have been used several times in Revelation.

Notice that the angel associates the judgements of God with His holiness *(16:5)*. Jehovah's Witnesses, in their self-delusion, insist that a truly "loving" God would not judge and certainly would not send anyone to hell. The heavenly angel disagrees. He sees the judgement of God to be a just thing driven by God's holiness.

16:6 ...for they poured out the blood of saints and prophets, and You have given them blood to drink. They deserve it. These evil men and women have *poured out the blood of saints and prophets (16:6)*. Now, using apocalyptic metaphor, God is giving them blood to drink in punishment for their sin. They are not drinking literal blood; they are drinking from the cup of God's wrath. He does it because *they deserve it (16:6)*. In other words, it is a just thing to do. There is a law of retribution found in the Bible; a person sows, then he reaps.

> *Whoever sheds man's blood, by man his blood shall be shed, for in the image of God He made man. (Genesis 9:6, NASB95)*

God requires that murderers be punished with the loss of their lives. If man in his self-righteousness refuses to do it, He will take the matter into His own hands.

An attorney asked one dispensational Arminian who was facing jury duty, if she was willing to support the death penalty if the person was convicted of murder. Her reply was she could not do that, for who knows, perhaps some day that person might get saved. She was unwilling to enforce the law of God (and man), fearing that the person would thereby go to hell. But if given an extra, and unscriptural chance, he might choose to accept Christ. The thought that Christ might had not chosen to accept *him* was never entertained. Regenerating choice was to be found in the hand of man, not God. This is lawless antinomianism.

16:7 And I heard the altar saying, "Yes, O Lord God, the Almighty, true and righteous are Your judgements." The phrase *I heard the altar (16:7)* would refer to the angel of the altar or temple, the one to which John referred to when he said; *then I heard a loud voice from the temple* (16:1). So, by way of confirmation of the righteousness of these judgements, another angel joins in and validates God's righteousness in these judgements upon Christ's enemies. "…inasmuch as the altar stands in the temple above, in the immediate presence of the Godhead, so confirmation from such a source shows at once that all is approved by the Court of Heaven."[585]

Fourth Bowl: Men Are Scorched

16:8 The fourth angel poured out his bowl upon the sun, and it was given to it to scorch men with fire. By way of correspondence, the fourth trumpet covers similar material.

> *The fourth angel sounded, and a third of the sun and a third of the moon and a third of the stars were struck, so that a third of them would be darkened and the day would not shine for a third of it, and the night in the same way. (Revelation 8:12, NASB95)*

In both judgements, the **sun (16:8)** is the object of our attention. The trumpet records the darkening of the sun, while the bowl records its scorching heat upon **men (16:8)**. The corresponding Exodus plague is found in Exodus 10:21-23.

> *Then the Lord said to Moses, "Stretch out your hand toward the sky, that there may be darkness over the land of Egypt, even a*

---

[585] Moses Stuart, vol. II, 311.

> *darkness which may be felt." 22 So Moses stretched out his hand toward the sky, and there was thick darkness in all the land of Egypt for three days. 23 They did not see one another, nor did anyone rise from his place for three days, but all the sons of Israel had light in their dwellings. (Exodus 10:21-23, NASB95)*

It too is associated with the sun in its judgement and like the trumpet it is a darkening of the sun.

As we saw in our study of the fourth trumpet, the heavenly symbols, sun, moon, stars signify political leaders. Israel was the object of the wrath not only of Vespasian and Titus, but often even more importantly, of their own leaders. These men headed up various factions within the city and thereby produced greater death and destruction on Jerusalem than even Rome did. Their rule truly did **scorch men with fire**.

16:9   Men were scorched with fierce heat; and they blasphemed the name of God who has the power over these plagues, and they did not repent so as to give Him glory. At first thought, it would seem that those under the curse of God would quickly **repent (16:9)** and throw themselves on the mercy of God, but not the inhabitants of Jerusalem. Instead, **they blasphemed the name of God (16:9)** and utterly refused to repent of their sins.

> But these men, and these only, <u>were incapable of repenting of the wickednesses they had been guilty of</u>; and separating their souls from their bodies, they used them both as if they belonged to other folks, and not to themselves. For no gentle affection could touch their souls, nor could any pain affect their bodies, since they could still tear the dead bodies of the people as dogs do, and fill the prisons with those that were sick.[586]

Fifth Bowl: Darkness and Pain

16:10-11   Then the fifth angel poured out his bowl on the throne of the beast, and his kingdom became darkened; and they gnawed their tongues because of pain, [11] and they

---

[586] Flavius Josephus, *Wars*, 5:12:4

blasphemed the God of heaven because of their pains and their sores; and they did not repent of their deeds. What is not specifically mentioned is which *beast (16:10)* is being discussed, the beast out of the sea, or the beast out of the land? The additional comments stating that *his kingdom became darkened (16:10)* could certainly refer to the religious kingdom of the Pharisees, Sadducees and priest at Jerusalem during this period. The further comment that *they gnawed their tongues because of pain (16:10)* would easily put us right in the middle of the siege of Jerusalem. This is especially an apt description of what the people went through during these months. One faction or the other, fighting for the internal control of Jerusalem, murdered many people. And, like those mentioned in 16:9, *they blasphemed the God of heaven because of their pains and their sores; and they did not repent of their deeds (16:11).* There was no revival in Jerusalem brought on by recognition that they had murdered the King of Glory. But in answer to the prayers of their fathers, *"His blood shall be on us and on our children"* (Matthew 27:25), they continued in the hardness of their hearts to their ultimate and final destruction.

Now let us look at the correspondence to the fifth trumpet and Egyptian plague.

> *Then the fifth angel sounded, and I saw a star from heaven which had fallen to the earth [land]; and the key of the bottomless pit was given to him. 2 He opened the bottomless pit, and smoke went up out of the pit, like the smoke of a great furnace; and the sun and the air were darkened by the smoke of the pit. 3 Then out of the smoke came locusts upon the earth [land], and power was given them, as the scorpions of the earth [land] have power. (Revelation 9:1-3, NASB95)*

The eighth plague of the Exodus also deals with locusts.

> *Then the Lord said to Moses, "Stretch out your hand over the land of Egypt for the locusts, that they may come up on the land of Egypt and eat every plant of the land, even all that the hail has left.... 15 For they covered the surface of the whole land, so that the land was darkened; and they ate every plant of the land and all the fruit of the trees that the hail had left. Thus nothing green was left on tree or plant of the field through all the land of Egypt. (Exodus 10:12,15, NASB95)*

The apparent similarity between these and the bowl judgements is that in the bowl judgement the beast's **kingdom became darkened (16:10)**, while *the sun and the air were darkened* (9:2) by the locusts of the trumpet judgement and *the land was darkened* (Exodus 10:15) by the plague of the Exodus. Darkness, therefore, is the theme of this judgement. Darkness signals death and destruction. Certainly the **kingdom (16:10)** of religious Judaism **became darkened (16:10)** as it entered its last days of life.

It is possible that the beast under discussion was not the second one out of the land, but the first one out of the sea or Rome. The use of the word **throne (16:10)** and **kingdom (16:10)** give credence to that opinion. The **throne (16:10)** would be Nero's and the **kingdom (16:10)** the Roman Empire. If that were the case here then the civil war during and after Nero's reign would fit the picture of darkness before us. "...this Egyptian plague of darkness symbolizes the anarchy and civil war that befell the Empire after the suicide of Nero in A.D. 68,[587]

Sixth Bowl: Euphrates Dried Up

16:12 The sixth angel poured out his bowl on the great river, the Euphrates; and its water was dried up, so that the way would be prepared for the kings from the east. The sixth Trumpet judgement also takes us to the Euphrates.

> *Then the sixth angel sounded, and I heard a voice from the four horns of the golden altar which is before God, 14 one saying to the sixth angel who had the trumpet, "Release the four angels who are bound at the great river Euphrates." 15 And the four angels, who had been prepared for the hour and day and month and year, were released, so that they would kill a third of mankind. (Revelation 9:13-15, NASB95)*

The drying up of the **Euphrates (16:12)** and the drying up of the Red Sea are similarly striking pictures. In the one, God intervenes to help Israel and punishes her enemies, in the other, God intervenes to punish Israel and help her enemies. Although, God certainly dried up the Red Sea—literally—

---

[587] Philip Carrington, 264.

that is not the picture here. The comparison is to enhance the metaphor. God is saying that He will make it easy for the enemies of Israel to come swiftly from the frontier camps of the Romans to attack Jerusalem.

> Translated into historical terms, this symbol represents the mobilizing of the forces of the Empire and of the kings of the neighboring nations for the Jewish war. The drying up of the Euphrates seems plainly to signify its being crossed with ease and speed...the drawing of troops from that quarter for the invasion of Judea. This we know from historical fact. Not only Roman legions from the frontier of the Euphrates, but auxiliary kings whose dominions lay in that region, such as Anticochus of Commagene and Sohemus of Sophene, most properly designated 'kings from the east,' followed the eagles of Rome to the siege of Jerusalem.[588]

Josephus speaks of the movement of troops from various locations to the battle in Jerusalem. One of those locations is the river *Euphrates (6:12).*

> ...he also moved himself, together with the rest; besides whom marched those auxiliaries that came from the kings, being now more in number than before, together with a considerable number that came to his assistance from Syria. (43) Those also that had been selected out of these four legions, and sent with Mucianus to Italy had their places filled up out of these soldiers that came out of Egypt with Titus, (44) who were two thousand men, chosen out of the armies at Alexandria. There followed him also three thousand drawn from those that guarded <u>the river Euphrates</u>....[589]

Indeed *kings (16:12)* did send considerable military help to the Romans and many of these *kings (16:12)* were from the *east (16:12)*. "...so that the whole army, including the auxiliaries sent by the <u>kings</u>, as well horsemen and footmen, when all were united together....[590]

---

[588] J. Stuart Russell, 479.

[589] Flavius Josephus, *Wars*, 5:1:6.

[590] Ibid., *Wars*, 3:4:2.

Armageddon

16:13 And I saw coming out of the mouth of the dragon and out of the mouth of the beast and out of the mouth of the false prophet, three unclean spirits like frogs.... Notice the picture of the unholy trinity of the ***dragon (16:13)***, ***beast (16:13)*** and ***false prophet (16:13)***. Just as the God of heaven performs signs and wonders, so this fraudulent trinity attracts followers to Satan by performing *signs* (16:14). This stands as a warning to the current Church, not all *signs* (16:14), not all wonders are from God.

Three unclean spirits like frogs (16:13). One of the curses upon Egypt was the curse of the *frogs (16:13)*.

> *But if you refuse to let them go, behold, I will smite your whole territory with frogs. 3 The Nile will swarm with frogs, which will come up and go into your house and into your bedroom and on your bed, and into the houses of your servants and on your people, and into your ovens and into your kneading bowls. 4 So the frogs will come up on you and your people and all your servants. (Exodus 8:2-4, NASB95)*

The similarities between these curses and the curses of the Exodus are given to make a point. That point is this, Jerusalem is the new Egypt. As God cursed Egypt of old, so He now curses the new Egypt, Jerusalem. That point was clearly made in Revelation chapter 11:

> *And their dead bodies will lie in the street of the great city which mystically is called Sodom and Egypt, where also their Lord was crucified. (Revelation 11:8, NASB95)*

16:14 ...for they are spirits of demons, performing signs, which go out to the kings of the whole world, to gather them together for the war of the great day of God, the Almighty. In the decade of the 60's A.D., Rome's history was a time when the Empire was experiencing both civil wars and foreign wars. It was not a time when it had firm control of its allies. It was a time when troops were at a premium because of their commitment to so many other engagements. That decade opened with the great revolt in Britain under Boudicca in A.D. 60 which almost lost the Province to Rome, and saw the total destruction of the cities of Colchester, St. Albans and London with the massacre of all Romans and Roman allies found in them. The whole decade was one of strife, leading to the crescendo of the great fire of Rome (A.D. 64), to the Jewish rebellion, the revolt of the Germanic legions, the death of Nero, and the "year of the four Emperors." This is a decade in which Rome does not appear to be in firm control of its Empire. Therefore, if any of the allies of Rome have doubts that would deter them in their commitment to support Rome in this war, then these **spirits of demons (16:14)**, which these **frogs (16:13)** represent, go forth performing **signs (16:14)**, which produce the loyalty and commitment needed to field a great army at Jerusalem.

The phrase **the great day of God, the Almighty (16:14)** is a variation on the Old Testament phrase "*the day of the LORD*." "The day of Jehovah...is everywhere in the O. Testament a name for a day of evil, and mostly one of sore punishment."[591]

> *Alas for the day!*
> *For the day of the Lord is near,*
> *And it will come as destruction from the Almighty. (Joel 1:15,*
> *NASB95)*

It is this passage that Peter is quoting in Acts.

> *But Peter, taking his stand with the eleven, raised his voice and declared to them: "Men of Judea and all you who live in Jerusalem, let this be known to you and give heed to my words. "For these men are not drunk, as you suppose, for it is only the third hour of the day; but this is what was spoken of through the prophet Joel: 'And it shall be in the last days,' God says, 'That I will pour forth of My Spirit on all mankind; And your sons and your daughters shall prophesy, And your young men shall see visions, And your old men shall dream dreams; Even on My bondslaves, both men and women, I will in those days pour forth of My Spirit And they shall prophesy. 'And I will grant wonders in the sky above And signs on the earth below, Blood, and fire, and vapor of smoke. The sun will be turned into darkness and the moon into blood, Before the great and glorious day of the*

---

[591] Moses Stuart, vol. II, 315.

*Lord shall come. 'And it shall be that everyone who calls on the
name of the Lord will be saved.' (Acts 2:14-21, NASB95)*

This passage in Acts is another one of those verses that make little sense to a
Dispensationalist. The best they can hope to do is make the passage
irrelevant by stating the "last days" have now lasted 2,000 years and
counting, making the years concluding Israel's era longer than the whole of
their national existence combined. But that is not the case. As Peter stated,
this end game started at Pentecost and, as John demonstrates, is now
concluding 40 years later in the destruction of Jerusalem.

**16:15 ("Behold, I am coming like a thief. Blessed is the one
who stays awake and keeps his clothes, so that he will not walk
about naked and men will not see his shame.")** Christ's seeming
delay and unexpected **coming (16:15)** was illustrated in Christ's parable
of the wedding feast.

> *Jesus spoke to them again in parables, saying, 2 "The kingdom of
> heaven may be compared to a king who gave a wedding feast for
> his son. 3 And he sent out his slaves to call those who had been
> invited to the wedding feast, and they were unwilling to come. 4
> Again he sent out other slaves saying, 'Tell those who have been
> invited, "Behold, I have prepared my dinner; my oxen and my
> fattened livestock are all butchered and everything is ready; come
> to the wedding feast."' 5 But they paid no attention and went
> their way, one to his own farm, another to his business, 6 and the
> rest seized his slaves and mistreated them and killed them. 7 But
> the king was enraged, and he sent his armies and destroyed those
> murderers and set their city on fire. (Matthew 22:1-7, NASB95)*

For nearly forty years now, from the death of Christ to the destruction of
Jerusalem, Christ's servants have been inviting the inhabitants of Judea to
the wedding feast, but they were unwilling to come. Indeed, they *seized*
some and *mistreated* and *killed* others. And now the enraged king has *sent
his armies and destroyed those murderers and set their city on fire.*

In the beginning of the Book of Revelation, here in the middle, and finally at
the end, the writer warns his readers of His soon coming in judgement.
Matthew made the same point.

> *Therefore be on the alert, for you do not know which day your Lord is coming. (Matthew 24:42, NASB95)*

> *But keep on the alert at all times, praying that you may have strength to escape all these things that are about to take place, and to stand before the Son of Man. (Luke 21:36, NASB95)*

These verses clearly teach the importance of alertness and preparation for the *quick* return of Christ. This was a first century message. The readers of Revelation would, no doubt, understand that this message was for them. It was they that must **stay awake (16:15)**. This is not to say that a future bodily return of Christ is not also impending, it certainly is, only that this passage and the ones in Matthew and Luke are not dealing with Christ's bodily return on the last day, but with His coming in judgement on Jerusalem in A.D. 70.

But what of the part about keeping his **clothes (16:15)** and being **naked (16:15)**? That certainly appears to be an esoteric element (one of many in Revelation). Interestingly, Edersheim tells of the role of the Temple guards in keeping watch during the night and how the captain of the guard would check on them during the watch. If he found any asleep, he would beat them. If he found them asleep a second time, he would set their clothes on fire. And remember, it was not uncommon for a person to own only one set of clothes in that day! Edersheim says,

> Perhaps one of the most striking instances of this kind is afforded by the words quoted at the head of this chapter—'Blessed is he that watcheth, and keepeth his garments.' They literally describe, as we learn from the Rabbis, the punishment awarded to the Temple-guards if found asleep at their posts; and the Rabbinical account of it is curiously confirmed by the somewhat naive confession of one of their number, that on a certain occasion his own maternal uncle had actually undergone the punishment of having his clothes set on fire by the captain of the Temple as he went his rounds at night.[592]

Presumably, he would take them off, burning as they were, as quickly as possible under those circumstances and thereby find himself **naked**

---

[592] Alfred Edersheim, The Temple Its Ministry and Services, 102.

(16:15). The message is one of watchfulness. The faithful watched and were not caught up in the destruction of Jerusalem. Others slept, while ostensibly guarding the things of God, the Temple, and are now being stripped of their country, city, clothes and lives as all are now burnt up in the fire, not to speak of the eternal damnation that awaits them.

16:16 *And they gathered them together to the place which in Hebrew is called Har-Magedon.* This is the only reference to **Har-Magedon (16:16)** or Armageddon found in the entire Bible. Let us look at the historical context of the passage.

Armageddon, a name found only in ***Rev. 16:16*** is described as the rallying place of the kings of the whole world who, led by the unclean spirits issuing from the mouth of the dragon, the beast, and the false prophet, assemble here for *the war of the great day of God, the Almighty* (Revelation 16:14).

> Although the author designates the name as Hebrew, ... its derivation is uncertain. The generally accepted view is that the word *har* means mountain (or mountains) and that *magedon* refers to Megiddo, the biblical city near which many notable battles were fought. Here the armies of Israel defeated Sisera and his host (Jgs. 5:19), and later it was the scene of the fatal struggle between Josiah and Pharaoh Neco (2 K. 23:29f; 2 Ch. 35:22). There was, therefore, a peculiar appropriateness in the choice of this as the arena of the last mighty struggle between the powers of good and evil....
>
> Because the phrase "mountains of Megiddo" does not occur elsewhere, some scholars have conjectured interpretations such as "city of Megiddo," "land of Megiddo," or "mount of assembly"; but none has met with general acceptance. "Mountains" seems to be the best translation for *har*. Megiddo itself was a hill town, and the district was in part mountainous....[593]

---

[593] Geoffrey W. Bromiley, ed, International Standard Bible Encyclopedia (Grand Rapids, MI: William B. Eerdmans Publishing Company, 2001), Armageddon, Vol. 1, 295.

Two things of importance need to be noted here. First, Megiddo was a place associated with indescribable grief to the Jew. It was here that one of their greatest and most godly kings died.

> *However, Josiah would not turn away from him, but disguised himself in order to make war with him; nor did he listen to the words of Neco from the mouth of God, but came to make war on the plain of Megiddo. The archers shot King Josiah, and the king said to his servants, "Take me away, for I am badly wounded." So his servants took him out of the chariot and carried him in the second chariot which he had, and brought him to Jerusalem where he died and was buried in the tombs of his fathers. All Judah and Jerusalem mourned for Josiah. Then Jeremiah chanted a lament for Josiah. And all the male and female singers speak about Josiah in their lamentations to this day. And they made them an ordinance in Israel; behold, they are also written in the Lamentations. (2 Chronicles 35:22-25, NASB95)*

This event made a lasting mark on the conscience of Israel. Associating grief and sorrow with Megiddo the Biblical writers used this reference to note that there would come another time in which such sorrow would strike Israel. Revelation 1:7 references Zechariah 12:10 which refers to Christ crucifixion and to Pentecost. Revelation 16 continues with that thought taking us to the conclusion of that mourning, to those people that did not respond in repentance and faith.

> *I will pour out on the house of David and on the inhabitants of Jerusalem, the Spirit of grace and of supplication, so that they will look on Me whom they have pierced; and they will mourn for Him, as one mourns for an only son, and they will weep bitterly over Him like the bitter weeping over a firstborn. In that day there will be great mourning in Jerusalem, <u>like the mourning of Hadadrimmon in the plain of Megiddo</u>. The land will mourn, every family by itself.... (Zechariah 12:10-12, NASB95)*

Reference is made to "Hadadrimmon." "The term refers to a place near Megiddo at which mourning for Josiah took place after his death in battle against Pharaoh Neco...."[594] Notice the phrase "like the mourning of

---

[594] Ibid., Vol. 2, Page 591.

Hadadrimmon." Revelation picks up this theme of mourning, speaking of this gathering at a place called **Har-Magedon (16:16)**. This is a gathering for a great mourning like the mourning Israel did for King Josiah when he died. However, in this mourning the Jews mourn for the death of Israel itself.

Second, Megiddo was a fortress town on one edge of the valley of Jezreel. It overlooked a great valley where armies often gathered to fight. Because it was so strategically located, it was a military necessity to take this fortress town if one wanted to dominate the battlefield. An army never gives the high ground to the enemy. As a result, Megiddo could be a precarious place to live. In other words, there was not a lot of security in being an inhabitant of Megiddo. It was the object of an invading army's immediate attention.

That being the case, if you wanted to create a picture of a great army gathering to attack and destroy a city set on a hill or mountain, could you pick a better one than by referring to **Har-Magedon (16:16)** or "Mount of Megiddo?" "This figure in the text of the apocalypse was employed not for the physical location but for the battle imagery."[595] This is a point of considerable significance. The Mount of Megiddo was not and is not the geographic center of our study here. It is Jerusalem. However, **Har-Magedon (16:16)** had one considerable contribution to make. It lent its considerable history to the crises Jerusalem was then facing. Jerusalem is set on a mountain as well. God is saying that it too is facing destruction by gathering armies. The image of **Har-Magedon (16:16)** as a city facing attack and destruction makes that point with flair. Jerusalem is the city set on a hill. Jerusalem, like **Har-Magedon (16:16)** so often before it, will now suffer attack and defeat.

The unholy trinity of the *dragon* (16:13), the *beast* (16:13) and the *false prophet* (16:13) are determined to destroy what they envision as "*the apple of His eye*" (Zechariah 2:8), not realizing it is He who has given Jerusalem up to destruction. This unholy trinity has succeeded in gathering the kings of the whole world to do this evil deed. But it is instead *the war of the great day of God, the Almighty* (Revelation 16:14).

Please take note: the battle of **Har-Magedon (16:16)** has already occurred; it was one and the same as the battle of Jerusalem in A.D. 70.

---

595 Foy E. Wallace, Jr., 335.

Seventh Bowl: The Earth Utterly Shaken

16:17 *Then the seventh angel poured out his bowl upon the air, and a loud voice came out of the temple from the throne, saying, "It is done."* This **voice (16:17)** from **out of the temple from the throne (16:17)** is "signifying God's control and approval."[596] "God himself is the speaker...in order to denote the full certainty of the destruction threatened...."[597] "The announcement, *It is done!* (v. 17) brings us to the long-anticipated culmination of what had seemed an endless stream of judgements."[598]

16:18 *And there were flashes of lightning and sounds and peals of thunder; and there was a great earthquake, such as there had not been since man came to be upon the earth, so great an earthquake was it, and so mighty.* This last bowl judgement **(16:18)** brings us back to the sixth seal, which was also the last seal. Again, this suggests the cyclic nature of the judgements in Revelation.

> *I looked when He broke the sixth seal, and there was a great earthquake; and the sun became black as sackcloth made of hair, and the whole moon became like blood; 13 and the stars of the sky fell to the earth [land], as a fig tree casts its unripe figs when shaken by a great wind. 14 The sky was split apart like a scroll when it is rolled up, and every mountain and island were moved out of their places. 15 Then the kings of the earth [land] and the great men and the commanders and the rich and the strong and every slave and free man hid themselves in the caves and among the rocks of the mountains; 16 and they said to the mountains and to the rocks, "Fall on us and hide us from the presence of Him who sits on the throne, and from the wrath of the Lamb; 17 for the great day of their wrath has come, and who is able to stand?* (Revelation 6:12-17, NASB95)

---

[596] David Chilton, The Great Tribulation, 412.

[597] Moses Stuart, vol. II, 317.

[598] Steve Gregg, 388.

An ***earthquake (16:18)*** was used as an illustration by Isaiah of the destruction that God would bring upon Jerusalem in its first destruction in 586 BC. He said,

> *From the Lord of hosts you will be punished with thunder and*
> *earthquake and loud noise, with whirlwind and tempest and the*
> *flame of a consuming fire. (Isaiah 29:6, NASB95)*

Of course, there was no actual earthquake during this period. But that was not necessary. It was not an actual earthquake that God is here threatening either. It is stylized language referring to the coming destruction upon Jerusalem. Ezekiel makes the same point,

> *In My zeal and in My blazing wrath I declare that on that day*
> *there will surely be a great earthquake in the land of Israel. The*
> *fish of the sea, the birds of the heavens, the beasts of the field, all*
> *the creeping things that creep on the earth [land], and all the men*
> *who are on the face of the earth [land] will shake at My presence;*
> *the mountains also will be thrown down, the steep pathways will*
> *collapse and every wall will fall to the ground. (Ezekiel 38:19-20,*
> *NASB95)*

"The earthquake is the symbol of revolution, the shaking up of the nations in their various places. It is the figure of the agitations, upheavals, resulting in the revolutions and wars.... It is the symbol of divine judgement on the nations persecuting the cause of the Lamb."[599] An earthquake is a prophetic word picture for the coming destruction of a society. That is the case here; Jerusalem is overthrown. The world has come to an end for the inhabitants of Jerusalem and Judea. So predicted the author of Hebrews.

> *This expression, "Yet once more," denotes the removing of those*
> *things which can be shaken, as of created things, so that those*
> *things which cannot be shaken may remain. Therefore, since we*
> *receive a kingdom which cannot be shaken, let us show gratitude,*
> *by which we may offer to God an acceptable service with*
> *reverence and awe; for our God is a consuming fire. (Hebrews*
> *12:27-29, NASB95)*

---

599 Foy E. Wallace, Jr., 153.

The things that can be shaken, apostate Israel, are indeed now shaken with the judgement of God. That which cannot be shaken, His Church, abides forever.

16:19 *The great city was split into three parts, and the cities of the nations fell. Babylon the great was remembered before God, to give her the cup of the wine of His fierce wrath.* This statement, ***the great city was split into three parts (16:19)***, could refer to the methods used by Titus in the destruction of Jerusalem; breaking in the ***city (16:19)*** in different places and cutting off the rebels into three parts.

Or, possibly, it refers to the internal divisions within the ***city (16:19)*** during the war.

> This refers to the division into three factions, which became acute after the return of Titus. While Titus was besieging it from without, the three leaders of rival factions were fighting fiercely within; but for this the city might have staved off defeat for a long time, even perhaps indefinitely, for no great army could support itself for long in those days in the neighborhood of Jerusalem; there was no water and no supplies. This fighting within the city delivered it quickly into the hands of Titus....[600]

"And now there were three treacherous factions in the city, the one parted from the other. Eleazar and his party, that kept the sacred first-fruits, came against John in their cups. Those that were with John plundered the populace, and went out with zeal against Simon. This Simon had his supply of provisions from the city, in opposition to the seditious."[601]

Or, it may very well refer in a similar way to what Ezekiel prophesied.

> *As for you, son of man, take a sharp sword; take and use it as a barber's razor on your head and beard. Then take scales for weighing and divide the hair. 2 One third you shall burn in the fire at the center of the city, when the days of the siege are*

---

[600] Philip Carrington, 266.

[601] Flavius Josephus, *Wars*, 5:1:4.

> *completed. Then you shall take one third and strike it with the
> sword all around the city, and one third you shall scatter to the
> wind; and I will unsheathe a sword behind them. (Ezekiel 5:1-2,
> NASB95)*

This position would refer to one-third dying in the city during the siege, probably from famine and disease. An additional one-third would die from the sword in the battles with the Romans, and a final one-third would be taken as prisoners and slaves or scattered among the nations.

> *One third of you will die by plague or be consumed by famine
> among you, one third will fall by the sword around you, and one
> third I will scatter to every wind, and I will unsheathe a sword
> behind them. (Ezekiel 5:12, NASB95)*

Notice how the phrases **great city (16:19)** and **cities of the nations (16:19)** are set in opposition to each other as distinct and separate entities. The point here is that Rome would not fit this distinction, for Rome was indeed a city of the nations, or gentiles, as it is often translated. However, Jerusalem fits very well and is indeed set apart from the **cities of the nations (16:19)**.

This phrase, **and the cities of the nations fell (16:19)**, at first glance just doesn't seem to fit here. Look at the context. The **great city (16:19)** is divided into **three parts (16:19)**, the cities of the nations **fell (16:19)**, Babylon the great was **remembered before God (16:19)**, every island fled away (16:20), mountains were not found (16:20), and huge hailstones (16:21) came down. Except for the islands (16:20) and the mountains (16:20) all the phrases refer directly to things that happened to Jerusalem. In the midst of these specific disasters that befall Jerusalem, three symbolic statements are made, one about islands (16:20), one about mountains (16:20) and one about gentile cities, *the nations* (16:19). The meaning of our difficult passage must be found in this context. The main point of the passage is Jerusalem is falling. This is explained in the points made. How does the phrase, cities of the nations fell (16:19), fit into this context? It fits in the same way islands (16:20) and mountains (16:20) fit. The removal of the islands (16:20) and mountains (16:20) is symbolic of the destruction of all that opposes God. Hebrews 12 brings this to light.

> *This expression, "Yet once more," denotes the removing of those
> things which can be shaken, as of created things, so that those*

things which cannot be shaken may remain. Therefore, since we
receive a kingdom which cannot be shaken, let us show gratitude,
by which we may offer to God an acceptable service with
reverence and awe; for our God is a consuming fire. (Hebrews
12:27-29, NASB95)

Cities in the ancient world were city-states or city-kingdoms. Here in Hebrews the author talks about a kingdom, which cannot be shaken—the new Jerusalem. This city is evident amongst those that can be shaken. The kingdoms and cities of this world can be shaken and they indeed do fall. Not only does the old Jerusalem fall in the presence of God's eternal kingdom but so do all the city-states, kingdoms, islands and mountains of this world. The new Jerusalem cannot be shaken and therefore does not fall.

Babylon the great (16:19) is the code name for Jerusalem in the Book of Revelation. John mentions Babylon earlier using the same wine symbolism.

And another angel, a second one, followed, saying, "Fallen, fallen
is Babylon the great, she who has made all the nations drink of
the wine of the passion of her immorality." 9 Then another angel,
a third one, followed them, saying with a loud voice, "If anyone
worships the beast and his image, and receives a mark on his
forehead or on his hand, 10 he also will drink of the wine of the
wrath of God, which is mixed in full strength in the cup of His
anger; and he will be tormented with fire and brimstone in the
presence of the holy angels and in the presence of the Lamb."
(Revelation 14:8-10, NASB95)

16:20 And every island fled away, and the mountains were not found. Again, this is symbolic language of the utter destruction of Israel. Jeremiah said something similar as he considered the coming destruction of Judah at the hands of Babylon.

I looked on the earth, and behold, it was formless and void;
And to the heavens, and they had no light.
24 I looked on the mountains, and behold, they were quaking,
And all the hills moved to and fro.
25 I looked, and behold, there was no man,

And all the birds of the heavens had fled.
26 I looked, and behold, the fruitful land was a wilderness,
And all its cities were pulled down
Before the Lord, before His fierce anger. (Jeremiah 4:23-26,
NASB95)

These word pictures do not describe literal islands and mountains, they describe the destruction of a people and a culture, a destruction so utterly thorough that the closest analogy he can imagine is the leveling of creation itself.

16:21 *And huge hailstones, about one hundred pounds each, came down from heaven upon men; and men blasphemed God because of the plague of the hail, because its plague was extremely severe.* "One might conjecture that the author had in mind not so much hail from heaven as the stones sent by catapults and other army equipment...."[602] Josephus gives an account of stones cast by Roman war engines that weighed a talent or about one hundred pounds. This very probably is what John is referring to here.

> The engines, that all the legions had ready prepared for them, were admirably contrived; but still more extraordinary ones belonged to the tenth legion: those that threw darts and those that threw stones, were more forcible and larger than the rest, by which they not only repelled the excursions of the Jews, but drove those away that were upon the walls also. (270) Now, the stones that were cast were of the weight of a talent, and were carried two furlongs and farther. The blow they gave was no way to be sustained, not only by those that stood first in the way, but by those that were beyond them for a great space. (271) As for the Jews, they at first watched the coming of the stone, for it was of a white color, and could therefore not only be perceived by the great noise it made, but could be seen also before it came by its brightness; (272) accordingly the watchmen that sat upon the towers gave them notice when the engine was let go, and the stone came from it, and cried out aloud in their own country language, "THE SON COMETH:" so those that were in its way stood off, and threw

---

[602] J. Massyngberde Ford, 265.

themselves down upon the ground; by which means, and by their thus guarding themselves, the stone fell down and did them no harm. (273) But the Romans contrived how to prevent that by blacking the stone, who then could aim at them with success, when the stone was not discerned beforehand, as it had been till then; and so they destroyed many of them at one blow.[603]

"A remarkable feature of the siege of Jerusalem was the artillery; a new kind of catapult was used which cast huge blocks of white limestone that did weigh a Talent."[604]

But what could that phrase "the son cometh" mean? Stuart Russell says this of this phrase.

It could not but be well known to the Jews that the great hope and faith of the Christians was the speedy coming of the Son. It was about this very time, according to Hegesippus, that St. James, the brother of our Lord, publicly testified in the temple that 'the Son of man was about to come in the clouds of heaven,' and then sealed his testimony with his blood. It seems highly probable that the Jews, in their defiant and desperate blasphemy, when they saw the white mass hurtling through the air, raised the ribald cry, 'The Son is coming,' in mockery of the Christian hope of the Parousia, to which they might trace a ludicrous resemblance in the strange appearance of the missile.[605]

In concluding this chapter, it is critical to note that John has gone to great lengths to make the point that Israel is now the object of the covenant curses. As He promised to *bring back on you all the diseases of Egypt*, so He has done. The Book of Revelation is clearly a covenant lawsuit.

If you are not careful to observe all the words of this law which are written in this book, to fear this honored and awesome name, the Lord your God, 59 then the Lord will bring extraordinary plagues on you and your descendants, even severe and lasting plagues, and miserable and chronic sicknesses. 60 He will bring

---

[603] Flavius Josephus, *Wars*, 5:6:3.

[604] Philip Carrington, 273.

[605] J. Stuart Russell, 482.

*back on you all the diseases of Egypt of which you were afraid,
and they will cling to you. 61 Also every sickness and every
plague which, not written in the book of this law, the Lord will
bring on you until you are destroyed. 62 Then you shall be left
few in number, whereas you were as numerous as the stars of
heaven, because you did not obey the Lord your God. 63 It shall
come about that as the Lord delighted over you to prosper you,
and multiply you, so the Lord will delight over you to make you
perish and destroy you; and you will be torn from the land where
you are entering to possess it. (Deuteronomy 28:58-63, NASB95)*

"...the author has followed carefully, albeit with ingenuity, the Levitical and Deuteronomic warnings, even to the point of portraying three-fold punishments as in Lev 26:18, 21, 24, and taking very literally the text of Deut 28:60-61, that if the Israelites do not obey "the words of this law" ... then Yahweh would turn all the plagues of Egypt back on them, and add even those not mentioned in the book of the law."[606]

---

[606] J. Massyngberde Ford, 282.

Chapter 17

Babylon Remembered

The Doom of Babylon

" ... **B**abylon the Harlot and Jerusalem the Bride are the two great figures in the concluding portion of the Apocalypse. The one must be overthrown before the other can appear in her full glory."[607] Chapters 17 and 18 give us full details of the Harlot's destruction. Chapter 19 introduces us to the new bride and the marriage supper of the lamb.

17:1 Then one of the seven angels who had the seven bowls came and spoke with me, saying, "Come here, I will show you the judgement of the great harlot who sits on many waters.... The word **judgement (17:1)** here is κρίμα (krímα). This word "...may mean lawsuit, judgement, judicial verdict, or sentence of condemnation."[608] Indeed, Israel is here experiencing the judicial result of a lawsuit by God against her for her harlotry. She has been found guilty and the sentence of condemnation is now being exercised against her.

Who is **the great harlot (17:1)**? There are two common positions. One, she is Rome; two, she is Jerusalem. A good case can be made, and is made, for either. Let us begin by focusing on the word **harlot (17:1)**.

> *How the faithful city has become a harlot,*
> *She who was full of justice!*
> *Righteousness once lodged in her,*
> *But now murderers. (Isaiah 1:21, NASB95)*

> *But come here, you sons of a sorceress,*
> *Offspring of an adulterer and a prostitute. (Isaiah 57:3, NASB95)*

> *For long ago I broke your yoke*
> *And tore off your bonds;*

---

[607] Milton S. Terry, <u>Biblical Apocalyptics</u>, 426.
[608] J. Massyngberde Ford, 277.

But you said, 'I will not serve!'
For on every high hill
And under every green tree
You have lain down as a harlot. (Jeremiah 2:20, NASB95)

But you trusted in your beauty and played the harlot because of
your fame, and you poured out your harlotries on every passer-
by who might be willing. (Ezekiel 16:15, NASB95)

In each case, the Scripture is referring to Israel or Jerusalem in these passages. Biblically, Jerusalem is a **harlot (17:1)** and appears to be the **harlot (17:1)** spoken of in this passage. Therefore, with Terry, we conclude "the Jerusalem and Judah which thus rejected the Christ of God were therefore guilty of the most criminal apostasy, and are appropriately called the great harlot."[609]

The next phrase, **who sits on many waters (17:1)**, is interpreted in verse 15. There we read *"The waters which you saw where the harlot sits, are peoples and multitudes and nations and tongues"* (17:15). Those that see the **harlot (17:1)** as Rome understand this to mean that Rome rules many nations.

On the other hand, those that see the **harlot (17:1)** as Jerusalem understand this to mean that Jerusalem extends its religious influence over a vast area and people. Acts chapter 2 makes the point in describing those that came to Jerusalem at Pentecost.

And how is it that we each hear them in our own language to
which we were born? 9 Parthians and Medes and Elamites, and
residents of Mesopotamia, Judea and Cappadocia, Pontus and
Asia, 10 Phrygia and Pamphylia, Egypt and the districts of Libya
around Cyrene, and visitors from Rome, both Jews and
proselytes, 11 Cretans and Arabs—we hear them in our own
tongues speaking of the mighty deeds of God. (Acts 2:8-11,
NASB95)

Again, one author records the extent of Jewish emigration and growth in these terms.

---

[609] Milton S. Terry, Biblical Apocalyptics, 427.

The Roman-Hellenistic period is characterized by an increase in the number of Jews throughout the civilized world. Hundreds of thousands of Jews lived in Babylon, Syria, Cyprus, Asia Minor, Egypt, Cyreaica, the Dodecanese Islands, Greece and Italy. Their number grew from generation to generation by the combined effect of natural increase, migration from Palestine and conversions to Judaism, which reached record proportions during the generation preceding the destruction of the Temple.[610]

One is reminded of Christ's statement to the Pharisees *"Woe to you, scribes and Pharisees, hypocrites, because you travel around on sea and land to make one proselyte; and when he becomes one, you make him twice as much a son of hell as yourselves* (Matthew 23:15). And indeed, the Jews had done just that across the known world. For this reason, Paul and others could go into most any city in the empire and find Jews and their proselytes to minister to. As Russell says, "The influence exercised by the Jewish race in all parts of the Roman Empire previous to the destruction of Jerusalem was immense; their synagogues were to be found in every city, and their colonies took root in every land."[611]

So in this sense, the idea of great influence, Jerusalem sat **on many waters (17:1)**.

17:2 ...with whom the kings of the earth [land] committed acts of immorality, and those who dwell on the earth [land] were made drunk with the wine of her immorality. First, if one were to view the word **earth (17:2)** as whole (known) world, and not land, then there actually was an international extent and influence held by Israel over the **kings of the earth (17:2)**. Josephus gives us some idea of the extend of the lands that the Jews ruled over saying of Jerusalem that this,

> ...royal city Jerusalem was the supreme, and presided over all the neighboring country, as the head does over the body. As to the other cities that were inferior to it, they presided over their several

---

[610] Benjamin Mazor and Moshe Davis, The Illustrated History of the Jews (New York, N.Y.: Harper and Row, 1963), 127.

[611] J. Stuart Russell, 503.

toparchies; (55) Gophna was the second of those cities, and next to that Acrabatta, after them Thamna, and Lydda, and Emmaus, and Pella, and Idumea, and Engaddi, and Herodium, and Jericho; (56) and after them came Jamnia, and Joppa, as presiding over the neighboring people; and besides these there was the region of Gamala, and Gaulanitis, and Batanea, and Trachonitis, which are also parts of the kingdom of Agrippa. (57) This [last] country begins at Mount Libanus, and the fountains of Jordan, and reaches breadthways to the lake of Tiberias; and in length is extended from a village called Arpha, as far as Julias.[612]

Philo adds valuable insight into this subject saying,

Concerning the holy city I must now say what is necessary. It, as I have already stated, is my native country, and the metropolis not only of the one country of Judaea but also of many, by reason of the colonies which it has sent out from time to time into the bordering districts of Egypt, Phoenicia, Syria in general, and especially that part of it which is called Coelo-Syria and also with those more distant regions of Pamphylia, Cilicia, the greater part of Asia Minor as far as Bithynia, and the furthermost corners of Pontus. And in the same manner into Europe, into Thessaly, and Boeotia, and Macedonia, and Aetolia, and Attica, and Argus, and Corinth and all the most fertile and wealthiest districts of Peloponnesus, (282) And not only are the continents full of Jewish colonies, but also all the most celebrated islands are so too; such as Euboea, and Cyprus, and Crete. "I say nothing of the countries beyond the Euphrates, for all of them except a very small portion, and Babylon, and all the satrapies around, which have any advantages whatever of soil or climate, have Jews settled in them.

(283) So that if my native land is, as it reasonably may be, looked upon as entitled to a share in your favour it is not one city only that would then be benefited by you, but ten thousand of them in every region of the habitable world, in Europe, in Asia, and in Africa, on the continent, in the islands, on the coasts, and in the inland parts. (284) And it corresponds well to the greatness of your good fortune, that, by conferring benefits on one city, you should also

---

[612] Flavius Josephus, *Wars*, 3:3:5.

benefit ten thousand others, so that your renown may be celebrated in every part of the habitable world, and many praises of you may be combined with thanksgiving.[613]

Second, if one were to view the word as *land* and not **earth (17:2)**, the religious community and priesthood of Israel have been in bed, figuratively and literally, with the kings in and of the land. The Sadducees, those that controlled the priesthood, were quite willing to work hand in glove with Rome and murder Christ, if that is what it would take to secure their position, power and prestige.

> *...nor do you take into account that it is expedient for you that one man die for the people, and that the whole nation not perish. (John 11:50, NASB95)*

In earlier Jewish history, the kings of Israel followed the Baals instead of Yahweh. Manasseh, working hand and glove with the priest of Jerusalem, was especially evil in his idolatry.

> *Manasseh ... did evil in the sight of the Lord according to the abominations of the nations whom the Lord dispossessed before the sons of Israel. 3 For he rebuilt the high places which Hezekiah his father had broken down; he also erected altars for the Baals and made Asherim, and worshiped all the host of heaven and served them. 4 He built altars in the house of the Lord of which the Lord had said, "My name shall be in Jerusalem forever." 5 For he built altars for all the host of heaven in the two courts of the house of the Lord. 6 He made his sons pass through the fire in the valley of Ben-hinnom; and he practiced witchcraft, used divination, practiced sorcery and dealt with mediums and spiritists. He did much evil in the sight of the Lord, provoking Him to anger. 7 Then he put the carved image of the idol which he had made in the house of God, of which God had said to David and to Solomon his son, "In this house and in Jerusalem, which I have chosen from all the tribes of Israel, I will put My name forever; 8 and I will not again remove the foot of Israel from the land which I have appointed for your fathers, if only they will observe to do*

---

[613] http://www.geocities.com/Paris/leftBank/5210/gaggripa.htm, Philo of Alexandria: On the Embassy to Gaius

> *all that I have commanded them according to all the law, the*
> *statutes and the ordinances given through Moses." 9 Thus*
> *Manasseh misled Judah and the inhabitants of Jerusalem to do*
> *more evil than the nations whom the Lord destroyed before the*
> *sons of Israel. (2 Chronicles 33:1-9)*

The point being, it was the kings of the **land (17:2)** of Israel that the religious crowd fornicated with. It was not Rome that was committing acts of immorality; it was Jerusalem that was the *harlot* (17:1). As has been noted, "In the OT the term זנה *zānâ*, 'fornicate, be a prostitute,' is frequently used in a figurative sense of Israel's faithless behavior toward Yahweh as manifested in her frequent lapses into idolatry. This is based on the analogy of the covenant between Yahweh and Israel and marriage contracts...."[614] "...the harlot in Rev 17 is Jerusalem, not Rome. Indeed, if it is the covenant relationship with Yahweh which makes Israel his special people, his bride, how could a non-Israelite nation be called "harlot" except in a much less precise sense? It is the covenant which makes the bride, the breaking of it which makes the adulteress."[615]

17:3 And he carried me away in the Spirit into a wilderness; and I saw a woman sitting on a scarlet beast, full of blasphemous names, having seven heads and ten horns. To find the harlot, John had to be taken to where she was. She was in the **wilderness (17:3)**. Hosea spoke of adulterous Israel this way:

> *... For she is not my wife, and I am not her husband; / and let her*
> *put away her harlotry from her face / and her adultery from*
> *between her breasts, / 3 or I will strip her naked / and expose her*
> *as on the day when she was born. / I will also make her like a*
> *<u>wilderness</u>, / make her like desert land / and slay her with thirst.*
> *(Hosea 2:2-3, NASB95)*

So here again Israel is located in a *desert land* or **wilderness (17:3)**, and for the same reason, harlotry. The **woman (17:3)**, as we indicated, is Israel. The **beast (17:3)** as we know from chapter 13 of Revelation is Rome.

---

[614] D. E. Aune, Vol. 52C: Revelation 17-22, Rev. 17:2.

[615] J. Massyngberde Ford, 285.

Then I saw a beast coming up out of the sea, having ten horns and seven heads, and on his horns were ten diadems, and on his heads were blasphemous names. (Revelation 13:1, NASB95)

The **woman (17:3)** sits on the **beast (17:3)**, which is Rome. Jerusalem is supported by and uses the beast for her own purposes. And what was their purpose? *"If we let Him go on like this, all men will believe in Him, and the Romans will come and take away both our place and our nation"* (John 11:48, NASB95). Their purpose was to continue in position, power and prestige at whatever cost.

The Jewish people, at the time this Apocalypse was written, had been dependent for their national existence a hundred years on Rome and for this reason it is said of her that she was **sitting on a scarlet beast (17:3)**.[616] "The prostitute's sitting on the beast (17:3) is ironic: It indicates not identity with Rome, but dependence on Rome. The image reminds us of Israel's past dependence on Rome so that she could attack Christ and his followers."[617] Along this line, Josephus speaks of "...all the honors that the Romans and their emperor paid to our nation, and of the leagues of mutual assistance they have made with it...."[618]

What does the **seven heads and ten horns (17:3)** refer to? The **seven heads (17:3)** refer to seven Roman emperors and the **ten horns (17:3)** refer to regional monarchs subject to Rome. We will look at this more carefully in 17:9.

17:4 The woman was clothed in purple and scarlet, and adorned with gold and precious stones and pearls, having in her hand a gold cup full of abominations and of the unclean things of her immorality.... The picture is of the garments and adornments of the high priest. The Scripture speaks of the priestly garments in this way,

---

[616] Milton S. Terry, Biblical Apocalyptics, 428.

[617] C. Marvin Pate, Editor, 78.

[618] Flavius Josephus, *Antiquities*, 14,10,7.

> *Moreover, from the blue and purple and scarlet material, they
> made finely woven garments for ministering in the holy place as
> well as the holy garments which were for Aaron, just as the Lord
> had commanded Moses. He made the ephod of gold, and of blue
> and purple and scarlet material, and fine twisted linen. Then
> they hammered out gold sheets and cut them into threads to be
> woven in with the blue and the purple and the scarlet material,
> and the fine linen, the work of a skillful workman. (Exodus 39:1-3,
> NASB95)*

"That the harlot is bedecked with gold and precious stones ... sounds like a perversion of the high priest's breastplate."[619]

> *He made the breastpiece, the work of a skillful workman, like the
> workmanship of the ephod: of gold and of blue and purple and
> scarlet material and fine twisted linen. It was square; they made
> the breastpiece folded double, a span long and a span wide when
> folded double. And they mounted four rows of stones on it. The
> first row was a row of ruby, topaz, and emerald; and the second
> row, a turquoise, a sapphire and a diamond; and the third row, a
> jacinth, an agate, and an amethyst; and the fourth row, a beryl,
> an onyx, and a jasper. They were set in gold filigree settings
> when they were mounted. (Exodus 39:8-13, NASB95)*

She is **clothed in purple and scarlet, and adorned with gold and precious stones and pearls (17:4)**. G. K. Beale mentions that this combination of words in the Greek is *identical* to the LXX description of the high priest's garments. The city is being represented as having the role of the high priest and associated with the Jewish priestly system.[620]

In addition, Josephus speaks of the veil of the Temple saying; "...but before these doors there was a veil of equal largeness with the doors. It was a Babylonian curtain, embroidered with blue, and fine linen, and scarlet, and purple, and of a contexture that was truly wonderful."[621]

---

[619] J. Massyngberde Ford, 278.

[620] G. K. Beale, The Book of Revelation: A Commentary on the Greek Text, *New International Greek Testament Commentary*, ed. I. Howard Marshall and Donald A. Hagner (Grand Rapids: Eerdmans, 1999), 858.

[621] Flavius Josephus, *Wars*, 5:5:4.

Next we read of her **having in her hand a gold cup full of abominations and of the unclean things of her immorality (17:4)**. The priesthood, full of murder and immorality, no longer serves God but evil instead.

> *Woe to you, scribes and Pharisees, hypocrites! For you clean the outside of the cup and of the dish, but inside they are full of robbery and self-indulgence. ... So you, too, outwardly appear righteous to men, but inwardly you are full of hypocrisy and lawlessness. (Matthew 23:28, NASB95)*

But instead of having in her hand a cup for a drink offering, it is a **cup full of abominations (17:4)**. Speaking to Jerusalem, Ezekiel says,

> *'You will be filled with drunkenness and sorrow, the <u>cup</u> of horror and desolation, the cup of your sister Samaria. You will drink it and drain it. Then you will gnaw its fragments and tear your breasts; for I have spoken,' declares the Lord God. Therefore, thus says the Lord God, 'Because you have forgotten Me and cast Me behind your back, bear now the punishment of your lewdness and your harlotries.' (Ezekiel 23:33-35, NASB95)*

Jeremiah comments in a similar vain referring to the Babylon of his day.

> *Babylon has been a golden <u>cup</u> in the hand of the Lord, intoxicating all the earth. The nations have drunk of her wine; therefore the nations are going mad. (Jeremiah 51:7, NASB95)*

Speaking even more directly and prophetically for the first century after Christ Zechariah says,

> *Behold, I am going to make Jerusalem a <u>cup</u> that causes reeling to all the peoples around; <u>and when the siege is against Jerusalem</u>, it will also be against Judah. (Zechariah 12:2, NASB95)*

Zechariah goes so far as to refer to the coming *siege against Jerusalem*. This is the very siege that John is now prophesying. Zechariah 12 is a critical prophetic passage that speaks not only of the coming siege but also refers to those that "*will look on Me whom they have pierced; and they will mourn for Him, as one mourns for an only son, and they will weep bitterly over Him like the bitter weeping over a firstborn"* (Zechariah 12:10). Some will mourn in repentance as at Pentecost while others simply mourn in fear for the coming judgement.

John makes these applications afresh to Jerusalem here in chapter 17 of Revelation. "To the uninitiated the religious system headquartered in Jerusalem appeared as holy and good, exemplified by the beauty of the temple and its ceremonies. But at its center the religion was corrupt, honoring God with its lips but with a heart that was far from Him...."[622]

17:5 ...and on her forehead a name was written, a mystery, "BABYLON THE GREAT, THE MOTHER OF HARLOTS AND OF THE ABOMINATIONS OF THE EARTH." The word **forehead (17:5)** here reminds us of Jeremiah chapter 3, which is in response to Jerusalem's harlotry with other gods.

> *Yet you had a harlot's forehead;*
> *You refused to be ashamed. (Jeremiah 3:3; NASB95)*

This of course is a perfect fit with the then current spiritual state of Jerusalem.

This city, **BABYLON (17:5)**, is called **great (17:5)**. It was called **great (17:5)** because it was a city of significance. Josephus refers to Jerusalem on several occasions saying, "This was the end which Jerusalem came to by the madness of those that were for innovations; a city otherwise of great magnificence, and of mighty fame among all mankind."[623] "And where is now that great city, the metropolis of the Jewish nation...."[624] "There are a people called Jews, who dwell in a city the strongest of all other cities, which the inhabitants call Jerusalem...."[625]

The identification of this harlot with the religion of Israel and its high priest is intensified with the name placed on her forehead. "There was placed on

---

[622] J. E. Leonard, Come Out of Her My People, 123.

[623] Flavius Josephus, *Wars*, 7:1:1.

[624] Ibid., *Wars*, 7:8:7.

[625] Ibid., Apion, 1,22.

the forehead of the high priest a golden plate engraved with a consecrating word."[626] That engraved word was "holiness."[627] On the forehead of the harlot, the metaphor of corrupt Jewish religion, is instead **BABYLON THE GREAT, THE MOTHER OF HARLOTS AND OF THE ABOMINATIONS OF THE EARTH (17:5)**. This is the third time we have met with the phrase **BABYLON THE GREAT (17:5)**.

> *And another angel, a second one, followed, saying, "Fallen, fallen is Babylon the great, she who has made all the nations drink of the wine of the passion of her immorality." (Revelation 14:8, NASB95)*

> *The great city was split into three parts, and the cities of the nations fell. Babylon the great was remembered before God, to give her the cup of the wine of His fierce wrath. (Revelation 16:19, NASB95)*

In each case, **Babylon the great (17:5)** refers to Jerusalem. Her harlotry, both physical and spiritual, is set forth as the basis of her judgement.

"In the picture of the adulteress what one may have is a parody of the high priest on the Day of Atonement wearing the vestments specially reserved for that occasion and holding the libation offering. However, instead of the sacred name upon his brow the "priest-harlot' bears the name Babylon, mother of harlots and the abominations of the earth...."[628]

17:6 And I saw the woman drunk with the blood of the saints, and with the blood of the witnesses of Jesus. When I saw her, I wondered greatly. Again, Rome can be imagined as the **woman (17:6)** because in time Rome was to martyr many saints and was therefore **drunk with the blood of the saints (17:6)**. However, the murderer par excellence of God's people has historically been Jerusalem. Christ said this to Jerusalem not Rome,

---

[626] J. Massyngberde Ford, 279.

[627] Ibid., 279.

[628] Ibid., 288.

Fill up, then, the measure of the guilt of your fathers. 33 You serpents, you brood of vipers, how will you escape the sentence of hell? 34 Therefore, behold, I am sending you prophets and wise men and scribes; some of them you will kill and crucify, and some of them you will scourge in your synagogues, and persecute from city to city, 35 so that upon you may fall the guilt of all the righteous blood shed on earth [land], from the blood of righteous Abel to the blood of Zechariah, the son of Berechiah, whom you murdered between the temple and the altar. 36 Truly I say to you, all these things will come upon this generation. Jerusalem, Jerusalem, who kills the prophets and stones those who are sent to her! How often I wanted to gather your children together, the way a hen gathers her chicks under her wings, and you were unwilling. (Matthew 23:32-37, NASB95)

...for it cannot be that a prophet would perish outside of Jerusalem. (Luke 13:33, NASB95)

Let's look at the evidence:

1) The woman is clothed with precious stones and expensive fabric, just like the priest of the Temple (Exodus 28). "The prostitute's array reflects the Jewish priestly colors of scarlet, purple, and gold (Ex. 28), indicating her priestly status with the temple in her midst...."[629]

2) She bears a gold cup answering to Christ comments: "*Woe to you, scribes and Pharisees, hypocrites! For you clean the outside of the cup and of the dish, but inside they are full of robbery and self-indulgence.*" (Matthew 23:25, NASB95)

3) She is called "*the mother of harlots*" in Revelation 17:5. This fits Jerusalem perfectly as the wife of Jehovah but Rome not at all. The harlot is "*drunk with the blood of the saints*" (Revelation 17:6). Although in time this will fit Rome to some degree, at this point, and especially time, it fits Jerusalem perfectly, "*Which one of the prophets did your fathers not persecute? They killed those who had previously announced the coming of*

---

[629] C. Marvin Pate, Editor, 76.

the Righteous One, whose betrayers and murderers you have now become..." (Acts 7:52, NASB95)."[630]

4) The harlot is sitting upon the beast (17:3). How can Rome be sitting upon Rome? If the first beast is clearly Rome, and it is, how then can the second beast be the same city?

We read that the beast hates *"the harlot and will make her desolate and naked, and will eat her flesh and will burn her up with fire"* (Revelation 17:16, NASB95). Surely, this is not Rome hating and burning Rome! It can only be Rome, the beast from the sea, destroying Jerusalem, the beast from the land. "...it is the Beast that destroys Babylon; and if Babylon is Rome then it is very odd that Rome should destroy Rome. It leads, in fact, to the hopeless confusion in which many commentaries have wallowed. The Beast is certainly Rome; the city it destroys is Jerusalem."[631]

5) We are told that this woman is *"the great city, which reigns over the kings of the earth [land]"* (Revelation 17:18, NASB95). In addition, we read *"And their dead bodies will lie* in the street of the great city which mystically is called Sodom and Egypt, where also their Lord was crucified" (Revelation 11:8, NASB95). What could be clearer? Only Jerusalem is called *the great city* in Scripture. Rome is never given this title.

6) However, there is one more comparison that should be made, one that Kenneth Gentry calls a "literary contrast."[632] He provides these insights.

A. The harlot and a bride are introduced in Revelation is a similar fashion.

Then one of the seven angels who had the seven bowls came and spoke with me, saying, "Come here...." (Revelation 17:1, NASB95)

---

[630] Acts 4:12; 5:18-33; 6:12; 7:54-60; 81ff; 9:1-4, 13, 23; 11:19; 12:1-3; 13:45-50; 14:2-5, 19; 16:23; 17:5-13; 18:12; 20:3, 19: 21:11, 27; 22:30; 23:12, 20, 27, 30; 24:5-9; 25:2-15; 25:24; 26:21; II Corinthians 11:24; II Thessalonians 2:14-15; Hebrews 10:32-34.

[631] Philip Carrington, 274.

[632] Kenneth L. Gentry, Jr., The Revelation of Jesus Christ, 15.

Then one of the seven angels who had the seven bowls full of the seven last plagues came and spoke with me, saying, "Come here...." (Revelation 21:9, NASB95)

B. The character of the two women is contrasted in Revelation.

Then one of the seven angels who had the seven bowls came and spoke with me, saying, "Come here, I will show you the judgement of the great <u>harlot</u> who sits on many waters...." (Revelation 17:1, NASB95)

Then one of the seven angels who had the seven bowls full of the seven last plagues came and spoke with me, saying, "Come here, I will show you the <u>bride</u>, the wife of the Lamb." (Revelation 21:9, NASB95)

C. The environment of the two women is contrasted in Revelation.

And he carried me away in the Spirit into a <u>wilderness</u>; and I saw a woman sitting on a scarlet beast, full of blasphemous names, having seven heads and ten horns. (Revelation 17:3, NASB95)

And he carried me away in the Spirit to a great and <u>high mountain</u>, and showed me the holy city, Jerusalem, coming down out of heaven from God.... (Revelation 21:10, NASB95)

D. The dress of the two women is contrasted in Revelation.

The woman was <u>clothed in purple and scarlet</u>, and adorned with gold and precious stones and pearls, having in her hand a gold cup full of abominations and of the unclean things of her immorality.... (Revelation 17:4, NASB95)

And to her was granted that she should be <u>arrayed in fine linen, clean and white</u>: for the fine linen is the righteousness of saints. (Revelation 19:8, KJV)

The evidence is overwhelming; the woman is the old Jerusalem; the bride is the new Jerusalem. This is a comparison between the two Jerusalems, the wife of Jehovah and the Bride of Christ, not between Rome and the new Jerusalem. For those two cities, there is no comparison here at all.

17:7 And the angel said to me, "Why do you wonder? I will tell you the mystery of the woman and of the beast that carries her, which has the seven heads and the ten horns." Notice the perplexity of verse six with the response of verse 7. It is not the intention of God or His angel to leave John or his readers confused. With that in mind the angel begins to remove the confusion that has overtaken John with clear explanation. Statements like these in Revelation drive home the point that God does not intend that this book remain closed to our understanding. So, in this next section the angel will give a divine interpretation of the passage.

17:8 The beast that you saw was, and is not, and is about to come up out of the abyss and go to destruction. And those who dwell on the earth [land], whose name has not been written in the book of life from the foundation of the world, will wonder when they see the beast, that he was and is not and will come. Notice the phrase, ***was, and is not, and will come (17:8).*** This is a demonic parody of Christ. We read this of Christ in Revelation:

> *John to the seven churches that are in Asia: Grace to you and peace, from <u>Him who is and who was and who is to come</u>.... (Revelation 1:4, NASB95)*

> *"I am the Alpha and the Omega," says the Lord God, "<u>who is and who was and who is to come</u>, the Almighty." (Revelation 1:8, NASB95)*

> *Holy, holy, holy is the Lord God, the Almighty, <u>who was and who is and who is to come</u>. (Revelation 4:8, NASB95)*

"If the name on the forehead of the harlot is a mockery of the sacred name on the high priest's miter, the character of the beast which 'was and is not' is a parody of the divine name...."[633] In addition to being a perverse parody on God's holy Name, we want to look for the historical context of the phrase as well. There are three other passages that contribute to an understanding of this verse; they are:

---

[633] J. Massyngberde Ford, 288.

I saw one of his heads as if it had been slain, and his fatal wound was healed. And the whole earth [land] was amazed and followed after the beast... (Revelation 13:3, NASB95)

And he deceives those who dwell on the earth [land] because of the signs which it was given him to perform in the presence of the beast, telling those who dwell on the earth [land] to make an image to the beast who had the wound of the sword and has come to life. (Revelation 13:14, NASB95)

The beast which was and is not, is himself also an eighth and is one of the seven, and he goes to destruction. (Revelation 17:11, NASB95)

From our study of Revelation 13, we know that *the beast who had the wound of the sword* was both Nero and the Roman Empire, the two being used interchangeably. "This is a picture of the beast of 13:1ff which the woman is riding, but no longer just the empire, but one of the emperors who died...."[634] When Nero died, the Roman Empire was thrown into chaos. It appeared the Roman Empire would tear apart and, indeed, was as good as dead going through a violent revolution and seeing three Emperors come to power and murdered in one year. "Rome, they thought, was o the verge of destruction by civil warfare; the empire was about to break up."[635] But the Empire was healed. Vespasian returned from his attack on Israel and revived the power of Rome. The Empire came back from the edge of destruction to live again. We will look at this further when we deal with 17:11.

These who dwell in the land are described as those **whose name has not been written in the book of life from the foundation of the world (17:8)**. Notice, it is the non-elect in Israel that wonders at the power of the beast, Rome. They wonder because that which would destroy any other nation will not destroy this beast. It comes back, as it were, from the grave.

This is in comparison to God's true children of whom it is said, "...*He chose us in Him before the foundation of the world, that we would be holy and*

---

[634] Archibald Thomas Robertson, Vol. VI, 431.

[635] F.F. Bruce, Israel & the Nations, 224.

blameless before Him" (Ephesians 1:4, NASB95). The people of Judea wonder, and indeed tremble, at the power and magnificence of Rome.

17:9 *Here is the mind which has wisdom. The seven heads are seven mountains on which the woman sits....* Basically, John is suggesting that the wise man will understand him at this point, **here is the** **mind which has wisdom (17:9)**, and by deduction, the fool will miss the point. So, this passage, or clue, wasn't considered particularly difficult by John. The **seven mountains (17:9)** or hills clearly refer to "...Rome, known widely as the 'city on Seven Hills' or, as it was called in antiquity, the *Septimontium.*"[636] This verse tells us that the **woman sits (17:9)** on these **seven mountains (17:9)**, it does not say that the woman is to be equated with these **seven mountains (17:9)** as some seem to think. They are separate and distinct entities. The **seven mountains (17:9)** equate to Rome and **the woman (17:9)** equates to Jerusalem who rides on, and is supported by Rome.

17:10 *...and they are seven kings; five have fallen, one is, the other has not yet come; and when he comes, he must remain a little while.* **Seven kings (17:10)** are mentioned, of these kings *five* **have fallen (17:10)**, died, **one is (17:10)** currently reining, Nero, and one will succeed him but will only reign for **a little while (17:10)**, a short period of time, Galba.

The Five That "*Have Fallen*"

Julius Caesar	49-44 B.C.
Augustus Caesar	31 BC-A.D.14
Tiberius Caesar	A.D. 14-37
Gaius Caligula	A.D. 37-41
Claudius	A.D. 41-54

The One That "*Is*"

Caesar Nero	A.D. 54-68

The One That Has "*Not Yet Come*"

Galba	A.D. June 68 to January 69

---

[636] R. C. Sproul, <u>The Last Days According to Jesus</u>, 186.

He reigned but "*a little while*"

Following these seven were:

Otho	A.D. 69
Vitellius	A.D. 69
Vespasian	A.D. 69-79
Titus	A.D. 79-81

This is another proof of the early date of Revelation. It had to be written during the reign of the one that *is (17:8)*. That person was Nero. He died A.D. June 8, 68. Revelation of necessity had to have been written before that date, possibly several years before his death.

17:11 The beast which was and is not, is himself also an eighth and is one of the seven, and he goes to destruction. There is an important point of grammar not to be missed in *(17:11)*. The definite article *the (17:11)* is seen before *beast (17:11)* and *seven (17:11)*, but before *eighth (17:11)* there is the indefinite, or implied article, *an (17:11)*. There is a reason. "The definite article that clearly and repetitively defined the chronological series of head/kings ('*the* five,' '*the* one,' '*the* one to come') vanishes before an eighth is mentioned. Thus, this eighth king is 'an eighth,' i.e. it refers not to any one particular individual, but to the revival of the Empire itself under one who is outside of the originally specified seven kings. The Roman Empire is arising from ruin."[637] *The* eighth was Galba but he was not *one of the seven (17:11)*, that is, he was not one of the emperors that maintained the glory of the Empire; Vespasian was. Vespasian was a true successor to *the seven (17:11)* and as a result although not "the" *eighth (17:11)* he was *an eighth (17:11)*, and therefore *one of the seven (17:11)*. He was not numerically or sequentially the *eighth (17:11)* but he was qualitatively *an eighth (17:11)*, one of the *kind* that were *the seven (17:11)*.

17:12 The ten horns which you saw are ten kings who have not yet received a kingdom, but they receive authority as kings with the beast for one hour. We have seen *the ten horns (17:12)* mentioned before:

---

[637] Kenneth Gentry, <u>The Beast of Revelation</u>, 76.

> *Then another sign appeared in heaven: and behold, a great red dragon having seven heads and ten horns, and on his heads were seven diadems. (Revelation 12:33, NASB95)*

> *And the dragon stood on the sand of the seashore. Then I saw a beast coming up out of the sea, having ten horns and seven heads, and on his horns were ten diadems, and on his heads were blasphemous names. (Revelation 13:11, NASB95)*

As stated by the text, these horns are *ten kings (17:12)*. They are sub monarchs under the Emperor of Rome and serve him but for a short time, *one hour (17:12)*. It is not literally one hour, but symbolically a short period. This would be a good opportunity to point out the impossibility of demanding that numbers in Revelation be interpreted literally. Is it literally *one hour (17:12)* that these *kings (17:12)* exercise *authority (17:12)*? Clearly, no, but is to be understood as simply a short period of time. This lesson should be remembered whenever any number is used in this book.

17:13 These have one purpose, and they give their power and authority to the beast. These kings have *one purpose (17:13)* which is to do *"...his purpose by having a common purpose, and by giving their kingdom to the beast, until the words of God will be fulfilled"* (Revelation 17:17, NASB95). They unite with Rome to destroy Jerusalem.

Victory for the Lamb

17:14 These will wage war against the Lamb, and the Lamb will overcome them, because He is Lord of lords and King of kings, and those who are with Him are the called and chosen and faithful. Remember, it was the aim of Rome to destroy not only Judaism, but Christianity as well. And indeed, Nero was the first and the greatest persecutor of the early church. However, in fighting against the Church, Rome is fighting against the *Lamb (17:14)*. The *Lamb (17:14)* cannot be defeated by the forces of earth or hell. He *will overcome them (17:14)*.

The Roman Emperors gave to themselves blasphemous names which were names ascribing deity to themselves.

And the dragon stood on the sand of the seashore. Then I saw a beast coming up out of the sea, having ten horns and seven heads, and on his horns were ten diadems, and on his heads were blasphemous names. (Revelation 13:11, NASB95)

In contrast to the blasphemous names the Emperors gave themselves, the Lamb is **Lord of lords and King of kings (17:14)**. "...this is a way of expressing the superlative 'The greatest Lord, the mightiest King,' 'the Lord and King of all.' "[638]

17:15 And he said to me, "The waters which you saw where the harlot sits, are peoples and multitudes and nations and tongues." In Revelation 17:1 we were introduced to *the great harlot who sits on many waters.* Here we are told that the **waters (17:15)** are **peoples and multitudes and nations and tongues (17:15)**. As we indicated in 17:1, these refer to the vast influence the Jews possessed across the world. As Russell says, "The authority exercised by the Jewish race in all parts of the Roman Empire previous to the destruction of Jerusalem was immense; their synagogues were to be found in every city, and their colonies took root in every land."[639] So in this sense, Jerusalem sat *on many waters.*

17:16 And the ten horns which you saw, and the beast, these will hate the harlot and will make her desolate and naked, and will eat her flesh and will burn her up with fire. The **ten horns (17:16)** are of course ten kings, which are in confederation with Rome in its war against Jerusalem. Israel's neighbors, then as now, hated her and delighted in doing her harm. As a result, they willingly join with the beast, Rome, in making war on her.

Take note of the word **desolate (17:16)** in this verse. Daniel, concerning the same event, also uses it.

Then after the sixty-two weeks the Messiah will be cut off and have nothing, <u>and the people of the prince who is to come will destroy the city and the sanctuary.</u> And its end will come with a

---

[638] Robert G. Bratcher, Rev. 17:14.

[639] J. Stuart Russell, 503.

flood; even to the end there will be war; <u>desolations are</u>
<u>determined</u>. "And he will make a firm covenant with the many
for one week, but in the middle of the week he will put a stop to
sacrifice and grain offering; and on the wing of abominations
will come one who makes <u>desolate</u>, even until <u>a complete</u>
<u>destruction</u>, one that is decreed, is poured out on the one who
makes <u>desolate</u>. (Daniel 9:26-27, NASB95)

As dogs ate Jezebel's ***flesh (17:16)*** (II Kings 9:30-37) so this vast army will figuratively do the same to Jerusalem. Ezekiel used similar language in his description of God's judgement on Jerusalem in 586 BC.

Thus says the Lord God, "Because your lewdness was poured out
and your nakedness uncovered through your harlotries with your
lovers and with all your detestable idols, and because of the blood
of your sons which you gave to idols, 37 therefore, behold, I will
gather all your lovers with whom you took pleasure, even all
those whom you loved and all those whom you hated. So I will
gather them against you from every direction and expose your
nakedness to them that they may see all your nakedness. 38 Thus
I will judge you like women who commit adultery or shed blood
are judged; and I will bring on you the blood of wrath and
jealousy. 39 I will also give you into the hands of your lovers, and
they will tear down your shrines, demolish your high places, strip
you of your clothing, take away your jewels, and will leave you
naked and bare. 40 They will incite a crowd against you and
they will stone you and cut you to pieces with their swords. 41
They will burn your houses with fire and execute judgements on
you in the sight of many women. Then I will stop you from
playing the harlot, and you will also no longer pay your lovers."
(Ezekiel 16:36-41, NASB95)

It should be noted that the punishment for the harlotry of a priest' daughter was burning by fire.

Also the daughter of any priest, if she profanes herself by
harlotry, she profanes her father; she shall be burned with fire.
(Leviticus 21:9, NASB95)

And here we have Jerusalem, the wife of Jehovah, guilty of harlotry therefore consigned to suffer the Biblical punishment, which will ***burn her***

up with fire (17:16). And last, look at what Jesus Christ Himself said about these people who mistreated and killed His servants.

> *The kingdom of heaven may be compared to a king who gave a wedding feast for his son. And he sent out his slaves to call those who had been invited to the wedding feast, and they were unwilling to come. Again he sent out other slaves saying, 'Tell those who have been invited, 'Behold, I have prepared my dinner; my oxen and my fattened livestock are all butchered and everything is ready; come to the wedding feast.'" But they paid no attention and went their way, one to his own farm, another to his business, and the rest seized his slaves and mistreated them and killed them. <u>But the king was enraged, and he sent his armies and destroyed those murderers and set their city on fire</u>. (Matthew 22:2-7, NASB95)*

And here we have the fulfillment of this passage.

17:17 For God has put it in their hearts to execute His purpose by having a common purpose, and by giving their kingdom to the beast, until the words of God will be fulfilled. As 17:13 noted *"These have one purpose, and they give their power and authority to the beast."* We are reminded of another **purpose (17:17)** of evil men.

> *Men of Israel, listen to these words: Jesus the Nazarene, a man attested to you by God with miracles and wonders and signs which God performed through Him in your midst, just as you yourselves know— 23 this Man, delivered over by the predetermined plan and foreknowledge of God, you nailed to a cross by the hands of godless men and put Him to death. 24 But God raised Him up again, putting an end to the agony of death, since it was impossible for Him to be held in its power. (Acts 2:22-24, NASB95)*

And yet in the death of Christ by evil men **the words of God will be fulfilled (17:17)**; so here in Jerusalem in A.D. 70, **God has put it in their hearts to execute His purpose (17:17)**. "...the expression 'to put into the heart' means to cause someone to decide, resolve, purpose. Here it is God who will make these ten kings decide to do what will actually be God's own plan, even though they are not aware of this. Without their knowing it, they will be God's instrument for achieving his purpose."[640] It was God's ***purpose (17:17)*** to destroy Jerusalem although the beast and his associates delighted in the task.

17:18 The woman whom you saw is the great city, which reigns over the kings of the earth [land]. Here John fully clarifies who this ***woman (17:18)*** is. He identifies her as ***the great city (17:18).*** From 11:8 we know that the ***great city (17:18)*** is Jerusalem,

> *And their dead bodies will lie in the street of <u>the great city</u> which mystically is called Sodom and Egypt, <u>where also their Lord was crucified</u>. (Revelation 11:8, NASB95)*

As Ragan Ewing says, "it is hard to imagine this reference not ringing in the ears of the original audience when they would arrive at 17:18."[641]

> It is clear that our Lord was crucified in Jerusalem, the city John calls ***the great city (17:18).*** This title is *never* given to Rome in Scripture. However, "there is in fact a fairly substantial precedent for similar hyperbolic language of exaltation for the city of Jerusalem in the Old Testament as well other early Jewish sources. For instance, in Ps 48:2, Jerusalem is said to be the 'exultation of all the earth" (מְשׂוֹשׂ כָּל־הָאָרֶץ) because it is the 'city of the great king' (קִרְיַת מֶלֶךְ רָב)."[642]

The Psalmist referrers to Jerusalem using a similar phrase "The city of the great King." The similarity is significant.

> *Beautiful in elevation, the joy of the whole earth,*
> *Is Mount Zion in the far north,*
> *The city of the great King. (Psalm 48:2; NASB95)*

---

[640] Robert G. Bratcher, Rev. 17:17.

[641] Ragan Ewing, <u>The Identification of Babylon the Harlot in the Book of Revelation</u>, chapter 4, www.christonomy.com

[642] Ibid., chapter 4, www.christonomy.com

In addition, notice how Josephus refers to Jerusalem:

> And where is now <u>that great city</u>, the metropolis of the Jewish nation, which was fortified by so many walls round about, which had so many fortresses and large towers to defend it, which could hardly contain the instruments prepared for the war, and which had so many ten thousands of men to fight for it? (376) Where is this city that was believed to have God himself inhabiting therein? It is now demolished to the very foundations....[643]

Can the ***great city (17:18)*** of Revelation be any other than Jerusalem? No.

---

[643] Flavius Josephus, *Wars*, 7:8:7.

Chapter 18
The Fall of Babylon

Babylon Is Fallen

18:1 After these things I saw another angel coming down from heaven, having great authority, and the earth [land] was illumined with his glory. We see in ***(18:1)*** "...in vivid contrast to the scarlet woman established upon the scarlet beast in ch. 17, ... an angel with great authority descends from heaven. His glory is so bright that the earth is filled with light. He seems to be no ordinary angel, for in this apocalypse 'glory,' Gr. doxa, is an attribute of only God and the Lamb...."[644]

We see a similar ***glory (18:1)*** reveled in Ezekiel:

> *Then he led me to the gate, the gate facing toward the east; and behold, the glory of the God of Israel was coming from the way of the east. And His voice was like the sound of many waters; and the earth shone with His <u>glory</u>. And it was like the appearance of the vision which I saw, like the vision which I saw <u>when He came to destroy the city</u>. (Ezekiel 43:1-3, NASB95)*

There this ***glory (18:1)*** of God was associated with the fall and destruction of Jerusalem; it is here as well. It is not Rome who is the object of God's attention; it is Jerusalem.

18:2 And he cried out with a mighty voice, saying, "Fallen, fallen is Babylon the great! She has become a dwelling place of demons and a prison of every unclean spirit, and a prison of every unclean and hateful bird." John takes the picture of Babylon as ***fallen (18:2)*** from Isaiah.

> *... And one said, "Fallen, fallen is Babylon; and all the images of her gods are shattered on the ground." (Isaiah 21:9, NASB95)*

---

[644] J. Massyngberde Ford, 300.

Just as Babylon of old was judged and destroyed for her idolatry, so now the new Babylon, Jerusalem, is being judged for her idolatry. John goes on to use a powerfully descriptive image of Jerusalem, *she has become a dwelling place of demons and a prison of every unclean spirit, and a prison of every unclean and hateful bird (18:2)*. Certainly this is a picture of great evil. Do the facts of the case support the charge? Josephus adds these words,

"I shall therefore speak my mind here at once briefly: —That neither did any other city ever suffer such miseries, nor did any age ever breed a generation more fruitful in wickedness that this was, from the beginning of the world."[645]

Again he says,

> ... indeed that was a time most fertile in all manner of wicked practices, insomuch that no kind of evil deeds were then left undone; nor could any one so much as devise any bad thing that was new, so deeply were they all infected, and strove with one another in their single capacity, and in their communities, who should run the greatest lengths in impiety towards God, and in unjust actions towards their neighbors, the men of power oppressing the multitude and the multitude earnestly laboring to destroy the men of power. The one part were desirous of tyrannizing over others; and the rest of offering violence to others, and of plundering such as were richer than themselves.[646]

He then comes to this astonishing conclusion,

> I suppose, that had the Romans made any longer delay in coming against these villains, the city would either have been swallowed up by the ground opening upon them, or been overflowed by water, or else been destroyed by such thunder as the country of Sodom perished by, for it had brought forth a generation of men much more atheistical than were those that suffered such punishments;

---

[645] Flavius Josephus, *Wars,* 5:10:5.

[646] Ibid., *Wars,* 7:8:1.

for by their madness it was that all the people came to be destroyed.[647]

Josephus' first hand account illustrates John's analysis. Truly Jerusalem had **become a dwelling place of demons (18:2)**.

18:3 For all the nations have drunk of the wine of the passion of her immorality, and the kings of the earth [land] have committed acts of immorality with her, and the merchants of the earth [land] have become rich by the wealth of her sensuality. Clearly, Revelation **18:3** has been influenced by Jeremiah, who wrote,

> *Flee from the midst of Babylon, and each of you save his life! Do not be destroyed in her punishment, for this is the Lord's time of vengeance; He is going to render recompense to her. Babylon has been a golden cup in the hand of the Lord, intoxicating all the earth. The nations have drunk of her wine; therefore the nations are going mad. Suddenly Babylon has fallen and been broken; wail over her! Bring balm for her pain; perhaps she may be healed. (Jeremiah 51:6-8, NASB95)*

This parallels John's statement in our passage, **for all the nations have drunk of the wine of the passion of her immorality (18:3)**. God used Babylon to judge Judah and many other nations of the earth. The nations of the period were made to drink from her cup; that is, they were attacked and destroyed by Babylon. Here the nations are attacked a different way. They are attacked and destroyed spiritually by imbibing from the heresy of unbiblical Judaism. Judah extended her influence throughout the known world through her religion.

Judah's immorality was in fornication with idols. The nations she comes into contact with are infected with her particularly evil spiritual practices. Judah was particularly evil because she mixed knowledge of the truth with Baal worship and the worship of many other pagan gods. Such a mixture is more deceptive and destructive than common paganism. This serves as a warning to modern Christianity that is so inclined to mix Christianity with

---

[647] Ibid., *Wars*, 5:13:6.

psychology, not believing that *"His divine power has granted to us everything pertaining to life and godliness, through the true knowledge of Him who called us by His own glory and excellence"* (II Peter 1:3, NASB95). With such an attitude it may soon be said of the Church that **all the nations have drunk of the wine of the passion of her immorality (18:3)** as we infect the world with powerless a psycho-babel gospel.

18:4 *I heard another voice from heaven, saying, "Come out of her, my people, so that you will not participate in her sins and receive of her plagues...."* This phrase **come out of her, my people (18:4)** closely resembles Jeremiah's *"flee from the midst of Babylon, and each of you save his life!"* (Jeremiah 51:6). Christ made the same point in His ministry adding that *these are days of vengeance.*

> *Then those who are in Judea must flee to the mountains, and those who are in the midst of the city must leave, and those who are in the country must not enter the city; because these are days of vengeance, so that all things which are written will be fulfilled. (Luke 21:21-22, NASB95)*

Jeremiah's comments include, *"For this is the Lord's time of vengeance; He is going to render recompense to her"* (Jeremiah 51:6, NASB95), which is exactly what Christ said in Luke. Of course the early church, not being Dispensationalists, remembered what Christ said and did flee Jerusalem, i.e. Babylon, and escaped the judgement of God coming through Rome. If they had been good Dispensationalists, they would have said, "That verse is not for us, that's for Christians two or three thousands years from now." And they would have all died!

The phrase **my people (18:4)** deserves our attention. " 'My people' could not be addressed to the Romans, for it is a covenant appellation...."[648] Although the **people (18:4)** referred to here could be living in any city, it does appear that the city under question is the city of or belonging to the people, Jerusalem.

---

[648] J. Massyngberde Ford, 302.

18:5 ...*for her sins have piled up as high as heaven, and God has remembered her iniquities.* This next phrase ***piled up (18:5)*** is a good English translation of a Greek word χολλάω (*kollaō*) that means to "cleave" or "cling." "Jerusalem's sins (not her love) have cleaved to God."[649] Again looking at Jeremiah 51, which so clearly influenced John, we read,

> *We applied healing to Babylon, but she was not healed; forsake her and let us each go to his own country, for her judgement has reached to heaven and towers up to the very skies. (Jeremiah 51:9, NASB95)*

We read in several places in the Old Testament that "God remembered." "...*God remembered Noah...*" (Genesis 8:1, NASB95), "...*God remembered Abraham, and sent Lot out of the midst of the overthrow...*" (Genesis 19:29, NASB95), "...*God remembered Rachel, and God gave heed to her...*" (Genesis 30:22, NASB95), "...*God heard their groaning; and God remembered His covenant with Abraham, Isaac, and Jacob*" (Exodus 2:24, NASB95). Now God remembers again; this time He remembers Jerusalem's iniquities. Because He remembers, He will now act.

18:6 *Pay her back even as she has paid, and give back to her double according to her deeds; in the cup which she has mixed, mix twice as much for her.* Here we are reminded of the Mosaic Law where Biblical restitution requires a multiple pay back for a criminal deed. For instance,

> *If what he stole is actually found alive in his possession, whether an ox or a donkey or a sheep, he shall pay <u>double</u>. (Exodus 22:4, NASB95)*

In addition, Jeremiah records that Israel is to receive a double repayment and a two-fold destruction for her sin.

> *I will first <u>doubly</u> repay their iniquity and their sin, because they have polluted My land; they have filled My inheritance with the carcasses of their detestable idols and with their abominations. (Jeremiah 16:18, NASB95)*

---

[649] Ibid., 302.

Let those who persecute me be put to shame, but as for me, let me not be put to shame; let them be dismayed, but let me not be dismayed. Bring on them a day of disaster, and crush them with <u>twofold</u> destruction! (Jeremiah 17:18, NASB95)

"The point is that her deeds have been doubly bad and, therefore, the punishment must be doubly bad."[650]

18:7 *To the degree that she glorified herself and lived sensuously, to the same degree give her torment and mourning; for she says in her heart, 'I SIT AS A QUEEN AND I AM NOT A WIDOW, and will never see mourning.'* Christ had spoken of a *"city set on a hill"* that should let its light shine so that others *"may see your good works, and glorify your Father who is in heaven"* (Matthew 5:14-16, NASB95). But instead of glorifying God, Jerusalem **glorified herself (18:7)**. "In the biblical tradition, δόξα, "glory, honor, praise, is something that one properly ascribes to God."[651] In glorifying herself, Jerusalem worshiped herself and thereby became the enemy of God.

In addition, we are told she **lived sensuously (18:7)**. Isaiah uses a similar term in his reference to Babylon saying, *"Now, then, hear this, you <u>sensual</u> one, who dwells securely, who says in your heart, 'I am, and there is no one besides me. <u>I will not sit as a widow</u>, nor know loss of children'"* (Isaiah 47:8). Interestingly, Isaiah includes the words *"I will not sit as a widow"* which John also refers to in our passage by saying *'I SIT AS A QUEEN AND <u>I AM NOT A WIDOW</u>, and will never see mourning (18:7).'* In both cases, the idea is that Babylon will never experience the loss of her greatness. In both cases they were wrong.

18:8 *For this reason in one day her plagues will come, pestilence and mourning and famine, and she will be burned up with fire; for the Lord God who judges her is strong.* The phrase, **one day (18:8)**, is not meant to identify a specific 24-hour period of judgement. Such literalism is foreign to Revelation; it is meant to identify

---

[650] Ibid., 298.

[651] D. E. Aune, Vol. 52C: Revelation 17-22, Rev. 18:7.

the suddenness of judgement. As we noted in Revelation 17:6, the punishment for the harlotry of a priest's daughter was burning by fire.

> *Also the daughter of any priest, if she profanes herself by*
> *harlotry, she profanes her father; she shall be burned with fire.*
> *(Leviticus 21:9)*

And here we have Jerusalem, the wife of Jehovah, guilty of harlotry therefore consigned to suffer the Biblical punishment of being burned with fire. "The form of her punishment is significant; she is to be burnt with fire. Burning was the punishment for adultery or harlotry only if the adulteress was a daughter of a priest."[652]

Lament for Babylon

18:9-10 *And the kings of the earth [land], who committed acts of immorality and lived sensuously with her, will weep and lament over her when they see the smoke of her burning, 10 standing at a distance because of the fear of her torment, saying, 'Woe, woe, the great city, Babylon, the strong city! For in one hour your judgement has come.* Three classes are identified as mourning over Jerusalem's destruction. They are **the kings of the earth [land] (18:9)**, *the merchants of the earth [land]* (18:11), and *every shipmaster and every passenger and sailor* (18:17).

The kings of the earth [land] (18:9) were the various leaders of the area of Israel who cooperated with the Jews for their own selfish benefit. "Herod the Great, e.g., and many other rulers of different parts of Palestine, introduced Hellenistic and Roman customs, contrary to orthodox Jewish beliefs."[653] They lament for they see their prosperity ruined in the destruction of Jerusalem. The religious crowd had the same concern. They put their problem this way concerning Jesus. *"If we let Him go on like this, all men will believe in Him, and the Romans will come and take away both our place and our nation"* (John 11:48, NASB95). "...the priestly aristocracy owed its very position of wealth and power to the Romans. As a result, in order to stay at the head of Jewish society, it had to collaborate

---

[652] J. Massyngberde Ford, 303.

[653] Ibid., 304.

with the Roman imperial system."[654]   They were concerned for their "place," that is, their honored position, and their privileged role in the nation. They needed the nation to provide them this place. They needed Rome's friendship to secure the nation. Here we have Rome's friendship turned to hatred and destruction. The nation is gone and their place with it. They *weep and lament (18:9)* over this loss. They don't have any particular affection for Israel, and certainly not any for God, their affection is for self and the comforts of life. With the destruction of Jerusalem, all this is gone.

18:11-17   And the merchants of the earth [land] weep and mourn over her, because no one buys their cargoes any more— 12 cargoes of gold and silver and precious stones and pearls and fine linen and purple and silk and scarlet, and every kind of citron wood and every article of ivory and every article made from very costly wood and bronze and iron and marble, 13 and cinnamon and spice and incense and perfume and frankincense and wine and olive oil and fine flour and wheat and cattle and sheep, and cargoes of horses and chariots and slaves and human lives· 14 "The fruit you long for has gone from you, and all things that were luxurious and splendid have passed away from you and men will no longer find them. 15 The merchants of these things, who became rich from her, will stand at a distance because of the fear of her torment, weeping and mourning, 16 saying, 'Woe, woe, the great city, she who was clothed in fine linen and purple and scarlet, and adorned with gold and precious stones and pearls; 17 for in one hour such great wealth has been laid waste!'

The merchants of the earth [land] (18:11) are the next group to lament over Jerusalem. Their concern is for the loss of trade that comes with the destruction of Judah and Jerusalem. Remember, Jerusalem was a very large city and as such had a very large trade associated with it. "There were camel caravans sometimes composed of about two hundred beasts passing from places like Tyre to Jerusalem...."[655]   Added to this large

---

654 Richard A. Horsley, 62.

655 Ibid., 305.

population were the hundreds of thousands of people that came to Jerusalem laden with cash every year for its various religious feasts.

Various authors comment on the riches of Jerusalem. "Their capital is Jerusalem. Here stood their Temple with its boundless riches...."[656] "The conclusion is reached that foreign trade had considerable importance for the Holy City. The Temple drew the largest share. For the rest, foreign trade consisted of food supplies, precious metals, luxury goods, and clothing materials."[657] "In fact the province of Syria, to which the province of Judaea really belonged, 'was the equal of Egypt, as far as commerce and industry was concerned, among the provinces of the Roman Empire.' So cultural conditions were favorable for commerce in Jerusalem."[658] "They also burnt down the treasury chambers, in which was an immense quantity of money, and an immense number of garments, and other precious goods, there reposited; and to speak all in a few words, there it was that the entire riches of the Jews were heaped up together, while the rich people had there built themselves chambers [to contain such furniture]."[659]

Jesus Himself had to deal with some from this merchant crowd.

> *And He made a scourge of cords, and drove them all out of the temple, with the sheep and the oxen; and He poured out the coins of the money changers and overturned their tables.... (John 2:15, NASB95)*

"The popularity of commerce among all classes in Jerusalem can be judged by the fact that merchants were held in such respect that even priests and scholars joined their ranks."[660] They lived for money and now, with the destruction of Jerusalem, are distraught beyond words.

18:17-18 And every shipmaster and every passenger and sailor, and as many as make their living by the sea, stood at a distance, [18] and were crying out as they saw the smoke of her

---

[656] Tacitus, Histories 5:8.

[657] Joachim Jeremias, Jerusalem in the Times of Jesus (Philadelphia, PA: Fortress, 1969), 38.

[658] Ibid., 51.

[659] Flavius Josephus, *Wars*, 6:5:2.

[660] J. Massyngberde Ford, 305.

burning, saying, 'What city is like the great city?'. Tens of thousands of visitors came to Jerusalem every year for its various feasts. A large portion of these would come by ship. In addition, the trading in Israel by way of the sea would by no means be small. Added to this were the economics of fishing in the Sea of Galilee and also the fact that many "men were employed in the brisk trade involving the salt industry at Qumran in the Dead Sea area."[661] In short, shipmasters, passengers and sailors from three different but large bodies of water would be hit hard by the destruction of Jerusalem.

18:19-20 And they threw dust on their heads and were crying out, weeping and mourning, saying, 'Woe, woe, the great city, in which all who had ships at sea became rich by her wealth, for in one hour she has been laid waste!' [20] *"Rejoice over her, O heaven, and you saints and apostles and prophets, because God has pronounced judgement for you against her."* While one group is *weeping and mourning (18:19)* over Jerusalem's destruction, another is told to *rejoice over her, O heaven, and you saints and apostles and prophets (18:20).* "The Church tabernacling in heaven—saints and apostles and prophets—had prayed for the destruction of the apostate, demonized City that led the world in rebellion against God and persecution of His children. As the smoke of the whole burnt offering ascends to heaven, the saints are to rejoice that their prayers have been answered...."[662]

> *...and they cried out with a loud voice, saying, "How long, O Lord, holy and true, will You refrain from judging and avenging our blood on those who dwell on the earth?" (Revelation 6:10, NASB95)*

But things are different today, so much so that the Church faces a danger in being so "good" that it loses its hatred of sin. How many Christians today could pray such prayers? To do so would quickly get you labeled as a "harsh" and "unloving" person lacking Christian compassion and certainly not the "winsome" person a Believer should be. Of course this is not a

---

[661] Ibid., 306.

[662] David Chilton, The Days of Vengeance, 458-459.

Christian goodness at all, but a weakness and sentimentality clothed in the garments of Christian virtue.

18:21   *Then a strong angel took up a stone like a great millstone and threw it into the sea, saying, "So will Babylon, the great city, be thrown down with violence, and will not be found any longer."* The metaphor of ***millstone (18:21)*** is interpreted in the next clause; the ***city (18:21)*** is destroyed with considerable violence. Josephus adds his observation of the destroyed city of Jerusalem, "... it was so thoroughly laid even with the ground by those that dug it up to the foundation, that there was left nothing to make those that came thither believe it had ever been inhabited."[663]

The phrase ***and will not be found any longer (18:21)*** is of importance. Obviously, the city itself was rebuilt. Then what was ***not found any longer (18:21)*** in Jerusalem? The answer must be the special presence of God. This particular Jerusalem is forever rejected. This geographic Jerusalem will never again be found to be spiritual Jerusalem. That distinction is reserved for another Jerusalem.

God was in covenant with Jerusalem. However, Jerusalem rejected her God and became in God's eyes a Sodom, an Egypt and a Babylon. The physical Jerusalem was rebuilt, but the Old Testament covenant Jerusalem will never be again. "It is *as the city of God* that she is fallen; it is *as the dwelling-place of Jehovah* that she is 'found no more at all,' it is as the *metropolis of the Jewish nation* that she is 'thrust down with violence'; and it is as '*the joy of the whole earth*,' that her 'smoke rises up for ever and ever.'"[664]

The Dispensationalists believe that God will again be in covenant with physical Israel. This passage teaches otherwise. God is now in covenant with his Church. The Church is the new Israel and new Jerusalem. The promises and the curses of the old Israel are now the promises and curses of the Church.

---

[663] Flavius Josephus, *Wars*, 7:1:1.

[664] Phillip S. Desprez, 405.

> *...you also, as living stones, are being built up as a spiritual house for a holy priesthood, to offer up spiritual sacrifices acceptable to God through Jesus Christ.... But you are A CHOSEN RACE, A royal PRIESTHOOD, A HOLY NATION, A PEOPLE FOR God's OWN POSSESSION...now you are THE PEOPLE OF GOD.... (I Peter 2:5, 9-10, NASB95)*

Paul confidently calls gentile Christians *"the Israel of God."*

> *And those who will walk by this rule, peace and mercy be upon them, and upon <u>the Israel of God</u>. (Galatians 6:16, NASB95)*

Here in Galatians Paul is addressing a Christian church, not a Jewish Synagogue. The point is he calls the members of this church, Jews and Gentiles alike, *"the Israel of God."*

The Church is Israel now.[665]

> *Therefore I say to you, the kingdom of God will be <u>taken away from you</u> and given to <u>a people</u>, producing the fruit of it. (Matthew 21:43, NASB95)*

18:22-23 And the sound of harpists and musicians and flute-players and trumpeters will not be heard in you any longer; and no craftsman of any craft will be found in you any longer; and the sound of a mill will not be heard in you any longer; 23 and the light of a lamp will not shine in you any longer; and the voice of the bridegroom and bride will not be heard in you any longer; for your merchants were the great men of the earth [land], because all the nations were deceived by your sorcery. Verses 22 and 23 are a description of the end of civilization in Jerusalem. And the reason for this destruction is given with the phrase beginning with **because (18:23)**. Jerusalem, who was to be a light to the gentiles and a witness to the world, has instead infected the world with her spiritual **sorcery (18:22)**.

---

[665] Romans 9:6; Galatians 3:7, 29; Philippians 3:3

18:24 *And in her was found the blood of prophets and of saints and of all who have been slain on the earth [land].* Verse 24 with its reference to **prophets (18:24)** provides one more proof that the city under discussion is indeed Jerusalem. Christ clarified this point saying,

> *Therefore, behold, I am sending you prophets and wise men and scribes; some of them you will kill and crucify, and some of them you will scourge in your synagogues, and persecute from city to city, 35 so that upon you may fall the guilt of all the righteous blood shed on earth [land], from the blood of righteous Abel to the blood of Zechariah, the son of Berechiah, whom you murdered between the temple and the altar. 36 Truly I say to you, all these things will come upon this generation. (Matthew 23:34-36, NASB95)*

All these things were to come upon this generation, not one in the distant future. "The language cannot be used of Rome or any other city. 'Only Jerusalem was guilty of "all the righteous blood shed on the earth,' from Abel onward."[666] "The writer seems to portray the whole land as an altar on which is poured the blood of the martyrs which is an offering more solemn than the blood of animal sacrifice."[667]

---

[666] David Chilton, The Days of Vengeance, 466.

[667] J. Massyngberde Ford, 307.

Chapter 19
The Heavenly Conqueror

The Fourfold Hallelujah

We begin chapter 19 of Revelation noting that Chapter 18 reads like a mournful dirge for the destruction of Jerusalem. Yet Chapter 19 will have a tone of rejoicing in it.

19:1 After these things I heard something like a loud voice of a great multitude in heaven, saying, "Hallelujah! Salvation and glory and power belong to our God.... **Hallelujah (19:1)** means "praise Yahweh" or "praise the LORD." There are five Hallelujahs in this chapter. One author says, they "have the appearance of OT battle prayers...."[668] God has engaged His enemy, apostate Israel, in battle. As God makes war on His enemy, the heavenly hosts praise God for His victory and Israel's destruction. "The songs ... are liturgical celebrations in heaven where God is praised because of the fall of the harlot and consequently the overcoming of evil and the establishment of His kingdom, i.e. the fulfillment of His plan."[669]

In addition, they appear to refer to the Hallel or hymn what was sung while the lamb was slain on the Passover. As Edersheim says, "every first line of a Psalm was repeated by the people, while to each of the others they responded by a 'Hallelujah,' or 'Praise ye the Lord' ... May it not be that this solemn and impressive 'hymn' corresponds the Alleluia song of the redeemed Church in heaven, as described in Revelation 19:1, 3, 4, 6?"[670] Edersheim rightly identifies the relationship between the Passover and the Lord's Supper. The marriage supper of the lamb is but the Lord's Supper, which is the New Testament counterpart and fulfillment to the Old Testament Passover.

---

[668] J. Massyngberde Ford, 316.

[669] Ibid., 309.

[670] Alfred Edersheim, 149-150.

There is something both frightening and exciting about *loud (19:1)* noises. On the one hand, noise can be freighting having the sound of judgement to it. On the other, it can be exciting having the sound of victory to it. The same sound will produce different effects on different audiences.

Hallelujah! Salvation and glory and power belong to our God...(19:1). As we indicated before, *Hallelujah* represents in Hebrew "Praise Yah," Yah is a shortened form of Yahweh. This expression, in its transliterated form, has entered several European languages.[671] "Salvation means deliverance of the church from its enemies.... [Glory] seems here to designate the divine attribute of majesty... power, has reference to God's omnipotence, as exerted in the overthrow of the enemies of the church.... The meaning is, that deliverance from enemies, and majesty, and might, are to be ascribed to God, and he is to be praised on account of them."[672]

19:2 BECAUSE HIS JUDGEMENTS ARE TRUE AND RIGHTEOUS; for He has judged the great harlot who was corrupting the earth [land] with her immorality, and HE HAS AVENGED THE BLOOD OF HIS BOND-SERVANTS ON HER. We left off chapter 18 with a description of "*...the blood of prophets and of saints and of all who have been slain on the earth [land]*" (18:24). Here we read that this *blood (19:2)* has been avenged and *judged (19:2)*. This is something only God has a right to do. We are forbidden to seek vengeance. "*Never take your own revenge, beloved, but leave room for the wrath of God, for it is written, 'Vengeance is Mine, I will repay,' says the Lord*" (Romans 12:19, NASB95). And in God's time He has repaid the great harlot for her sin against the saints. "Jerusalem, the unfaithful wife of God, suffers capital punishment as a spiritual adulteress for denying her Messiah.... Her destruction avenges 'the blood of his servants'...causing the saints to rejoice in witnessing the conquering of the first great enemy of Christ and his people."[673]

19:3 And a second time they said, "Hallelujah! HER SMOKE RISES UP FOREVER AND EVER." In 18:21 we read that Babylon would be *thrown down with violence, and will not be found any longer.* We noted at that time that this had reference to the fact that geographic Jerusalem

---

[671] Robert G. Bratcher, Rev. 19:1.

[672] Moses Stuart, 341.

[673] C. Marvin Pate, Editor, 79.

would never again be the place of God's special presence. Here is a similar thought; *HER SMOKE RISES UP FOREVER AND EVER (19:3)*. It could not be said that a geographic city called Jerusalem that *HER SMOKE RISES UP FOREVER AND EVER*. However, that could be said of the old wife of Yahweh, spiritual Jerusalem. "It is here used to indicate the permanent nature of Babylon's fall.... The actual flames that consumed 'Babylon' burned out long ago; but her punishment was eternal. She will never be resurrected."[674] Spiritual Jerusalem exists only in the Church and in heaven—where God's saints are found.

19:4 And the twenty-four elders and the four living creatures fell down and worshiped God who sits on the throne saying, "Amen. Hallelujah!" This is our third *Hallelujah (19:4)*. This is also the fifth and last mention of *the twenty-four elders (19:4)* in the book of Revelation.[675] Here we see the church, the true Israel, led by its leaders praising God for the destruction of Babylon.

19:5 And a voice came from the throne, saying, "Give praise to our God, all you His bond-servants, you who fear Him, the small and the great." From the throne of God itself there proceeds a voice that encourages His *bond-servants (19:5)* to *give praise to our God (19:5)*. Through most of history the *small (19:5)* have little to say about world events. In time, God gives them voice. All, *the small and the great (19:5)*, are to praise God for his judgements.

19:6 Then I heard something like the voice of a great multitude and like the sound of many waters and like the sound of mighty peals of thunder, saying, "Hallelujah! For the Lord our God, the Almighty, reigns." This is our fourth *Hallelujah (19:6)*. Here *a great multitude (19:6)* in heaven joins in praise to God for His judgement on the harlot.

The full establishment of Christ's Kingdom as expressed in His Church is publicly secured and instituted at this point in the destruction of the Church's first great enemy and Christ's unfaithful wife, Judaism, with these words: *For the Lord our God, the Almighty, reigns (19:6)*.

---

[674] David Chilton, The Days of Vengeance, 472.

[675] Revelation 4:4; 4:10; 5:8; 11:16; 19:4

And Jesus was saying to them, "Truly I say to you, there are some of those who are standing here who will not taste death until they see the kingdom of God after it has come with power." (Mark 9:1, NASB95)

Marriage of the Lamb

The unfaithful first wife has been judged. A new marriage now takes place replacing the old adulterous wife with a new bride. "It is naturally the thesis of the *Revelation* that the Christian churches form the true Israel. The Harlot has disappeared, and the Bride is taking her place. ...the antithesis must lie between the old Israel and the new, the false Israel and the true, the Israel that is to appear so soon as the New Jerusalem."[676]

19:7 Let us rejoice and be glad and give the glory to Him, for the marriage of the Lamb has come and His bride has made herself ready. The topic is the **marriage (19:7)** of Christ to His Church. "In the O.T. God is the Bridegroom of Israel...."[677] We see that in these verses,

> *Thus says the Lord, "where is the certificate of divorce by which I have sent your mother away? Or to whom of My creditors did I sell you? Behold, you were sold for your iniquities, and for your transgressions your mother was sent away." (Isaiah 50:1, NASB95)*

> *"For your husband is your Maker, whose name is the Lord of hosts; and your Redeemer is the Holy One of Israel, who is called the God of all the earth. For the Lord has called you, like a wife forsaken and grieved in spirit, even like a wife of one's youth when she is rejected," says your God. (Isaiah 54:5-6, NASB95)*

> *"I made you numerous like plants of the field. Then you grew up, became tall and reached the age for fine ornaments; your breasts were formed and your hair had grown. Yet you were naked and*

---

[676] Philip Carrington, 294.

[677] Archibald Thomas Robertson, Vol. VI, 449.

> *bare. Then I passed by you and saw you, and behold, you were at the time for love; so I spread My skirt over you and covered your nakedness. I also swore to you and entered into a covenant with you so that you became Mine," declares the Lord God. (Ezekiel 16:7-8, NASB95)*

> *I will betroth you to Me forever; yes, I will betroth you to Me in righteousness and in justice, in lovingkindness and in compassion, and I will betroth you to Me in faithfulness. Then you will know the Lord. (Hosea 2:19-20, NASB95)*

However, God has divorced Israel and Judah and now takes a new bride. Dispensationalists hold that the marriage of the Lamb is to be at the end of time. However, there are problems with this position. First, the marriage supper is supposed to take place when the marriage takes place. For the Church, that began at Pentecost and continues with each new soul added to the Kingdom. Second, Israel was also wedded to Yahweh. The celebration of that wedding did not take place at the end of the relationship, but at the beginning in the various feasts set aside by God for worship, very similar to our Lord's Supper, which is the marriage supper spoken of here. Third, our passage here brings us to the end of Yahweh's marriage to Israel, through these divorce proceedings and the judgement of the unfaithful wife. The next step is God's marriage to the Church. The New Covenant and Church age has been in transition in coming as the Mosaic Covenant and Judaic age has been passing away. The culmination has arrived. The Church has now, with the destruction of Jerusalem, fully become the Bride of Christ—not will someday become the Bride of Christ at the end of time.

> The destruction of the Harlot and the marriage of the Lamb and the Bride—the divorce and the wedding—are correlative events. The existence of the Church as the congregation of the New Covenant marks an entirely new epoch in the history of redemption. God was not now merely taking Gentile believers into the Old Covenant (as He had often done under the Old Testament economy). Rather, He was bringing in "the age to come" (Heb. 2:5; 6:5), the age of fulfillment, during these Last Days. Pentecost was the inception of a New Covenant. With the final divorce and destruction of the unfaithful wife in A.D. 70, the marriage of the Church to her Lord was firmly established; *the Eucharistic*

celebration of the Church was fully revealed in its true nature as
"the Marriage Supper of the Lamb"(v.9).[678]

"The marriage union of Christ and the church is not a single act or thing. Every union of a believer with Christ in baptism is marriage to Christ, and is representative of the whole relation."[679] So, the marriage supper of the lamb is not something that will happen at the end of time at the coming of the Lord. That is not where this passage fits in the Book of Revelation. It fits right after the destruction of Jerusalem. Israel, the wife of Jehovah, is dead. She was the object of God's righteous judgement for her many sins, especially for murdering Christ and rejecting His call for forty years following His resurrection. At this point, the marriage supper of the lamb is mentioned to make it clear that God has never been without His bride. The Church takes the place of Old Testament Israel and becomes the new Israel of God, and God's people continue to be married to Him.

"The marriage supper is a metaphor for the final repudiation of the harlot and the introduction of the bride. This is the covenant meal or marriage supper, which seals the new relationship. It is accomplished when the Bridegroom overthrows the unfaithful wife and punishes her lovers, the kings of the land with whom she has committed adultery."[680] Christ predicted this moment.

> *I say to you that many will come from east and west, and recline*
> *at the table with Abraham, Isaac and Jacob in the kingdom of*
> *heaven; but the sons of the kingdom will be cast out into the outer*
> *darkness; in that place there will be weeping and gnashing of*
> *teeth. (Matthew 8:11-12, NASB95)*

The marriage of the Lamb is the union of Christ with believers, and is therefore essentially a fact of spiritual life. The feast or supper of that marriage is a figure for the delightful fellowship, the blessed entertainment and fruition of such vital union with the Prince of life. The marriage of the Lamb is a process continually going on as

---

[678] David Chilton, <u>The Days of Vengeance</u>, 473.

[679] Foy E. Wallace, Jr., 388.

[680] J. E. Leonard, <u>Come Out of Her My People</u>, 139.

long as such unions of Christ and his beloved and elect ones continue to be consummated.[681]

Jesus discusses this wedding banquet and His relationship to Israel in some detail in Matthew.

> *Jesus spoke to them again in parables, saying: "The kingdom of heaven is like a king who prepared a wedding banquet for his son. He sent his servants to those who had been invited to the banquet to tell them to come, but they refused to come. Then he sent some more servants and said, 'Tell those who have been invited that I have prepared my dinner: My oxen and fattened cattle have been butchered, and everything is ready. Come to the wedding banquet.' But they paid no attention and went off—one to his field, another to his business. The rest seized his servants, mistreated them and killed them. The king was enraged. He sent his army and destroyed those murderers and burned their city."* (Matthew 22:1-7, NIV)

The banquet takes place nevertheless. Only Israel is not there, having been destroyed by God. But the wedding goes on with anyone that would hear the call of the master with the result that "*the wedding hall was filled with guests*" (Matthew 22:10, NASB95).

19:8 It was given to her to clothe herself in fine linen, bright and clean; for the fine linen is the righteous acts of the saints. The meaning of **19:8** is considerably impacted by one's understanding of the words **righteous acts (19:8)**. Perhaps a better translation is found in the *King James Version*.

> *And to her was granted that she should be arrayed in fine linen, clean and white: for the fine linen is the righteousness of saints.* (Revelation 19:8, KJV)

Every "modern" version, including even the NKJV, reads this as "the righteous acts or deeds of the saints." This may be interpretation and conjecture, intruding a doctrinal reading into the Bible, with no authority in

---

[681] Milton S. Terry, <u>Biblical Apocalyptics</u>, 441.

the original. As Moses Stuart says, "This plainly does not designate the good deeds and virtuous actions, simply or principally, of the saints; for it is something given to them."[682]

> *...and may be found in Him, not having a righteousness of my own derived from the Law, but that which is through faith in Christ, the righteousness which comes from God on the basis of faith.... (Philippians 3:9, NASB95)*

And what are the results of deeds, acts or works? The saints of God, the totality of the elect, appear in heaven before the Almighty clothed with their own righteous deeds! This suggests that the righteousness that clothes the believer will be their deeds, which is a works righteousness. Indeed this is exactly what the Roman Catholic Church teaches. "Catholic scholars appeal to Revelation 19:8 to support the idea of a storehouse or collection of the good deeds of the saints. This Treasury of Merit ... is supposedly based on the idea that the white robes of the saints means "the righteous acts of the saints."[683] It does not. Instead, John is teaching an *imputed righteousness of Christ*, without the works or the merits of the saints.[684]

19:9 Then he said to me, "Write, 'Blessed are those who are invited to the marriage supper of the Lamb.' And he said to me, 'These are true words of God.'" Here the speaker changes the symbol. In the last verse the Church was the Bride of Christ. In this verse they are guests **invited (19:9)** to the **marriage supper (19:9)**. "The idea of a feast, as an image of the happiness of heaven, was a familiar one with the Jews...."[685] Christ gave a parable of a wedding and although many were *invited to the marriage, they were unwilling to come*.

> *Jesus spoke to them again in parables, saying, "The kingdom of heaven may be compared to a king who gave a wedding feast for his son. And he sent out his slaves to call those who had been*

---

[682] Moses Stuart, 343.

[683] Norman L. Geisler, and Ron Rhodes, 310.

[684] Valued insight based on a conversation with, and notes from Dr. Stephen Westcott, Bristol, England.

[685] Moses Stuart, 344.

> *invited to the wedding feast, and they were unwilling to come."*
> *(Matthew 22:1-3, NASB95)*

Those that were *unwilling to come* were, of course, the Jews who had rejected Christ. Paul and Barnabas had a similar experience.

> *Paul and Barnabas spoke out boldly and said, "It was necessary*
> *that the word of God be spoken to you first; since you repudiate it*
> *and judge yourselves unworthy of eternal life, behold, we are*
> *turning to the Gentiles." (Acts 13:46, NASB95)*

As Paul said of their unwillingness, *you repudiate it and judge yourselves unworthy of eternal life.*

19:10 *Then I fell at his feet to worship him. But he said to me,* **"*Do not do that; I am a fellow servant of yours and your* *brethren who hold the testimony of Jesus; worship God. For* *the testimony of Jesus is the spirit of prophecy."*** Although religious leaders like the Pope and others will willingly allow people to bow before their *feet (19:10)*, this exalted and holy being will not do so. Compare this to the ***worship (19:10)*** that was accorded Jesus on this earth. But, "how comes it that Jesus, if merely human, never checked any of his worshippers in this way?"[686] This is not a trick question; it is a fill in the blank question. The answer is because

_____.

The testimony of Jesus (19:10) can bear either of two meanings. 1) It can mean *the witness, which the Christian bears to Jesus Christ.* 2) It can equally mean *the witness, which Jesus Christ gives to men.* On that interpretation the phrase will mean that no man can speak to men until he has listened to Jesus Christ.[687]

The Coming of Christ

There are in the Book of Revelation several places in which something like a conclusion or Coming is described.

---

[686] Ibid., 345.

[687] William Barclay, Vol. 2, Chapters 6-22, Re 19:10b.

Now, of course, these "comings" cannot all be conclusions to the Book of Revelation or each *the* Second Coming. However, they may be several different descriptions of one "Judgement Coming" of Christ against Jerusalem. In other words, John may, in the Book of Revelation, tell his story of God's judgement on Jerusalem in several cycles, each section ending with His judgement coming on Jerusalem.

Dispensationalists delight in affirming that this is The Second Coming of Christ to conquer His enemies and set up His millennial kingdom. However, there are several problems with this view.

1) Here Christ comes on a white horse as a conquering warrior. He did not leave on a white horse slaying His enemies as He went. And since He said He would come in the same way He left, this could not be His Second Coming.

> *They also said, "Men of Galilee, why do you stand looking into the sky? This Jesus, who has been taken up from you into heaven, will come in just the same way as you have watched Him go into heaven." (Acts 1:11, NASB95)*

2) It does not say here that He comes "with His saints" as the Dispensationalists insist that He will do at His Second Coming. Instead, it says that *"the armies which are in heave"* (Revelation 19:14) come with him, and they to make war. It is said of His holy angels that they make war, but never of the Church.

3) And very importantly, where is the Bride? The Scripture says, *"...for the marriage of the Lamb has come and His bride has made herself ready"* (Revelation 19:7). The Bride did not come *with* Christ; the Bride having *made herself ready* was waiting *on* Christ. He came *to* her, not *with* her. This is an insurmountable problem for Dispensationalism who reverse these points and insists that at the Second Coming Christ comes with the Church, having raptured the Church seven years earlier at the beginning of the Great Tribulation. Not!

However, this, like the other "comings" in the Book of Revelation, is a judgement coming, not the Second Coming. And I might add, another illustration of Dispensational error.

19:11 And I saw heaven opened, and behold, a white horse, and He who sat on it is called Faithful and True, and in righteousness He judges and wages war. Again, is this *the* Second Coming? No, I repeat myself; the angels made it clear in Acts 1:11, Christ would come as He went.

He did not go galloping off to heaven on a horse slaying His enemies as He went. He will not so come. This is *a* Judgement Coming, not *the* Second Coming. "That this does not describe a physical coming such as the second advent is apparent.... Christ is nowhere else said to return upon a *horse*. He did not ascend this way, and he is to return *as he ascended*. The whole idea of a physical horse connected with the final return is foreign to Scripture. The horse was the emblem of war. That is its emblematic purpose here."[688]

In chapter 1 we looked at a verse, which reads:

> BEHOLD, HE IS COMING WITH THE CLOUDS, *and every eye will see Him, even those who pierced Him; and all the tribes of the earth [land] will mourn over Him. (Revelation 1:7, NASB95)*

At that time, we noted that there are mentioned several judgement comings in the Old Testament and this is another. Here is a selection of "comings" in the Old Testament.

> *Behold, the* LORD *is riding on a swift <u>cloud</u> and is about to <u>come</u> to Egypt; / The idols of Egypt will tremble at His presence, / And the heart of the Egyptians will melt within them. (Isaiah 19:1, NASB95)*

> *Then the earth shook and quaked;*
> *And the foundations of the mountains were trembling*
> *And were shaken, because He was angry.*
> *8 Smoke went up out of His nostrils,*
> *And fire from His mouth devoured;*
> *Coals were kindled by it.*
> *9 He bowed the heavens also, and <u>came</u> down*

---

[688] Jay E. Adams, <u>The Time is at Hand</u>, 81.

With thick darkness under His feet.
10 He rode upon a cherub and flew;
And He sped upon the wings of the wind.
11 He made darkness His hiding place, His canopy around Him,
Darkness of waters, thick <u>clouds</u> of the skies.
12 From the brightness before Him passed His thick <u>clouds</u>,
Hailstones and coals of fire.
13 The LORD also thundered in the heavens,
And the Most High uttered His voice,
Hailstones and coals of fire.
14 He sent out His arrows, and scattered them,
And lightning flashes in abundance, and routed them.
15 Then the channels of water appeared,
And the foundations of the world were laid bare
At Your rebuke, O LORD,
At the blast of the breath of Your nostrils. (Psalms 18:7-15,
NASB95)

"For the day is near,
Even the day of the LORD is near;
It will be a day of <u>clouds</u>,
A time of doom for the nations.
4 "A sword will <u>come</u> upon Egypt,
And anguish will be in Ethiopia;
When the slain fall in Egypt,
They take away her wealth,
And her foundations are torn down. (Ezekiel 30:3-4, NASB95)

This *coming with clouds* in Revelation chapter 1 does not refer to the Second Coming. None of the previous "*coming with clouds*" mentioned above from the Old Testament has been the Second Coming either. *Like the others*, this one is a coming by God in judgement.

So, Christ did come in A.D. 70 in judgement, just as He came in judgement at other times in the Old Testament against Egypt, Assyria, Babylon, and Israel itself. But *the* Second Coming is yet in the future.

Next we read, **behold, a white horse (19:11)**. Another question comes to mind—is this the same person found in Revelation 6:2? It does not appear so. In our previous passage the person described there is potentially one of four different figures, one of which is Christ and another possibility is

Vespasian. However, the best option is that he is simply one of four riders on a mission from God, and thereby given no particular identification. Certainly, however, in this passage, the person described here is none other than Jesus Christ.

Jesus identified Himself as the **Faithful and True (19:11)** earlier in our book, *"To the angel of the church in Laodicea write: The Amen, the faithful and true Witness, the Beginning of the creation of God..."* (Revelation 3:14, NASB95).

We have echoes of the phrase **and in righteousness He judges and wages war (19:11)** in the Old Testament. Interestingly, this is the very type of Messiah the Jews were waiting for at His first Advent. At that time He came, not as a conquering warrior, but as a suffering savior. The Jews were not interested in such a Messiah. Now, 40 years later, He comes as they envisioned.

> *Before the Lord, for He is coming, for He is coming to judge the earth. He will judge the world in righteousness and the peoples in His faithfulness. (Psalm 96:13, NASB95)*

> *And He will delight in the fear of the Lord, and He will not judge by what His eyes see, nor make a decision by what His ears hear; but with righteousness He will judge the poor, and decide with fairness for the afflicted of the earth; and He will strike the earth with the rod of His mouth, and with the breath of His lips He will slay the wicked. (Isaiah 11:3-4, NASB95)*

This was their concept of Messiah, judging the enemies of Israel! Ironically, however, when He does come fulfilling these prophecies by judging the enemies of Israel, it is the Jews who are the object of His attack, for it is the Jews who are the enemies of Israel! For the old Israel, both the ten Northern tribes and the two Southern tribes, has rejected the Holy One of Israel. Therefore old branches were broken off and new branches were grafted in to the one olive root (Romans 11). But, the Israel of God, the Israel by faith, still serves the living God; it is the Church of Jesus Christ.

19:12 His eyes are a flame of fire, and on His head are many diadems; and He has a name written on Him which no one knows except Himself. The phrase **His eyes are a flame of fire**

(19:12) "...signify that his judgement is incapable of deception or fraud, i.e. it penetrates all things, even the secrets of the heart, and consumes his enemies...."[689] We read earlier of Christ, *"His head and His hair were white like white wool, like snow; and His eyes were like a flame of fire"* (Revelation 1:14).

What is this name that *no one knows except Himself (19:12)*? Indeed, should we be asking that question? If no one knows it, what is the point in discussing it?

> ...the New Testament use of the words for know (ginosko and oida) is influenced by a Hebrew idiom, in which the verb *to know* acquires related meanings: *to acknowledge, to acknowledge as one's own,* and *to own. ....* Thus, the point in this verse is not that no one can know what the name is (for in fact, as we shall see, we do "know" the name, in the cognitive sense), but that He alone properly owns the name; it belongs only to Him.[690]

So, what is this name that belongs only to Him and *no one knows (19:12)*, that is owns, *except Himself (19:12)*? In the next verse we are given that name: *His name is called "The Word of God" (19:13)*. And in the 16th verse we are given another unique name of Christ: *KING OF KINGS, AND LORD OF LORDS (19:16)*. It would seem that one or both of these names would apply here.

19:13 He is clothed with a robe dipped in blood, and His name is called The Word of God. Next we read, *He is clothed with a robe dipped [sprinkled]*[691] *in blood (19:13)*. The warrior King clearly did not dip His robe in blood. It was however, sprinkled with blood as Isaiah clarifies and as any picture of war would illustrate.

> *I have trodden the wine trough alone, and from the peoples there was no man with Me. I also trod them in My anger and trampled them in My wrath; and their lifeblood is <u>sprinkled</u> on My*

---

[689] J. Massyngberde Ford, 313.

[690] David Chilton, <u>The Days of Vengeance</u>, 483.

[691] Ralph E. Bass, Jr., <u>What About Baptism? A Discussion on the Mode, Candidate, and Purpose of Christian Baptism</u> (Naples, FL: Nicene Press, Inc., 1999), 33-34.

> *garments, and I stained all My raiment. For the day of vengeance was in My heart, and My year of redemption has come. (Isaiah 63:3-4, NASB95)*

A. T. Robertson, the Baptist scholar says of this passage, "Probably (sprinkled) is correct, because the picture comes from Is. 63:3...."[692] The picture is one of war. Christ is attacking His enemies. The Day of the Lord has come. Judgement has now fallen. The blood of the enemies of God is liberally shed and indeed sprinkled or spattered on Christ's robe as He engages in war with them.

In this verse we note that here John uses his special name for Christ found in his Gospel, **The Word of God (19:13)**. *"In the beginning was the Word, and the Word was with God, and the Word was God"* (John 1:1). This is another indication that the apostle John is the John of Revelation.

19:14 And the armies which are in heaven, clothed in fine linen, white and clean, were following Him on white horses. The armies (19:14) of God consist of angelic beings; that is the case here. It is not the Church that is coming with Christ slaying His enemies; that is not a function of the Church. Plus, as we noted earlier, the Church, the bride, was waiting on Christ when He came.

19:15 From His mouth comes a sharp sword, so that with it He may strike down the nations, and He will rule them with a rod of iron; and He treads the wine press of the fierce wrath of God, the Almighty. God brought the world into existence with a word *from His mouth (19:15)*. All discussions of His military might are but metaphors of the power of His word. "In the war between Christ and the emperor there is no sword in the hand of Christ, but only in his mouth; it is his Word that is going to run sharply and swiftly through the world and destroy all that is false."[693]

---

[692] Archibald Thomas Robertson, Vol. VI, 452.

[693] Philip Carrington, 322.

He does not need to physically engage His enemies. He needs but to speak.

> *For the word of God is living and active and sharper than any*
> *two-edged sword, and piercing as far as the division of soul and*
> *spirit, of both joints and marrow, and able to judge the thoughts*
> *and intentions of the heart. And there is no creature hidden from*
> *His sight, but all things are open and laid bare to the eyes of Him*
> *with whom we have to do. (Hebrews 4:12-13, NASB95)*

It is not simply Israel that must suffer His judgement for their sin, but all His creation must acknowledge His authority. *"For He must reign until He has put all His enemies under His feet"* (1 Corinthians 15:25). In heaven, His children bow the knee willingly. But here He rules *with a rod of iron.* This is not a picture of heaven. This is a picture of the providential rule of Christ in the lives of unbelievers.

The judgement of Jerusalem by Christ is now in the culmination stage and in its conclusion **He treads the wine press of the fierce wrath of God, the Almighty (19:15).**

19:16   And on His robe and on His thigh He has a name written, "KING OF KINGS, AND LORD OF LORDS." In verse 12 we read of a name of Christ that *no one knows except Himself.* There we saw that the use of "know" can have the meaning of knowing intimately to possess knowledge thoroughly and thereby to own that knowledge. It is in this sense that *no one knows* this name *except Himself?* The name so known is **KING OF KINGS, AND LORD OF LORDS (19:16).**

19:17   Then I saw an angel standing in the sun, and he cried out with a loud voice, saying to all the birds which fly in midheaven, "Come, assemble for the great supper of God...." This **great supper of God (19:17)** is not to be confused with the **marriage supper of the Lamb (19:7,9).** The marriage supper of the Lamb is a worship feast that takes place with God's own people. This supper is very different.

19:18 *...so that you may eat the flesh of kings and the flesh of commanders and the flesh of mighty men and the flesh of horses and of those who sit on them and the flesh of all men, both free men and slaves, and small and great.*[694] This supper is for the beasts of the air and of the field. Here they are invited to eat the flesh of **commanders** and **mighty men** and **horses (19:18)** and those that **sit on them (19:18)**. Here is a picture of slaughter where the dead are many, the survivors are gone into slavery, and the victors are indifferent to the bodies of the slain. None are left who are able or willing to care for the dead. Here God invites the birds to this special supper in order that one more indignity might be visited upon the enemies of God, the Jews of Jerusalem. Here is one more prophecy of covenant curses promised by God.

> *Your carcasses will be food to all birds of the sky and to the beasts of the earth, and there will be no one to frighten them away. (Deuteronomy 28:26, NASB95)*

> *As for you, son of man, thus says the Lord God, "Speak to every kind of bird and to every beast of the field, Assemble and come, gather from every side to My sacrifice which I am going to sacrifice for you, as a great sacrifice on the mountains of Israel, that you may eat flesh and drink blood. 18 You will eat the flesh of mighty men and drink the blood of the princes of the earth, as though they were rams, lambs, goats and bulls, all of them fatlings of Bashan. 19 So you will eat fat until you are glutted, and drink blood until you are drunk, from My sacrifice which I have sacrificed for you. 20 You will be glutted at My table with horses and charioteers, with mighty men and all the men of war," declares the Lord God. (Ezekiel 39:17-20, NASB95)*

"The slaughter seems to include all classes in society and the horror lies in the fact that they will not be buried, a matter of great shame to the ancients and sometimes thought to exclude people from the resurrection."[695]

---

[694] This is the language of covenant curses. See Isaiah 34:13b-15; Isaiah 51:17; Jeremiah 25:15, 17, 28; Deuteronomy 28:26; Jeremiah 7:33; Jeremiah 16:4.

[695] J. Massyngberde Ford, 324.

19:19 And I saw the beast and the kings of the earth and their armies assembled to make war against Him who sat on the horse and against His army. As we saw earlier, ***the beast (19:19)*** (out of the sea) is referred to both as Rome and, Rome's emperor, Nero.

We see here that not only were ***the beast and the kings of the earth [land] (19:19)*** enemies of Israel, they are also enemies of God. Just because God uses them in His plan for Jerusalem, does not mean that these are godly people. On the contrary, they are evil and oppose Christ Himself. Their hope is in not only destroying Judaism but Christianity as well. The fact that they freed Christianity from the corruption of apostate Judaism does not go to their credit. They meant it for evil, not good. Titus greatly opposed Christianity and "expressed the opinion that the temple ought most certainly to be destroyed, in order that the Jewish and Christian religions might more completely be abolished; for although these religions were hostile to each other, they had nevertheless sprung from the same founders; the Christians were an offshoot of the Jews, and if the root were taken away the whole plant would soon perish."[696]

Their ***armies assembled (19:19)*** to make war against Jerusalem, and God and His people. In their first endeavor, God allows them to be successful. In their second, He brings them defeat.

The Doom of the Beast and False Prophet

19:20 And the beast was seized, and with him the false prophet who performed the signs in his presence, by which he deceived those who had received the mark of the beast and those who worshiped his image; these two were thrown alive into the lake of fire which burns with brimstone. Verse ***20*** reminds us of the story of Korah, Dathan and Abiram found in the book of Numbers.

> "But if the Lord brings about an entirely new thing and the
> ground opens its mouth and swallows them up with all that is
> theirs, and they descend alive into Sheol, then you will understand
> that these men have spurned the Lord." As he finished speaking

---

[696] F.F. Bruce, <u>Israel & the Nations</u>, citing the Qumran commentator on Habakkuk 1:16, 226.

> *all these words, the ground that was under them split open; and the earth opened its mouth and swallowed them up, and their households, and all the men who belonged to Korah with their possessions. So they and all that belonged to them went down alive to Sheol; and the earth closed over them, and they perished from the midst of the assembly. (Numbers 16:30-33, NASB95)*

Now Nero and the High Priest of Jerusalem clearly died in and around the time of the destruction of Jerusalem. In addition, it can be said that in time both Jerusalem and Rome were destroyed. However, to the best of our knowledge, they were not ***thrown alive into the lake of fire which burns with brimstone (19:20)***. There are a few of possibilities for this, 1) Nero and the high priest in Jerusalem were indeed in bodily form ***thrown alive into the fire which burns with brimstone (19:20)***. However, there is no historical record that this took place. But then again, would there be a "historical" record of such an event? Not likely. 2) They were indeed ***thrown alive into the lake of fire (19:20)***, but what is referred to is their soul. 3) This will happen in the future. It has not yet been fulfilled. If we take this position, then we remove historic Jerusalem and Rome of the first century from our current interpretation and look for another interpretation at a different time in history. 4) This passage is metaphor or symbol. As such, we should not look for a literal fulfillment but one in keeping with the metaphor.

> St. John's point, therefore, is not to provide a detailed personal eschatology of the Beast and the False Prophet; still less is he attempting to describe the Fall of Rome 410 or 476. Rather, the Lake of Fire is his symbolic description of the utter defeat and complete destruction of these enemies in their attempt to seize the Kingdom: The evil personifications of pagan Rome, like Sodom, is destroyed by fire and brimstone; Israel's false prophets, like Korah, Dathan, and Abiram, are swallowed up alive.[697]

What we would then have is a use of Old Testament imagery by John, drawn from Korah, Dathan, and Abiram, to make a point that God will judge Jerusalem and Rome decisively and with utter violence. And indeed, both Nero and the false prophet will die miserable deaths at the very hand of God for their sins against Christ and His Church. And they both did.

---

[697] David Chilton, The Days of Vengeance, 491.

19:21 *And the rest were killed with the sword which came from the mouth of Him who sat on the horse, and all the birds were filled with their flesh.* The symbolic figure of metaphor is strengthened with this scene. Although the Roman armies are credited with literally killing the enemies of God in Jerusalem, here we are told that the victory was *from the mouth of Him who sat on the horse (19:21)*.

With these comments the story of Jerusalem's destruction is complete.

"This was the end of the Jewish affairs and happened as predicted by Jesus in the Gospels. All these things came to pass in the very same generation that heard Jesus speak them, exactly as they were recorded in the Gospels ... and graphically elaborated on by John in the book of Revelation."[698]

---

[698] James Ussher, <u>The Annals of the World</u> (Green Forest, AR: Master Books, 2003, 1658), 882.

Chapter 20
The Millennium

Satan Bound

C hrist, Calvary, His resurrection and the destruction of His great enemy, apostate Israel, result in a special blessing upon the whole world, the binding of Satan. This binding is the immediate product of the defeat of Christ's enemies. He is now bound and will be so for the duration of the Church age. We will learn, in the verses that follow, the purpose of this binding and just how restrictive it is. The point to remember is that all this took place in the life, death, resurrection and judgement coming of Christ in A.D. 70, and is not something that will take place thousands of years in the future.

20:1 Then I saw an angel coming down from heaven, holding the key of the abyss and a great chain in his hand. Dealing with the word ***then (20:1)***, Gregg gives the position of Premillennialism at this point saying, "Then (v. 1) suggest a chronological sequence following the events in chapter 19:10ff., where Christ was seen in His Second Coming upon a white horse, subduing His enemies and defeating the Antichrist and the False Prophet. Hence, the events of which we now read are to occur after the Second Coming of Christ."[699] The only point that I could differ with here is the phrase "the Second Coming." If he were to speak of Christ's "judgement coming" in the clouds at this point, there would be nothing to disagree with at all. Clearly Christ has come in chapter 19. The material before us follows immediately upon the heels of that coming.

Whether this ***angel (20:1)*** is Christ or His envoy is not stated. What is stated is that he has a ***key (20:1)*** and ***chain (20:1)***. This is the fourth time in Revelation that keys have been mentioned. Christ *"has the keys of death and of Hades"* (Revelation 1:18, NASB95), and He *"has the key of David, who opens and no one will shut, and who shuts and no one opens"* (Revelation 3:7, NASB95). However, we are told that a *"star"* from heaven fell *"to the earth,"* and a *"key of the bottomless pit was given to him"*

---

[699] Steve Gregg, 460.

431

(Revelation 9:1, NASB95). In Revelation 9, the person mentioned is Satan. He is given authority in that he is given keys. He did not possess this authority in his own right. It was *given* to him. On the other hand Christ *has* these keys of authority; they are His by natural right. "The key, in the Scriptures, is a symbol of sovereignty and power."[700]

20:2 And he laid hold of the dragon, the serpent of old, who is the devil and Satan, and bound him for a thousand years.... In order to make his point most clear, John uses several names of the one that is here bound; he is **the dragon (20:2), the serpent of old (20:2), the devil and Satan (20:2)**.

We are specifically here told that Satan is **bound (20:2)**. Now of course, God does not bind spiritual beings with physical chains. Because we are material beings, we need material symbols to grasp spiritual lessons. The point is clear; however, this is a verbal picture that describes severe limitations placed on Satan by God. But, when did or does this occur? It occurred during the first century. Christ said,

> *Or how can anyone enter the strong man's house and carry off his property, unless he first <u>binds</u> the strong man? And then he will plunder his house. (Matthew 12:29, NASB95)*

Of course, Christ was making the point that it was He who had bound the strong man and plundered his house of souls held in bondage. He again addressed the same subject in Luke when he said,

> *When a strong man, fully armed, guards his own house, his possessions are undisturbed. But when someone stronger than he attacks him and <u>overpowers</u> him, he takes away from him all his armor on which he had relied and distributes his plunder. (Luke 11:21-22, NASB95)*

The point is made again; Christ has overpowered the strong man. It is He who plunders Satan's possessions. We are not in the habit to thinking that Christ did this at His first advent. It is assumed that this will someday

---

[700] J. Marcellus Kik, 192.

become true when He returns. However, Christ was not speaking prophetically; He was speaking of His then current ministry.

> *But if I cast out demons by the Spirit of God, then the kingdom of God has come upon you. (Matthew 12:28, NASB95)*

That was the point He was trying to make, the kingdom of God had indeed come upon them. The proof: He cast out demons. But to do that He had to first bind the strong man. Again, He cast out demons therefore He bound Satan. Of course to bind Satan He would have to be G_ _. They were expected to fill in the blanks.

John, the writer of Revelation, in his gospel uses a similar, but not identical, metaphor when he says,

> *Now judgement is upon this world; now the ruler of this world will be cast out. (John 12:31, NASB95)*

"The casting out of Satan was not to wait the second coming but was now."[701] Luke records something similar saying,

> *The seventy returned with joy, saying, "Lord, even the demons are subject to us in Your name." And He said to them, "I was watching Satan fall from heaven like lightning." (Luke 10:17-18, NASB95)*

Paul also commented on this saying,

> *And having <u>disarmed</u> the powers and authorities, he made a public spectacle of them, triumphing over them by the cross. (Colossians 2:15, NIV)*

The author of Hebrews enters the discussion saying,

> *Therefore, since the children share in flesh and blood, He Himself likewise also partook of the same, that through death He might render <u>powerless</u> him who had the power of death, that is, the devil.... (Hebrews 2:14, NASB95)*

---

[701] Ibid., 193.

433

Steve Gregg gives a general summary of these ideas, but not necessarily his own personal opinion, saying, "The meaning of this binding of Satan then, is that Christ, at His first advent, brought about a conclusive victory, leaving Satan impotent to prevent the success of God's kingdom."[702]

20:3 ...and he threw him into the abyss, and shut it and sealed it over him, so that he would not deceive the nations any longer, until the thousand years were completed; after these things he must be released for a short time. But in what sense was Satan bound? The text reads **that he would not deceive the nations any longer (20:3).** Up till the time of Christ's first advent, there was but one nation on earth that possessed a true knowledge of God; that was Israel. With His first coming that condition was to change. Satan had **deceived the nations (20:3)** for several thousand years. Outside of Israel, the world was for the most part ignorant of God. But now that the strong man was bound at Christ's first coming, **he would not deceive the nations any longer (20:3).** With the proclamation of the good news of Christ, the nations heard and responded to the gospel. The strong man no longer held them, a stronger than he had come. Souls were now being snatched from the fire from every tribe, tongue and nation. The gospel was to progress across the globe. Now some see the binding of Satan as the complete subjugation of all evil. But that is not at all what the text says here. As James Jordan says, "This does not mean Satan can do nothing, but that he can no longer deceive the nations and keep the Kingdom from them. ... He is bound from deceiving all the nations fully and simultaneously."[703] In saying this we "...neither believe nor teach that the binding of Satan means that all his activity is curtailed."[704] He is certainly alive and well on planet earth, but he can no longer keep the **nations (20:3)** in bondage. From this, he is *bound.* As a result, souls are coming to Christ from every nation on the globe, unlike what happened before His incarnation.

> The "binding" of Satan in a way that keeps him from "deceiving the nations" (Rev. 20:2-3) serves well as a description of the present age, in which the gospel is being spread to all the peoples of the

---

[702] Steve Gregg, 464.

[703] James B. Jordan, 48.

[704] Jay E. Adams, The Time is at Hand, 84.

world.   In previous ages, the message of redemption was essentially confined to the borders of a single nation of the world, but now all nations are the privileged possessors of God's saving graces.[705]

We are told that Satan was to be bound *until the thousand years were completed (20:3)*. It is from this word, thousand, that we get the words chiliasm (Greek) and millennium (Latin).

This is the only book in the Bible that this *thousand years (20:3)* period is specifically mentioned. Indeed, this is the only chapter in this book that this *thousand years (20:3)* period is mentioned. As options go, we have at least two to explain this period. One, it refers to a literal thousand years, no more, no less. The Premillennialists hold to this position and some Postmillennialists as well. For the Dispensationalists, the millenium will come after the rapture, the great tribulation and, finally, the Second Coming of Christ. For the Postmillennialist, a triumphal Church will usher in the millenium. The Church will be victorious in time and will usher in a period of indescribable blessing and prosperity upon this earth, and this period will be for one thousand years.

There is a second possibility, however, one that considers this as simply a large number or an undefined long period of time. Historically, perhaps socially as well, ten has been recognized as the perfect whole number. Our decimal system is based on the significance of ten. Perhaps the origin of ten as the perfect number came from our ten fingers and ten toes. A full ten fingers allows a person to do his work properly and a full ten toes allows a person to walk and use his legs properly. When this number is cubed, it becomes the ultimate symbolic number of quantitative perfection. In fact, the Scripture uses one thousand in just this way. Consider these verses:

> *Know therefore that the Lord your God, He is God, the faithful*
> *God, who keeps His covenant and His lovingkindness to a*
> *thousandth generation with those who love Him and keep His*
> *commandments.... (Deuteronomy 7:9, NASB95)*

Of course, there probably have not been a thousand generations since creation till today, and even fewer at the time Deuteronomy was written;

---

[705] O. Palmer Robertson, 161.

three hundred generations would be a reasonable guess to the present time. But we must ask, if the Lord tarries, will He stop keeping covenant after one thousand generations? That does not seem to be the point of the passage. So, are we to understand that this refers literally to a thousand generations? Or is it more likely, that this means that God's faithfulness is perfect and immeasurable? The second option is clearly the correct one. So, is the thousand mentioned in Deuteronomy a literal thousand? No, it is not.

> *For every beast of the forest is Mine, the cattle on a thousand hills.*
> *(Psalm 50:10, NASB95)*

Are the cattle on the many other thousands of hills someone else's other than God's? No? But what of our literal interpretation, is it not required? Obviously it is not. God owns the cattle on all hills. Thousand, used as a metaphor, is here used as an indeterminate large and perfect number to include all hills, millions of them, not simply a thousand.

> *One of your men puts to flight a thousand, for the Lord your God*
> *is He who fights for you, just as He promised you. (Joshua 23:10)*

Is it perhaps possible that one of the men put to flight 900 or 1,100, or some other number? Yes, of course it is. But, what of the use of "one thousand," must it be interpreted literally? No, it simply means a large perfect number. The perfect victory of God's people is illustrated with the use of the perfect number. It would not be "honoring God" to demand one thousand and only one thousand in the battle mentioned. Indeed, such an attitude might be viewed as making the Bible look foolish.

> *A thousand may fall at your side and ten thousand at your right*
> *hand, but it shall not approach you. (Psalm 91:7, NASB95)*

Perhaps only 800 fell at his side or 9,000 at his right hand; is the Scripture here in error? No, in poetic and apocalyptic literature it is often not a virtue but a vice to take words "literally." Literature must be interpreted in keeping with the genre of the literature of which it is a class. Metaphor and symbol are common in prophecy and poetry alike.[706]

---

[706] Consider these uses of one thousand in Scripture also: Exodus 20:6; Deuteronomy 1:11; 32:30; Joshua 23:10; Job 9:3; Psalms 50:10; 84:10; 90:4; 105:8; Ecclesiastes 7:28; Isaiah 7:23; 30:17; 60:22; 2 Peter 3:8.

The Scripture is famous for using numbers symbolically. In Revelation we read of the *seven Spirits of God.*[707] Yet we know there is but one Holy Spirit. But the number seven conveys both the completeness of the work of the Holy Spirit, and most importantly, His Trinitarian role in establishing and enforcing the covenant entered into by God and man. Twelve is a number used collectively of God's people, i.e. the twelve tribes of Israel and the twelve Disciples of Christ being examples. A number squared brings that number and concept to perfection. Twelve times twelve is 144; when combined with the perfect number one thousand we have a symbolic number for the totality of God's people which is referred to in Revelation 7 and 14. We will see this thought again soon in the dimensions of the New Jerusalem.

So, the point is well taken, "thousand" in Scripture is certainly used poetically and metaphorically as simply a large number, and it is used here in these verses as a large and complete number as well. The strong man has bound Satan for a long period of time, the complete period needed for God to do what He has planned through the Church. "The term *thousand years* in Revelation twenty is a figurative expression used to describe the period of the Messianic Kingdom upon earth. It is that period from the first Advent of Christ until His Second Coming. It is the total or complete period of Christ's Kingdom upon earth."[708]

In verse *3* we are told that Satan is thrown into the ***abyss (20:3)*** or as it is sometimes translated a bottomless pit. The ***abyss (20:3)*** is

> ...an extremely deep place. It occurs only twice outside the book of Revelation (Rom. 10:7, simply the abode of the dead; Luke 8:31, the prison destined for evil spirits). In Rev. 9:1, 2; 11:7; 17:8; 20:1, 3, it is a prison in which evil powers are confined and out of which they can at times be let loose. It is not the lake of fire (Rev. 20:2, 10); nor is Satan regarded as being cast into this prison forever, but only to be so cast for one thousand years (Rev. 20:1, 2).[709]

---

[707] Revelation 1:4; 3:1; 4:5; 5:6.

[708] J. Marcellus Kik, 205.

[709] Spiros Zodhiates, S., The Complete Word Study Dictionary: New Testament - electronic ed. (Chattanooga, TN: AMG Publishers, 2000, c1992, c1993), βυσσος,

As we said, in this **abyss (20:3)** Satan is no longer able to **deceive the nations (20:3)**. This does not mean that demonic forces are not at work in our world, or that our own fallen nature is not driving us to sin, only that Satan is no longer able to keep the gospel from the whole world, as he once did. "...Satan being cast into the abyss does not mean a cessation of his activity upon earth. He will remain active in a limited degree until the second coming of our Lord when he will be cast into the lake of fire and brimstone and where he will remain forever."[710]

20:4   Then I saw thrones, and they sat on them, and judgement was given to them. And I saw the souls of those who had been beheaded because of their testimony of Jesus and because of the word of God, and those who had not worshiped the beast or his image, and had not received the mark on their forehead and on their hand; and they came to life and reigned with Christ for a thousand years. The reference to the **beast (20:4)** and his **mark (20:4)** make it clear, this material is part and parcel with the chapters that have preceded it. This is a critical point. Many want to separate this chapter from chapters 19 by a thousand years. But the result would be a disjoined and confused work.

The result of the faithfulness of God's martyrs and their immediate condition is now brought to our attention. These saints will now reign with Christ in heaven during the Church age.

Then I saw thrones, and they sat on them, and judgement was given to them (20:4). This passage reminds us of two additional verses.

> *Or do you not know that the saints will judge the world? If the world is judged by you, are you not competent to constitute the smallest law courts? (1 Corinthians 6:2, NASB95)*

> *And Jesus said to them, "Truly I say to you, that you who have followed Me, in the regeneration when the Son of Man will sit on His glorious throne, you also shall sit upon twelve thrones, judging the twelve tribes of Israel." (Matthew 19:28, NASB95)*

---

[710] J. Marcellus Kik, 208.

The **thrones (20:4)** mentioned are plural. Here we have a judgement scene. Who is being judged and who is doing the judging? We are not explicitly told. The next thing mentioned is **the souls of those who had been beheaded because of their testimony of Jesus (20:4)**. It is not their bodies that are seen, just their souls. If this is **beheaded (20:4)** believers only, then this is a somewhat small audience. But are they perhaps representative off all martyrs? "But plainly it was not the writer's intention to confine the rewards of martyrs merely to those who suffered death in this particular way; for this specific and ignominious method of punishment is designated merely as the symbol of any and ever kind of martyrdom."[711] Are they, indeed, representative of all believers? Although the answer is not certainly known, there is a good reason to believe that they are representatives of all believers that have slept in Christ during the Great Tribulation that has just concluded.

Of this group, we are told that **they came to life (20:4)**. That is they came back to life at the very same time that they died. There is no soul sleep here. Just as quickly as they die, they come to life. Does this mean that they were bodily resurrected and united with their bodies? It does not appear to mean that. Coming to **life (20:4)** and reigning with **Christ (20:4)** may mean nothing more than, having closed their eyes on earth; they opened them in eternity. Doing this for the **thousand years (20:4)** then would mean they have, since the first century, **reigned (20:4)** with Him in Heaven waiting for the last judgement.

> It is a trustworthy statement: For if we died with Him, we will also live with Him; if we endure, we will also reign with Him.... (2 Timothy 2:11-12, NASB95)

However, we may also consider this coming to life as descriptive of the new birth. "...the Christian's experience of regeneration is frequently spoken of in terms of a spiritual rising from death to life...."[712] Consider these verses:

> Truly, truly, I say to you, he who hears My word, and believes Him who sent Me, has eternal life, and does not come into judgement, but has passed out of death into life. (John 5:24, NASB95)

---

[711] Moses Stuart, 359.

[712] Steve Gregg, 470.

*And you were dead in your trespasses and sins, 2 in which you
formerly walked according to the course of this world, according
to the prince of the power of the air, of the spirit that is now
working in the sons of disobedience.... 4 But God, being rich in
mercy, because of His great love with which He loved us, 5 even
when we were dead in our transgressions, made us alive together
with Christ (by grace you have been saved), 6 and raised us up
with Him, and seated us with Him in the heavenly places in Christ
Jesus.... (Ephesians 2:1-2, 4-6)*

*When you were dead in your transgressions and the
uncircumcision of your flesh, He made you alive together with
Him, having forgiven us all our transgressions.... (Colossians
2:13, NASB95)*

*Therefore if you have been raised up with Christ, keep seeking the
things above, where Christ is, seated at the right hand of God.
(Colossians 3:1, NASB95)*

*...and do not go on presenting the members of your body to sin as
instruments of unrighteousness; but present yourselves to God as
those alive from the dead, and your members as instruments of
righteousness to God. (Romans 6:13, NASB95)*

These verses all make the point that the new birth and being alive from the
dead are one and the same thing. Now whether our passage here in
Revelation is teaching this doctrine, or is simply making the point that there
is no soul sleep, is open to discussion.

**20:5   The rest of the dead did not come to life until the
thousand years were completed. This is the first resurrection.**
The rest (20:5) that **did not come to life (20:5)** would be the unsaved
dead. They would stay in this condition of death until the final judgement
day. The **first resurrection (20:5)** refers to our condition with Christ
after our death on earth, or, possibly, after the new birth, at which point we
are resurrected to be with Him until the last day. "The 'first resurrection'
(Rev. 20:4-6) associated with the millennium is best understood as

referring either to the renewal of life that occurs at conversion or to the transfer of the believer's soul from earth to heaven at death."[713] Steve Gregg makes this observation, "...while the saints enjoy two resurrections (the first being spiritual re-birth and the second being the physical resurrection at the end of time), the lost know no such "first resurrection" and have only the physical resurrection ahead of them at the end of the present dispensation (a "resurrection of condemnation," according to Christ—John 5:29)."[714]

20:6 Blessed and holy is the one who has a part in the first resurrection; over these the second death has no power, but they will be priests of God and of Christ and will reign with Him for a thousand years. If, having died, we are "*...absent from the body and ... at home with the Lord*" (2 Corinthians 5:8, NASB95), then we are **blessed and holy (20:6)** indeed. For such people, having died in Christ and now a part of the *first resurrection*, **the second death has no power (20:6)**.

> *Therefore there is now no condemnation for those who are in Christ Jesus. (Romans 8:1, NASB95)*

We are told we are to reign with Him for a thousand years. This does not limit our reign per se to just a thousand years, but to an indeterminable long period of time. This reign is limited to the time our soul is with Him in heaven without resurrected bodies. At the last day, when our bodies are resurrected we will continue our reign but in a more perfect state.

If you take part in the *first resurrection (20:6)*, then you will not take part in the **second death (20:6)**.

> *Then death and Hades were thrown into the lake of fire. This is the second death, the lake of fire. (Revelation 20:14, NASB95)*

> *But for the cowardly and unbelieving and abominable and murderers and immoral persons and sorcerers and idolaters and all liars, their part will be in the lake that burns with fire and brimstone, which is the second death. (Revelation 21:8, NASB95)*

---

[713] O. Palmer Robertson, 163.

[714] Steve Gregg, 471-472.

Let us take another look at 20:1-6. These verses are the cornerstone of the premillennial doctrine. The verses are quoted as teaching; 1. the second coming of Christ, 2. a bodily resurrection, 3. a reign on earth, 4. a literal throne of David, 5. Jerusalem in Palestine, 6. we will reign, and 7. Christ physically on earth. Now read these six verses. You will find the following <u>NOT</u> mentioned anywhere in these verses: 1. the second coming of Christ, 2. a bodily resurrection, 3. a reign on earth, 4. a literal throne of David, 5. Jerusalem in Palestine, 6. we will reign, and 7. Christ physically on earth.[715]

It is important to note that Premillennialists believe that this is the point in time in which Christ returns to earth at His Second Coming and brings the Church with Him, the Church that they believe was raptured at the beginning of Revelation chapter 4. So, for them, this is where the Millennium will begin, and earthly and heavenly beings will live together on earth for a thousand years.

As to the notion of a descent to the earth by Christ and the martyrs, and their visible reign here, there is not a word in the text, nor even an implication; at least I can find none. What a gross conception it would be, to mingle celestial and terrestrial beings in one common mass! ... it is utterly improbable, on any ground, that the triumph and exaltation of the martyrs are to consist in their being sent back to the earth, in order to resume a terrestrial existence, surrounded with sufferings and sorrows. ... the idea of spiritual beings, as descending from the heavenly world to this, and spending a thousand years in a material world whose organization is not substantially changed, can have no foundation but in the phantasy of the brain.[716]

The things written prior to this in the Book of Revelation are the story of God's destruction of Jerusalem, and the final end of the old covenant. That period of transition between the death of Christ and the destruction of Jerusalem has been completed. The new covenant is now fully in place. The harlot wife of Yahweh has been divorced and put to death for her sins;

---

[715] Gene Fadeley, 73.

[716] Moses Stuart, 361-362.

the new wife, the bride of Christ has been married. For two thousand years now the new covenant has been in place, fulfilling God's plan for this age.

The subject before us now is the thousand-year period known as the millenium.

In the introduction to this book we talked about the four ways that chapters 4 through 19 of the Book of Revelation could be considered. They were the Futurists, the Historicists, the Spiritualists, and the Preterists. Beginning with chapter 20, these categories no longer, necessarily, apply.

There is an orthodox Preterist position that sees most all of Revelation in Preterists terms. They do recognize the end time teachings of chapter 20, but they see that section as a parenthetic section, and when that is complete, the book returns from a Preterist focus to a Preterist/Futurists focus. Now there are non-orthodox Preterist theologies that deny the future second coming of Christ, the bodily resurrection of the saved and the lost, the damnation of the lost and the eternal heavenly reward of the saved. Chapter 20 of Revelation and the overwhelming instructions of the Bible as a whole teach to the contrary and we therefore refer to this position as non-orthodox, or simply unscriptural.

However, most students of eschatology define themselves in terms of how they view the Millenium. Each looks at these chapters in light of this new element. As a result, most students of chapter 20 fall into one of three millennial categories.

Amillennialism. Not all like this term, as it actually states what is not believed by this group. It states that there is no millennium. "Amillennialists simply are not amillennialists!"[717] Amillennialists certainly believe in a millennium, and for that reason another term has been suggested that reflects their system better. "Accurately speaking, the biblical system may be distinguished from the two other systems as realized millennialism."[718]

This position sees the millennium as a symbolic period referencing a long but undetermined period of time; this period is the Church age. For them

---

[717] Jay E. Adams, The Time is at Hand, 8.
[718] Ibid., 9.

the millennium began with Christ's first advent, or with the destruction of Jerusalem, and will end with Christ's return and is therefore in progress now. "Thus the binding of Satan at the beginning of the Millennium is associated with the first Coming of Christ, and the "fire from heaven" at the end of the Millenium is associated with His Second Coming."[719] Amillennialism does not mean that there is no millenium, simply that it is not necessarily limited to one thousand years and that it is not a period in which sin has virtually ceased from the earth. Instead, it is the Church age. Christ reigns during this age through His Church. However, for them the Church is not successful in evangelizing the world during this period. Christ will, after this period, rapture the Church and will then immediately return to earth with the Church. At this time He will judge saints and sinners alike, an event which will institute the eternal state of the redeemed in heaven and the lost in hell.

Postmillennialism. For them, the Millennium is a period that begins with the Church's successful mission to evangelize the nations. This success manifests itself toward the end of the Church age. During the Millennium, Christ does not physically reign on earth; He reigns through His Church. During this period "*...the earth will be full of the knowledge of the Lord as the waters cover the sea*" (Isaiah 11:9).

> The world will become *christianized*, either as the result of worldwide revival and mass conversions, or through the imposition of Christian ideals by converted rulers and Christian governments—or both. The former prospect was suggested by Jonathan Edwards and most early *postmillennialists*, while the latter is emphasized by many modern *postmillennialists*, especially of the Christian Reconstructionist variety.[720]

After the millennium, Christ comes and the saints are resurrected. Some Postmillennialists would say that He first raptures the Church and then immediately returns to earth. A great battle with Satan will ensue and the final judgements will take place. It should be noted that a person could subscribe to any one of the three mentioned millennial positions, except for Dispensational Premillennialism, and still be a Preterist.

---

[719] Steve Gregg, 459.

[720] Steve Gregg, 459.

Historic Premillennialists. This position holds to a literal thousand-year age in which Christ comes physically to the earth. He comes after a future Great Tribulation and at the beginning of the millennium, raptures the Church and then immediately returns with the Church to reign physically on the earth. Satan is bound in the abyss during this period. As a result, righteousness reigns and sin is reduced to a minimum. After the millenium when Satan is released, a great battle will ensue in which Satan is once again defeated, this time forever, followed by the final judgements of saints and sinners. The eternal state will follow. This is known as historic Premillennialism. The bodily return of Christ will be after the Church age but before the millenium begins.

Dispensational Premillennialists. They differ from historic Premillennialists in that Dispensationalists believe Christ will rapture the Church seven years before the millenium, thereby removing the Church from the Great Tribulation. He will return after the Great Tribulation with the Church to set up His Kingdom.

> Another doctrine, a rather new one, to examine is the 'pre-tribulation rapture.' This teaches that Christians, in the future, will be taken from the earth before the supposed future seven year great tribulation prior to the millennial reign of Christ. This doctrine is foreign to the Bible. The word 'rapture' is not even found in the Bible. The oldest reference to the 'pre-tribulation rapture' that this writer can find originated in the year 1812, by Emmanuel Lacunza, a Jesuit Priest in Chile. His notes, which were after his death entitled, *'The Coming of Messiah in Glory and Majesty,'* were translated into English in London in 1827. His teaching became widely embraced and is now, in less than 200 years, taught by many churches.[721]

Edward Irving and John Nelson Darby picked up on Lacunza's work and, without mentioning him at all, popularized his theory.

In addition, concerning the point about the pre-tribulation rapture, we should note that Dispensationalists believe that at this time the Jewish nation will again be God's tool of evangelism on earth, and the Old Testament kingdom of Israel will be re-instituted. They believe there will be

---

[721] Gene Fadeley, 74.

a restored Kingdom of David and a Temple in Jerusalem and that a Levitical priesthood will offer animal sacrifices as a memorial to Christ. Interestingly though, nothing at all is said in Revelation about any special role Jews are to play in the end times. "This absence of a distinctive role for Israel in the coming of the consummate kingdom of the Messiah characterizes the whole book of Revelation. Nowhere in this book are the Jewish people described as having a distinctive part in this kingdom."[722]

All this culminates with the return of Christ with the raptured saints to live with the un-raptured saints on this earth. They also live with the unregenerate people of this world for these one thousand years as well. This is a very strange position. "What shall we say of a divine program which, after glorifying the spirit in heaven, resurrects the body, reunites it to the spirit, and then consigns the now-completely glorified believer to-not another one hundred years, but-one thousand years of life in the same sinful world he longed to leave?"[723] It is hard to imagine such a world with saved, unsaved, and resurrected and unresurrected people living together. "It is unthinkable that those who experience the heavenly joys described in Revelation 7:15-17 should be torn from them, and demoted to the premillennialist powder-keg millennium!"[724] Excellent points indeed!

As already indicated, Dispensational Premillennialism is a recent deviation in the Church developed in the 1830's by two British pastors, Edward Irving and John Nelson Darby (Although Darby would not like being called a "pastor," in fact, he was.). As pointed out, Dispensationalists differ from historic Premillennialism in that they have a pre-tribulation rapture at the beginning of chapter 4 of the book of Revelation and see the millennium as a period in which Israel picks up its favored people status with God after a parenthesis in which the Church age occurred.

> Ultimately, according to Scofield, the Jewish plan will be restored to its primacy, with the temple and sacrifice re-established. Such a system is a practical denial of the Christian faith, a revival of the Phariseeism which crucified Christ, and an offense to the Saviour who came, not to establish a Jewish kingdom, but as the Lamb

---

[722] O. Palmer Robertson, 165.

[723] Jay E. Adams, The Time is at Hand, 12-13.

[724] Ibid. 13.

slain from the foundation of the world, come to give His life a ransom for many.[725]

Because of its recent origin, most of the historic Christian church has not heard of this theory. But in the last one hundred and seventy-five years it has become the dominant explanation of things to come. However, it is foreign to historic Christianity, it is based on a view of Scripture, dispensational, that is unmistakably not taught in the Bible. And although it claims to be the only "literal" interpretation of the Book of Revelation, in reality, it is filled with Cobra helicopters, nuclear war, and fantasy explanations of the various scenes of Revelation. Clearly, it is certainly no more "literal" than any other view of the book; indeed, it is far less literal than Preterism, which takes the Book of Revelation quite seriously as a literal message to its then current audience.

Satan Freed, Doomed

At this point in Revelation, John having accomplished his purpose, in instructing us on the forthcoming satanic rebellion at the end of time and the Great White Throne judgement that will follow, he will return us in chapter 21 to our present, or current point in the story of the fall of the old covenant and the establishment of the new.

Clearly, this rebellion takes place after the millenium, that is, the Church age.

20:7 *When the thousand years are completed, Satan will be released from his prison....* At this point, John momentarily moves us past the Church age to the end of time. He will return to the Church age in a moment. The completion of ***the thousand years (20:7)*** would refer to the end of the Church age. At this time Satan is released and what he could not do before, *deceive the nations*, he can now do again.

20:8 *...and will come out to deceive the nations which are in the four corners of the earth, Gog and Magog, to gather them together for the war; the number of them is like the sand of the seashore.* We see that Satan loses no time in using his freedom to attack

---

[725] John Rousas Rushdoony, <u>Thy Kingdom Come</u>, 210.

the nations (20:8) and is, indeed, amazingly successful. "Clearly then the millennium, whatever it is, does not mean a period when Satan has no following on earth, for this vast host rallies at once to his standard."[726]

Next mentioned are *Gog and Magog (20:8)*. Grammatically, they are in apposition[727] (not opposition) to *the nations (20:8)*; that is, they are one and the same. This means that *God and Magog (20:8)* are used grammatically and symbolically to mean *nations (20:8)*, specifically hostile nations to God's people.

Gog and Magog (20:8) have been the object of much confusion in prophetic studies. John's source is of course Ezekiel chapters 38 and 39. Although at first reading, it would appear that Revelation 20:8 is an expansion of Ezekiel, that actually is not the case. The word *Gog (20:8)* simply provides the Old Testament imagery that John is looking for and is not a specific reference to a people or person called Gog. It is not uncommon for the imagery of Revelation to be based on Old Testament subjects or places. Consider John's use of other Old Testament proper names. The 'Jezebel' of Revelation is not the same woman as in the Book of Kings. The 'Sodom' in Revelation is not the same Sodom as in Genesis. The 'Egypt' in Revelation is not the same Egypt as in Egypt. The 'Babylon' in Revelation is not the Babylon of Daniel. The 'New Jerusalem' in Revelation is not the old Jerusalem in Israel. But, in each instance, the former serves as a *type*.[728] That is the case before us here, the Gog of Revelation is not the Gog of Ezekiel either. However, it is so much like Ezekiel's Gog that it serves John's purpose perfectly as Jezebel, Sodom, Egypt and Babylon served John's purpose by their proximate character as well.

Gog and Magog (20:8) serve very well as a type. Jewish literature is replete with eschatological stories of this enemy of God.

> ...here we come on a picture which etched itself deeply, if mysteriously, on Jewish thought, the picture of Gog and Magog.

---

[726] Archibald Thomas Robertson, Vol. VI, 461.

[727] "A grammatical construction in which two usually adjacent nouns having the same referent stand in the same syntactical relation to the rest of a sentence (as *the poet* and *Burns* in 'a biography of the poet Burns')."

www.m-w.com/ cgi-bin/dictionary?book=Dictionary&va=apposition

[728] David Chilton, <u>The Days of Vengeance</u>, 523.

We find it first in Ezekiel 38 and 39. There Gog of the land of Magog, the chief prince of Meshech and of Tubal, is to launch the great attack upon Israel and is to be in the end utterly destroyed. It may be that originally Gog was connected with the Scythians whose invasions all men feared. As time went on, in Jewish thought Gog and Magog came to stand for everything that is against God. The rabbis taught that Gog and Magog would assemble themselves and their forces against Jerusalem, and would fall by the hand of the Messiah.[729]

So, it would appear that John took advantage of existing judgement motifs in Jewish and Biblical writings. **Gog and Magog (20:8)** are simply **the nations (20:8)** and are here used much like the way we used go use the word "Communists" a few years back—"The communists are coming!" In the same sense he is saying, "Gog and Magog are coming!" In both cases, they engender fear.

One other point, "In Ezekiel 39, Gog is completely destroyed before the kingdom era. In Revelation, Gog is destroyed after the 1,000 years. Either Ezekiel's kingdom is not the same as the 1,000 years, or neither account gives us chronology but doctrine."[730]

> Ezekiel's picture of the destruction of Gog is one of complete annihilation; and this destruction proceeds the kingdom age. Yet in the Apocalypse the destruction of Gog follows the thousand years. Is Gog to be destroyed forever, and then brought to life again to fight a last great battle against Messiah and the saints? Or, are there two Gogs? Or, are we to reverse the sequence of events in Ezekiel? Or in Revelation?[731]

Or better yet, is John simply availing himself of the baggage that comes with the word **Gog (20:8)** to create the emotional atmosphere he seeks here? He is indeed.

---

[729] W. Barclay, *Volume 2.*, Re 20:11.

[730] Rousas John Rushdoony, Thy Kingdom Come, 214.

[731] Oswald T. Allis, 27-28.

20:9 *And they came up on the broad plain of the earth and surrounded the camp of the saints and the beloved city, and fire came down from heaven and devoured them.* An important question at this point is this, is the **beloved city (20:9)** a rebuilt Jerusalem? The presence of a rebuilt Jerusalem is a critical part of dispensational premillennialism, although that in itself certainly does not prove the dispensational system.

But to our question, is it a literal city? On the plus side is 1) the term **beloved city (20:8)**. Although never specifically used of Jerusalem, this term is nevertheless close to other affectionate terms used in Scripture to describe Jerusalem. And indeed, the phrase is used in extrabiblical literature for Jerusalem. 2) Jerusalem has indeed been rebuilt today, although it exists in unbelief.

On the negative side are 1) as of chapter 19 in Revelation, Jerusalem is thoroughly destroyed and does not appear to have any earthly future in God's plan for His people. 2) The heavenly Jerusalem spoken of fondly in Revelation is said to descend to earth in Revelation 21:2. Although that passage is future to our current place in the text, we will find that in fact, it is not future to this battle we are studying here.

In addition to these points, I think we need to deal with the phrase **the number of them is like the sand of the seashore (20:8)** in the previous verse. These are the enemies of God that come upon **the saints (20:8)**. Their leader is **Satan (20:8)** who ...**will come out to deceive the nations which are in the four corners of the earth (20:8)**. The implication is that millions of people will gather to this place. Now the question comes to mind, is the area around Israel large enough to host such a great army? The answer is no. Of course, the greater the area considered, the more likely it is that millions of people would fit. But at first reading, it does not seem probable. So, there is some question as to the literalness of this passage. In fact, wars of this magnitude would no longer be fought with such huge armies; nuclear weapons would be the method of choice.

The phrase **the camp of the saints (20:9)** used in this passage is equivalent to **the beloved city (20:9)**. That can provide us some insight here. **Camp (20:9)**, of course, refers to Israel's wilderness wandering days. They traveled and camped in a specific order, and it was there that God walked and communed with them.

> *Since the Lord your God walks in the midst of your camp to*
> *deliver you and to defeat your enemies before you, therefore your*
> *camp must be holy; and He must not see anything indecent*
> *among you or He will turn away from you. (Deuteronomy 23:14,*
> *NASB95)*

Having established this point, now let us return to our text. Is there to be a rebuilt **camp of the saints (20:9)** in this millennial/postmillennial period? Of course, that point is easily passed over in getting to **the beloved city (20:9)** issue. But the fact is critical. One equals the other. Probably no commentator, dispensational or otherwise, believes that this is a "rebuilt" literal **camp (20:9)** of Israelites. If we do not have a literal rebuilt **camp (20:9)** here in this passage, then probably we do not have a literal rebuilt **beloved city (20:9)** here either. If not that, then what? One author addresses the issue saying, "...wherever the people of God are, there the city of God is."[732] The enemies of God attack the people of God, the Church. God intervenes and defeats Satan. A literal beloved city is not the point here. That is a term to designate the people of God or the bride of Christ, the New Jerusalem, the Church. It is the Church that is the New Jerusalem and therefore the **beloved city (20:9)**. The Church is the object of Satan's attack.

However, keep in mind that our passage here in chapter 20 is taking us far in the future, far from our starting place at the destruction of Jerusalem in A.D. 70. John will return us to that point in a moment, then he will explain in far greater detail just what the new Jerusalem is that he is referring to here. We will find that this new Jerusalem is the New Covenant people, the Church of Jesus Christ. It is the Church that is the object of Satan's evil efforts. His attack is spoken of in military terminology, very similar to what we have experienced in the earlier chapters of Revelation. Using these symbols, John tells us the worldwide Kingdom and Church of Christ will be attacked in a most violent way in the last days. He also explains that Christ will make short work of Satan's evil efforts. The victory is assured to the Church.

...and fire came down from heaven and devoured them (20:9). The destruction of the wicked on the last day is a universal teaching of

---

[732] D. E. Aune, *Revelation 17-22*, Re 20:10.

apocalyptic literature. That scene is before us now. *This* is the Lord's Second Coming that we have made reference to so often in this book. The Second Coming is not "the" theme of Revelation and has therefore not been the object of John's attention. However, he now addresses it succinctly in the ultimate coming of God in judgement. Paul speaks of this very point saying,

> *For after all it is only just for God to repay with affliction those who afflict you, 7 and to give relief to you who are afflicted and to us as well when <u>the Lord Jesus will be revealed from heaven with His mighty angels in flaming fire, 8 dealing out retribution to those who do not know God</u> and to those who do not obey the gospel of our Lord Jesus. (2 Thessalonians 1:6-8, NASB95)*

This would be a good time to make an observation—there is no rapture mentioned anywhere in the Book of Revelation.

> No mention is made of the παρουσία [presence, coming, advent] or ἐπιφάνεια [an appearing, appearance] of the Lord, and though ἔρχομαι [to come, to go] and the response ἔρχου [come] are watchwords in this book, the "coming" intended, in some instances at least, is not the final Advent, but the visitation of a Church or an individual. Moreover, there is no one vision which answers altogether to the conception of the Return, as it is presented in our Lord's teaching and in the Epistles. We look for such an appearance immediately before the general resurrection and judgement (xx. II ff.), or in connexion with the descent of the Bride, but it is absent. Perhaps the Reaper on the white cloud, and the crowned warrior on the White horse, may describe, each in its own way, the Last Coming, but neither of these visions exhausts the conception, or occupies the position which the Parousia might have been expected to fill.[733]

Yet, we know there is a rapture for Paul talks about the very situation before us saying,

> *For the Lord Himself will descend from heaven with a shout, with the voice of the archangel and with the trumpet of God, and the*

---

[733] Henry Barclay Swete, cixxi.

> *dead in Christ will rise first. Then we who are alive and remain*
> *will be caught up together with them in the clouds to <u>meet</u> the*
> *Lord in the air, and so we shall always be with the Lord. (1*
> *Thessalonians 4:16-17, NASB95)*

I especially want to draw your attention to the word "meet." It is the Greek word ἀπάντησις, *apántēsis*; Paul uses this same word in Acts:

> *And the brethren, when they heard about us, came from there as*
> *far as the Market of Appius and Three Inns to <u>meet</u> us; and when*
> *Paul saw them, he thanked God and took courage. (Acts 28:15,*
> *NASB95)*

In Acts, the church met Paul some miles from Rome and then immediately returned to Rome accompanying Paul.

Matthew uses the same Greek word where wise and foolish virgins are contrasted.

> *But at midnight there was a shout, 'Behold, the bridegroom!*
> *Come out to <u>meet</u> him.' (Matthew 25:6, NASB95)*

> How did the wise virgins respond? They went out as a welcoming
> party and met him somewhere outside the place where the
> marriage feast was to take place. They then turned around and
> accompanied or escorted him to the marriage feast. Presumably
> they did not interrupt the bridegroom's progress or reverse his
> direction; they and he did not depart to some other place for an
> interlude after which they returned together.[734]

The Acts and Matthew verses are the only other places in the New Testament in which this word is used. My point is, on this last day, we are caught up in the clouds to <u>meet</u> Him, and then we immediately return with Him to the earth. This interpretation is in full harmony with the way it is used in Acts and Matthew. In these books, as well as in life in general, important people will be met with delegations on the outskirts of town or at the airport and escorted into the community, to a banquette, the White

---

[734] Millard J. Erickson, <u>Contemporary Options in Eschatology</u> (Grand Rapids, MI: Baker Book House, 1977), 156-157.

House, etc. In just this way Christ is met with the delegation of His Church to escort Him in Triumph to earth. In other words, there is no seven-year period between the rapture and our return with Christ to this earth. The return is immediate in Thessalonians as it is in Acts and Matthew. You might note that the passage says, "...*so we shall always be with the Lord.*" So, if the Lord is coming to earth to judge his creatures, then that is where we must also immediately go if we are to "*always be with the Lord.*"

So, the rapture and His second coming occur at the end of the Church age and therefore at the end of the Millenium. The rapture of the Church and His bodily Second Coming to the earth are at one and the same time and both after the Church age are, therefore Post-Millennial.

20:10 And the devil who deceived them was thrown into the lake of fire and brimstone, where the beast and the false prophet are also; and they will be tormented day and night forever and ever. We read earlier that the beast and the false prophet were thrown into the lake of fire.

> *And the beast was seized, and with him the false prophet who performed the signs in his presence, by which he deceived those who had received the mark of the beast and those who worshiped his image; these two were thrown alive into the lake of fire which burns with brimstone. (Revelation 19:20, NASB95)*

However, Satan was not consigned to the **lake of fire (20:10)** at that time. Instead, he was thrown into the *abyss*.

> *And he threw him into the abyss, and shut it and sealed it over him, so that he would not deceive the nations any longer, until the thousand years were completed; after these things he must be released for a short time. (Revelation 20:3, NASB95)*

His freedom to do his worst was but for *a short time*. That time having now come and gone he is now **thrown into the lake of fire and brimstone (20:10)**. His fate is not now simply for a thousand years, as was his stay in the abyss. It is instead **forever and ever (20:10)**.

Judgement at the Throne of God

20:11 *Then I saw a great white throne and Him who sat upon it, from whose presence earth and heaven fled away, and no place was found for them.* The scene experiences a dramatic shift. We are no longer on earth; we are now in heaven. John sees ***a great white throne (20:11).*** This is the only place in the Bible this phrase is used, although the word throne is used 37 times in Revelation. The throne of God with all its implied majesty and power is a major theme of Revelation.

Who is sitting upon this throne, the Father or the Son? In the gospel John says of Christ, "*He gave Him authority to execute judgement*" (John 5:27, NASB95). Matthew says, "*But when the Son of Man comes in His glory, and all the angels with Him, then He will sit on His glorious throne*" (Matthew 25:31, NASB95). Paul says to Timothy, "*I solemnly charge you in the presence of God and of Christ Jesus, who is to judge the living and the dead, and by His appearing and His kingdom*" (2 Timothy 4:1, NASB95). The answer is Jesus Christ.

The phrase ***from whose presence earth and heaven fled away (20:11)*** suggest that heaven and earth at this point no longer exist. Although this is possible, it is not necessarily the case. "The fleeing away of heaven and earth is a poetic portraiture of the effects of the divine presence. Even the natural creation shrinks back with awe and seeks to hide itself...."[735]

20:12 *And I saw the dead, the great and the small, standing before the throne, and books were opened; and another book was opened, which is the book of life; and the dead were judged from the things which were written in the books, according to their deeds.* We are now presented with a picture of **the dead, the great and the small (20:12)** that are now before the throne of God. No one is missing, no one is able to hide, all are there.

Punishment of the lost is not all of the same quality or quantity but is ***according to their deeds (20:12).*** It is based on the nature of a person's behavior or life. "...there is an implication here, that different

---

[735] Moses Stuart, 370.

degrees of punishment and of reward will be the consequence of final judgement."[736]

> *And that slave who knew his master's will and did not get ready or act in accord with his will, will receive many lashes, but the one who did not know it, and committed deeds worthy of a flogging, will receive but few. From everyone who has been given much, much will be required; and to whom they entrusted much, of him they will ask all the more. (Luke 12:47-48, NASB95)*

The question is often asked if there is one or several judgements. The dispensationalists insist there are several, so many in fact that it is hard to determine how many. However, the universal opinion of the Church has generally supported just one. "The Bible everywhere affirms that the righteous and the wicked will be resurrected at the same time...and face judgement on the same occasion."[737]

Christ speaks of two resurrections but both occur in one hour. At that time, "all" who are in the tombs come forth.

> *Do not marvel at this; for an hour is coming, in which <u>all</u> who are in the tombs will hear His voice, and will come forth; those who did the good deeds to a resurrection of life, those who committed the evil deeds to a resurrection of judgement. (John 5:28-29, NASB95)*

In Matthew, Jesus talks of the tares and wheat. The slave wants to separate one from the other now, but the master forbids it and says that both are to be allowed to grow till the harvest when both are reaped at one time.

> *But when the wheat sprouted and bore grain, then the tares became evident also. The slaves of the landowner came and said to him, 'Sir, did you not sow good seed in your field? How then does it have tares?' And he said to them, 'An enemy has done this!' The slaves said to him, 'Do you want us, then, to go and gather them up?' But he said, 'No; for while you are gathering up the tares, you may uproot the wheat with them. 'Allow both to grow*

---

[736] Ibid., 371.

[737] Steve Gregg, 481.

> *together until the harvest; and in the time of the harvest I will say*
> *to the reapers, First gather up the tares and bind them in bundles*
> *to burn them up; but gather the wheat into my barn.' (Matthew*
> *13:26-30, NASB95)*

Again in Matthew, Jesus speaks of the end of the age when the good and bad fish are separated out at one time.

> *Again, the kingdom of heaven is like a dragnet cast into the sea,*
> *and gathering fish of every kind; and when it was filled, they*
> *drew it up on the beach; and they sat down and gathered the*
> *good fish into containers, but the bad they threw away. So it will*
> *be at the end of the age; the angels will come forth and take out*
> *the wicked from among the righteous, and will throw them into*
> *the furnace of fire; in that place there will be weeping and*
> *gnashing of teeth. (Matthew 13:47-50, NASB95)*

And in a discussion of the nations, Jesus says that the sheep and the goats will be separated at the same time, one on His right and the other on His left.

> *All the nations will be gathered before Him; and He will separate*
> *them from one another, as the shepherd separates the sheep from*
> *the goats; and He will put the sheep on His right, and the goats on*
> *the left. (Matthew 25:32-33, NASB95)*

There really is no reason to believe in multiple judgements of saved, lost, gentiles, Jews, Old Testament believers, New Testament believers, those that died before the rapture, those that died after the rapture, those that died in the Tribulation, those that died during the millenium, etc, etc. It is simply not taught in the Bible.

The books, containing the record of human deeds, **were opened (20:12)**. "The representation is, that all that men have done is recorded, and that it will be exhibited on the final trial, and will constitute the basis of the last judgement."[738]

---

[738] Albert Barnes, <u>Notes on the New Testament, Revelation</u> (Grand Rapids, MI: Baker Book House, 1951), 439.

Daniel says this about the opening of the books.

> *A river of fire was flowing and coming out from before Him;*
> *thousands upon thousands were attending Him, and myriads*
> *upon myriads were standing before Him; the court sat, and the*
> *books were opened. (Daniel 7:10, NASB95)*

How sad that day will be and how moving are the words of the unnamed poet.

> The moving finger writes, and having writ
> Moves on; nor all thy piety or wit
> Can lure it back to cancel half a line,
> Or all thy tears wash out a word of it.[739]

Fortunately we read that **another book was opened, which is the book of life (20:12).** Without this other book, and with only our works to be judged, all would be lost. However, there is a **book of life (20:12)**, the book in which God has listed the names of His redeemed from the foundation of the world.

> *...just as He chose us in Him before the foundation of the world,*
> *that we would be holy and blameless before Him. (Ephesians 1:4,*
> *NASB95)*

20:13 And the sea gave up the dead which were in it, and death and Hades gave up the dead which were in them; and they were judged, every one of them according to their deeds. So here we have before us the resurrection on the last day. The world has come to an end. Now the works of men will be judged and an eternal destiny assigned to the saved and the lost.

These comments about **the sea (20:13)**, **death (20:13)** and **Hades (20:13)** giving up their **dead (20:13)** is another strong indicator that both believers and the lost are resurrected at this time. "The Bible everywhere

---

[739] Philip Carrington, 328.

affirms that the righteous and the wicked will be resurrected at the same time...and the same is taught here."[740]

20:14 Then death and Hades were thrown into the lake of fire. This is the second death, the lake of fire. Finally, **death (20:14)** and **Hades (20:14)**, (that is, the grave) are cast into **the lake of fire (20:14)**, signaling the end of the mortal era.[741]

> *The last enemy that will be abolished is death. (1 Corinthians 15:26, NASB95)*

"...death and Hades are ultimately as powerless as the other forces of evil. Finally there is no power but that of God. All else is completely impotent."[742]

The first death is of course the death of our flesh. **The second death (20:14)** is the damnation of the lost in the lake of fire.

> *Blessed and holy is the one who has a part in the first resurrection; over these the second death has no power....*
> *(Revelation 20:6, NASB95)*

20:15 And if anyone's name was not found written in the book of life, he was thrown into the lake of fire. Earlier we read,

> *And I saw the dead, the great and the small, standing before the throne, and books were opened; and another book was opened, which is the book of life; and the dead were judged from the things which were written in the books, according to their deeds. (Revelation 20:12, NASB95)*

"The books" refer to the record of all human deeds and all sin that must be assigned a punishment in the lake of fire. However, if one has his or her

---

[740] Steve Gregg, 481.

[741] J. Massyngberde Ford, 359.

[742] Leon Morris, <u>The Revelation of St. John</u> (Grand Rapids, MI: William B. Eerdmans Publishing Co., 1969), 241f.

name written in *the book of life (20:15)*, then those sins are punished already in the person of Christ.

"In this short sentence the doom is told of all who are out of Christ, for they too follow the devil and the two beasts into the lake of fire.... There is no room here for soul sleeping, for an intermediate state, for a second chance, or for annihilation of the wicked."[743] "The sufferings of those who undergo the second death, cannot be alleviated by expiring; for there is no expiring. Pardon, moreover, is now too late."[744]

Earth's history, as we know it, has now come to an end. The Millenium is over; the eternal state now begins.

SUMMARY:

By way of summary, let us look at the events that occur in the Bible following the Millenium. At the end of the Millenium there is 1) a rebellion (20:7). 2) A battle is fought (20:8). 3) Fire falls from heaven and consumes the enemy (20:9). 4) A resurrection occurs (20:13). 5) Finally, a judgement takes place (20:12, 14).

Amillennialism: The Amillennialists believe that the Church era is the Millennium spoken of here in Revelation. At the end of the Church age, the events of Revelation 20 occur, the Lord will return, rapture the living saints, resurrect the dead and judge all before His throne.

Postmillennialism: It should be noted that many, but not all, postmillennialists have a literal millennium as do the dispensationalists. Others agree with the Amillennialists and believe that the millennium is the realized Church age. Most postmillennialists believe the millennium will be ushered in gradually by the progressive expansion of the church, empowered by the Holy Spirit, as it proclaims the gospel of Christ. Then the events of Revelation 20 will take place. Some embrace something of a cataclysmic Postmillennialism in which the world will suffer moral decay, much as the Premillennialist teach, and at the end of this process there will be a cataclysmic crash of civilization. From the ashes of this cataclysm the

---

[743] Archibald Thomas Robertson, Vol. VI, 465.

[744] Moses Stuart, 373.

Church will rise, empowered by the Holy Spirit, to successfully evangelize the world. This would usher in the Millennium.

Premillennialism: But in the dispensational system, all these events mentioned that follow the millennium: 1) a rebellion (20:7). 2) a battle is fought (20:8). 3) fire falls from heaven and consumes the enemy (20:9). 4) a resurrection occurs (20:13). 5) finally, a judgement takes place (20:12, 14), take place at the end of the Great Tribulation and thereby usher in the beginning of the Millenium. But, then at the end of the Millenium, we see these same events all over again.

Notice that for the Dispensationalists these "...unique factors are repeated precisely at both the beginning and at the end of the thousand years. Do you not begin to wonder whether the millennium and the church age are distinct periods of time after all?"[745] Indeed does the Bible actually teach all this occurs twice? No, it does not.

---

[745] Jay E. Adams, The Time is at Hand, 21.

Chapter 21
All Things Made New

The New Heaven and Earth

At this point, John returns us to where he left off just prior to
parenthetically taking the reader forward in time to the end of the
world. He returns the reader to that period just at and after the destruction
of Jerusalem in Revelation 20:6. Revelation 21 picks up at this point. The
old Jerusalem has just been destroyed. John now describes its
replacement, the New Jerusalem. "St. John saw the fall of Jerusalem, and
recognized in it the hand of God; it was not an accident, but a judgement of
God; it was a visitation, a Coming of the Son of Man."[746]

This new Jerusalem, a synonym for the new covenant, came into existence
at the Lord's Supper in the upper room just before Christ's crucifixion.
However, it has been in transition from that point to the point before us. At
this time, with the old Jerusalem fully destroyed, and the old covenant fully
fulfilled, the new community of faith now takes its full and sole right to the
elevated term Jerusalem. The picture of the establishment of the new
Jerusalem, the Church, is highly picturesque. It uses symbol, metaphor and
highly developed imagery to draw us this picture of the bride of Christ, the
new covenant replacement of the old covenant wife of Jehovah.

**21:1 Then I saw a new heaven and a new earth; for the first
heaven and the first earth passed away, and there is no longer
any sea.** We are told that **the first heaven and the first earth
passed away (21:1)**. Peter gives us some detail concerning this event.

> But the day of the Lord will come like a thief, in which the heavens
> will pass away with a roar and the elements will be destroyed
> with intense heat, and the earth and its works will be burned up.
> Since all these things are to be destroyed in this way, what sort of
> people ought you to be in holy conduct and godliness, looking for
> and hastening the coming of the day of God, because of which the

---

[746] Philip Carrington, 308.

> *heavens will be destroyed by burning, and the elements will melt
> with intense heat! But according to His promise we are looking
> for new heavens and a new earth, in which righteousness dwells.
> (2 Peter 3:10-13, NASB95)*

Now the question is this, is this a physical destruction of the earth? It certainly could be construed that way, and indeed many, probably most, good people do just that.[747] However, note the similarity of this passage with another in the early chapters of Revelation.

> *I looked when He broke the sixth seal, and there was a great
> earthquake; and the sun became black as sackcloth made of hair,
> and the whole moon became like blood; and the stars of the sky
> fell to the earth, as a fig tree casts its unripe figs when shaken by a
> great wind. The sky was split apart like a scroll when it is rolled
> up, and every mountain and island were moved out of their
> places. (Revelation 6:12-14, NASB95)*

"...St. Peter, speaking of that day of the Lord, says, "the heavens shall pass away (παρελεύσεται) with a great noise, and the elements shall melt with fervent heat, the earth also, and the works that are therein shall be burnt up." Our Lord said the same respecting his coming, "Heaven and earth shall pass away" (παρελεύσεται), "but my words shall not pass away." "[748] Consider also Isaiah,

> *And all the host of heaven will wear away, and the sky will be
> rolled up like a scroll; all their hosts will also wither away as a
> leaf withers from the vine, or as one withers from the fig tree. For
> My sword is satiated in heaven, behold it shall descend for
> judgement upon Edom and upon the people whom I have devoted
> to destruction. (Isaiah 34:4-5, NASB95)*

And Ezekiel says,

> *And when I extinguish you, I will cover the heavens and darken
> their stars; I will cover the sun with a cloud and the moon will not
> give its light. (Ezekiel 32:7, NASB95)*

---

[747] Jay E. Adams, Preterism: Orthodox or Unorthodox?, 50.
[748] Phillip S. Desprez, 436.

This is de-creation language. The world that the Jews then knew was being uncreated. The heaven and earth that they were familiar with, their world, was passing away, and indeed, as John put it, **the first heaven and the first earth (21:1)** did pass away. Judaism no longer existed. Something new was created in its place, a new heaven and a new earth. Here creation language is used to describe what would take the place of the old order. The new order would be so unique and the ways of God with men so different that only the phrase **a new heaven and a new earth (21:1)** could describe it. The replacement for the old Jewish order would be the New Kingdom and Church of Jesus Christ. In this phrase we can see "the defunct Old Covenant system of Judaism as the older "creation," now replaced with the new order under Christ."[749]

> *When He said, "A new covenant," He has made the first obsolete.*
> *But whatever is becoming obsolete and growing old is ready to*
> *disappear. (Hebrews 8:13, NASB95)*

And it did disappear.

This **new heaven and new earth (21:1)** phrase is otherwise found only in Isaiah 65 and 66. Interestingly, this Isaiah passage is liberally applied in the New Testament to the current age and to the new Church.[750] The allusions are often faint, but they have a collective force demonstrating the application of the Old Testament imagery of a millennial state to today's New Testament Church.

"They will not labor in vain, or bear children for calamity; for they are the offspring of those blessed by the Lord, and their descendants with them." (Isaiah 65:23, NASB95)	*"Therefore, my beloved brethren, be steadfast, immovable, always abounding in the work of the Lord, knowing that your toil is not in vain in the Lord." (1 Corinthians 15:58, NASB95)*

---

[749] Steve Gregg, 488.
[750] Ibid., 506.

"The wolf and the lamb will graze together, and the lion will eat straw like the ox; and dust will be the serpent's food. <u>They will do no evil or harm</u> in all My holy mountain," says the Lord." (Isaiah 65:25, NASB95)	"Behold, I have given you authority to tread on serpents and scorpions, and over all the power of the enemy, and <u>nothing will injure you</u>." (Luke 10:19, NASB95)
"Thus says the Lord, "Heaven is My throne and the earth is My footstool. Where then is a house you could build for Me? And where is a place that I may rest? For My hand made all these things, thus all these things came into being," declares the Lord. <u>"But to this one I will look, to him who is humble and contrite of spirit, and who trembles at My word</u>." (Isaiah 66:1-2, NASB95)	"...but in case I am delayed, I write so that you will know how one ought to conduct himself in <u>the household of God</u>, which is <u>the church of the living God</u>, the pillar and support of the truth." (1 Timothy 3:15, NASB95)
"That you may nurse and be <u>satisfied</u> with her comforting breasts, that you may suck and be delighted with her bountiful bosom." (Isaiah 66:11, NASB95)	"Blessed are those who hunger and thirst for righteousness, for they shall be <u>satisfied</u>." (Matthew 5:6, NASB95)
"For thus says the Lord, <u>behold, I extend peace to her like a river</u>, and the glory of the nations like an overflowing stream; and you will be nursed, you will be carried on the hip and fondled on the knees." (Isaiah 66:12, NASB95)	<u>"Peace I leave with you; My peace I give to you</u>; not as the world gives do I give to you. Do not let your heart be troubled, nor let it be fearful." (John 14:27, NASB95)

"For behold, the Lord will come in <u>fire</u> and His chariots like the whirlwind, to render His <u>anger with fury</u>, and His rebuke with flames of <u>fire</u>. For the Lord will <u>execute judgement</u> by <u>fire</u> and by His sword on all flesh, and those slain by the Lord will be many." (Isaiah 66:15-16, NASB95)	*"But the king was <u>enraged</u>, and he sent his armies and <u>destroyed those murderers</u> and set their city on <u>fire</u>."* (Matthew 22:7, NASB95)
"For I know their works and their thoughts; <u>the time is coming to gather all nations and tongues.</u> And <u>they shall come</u> and see <u>My glory</u>." (Isaiah 66:18, NASB95)	*"I say to you that <u>many will come from east and west,</u> and recline at the table with Abraham, Isaac and Jacob in the <u>kingdom of heaven</u>...."* (Matthew 8:11, NASB95)
"I will set a sign among them and will send survivors from them to the nations: Tarshish, Put, Lud, Meshech, Rosh, Tubal and Javan, to the distant coastlands that have neither heard My fame nor seen My glory. <u>And they will declare My glory among the nations</u>." (Isaiah 66:19, NASB95)	*"...to whom God willed to make known what is <u>the riches of the glory of this mystery among the Gentiles</u>, which is Christ in you, the hope of glory."* (Colossians 1:27, NASB95) *"To me, the very least of all saints, this grace was given, <u>to preach to the Gentiles the unfathomable riches of Christ</u>...."* (Ephesians 3:8, NASB95)
"Then they shall bring all your brethren <u>from all the nations as a grain offering to the Lord</u>, on horses, in chariots, in litters, on mules and on camels, to My holy mountain Jerusalem," says the Lord, "just as the sons of Israel bring their grain offering in a clean vessel to the house of the Lord." (Isaiah 66:20, NASB95)	*"...to be a minister of Christ Jesus to the Gentiles, ministering as a priest the gospel of God, so that <u>my offering of the Gentiles</u> may become acceptable, sanctified by the Holy Spirit."* (Romans 15:16, NASB95)

We are also told that there is **no longer any sea (21:1)**. To comprehend what John is saying you must understand that **sea (21:1)** in Scripture often refers to unregenerate gentiles. "The Sea appears to stand for all that separates and hinders; we remember that it has often symbolized the ancient enemy of God."[751] "The word, *sea,* is frequently used in Scripture to depict Gentile nations."[752]

> *Alas, the uproar of many peoples who roar like the roaring of the seas, and the rumbling of nations who rush on like the rumbling of mighty waters! The nations rumble on like the rumbling of many waters, but He will rebuke them and they will flee far away, and be chased like chaff in the mountains before the wind, or like whirling dust before a gale. (Isaiah 17:12-13, NASB95)*

> *Who stills the roaring of the seas, the roaring of their waves, and the tumult of the peoples. (Psalm 65:7, NASB95)*[753]

In addition, we see John himself using *waters* in the same way the word **sea (21:1)** is here used.

> *And he said to me, "The waters which you saw where the harlot sits, are peoples and multitudes and nations and tongues." (Revelation 17:15, NASB95)*

The result of this understanding of the word, **sea (21:1)**, is that there would be, in the ultimate completion of this new heaven and new earth, no pagan world, only spiritual Israel. This is of course a picture of the final victory of the church.

> *They will not hurt or destroy in all My holy mountain, for the earth will be full of the knowledge of the Lord as the waters cover the sea. (Isaiah 11:9, NASB95)*

The symbolic nature of the context favors this idea. The gentiles were to the Jewish nation unclean people to be avoided at all cost. But that attitude

---

[751] Philip Carrington, 333.

[752] J. E. Leonard, Come Out of Her My People, 101.

[753] See also Isaiah 5:26-30; 8:7-8; 57:20; Jeremiah 6:22-23; and Ezekiel 26:3.

would not do. There would no longer be an unclean gentile world to be avoided.

> *And he said to them, "You yourselves know how unlawful it is for a man who is a Jew to associate with a foreigner or to visit him; and yet God has shown me that I should not call any man unholy or unclean." (Acts 10:28, NASB95)*

The mission of the church became the conversion of the world. And in converting the world to Christ, there will no longer be a **sea (21:1)**.

> *And Jesus came up and spoke to them, saying, "All authority has been given to Me in heaven and on earth. Go therefore and make disciples of all the nations, baptizing them in the name of the Father and the Son and the Holy Spirit, teaching them to observe all that I commanded you; and lo, I am with you always, even to the end of the age." (Matthew 28:18-20, NASB95)*

21:2 And I saw the holy city, new Jerusalem, coming down out of heaven from God, made ready as a bride adorned for her husband. This new earth is to have a new capital, a **holy city (21:1)**, a **new Jerusalem (21:2)**. Notice how John identifies the **holy city (21:1)** and the **bride (21:2)** as one entity. "... it is not the first time the images of a city and a woman have been joined in describing one entity. In Revelation 17, the great harlot was also Babylon, and a divine interpreter explained that "the woman whom you saw is that great city" (17:18)."[754] As the old Jerusalem was the harlot wife of Jehovah, so the **new Jerusalem (21:2)** is the adorned **bride (21:2)** of Christ. The one has passed away; the other now takes its place.

In chapter 19, we saw the announcement of the marriage of the Lamb. Here in chapter 21, we continue with this subject. The proximity between the same subject in both chapters shows us that the author has returned to where he left off in chapter 19 testifying to the proximity of time as well. "The vision seems to pick up where that one left off, for here we see the procession of the bride in her readiness to be joined to her husband."[755]

---

[754] Steve Gregg, 489.

[755] Ibid., 490.

This is the city Abraham was looking for "*for he was looking for the city which has foundations, whose architect and builder is God*" (Hebrews 11:10, NASB95). Paul talked of this city saying, "*But the Jerusalem above is free; she is our mother*" (Galatians 4:26, NASB95). The writer of Hebrews again addresses our topic, "*But you have come to Mount Zion and to the city of the living God, the heavenly Jerusalem, and to myriads of angels*" (Hebrews 12:22, NASB95). Now that "*heavenly Jerusalem*" which was "*above*" has now come down to man.

The significance of this descent from heaven to the new earth is found in the role Jerusalem plays in the war with God's enemies. "Jerusalem is not simply the capital of a kingdom that must fight against other kingdoms of the world for survival. It is the city of God, and there is a cosmic, satanic opposition against God and against His redemptive purpose."[756] In the world of war, one protects ones capital at any cost. And so the heavenly Jerusalem has been under God's divine care. However, as a result of Calvary, the war has been won and there is no need to give it special protection. Its descent to earth demonstrates the total victory of God over His enemies. We are now in a mopping up operation to expand the limits of the Kingdom across the globe.

21:3 *And I heard a loud voice from the throne, saying, "Behold, the tabernacle of God is among men, and He will dwell among them, and they shall be His people, and God Himself will be among them...."* In the Old Testament, **the tabernacle of God (21:3)** made reference to the tent, and later the temple, in which God dwelt. But a deeper meaning of God tabernacling amongst His people was even understood then.

> *Moreover, I will make My dwelling among you, and My soul will not reject you. I will also walk among you and be your God, and you shall be My people. (Leviticus 26:11-12, NASB95)*

---

[756] G. W. Bromiley, Vol. 2, Page 1031.

John gives us the fullness of that meaning in his Gospel when he wrote,

> *And the Word became flesh, and dwelt [tabernacled, σκηνόω (skēnoó)] among us, and we saw His glory, glory as of the only begotten from the Father, full of grace and truth. (John 1:14, NASB95)*

The tabernacle of God is now Christ Himself. It is He who **will dwell among them (21:3)**.

> *Jesus answered and said to him, "If anyone loves Me, he will keep My word; and My Father will love him, and We will come to him and make Our abode with him." (John 14:23, NASB95)*

The phrase **they shall be His people, and God Himself will be among them (21:3)** is a covenant phrase. God again renews the covenant with us. He swears by Himself, for there is no greater than He to swear by, that we **shall be His people (21:3)**.

21:4 ...and He will wipe away every tear from their eyes; and there will no longer be any death; there will no longer be any mourning, or crying, or pain; the first things have passed away." This verse has been of indescribable comfort to the Church. There is coming a time when there will be no more tears, death, mourning or pain. This will happen only when the mission of the Church has been fully completed and the idealized picture of the new heaven and new earth becomes an eternal reality after the resurrection. This will happen when **the first things have passed away (21:4)**, which means not only the first covenant described as the first heaven and earth but when the first world ends at the resurrection and final judgement.

> *He will swallow up death for all time, and the Lord God will wipe tears away from all faces, and He will remove the reproach of His people from all the earth; for the Lord has spoken. (Isaiah 25:8, NASB95)*

Earlier John had spoken in like vein when he said,

> *The world is passing away, and also its lusts; but the one who does the will of God lives forever. (1 John 2:17, NASB95)*

Paul likewise made similar remarks demonstrating the present reality of the New Jerusalem.

> *Therefore if anyone is in Christ, he is a new creature; the old things passed away; behold, new things have come. (2 Corinthians 5:17, NASB95)*

"With the emphasis upon "all things," he points out that the Christian is not simply given a ticket to heaven and a new set of religious rituals, but every area of his life is targeted for renewal as the result of his participation in the new life."[757]

21:5 *And He who sits on the throne said, "Behold, I am making all things new." And He said, "Write, for these words are faithful and true."* The phrase, ***behold, I am making all things new (21:5)*** is interpreted by most as the beginning of the eternal state. This brings us to ask the Premillennialists how an eternal state, here called the new heaven and new earth, is different from their previous millenium? They posit a previous millenium that looks suspiciously like the eternal state. We posit a millenium, which moves the world increasingly toward this eternal state with the increasing victory of the Church, but does not ultimately confuse the one with the other. Symbolic language pictures our spiritual victories and looks forward to material benefits in earthly prosperity and health. But the earthly millenium is never to be confused with heaven itself. For the Dispensationalists there,

> ...is pointless duplication. Both are golden ages, the first partial to be sure, the other perfect. Negatively they are the same: in one, the curse, pain, and sin are partially removed (Rom. 8), in the other, the curse, pain and sin are removed (Rev. 21:22). Nor is there a positive difference: In the millennium peace, righteousness and the reign of the saints are instituted. In the new heavens and earth peace righteousness and the reign of the saints are reinstituted. In the former, the saints are supposed to reign on earth; in the latter, the New Jerusalem and the tabernacle of God descend and the saints reign on earth. In the millennium, the nations are to bring

---

[757] Steve Gregg, 491.

their glory, wealth and honor into Jerusalem (Isa. 60); in the new heaven and earth the nations are to do the same (Rev. 21:24-26).[758]

It would appear that they have confused the one with the other.

Christ is making this new heaven and earth, as He made the old one. He is both creator and re-creator.

21:6 Then He said to me, "It is done. I am the Alpha and the Omega, the beginning and the end. I will give to the one who thirsts from the spring of the water of life without cost. What is **done (21:6)**? Everything planned from before the foundation of the world for this new creation. It is completed; **it is done (21:6)**. Calvary and the establishment of the Church have come to their fullness. Eternal salvation is offered, not simply to Jews, but to everyone. Christ gives to every one **the water of life without cost (21:6)**. Jesus began this book identifying Himself saying, " '*I am the Alpha and the Omega,' says the Lord God, 'who is and who was and who is to come, the Almighty*' " (Revelation 1:8, NASB95). He now ends the book the same way. This fact demonstrates a continuity of content. The material before us is a part of the material found in Revelation chapter 1. There is one message, experiencing fulfillment at one time.

This phrase **I will give to the one who thirsts from the spring of the water of life without cost (21:6)** is a familiar one. We are first introduced to it in Isaiah,

> *Ho! Every one who thirsts, come to the waters; and you who have no money come, buy and eat. Come, buy wine and milk without money and without cost. (Isaiah 55:1, NASB95).*

And Christ in His earthly ministry said, and John himself recorded it,

> *...but whoever drinks of the water that I will give him shall never thirst; but the water that I will give him will become in him a well of water springing up to eternal life. (John 4:14, NASB95)*

---

[758] Jay E. Adams, <u>The Time is at Hand</u>, 19.

Now on the last day, the great day of the feast, Jesus stood and cried out, saying, "If anyone is thirsty, let him come to Me and drink. He who believes in Me, as the Scripture said, 'From his innermost being will flow rivers of living water.'" But this He spoke of the Spirit, whom those who believed in Him were to receive; for the Spirit was not yet given, because Jesus was not yet glorified. (John 7:37-39, NASB95)

"Like the oriental thrones, which have a fountain of cool water springing up near by, so the throne on which the Redeemer sits, is regarded as furnished with a like fountain of water; and from this his friends and followers, who are admitted to his presence, drink."[759]

The phrase **without cost (21:6)** drives home the great truth of the free grace of God in salvation. *"He who did not spare His own Son, but delivered Him over for us all, how will He not also with Him freely give us all things?"* (Romans 8:32, NASB95). Every religion on earth is a "works salvation" religion. Not only do they criticize Christians for "doing nothing" in their own salvation, they boast of their work and merit in obtaining salvation. But such "merit" is an affront to God. It is impossible to earn eternal life; it can only be obtained *"...by grace ... through faith..."* (Ephesians 2:8-9, NASB95).

21:7 He who overcomes will inherit these things, and I will be his God and he will be My son. Salvation is promised to **he who overcomes (21:7)**.

He who has an ear, let him hear what the Spirit says to the churches. To him who overcomes, I will grant to eat of the tree of life which is in the Paradise of God. (Revelation 2:7, NASB95)

For those that overcome, God identifies Himself as their God and they as His children. The John that wrote this passage also penned these words about overcoming.

For this is the love of God, that we keep His commandments; and His commandments are not burdensome. For whatever is born

---

759 Moses Stuart, vol. II, 376.

of God overcomes the world; and this is the victory that has overcome the world—our faith. Who is the one who overcomes the world, but he who believes that Jesus is the Son of God? (1 John 5:3-5, NASB95)

To be a Christian is to be an overcomer. More specifically to our context however, overcomers are martyrs.

And they overcame him because of the blood of the Lamb and because of the word of their testimony, and they did not love their life even when faced with death. (Revelation 12:11, NASB95)

But what of the others? Shallow conversions and worldly lifestyles are common in many churches today. Will this faith overcome? It will not.

At this point, we are given a list of the sinful characteristics of those that do not overcome. It is not exhaustive, simply representative of those that do not persevere.

21:8 But for the cowardly and unbelieving and abominable and murderers and immoral persons and sorcerers and idolaters and all liars, their part will be in the lake that burns with fire and brimstone, which is the second death. The first mentioned here are the **cowardly (21:8)**. I don't think we really expect this word here. The other words certainly but cowardly, how does that behavior fit such a terrible destiny? I mean, who is not frightened from time to time? But these are not simply frightened people. These are traitors to Christ! These are "...the timid Christians, who, moved by persecution, leave the ranks of believers...."[760] They "...are in contrast to those who have been faithful unto death."[761] Christ used this very word in rebuking His disciples *"He said to them, "Why are you afraid, you men of little faith?" Then He got up and rebuked the winds and the sea, and it became perfectly calm"* (Matthew 8:26, NASB95). Clearly, faith and fearfulness are not a mix approved by God. *"The cowardly (v. 8)* are in contrast to those who have been faithful unto death. Thus the cowardly are equated ... with apostates, who defect from the gospel rather than enduring hardship as

---

[760] Ibid., vol. II, 377.
[761] Steve Gregg, 492.

good soldiers of Jesus Christ."[762]   Indeed, fearfulness, or the ***cowardly (21:8)***, finds a better mix with the *unbelieving*, those that reject Christ as Lord and Savior.   "...the speaker excludes from the abode of the blessed such as apostatize from the Christian faith."[763]

Our next word, ***abominable (21:8)***, comes from a word meaning, "to stink."[764] Those that reject Christ in unbelief are an aroma from death to death, while those that look to the offering of Christ Himself for our sins are an aroma from life to life.

> *But thanks be to God, who always leads us in triumph in Christ,*
> *and manifests through us the sweet aroma of the knowledge of*
> *Him in every place. For we are a fragrance of Christ to God*
> *among those who are being saved and among those who are*
> *perishing; to the one an aroma from death to death, to the other*
> *an aroma from life to life. And who is adequate for these things?*
> *(2 Corinthians 2:14-16, NASB95)*

These are an abomination to God. They are a stink in His nostrils.

The Greek word for ***murderers (21:8)*** refers to "...one who deliberately takes the life of another human being for personal and evil reasons."[765] We are not here referring to capital punishment, accidental deaths or war, but to all others that intentionally take the life of another. In particular, the current context refers to those who are the murders of the saints.

Next we have ***immoral persons (21:8)***, which has specific reference to sexual immorality of any kind. Idol worship and immorality went hand and glove in the ancient world. Immorality is "in" in the world today as well. But God will cast "out" those who do so.

> *For this is the will of God, your sanctification; that is, that you*
> *abstain from sexual immorality; that each of you know how to*
> *possess his own vessel in sanctification and honor, not in lustful*
> *passion, like the Gentiles who do not know God; and that no man*

---

[762] Ibid., 492.

[763] Moses Stuart, vol. II, 377.

[764] Thoralf Gilbrant, Vol. Alpha-Gamma, 548.

[765] Ibid., Vol. Sigma-Omega, 447.

transgress and defraud his brother in the matter because the Lord is the avenger in all these things, just as we also told you before and solemnly warned you. (1 Thessalonians 4:3-6, NASB95)

The word, **sorcerers (21:8)**, is interesting. "It refers to one who practices magical arts, such as mixing potions and exotic ingredients and muttering magical formulas or charms."[766] Its reference would be primarily to the occult. We get the English word pharmacology from this very Greek work φάρμακος [*phármakos*] used here.

In addition to the occult applications of this word, there are two others to consider. First, it was the **sorcerers (21:8)** that provided the needed, but secret, formula that induced abortions in the ancient world. We have something of the same thing going on in our current world with prescriptions for drugs that induce abortions.[767] Second, from distant ages man has taken drugs, provided by the community **sorcerers (21:8)** or witch doctor, which allowed him to "get high." These were taken for a number of reasons: to have a god experience, to obtain a mission from god, to deal with a heavy heart, to forget problems, to deal with depression. For the most part, many still use drugs for the same reasons. Such behavior demonstrates how far modern medicine has advanced, and how far Christian people have fallen from the faith of the Bible. Christians today are far more likely to seek counsel and pharmakos (drugs) from their local witch doctor than they are to seek counsel from their pastor.

The Greek word for **idolaters (21:8)** is made up of two other words, "image" and "service." So, in its most limited sense it means "giving service to an image," bowing, praying, sacrificial offerings, etc. However, this word is used in a broader sense in the New Testament. It is "...specifically linked to monetary greed in the New Testament as well as other literature.... Very simply, ειδολολατρεια [*eidōlolatría*], idolatry, is active rejection of God by willful participation in sin. Allegiance is sworn to sin rather than to God."[768]

---

[766] Ibid., Vol. Sigma-Omega, 413.

[767] J. Massyngberde Ford, 345.

[768] Thoralf Gilbrant, Vol. Delta-Epsilon, 247.

Therefore consider the members of your earthly body as dead to immorality, impurity, passion, evil desire, and greed, which amounts to idolatry. (Colossians 3:5, NASB95)

The word, **liars (21:8)**, is a simple word with an unambiguous meaning. It means "false, lying, liar."[769] "So the *liars* are those who invented and propagated false doctrines among the heathen."[770]

Who is the liar but the one who denies that Jesus is the Christ?
This is the antichrist, the one who denies the Father and the Son.
(1 John 2:22, NASB95)

We are told of those that practice these vices that **their part will be in the lake that burns with fire and brimstone, which is the second death (21:8)**. We were earlier introduced to this lake with the description that it is "... *the lake of fire which burns with brimstone*" (Revelation 19:20, NASB95). Here we have the added information that this is **the second death (21:8)**. The first death is the death of the body; the second is the death of the resurrected body and the soul in hell for eternity.

21:9 Then one of the seven angels who had the seven bowls full of the seven last plagues came and spoke with me, saying, "Come here, I will show you the bride, the wife of the Lamb." We read a phrase very similar to this in chapter 17 demonstrating the continuity of these two sections.

Then one of the seven angels who had the seven bowls came and spoke with me, saying, "Come here, I will show you the judgement of the great harlot who sits on many waters.... (Revelation 17:1, NASB95)

In evaluating this section let us notice that "These two extensive textual units use antithetical female imagery: the first (17:1–19:10) focuses on Rome-Babylon under the dominating metaphor of a prostitute, while the second (21:9–22:9) focuses on the eschatological city of God, the New

---

[769] Ibid., Vol. Sigma-Omega, 543.

[770] Moses Stuart, vol. II, 377.

Jerusalem, under the metaphor of the bride, the wife of the Lamb."[771] We have a comparison between two women; the first is the harlot, the second is the bride. The harlot, Jerusalem, is judged, divorced, and burned with fire. The Church, is praised, married and established for eternity.

The New Jerusalem

"...the rejection of the old Israel is followed by the union of Christ with the new Israel."[772]

21:10 And he carried me away in the Spirit to a great and high mountain, and showed me the holy city, Jerusalem, coming down out of heaven from God.... We were told in the last verse that we were to see *the bride, the wife of the Lamb* (21:9). But what we see is **the holy city, Jerusalem (21:10)**. This is significant. This tells us that what we are about to see is not in John's distant future but in his immediate future. Just as the Church of Jesus Christ, the bride of Christ, is a present reality, so is this Jerusalem a present reality. Indeed, they are one and the same. "The false religion having been destroyed, its place is taken by the true; the old Jerusalem goes and the new comes. The Bride takes the place of the Harlot; Israel is gone and the Christian Church flourishes."[773]

Again, Carrington says of this passage, "This follows the introduction of the vision of the Great Harlot almost word for word, except that the prophet goes to a Mountain, not to the Desert; the Bride is the antithesis of the Harlot; the New Jerusalem takes the place of the Old. The whole literary framework of the book becomes clear and simple once the Harlot Babylon is identified with Jerusalem."[774] This comment about the word for word comparison to the vision of the Great Harlot in Revelation 17:3 is of immense importance. This is a major key in understanding Revelation. Revelation is about the divorce and death of the Harlot wife of Jehovah and His remarriage to the Bride of Christ. What we have before us now is God's replacement for the unfaithful wife of Jehovah. It is an idealized picture of

---

[771] D. E. Aune, Vol. 52C: *Revelation 17-22*, Re 21:9.

[772] Philip Carrington, 306-307.

[773] Ibid., 301.

[774] Ibid., 345.

the Church; it is a picture of what the Church is and what it will be in its perfections at the end of time.

What we have before us now is the descent of the Church, the bride of Christ. The figure used in the place of the word Church is of ***the holy city (21:10)*** because this is the home of the bride. This is known as metonymy,[775] a figure of speech in which one word or phrase is substituted for another with which it is closely associated.

John now returns to his subject, the descent of the heavenly Jerusalem to earth, and begins a detailed external description of it.

21:11 ...having the glory of God. Her brilliance was like a very costly stone, as a stone of crystal-clear jasper. The Shekinah ***the glory of God (21:11)***, that once rested upon the temple in earthly Jerusalem has departed from that institution and come to alight upon the church, the new temple of the Holy Spirit and the new City of God.[776]

Her brilliance was like a very costly stone (21:11). "The emphasis on the wealth of the new Jerusalem would remind older Jewish readers of the glory of the temple, whose gates had been adorned with gold and silver; John declares that the whole city will share the glory of the temple."[777] The particular stone here is identified as ***jasper (21:11)***. However, "In antiquity the name was not limited to the variety of quartz now called jasper, but could designate any opaque precious stone."[778] The ***crystal-clear (21:11)*** description of the stone, not opaque, would incline us to see here something closer to a modern day diamond.

In other words, the Church, the New Jerusalem, is of great beauty and value. "The believing remnant is likened to jewels in the Old Testament. In

---

[775] "...a figure of speech consisting of the use of the name of one thing for that of another of which it is an attribute or with which it is associated (as "crown" in "lands belonging to the crown")."
www.m-w.com/cgi-bin/dictionary?book= Dictionary&va=metonymy

[776] Steve Gregg, 493.

[777] C.S. Keener, The IVP Bible Background Commentary: New Testament (Downers Grove, Ill.: InterVarsity Press, 1993), Rev. 21:11.

[778] William Arndt, A Greek-English lexicon of the New Testament and other early Christian literature (Chicago, IL: University of Chicago Press, 1996, c1979), ἴασπις.

Malachi 3:16-17, it is said that those who fear the Lord and meditate on His name, 'They shall be Mine,' says the LORD of hosts, 'on the day that I make them my jewels.' The context in Malachi suggests that the reference is to the Jewish believers in Christ, who escaped the desolation of the capital city in A.D. 70."779

21:12 It had a great and high wall, with twelve gates, and at the gates twelve angels; and names were written on them, which are the names of the twelve tribes of the sons of Israel. Although we are not specifically told why there are **angels (21:12)** at the **gates (21:12)**, we are reminded of the Garden of Eden.

> *So He drove the man out; and at the east of the Garden of Eden He stationed the cherubim and the flaming sword which turned every direction to guard the way to the tree of life. (Genesis 3:24, NASB95).*

Perhaps that is the purpose of these angels as well. The true Jerusalem, the bride of Christ, will not be populated by rebels but only by the redeemed.

As the twelve tribes of Israel were stationed around the Tabernacle in a special order, so here, the tribes of Israel are remembered by having the **twelve gates (21:12)** named in honor of them. No doubt this is to remind us that Christianity did not spring from unplowed ground but is deeply rooted in the faith of Abraham and Moses, indeed, it is the only true faith of Israel, for the true Israel is now the true Church. "The attachment of the tribal names to the gates may suggest that through Israel God made a way for the world to enter the City of God, for 'salvation is of the Jews' (John 4:22). Of course, this in only another way of saying that salvation is through Jesus Christ, who sprang from the Jewish race."780

21:13 There were three gates on the east and three gates on the north and three gates on the south and three gates on the west. As Luke says,

---

779 Steve Gregg, 494.
780 Ibid., 494.

> *And they will come from east and west and from north and south,*
> *and will recline at the table in the kingdom of God. (Luke 13:29,*
> *NASB95)*

**21:14 And the wall of the city had twelve foundation stones,
and on them were the twelve names of the twelve apostles of
the Lamb.** Paul says something similar.

> *So then you are no longer strangers and aliens, but you are fellow*
> *citizens with the saints, and are of God's household, <u>having been</u>*
> *<u>built on the foundation of the apostles and prophets</u>, Christ Jesus*
> *Himself being the corner stone, in whom the whole building,*
> *being fitted together, is growing into a holy temple in the Lord, in*
> *whom you also are being built together into a dwelling of God in*
> *the Spirit. (Ephesians 2:19-22, NASB95)*

"Further evidence for identifying the city with the church is seen in the city
foundations that have upon them the names of the twelve apostles of the
Lamb (v. 14)."[781] So, the Church's heritage is rooted not only in the Old
Testament but is founded on the New Testament counterpoint to the Old
Testament prophets, the Apostles of Christ. This is the city that Abraham
was seeking.

> *...for he was looking for the city which has foundations, whose*
> *architect and builder is God. (Hebrews 11:10, NASB95)*

This is a beautiful symbolic portrait of the unity of the bride of Christ
composed of both Old Testament and New Testament believers.   The
dispensational claim that the body of Christ consists only of believers in this
age, and that Old Testament believers are not part of the body of Christ,
does not stand the test of Scripture.[782] This is an important point;
Dispensationalists make a determined effort to point out the utter
separateness of Israel and the Church. John has made a determined effort
to point out their utter commonality and unity. I wonder which one is
right?

---

[781] Ibid., 494.

[782] Keith A. Mathison, 35-36.

21:15 *The one who spoke with me had a gold measuring rod to measure the city, and its gates and its wall.* The purpose of **measuring (21:15)** is to set apart something, either for destruction or for preservation. This city, the new Jerusalem, is set apart by God and preserved for eternity.

21:16 *The city is laid out as a square, and its length is as great as the width; and he measured the city with the rod, fifteen hundred miles; its length and width and height are equal.* This is the way the Holy of Holies was laid out in the Temple, a cube. What John appears to be telling us in **verse 16** is that God's new Jerusalem is in its entirety the Holy of Holies. So all the Church, the bride of Christ, is to God as the holy of Holies was in the Old Testament. The Holy of Holies in Solomon's temple was a cube as is the new Jerusalem.

> *The inner sanctuary was twenty cubits in length, twenty cubits in width, and twenty cubits in height, and he overlaid it with pure gold. He also overlaid the altar with cedar. (1 Kings 6:20, NASB95).*

The numbers are staggering; the new Jerusalem is a **fifteen-hundred miles (21:16)** cube. These numbers do not suggest a literal meaning. For instance, the distance between Jerusalem and Rome is 1,428 miles, not quite the fifteen hundred miles mentioned here, and that would only be one leg of the base! A literal fifteen hundred-mile square for one city is inconceivable. And that does not take into account the fifteen hundred-mile elevation of the city. Outer space as we know it begins about 100 miles above the earth's surface. Atmosphere becomes dangerously thin for human life in excess of about three miles. In addition, temperatures fall drastically above one mile. So, do we have a literal megalith city of staggering proportions or is this symbolic language, like so much of Revelation?

Clearly this is symbolic language for the perfection of God's Church. Our translation says fifteen hundred miles, but the Greek text tells us it is 12,000 stadia. Notice the symbolic 12 used here. Twelve, the number of the tribes of Israel and the Apostles of the Church, is multiplied by 1,000, the number of immeasurable greatness and perfection. All this is multiplied by 3, the number of God. The size of the city is not the issue; that is purely incidental.

The 12, the 1000 and the 3 are what's important. These holy numbers produce a perfect Holy City or community of God's people.

21:17 And he measured its wall, seventy-two yards, according to human measurements, which are also angelic measurements. The fact that the wall is only ***seventy-two yards (21:17)*** high, but the city itself is fifteen-hundred miles high is suspicious and again suggests that these are not actual measurements but have instead symbolic significance, not military significance.

Again, our translation lets us down at this point as it did in the last verse. The Greek text tells us the wall is 144 cubits. But again the actual height is not the issue. It is the symbolic number 144 that is the critical point. As God's protection of the holy seed was described symbolically as the 144,000, so here 144 shows up again in that protective role, the wall that protects the city of God. God's holy community, his bride, is always the object of his protective care.

21:18 The material of the wall was jasper; and the city was pure gold, like clear glass. The city itself is of ***pure gold, like clear glass (21:18)***. Gold, of course, is not clear but yellow. As a result, it would seem that a metaphor is used here to drive home two points, the purity and immense value of Christ's bride.

21:19-20 The foundation stones of the city wall were adorned with every kind of precious stone. The first foundation stone was jasper; the second, sapphire; the third, chalcedony; the fourth, emerald, the fifth, sardonyx; the sixth, sardius; the seventh, chrysolite; the eighth, beryl; the ninth, topaz; the tenth, chrysoprase; the eleventh, jacinth; the twelfth, amethyst. In the Old Testament, the High priest was to wear a garment with twelve stones on it representing the twelve tribes of Israel. The new Jerusalem is also adorned with precious jewels on its twelve ***foundation stones (21:19)***. They are not the same as worn by the High Priest, but they have a similar mission, to magnify that which it adorns.

> *You shall make a breastpiece of judgement, the work of a skillful*
> *workman; like the work of the ephod you shall make it: of gold, of*
> *blue and purple and scarlet material and fine twisted linen you*
> *shall make it. It shall be square and folded double, a span in*

length and a span in width. You shall mount on it four rows of stones; the first row shall be a row of ruby, topaz and emerald; and the second row a turquoise, a sapphire and a diamond; and the third row a jacinth, an agate and an amethyst; and the fourth row a beryl and an onyx and a jasper; they shall be set in gold filigree. (Exodus 28:15-20, NASB95)

In addition, we read in Isaiah,

O afflicted one, storm-tossed, and not comforted, behold, I will set your stones in antimony, and your foundations I will lay in sapphires. Moreover, I will make your battlements of rubies, and your gates of crystal, and your entire wall of precious stones. (Isaiah 54:11-12, NASB95)

"That the church is here pictured seems a necessary conclusion ... and his application of it to the Gentiles of the New Covenant church."[783]

21:21 And the twelve gates were twelve pearls; each one of the gates was a single pearl. And the street of the city was pure gold, like transparent glass. A *pearl (21:21)* large enough to serve as a *gate (21:21)* is staggering. You can only wonder what the oyster looked like! Again, we should be looking at this *pearl (21:21)* as symbolic. We were introduced to the *twelve gates (21:21)* earlier; they represented the twelve tribes of Israel. In 21:12 we read of the "*...twelve gates, and at the gates twelve angels; and names were written on them, which are the names of the twelve tribes of the sons of Israel.*"

Unlike the previously named gems, pearls are created organically. A rough grain of sand irritating the tissues of the oyster causes the secretion of a substance that transforms the source of irritation into a pearl. The pearl thus may stand for affliction turned to benefit, even as silver and gold refined by fire are used in scripture for the same concept. The gates are the means of entry into the city. If the pearl is understood in this light, we have a picture of

---

[783] Ibid., 506.

one of Paul's preaching themes: We must through many tribulations enter the kingdom of God" (Acts 14:22).[784]

We just read of gold in 21:18, *"and the city was pure gold, like clear glass."* Now we are told that the streets are also made of this *pure gold, like transparent glass (21:21)*. All of these things are designed to draw our attention to the unique beauty and value of the bride, the new Jerusalem.

It comes somewhat as a surprise to read, *I saw no temple in it (21:22)*. Since we saw the temple in heaven (7:15) we might expect it to descend with the new Jerusalem. It does not. The church at Philadelphia received a promise,

> *He who overcomes, I will make him a pillar in the temple of My God, and he will not go out from it anymore; and I will write on him the name of My God, and the name of the city of My God, the new Jerusalem, which comes down out of heaven from My God, and My new name. (Revelation 3:12, NASB95)*

Notice how the new Jerusalem was anticipated in chapter 3. In addition, notice how the church at Philadelphia is offered membership in it 2,000 years ago.

21:22 *I saw no temple in it, for the Lord God the Almighty and the Lamb are its temple.* The fact that there is no temple in the new Jerusalem is proof that this is not a heavenly picture. The temple is in heaven. But this is on earth where **the Lord God the Almighty and the Lamb are its temple (21:22)**. The Holy of Holies in the Church of Jesus Christ is Jesus Himself. He dwells in His Church.

21:23 *And the city has no need of the sun or of the moon to shine on it, for the glory of God has illumined it, and its lamp is the Lamb.* It would seem that this is one more indicator of the symbolic nature of this new Jerusalem. Although our physical world has a *sun (21:23)* and *moon (21:23)*, this spiritual one, the Church, needs only the presence of *the Lamb (21:23)* to provide light.

---

[784] Ibid., 496.

> *Then Jesus again spoke to them, saying, "I am the Light of the world; he who follows Me will not walk in the darkness, but will have the Light of life." (John 8:12, NASB95)*

21:24 The nations will walk by its light, and the kings of the earth will bring their glory into it. The fact that there are **nations (21:24)** and **kings of the earth (21:24)** tells us that this is not the eternal state, but a temporal one. John appears to be making reference to Isaiah 60 at this point.

> *Nations will come to your light, and kings to the brightness of your rising.... Your gates will be open continually; they will not be closed day or night, so that men may bring to you the wealth of the nations, with their kings led in procession.... No longer will you have the sun for light by day, nor for brightness will the moon give you light; but you will have the Lord for an everlasting light, and your God for your glory. Your sun will no longer set, nor will your moon wane; for you will have the Lord for an everlasting light, and the days of your mourning will be over. (Isaiah 60:3, 11, 19-20, NASB95)*

Nations (21:24) and **kings (21:24)** have bowed the knee to Christ, and will again.

21:25 In the daytime (for there will be no night there) its gates will never be closed.... As we just read in Isaiah,

> *Your gates will be open continually; they will not be closed day or night.... (Isaiah 60:11 NASB95).*

The fact that **its gates will never be closed (21:25)** is testimony to the eternal peace that inhabits the land. God protects His bride with the perfect protection implied by the wall of 144 cubits. It also implies that opportunity for repentance and faith in Christ is still before the nations, thus a temporal state, not an eternal one.

21:26 ...and they will bring the glory and the honor of the nations into it....

*Then you will see and be radiant, and your heart will thrill and
rejoice; because the abundance of the sea will be turned to you,
the wealth of the nations will come to you. (Isaiah 60:5, NASB95)*

Before the New Testament Church only one nation enjoyed God's special
redemptive care, which now changes, for all the nations will now respond
with souls for the Kingdom.

**21:27 ...and nothing unclean, and no one who practices
abomination and lying, shall ever come into it, but only those
whose names are written in the Lamb's book of life.** Earlier we
read of those who practice **abomination and lying (21:27)** *"... their
part will be in the lake that burns with fire and brimstone, which is the
second death" (Revelation 21:8, NASB95)*.

The new Jerusalem is only for those **whose names are written in the
Lamb's book of life (21:27)**. We read that fellow workers in the gospel
are those *"whose names are in the book of life"* (Philippians 4:3, NASB95).
To those who overcome Christ says, *"I will not erase his name from the
book of life..."* (Revelation 3:5, NASB95). Those that worship the beast are
those *"whose name has not been written from the foundation of the world
in the book of life of the Lamb who has been slain"* (Revelation 13:8,
NASB95). On that last day we read, *"And I saw the dead, the great and the
small, standing before the throne, and books were opened; and another
book was opened, which is the book of life; and the dead were judged from
the things which were written in the books, according to their deeds"*
(Revelation 20:12, NASB95). And lastly Scripture says, *"And if anyone's
name was not found written in the book of life, he was thrown into the
lake of fire"* (Revelation 20:15, NASB95).

Membership in the true Church is guarded by Christ. None but the elect
obtain entrance. Compare Isaiah 60 with Revelation 21.

In Isaiah 60, all of this is precipitated by the dawning of the glory of
the Lord in a glorious new day (Isa. 60:1-3). This day was seen to
dawn with the birth of John the Baptist and Jesus (cf. Luke 1:76-
78; Matt. 4:13-16). Both passages then would appear to speak,
albeit in symbolic terms, of the realities of the New Covenant age.
The coming of the Gentiles into the church and the submission of

the kings to Christ has been in progress for nearly two thousand years now.[785]

"No longer will you have the sun for light by day, nor for brightness will the moon give you light; but you will have the Lord for an everlasting light, and your God for your glory." (Isaiah 60:19, NASB95)	*"And the city has no need of the sun or of the moon to shine on it, for the glory of God has illumined it, and its lamp is the Lamb." (Revelation 21:23, NASB95)*
"Nations will come to your light...." (Isaiah 60:3, NASB95)	*"The nations will walk by its light...." (Revelation 21:24, NASB95)*
"And kings to the brightness of your rising." (Isaiah 60:3, NASB95) *"And their kings will minister to you..." (Isaiah 60:10, NASB95)*	*"... and the kings of the earth will bring their glory into it. " (Revelation 21:24, NASB95)*
"Your gates will be open continually; they will not be closed day or night...." (Isaiah 60:11, NASB95)	*"In the daytime (for there will be no night there) its gates will never be closed...." (Revelation 21:25, NASB95)*
"So that men may bring to you the wealth of the nations, with their kings led in procession." (Isaiah 60:11, NASB95) *"The wealth of the nations will come to you." (Isaiah 60:5, NASB95)*	*"...and they will bring the glory and the honor of the nations into it....; " (Revelation 21:26, NASB95)*
"Then all your people will be righteous...." (Isaiah 60:21, NASB95)	*"...and nothing unclean, and no one who practices abomination and lying, shall ever come into it...." (Revelation 21:27, NASB95)*

The new Jerusalem, the Church of Jesus Christ is the millenium of Isaiah chapter 60.

---

[785] Ibid., 497.

Chapter 22
Eternal Reign in Glory

The River and the Tree of Life

This section through verse 9 of chapter 22 continues and concludes the description of the new creation found in chapter 21. The chapter division is unfortunate.

22:1 Then he showed me a river of the water of life, clear as crystal, coming from the throne of God and of the Lamb....
Earlier we read where Christ offers *"the spring of the water of life without cost"* (21:6). Here we are given greater detail about this water. Its origin is ***the throne of God and of the Lamb (22:1)***. The picture of a river of water has its origin in Genesis chapter 2. *"Now a river flowed out of Eden to water the garden..."* (Genesis 2:10, NASB95). This picture is expanded considerably by Ezekiel.

> *Then he brought me back to the door of the house; and behold, water was flowing from under the threshold of the house toward the east, for the house faced east. And the water was flowing down from under, from the right side of the house, from south of the altar..... 7 Now when I had returned, behold, on the bank of the river there were very many trees on the one side and on the other. .... 12 By the river on its bank, on one side and on the other, will grow all kinds of trees for food. Their leaves will not wither and their fruit will not fail. They will bear every month because their water flows from the sanctuary, and their fruit will be for food and their leaves for healing. (Ezekiel 47:1, 7, 12, NASB95)*

In Ezekiel the house under discussion is the Temple. However, here in Revelation there is no Temple. *"I saw no temple in it, for the Lord God the Almighty and the Lamb are its temple"* (21:22). The difference between Ezekiel's passage and this one clearly demonstrates that John is not trying to portray his work as a further fulfillment of Ezekiel's, but is instead simply making use of Ezekiel's categories and vocabulary. Ezekiel spoke of the future of Israel and the Temple that would soon be rebuilt in Jerusalem. John speaks of a greater new Jerusalem and a greater Temple *"for the Lord*

God the Almighty and the Lamb are its temple" (21:22). Jesus addressed this life giving water Himself.

> *Jesus answered and said to her, "Everyone who drinks of this water will thirst again; but whoever drinks of the water that I will give him shall never thirst; but the water that I will give him will become in him a well of water springing up to eternal life."*
> *(John 4:13-14, NASB95)*

The Psalmist also addresses this topic saying,

> *There is a river whose streams make glad the city of God, the holy dwelling places of the Most High. (Psalm 46:4, NASB95)*

22:2 ...in the middle of its street. On either side of the river was the tree of life, bearing twelve kinds of fruit, yielding its fruit every month; and the leaves of the tree were for the healing of the nations. Again, as Ezekiel noted, *"...and their fruit will be for food and their leaves for healing"* (Ezekiel 47:12, NASB95). "...not a single tree only, but forests of Tree-of-Life lining the riverbanks. The blessing which Adam forfeited has been restored in overwhelming superabundance, for what we have gained in Christ is, as St. Paul said, "much more" than what we lost in Adam."[786]

"The writer conceives here of the river as running through the whole city; then of streets parallel to it on each side; and then, on the banks of the river, between the water and the street, the whole stream is lined on each side with two rows of the *tree of life*."[787]

John adds, **yielding its fruit every month (22:2)**. The growing season is monthly, not yearly. The Church grows continually. Souls are added to the Body of Christ every month. Fruit is produced as Believers evidence the fruits of God's Spirit in their lives and souls are added to the kingdom.

---

[786] David Chilton, The Days of Vengeance, 567.

[787] Moses Stuart, vol. II, 377.

22:3 *There will no longer be any curse; and the throne of God and of the Lamb will be in it, and His bond-servants will serve Him....* The **curse (22:3)** has been removed; and how was it removed?

> *Christ redeemed us from the curse of the Law, having become a curse for us—for it is written, "Cursed is everyone who hangs on a tree...." (Galatians 3:13, NASB95)*

22:4 *...they will see His face, and His name will be on their foreheads.* The comment, **and His name will be on their foreheads (22:4)**, reminds us of two other places in Revelation where names or marks were places on *foreheads*.

> *And he causes all, the small and the great, and the rich and the poor, and the free men and the slaves, to be given a mark on their right hand or on their forehead.... (Revelation 13:16, NASB95)*

> *Then I looked, and behold, the Lamb was standing on Mount Zion, and with Him one hundred and forty-four thousand, having His name and the name of His Father written on their foreheads. (Revelation 14:1, NASB95)*

In one case, Satan is marking his servants, in the other God is marking His servants. Now God marks all his Church for His protection and blessing.

22:5 *And there will no longer be any night; and they will not have need of the light of a lamp nor the light of the sun, because the Lord God will illumine them; and they will reign forever and ever.* John has already told us that *"there will be no night"* (21:25) in the New Jerusalem. In **22:5** John gives us greater detail.

The one who said of Himself *"I am the Light of the world; he who follows Me will not walk in the darkness, but will have the Light of life"* (John 8:12, NASB95) is the one that brings light to His Church. Not only will Christ reign throughout eternity but His children **will reign forever and ever (22:5)** as well.

> *If we endure, we will also reign with Him.... (2 Timothy 2:12, NASB95)*

22:6-7 *And he said to me, "These words are faithful and true"; and the Lord, the God of the spirits of the prophets, sent His angel to show to His bond-servants the things which must soon take place. "And behold, I am coming quickly. Blessed is he who heeds the words of the prophecy of this book."* The fact that John now records Christ's promise of **coming quickly (22:7)** shows how integral chapter 22 is to the earlier parts of the book. This is not simply a picture of heaven to come, some day. This is a picture of the victory and glory of the Church, the bride of Christ, now.

We began our study in Revelation reading of "*... the things which must soon take place...*" (1:1), being told that "*the time is near...*" (1:3), being informed of "*the things which will [are about to] take place after these things...*" (1:19), and hearing of an "*...hour which is about to come upon the whole world...*" (3:10).

Now we end the book reading of **the things which must soon take place (22:6)**, being told, **...behold, I am coming quickly (22:7)**, instructed, "*Do not seal up the words of the prophecy of this book, for the time is near*" (22:10), again told "*Behold, I am coming quickly*" (22:12), and yet again assured "*Yes, I am coming quickly*" (22:20).

Can such a beginning and an ending mean that two thousand plus years will exists between John's vision and its fulfillment? Not if words have meaning it cannot.

22:8 *I, John, am the one who heard and saw these things. And when I heard and saw, I fell down to worship at the feet of the angel who showed me these things.* John **(22:8)** again identifies himself as the earthly author of this book, the one who **saw these things (22:8)**.

John was awed. The message of the angel was both horrific and terrific. In this state of wonder he falls at the angel's feet as he did at the conclusion of the story of Jerusalem's destruction.

> *Then I fell at his feet to worship him. But he said to me, "Do not do that; I am a fellow servant of yours and your brethren who hold the testimony of Jesus; worship God. For the testimony of Jesus is the spirit of prophecy. (Revelation 19:10, NASB95)*

***22:9 But he said to me, "Do not do that. I am a fellow servant
of yours and of your brethren the prophets and of those who
heed the words of this book. Worship God."*** Again, he is told **do
not do that (22:9)** which is not at all like what those in the Roman
Catholic Church are told when they fall at the feet of their Bishops and
Pope. Instead, John is to **worship God (22:9)**, not angels, and certainly
not man.

The Final Message

***22:10 And he said to me, "Do not seal up the words of the
prophecy of this book, for the time is near."*** Daniel on the other
hand was told, *"But as for you, Daniel, <u>conceal these words</u> and <u>seal up the
book</u> until the end of time..."* (Daniel 12:4, NASB95). And these words as
well, *"Go your way, Daniel, for these words are <u>concealed</u> and <u>sealed</u> up
until the end time"* (Daniel 12:9, NASB95).

Why is Daniel to *seal* but John is told **do not seal (22:10)**? Daniel was to
"conceal these words" and "seal up the book" because it would be a
considerable amount of time before his prophecies are to be fulfilled; they
were not relevant to his immediate audience. Daniel was written about 530
BC. These concluding words from Daniel refer to Antiochus Epiphanes
who appeared on the scene about 168 BC, the Roman Empire which began
to make its presence felt in Israel about 63 BC, and the death of Christ about
A.D. 28-29. So there was a delay of between 344 to 558 years before the
events were to transpire. This being such a long time, and having no
immediate relevance to Daniel's current audience, he is told to *"seal up the
book"* until a later date when all this would come to pass and thereby have
relevance.

On the other hand, the book of Revelation is nearly 2000 years old and,
according to some, we have yet to see the first prophecy fulfilled, even
though we are told **<u>do not seal up the words</u> of the prophecy of this
book, for <u>the time is near</u> (22:10)**. Something is radically wrong here.
If 344 to 558 years were so long as to demand a sealing of the book, would
not 2000 years require an even stronger message to conceal and seal the
book? It would. But the message is the opposite; we are not to seal the
book because **the time is near (22:10)**. "Unlike John's, Daniel's
prophecy did not constitute a 'contemporary' message, and was therefore

sealed until the times of which he wrote. In direct contrast, Jesus told John not to seal the Apocalypse, for the matters it concerns were '*at hand.*'"[788]

22:11 Let the one who does wrong, still do wrong; and the one who is filthy, still be filthy; and let the one who is righteous, still practice righteousness; and the one who is holy, still keep himself holy. The implication here is that the time is so short that there is no time to change. Certainly two thousand years would be time to change. That shortness of time is the meaning is made clear by the fact that this passage is between verses 10 and 12, both of which refer to His soon coming.

22:12-13 Behold, I am coming quickly, and My reward is with Me, to render to every man according to what he has done. 13 "I am the Alpha and the Omega, the first and the last, the beginning and the end." Once again, He says, **I am coming quickly (22:12)**. The **reward (22:12)** spoken of here is not the reward given out on that last day. This is a reward enforced with judgement on some and on deliverance from the Great Tribulation on others.

> Behold, the Lord God will come with might, with His arm ruling for Him. Behold, His reward is with Him and His recompense before Him. (Isaiah 40:10, NASB95)

As Christ the giver of the Revelation made clear in His introduction, so now He reiterates once more, it is He who is **the Alpha and Omega (22:13)**. The deity of Christ is again made abundantly clear.

> "I am the Alpha and the Omega," says the Lord God, "who is and who was and who is to come, the Almighty." (Revelation 1:8, NASB95)

> And He placed His right hand on me, saying, "Do not be afraid; I am the first and the last...." (Revelation 1:17, NASB95)

> Then He said to me, "It is done. I am the Alpha and the Omega, the beginning and the end." (Revelation 21:6, NASB95)

---

[788] Jay E. Adams, The Time is at Hand, 52.

If there was any question as to who was speaking in these four verses, the Father or the Son, **22:12-13** clarifies it for us. The speaker is the one who is **coming (22:12)**. That can be none other but Jesus Christ.

22:14 Blessed are those who wash their robes, so that they may have the right to the tree of life, and may enter by the gates into the city. How does a person **wash (22:14)** his or her **robes (22:14)**? Earlier we read a similar statement "*...they have washed their robes and made them white in the blood of the Lamb*" (Revelation 7:14, NASB95). It is the *blood of the Lamb* that washes from sin, nothing else. William Cowper the great hymn writer wrote the song, <u>*There is a Fountain*</u>, which so beautifully makes this point.

> *There is a fountain filled with blood*
> *Drawn from Immanuel's veins;*
> *And sinners plunged beneath that flood*
> *Lose all their guilty stains;*
> *Lose all their guilty stains;*
> *Lose all their guilty stains;*
> *And sinners plunged beneath that flood*
> *Lose all their guilty stains.*
>
> *The dying thief rejoiced to see*
> *That fountain in His day;*
> *And there may I, though vile as he,*
> *Wash all my sins away;*
> *Wash all my sins away;*
> *Wash all my sins away;*
> *And there may I, though vile as he,*
> *Wash all my sins away.*
>
> *Dear dying Lamb, Thy precious blood*
> *Shall never lose its pow'r*
> *Till all the ransomed church of God*
> *Be saved to sin no more;*
> *Be saved to sin no more;*
> *Be saved to sin no more;*
> *Till all the ransomed church of God*
> *Be saved to sin no more.*

E'er since by faith I saw the stream
Thy flowing wounds supply,
Redeeming love has been my theme,
And shall be till I die;
And shall be till I die;
And shall be till I die;
Redeeming love has been my theme
And shall be till I die.[789]

It is only these blood washed ones that **have the right to the tree of life (22:14)**. All others have been driven from God's garden, never to return.

So He drove the man out; and at the east of the garden of Eden
He stationed the cherubim and the flaming sword which turned
every direction to guard the way to the tree of life. (Genesis 3:24,
NASB95)

22:15 Outside are the dogs and the sorcerers and the immoral persons and the murderers and the idolaters, and everyone who loves and practices lying. The city of God, the new Jerusalem, serves as a symbolic description of heaven. Those in the city are in heaven; those outside it are in hell. The blood-washed are inside. Who are outside? This list is similar to 20:8 except for the addition of **dogs (22:15)**. "...Oriental cities were full of dirty, mangy curs of the jackal type who fed on garbage. There will naturally be none of these in the Holy City; and they symbolize the men and women who nourish their souls on what is filthy and false."[790]

The term is also used in Deuteronomy to refer to prostitutes and sodomites who also nourish their souls and bodies on what is filthy and false. It is interesting that so many "churches" are making such prodigious efforts to make sure **dogs (22:15)**, sodomites and prostitutes, are indeed a part of their church. Of course their church is not the Church of Jesus Christ.

---

[789] Logos Hymnal (Oak Harbor, WA: Logos Research Systems, Inc., 1995).
[790] Philip Carrington, 352.

You shall not bring the hire of a harlot or the wages of a <u>dog</u> into the house of the Lord your God for any votive offering, for both of these are an abomination to the Lord your God. (Deuteronomy 23:18, NASB95)

22:16 I, Jesus, have sent My angel to testify to you these things for the churches. I am the root and the descendant of David, the bright morning star. Identifying Himself as **the root and the descendant of David (22:16)** clarifies His role and authority in passing these judgements on Israel. As the promised Son of David He has the authority to speak to the children of **David (22:16)** in the Role of King.

In addition, He is **the bright morning star (22:16)**. Peter speaks of Him this way,

So we have the prophetic word made more sure, to which you do well to pay attention as to a lamp shining in a dark place, until the day dawns and the morning star arises in your hearts. (2 Peter 1:19, NASB95)

In our death, it appears that the sun has set forever. But the night passes and the last star, the morning star, arises proclaiming the dawn of a new day. So, the eternal dawn has come and in the resurrection of our bodies the morning star has arisen in the hearts of His children. A new eternal dawn proclaims an eternal day of rest for the children of God.

22:17 The Spirit and the bride say, "Come." And let the one who hears say, "Come." And let the one who is thirsty come; let the one who wishes take the water of life without cost. Notice that it is the **Spirit (22:17)** working through His Church, the **bride (22:17)**, which calls sinners to the safety of salvation. This not the eternal state. This is a time in which sinners can hear the gospel message, repent and **come (22:17)** to Jesus.

Then He said to me, "It is done. I am the Alpha and the Omega, the beginning and the end. I will give to the one who thirsts from the spring of the water of life without cost." (Revelation 21:6, NASB95)

"This gracious and wide invitation is cheering after the gloomy picture of the doomed and the damned."[791]

22:18 *I testify to everyone who hears the words of the prophecy of this book: if anyone adds to them, God will add to him the plagues which are written in this book....* Although many people believe that several books of the New Testament were written after A.D. 70, the fact is there is no mention or allusion to the fall of Jerusalem, which occurred at that time, in any of them. The absence of a comment concerning this indescribable event strongly suggests that most, if not all, of the books of the New Testament were written prior to this event. Now some books were possibly written after Revelation, II Timothy for instance, yet as Rushdoony says, "In a very real sense, Revelation concludes Scripture. It speaks deliberately as a final word."[792] And in the providence of God, it is placed last in our Bible.

> *You shall not add to the word which I am commanding you, nor take away from it, that you may keep the commandments of the Lord your God which I command you. (Deuteronomy 4:2, NASB95)*

22:19 *...and if anyone takes away from the words of the book of this prophecy, God will take away his part from the tree of life and from the holy city, which are written in this book.* The question is asked, does this mean a person can lose his or her salvation? Hard passages, as this one is, can best be understood in the light of those passages which are clear.

> *My sheep hear My voice, and I know them, and they follow Me; and I give eternal life to them, and they will never perish; and no one will snatch them out of My hand. My Father, who has given them to Me, is greater than all; and no one is able to snatch them out of the Father's hand. I and the Father are one. (John 10:27-30, NASB95)*

---

[791] Archibald Thomas Robertson, Vol. VI, 486.

[792] Rousas John Rushdoony, <u>Thy Kingdom Come</u>, 225.

All that the Father gives Me will come to Me, and the one who comes to Me I will certainly not cast out. For I have come down from heaven, not to do My own will, but the will of Him who sent Me. This is the will of Him who sent Me, that of all that He has given Me I lose nothing, but raise it up on the last day. For this is the will of My Father, that everyone who beholds the Son and believes in Him will have eternal life, and I Myself will raise him up on the last day. (John 6:37-40, NASB95)

In the light of these and other clear passages, we must understand that this verse is making a hypothetical statement, which can never happen. No true believer would ever do damage to the Word of God. Those that do attack this book are not true believers, not really regenerate, and their *part from the tree of life (22:19)*, which is only apparent but not real, is taken away.

This topic opens the door to the issue of textual critics that remove and change much of the text found in the majority of the existing manuscripts of the Bible.[793] Such work must be handled with great care.

For we are not like many, peddling the word of God, but as from sincerity, but as from God, we speak in Christ in the sight of God. (2 Corinthians 2:17, NASB95)

...but we have renounced the things hidden because of shame, not walking in craftiness or adulterating the word of God, but by the manifestation of truth commending ourselves to every man's conscience in the sight of God. (2 Corinthians 4:2, NASB95)

22:20 He who testifies to these things says, "Yes, I am coming quickly." Amen. Come, Lord Jesus. This is a last reminder that thousands of years will not pass before the prophecies of this book are substantially fulfilled.

---

[793] Wilbur N. Pickering, The Identity of the New Testament Text (Nashville, TN: Thomas Nelson, 1977). John William Burgon, The Revision Revised (Paradise, PA; Conservative Classics, 1883).

22:21 *The grace of the Lord Jesus be with all. Amen.*

The God of peace will soon crush Satan under your feet. The grace of our Lord Jesus be with you. (Romans 16:20, NASB95)

Conclusion

We have presented to the reader an interpretation of the Book of Revelation that is based on the presupposition that we, as readers of the book two thousand years after it was written, can only hope to understand it if we first ask the question, "How did its original readers interpret the message?" One thing is certain, the original readers of this book did not say to themselves, "This book is not for us, it contains a prophecy of what the church will someday experience hundreds, even thousands of years in the future." No, they immediately sought to interpret the symbols found in this book in terms of their environment and discovered applications to their age substantially as we unfolded it in this commentary.

As David Clark said, "Any interpretation therefore that makes the body of a book unintelligible to those addressed is to be rejected."[794] And perhaps it can be said, any interpretation that outright rejects Biblical Preterism is not able to instruct the reader in the message of the Book of Revelation as understood by its original audience.

> If the seven churches of Asia to whom John wrote this entire book (1:4) could not understand the main and vital things it contains, then it was to them in just so far a dead letter—a book written in vain as to any effect upon them—a 'revelation' that *revealed* nothing. The notion that the great body of this prophetic book was unintelligible to its first readers and therefore may be interpreted today to mean things which they could never have imagined, must be for every reason rejected.[795]

So, in conclusion, let us remind ourselves again of the message, purpose or theme of this book. Fortunately for us, the Book of Revelation tells us up front just what its theme is:

---

[794] David S. Clark, 14.

[795] Henry Cowles, The Revelation of John (New York: Appleton, 1871. (Republished by Alethea In Heart, Fenwick, MI, 2002), 51.

Behold, <u>He is coming with the clouds</u>, and every eye will see Him, even those who pierced Him; and all the tribes of the earth [land] will mourn over Him. So it is to be. Amen. (Revelation 1:7, NASB95)

The theme of the Book of Revelation is the judgement coming of Jesus Christ.

A Coming Judgement Against Israel

Jesus Himself made this very point that He was coming in judgement against Israel in His earthly ministry.

Therefore when the owner of the vineyard <u>comes</u>, what will he do to those vine-growers? They said to Him, "He will bring those wretches to a wretched end, and will rent out the vineyard to other vine-growers who will pay him the proceeds at the proper seasons." .... Therefore I say to you, the kingdom of God will be <u>taken away from you</u> and <u>given to a people, producing the fruit of it</u>. And he who falls on this stone will be broken to pieces; but on whomever it falls, it will scatter him like dust. When the chief priests and the Pharisees heard His parables, <u>they understood that He was speaking about them</u>. (Matthew 21:40-41; 43-45, NASB95)

"Our Lord here causes them to pass that sentence of destruction upon themselves which was literally executed about forty years afterwards by the Roman armies."[796] Consider also these passages.

...and the rest seized his slaves and mistreated them and killed them. But the king was enraged, and he sent his armies and destroyed those murderers and set their city on fire. (Matthew 22:6-7, NASB95)

---

[796] <u>The Treasury of Scripture Knowledge</u>, Mt 21:41.

Which is exactly what He did in A.D. 70 with the destruction of Jerusalem.

> *You serpents, you brood of vipers, how will you escape the*
> *sentence of hell? Therefore, behold, I am sending you prophets*
> *and wise men and scribes; some of them you will kill and crucify,*
> *and some of them you will scourge in your synagogues, and*
> *persecute from city to city, so that upon you may fall the guilt of*
> *all the righteous blood shed on earth [land], from the blood of*
> *righteous Abel to the blood of Zechariah, the son of Berechiah,*
> *whom you murdered between the temple and the altar. Truly I*
> *say to you, <u>all these things will come upon this generation</u>.*
> *Jerusalem, Jerusalem, who kills the prophets and stones those*
> *who are sent to her! How often I wanted to gather your children*
> *together, the way a hen gathers her chicks under her wings, and*
> *you were unwilling. <u>Behold, your house is being left to you</u>*
> *<u>desolate!</u> For I say to you, from now on you will not see Me until*
> *you say, 'Blessed is He who comes in the name of the Lord!'*
> *(Matthew 23:33-39, NASB95)*

In summary, Revelation is about the coming of Jesus Christ in judgement against Israel. The reader should study the commentary section at Revelation 1:7 for greater detail on this point.

The Purposes of this Judgement Coming

IT CLOSES THE OLD COVENANT AND IMPLEMENTS THE NEW COVENANT

First, the Book of Revelation is about the close of the old covenant and the full implementation of the new. Christ alluded to this in His conversation to the woman at the well.

> *Our fathers worshiped in this mountain, and you people say that*
> *in Jerusalem is the place where men ought to worship. Jesus said*
> *to her, "Woman, believe Me, an hour is coming when neither in*
> *this mountain nor in Jerusalem will you worship the Father. You*
> *worship what you do not know; we worship what we know, for*
> *salvation is from the Jews. But an hour is coming, and now is,*
> *when the true worshipers will worship the Father in spirit and*

truth; for such people the Father seeks to be His worshipers."
(John 4:20-23, NASB95)

The writer of Hebrews speaks of *"removing of those things which can be shaken"* *"so that those things which cannot be shaken may remain."* That which can be shaken is old Israel. That which cannot be shaken is the true worship of Christ in the New Covenant.

> *See to it that you do not refuse Him who is speaking. For if those did not escape when they refused him who warned them on earth [land], much less will we escape who turn away from Him who warns from heaven. And His voice shook the earth [land] then, but now He has promised, saying, "Yet once more I will shake not only the earth [land], but also the heaven." This expression, "Yet once more," denotes the removing of those things which can be shaken, as of created things, so that those things which cannot be shaken may remain. Therefore, since we receive a kingdom which cannot be shaken, let us show gratitude, by which we may offer to God an acceptable service with reverence and awe; for our God is a consuming fire. (Hebrews 12:25-29, NASB95)*

Notice that the writer of Hebrews expressly states that believers *receive a kingdom.* The New Testament authors were not looking for a kingdom some day in the distant future by means of an earthly mellinium; they were already in the kingdom by their own testimony.

> *When He said, "A new covenant," He has made the first obsolete. But whatever is becoming obsolete and growing old is <u>ready to disappear</u>. (Hebrews 8:13, NASB95)*

This passage in Hebrews 8 is critical to understanding New Testament theology. Although the new covenant had come with its institution by Christ at the Lord's Supper, yet the old covenant was also in force in this age of transition. But this age would only last one generation, for Christ had *made the first obsolete* and it was therefore *ready to disappear.* Revelation is the story of how God made it disappear.

IT REVEALS THE LORD'S DIVORCE OF ISRAEL AND THE TAKING OF A NEW BRIDE – THE CHURCH

Second, Revelation is about Christ' judgement coming to punish of Israel, His former wife, for her harlotry, and the establishment of the new covenant in His marriage to a new bride, the Church. God's relationship to Israel is the same as God's relationship to the Church. In both He is the husband of his bride or wife. In the Old Testament we read these passages that make that point with clarity:[797]

> *"Then I passed by you and saw you, and behold, you were at the time for love; so I spread My skirt over you and covered your nakedness. I also swore to you and entered into a [marriage] covenant with you so that you became Mine," declares the Lord God. (Ezekiel 16:8, NASB95)*

> *"How languishing is your heart," declares the Lord God, "while you do all these things, the actions of a bold-faced harlot. When you built your shrine at the beginning of every street and made your high place in every square, in disdaining money, you were not like a harlot. You adulteress wife, who takes strangers instead of her husband!" (Ezekiel 16:30-32, NASB95)*

Isaiah, speaking at a time before God divorced Israel says,

> *Thus says the Lord, "Where is the certificate of divorce by which I have sent your mother away? Or to whom of My creditors did I sell you? Behold, you were sold for your iniquities, and for your transgressions your mother was sent away." (Isaiah 50:1, NASB95)*

> *For your husband is your Maker, whose name is the Lord of hosts; and your Redeemer is the Holy One of Israel, who is called the God of all the earth [land]. (Isaiah 54:5, NASB95)*

> *"...not like the covenant which I made with their fathers in the day I took them by the hand to bring them out of the land of Egypt,*

---

[797] See also Isaiah 62:4; Jeremiah 3:14, 20; Hosea 1:2; 2:2, 7, 16; 5:4, 9:1.

My covenant which they broke, although I was a husband to them," declares the Lord. (Jeremiah 31:32, NASB95)

In time, God divorced the ten northern tribes called Israel. God brought a covenant lawsuit against the ten tribes, found her guilty, divorced her, and put her to death for breaking the covenant through her spiritual adulteries. He did so by destroying her as a nation, and sending her survivors into captivity and exile.

And I saw that for all the adulteries of faithless Israel, I had sent her away and given her a writ of divorce, yet her treacherous sister Judah did not fear; but she went and was a harlot also. (Jeremiah 3:8, NASB95)

Therefore, I gave her into the hand of her lovers, into the hand of the Assyrians, after whom she lusted. They uncovered her nakedness; they took her sons and her daughters, but they slew her with the sword. Thus she became a byword among women, and they executed judgements on her. (Ezekiel 23:9-10, NASB95)

The penalty for harlotry in Scripture is death. In the Book of Revelation, that sentence is now carried out on Judah as it was earlier on the ten northern tribes. The nation, city, and the temple are being destroyed. Old Testament Israel no longer exists; the old covenant is abolished. God is now married to another, the Church; the new covenant is fully instituted. The Book of Revelation "...predicts the curses which are about to be brought upon the Judaistic system and its people because of their violations of the covenant."[798] "Thus, the theme of Revelation is the execution of God's divorce decree against Israel, her subsequent capital punishment and cremation, followed by his turning to take a new bride, the Church."[799]

But if you or your sons indeed turn away from following Me, and do not keep My commandments and My statutes which I have set before you, and go and serve other gods and worship them, then I will cut off Israel from the land which I have given them, and the house which I have consecrated for My name, I will cast out of My sight. So Israel will become a proverb and a byword among

---

[798] J. E. Leonard, I Will Be Their God, 152.

[799] Kenneth L. Gentry, Jr., The Revelation of Jesus Christ, 20.

all peoples. And this house will become a heap of ruins; everyone who passes by will be astonished and hiss and say, 'Why has the Lord done thus to this land and to this house?' And they will say, 'Because they forsook the Lord their God, who brought their fathers out of the land of Egypt, and adopted other gods and worshiped them and served them, therefore the Lord has brought all this adversity on them.' (1 Kings 9:6-9, NASB95)

IT COMMUNICATES HOPE TO THE CHURCH ON THE VERGE OF PERSECUTION

Third, it is a message of hope to the church. "At bottom the book of Revelation is a message of encouragement and exhortation to the churches of Asia Minor in view of portending persecutions of great magnitude."[800] On the verge of persecutions that will prove to be vicious beyond comprehension, the church is forewarned and assured that God is in charge and will from the misery and chaos bring victory to His church. "By predicting events shortly to come in great detail—events they will see transpire before their very eyes exactly as predicted—thy will recognize that God is in control of history."[801]

Adams points out an important verse in Daniel that focuses on what God is doing in the period of Revelation.

I kept looking, and that horn was waging war with the saints and overpowering them until the Ancient of Days came and judgement was passed in favor of the saints of the Highest One, and the time arrived when the saints took possession of the kingdom. (Daniel 7:21-22, NASB95)

"The three things mentioned in that passage are primary in Revelation. The brief successful persecution of the church; God's vindication of his suffering people by the judgement of the persecutor, and the establishment of the new kingdom of God."[802] Revelation is Daniel 7 come to fulfillment.

---

[800] Jay E. Adams, <u>The Time is at Hand</u>, 46.

[801] Jay E. Adams, and Michael W. Carroll, <u>Visions of the Revelation</u>, 22.

[802] Jay E. Adams, <u>The Time is at Hand</u>, 48.

IT PREDICTS THE POURING OUT OF GOD'S WRATH ON ISRAEL FOR MURDERING HIS SON

Fourth, Revelation is a pouring out of God's wrath on Israel for murdering His Son. The Jews demanded Christ's crucifixion and are directly responsible for his murder. That act will not go without consequence.[803] The Book of Revelation is that consequence.

> *...let it be known to all of you and to all the people of Israel, that by the name of Jesus Christ the Nazarene, whom you crucified, whom God raised from the dead—by this name this man stands here before you in good health. (Acts 4:10, NASB95)*

> *So when the chief priests and the officers saw Him, they cried out saying, "Crucify, crucify!" Pilate said to them, "Take Him yourselves and crucify Him, for I find no guilt in Him." (John 19:6, NASB95)*

> *As a result of this Pilate made efforts to release Him, but the Jews cried out saying, "If you release this Man, you are no friend of Caesar; everyone who makes himself out to be a king opposes Caesar." (John 19:12, NASB95)*

> *And he said to the Jews, "Behold, your King!" So they cried out, "Away with Him, away with Him, crucify Him!" Pilate said to them, "Shall I crucify your King?" The chief priests answered, "We have no king but Caesar." (John 19:14-15, NASB95)*

IT PICTURES THE CONSUMMATION OF THE AGES – THE ENDING OF THE JEWISH ERA

Fifth, the destruction of Jerusalem, the theme of the Book of Revelation is a sovereign act by God closing down the Old Testament sacrificial system. See Hebrews 8-10.

> *... but now once at the consummation of the ages He has been manifested to put away sin by the sacrifice of Himself. (Hebrews 9:26, NASB95)*

---

[803] Acts 2:22, 23, 36; 3:14, 15; 4:8-10; 5:30; 10:39; I Thessalonians 2:14-16.

508

The Jewish age is about to end. The writer of the book of Hebrews describes his time as *the consummation of the ages*. This is not the end of the world. That is not what he was talking about, but the end of the Jewish era. The sacrificial system is not longer required or even appropriate with the finished work of Christ.

IT PROMOTES THE WORLDWIDE FOCUS OF THE GREAT COMMISSION

Sixth, the destruction of Jerusalem frees Christianity from Judaism, allowing it to turn its focus worldwide in fulfilling its great commission.

> *And Jesus came up and spoke to them, saying, "All authority has been given to Me in heaven and on earth. Go therefore and make disciples of all the nations, baptizing them in the name of the Father and the Son and the Holy Spirit, teaching them to observe all that I commanded you; and lo, I am with you always, even to the end of the age." (Matthew 28:18-20, NASB95)*

> *For He Himself is our peace, who made both groups into one and broke down the barrier of the dividing wall, by abolishing in His flesh the enmity, which is the Law of commandments contained in ordinances, so that in Himself He might make the two into one new man, thus establishing peace, and might reconcile them both in one body to God through the cross, by it having put to death the enmity. (Ephesians 2:14-16, NASB95)*

In conclusion, although the purposes of Revelation are multifaceted, they are summed up with admirable simplicity in Revelation 1:7.

> *Behold, <u>He is coming with the clouds</u>, and every eye will see Him, even those who pierced Him; and all the tribes of the earth [land] will mourn over Him. So it is to be. Amen. (Revelation 1:7, NASB95)*

But Preterism Robs the Church of its Eschatology

This is a criticism of Preterism by many. If Revelation is substantially fulfilled in the first century, then it is for us no longer prophecy. Therefore the Church is robbed of its doctrine of end times. Dr. Merrill Tenney puts it this way, "The preterist viewpoint does not do justice to the predictive element in Revelation. If its premises are accepted, the book is directed only to the day in which it was written, and has no real significance for the succeeding centuries...."[804]

There are several things that need to be said in reference to this objection.

MOST OF THE PROPHECY IN THE BIBLE IS NOT ABOUT THE END-OF-THE-WORLD.

Most prophecy in the Bible is about either, Christ and Calvary, or about the founding and growth of the Church or about Israel and the various judgements facing it from Assyria, Babylon or other enemies. The book of Revelation is no different than many of the other books of the Bible. It too is primarily about Christ, the Church, and God's judgement on Israel. Although there is some material on end-of-the-world issues in Revelation, like the other books of the Bible, this is not its primary theme.

MOST PROPHECY IN THE BOOKS OF THE BIBLE IS NOW FULFILLED PROPHECY, NOT JUST THE PROPHECY OF REVELATION.

Because most prophecy is about Christ, the Church and Israel's temporal judgements, it is now fulfilled prophecy because these events are now behind us. The norm for most of the prophetic material of the Bible is that it would soon come to pass, and it did. The great majority of prophecy in the Bible was fulfilled in the following generations after it was given. The same is true of the Book of Revelation. Therefore these Old Testament prophetic themes and the book of Revelation itself are no longer unfulfilled prophecy.

THE CHURCH HAS AS MUCH OR MORE END-OF-THE-WORLD PROPHECY NOW AS IT HAS EVER HAD.

What are the major end times themes that have been covered in Scripture? They include the Second Coming at the end-of-the-world, the rapture of the Church, the resurrection of the dead, the Great White Throne Judgement,

---

[804] Merrill C. Tenney, 145-146.

the damnation of the lost and the eternal bliss of the saved. Biblical Preterism in no way denies these teaching, indeed, it insists on them.

Therefore, the Church has as much end-of-the-world prophecy as it ever has. And with the material found in chapter 20, it has that material in greater clarity. The fact that it has no more end-of-the-world prophecy in Revelation is simply because that was not the purpose for which it was written.

Eschatology Affects your Worldview

If you believe the world is "going to hell in a handbasket" and that Christians should not be "polishing brass on a sinking ship" then you will withdraw yourself from society and culture in some kind of holy huddle and wait for Jesus to bail you out of this mess. Your great hope will be the late great coming escape of the rapture. However, you will begin the process by bailing out of culture long before the glorious escapism of the rapture. You will marginalize yourself, seeing no sense in fighting a battle you cannot win. As such, society will go unchallenged by your faith and unbenefited by Christianity. "Thus, premillennialism is more than just 'pessi'-millennialism. Because it leads many Christians to have a short-termed, pessimistic predestined, mentally confused view of the future; it leads to absolute paralysis in the Christianity community with regard to how we should relate to the society around us. Beyond pessimillennialism it is, in fact, 'paralysimillennialism."[805]

If, on the other hand, you believe that God's intention is to redeem his creation in time as well as eternity, then you will evidence a sense of obligation to impact the world and its culture for God. As such, you will not marginalize yourself from society but seek to involve yourself and your message in society. You will challenge its behavior, faith, and laws, seeking the Lordship of Christ over all these things.

Your eschatology does make a difference. You will either be useful or useless in time, based on your view of the end-of-the-world. Although in and by itself, Preterism does not require either an optimistic or pessimistic view of the mission of the Church, still it does deny that the rapture is in

---

[805] Joseph R. Balyeat, 22-23.

chapter 4 of Revelation and thereby denies that the Church can expect to be bailed out of the world. That being the case, Preterism lends itself to eschatologies of hope in the victory of the Church in time and eternity, instead of the defeat of the Church in this world.

Appendix A

A Study in Greek Vocabulary

We have in Revelation several words that appear to demand a quick coming of Christ. Let's summarize these words and see if they tell a common story. The Greek text divides the time-frame references of Revelation into three categories.

The first Greek word is τάχος (*táchos*) and means "shortly" or "quickly." "In classical Greek, from Homer on, this word means 'quickness' or 'speed.'[806] Some illustrations are:

> *The Revelation of Jesus Christ, which God gave Him to show to His bond-servants, the things which must soon take place; and He sent and communicated it by His angel to His bond-servant John.... (Revelation 1:1, NASB95)*

> *Repent therefore! Otherwise, I will soon come to you and will fight against them with the sword of my mouth. (Revelation 2:16, NASB95)*

> *I am coming soon. Hold on to what you have, so that no one will take your crown. (Revelation 3:11, NASB95)*

> *And he said to me, "These words are faithful and true"; and the Lord, the God of the spirits of the prophets, sent His angel to show to His bond-servants the things which must soon take place. (Revelation 22:6, NASB95)*

> *And behold, I am coming quickly. Blessed is he who heeds the words of the prophecy of this book. (Revelation 22:7, NASB95)*

> *Behold, I am coming quickly, and My reward is with Me, to render to every man according to what he has done. (Revelation 22:12, NASB95)*

---

[806] Thoralf Gilbrant, Vol. Sigma-Omega, 259.

> *He who testifies to these things says, "Yes, I am coming quickly."*
> *Amen. Come, Lord Jesus. (Revelation 22:20, NASB95)*

The second word is ἐγγύς (*eggús*) and is translated "near," "close to," or "at hand."

> *Blessed is he who reads and those who hear the words of the prophecy, and heed the things which are written in it; for the time is near. (Revelation 1:3, NASB95)*

> *And he said to me, "Do not seal up the words of the prophecy of this book, for the time is near."(Revelation 22:10, NASB95)*

The third word is μελλώ (*mellō*) and is translated "be about to," "be on the point of."

> *Therefore write the things which you have seen, and the things which are, and the things which will [is about to] take place after these things. (Revelation 1:19, NASB95)*

> *Because you have kept the word of My perseverance, I also will keep you from the hour of testing, that hour which is about to come upon the whole world, to test those who dwell on the earth. (Revelation 3:10, NASB95)*

So we can see that these several Greek words tell a common story; the Lord is coming soon. "In harmony with the utterances of our Lord and his apostles, we are told that the content of the *Revelation* is *bound to happen shortly*. This statement, so frequently repeated, cuts out altogether the idea of an outline or survey of many centuries of future history. What is revealed is shortly to come to pass."[807]

---

[807] Philip Carrington, 72.

Appendix B

The Mark of the Beast
and the Number of the Name?
by
Dr. Stephen P. Westcott
Bristol, England.

As we stand at the opening of the 21st Century, we have twenty centuries of professing Christianity stretching behind us, with all the apostasies and reformations, the declensions and revivals, the errors, heresies, and doctrinal clarifications of our long ecclesiastical history. We must be constantly alert to the culture gulf between ourselves and the Apostles, and be willing to make the necessary effort to place ourselves, so far as we can, in the mindset of the 1st Century Jewish world within which our faith was born and nurtured. This-more easily said than done-is sometimes called the 'Timothy factor.' This 'Timothy factor' indicates that Paul's young companion Timothy was an inhabitant of the Mediterranean world in the 1st Century Roman Empire, was a Koiné Greek speaker, and had been brought up from a child in knowledge of the Hebrew Bible and the customs of the Jewish dispersion among the gentiles. No one has this background or these advantages today! That is why pastors must attend Seminary, work hard at their Hebrew and Greek, and study ecclesiastical history and archaeology. All to get somewhere near what Timothy took for granted. Fail to appreciate this and do the necessary work, and the Bible-the *whole* Bible-becomes a modern Western oriented book, recast in our own image, and the faith undergoes evolution along with it, and at the same time fragments. History is thus *vital* to interpretation, archaeology to exegesis. We must see first of all what a text meant to its original recipients, in their real 'flesh-and-blood' 'world-and-life' reality, and then, secondly, extract the lasting messages for all time thereafter.

These factors must also apply to the vexed questions of the 'Mark of the Beast' and 'the number of his name', if we make the effort to dissociate ourselves from our own world, and try to see and think and feel as the 1st Century Jews did. Here is at least an intriguing *possible* alternative explanation to the number of his name.

Judaea was under Roman occupation and rule. The Herodian dynasties were client rulers and 'Hellenistic': collaborators with the Empire, and the land moved towards being a Roman Province. Worst of all for religious Jews the Romans were pagans and idolaters, and their abominations (statues, standards, uniforms, altars, milestones, and inscriptions) defiled the land at every turn. The Caesars were worshipped as Gods, and all good citizens must identify themselves with the cult of 'Rome & the Emperor'. Gaius Caligula was narrowly prevented from placing his statue within the Jerusalem Temple and sparking off a rebellion in A.D. 40. All throughout Palestine orthodox Jews fretted and chafed under the pagan rule, and one day soon would be goaded into that outright rebellion that saw the destruction of Jerusalem and the Temple, disasters unparalleled for the people-and the emergence of world-wide Christianity from its Jewish nurturing place. But what angered and frustrated the people most under Roman rule was the tribute, the *taxation* they had to pay to the occupying power. In all Provinces taxation was a grievance as syndicates of 'publicani' vied for contracts for the collection of taxes, and proceeded to fleece the provincials for their own profit as well as filling the Imperial treasury. The Roman Historian Tacitus records how the Frisii on the lower Rhine were driven into revolt by excessive taxation in A.D.28[1], whilst the newly organized province of Britannia flared into bloody revolt over the question of burdensome taxes and shady financial dealings (in which the Stoic philosopher Seneca was deeply involved), and the Romanized cities of Verulamium (St. Albans), Camulodunum (Colchester) and Londinium (London) were destroyed in flames and massacre by irate tribes under the leadership of Queen Boudicca in A.D. 61.

But for the Jews there was far more than mere resentment of being fleeced by unjustly high taxation. The levy, the tax, went to support that very *paganism*, the idolatry and blasphemy that Jews abominated. We should remember how all pervading this tax system was: even Christ's birth at Bethlehem came about because: *"It came to pass in those days that there went out a decree from Caesar Augustus that all the world (i.e. Roman Empire) should be taxed. (And this taxing was first made when Quirinius was governor of Syria.) And all went to be taxed, every one into his own city. And Joseph also went up from Galilee, out of the city of Nazareth in Judaea, unto the city of David, to be taxed with Mary his espoused wife, being great with child."* (Luke 19:2 KJV). The background to this is that the Emperor Augustus (A.D. 27-14) required a full census of the Empire for taxation purposes, at an indeterminate date in his reign. For Judaea this census was apparently carried out in 5-4 B.C., not long before the death of the client King Herod ('The Great') in March of 4. B.C., and the first taxes under it were collected in A.D. 6-9, when Copronius was Governor of

Judaea, but under the authority of the larger Province of Syria, and its Legate P. Sulpicius Quirinus. As the tax began to be applied there was immediate resistance: the historian Josephus records that "A Galilean named Judas tried to stir up the natives to revolt, saying that they were cowards to submit to paying taxes to the Romans."[2]. The New Testament confirms this: "*After this there rose up Judas of Galilee in the days of the taxing, and drew away much people after him: he also perished; and all, even as many as obeyed him, were dispersed*" (Acts 5:37). From then on the question of whether it was "*lawful to pay tribute unto Caesar*" (Luke 20:22) was an ever present one, and payment was only enforced against the consciences of the people. Apart from the capitation or poll tax many local taxes and dues on imports and exports, licenses and taxes on goods and manufacturers were progressively enforced. No one can read the Gospels without being struck with the contempt and hatred with which the tax-gatherers or 'Publicani' were regarded by the people. Here were the arch-traitors, the ultimate collaborators, Jews who for lucre's sake were helping the heathen trample on all that was holy. "Publicans and sinners," the vilest and lowest of sinners, are near synonymous terms, ("Publicans and harlots" Matthew 21:32, Luke 7:34). To eat with a Publican was to incur pollution, the Jews were forbade their daughters to marry them, and Christ, himself classed them with "heathen men" (Matthew 18:17.). Christ scandalized the Pharisees because he was willing to evangelize tax gatherers for "many publicans and sinners came and sat down with him and his disciples" (Matthew 9:10, Mark 2:15) and this became a leading accusation against him as being "a friend of publicans and sinners" (Matthew 11:19) and his gracious contacts were classed with his touching lepers. The conversions of Matthew 'The Publican', who gathered taxes at Caparnaum from traffic on the Sea of Galilee (Matthew 9:9, Mark 2:14), and Zachaeus "which was chief of the publicans and he was rich" (Luke 19:2) are recorded as outstanding monuments of grace abounding indeed! Imagine, then, the humiliation of the religious Jew as his tax was taken, and his goods or documents marked to show that he had paid his dues to Caesar. But if that mark, showing his acceptance of taxation, was in itself 'idolatrous' and the brand of submission to the pagan 'beast' of Rome, and yet nothing could be bought or sold, pass the borders or cross the sea of Galilee without toll and tribute, it would indeed seem to the religious Jew (and Jewish Christian) that no work by head or hand could be accomplished without this payment to the beast, and acceptance of his mark, the receipt for taxes paid to pagan Rome. Can this be the concept behind Revelation 13:16-17: "*And he causeth all, both small and great, rich and poor, free and bond, to receive a mark in their right hand, or in their foreheads: and that no man might buy or sell, save he that had the mark, or the name of the beast, or the number of his name"*? Note that no-one might trade, *buy or sell*, unless he had the mark (tax receipt?) with the name of the beast (Roman Emperor), and the number of his name (see below). Right hand (or rather forearm) and forehead were, and are, where orthodox Jews wear phylacteries, demonstrating their obedience to God and His laws. Here was a pagan power demanding tokens of submission over the fruits of all labor, mental or physical, over minds and bodies, and its pagan bureaucracy recording receipt of the tribute.

This double factor of a) crushingly high and unfair taxation, and b) its idolatrous import, were certainly a major factors in the outbreak of the great Jewish revolt of A.D. 66 to A.D. 70. Josephus records King Agrippa as protesting: "You have acted as if you are already at war with Rome: you have paid no tribute to Caesar. The magistrates and councilors went to the various villages and collected the tribute, quickly getting together the forty talents due. The king...sent magistrates and influential citizens to Florus at Caesarea, to collect tribute from the countryside."[3] A major factor in the Jews' case against Christ, in order to turn the Roman authorities against him, was the accusation that he incited the people to withhold their taxes; *"We found this fellow perverting the nation and forbidding to give tribute to Caesar, saying that he himself is Christ a king"* (Luke 5:46-7). If taxation to Rome and its servants was thus a major factor in Jewish unrest and underlay the great revolt, and if, as we have seen, the prime theme of the Book of Revelation is that revolt and the consequent destruction of the city and Temple and breakup of the Jewish polity (and breakout of worldwide Christianity from its Jewish cradle) then we should expect to see references to this very actor in the symbolism of the Apocalypse. Can we find it?

Nothing of course is so predictable, or comes around so regularly, as taxes. And, naturally, when you pay your dues this year, today's receipt will avail you nothing when next year comes around. Do we know, at this distance in time, the 'tax-paid' stamp of receipt that so defiled Jewish goods and paperwork? Well, yes, archaeology can help us here, and keep us in the real world of the gospels. Here is a copy of a limestone stamp dating from the reign of the Emperor Augustus, dating to A.D. 5-6.

The circular legend reads LE KAISAROS, that is, the 35th year of the Emperor, equating to taxes paid for the year A.D. 5-6. Naturally this receipt would be no longer valid in the following tax year, A.D. 6-7, 36th year of Augustus. We do not have a complete run of these artifacts, but the sequence is easily worked out, from examples such as that shown above. We must assume that as time went by and Emperors came and went in quicker succession, it would be found necessary to identify the Emperor by his initial.

For the sake of argument let us envisage a tax stamp in this archaeologically identified series from, let us say, the 14th year of the Emperor Nero. It would have read ID N KAISAROS. That is ID (14) N (Nero) KAISAROS (Caesar).

Now let us add up the 'number weighting' of these Greek letters:

I	10
D	4
N	50
K	20
A	1
I	10
S	200
A	1
R	100
O	70
S	200

666	

So anyone in that situation and era, looking at the 'mark of the beast' customs stamps on their goods or paperwork, would easily be able to determine when the 'number of the name' would reach the figure of 666. It would be the 14th year of Nero. And is there significance in that? Well we must look to see what year was the 14th of Nero's reign, and what happened in that very year.

Nero's 14th year equates to A.D. 68.

A.D. 68 is the very year in which Nero was finally overthrown and slain.

It is the very year in which the fatal siege of Jerusalem began. Half way exactly through the Jewish war of A.D. 66-A.D. 70 when the Christians fled the city to safety, 'divinely warned.'

Is this a coincidence, or a date marker revealing the *very year* in which these things were to come to pass? It certainly fits the historic reality of the situation, rather than modern speculation and guesswork. Things that were central to the thinking and concerns of first century Jews and Christians are by no means so obvious to us today, and need some archaeological and historical research (the 'Timothy factor' again!) to see things with their eyes. We cannot be absolutely certain. The reader must make up his or her own mind.

* An alternative reading of Revelation 13:18 reads 616 rather than 666. A limestone stamp as above but omitting the initial 'N' for Nero would lack the numeral for the figure 50. 50 less than 666 is, of course, 616.

1 Tacitus 'Annals of Imperial Rome' iv. 72.
2 Josephus, Jewish War, Book II, Cap.7
3 Jewish War, Book II, Cap.8.

Bibliography

Abanes, Richard, End Time Visions: The Doomsday Obsession (Nashville, TN: Broadman & Holman Publishers, 1998).

Adams, Jay E., Preterism: Orthodox or Unorthodox? (Stanley, NC: Timeless Texts, 2003).

Adams, Jay E., Signs & Wonders In the Last Days (Woodruff, SC: Timeless Texts, 1977)

Adams, Jay E., The Time is at Hand (Greenville, SC: A Press, 1987).

Adams, Jay E. and Milton C. Fisher, The Time of the End (Woodruff, SC: Timeless Texts, 2000).

Adams, Jay E. and Carroll, Michael W., Visions of the Revelation (Virginia Beach, VA: The Donning Company Publishers, 1991).

Alexander, J. A., Acts of the Apostles (London: Banner of Truth Trust, 1857, 1963).

Alford, Henry, The Greek New Testament, 4 vols. (Chicago, IL: Moody Press, 1958 [1849-1861]).

Allis, Oswald T., Prophecy and the Church (Nutley, NJ: The Presbyterian and Reformed Publishing Co., 1974).

Arndt, William; Bauer, Walter; Gingrich, F. Wilbur; and Danker, Frederick W., A Greek-English Lexicon of the New Testament and Other Early Christian Literature (Chicago, IL: University of Chicago Press, 1979, 2000).

Ashcraft, Morris, Hebrews - Revelation in The Broadman Bible Commentary; Clifton J. Allen, Gen. ed., vol. 12 (Nashville: Broadman Press, 1972).

Auberlen, Karl August, Daniel and Revelation in Their Mutual Relation (Andover: 1857).

Aune, David, Word Biblical Commentary (Dallas, Texas: Word Books Publisher, 1998).

Bahnsen, Greg L., The Book of Revelation: Its Setting (unpublished paper, 1984).

Balyeat, Joseph R., Babylon, The Great City of God (Sevierville, TN: Covenant House Books, 1991, 1995).

Barclay, William, <u>Daily Study Bible Series: The Revelation of John</u>, Revised Edition (Louisville, KY: Westminster John Knox Press, 2000, c1976).

Barnes, Albert, <u>Notes on the New Testament, Revelation</u> (Grand Rapid, MI: Baker Book House, 1951).

Barnes, Arthur Stapylton, <u>Christianity at Rome in the Apostolic Age</u> (Westport, CT: Greenwood, [1938] 1971).

Bartlet, James Vernon, <u>The Apostolic Age: Its Life, Doctrine, Worship, and Polity</u>, Book 2 (Edinburgh: T. & T. Clark, [1899] 1963).

Bass, Clarence B., <u>Backgrounds to Dispensationalism</u> (Grand Rapids, MI: Baker Book House, 1960).

Bass, Ralph E. Jr., <u>Hope For Today's Problems</u>, (Greenville, SC: Living Hope Press, 2002).

Bass, Ralph E, Jr., <u>What About Baptism? A Discussion on the Mode, Candidate, and Purpose of Christian Baptism</u>, (Naples, FL: Nicene Press, Inc., 1999)

Baur, Ferdinand Christian, <u>Church History of the First Three Centuries</u>, 3rd ed. (Tubingen: 1863).

Beale, G. K., <u>The Book of Revelation: A Commentary on the Greek Text</u>, *New International Greek Testament Commentary*, ed. I. Howard Marshall and Donald A. Hagner (Grand Rapids: Eerdmans, 1999).

Beasley-Murray, G.R., <u>Jesus and the Kingdom of God</u> (Grand Rapids: Eerdmans, 1986).

Beasley-Murray, G.R., "The Kingdom Of God In The Teaching Of Jesus," *Journal of the Evangelical Theological Society*, 35.1 (1992).

Beasley-Murray, G.R., "Jesus and the Kingdom of God," *Baptist Quarterly* 32 (1987).

Bell, Jr., Albert A., <u>The Date of John's Apocalypse. The Evidence of Some Roman Historians Reconsidered</u> (New Testament Studies 25, 1978).

Benware, Paul N., <u>Understanding an End Times Comprehensive Prophecy Approach</u> (Chicago: Moody Press, 1995).

Beyschlag, Willibald, <u>New Testament Theology</u>, trans. Neil Buchanan, 2nd Eng. ed. (Edinburgh: T. &T. Clark, 1896).

Bigg, Charles, The Origins of Christianity, ed. by T. B. Strong (Oxford: Clarendon, 1909).

Boring, M. Eugene, Revelation. Interpretation, A Bible Commentary for Teaching and Preaching (Louisville, KY: John Knox Press, 1989).

Boyer, Paul., When Time Shall Be No More: Prophecy Belief in Modern American Culture (Cambridge, Massachusetts and London: Harvard University Press, 1992).

Bratcher, Robert G., and Hatton, Howard, A Handbook on the Revelation to John. UBS handbook series (New York, NY: United Bible Societies, 1993).

Bromiley, Geoffrey W., ed, International Standard Bible Encyclopedia (Grand Rapids, MI: William B. Eerdmans Publishing Company, 2001, c1988).

Brown, John, Discourses and Sayings of Our Lord, 3 vols. (Edinburgh: The Banner of Truth Trust, [1852] 1990).

Boatman, Russell, What the Bible Says About the End Time (Joplin, MO: College Press, 1980).

Boettner, Loraine, The Millennium (Phillipsburg, NJ: Presbyterian and Reformed Publishing, 1957).

Bruce, F.F., Israel & the Nation, (Downers Grove, IL: Intervarsity Press, 1997).

Bruce, F.F., New Testament History (Garden City, NY: Anchor Books, 1969).

Burgon, John William, The Revision Revised (Paradise, PA: Conservative Classics, 1883).

Caird, G.B., The Revelation of St. John the Divine (New York, NY: Harper and Row Publishers, 1966).

Carey, John, Eyewitness to History, Remarkable First-Hand Accounts of the Events that Shaped Civilization: From the Siege of Jerusalem (N.Y.: Avon Pub., 1990).

Carpenter, W. Boyd, The Revelation of St. John, in vol. 8 of Charles Ellicott, cd., *Ellicott's Commentary on the Whole Bible* (Grand Rapids: Zondervan, rep. n.d.).

Carrington, Philip, The Meaning of the Revelation (London, England: SPCK, 1931).

Chafer, Lewis Sperry, Major Bible Themes, (Chicago, Il; Moody Press, 1944).

Charles, R. H., A Critical and Exegetical Commentary on the Revelation of St. John (Edinburgh, Scotland: T. & T. Clark, 1920).

Cheetham, S., A History of the Christian Church (London: Macmillan, 1894).

Chilton, David, The Days of Vengeance (Tyler, TX: Dominion Press, 1987).

Chilton, David, Paradise Restored (Tyler, TX: Dominion Press, 1985).

Chilton, David, The Great Tribulation (Tyler, TX: Institute for Christian Economics, 1997).

Clark, David S., The Message from Patmos: A Postmillennial Commentary on the Book of Revelation (Grand Rapids: Baker Book House, 1989).

Clarke, Adam, Commentary on the Whole Bible, vol. 6 (Nashville: Abingdon, rep. n.d.).

Clarke, William Newton, An Outline of Christian Theology (New York: Scribners, 1903).

Clouse, Robert G., Editior, The Meaning of the Millennium (Downers Grove, IL: InterVarsity Press, 1977).

Cowles, Henry, The Revelation of St. John (New York: Appleton, 1871. Republished by *Alethea In Heart*, Fenwick, MI, 2002).

Crampton, W. Gary, Biblical Hermeneutics (n. p.: by the author, 1986).

Crebs, Berry Stewart, The Seventh Angel (Grand Rapids: Eerdmans, 1938).

Crowne, John, The Destruction of Jerusalem by Titus Vespasian (London, 1677).

DeMar, Gary, Is Jesus Coming Soon? (Powder Springs, GA: American Vision, 1990).

DeMar, Gary, Last Days Madness: Obsession of the Modern Church (Atlanta: American Vision, 1994).

DeMar, Gary, End Times Fiction: A Biblical Consideration of the Left Behind Theology (Nashville, TN: Thomas Nelson Publishers, 2001).

Desprez, Phillip S., The Apocalypse Fulfilled (London, England: Longman, Brown, Green and Longmans, 1854).

De Pressense, Edmund, The Early Years of Christianity, trans. Annie Harwood (New York: Philips and Hunt, 1879).

Donahue, John, http://www.roman-emperors.org/domitian.htm

Douglas, J. D., Editor, The New Bible Dictionary, Third Edition, Logos electronic edition (Wheaton, Illinois: Tyndale House Publishers, Inc. 1962).

Dusterdieck, Friedrich, Critical and Exegetical Handbook to the Revelation of John, 3rd ed., trans. Henry E. Jacobs (New York: Funk and Wagnalls, 1886).

Early Church Fathers - Nicene/Post Nicene Part 2, Volume One (Garland, TX: Galaxie Software, 1999).

Edersheim, Alfred, The Temple Its Ministry and Services (Garland, Texas: Electronic edition by Galaxie Software, 2000).

Edersheim, Alfred, The Temple, (Grand Rapids, MI: Kregel Publications, 1874, 1997).

Edmundson, George, The Church in Rome in the First Century (London: Longman's and Green, 1913).

Enhanced Strong's Lexicon (Oak Harbor, WA: Logos Research Systems, Inc., 1995).

Ephesians Four Group, Greek Dictionary, electronic ed., (Oak Harbor, WA: Logos Research Systems, Inc., 1997).

Erickson, Millard J., Contemporary Options in Eschatology (Grand Rapids, MI: Baker Book House, 1977).

Ewing, D. Ragan, The Identification of Babylon the Harlot in the Book of Revelation, www.christonomy.com

Fadeley, Gene, Revelation: Kingdoms in Conflict (Waxhaw, NC: Anchor Publishing, 1995).

Fairbairn, Patrick, The Interpretation of Prophecy (London: The Banner of Truth, 1856).

Farrar, Frederic W., The Early Days of Christianity (New York: E.P. Dutton & Co, 1882).

Fenley, Ward, The Second Coming of Christ Already Happened! (1998).

Fisher, George P., The Beginnings of Christianity, with a View to the State of the Roman World at the Birth of Christ (New York: Scribners, 1916).

Fitzmeyer, J. A., "Review of John A. T. Robinson's Redating the New Testament" (1977-78).

Ford, J. Massyngberde, Revelation (New York, NY: The Anchor Bible, Doubleday, 1975).

Frost, Samuel M., Misplaced Hope (Bimillennial Press, CO Springs, 2002).

Fuller, Robert, Naming the Antichrist: The History of an American Obsession (New York and Oxford: Oxford University Press, 1995).

Furneaux, Rupert, The Roman Siege of Jerusalem (N.Y., David McKay, 1972).

Gaebelein, Arno C., The Prophet Ezekiel (New York, NY: Our Hope Publishers, 1911).

Gebhardt, Hermann, The Doctrine of the Apocalypse, trans. John Jefferson (Edinburgh: T. & T. Clark, 1878).

Geisler, Norman L., and Ron Rhodes, When Cultists Ask: A Popular Handbook on Cultic Misinterpretations (Grand Rapids, Mich.: Baker Books, 1997).

Gentry, Kenneth L., Jr., Before Jerusalem Fell (Atlanta, GA: American Visions Publishers, 1998).

Gentry, Kenneth L., Jr., Lord of the Saved (Phillipsburg, NJ: P&R Publishing, 1992).

Gentry, Kenneth L., Jr., Perilous Times: A Study in Eschatological Evil (Texarkana, AR: Covenant Media Press, 1973).

Gentry, Kenneth L, Jr., The Beast of Revelation (Tyler, TX: Institute for Christian Economics, 1989).

Gentry, Kenneth L., Jr., The Revelation of Jesus Christ, *Biblical Issues Series* (NP, 2001).

Giblin, C.H., The Destruction of Jerusalem according to Luke's Gospel Analecta Biblica - AB 107 (Biblical Institute Press / Editrice Pontificio Istituto Biblico, 1985).

Gibbs, Jeffrey, Jerusalem and Parousia (Concordia Publishing House, 2001).

Gilbrant, Thoralf, International Editor, The New Testament Greek-English Dictionary (Springfield, MO: The Complete Biblical Library, 1991).

Gill, John, Expositions of the New Testament, 3 vols. (Paris, AR: The Baptist Standard Bearer, [1809] 1989).

Glasgow, James, The Apocalypse Translated and Expounded (Edinburgh: 1872).

Grant, Robert McQueen, <u>A Historical Introduction to the New Testament</u> (New York: Harper & Row, 1963).

Gray, James Comper, <u>Adams' Bible Commentary</u>, vol. V (Grand Rapids: Zondervan, [1903] rep. n.d.).

Green, Samuel G., <u>A Handbook of Church History from the Apostolic Era to the Dawn of the Reformation</u> (London: Religious Tract Society, 1904).

Gregg, Steve, <u>Revelation – Four Views</u> (Nashville, TN: Thomas Nelson Publishers, 1997).

Guenke, Heinrich Ernst Ferdinand, <u>Introduction to the New Testament</u> (Boston: Halliday, 1843).

Guenke, Heinrich Ernst Ferdinand, <u>Manual of Church History</u>, trans. W. G. T. Shedd (Boston: Halliday, 1874).

Gwatkin, Henry Melville, <u>Early Church History to A.D. 313</u>, vol. 1 (London: Macmillan).

Hase, Karl August von, <u>A History of the Christian Church</u>, 7th cd., trans. Charles E. Blumenthal and Conway P. Wing (New York: Appleston, 1878).

Hayhow, Stephen F., "Matthew 24, Luke 17 and the Destruction of Jerusalem," *Christianity and Society* 4:2 (April, 1994)

Hemer, C. J., *Seven Cities of Asia Minor*, in R. K. Harrison, ed., <u>Major Cities of the Biblical World</u> (Nashville, TN: Thomas Nelson Publishers, 1985).

Hendriksen, William, <u>More Than Conquerors</u> (Grand Rapids, MI: Baker Books, 1940, 1967).

Hill, David, <u>New Testament Prophecy</u> (Atlanta: John Knox, 1979).

Holford, George Peter, <u>The Destruction of Jerusalem</u> (NP: 1803)

Horsley, Richard A., <u>Bandits, Prophets & Messiahs</u> (Harrisburg, PA: Trinity Press International, PA,1999).

Hort, F. J. A., <u>The Apocalypse of St. John</u> (London: Macmillan, 1908).

Hort, F. J. A, <u>Judaistic Christianity</u> (London: Macmillan, 1894).

Hug, John Leonhard, <u>Introduction to the New Testament</u>, trans. David Fosdick, Jr. (Andover: Gould and Newman, 1836).

Hurte, William, A Catechetical Commentary on the New Testament (St. Louis: John Burns, 1889).

Ice, Thomas and Gentry, Kenneth, The Great Tribulation: Past or Future? Two Evangelicals Debate the Question (Grand Rapids, MI: Kregel Publications, 1999).

Immer, A., Hermeneutics of the New Testament, trans. A. H. Newman (Andover: Draper, 1890).

Israel, Gerard and Jacques Lebar, When Jerusalem Burned: The Catasrophic Day When the Romans Destroyed the Great Temple and Jerusalem Itself (N.Y.: William Morrow, 1973).

Jeremias, Joachim, Jerusalem in the Times of Jesus (Philadelphia, PA: Fortress Press, 1969).

Jones, R. Bradley, The Great Tribulation (Grand Rapids, MI: Baker Book House, 1980).

Jordan, James B., A Brief Reader's Guide to Revelation (Niceville, FL: Transfiguration Press, 1999).

Josephus, Flavius, The Works of Josephus (Oak Harbor, WA: Logos Research Systems, Inc., 1997).

Kaiser, W. C., Hard Sayings of the Bible (Downers Grove, IL: InterVarsity Press, 1997, c1996).

Keener, Graig S., The NIV Application Commentary (Grand Rapids, MI: Zondervan Publishing House, 2000).

Keener, G. S., The IVP Bible Background Commentary: New Testament (Downers Grove, Ill.: InterVarsity Press, 1993).

Kik, J. Marcellus, An Eschatology of Victory (Nutley, NJ: The Presbyterian and Reformed Publishing Co., 1971).

King, Max R., The Spirit of Prophecy (Warren, OH: by the author, 1971).

King, Max R., The Cross and the Parousia of Christ (Warren, OH.: Writing and Research Ministry sponsored by the Parkman Road Church of Christ, 1987).

King, Max R., Old Testament Israel and New Testament Salvation (Warren, OH: 1990).

Simon J. Kistemaker, and William Hendriksen, <u>New Testament Commentary: Exposition of the Book of Revelation</u>. (Grand Rapids: Baker Book House, 1953-2001).

Kittel, Gerhard; Friedrich, Gerhard, <u>The Theological Dictionary of the New Testament</u> (Grand Rapids, MI: Wm. B. Eerdmans Publishing Company, 2000, c1964).

Koppe, Theodor, <u>History of Jesus of Nazareth,</u> 2nd ed., trans. Arthur Ransom (London: William and Norgate, 1883).

Kurtz, Johann Heinrich, <u>Church History,</u> 9th ed., trans. John McPherson (New York: Funk and Wagnalls, 1888).

Kyle, Richard, <u>The Last Days Are Here Again: A History of the End Time</u> (Grand Rapids, MI: Wm. B. Erdmans Publishing Company, [1993] 1995).

Lagass, Paul and Columbia University, <u>The Columbia Encyclopedia</u>. 6th ed. (New York, Detroit: Columbia University Press, 2000).

Lechler, Victor, <u>The Apostolic and Post-Apostolic Times: Their Diversity and Union Ltfe and Doctrine</u>, 3rd ed., vol. 2, trans. A. J. K. Davidson (Edinburgh: T. & T. Clark, 1886).

Lee, Francis Nigel, <u>Revelation and Jerusalem</u> (Brisbane, Australia: 1985).

Leonard, J.E., <u>I Will Be Their God</u> (Chicago, IL: Laudemont Press, 1992).

Leonard, J.E., <u>Come Out of Her My People</u> (Arlington Heights, IL: Laudemont Press, 1991).

Lewis, Daniel J., <u>3 Crucial Questions about the Last Days</u> (Grand Rapids, MI: Baker Books, 1998).

Lightfoot, Joseph B., "Galatians"; *Biblical Essays* (London: Macmillan, 1893).

Louw, Johannes P. and Nida, Eugene A., <u>Greek-English Lexicon of the New Testament based on Semantic Domains</u>, Logos Library System (New York, NY: United Bible Societies 1988, 1989).

Macdonald, James M., <u>The Life and Writings of St. John</u> (London: Hodder & Stoughton, 1877).

Mathison, Keith A., <u>Dispensationalism</u> (Phillipsburg, NJ: P&R Publishing, 1999).

Mathison, Keith A., Editor, <u>When Shall These Things Be? A Reformed Response to Hyper-Preterism</u> (Phillipsburg, NJ: P&R Publishing, 2004).

Martin, Ernest L., The Birth of Christ Recalculated (Pasadena, CA: Foundation for Biblical Research, 2nd. Ed., 1980).

Maurice, Frederick Denisen, Lectures on the Apocalypse, 2nd ed. (London: Macmillan, 1885).

Mathison, Keith A., Dispensationalism, Rightly Dividing the People of God, (Phillipsburg, NY: P&R Publishing, 1995).

Mazor, Benjamin and Davis, Moshe, The Illustrated History of the Jews (New York, N.Y.: Harper and Row, 1963).

Metzger, Bruce, M., A Textual Commentary on the Greek New Testament, (Stuttgart: United Bible Societies, 1975).

Milligan, William, The Book of Revelation, *The Expositor's Bible* (London: Hodder and Stoughton, 1889).

M'Ilvaine, Charles Pettit, The Evidences of Christianity (Philadelphia: Smith, English & Co., 1861).

Morgan, Charles Herbert, et. al., Studies in the Apostolic Church (New York: Eaton and Mains, 1902).

Morris, Leon, The Revelation of St. John (Grand Rapids, MI: William B. Eerdmans Publishing Co., 1969).

Moule, C. F. D., The Birth of the New Testament, 3rd ed. (New York: Harper & Row, 1982)

Mounce, Robert H., The Book of Revelation (Grand Rapids, MI: Eerdmans Publishing Co. 1977).

Neander, John Augustus Wilhelm, The History of the Planting and Training of the Christian Church by the Apostles, trans. J. E. Ryland (Philadelphia: James M. Campbell, 1844).

Newcombe, Jerry, Coming Again, But When? (Colorado Springs: Chariot Victor, 1999).

Newton, Sir Isaac, Observation Upon the Prophacies of Daniel, and the Apocalypse of St. John (London: 1732).

Newton, Bishop Thomas, A Dissertation on the Prophecies Which Have Remarkably Been Fulfilled, and at This Time Are Fulfilling in the World (London: J.F. Dove, 1754).

Nisbett, N, The Prophecy of the Destruction of Jerusalem (1787).

Noe, John, Beyond the End Times (Bradford, PA.: IPA, 1999).

North, Stafford, Armageddon Again? A Reply to Hal Lindsey (Oklahoma City, OK: By the author, 1991).

The NET Bible Notes, electronic edition (Dallas, TX: Biblical Studies Press, 1998).

New American Standard Bible: 1995 update (LaHabra, CA: The Lockman Foundation, 1995).

North, Gary, The Dominion Covenant: Genesis (Tyler, TX: Institute for Christian Economics, 1982).

Ogden, Arthur M., The Avenging of the Apostles & Prophets (Somerset, KY: Ogden Publications, 1991).

Otto, Randall E., Coming in the Clouds: An Evangelical Case for the Invisibility of Christ at his Second Coming (Lanham, MD: University Press of America, 1994).

Owen, John, The Works of John Owen, 16 vols. (London: The Banner of Truth Trust, 1965-68).

Paher, Stanley, Matthew 24: First Century Fulfillment or End-Time Expectation? (Las Vegas, NV: Nevada Publications, 1996).

Pate, C. Marvin, General Editor, Four Views on the Book of Revelation (Grand Rapids, MI: Zondervan Publishing House, 1998).

Pate, C. Marvin and Haines, Calvin, Doomsday Delusions: What's Wrong with Predictions About the End of the World (Downers Grove, IL: Intervarsity Press, 1995).

Pentecost, J. Dwight, Things to Come (Grand Rapids, MI: Dunham Publishing Co, 1958).

Pickering, Wilbur N., The Identity of the New Testament Text (Nashville, TN: Thomas Nelson, 1977).

Pierce, Robert L., The Rapture Cult (Signal Mtn., TN: Signal Point Press, 1986).

Plumtree, Edward Hayes, A Popular Exposition of the Epistles to the Seven Churches of Asia, 2nd ed. (London: Hodder and Stoughton, 1879).

Poythress, Vern S., Understanding Dispensationalists (Phillipsburg, NJ.: P&R Publishing, 1987, 1994).

Provan, Charles D., The Church is Israel Now (Vallecito, CA: Ross House Books, 1987).

Ramsey, W.M., The Letters to the Seven Churches (Peabody, Mass: Hendrickson Publishers, 1994).

Randell, T., Revelation in H. D. M. Spence &Joseph S. Exell, eds., *The Pulpit Commentary*, vol. 22 (Grand Rapids: Eerdmans, rep. 1950).

Ratton, James J. L., The Apocalypse of St. John (London: R. & T. Washbourne, 1912).

Reuss, Eduard Wilhelm Eugen, History of the Sacred Scriptures of the New Testament (Edinburgh: T. &T. Clark, 1884).

Revelation Its Grand Climax At Hand! (Brooklyn, NY: Watchtower Bible and tract Society, 1988).

Roberts, J. W., The Revelation to John (Austin, TX: Sweet, 1974).

Robertson, Archibard Thomas, Word Pictures in the New Testament (Nashville, TN: Broadman Press, 1933).

Robertson, O. Palmer, The Israel of God (Phillipsburg, NY, P&R Publishing Co, 2000).

Robinson, John A. T., Redating the New Testament (Philadelphia, PA: Westminster, 1976).

Rushdoony, R. J., *Chalcedon Report*, Vallecito, CA, August 2002.

Rushdoony, Rousas John, Thy Kingdom Come (Nutley, NJ: Presbyterian and Reformed Publishing Co, 1971).

Russell, D.S., The Method and Message of Jewish Apocalyptic (Philadelphia, PA: Westminster, 1964).

Russell, J. Stuart, The Parousia (Grand Rapids, MI: Baker Books, 1887, 1999).

Ryrie, Charles C., The Ryrie Study Bible (Chicago, Il: Moody Press, 1976).

Schaff, Philip, The Ante-Nicene Fathers, electronic ed. (Garland, TX: Galaxie Software, 2000).

Schaff, Philip, History of the Christian Church, 3rd cd., vol. 1: *Apostolic Christianity* (Grand Rapids: Eerdmans, [1910] 1950).

Schaff, Philip, The New Schaff-Herzog Encyclopedia of Religious Knowledge, ed. by Samuel Macauley Jackson (Grand Rapids, MI: Baker Book House, 1951).

Scott, J.J., The Apocalypse, or Revelation of S. John the Divine (London: John Murray, 1909).

Seargent, David, Millennium Now (ImprintBooks, 2003)

Selwyn, Edward Condon, The Christian Prophets and the Apocalypse (Cambridge: 1900).

Seraiah, C. Jonathin, The End of All Things, A Defense of the Future (Moscow, Idaho: Cannon Press, 1999).

Sheldon, Henry C., The Early Church, *vol. 1* of *History of the Christian Church* (New York: Thomas Y. Crowell, 1894).

Simcox, William Henry, The Revelation of St. John Divine, *The Cambridge Bible for Schools and Colleges* (Cambridge: Cambridge University, 1893).

Smith, Daniel, The Destruction of Jerusalem (New York: T. Mason & G. Lane, 1840).

Smith, D. Moody, *"A Review of John A. T. Robinson's Redating the New Testament,"* Duke Divinity School Review 42 (1977): 193-205.

Smith, Jerome H., editor, The New Treasury of Scripture Knowledge, electronic, Logos Library System (Nashville, TN: Thomas Nelson, 1997, c1992).

Sproul, R. C., New Geneva Study Bible (Nashville, TN: Thomas Nelson Publishers, 1995).

Sproul, R. C., The Last Days According to Jesus (Grand Rapids, MI: Baker Books, 1998).

Stanley, Arthur Penrhyn, Sermons and Essays on the Apostolic Age (3rd ed: Oxford and London: 1874).

Strauss, Lehman, The Book of Revelation (Neptune, NY: Loizeaux Brothers, 1964).

Stevens, Ed, Stevens' Response to Gentry (Bradford, PA: Kingdom Publications).

Stevens, Ed, What Happened in 70 A. D.? (Bradford, PA: Kingdom Publications).

Strong, Augustus H., Systematic Theology (Old Tappan, NJ: Revell, [1907] 1970).

Strong, James, The Exhaustive Concordance of the Bible: electronic ed. (Ontario, Canada: Woodside Bible Fellowship, 1996).

Stuart, Moses, Commentary on the Apocalypse, 2 vols. (New York, NY: Allen, Mornll, and Wardwell, 1845).

Sutton, Ray R., That You May Prosper (Tyler, TX: Institute for Christian Economics, 1987).

Swanson, J., Dictionary of Biblical Languages with Semantic Domains: Greek New Testament (Oak Harbor, WA: Logos Research Systems, Inc., 1997).

Swete, Henry Barclay, The Apocalypse of St. John (Grand Rapids, MI: Wm. B. Eerdmans Publishing Co., 1906).

Tacitus, The Complete Word of Tacitus, Edited by Moses Hadas (New York, NY: Random House, Inc., 1942).

Taylor, Charles, Commentary On Revelation - Things Which Must Shortly Come to Pass (Lenoir City, Tennessee: Netadvantage Christian Publishers, 1997).

Tenney, Merrill C., Interpreting Revelation (Grand Rapids, MI: Wm. B. Eerdmans Publishing Co., 1957).

Tense Voice Mood, (Ontario, Canada: Woodside Bible Fellowship, 1994).

Terry, Milton S., Biblical Apocalyptics: A Study of the Most Notable Revelations of God and of Christ (New York, NY: Curts & Jennings, 1898).

Terry, Milton S., Biblical Hermeneutics (Grand Rapids, MI: Academie Books, Zondervan Publishing, rep. 1974).

The Treasury of Scripture Knowledge: Introduction by R.A. Torrey (Oak Harbor, WA: Logos Research Systems, Inc., 1995).

Torrey, Charles Cutler, Documents of the Primitive Church, ch. 5 (New Haven: Yale, 1958).

Torrey, Charles Cutler, The Apocalypse of John (New Haven: Yale, 1958).

Ussher, James, The Annals of the World (Green Forest, AR: Master Books, 2003, 1658).

Vanderwaal, Cornelis, Hal Lindsey and Biblical Prophcey (St. Catharine's, Ontario: Paideia, 1978).

Vanderwaal, Cornelis, Search the Scriptures, vol. 10 (St. Cathannes, Ontario: Paideia, 1979).

VanGemeren, Willem A., Interpreting the Prophetic Word (Grand Rapids, MI.: Zondervan, 1990).

Wainwright, Arthur, The Mysterious Apocalypse: Interpreting the Book of Revelation (Nashville, TN: Abingdon Press, 1993)

Wallace, Foy E., Jr., The Book of Revelation (Fort Smith, AR: Foy E. Wallace, Jr. Publications, Inc., 1997).

Warfield, Benjamin B., Selected Shorter Writings of Benjamin B. Warfield (Nutley, NJ: Presbyterian and Reformed Publishing Co., 1973).

Weigall, Arthur, Nero: Emperor of Rome (London: Thornton Butterworth, 1930).

Weiss, Bernhard, A Commentary on the New Testament, 2nd cd., vol. 4., trans. G. H. Schodde and E. Wilson (NY: Funk and Wagnalls, 1906).

Wessinger, Catherine, "Millennialism With and Without the Mayhem" in Thomas Robbins and Susan J. Palmer (eds.), Millennium, Messiahs, and Mayhem: Contemporary Apocalyptic Movements (New York and London: Routledge, 1997).

Westcott, Brooke Foss, The Gospel According to St. John (Grand Rapids, MI: Eerdmans, [1882] 1954).

Wilson, S.G., Related Strangers: Jews and Christians 70-170 C.E. (Minneapolis, MN: Fortress Press, 1995).

Workman, Herbert B., Persecution in the Early Church (London: Oxford, [1906] 1980).

Wright, Charles Henry Hamilton, Zechariah and His Prophecies (Minneapolis, MN: Klock and Klock, [1879] 1980).

Wright, N.T., Jesus and the Victory of God (Fortress, 1996).

Young, Robert, Commentary on the Book of Revelation; *Critical Comments on the Holy Bible* (London: Pickering & Inglis, 1885).

Zodhiates, Spiros, The Complete Word Study Dictionary: New Testament, electronic ed. (Chattanooga, TN: AMG Publishers, 2000, c1992, c1993).

The Author

Ralph E. Bass, Jr. has an undergraduate degree, BA, in Bible from *Bob Jones University*, and graduate degrees: a M.A. in Counseling from *Webster University*, a M.Div. in divinity studies from *Erskine Theological Seminary*, a Th.M. in theological studies from *Greenville Presbyterian Theological Seminary,* and a Th.D. in theological studies from *Reformation International Theological Seminary.*

An experienced biblical counselor, Dr. Bass is a member of the *International Association of Biblical Counselors*. He has a number of years of experience as a biblical counselor, a pastor, and as a teacher and school administrator in several Christian schools. He is married and has five children and fourteen grandchildren.

Books by the author:

What About Baptism? A Discussion on the Mode, Candidate, And Purpose of Christian Baptism

Hope For Today's Problems - The How To Book Of Christian Living

Back to the Future – A Study in the Book of Revelation

Soon to be released

Tell Me About Presbyterians – Just What Do They Believe

Notes

Notes

Notes

Notes

Notes

www.ingramcontent.com/pod-product-compliance
Lightning Source LLC
Chambersburg PA
CBHW060424100426
42812CB00030B/3294/J